CONSUMERS AND THE LAW

LAW IN CONTEXT

Editors: Robert Stevens (Haverford College, Pennsylvania),
William Twining (University College London) and
Christopher McCrudden (Lincoln College, Oxford)

Consumers and the Law

Second Edition

ROSS CRANSTON

WEIDENFELD AND NICOLSON
London

For my Mother and Father

Weidenfeld and Nicolson
91 Clapham High St London sw4

isbn 0 297 78272 x cased
isbn 0 297 78273 8 paperback

Photoset by Deltatype, Ellesmere Port
Printed in Great Britain by
Butler & Tanner Ltd,
Frome and London

CONTENTS

PART III   PUBLIC CONTROL

STATUTES

OTHER JURISDICTIONS

Alberta

Australia

STATUTORY INSTRUMENTS

CASES

PREFACE TO THE SECOND EDITION

When the first edition of this book was being written in 1976 and 1977, the economic and political conditions still seemed reasonably favourable to consumer protection measures.[1] In particular, many politicians recognized 'consumerism' as an effective political force and saw consumer protection measures as an attractive, non-divisive electoral issue. No doubt many also accepted that in modern society the formal equality of the market place masks substantive inequality in practice and that they ought to use law to redress the balance. There were sceptics, but they were without great political clout. By 1983, however, the mood has changed. Politically, the 'New Right' is triumphant on both sides of the Atlantic. To its theorists much consumer protection law is objectionable because it interferes with the efficiency of the market. (In practice not a great deal of consumer protection law has been rolled back so far, although various new initiatives have been thwarted.) Business interests have also been campaigning against consumer protection legislation, on the basis of what they say are its enormous costs. For example, an estimate for 1978 was that consumer protection law in Britain cost in excess of £150 million – the direct costs of administering the legislation and the indirect costs including the diversion of management and staff time, the additional material and operational costs, and the new capital equipment costs.[2] The recession in western industrial countries has made the criticism about cost especially potent. Further, even relatively sympathetic observers of the consumer protection law of recent decades suggest that it is time to take stock, that, for instance, the limitations on the law's efficacy as an instrument of consumer protection have often been overlooked, that the costs of consumer protection law have been too readily neglected, and that the law ought to be premised on a greater degree of individual responsibility.[3] Proposals for a 'new' consumer protection law purport to offer a non-paternalistic, less costly and more efficient strategy, in which businesses are provided with market incentives to build and maintain consumer goodwill. The focus is on steps such as ensuring consumers are furnished with more information and restructuring the market through competition (anti-trust) policy.[4]

My objections to 'New Right' economic theory are outlined in Chapter I and set out at greater length elsewhere.[5] Arguments against consumer protection based on its costs are often spurious. Since the estimates used for these calculations come from business itself, distortion is possible. Businesses might also include matters which ought not to be regarded as regulatory costs. Indeed, businesses might have to incur certain so-called 'compliance costs' irrespective of regulation, for the 'paper work' required may be part of any efficient managerial system. Critics have reduced such cost estimates substantially by excluding the costs associated with certain types of regulation (for example, that which clearly benefits business), and by taking into account the fact that many businesses would meet the legal standards adopted irrespective of regulation.[6] Most importantly, attacks on the cost of consumer protection law frequently ignore that it has benefits. Indeed it might be that during a recession the benefits of consumer protection are even greater because more businesses are closer to the margin and therefore tempted to engage in unconscionable practices to make sales.[7] And even if consumer protection law involves net costs, this is not a conclusive argument that it should be abandoned, for people might be prepared to incur these costs because of their preferences or values.

None of this means that the market does not have a role in consumer protection policy, that business regulation is costless or that where the benefits of consumer protection law outweigh the costs the net benefit cannot be increased by reform. Elsewhere I have written about 'regulatory failure', in other words why regulation such as that involved in consumer protection law is ineffective. The causes of so-called 'regulatory failure' lie with the forces behind the emergence of business regulation; its actual form 'on the books'; the implementation of regulatory standards by the relevant agencies and by the courts; and the impact of business regulation in its social and economic context. It quickly becomes apparent on examining these four factors why business regulation might be thought to have 'failed'. An examination of the way business regulation emerges might show that it was designed to advance business interests, so that it should not be surprising if it 'fails' to achieve a more general public benefit. Regulatory failure might also derive from the form taken by the legislation: there might be deficiencies with the techniques used; its substantive provisions might not be commensurate with what is generally conceived of as its purpose; and the discretion devolved to the relevant agencies might be so wide that they can subvert the legislative purpose. In addition to the design of regulatory legislation, another major source of regulatory failure might be with the agency responsible for implementing it. The law-makers might be to blame here – at least in the first instance – for giving an agency limited powers, for not providing the agency with sufficient resources, for the appointments they make at the senior level of the agency, or for not supporting the agency because of pressure exerted by the regulated. However, regulatory failure might also be attributed to the context within which regulatory agencies operate, and the way this affects the impact of regulatory legislation, rather than to the agencies themselves. For example, businesses might fail to implement regulatory standards because competitive pressures oblige them to adopt production or marketing schemes in which legal obligations are secondary.[8]

None the less, I adhere to a major theme of the first edition, that generally speaking ordinary consumers are better protected by public law measures than by business self-regulation or the private law. '[M]ost lawyers take the view that consumers are better protected by private law remedies than by public law measures. My argument is that only the articulate, educated, better-off sections of society can invoke private law remedies without assistance.'[9] The contention is not that public law measures are the only avenue for consumer protection. Market conditions might induce a business to be especially responsive to consumer complaints. (If this occurs it will generally be without reference to legal norms.) Consumer organizations, in transcending individual grievances, have a potential for acting effectively in relation to the practices of particular businesses or public enterprises, test case litigation and lobbying for law reform.[10] Small claims courts, class actions, and the mass restitution suit are mechanisms, discussed in Chapter 3, which bolster the efficacy of consumers in the sphere of private law. Mention can also be made of other mechanisms such as the public interest action in which consumer organizations are empowered to litigate on behalf of consumers, and consumer collection agencies to whom consumers assign their claims.[11] Measures such as these might lead to the redress of individual grievances and might also have an impact on business activity. In particular, the mass restitution suit conceptualizes the grievances of individuals as a collective grievance, worthy of the intervention of a public agency. Conversely, public law measures are far from effective in certain circumstances. Legislation might be largely 'symbolic' in character, with no intention that it will be effective in practice. At the level of legislative technique, for example, Chapter 9 argues that information disclosure as a means of consumer protection has less impact than is often thought. Reference has already been made to 'regulatory failure' in the enforcement of public law standards. These arguments at various points in the book about the relative efficacy of the different means of consumer protection, in particular the role of public law, are brought together in the Conclusion.

Since the first edition of this book a number of important developments have occurred. In the legal area there are decisions such as *Lambert* v. *Lewis*,[12] *Junior Books Ltd* v. *Veitchi Co. Ltd*[13] and *Parkdale Custom Built Furniture Pty Ltd* v. *Puxu Pty Ltd*,[14] along with legislation such as the Supply of Goods and Services Act 1982, the Consumer Safety Act 1978 and the Price Marking (Bargain Offers) Order (as amended).[15] At the time of writing, the Law Commission is about to publish a working paper on the implied terms in the Sale of Goods Act 1979; the Commission also has implied terms as to the supply of services under review. In the non-legal area, changes such as the fading of consumer advice centres have not always been for the better. As well as taking such developments into account, the preparation of this edition has involved general editing and updating. Following the advice of at least one reviewer, I have also added material on certain legal matters such as the Unfair Contract Terms Act 1977 and the Trade Descriptions Act 1968. Moreover, there is new discussion about, for instance, competition and consumer protection (Chapter 1). To keep the volume within bounds, there have been compensating reductions in some parts, notably in Chapters 9, 11 and 12. As in the first edition, there is frequent reference to developments in Australia, Canada and the United States. In particular, the discussion of broad statutory standards

(Chapter 9) draws freely on the Australian Trade Practices Act 1974, which has generated a substantial volume of relevant litigation.

In preparing this edition I have incurred various debts of gratitude. I am especially grateful to a number of people who have taken the time to read and comment on various parts of the manuscript. In doing so they have saved me from various errors and drawn my attention to additional references and arguments. They are: the Editors, Professor R. M. Goode, Geoffrey Lindell, Jack McEwen, Professor C. J. Miller, F. M. B. Reynolds, Thomas Sharpe and Graham Stephenson. Both Sir Gordon Borrie (the Director General of Fair Trading) and Richard Thomas (National Consumer Council) have provided me with useful information. I must also thank those who assisted with various aspects of the book's production: at the Australian National University, Di Edwards and Carolyn McCusker, and at the publishers, Benjamin Buchan and Robert Baldock.

I

Introduction: the context of consumer protection

PROBLEMS FACING CONSUMERS

The advent of mass consumption has resulted in consumers facing an information gap when they enter transactions involving the purchase of products or the provision of services. Products are now being marketed in such number and in such a manner that it is more difficult for consumers to judge their qualities adequately. The advance of technology means that many consumer products are quite complex. Quite apart from questions of judgement, style and taste, expert knowledge is essential to appreciate the features of many modern products which fall below the threshold of perception of the ordinary consumer. In the nineteenth century innovation and technical changes were concerned mainly with making existing products more efficiently (the means of production) rather than with making new commodities (the means of consumption). Then there was a quickening of the pace around the turn of the century (with telephones, motorcycles, canned foods, and so on) and its subsequent acceleration, with the 1950s witnessing a range of new products (including television, synthetic fibres, detergents, frozen foods, motorscooters, long-playing records, colour film, magnetic recording, ballpoint pens and polythene).[1] The present is the age of the microchip. Mitchell comments that the course in innovations has thus quickly dated consumers' experience and knowledge; for example, what was known about natural fibres like wool and cotton has little bearing on the characteristics and performance of nylon.[2] Certainly a non-expert examination will not reveal many important characteristics of modern products, and the retailer is frequently unable to offer advice on them. Mark Green remarks how consumers, even the most sophisticated, can face difficulties:

How does an average consumer know how much unhealthy radiation is being emitted from a microwave oven, or from his dentist's x-ray machine? Should we assume a car buyer can know whether his purchase's motor mounts will fail, or when; or whether tasteless and odorless carbon monoxide is seeping into the passenger compartment from the exhaust system; or whether the drug he purchases is effective or toxic?[3]

Similarly with services: for example, the average consumer is not in a position to evaluate critically the detailed provisions of different insurance policies. There are developments such as the profusion of professional advisers, computer scanning in supermarkets (to price goods) and electronic funds' transfers. For example, the latter – the process of money, etc. exchange by use of electronic devices – raises consumer concerns such as consumers' liability when cards are lost, the elimination of alternative facilities for payment, the possible exclusion of poor consumers, the reversibility of payments (cf. the present position with cheques), the vulnerability of consumer assets to garnishment, and privacy.[4]

Advertising often fails to inform consumers, and in addition raises expectations beyond what can be fulfilled by a product or service.[5] A later chapter will consider advertising at some length, but at this point it need only be noted that it is no answer to say that consumers can only be sold what they need. An interesting empirical study of the purchase and use of electrical ranges and sewing machines found that while the equipment was used and used correctly, many respondents said that it was without utility, and for each device quite a large proportion did not use it.[6] Other factors raising consumers' expectations besides advertising have been the increase in real incomes and the widened choice of products and services. Frequently consumers' expectations are disappointed because of factors such as the real or planned obsolescence of consumer products. Economic factors are also involved because many cannot effectively participate in the consumption stimulated by advertising, at least at the level to which they aspire. In recent years inflation has made it even more desirable that consumers properly evaluate products and services. Inflation presses especially hard on the poor.[7]

When consumers have cause to complain about a product or

service there is no guarantee that they will obtain satisfaction. Many businesses adopt a positive attitude to consumer grievances, particularly with the growth of consumer concern in the last decades. Some large businesses have created customer relations departments to supervise the handling of grievances and to incorporate a consumer orientation into company decisions.[8] Whether these moves are successful is another matter. Other businesses are less responsive, however, either as a matter of policy or for other reasons such as inefficiency. Ralph Nader argues that in the United States a negative attitude is endemic to businesses and is not just an aberration of the minority: '[C]onsumers are being manipulated, defrauded, and injured not just by marginal businesses or fly-by-night hucksters, but by the US blue-chip business firms. . . .'[9]

But there is an <u>imbalance of power</u> when consumers confront a business with a grievance, even if it is favourably disposed to consumers. Consumers are typically in a weak bargaining position because of the disparity in knowledge and resources between the parties, which narrows the consumer's access to a remedy.

> Competition works to the benefit of the consumer, but we know that too often the balance of power is weighted in favour of traders, with their expert advisers – legal, commercial, public relations; with their organized trade and professional associates paid to represent their point of view in any and every dialogue with government or trade unions. Traders spend the whole of their working day on their business. In contrast, spending money is only one aspect of most people's lives – jobs, children education, recreation may take more time and more interest.[10]

Legal remedies may be available to consumers in the event of a business proving obstreperous, but the evidence demonstrates that many consumers are ignorant of their legal rights and/or either unwilling or unable to pursue them.[11] For this and other reasons the view is advanced in this book that public control is frequently the only way that consumers will be protected by law.

The poor consumer

The problems mentioned bear particularly heavily on the poor. Publication of Caplovitz's *The Poor Pay More* highlighted the point that consumer protection is not simply a middle-class issue but a matter of vital importance for the less well-off members of society.[12] Their interests are somewhat different, however, from what has been conventionally regarded as the main concern of consumer protection. There is still the need that the products and services they obtain should be merchantable and value for money, but low-income consumers are more concerned with the essentials of life.

As the title of Caplovitz's book suggests, the evidence is that the poor tend to pay more for what they purchase. The price levels in comparable stores in low-income and higher-income neighbourhoods are similar, but prices are higher in the smaller outlets prevalent in low-income areas. The crucial point is that although considerable numbers of poorer citizens venture outside their neighbourhoods to shop, many continue to patronize these smaller stores despite higher prices.[13] And there are compelling reasons for them to do so. There are fewer modern shops in the less affluent areas – they either have never existed, or the stores there have not been modernized – and many low-income families lack the mobility to shop elsewhere. Their immobility may reflect the inadequacy of private or public transport, or the problems of old age or of being a woman with young children. Other factors may also enter, such as the non-availability of credit facilities at stores outside the area. The lack of financial resources or storage facilities may necessitate the constant purchase of small quantities, which means buying at a local store.

Another difficulty which the less well-off experience, at least with consumer durables, is that they do not seem to be as well informed about price differences and the cost of credit. Yet credit is particularly important for the less affluent, since it permits them to enjoy benefits of the consumer society which their poverty would otherwise prevent. Many low-income families are frozen out of the normal credit market and are compelled to accept credit in its most expensive form.[14] They cannot obtain a bank loan, and hence they cannot shop around for the lowest price and obtain a cash discount. The argument is that there is a greater risk of default by poorer borrowers – and thus higher rates of interest are justified – because of factors like unemployment or a history of bad debts. Many poor consumers are branded as poor credit risks when there is no justification.[15] Consumers' Association has carried out a crude survey of interest rates. Visiting some 165 shops in the country, and classifying them roughly as to whether they served a professional or a working-class clientele or both, they found that the former charged rates nearly one half of those in shops whose customers were mainly working-class on the purchase of six common consumer durables.[16]

	Rate of interest
Professional customers	18%
Professional and working-class customers	28%
Working-class customers	34%

Questionable marketing techniques seem to affect less well-off consumers disproportionately. Caplovitz found numerous abuses in New York City. Price tags were generally absent so consumers paid high prices if they were perceived as a poor credit risk or naive, or if they were referred by another businessman to whom a commission had to be paid.[17] Another abuse was the 'T.O. system' whereby reluctant consumers were 'turned over' to another salesman who purported to be a supervisor or manager and who would convince consumers to enter transactions with promises of easier terms than hitherto discussed.[18] Evidence of similar practices elsewhere is not systematic, but there is little doubt that they exist. Well-publicized examples have been the exploitation of the less affluent in the inner urban areas of London and Birmingham through pyramid selling and second-mortgage rackets. For example the National Consumer Council document *For Richer, For Poorer* says about second mortgages in the London Borough of Lambeth:

[There are] many complaints, particularly from West Indians. Several of them had been visited by doorstep salesmen from a building contractor offering to undertake improvements to their homes. When they showed readiness, they were offered a choice between cash and credit, the estimated costs varying between £320 and £730. Many opted for the credit which the salesmen offered to arrange through a broker for second mortgages. Soon after, a cheque came from the finance company involved and soon after that came a visit from the representative of the contractor. He said the cheque was needed at once to purchase materials; his, he said, was a very small firm. It is not known how the contractor knew when the cheques from the finance company would be sent. The work was then either started and left incomplete or not started at all. In that same district a salesman of another kind, for a central heating firm also encouraging second mortgages, told another investigator that it was a good pitch for him. 'We sell to Jamaicans, the coloured boys . . . it's good samboland.' The rate of interest on the mortgage, at 28 per cent, was not so much the cause of complaint as the manner in which the borrowers were dealt with, or not dealt with, by this combination of lender and contractor.[19]

The document also records that 'tallymen' (door-to-door traders with regular rounds) had recently encouraged women on certain council housing estates to over-commit themselves financially and then had threatened to tell their husband if they did not repay the credit.[20]

Added to these problems is the fact that poorer consumers are less likely to utilize their legal rights as consumers. An American study found that it was mostly white, middle-class persons who complained to a consumer protection agency in one area, while a British survey of the users of various kinds of advice services detected an under-representation of those from the lowest socio-economic groups.[21] Knowledge and understanding of the legal position and of where to seek assistance declines as one progresses down the socio-economic scale. Surveys have constantly shown that the higher and not the lower socio-economic groups receive the information in publications like *Consumer Reports* (US), *Which?* (Britain), *Test* (West Germany), *Canadian Consumer* and *Choice* (Australia). Thus an NOP survey in Britain in 1975 found that 22 per cent of the highest social class read *Which?* compared with 1 per cent of the lowest social class. In the population as a whole, 8 per cent read it.[22] A study of consumer activism in Australia, which used membership of consumer groups or complaining to retailers or consumer protection agencies as indices of activism, revealed that the activists tended to be younger, better educated and more affluent.[23]

In addition to a deficiency in knowledge, lack of confidence is another explanation why the less affluent do not take advantage of their legal rights. It may be that the poor resign themselves to injustice and hardship as a matter of course because of a low expectation of success if they complain. Alternatively, they may be unwilling to jeopardize their relations with a business by complaining, for example, if it is their sole source of credit. To generalize this last point, it might be that poorer consumers are worse off because of the markets they are forced by circumstances to patronize.[24]

The consumer as citizen

The present work adopts a narrow view of the consumer interest and focuses mainly on citizens entering transactions to obtain products and services from commercial enterprises. Transactions involving land are mentioned only incidentally. In this sense the scope of the book coincides with what is generally regarded as the thrust of consumer protection legislation; such legislation confines itself to transactions involving 'goods' and 'services'. The meaning of 'goods' does not extend to matters concerning tenancy agreements or social welfare benefits,[25] although the definition of services is more extensive, encompassing work, including work of a professional nature (but not under a contract of employment).[26] In another way most consumer protection legislation has a wider ambit than the present work, since it applies to transactions between commercial parties as well as to consumer transactions. In this sense the present book is about what the Germans call the *Endverbraucher* – the ultimate consumer. Some recent legislation is specifically confined to *consumer* transactions. For example, certain exemption clauses are nullified by the Unfair Contract Terms Act 1977 as against a person dealing as a *consumer* but not automatically in commercial transactions.[27] Statutory orders can be made under the Fair Trading Act 1973 if the economic interests of *consumers* are prejudiced. In general terms a 'consumer' is defined in the Fair Trading Act 1973 as one who does not contract in the course of a business carried on by him but who deals with someone who does.[28]

But there is a wider view of the consumer interest: the term 'consumer' is virtually equated with the term 'citizen'. It is said that the consumer interest is involved when citizens enter exchange relationships with institutions like hospitals, libraries, police forces and various government agencies, as well as with businesses.[29] When the National Consumer Council was established in Britain in 1975, the first chairman made it clear that it would be concerned with users of public services as well as with users of commercial services, and with their rights to full information, to choice whenever possible, and to treatment with full consideration. For example, the National Consumer Council has published a number of reports on the difficulties facing tenants in council (local government) housing, the criteria used in allocating it, the nature of the tenancy agreements and the approach of the authorities to rent arrears and repairs.[30]

Ralph Nader in the United States has done much to equate the term consumer with citizen. Originally he began with a narrow focus similar to that adopted in the present work. Quickly he became aware that the cause of consumer protection narrowly defined was inextricably linked with the cause of the consumer as citizen. The Nader organization adopted the philosophy:

There can be no daily democracy without daily citizenship. If we do not exercise our civic rights, who will? If we do not perform our civic duties, who can? The fibre of a just society in pursuit of happiness is a thinking active citizenry.

A Nader report on Congress was undertaken with a view to evaluating the standards of legislative representation provided for citizens. A study of legal education and lawyers was designed to uncover the assumptions and standards of those who often play a key role in American society.

Even the concept of the consumer as citizen is limited, because it implicitly accepts the existing order of things. Much has been written about how advertising creates needs, generates consumption and thus perpetuates modern capitalism – a view given wide currency by Galbraith. Curbing advertising abuse does not affect this fact. The notion of consumer protection can mask deprivation and the divisions in society. Moreover, consumer protection does not really address issues such as the satisfaction (or non-satisfaction) of genuine needs and the distribution of wealth in society. There can also be a distortion of values so that the main emphasis is placed on the quality of private consumption. 'Free trade', for example, might be espoused without any apparent concern for the catastrophic effects this can have on the employment of ordinary people. Writers like Illich see an all-pervading societal domination over people's lives; in the area of consumption products, rather than non-industrial ways of satisfying needs, dominate. Consumer protection in this view is a mere palliative to such domination, for it perpetuates it, perhaps with slight modification. Illich expresses the point thus:

> Consumers cannot do without cars. They buy different makes. They discover that most cars are unsafe at any speed. So they organize to get safer, better and more durable cars and to get more as well as wider and safer roads. Yet when consumers gain more confidence in cars, the victory only increases society's dependence on high-powered vehicles – public or private – and frustrates even more those who have to, or would prefer to, walk.[31]

While the present work accepts that this analysis is valid, it does not reject present society for some unrealizable ideal, but proceeds on the basis that social engineering within the system is worth while and can be achieved.

CONSUMER PROTECTION AND THE THIRD WORLD

Developing countries have laws which fall within the consumer protection rubric. Some have even introduced comprehensive consumer protection legislation covering matters such as weights and measures, food and prices. Where there are laws on the books, however, the <u>administrative infrastructure</u> for their implementation and enforcement is often rudimentary.[32] This does not mean that governments in developing countries are helpless to achieve change of benefit to consumers. One specific example relates to the important concern in the last decade that transnational corporations have extensively promoted powdered milk for infant feeding in the Third World. Its use increases the risk of infant mortality and malnutrition when mixed with contaminated water and administered by illiterate mothers who did not know how to use it properly. Papua New Guinea was one of the few countries to take legislative action, in the form of the Baby Feed Supplies (Control) Act 1977. The Act and its attendant regulations prohibited advertisements whose intention or likely result was to encourage the bottle feeding of babies and the purchase or use of certain products and articles associated with it. A survey for the World Health Organisation concluded that the legislation seemed to have had positive effects: the number of infants reported as suffering from diarrhoea, gastroenteritis and other signs of malnutrition dropped dramatically and the proportion of artificially fed infants below 80 per cent weight for age fell to half of what it had been previously.[33]

This example raises the issue of the role of transnational corporations in the Third World and whether their home governments should impose legal controls over their activities. In particular, transnationals operating in the Third World have vigorously promoted certain products (e.g. high tar cigarettes, drugs) in a manner which would be prohibited in the developed countries. The companies argue that consumers in the Third World choose freely to purchase these products and that they are not in breach of local legislation. Critics point out that transnationals create demand by advertising and marketing methods which are sometimes blatantly false and bordering on the corrupt, and that because Third World countries lack the resources and experience they do not have the legal controls which are taken for granted in developed countries.[34] A first step legally would be that products which the law in developed countries has classified as unsafe should not generally be exported to the Third World.[35] Exceptionally, it might be possible for a company to demonstrate that the nature of the risk varies in the Third World and that therefore export should be permitted. Secondly, developed countries might do more at the international level in the way of codes of behaviour to which transnationals would be expected to conform. With voluntary codes problems of content and enforcement loom large, however, while the experience in international organizations such as the W.H.O. has been that developed countries with important transnationals are not always inclined to altruism. Thirdly, information can be made available to the Third World, for example, about unsafe products, to enable them to take action themselves.

CONSUMER GROUPS AND THE CONSUMER INTEREST

Before discussing legal safeguards for the consumer interest it is appropriate to throw some light on the non-legal ways in which consumer protection is advanced. Not everyone agrees that legal measures are necessary or even desirable. The assumption of some is that consumers can exercise a good deal of influence by banding together into pressure groups. Others say that consumer protection is achieved through the operation of the market and that other mechanisms are secondary. These contentions are briefly dealt with in the remaining sections of this introductory chapter. Then in the next chapter attention is directed to the contention that businesses can discipline themselves in the interests of consumers.

A theory of consumer groups

Pressure groups are a well-accepted feature of the politics of western society, and among the strongest are those representing commerce and industry. If individual consumers combined in groups they could more effectively pursue their interests like other pressure groups. Other consumers could be sensitized to consumer problems and educated about their rights; resources and support could be given for consumers to enforce their rights; and pressure for change could be exerted on businesses and government. Test cases might be taken in the courts, for costs could be distributed and the precedent value of decisions given greater weight than if individuals were bringing them. Even if test case litigation were ultimately unsuccessful it could be used to delay objectionable behaviour or to gain favourable publicity.

But are pressure groups representing the consumer interest a likely feature of the political scene? A number of writers take the view that consumer groups will spring up automatically to counter the power of business interests. A writer in the *Canadian Bar Review* puts this notion of countervailing power as follows:

> Whenever there is a substantial concentration of power . . . there is likely to develop a countervailing force representing an aggregation of individual interests. 'Consumer' groups will have their effect both in direct relations with suppliers and in influencing new government policy to regulate the corporations or other business organizations with respect to which the consumer groups may have conflicting interests.[36]

By contrast, there are those who say that the consumer interest will always be poorly represented in society. Everyone is a consumer, and since the consumer interest is so diffuse and widely shared it should not be surprising that people have difficulty agreeing on what the consumer interest entails.[37] In addition, people lack self-awareness of their role as consumers. Anthony Downs argues that people feel more intense about their role as income-earners because they earn their income in one area but spend it in many.[38] Since those who stand to gain most in an area are those who earn their incomes there, they will be the ones prepared to invest the money and expertise to influence government. And in most cases those who are prepared to invest the money and expertise to influence government policy in an area of production can deduct the cost from taxable income. Thus a business affected by a particular measure can afford to bring pressure to bear, but consumers with many other interests will have no over-riding concern impelling them to act. For this reason government might fund a special office to represent the consumer interest at the national level.

Furthermore, it is said that rational and self-interested individuals will not join a group purporting to represent the consumer interest, even if the collective benefits to be gained are greater than the total individual costs. An exception is if the group is small or if there is coercion or some other incentive to make them act in common. The 'free-rider' problem, as it is called, results because in large groups the contribution any one individual must make is most probably greater than the benefits to be received, and because in groups with many members it is unlikely that an individual contribution will make a difference. Olson writes:

> Virtually no one would be so absurd as to expect that the individuals in an economic system would voluntarily curtail their spending to halt an inflation, however much they would, as a group, gain from doing this. Yet it is typically taken for granted that the same individuals in a political or social context will organize and act to further their collective interests. The rational individual in the economic system does not curtail his spending to prevent inflation (or increase it to prevent depression) because he knows, first, that his own efforts would not have a noticeable effect, and second, that he would get the benefits of any price stability that others achieved in any case. For the same two reasons, the rational individual in the large group in a socio-political context will not be willing to make any sacrifices to achieve the objectives he shares with others.[39]

The truth probably lies somewhere between the proponents of countervailing power and those arguing that consumer bodies will never coalesce and have an influence. Certainly, consumer bodies are comparatively small in relation to their potential clientele; they lack resources when compared with pressure groups representing business interests; and the very broadness of the consumer interest explains in part the existence of several competing bodies each claiming to represent it.[40] On the other hand a number of factors mean that the position is not totally without hope. People are not always completely self-interested. The very existence of some consumer groups testifies to the fact that there are individuals who are prepared to band together to further the consumer cause. There may be a number of conflicting consumer interests but representation is not impossible. Consumers have a number of identifiable interests in common: economic efficiency, diversity of purchasing choice, avoidance of monopoly profits and consumer fraud, optimal purchasing information and good quality products and services in relation to price. That consumer interests can conflict is hardly a conclusive argument that they cannot be reconciled or adequately represented.

There are incentives impelling representation of the consumer interest. Consumer organizations which do comparative testing, like the Consumers' Association, recruit members because they offer a benefit, in the form of information, which otherwise would be very costly for individuals to obtain. Income from the publication of *Which?*

enables the Consumers' Association to carry on many other activities of benefit to customers. It is entirely rational for independent consumer advocates like Ralph Nader, who are financed from private sources and can make money from their publications on consumer protection, to devote their effort to exerting influence on behalf of consumers as a whole. In effect their motivation comes from their career orientation.

Representation of the consumer interest has also been fostered by government. One interpretation is that the consumer movement has had an impact on government because political parties have seen the issue as a vote-winner.[41] Recognizing that consumer protection measures do not require a large public expenditure, the parties competed with one another in new initiatives.[42] Another interpretation is that consumer protection measures have often coincided with the economic policies of various governments which have been keen to further competition, to eliminate restrictive trade practices and to reduce inflation.[43] As a corollary governments need the consumer viewpoint to be presented as a counter to business and trade-union pressure when they make policy in the areas of economic planning. Inherent in both interpretations is that the furtherance of the consumer interest has been largely dependent on political decisions.

Consumer groups in practice

Private organizations representing the consumer interest fall roughly into two categories: comparative testing groups, like the Consumers' Association, and the voluntary consumer groups operating at the local level. Other private organizations claim to represent the consumer interest but they cannot be regarded as an integral part of the consumer movement. Thus trade unions sometimes express pro-consumer sentiments. In Britain they were instrumental in the introduction of direct food subsidies in 1974 and have looked favourably on consumer legislation. The Australian Council of Trade Unions has moved to sponsor consumer-oriented services to provide lower prices and as a force against existing restrictive and monopoly practices. Trade unions in Europe have a long history of such activity. But trade unions are concerned mainly with the working conditions of their members and not with their problems as consumers.[44]

The consumer cooperatives, in which consumers are actually members of a retail organization, are in theory aligned with the consumer movement. The political wing of consumer cooperatives in Britain, the Cooperative Party, has sponsored Labour Party M.P.s and on occasions advocated consumer sovereignty as the only true classless way.[45] Quite strong as a retail group in Britain, the cooperatives have not been in the forefront of the consumer movement precisely because they have been preoccupied with business and have failed to resolve the conflict between this and the consumer interest. Business achievements are much easier to demonstrate for those running the cooperatives than advances in a particular philosophy.

The Consumers Associations have been primarily concerned with publishing information about products and services on a commercial basis. The information consists mainly of the results of comparative tests on products and of the systematic assessment of consumer experiences in relation to the durability, reliability and servicing of products.[46] Critics point out that comparative test surveys of Consumers Associations are often not comprehensive and that there are time-lags in providing information about modified or new products after they have been marketed. Limitations of finance and the wide range of products and services on the market are obvious explanations for these drawbacks. Members of Consumers Associations have an impact on the market by channeling demand for products and services. Following the publication of favourable reports by Consumers' Union in the United States, for example, sales figures for particular products have risen, although the converse drop after unfavourable reports has not been as dramatic.[47]

The Consumers Associations have also concerned themselves with representing the consumer interest in public policy-making. Thus the Consumers' Association in Britain has played an important role in the drafting of consumer legislation, acted as a catalyst for other consumer groups by making financial support available, and promoted the introduction of High Street consumer advice centres to widen the access of citizens to advice on consumer matters. Yet Consumers Associations face limitations on their advocacy role because their main focus is publishing information of immediate benefit to their members, their membership is not representative of the population and because of financial constraints.

The other major representatives of the consumer interest are the voluntary consumer groups. Mainly these operate at the grass-roots level and revolve around assessing local services and products. Most produce a magazine or newsletter. The National Federation of

Consumer Groups in Britain has coordinated some national surveys by member groups but its effort is largely devoted to serving member groups by collecting their publications and assisting them in conducting local surveys. The legislative committee of the Federation has made representations to the government on various consumer matters and Federation members are appointed, in individual capacities, to various bodies to represent the consumer interest.

A further step in representing the consumer interest has been taken in the United States by consumer advocates. Consumer advocates expose business malfeasance and actively represent the consumer interest by research, media publicity and appearances before legislatures, courts and regulatory bodies. The public interest research groups in other countries are a pale imitation of the American development. Finance seems to be the major problem and few private foundations are willing to fund a large-scale venture. A hurdle facing consumer advocates – indeed all consumer groups – is whether they have a mandate to speak for the consumer interest. One view is that, unlike other public interests such as education, citizens know so little about what their welfare requires in the area of consumer protection that consumer advocates can quite properly represent their interests.[48] On the other hand some say this view is patronizing and that consumer advocates are unrepresentative.

A new representative of the consumer interest in Britain was established in 1975 in the form of the National Consumer Council. The National Consumer Council – there are Councils also in Scotland and Wales – is similar to its predecessor, the Consumer Council, which operated between 1964 and 1971. Its members are appointed by the government, and have mainly consumer, social or voluntary work backgrounds. There is a full-time staff. Funded by the government but non-statutory in form, the National Consumer Council has no executive powers and does not deal directly with individual consumer problems. Rather, its role is to campaign on more general issues and in particular to represent the consumer interest in a partisan fashion at the national level. In the terms of the White Paper heralding its formation it is to make representations on consumer law, advertising standards, consumer advice at the local level and consumer representation in the nationalized industries, as well as to represent the consumer on appropriate government and other bodies.[49] The N.C.C. has taken the initiative in several areas which other consumer groups have ignored. For example, it has promoted bulk buying of food for poorer people, and it has funded an advice centre in a depressed area of Manchester on an action-research basis, to assist those applying for means-tested benefits.[50] Bodies similar to the National Consumer Council exist in a number of European countries. Like it they were nurtured by the state yet have no executive role in formulating consumer policy.

The law and consumer groups

The law has little to say about the activities of consumer groups. Certainly it has some relevance to their formation and operation as distinct entities; for example, one reason why the Credit Unions have had such a slow growth in Britain is that until recently there was no suitable legislation as in other countries, giving them a separate legal identity, and providing the framework within which they could be registered and supervised. The law can also facilitate the growth of consumer groups by economic measures such as tax concessions. In countries such as West Germany organizations like the Consumers' Association actually receive state subsidies to enable them to continue their work on the comparative testing of products and the evaluation of services.

The representation function of organized consumer bodies has been strengthened in Britain over the last decade. The government now regularly consults organizations like the Consumers' Association and the National Consumer Councils before introducing consumer protection measures. Occasionally legislation recognizes this and some statutory regulations cannot be made until consultation has taken place.[51] Legislation also provides for the appointment of representatives of recognized consumer organizations to bodies like the Consumer Protection Advisory Committee, which must consider statutory orders proposed to be made under the Fair Trading Act 1973.[52] More extensive use could be made of a provision obliging the appointment of representatives from recognized consumer organizations. Legislation for establishing advisory committees for the Independent Broadcasting Authority and consumer consultative councils of the nationalized industries[53] give the relevant authorities too wide a discretion to appoint anyone they want to represent the consumer viewpoint. Important organizations like the Medicines Commission and the Food Standards Committee need contain no consumer representatives at all, although they make recommendations which often become law.

Consumer groups lack some of the legal privileges conferred on trade unions, although both types of organization are in similar positions of opposing the economically powerful. Members of a local consumer group organizing a boycott, a black list or a picket against a business notorious for its malpractices could be the subject of an injunction, or be sued for damages, for committing torts such as conspiracy, defamation, trespass or private nuisance. Trade unions have a degree of immunity when they act in a similar manner in the furtherance of a trade dispute.[54] The position of consumer and similar groups is nicely illustrated by the decision in *Hubbard* v. *Pitt*.[55] A local tenants' group disapproved of the activity of an estate agent in changing the social character of a neighbourhood and began a small, peaceful picket outside the estate agent's offices, involving the distribution of leaflets explaining their case. The majority of the Court of Appeal held that the estate agent was entitled to an interlocutory injunction, preventing the group from continuing the picket, on the basis that there was a serious issue to be tried whether they were committing the tort of private nuisance by interfering with the enjoyment of the plaintiff's premises. Lord Denning dissented on the grounds that picketing was not a private nuisance in itself if it were directed to obtaining or to communicating information, or peacefully to persuading, so long as it was not associated with obstruction, threats or violence. Despite the decision, consumer groups will not automatically be restrained by an interlocutory injunction from distributing leaflets or displaying placards which a business alleges are defamatory if this is done elsewhere than outside the business's premises. In *Crest Homes Ltd* v. *Ascott*[56] a consumer was angry because he thought some builders had made his front door very badly, so he took the door, attached it to his car and drove around the streets. It bore the words: 'This door is typical of the poor materials used. Be warned.' The Court of Appeal refused to uphold an interlocutory injunction because the plaintiff could not show that the defence of justification would fail at trial of the alleged defamation. However, words such as these might be defamatory, and a business might be successful in later claiming damages from a consumer who publishes them. It seems that consumer boycotts might be unlawful on the basis that they constitute the tort of interference with contractual relations.[57]

COMPETITION, MARKET ECONOMICS AND CONSUMER PROTECTION

Competition has a role in protecting consumers. Where it is effective, consumers will have a choice of products and services, and information in relation to these products and services which producers provide in seeking consumer patronage. Competition is generally more effective in the case of products and services which are purchased frequently, the quality and performance of which are readily identifiable, and whose characteristics are fairly stable. By contrast, competition is weak in markets which involve substantial information gaps and markets where there are 'fly-by-night' businesses which are not interested in building and maintaining goodwill.[58]

After a brief examination of the role of competition (anti-trust) policy in consumer protection, the remainder of this Part directs attention to a strong school of thought which believes that recent consumer protection legislation is an undesirable departure from *caveat emptor*. It believes government regulation in the consumer interest is mostly superfluous and that consumers are afforded adequate protection through the operation of the market and the common law system. As the economics editor of *The Times* put it: 'The consumers' only true protection is and should be through the extension and strength of markets.'[59] The argument is by no means new, as illustrated by the following exchange between a solicitor (who was also the chairman of a local board of health) and a member of the Select Committee on the Adulteration of Food, which was considering the need for the public control of food quality in the 1850s.[60]

2520. Does your opinion go to this extent; that supposing a man having purchased a pound of coffee, goes into another shop, asking for the same article, and gets 75 per cent of chicory, that is one of the innocent adulterations of which you speak as being the result of competition? – Certainly; and for this reason, there is no standard of the value of any article; there is nothing to represent the fact that any article shall be sold for a certain price.

2521. Is there not an understanding between the public and the seller that the seller shall give to you what you ask for? – I think not; neither do I think it beneficial that it should be so. The same machinery which fixes the price of the one article fixes the price of the other; and you cannot draw a distinction, nor show any reason why competition should not regulate the price of a mixture of coffee and chicory, just as it does the price of coffee alone or any other article.

2522. A man purchases a pound of coffee for 1s.; he goes to the next shop and purchases a pound of what purports to be coffee, but which is adulterated with 75 per cent of chicory, and he pays 1s. for it; do you think there is any injustice in that? – I believe it should be left to regulate itself . . .

It should not be thought, however, that proponents of the market see no role for public control. Even the most rigid sometimes support legislation against marketing fraud or to ensure that businesses impart information to consumers. At the same time opponents of the market economists should not be taken to believe that there is no role for competition in consumer protection.

Competition policy and consumer protection

In many jurisdictions consumer protection and competition policy are incorporated in the same legislation and administered by the same department or agency. Often this is a matter of convenience and the two could just as well have been set out in different legislation and administered separately. Where the two are combined they might well conflict, for example, if preference is given to the indirect and intangible benefits of competition over the specific protection conferred by consumer protection measures. Mainly it will be possible to handle the two compatibly, by accepting that legislative policy is 'that the interests of a consumer of goods or services will best be served when manufacturers compete vigorously without adopting restrictive practices and observe prescribed standards of conduct in their dealings with consumers.'[61]

The details of competition policy are beyond the scope of this work.[62] It need simply be noted that whereas in some countries competition law acts generally by prohibiting conduct which is thought will inhibit competition, in others it operates mainly by means of *ad hoc* inquiry and investigation to determine whether action should be taken against particular practices, agreements or take-overs. Anti-trust law in the United States reflects the first approach, the United Kingdom tends towards the other, while other countries such as Australia fall along the spectrum between the two. The main concerns of competition policy can be conveniently divided into restrictive trading agreements, in which parties accept restrictions on their freedom to compete by fixing prices, dividing the market, establishing uniform terms and conditions and so on; monopolistic and anti-competitive practices, where a business uses its market power to engage in monopolistic pricing, exclusive dealing, tie-in sales, full-line forcing and so on with the objective of excluding competitors or inhibiting entry into the market; and mergers and takeovers, which may significantly reduce competition. The United Kingdom Competition Act 1980 provides a further form of investigation, into whether public enterprises are efficient or are abusing a monopoly position. Following an adverse report an order can be made remedying the adverse effects of conduct which have been found to operate against the public interest and/or the enterprise can be required to produce a plan for that purpose.[63]

Basically, the consumer case for competition policy is that it widens choice, means prices are lower than would otherwise obtain, and makes for a stimulus to industry to remain alert to consumer requirements and in tune with changing needs. Competition policy is said to be especially necessary in the consumer goods market given factors such as its relative concentration, product differentiation and other forms of non-price competition (which make comparisons more difficult), and the absence of objective information about products. Since perfect competition is an unrealistic goal to pursue, it is said that the consumer interest is more likely to be enhanced by a policy of seeking effective competition. Policies appropriate to this have been identified as increasing and preserving competition by the traditional means of competition policy, such as the proscription of price-fixing cartels, coupled with more radical action such as the forcible breaking up of dominant firms, assisting new entrants by means of subsidies, improving the quality of competition, monitoring and regulating existing monopolies, and increasing the market power of consumers.[64]

The case for competition policy often assumes a taken-for-granted character as far as the benefits to consumers are concerned. Certainly the criteria set out in competition law might include taking into account the consumer interest, but this by no means stands alone or is necessarily paramount. There are specific instances where competition policy has led to definite benefits to consumers in the way, for example, of lower prices.[65] Indeed, in a world of less than perfect competition there is a clear distinction in economic terms between competition policies which are aimed to improving allocative efficiency and those which seek to enhance the position of consumers (e.g. improving price competition). As Sharpe notes:

There is a distinction between laws which protect or enhance 'competition' in the sense of providing or increasing money gains to *consumers*, and laws which seek to increase economic efficiency, which may provide no direct benefit to consumers at all: any gains from efficiency could be appropriated, for example, by shareholders or employees. Conversely, any attempt to increase money gains to consumers might reduce economic efficiency in that the benefits to consumers might be at the expense of misallocating resources of rival producers or some other group.[66]

Moreover, even where competition policy is aimed directly at benefiting consumers the result does not automatically follow. For example, a wider choice for consumers might be spurious because of product differentiation, which is also wasteful of resources; more competition might mean a reduction in the number of outlets and thus more difficult access for consumers; lower prices might be at the expense of quality; and other legal measures might be more effective in making business responsive to consumers. Conversely, it is often overlooked that consumer protection measures might be good for competition by correcting market failures.[67] Information deficiencies might be reduced because the law requires businesses to disclose information in relation to their products or services or to their activities. The same result might be achieved, and more effectively, by the law fixing a standard, for although this restricts choice it provides consumers with information which does not require significant processing effort. Similarly, by uncovering deceptive and misleading conduct in the market-place, consumer protection agencies might reduce the average cost to consumers of doing so compared with the costs of organizing themselves as a group and overcoming 'free-rider' problems.

The Chicago approach in outline

The strongest advocates of the market system these days are members of the Chicago school of economists and their adherents in various parts of the world. Of major importance in their outlook are at least two assumptions: that the individual is a rational maximizer of satisfaction and that the market operates as an influence on producers. Consumers, it is said, can discipline producers through the market so that the latter cannot behave in an autonomous manner. For example, if consumers are dissatisfied with the quality of a product, in the light of its price, they will inform other consumers and no longer purchase it themselves. Finding that a product is no longer patronized, a business may reduce its price, modify the design or the quality control of its manufacture, or abandon its production completely. Similarly, competition among businesses is a curb on misleading trade practices for if consumers are misled on one occasion, for example by advertising, they will learn from experience and never again enter transactions with the business. Such businesses will quickly modify their trade practices for otherwise they will lose patronage to rivals, at least those who depend heavily on repeated sales of the same products or services to the same consumers, or who find it costly to liquidate their businesses at short notice.[68] A third example of faith in the market is in the discussion of standard form contracts. Contrary to accepted belief that these are onerous for consumers, the Chicago school says that if a business offers unattractive terms to consumers, competitors will come forward with better terms. 'Thus, the purchaser who is offered a printed contract on a take-it-or-leave-it basis does have a real choice: he can refuse to sign, knowing that if better terms are possible another seller will offer them to him.'[69]

The preference for the market and the common law over state regulation derives from various arguments. The market and common law methods, it is said, bring about more efficient results than government regulation. When the market fails to allocate resources efficiently, the common law comes into play and operates in a manner comparable to a market. It relies on the actions of private self-interested individuals acting in competition with each other, and its remedies such as damages are similar to those that would be generated by market forces. At a general level the legislative process is said to exhibit a less pervasive concern with efficiency and a much greater concern with wealth distribution. Unlike the situation in the courts, where the question of relative cost is always close to the surface, legislatures take relative deservedness into consideration on a regular basis. Moreover, in legislatures coalitions of special interest groups can often secure what are inefficient programmes at the expense of unrepresented large, generalized interest groups such as consumers which, because of free-loader problems, have difficulty in influencing legislation.[70]

With reference to consumer products it is assumed that the state cannot determine the quality of products which will maximize efficiency. Even if government selects an efficient point for production, this will not necessarily coincide with the preferences of individuals. Were standards to be set for consumer products, consumers would take less care in using them with the result that they would wear out more quickly or that accidents would rise. Total costs would increase because preventing these outcomes would not be done by those having the comparative advantage. The increased costs would be paid in the main by consumers in the form of higher prices. On the other hand leaving it to the market limits information costs about what degree of product liability is economical because consumers are in a better position than government to know the exact uses they plan for products and what degree of quality is appropriate.[71] This knowledge is transmitted through the existing market system where consumers can register their preferences as regards cost and quality. Producers respond to these in terms of the prices they charge, the quality of the products they market or the policies they adopt when consumers return dissatisfied. Moreover, government regulation restricts choice and consumers are no longer able to bear the risks which they had previously indicated a willingness to shoulder. By eliminating 'mutually advantageous exchanges' economic welfare is diminished. The poor are hardest hit because they are obliged to purchase better quality but more expensive products.

Failure of the market and the common law

The analysis of the Chicago school is subject to strong qualifications. Generally speaking, it fails to take adequate account of the severe deficiencies in the operation of the market and common law system. Based on questionable premises, the conclusions are demonstrably inaccurate.[72]

At the outset, it should be noted that just because consumers choose in a particular manner in no way indicates that that is their preference – they might choose from habit or they might regret the choice once made. It cannot be assumed that 'free choice' automatically leads to consumer welfare.[73] Members of the Chicago school continue to believe that markets are competitive and offer protection to consumers despite the fact that neoclassical economists as early as the 1930s recognized oligopoly as a prevalent form of market organization. Now it may be that consumers are able to protect themselves if, say, defects in consumer products are patent, their impact is small and the products are inexpensive and purchased frequently.[74] Many consumer products, however, are complex and costly and it is unreal to think that consumers can protect themselves. The 'search' qualities of products are such that it is often impossible to ascertain them prior to purchase, and even if 'experience' qualities can be discovered it may be a long time afterwards or the consumer may be unable to use the knowledge acquired because an occasional purchase is involved.[75] The Thalidomide children and their parents would have difficulty appreciating an argument against government regulation of drug quality premised on the assumption that consumers can acquire information from repeated purchases.[76]

Then it is assumed that competition among sellers generates product information for consumers – that the seller whose product is superior has an incentive to inform consumers.[77] (There are admitted exceptions, as where a fraudulent seller diverts only a small amount of trade from any of his rivals so that none has an inclination to correct his misrepresentation; or where information about a product applies equally to all kinds – e.g. no cigarette manufacturer will profit from an advertisement that cigarettes are dangerous to health.) The assumption, however, flies in the face of current advertising practice. Modern advertising does not function in a competitive manner but, rather, in a superficial way presents only the advantages of a product and not the disadvantages of those marketed by competitors.[78] It frequently excludes or distorts information which consumers need, such as useful information about value or performance, to concentrate on image appeal. Competitors may fail to publicize damaging information about one another, partly because of sympathy and partly because of a fear of retaliation.

A similar assertion is that 'information brokers' such as department stores, doctors, newspapers and travel agents function to inform the consumer about the merits of particular products, as well as to search for superior products and to guarantee their quality. Although 'information brokers' do not exist primarily to prevent deception, they are said to have that effect. More importantly, they supposedly reduce the cost which the consumer must invest in discovering facts about products being marketed. However, the argument about 'information brokers' neglects the realities. Retailers, for example, are often as ignorant about products as are consumers, and the lack of training of their employees means that they are hardly capable of an information-giving role. Evidence mentioned in Chapter 12 shows that the most important influence over a doctor's prescription of drugs is the manufacturer's commercial traveller and not any objective information about quality.

The criticism that consumer protection works to the detriment of the poor by pricing them out of markets overlooks that they might benefit relatively more than others because they are more exposed to deceptive or unfair practices. For example, if they are isolated from shops or other facilities (geographical location, transport costs, physical or social immobility), they are more susceptible to the high-pressure tactics of some door-to-door salesmen. Similarly, if because of higher charges the poor pay more in real terms for measures such as credit the benefits to them of regulation might be greater because, say, they are more likely to default and therefore to need protection in these circumstances.[79]

Apart from deficiencies in the market, there are limits to the effectiveness of the common law in protecting consumers. A general feature of common law is that consumers must take the initiative to enforce their legal rights. The assumption is that consumers know their rights and are sufficiently motivated to press them. If they are harmed because a business infringes their rights, economic self-interest will impel them to take action, including court action if a settlement cannot be achieved.

By creating economic incentives for private individuals and firms to investigate accidents and bring them to the attention of the courts, the system enables society to dispense with the elaborate governmental apparatus that would be necessary for gathering information about the extent and causes of accidents had the parties no incentive to report and investigate them exhaustively.[80]

Of course consumers frequently fail to utilize their legal rights in this way. As has been mentioned already, consumers may not know of their rights or fail to take advantage of them.

A characteristic of certain consumer offences is that they are complex, diffused over time and unpublicized. Consumers may not recognize that they have been adversely affected by an unlawful practice and thus lack sufficient incentive to complain. In many cases where the impact of wrong-doing occurs in the future, there are no victims to complain in the present. The adverse effects of some food additives and drugs are cases in point, for their effects are not manifest until after use over a period. Where large numbers of the public are mildly affected by an activity no one may suffer sufficient deprivation to complain. A specific example is that the consumer overcharged a small amount may think it trivial, but viewed from another perspective – the illegal profits accruing to business – the effect is more serious.

Furthermore, consumers may not be cognizant of their legal rights and the remedies by means of which their grievances can be redressed. They may not connect their problems with a legal obligation on the part of businesses to provide a solution. Thus a number of surveys indicate that consumers who in their own view have cause to complain do not do so, that consumers mistakenly think that manufacturers and not retailers are liable for defective products and that few consumers know whom to contact when they strike difficulties.

Since the frequent inefficiency of consumer action cannot be denied, the tack taken by the Chicago school is twofold. First it is said that there are existing mechanisms for aggregating small consumer claims. Retailers are supposed to perform this function with respect to the claims of their customers against the manufacturers whose products are sold.[81] The store replaces the product or refunds the customer's money and, if several customers complain, pools the complaints and presents them to the manufacturer. The store obtains reimbursement for its costs in responding to the customer's complaint because it has a credible threat of legal action against the manufacturer. In practice, however, the role of retailers is more complex and depends, for one, on the retailer's size relative to manufacturers. A powerful retailer may be in a strong position to claim against a manufacturer if it supplies defective products. On the other hand many retailers lack bargaining power with their suppliers and, because they bear the burden of any costs themselves, tend to be unsympathetic to consumers.

A second argument is that even if there are failures in the market and the common law system, public regulation need not follow inevitably because there is the possibility of improving these self-regulating mechanisms.

Defrauded consumers could be permitted to obtain their legal fees, plus a penalty as an additional incentive to sue, in any successful action against the seller. Consumer class actions, which permit a number of insignificant individual claims to be aggregated into a single large claim, could be encouraged.[82]

Improvements such as class actions are discussed at length in subsequent chapters. Even if they are introduced, there are still the many handicaps of the common law system: people must know their rights and act; a claim must be established in accordance with certain standards of evidence (an example is the burden of establishing negligence against a manufacturer of consumer products); and the courts are of limited competence to gather information to deal with technical issues and to enforce judgments requiring supervision.

Perhaps the fundamental failing of the Chicago approach is that it underplays the fact that the provision or reform of a market or a common law mechanism involves costs.[83] Yet once this is recognized it may be that empirically government regulation is less expensive and more likely to produce the correct outcome than modifying a market or common law mechanism. It is a question of comparing how the two would work out in the particular circumstances. The important point is that the optimal result is not the same as if transactions were costless. As Calabresi puts it, the actual optimum is not necessarily 'the one an unaided market would reach. Further, market improvements may well be prohibitive at a stage where laws and their enforcement are still a relatively cheap way of getting near the goal.'[84] Moreover, government action may be justified because it alone will achieve goals other than efficient resource allocation, such as wealth distribution or a change in the power structure, which are desirable for separate, non-economic reasons.

Another Chicago contention is that government regulation has failed: regulatory bodies have become lethargic, inefficient and more concerned with the interests they are designed to regulate than with the consumer interest. I have already said that the allegations contain an element of truth. On the other hand it is easy to paint too black a picture, and certainly these factors are no argument for the abolition or even for a substantial reduction of such agencies. Rather they indicate the need for reform.

One of the strong arguments behind government intervention is to protect values other than the maximization of output and efficient resource allocation. Economic analysis of the Chicago mould neglects values of justice and fairness, which are highly relevant to ordinary behaviour. Once government intervention is eschewed in favour of the market, particular distributions of power and wealth are obviously being favoured. The market is not unbiased in its effects; in treating unequals equally – by putting businesses on the same footing as consumers – it allows the stronger to dominate the weaker.[85] The reality of standard form contracts is not of sellers competing to offer favourable terms to consumers but of consumers being forced to accept contracts with disadvantageous terms, those terms being

contained in the main in all contracts of a particular nature.[86]
Further, the legal system is not neutral. Judges make law, and their
decisions are based on certain values so that in a sense they are
comparable to legislators. The existing legal system also sanctions a
situation where detriments can be imposed on certain groups like
consumers without their having an efficient means of redress.[87]
Businesses can continue to produce defective products, for example,
secure in the knowledge that few consumers will pursue the matter. It
cannot be said, then, that in using an economic model the sole
concern is efficiency and that other values, such as wealth distribution, are being ignored.

PART I
Business self-regulation

2
Business self-regulation

Business self-regulation has been advanced as a technique which, when supplemented by legal provisions, can make a major contribution to consumer protection. In recent years it has blossomed as individual firms and trade associations have announced moves to assist consumers. One result is that some businesses voluntarily label their products beyond legal requirements to provide consumers with information. Businesses have also launched codes of ethics and social practice; those with the imprimatur of the Office of Fair Trading are examined in the next section. Particularly important codes are the ones covering advertising; these are the subject of the second section of this chapter, where their operation is compared with the regulation of advertising in other countries by legal mechanisms. The final section of the chapter offers a general critique of business self-regulation.

CODES OF PRACTICE

Codes of ethics and social responsibility have sprouted in recent years as the business community has sought to demonstrate its sense of social responsibility.[1] There are a number of international codes of practice governing aspects of marketing such as market research, sales promotion and advertising.[2] At the national level codes of practice can be traced back to the attempts of the guilds to regulate the standards of their members, and even in the days of unbridled capitalism there were always individual capitalists who proclaimed the idea that there were acceptable standards which businesses should meet. The notion that companies are 'good corporate citizens' is of course very prominent in the current mythology of capitalism, although there are still those who look to the days of *laissez-faire* quite unrepentantly. Thus Milton Friedman takes the extreme view that companies have the sole responsibility to generate as much profit for their owners as possible, while conforming to the basic rules of society.

Few trends could so thoroughly undermine the very foundation of our free society as the acceptance by corporate officials of a social responsibility other than to make as much money for their shareholders as possible. This is a fundamentally subversive doctrine.[3]

The more general view is that businesses should not simply pursue profit but should have a number of objectives of which that is only one. One survey of chief executives found that 90 per cent thought that companies had obligations beyond simple profit-making, although in practice these manifested themselves in different ways – from vague expressions of social responsibility through to a concern to improve industrial relations, to quite specific acts like the loan of manpower for social projects, donations to charity or the financial sponsorship of community projects.[4] Codes of practice are thus only one way in which the notion of the company as a 'good corporate citizen' takes shape, and it is of some interest that a survey in 1976 of 130 companies found that sixty thought that there was no need for a code of practice. The same survey revealed that of the codes of practice which were examined, the main areas of responsibility were employees (30), consumers (26), the environment (19), the local community and society (18) and shareholders (16).[5]

The focus of this section is on the codes of practice approved by the Office of Fair Trading.[6] Section 124(3) of the Fair Trading Act 1973 imposes a duty on the Director General of Fair Trading to encourage trade associations to prepare codes of practice for guidance in safeguarding and promoting the interests of consumers. Some twenty codes of practice have been approved by the Office of Fair Trading since 1974, covering matters such as cars, domestic appliances, footwear, dry cleaning, funerals, mail order, photography and travel. A summary of some of these codes is contained in Table 2.1.

The Office of Fair Trading is particularly concerned to encourage suitable codes of practice, since the process of issuing statutory orders under Part II of the Fair Trading Act 1973, to control trade practices

Table 2.1   Codes approved by the Office of Fair Trading

Code	Trade association	Main provisions
Principles for Domestic Electrical Appliance Servicing (AMDEA Code)	Association of Manufacturers of Domestic Electrical Appliances	service within 3 working days at reasonable cost; adequate stocks of spares; estimates to be given; guarantees for repairs; internal complaints procedure; conciliation & arbitration scheme
Codes of Conduct (Tour Operators; Retail Agents) (Updated 1979 and 1980 resp.)	Association of British Travel Agents	clear and comprehensive brochures (e.g. on surcharges); exclusion clauses banned; comparable alternative arrangements or full refund if cancellation, alteration or overbooking by operators, etc.; cancellation fees for clients to be stated in booking conditions; agents to provide impartial and adequate information & to ensure tours compatible with requirements; arbitration scheme
Code of Practice for Motor Industry (revised 1981)	Motor Agents Association; Society of Motor Manufacturers and Traders; Scottish Motor Trade Association	new cars: dealers who carry out manufacturers' pre-delivery inspection to give copy of check list to customer; terms and conditions in order forms to be fair, reasonable, clear (esp. cancellation and total price); manufacturer's guarantee transferable and rectification by any franchised dealer; used cars: defects to be revealed on approved checklist; checklist to be prominently displayed and given to customer; reasonable

		steps to verify mileage and unless satisfied as to accuracy, customer to be informed that cannot be verified; repairs: spares to be reasonably available by manufacturer; estimate, or written quotation if possible; replaced parts to be generally available; repairs to be guaranteed; complaints: conciliation and arbitration.
Code of Practice for Vehicle Body Repair (VBRA Code)	Vehicle Builders & Repairers Association	fair prices; internal complaints procedure; repairs as above but guarantee for parts only (6 months/6000 miles); conciliation and arbitration scheme
Code of Practice for Shoe Repairs	National Association of Shoe Repair Factories, St Crispin's Boot Trades Association	stocks to meet demand; 'worth', etc. claims banned; prices to be clearly displayed; estimated time of collection; exclusion clauses banned; refund if non-delivery in 7 days; independent test report scheme
Footwear Code	Footwear Distributors Federation	staff to be informed/trained; shops with children's shoes to have facilities; prices, sizes, composition to be clear; refund if non-delivery in 7 days; Independant Footwear Testing Centre established
Code of Practice for Domestic Laundry & Cleaning Services (ABLC Code)	Association of British Launderers and Cleaners Ltd	standard prices to be clearly displayed; exclusion clauses banned; redress for articles lost/damaged and for bad workmanship; staff training; internal complaints procedure; conciliation and independent test report scheme

RETRA Code of Practice	Radio, Electrical & Television Retailers' Association	'worth', etc. claims banned; cash price, discount offers, additional costs for delivery, etc. to be clearly stated; 12 months parts and labour guarantee for new goods; loan item if repairs under guarantee take longer than 15 days; other repair guaranteed 3 months; service calls; complaints procedure; conciliation and conciliation panel
Direct Sales Code of Practice	Direct Sales & Service Association	public and product liability to be adequately covered and hostesses of selling parties to be indemnified against valid claims; direct sellers identify themselves immediately; customers to be informed of rights of cancellation; guarantees; no payment in full when order is placed; 14 days cancellation period; complaints procedure
Voluntary Code of Practice for Furniture	Branded Furniture Society; British Furniture Manufacturers Federated Assoc.; National Assoc. of Retail Furnishers; National Bedding Federation; Scottish House Furnishers Assoc.	full information re goods, prices and credit facilities; realistic delivery dates given and adhered to (or deposit refunded); discounts to be based on fair comparisons of prices; retailers must advise consumers where the price to be charged will be that at time of delivery; adequate information on construction, care, dimensions, price (e.g. by label); quotes for repairs; conciliation and arbitration
Code of Practice for Postal Services	Post Office	limited compensation for loss or damage in post; no consequential losses but

		sympathetic consideration for reasonable cost of inquiries about lost or damaged postal packets; complaints procedure
Code of Ethical Practice	Glass and Glazing Federation	restrictions on misleading sales promotions and advertising; confidential information not to be disclosed; members to ensure that customers are able to meet financial commitments; when price increased, customer to be able to cancel; deposit indemnity found where work cannot be carried out; quotations in writing; installation times to be specified; complaints: conciliation and arbitration

which are against the economic interests of consumers, is moribund. In addition, the Office of Fair Trading believes that businesses are more resistant to legal controls to improve trading standards than to voluntary efforts. A statutory power possessed by the Director General proves useful in ensuring that codes of practice suit the interests of consumers. The Restrictive Trade Practices Act 1976 equates the recommendations of trade associations, such as codes of practice, with agreements which might be registerable with the Director General of Fair Trading.[7] The Director General can refer restrictive agreements to the Restrictive Practices Court, which determines whether they are against the public interest and therefore void.[8] However, he may be relieved of his duty to do so if the restrictions are not of such significance as to call for investigation by the Court.[9] Where restrictions take the form of requirements or recommendations to use a standard form contract the Director General insists that the terms are fair to both parties, are not likely to mislead those who will use them, and do not unnecessarily exclude variation to meet special circumstances and requirements. Since the Unfair Contract Terms Act 1977 he has also insisted on the removal of terms that are void under that Act and has asked associations to justify terms that are subject to the reasonableness test under the Act.

In some respects the codes of practice approved by the Office of Fair Trading are in advance of the law, in that they cover trade practices for which legal measures might have been suggested but have not yet been adopted. Some codes ban exclusion clauses and allow cancellation when this is not mandatory. Written document-ation (e.g. cost estimates) is required in other cases. A number of codes oblige businesses to display prices clearly and prominently when this is not a legal obligation. It cannot be said, however, that the codes of practice embrace all possible reforms. Yet even with the latter there have been failings; for example, under the Code of Practice for the Motor Industry, the rather uncertain rules are left unchanged as to whether consumers can obtain a loan car or a contribution to hiring charges when their new car is off the road for repair under warranty. In recognition of this several codes have been redrafted to overcome deficiencies. Precisely because the codes of practice are in some respects in advance of the law, it is anticipated that they will channel its development. The Office of Fair Trading hopes that, in considering whether a business has fulfilled a consumer contract, the courts will refer to the relevant code of practice as containing the customary terms and the usage of a trade.[10]

Codes of practice are useful in areas which are ill-suited to statutory control. The Office of Fair Trading thought that codes are especially adept in improving the standard of services, which it said cannot easily be achieved by legislation.[11] Examples of code provisions which are probably not the stuff of legislation and perhaps should not give rise to legal liability are the undertakings to deal expeditiously with complaints, those to ensure that people handling complaints are adequately trained and those to offer delivery of an item or a service within a definite number of days. Codes of practice also provide a flexibility which is sometimes difficult to incorporate in legislation. One example is the provision in the Tour Operators' Code of Conduct which enables consumers generally to have an alternative holiday or a refund if a tour operator has to cancel or alter the holiday originally booked or if the facilities to be used are over-booked. Another example is the Code of Practice for Funeral Directors, where members undertake not to conduct themselves in a manner likely to prejudice their professional status or reputation, in particular, 'When two Funeral Directors are called at the same time to attend the same

Table 2.2   Nature of Consumer Complaints, 1980–81

	No. of complaints 1980–81	Complaints per £m spent 1980–81
Goods		
Food and drink	36,384*	1.03
Footwear	24,934	14.01
Clothing and textiles	53,729	5.60
Furniture and floor covering	58,013	16.86
Household appliances	70,251	27.46
Toilet requisites, soaps, detergents, etc.	1,802	1.20
Toys, games, sports goods, etc.	8,873	10.50
Solid and liquid fuels	6,818	1.06
Motor vehicles and accessories	60,715	9.38
Other consumer goods	80,040	—
Non-consumer goods	3,153	—
Land, including houses	1,491	—
Services		
Home repairs and improvements	14,363	3.51
Repairs and servicing to domestic electrical appliances (excluding radio and TV)	4,475	21.00
Repairs and servicing to motor vehicles	10,898	8.31
Other repairs and servicing	12,157	28.91
Cleaning	7,475	29.09
Public utilities and transport	13,727	0.74
Consumer credit	7,159	—
Entertainment and accommodation	11,059*	1.32
Holidays	7,670	2.32
Professional services	12,935	2.16
General services, etc.	18,187	—

* Includes complaints recorded by Environmental Health Officers as follows:

Food and drink	16,001
Entertainment and accommodation	6,574

case both should show a willingness to withdraw leaving the choice with the family.' It is difficult to envisage these provisions in legislation for the courts are not used to making orders of specific performance of this nature. Codes may also be useful where abuse is confined to one area of the market place and it is not worthwhile to bring to bear the whole legislative machinery to deal with the problem.

Trade associations have been well disposed to codes approved by the Office of Fair Trading. Codes attract favourable publicity for an industry because of the impression that it is introducing voluntary consumer protection measures. It is no surprise that codes approved by the Office of Fair Trading are concentrated in fields where there have been high levels of consumer dissatisfaction. Table 2.2 is reproduced from the Office of Fair Trading Annual Report and shows the nature of consumer complaints to consumer protection (trading standards) departments and other bodies like citizens advice bureaux.

Codes of practice approved by the Office of Fair Trading are fairly comprehensive in the coverage of particular trades, although it is possible that non-adherents may be the worst offenders when it comes to complying with acceptable standards. Below are some estimates of coverage announced publicly.

ABTA Code: 90 per cent of all package holiday business.
Motor Industry Code: 85 per cent garage trade.
Footwear Code: 60 per cent of business in shoe retailing trade.
ABLC Code: 80 per cent of professional launderers and dry cleaners.
Mail Order Publishers' Authority Code: approx. 75 per cent of market.

The hope is that once the codes are publicized, non-members will find it commercially advantageous to join. Some of the sponsoring trade associations have engaged in recruitment drives since launching their codes of practice. Monitoring has found that in some cases the standards of non-members had also improved after introduction of the relevant code. This might indicate that the adoption of a code of practice by the greater proportion of a trade actually induces higher standards throughout the trade as a whole. In particular cases other factors might be involved, for example economic forces such as the need to improve trading practices in order to meet weaker consumer demand. The fact remains, however, that the codes can never guarantee to apply across the board like the law.]

Most of the codes establish conciliation and arbitration procedures, funded mainly by the sponsoring trade associations, to assist
in the resolution of any consumer complaints against member
organizations. Initially a trade association will use its good offices to
try to settle a complaint informally if the consumer has already taken
up the matter with the business involved. Under the codes, adherents
undertake to expedite the settlement of genuine complaints. The aim
is to reach a settlement – without any close attention to the
consumer's entitlement at law. This approach cuts both ways: on the
one hand the consumer may be disadvantaged by a compromise
solution, but on the other hand conciliation can deal with matters like
dilatoriness, erroneous billing and poor service, which may not
amount to legal wrongs.

If conciliation fails consumers can ask that a matter be referred to
arbitration, which is provided for in almost all the codes of practice
approved by the Office of Fair Trading as a method of resolving the
more intractable complaints.[12] Arbitration is conducted under the
provisions of the Arbitration Act 1979 by an independent arbitrator, a
member of the Chartered Institute of Arbitrators. Arbitrators may be
assisted by expert assessors, who are members of the sponsoring trade
association, and they may obtain an independent report if necessary.
Consumers must pay a fee but this is usually the limit of their liability
and the fee is refundable at the discretion of the arbitrator. The trade
association bears the remaining cost of any arbitration. To reduce
costs, in particular to consumers who lose, arbitration is almost
invariably conducted on documents submitted by the parties, in
which they present points of claim and defence, although the
arbitrator can call on them to appear in person in exceptional
circumstances. Arbitrators can award sums of money or order a
business to take specific action (e.g. to replace goods).

Arbitration under the codes of conduct provides a quick and
relatively inexpensive means of resolving consumer complaints and
also relieves the state of the burden of funding tribunals or judicial
machinery. It is especially valuable because of defects in the small
claims procedure in the county court. It is estimated that during the
six years to December 1981 some 1750 cases were settled by
arbitration under codes of practice, the great majority being concerned with car or package holiday disputes. At the same time
arbitration under the codes has a number of limitations. Criticism has

been voiced on matters such as delays and the absence of reasons by arbitrators. Arbitration under the codes loses credibility, it is said, because it is conducted in private, in the absence of complainants, under the auspices of trade associations and without close supervision by a government agency.[13] In some cases arbitration is limited in scope: thus some codes exclude arbitration for personal injury claims, although minor claims of this nature might usefully be dealt with by this type of procedure. There is an absence of any appellate structure, for the basis on which consumers can appeal a matter to the courts is limited.[14]

Some codes recognize the possibility of trade associations imposing 'fines' on their members if they fail to observe the obligations.[15] This is a relatively simple means of disciplining members and inducing them to pay close attention to proper practices. The alternative procedure is to issue a reprimand, which lacks the bite of a fine. The ultimate sanction behind the codes is that sponsoring trade associations can expel members who persistently breach the terms. Expulsion may be a serious threat with a prestigious trade association, or one which confers important benefits on members. Trade associations hope that adherence to a code of practice will eventually become an important benefit to businesses as consumers become familiar with its existence and choose to patronize businesses which indicate adherence to its terms, for example by displaying an appropriate symbol.

These sanctions have drawbacks in that few trade associations seem prepared to invoke them. They adopt a relatively lenient attitude to transgressions, although the Office of Fair Trading requires them to undertake systematic monitoring of members' trade practices which is necessary if there is to be a real threat. Moreover, once a trade association takes a hard line and expels a member, its sanctions are expended and the business can continue operating in defiance of the code unless membership is a condition of operating. The only consolation to consumers is that a trade association may undertake to pay redress in those circumstances where a business has failed to pay compensation as required when it was a member. One glimmer of hope is that the Office of Fair Trading might use its powers under Part III of the Fair Trading Act 1973. In one case the assurance a business gave to the Restrictive Practices Court under that Part included a clause in which it undertook to use reasonable precautions and due diligence to comply with the relevant code of practice in the trade.[16] Persistent breach of a code could be made an explicit basis for the Director General to seek a cease and desist order.

Without independent monitoring it is difficult to say whether the codes of practice are being implemented. Trade associations work from the complaints they receive and conclude that things are quite satisfactory. The Consumers' Association research is of value because it involves independent monitoring of complaints, but it has the drawback that the standards expected by the Consumers' Association, and the experiences of its members, may not be representative of consumers as a whole. The Office of Fair Trading has a monitoring programme involving the codes. Complaints received by citizens advice bureaux and consumer protection departments are analysed and related to adherence to a code; independent research has been commissioned of consumers' experience; and complaints to trade associations are examined.

Monitoring of the codes by the Office of Fair Trading has found that in general the majority of businesses are adhering to them and have, on average, higher standards than non-members.[17] Perhaps more significantly, where subsequent monitoring has occurred, standards have with exceptions improved – members seem to have taken steps to support the provisions of the codes and the complaints mechanisms they provide. Consequently, a number of objectionable trading practices in use when the codes came into force have now been virtually abandoned. Particular obligations in particular codes have higher rates of non-compliance than others – some over 50 per cent, and often those which are of considerable benefit to consumers. Compliance with a few codes has proved quite disappointing, especially when set against the standards obtained by those covered by parallel codes and by non-members. As a result of its monitoring the Office of Fair Trading has evolved specific recommendations for improvements in existing codes or in trading practices. In some cases unsatisfactory trading practices really point beyond a code, for example, to the poor quality of products manufactured.

ADVERTISING

The nature of advertising

Rather than being blatantly misleading, modern advertising claims are more likely to verge on the half-truth, the ambiguous or the exaggerated. Claims which are literally true can, of course, be misleading because they omit factors which would influence consumers' attitudes. A good illustration is the advertisement for 'Lite Diet' bread, which an advertiser claimed would help weight control since it contained fewer calories per slice. The only reason this was true was because it was sliced thinner than other breads.[18] Ambiguity is another way that advertisements can mislead consumers, for although one interpretation may render an advertisement literally true, another interpretation will lead to a completely different impression.[19] Advertisements which give undue emphasis to certain information can also be misleading. They may highlight some features at the expense of others, give certain information in an unclear way, or present irrelevant information which has no real connection with the product, but inclusion of which gives a false impression. Exaggeration can sometimes make a claim appear true when it is not. A survey by the Bureau Européen Des Unions de Consommateurs of advertisements in Britain in 1974 considered exaggeration - even omitting 'best' or 'finest' claims – to be the largest category of misleading advertisements.[20] Exaggeration is often defended because consumers can see through it, but if it creates no impression on consumers it is difficult to see why it is used.

Consumers regard much modern advertising as misleading. In a nationwide survey of 1067 people in 1976, 28 per cent said that they were often misled by advertising and 67 per cent thought that advertising often misleads.[21] However, few (6 per cent) consumers spontaneously mentioned advertising as a problem (as opposed to government, trade unions, family life, etc.); fewer (3 per cent) had strong opinions about it; and still fewer (2 per cent) thought it needed fundamental change. Moreover, 73 per cent of the sample said they approved it. The Advertising Association concluded from the high approval rate that there was little cause for concern and that the statements about the misleading character of advertisements should be discounted because they probably expressed consumers' opinions about the effects of advertising on others and not on themselves. Another interpretation of the figures is that most consumers approve advertising in the abstract as a means of conveying information about products and services, but that they disapprove current advertising because it misleads. A survey based on interviews with nearly 9500

consumers throughout the EEC confirms that although many
consumers believe that advertising provides useful information, they
are still highly sceptical of it (see Table 2.3).[22]

Table 2.3   Opinions on Advertising in Europe

	Agree entirely	Agree on the whole	Disagree on the whole	Disagree entirely	Don't know/ no reply	Total
Advertising provides consumers with useful information	10%	40%	29%	17%	4%	100%
Advertising often makes consumers buy goods which they do not really need	38%	39%	14%	6%	3%	100%
Advertising often misleads consumers as to the quality of the products	38%	38%	15%	3%	6%	100%

The social and economic impact of advertising is largely untouched
by present-day voluntary or legal controls. Criticism is voiced of the
persuasive powers of advertising and critics believe that consumers
are brainwashed into purchasing what they do not really want. It is
also said that advertising creates illusions far removed from reality
which render people less able to adjust to real life. Another argument
that the Pilkington Committee found persuasive is that advertising is
exploitive because it plays on human weaknesses – hope, anxiety,
insecurity and aspiration.[23] A constant criticism has been that
advertising generates unacceptable values. Religious groups have
always objected to certain advertising as offensive in its use of sexual
images. In recent years there have been objections to the portrayal of
women, for example as housewives, because this causes undesirable
attitudes of sexism. Some members of the Annan Committee took
exception to the trivializing effects of advertising and to the way it
lowered the quality of the media, especially of television.[24] There is
also the charge that advertising fosters materialism. Other social

effects of advertising include an undue dependence on advertising revenue by the mass media and the possibility that this can expose it to undesirable pressure.

It is one thing to conclude that there should be controls on matters like excessive repetition, exaggeration, preying on consumers' susceptibility, and illusions. The difficult problem is to frame satisfactory controls in the absence of a wide public consensus. Certainly existing controls could be strengthened; we return to this below. Certain advertising could be banned completely, for example, for products like cigarettes and alcohol or to certain audiences such as children.

From the viewpoint of the present discussion, the most important economic aspect of advertising is whether it fosters market power by raising marketing costs and creating barriers to new entrants. Statistical studies over a number of industries disagree on the degree of association between advertising intensity and market concentration.[25] How far there is an association depends on the product and industry involved. For example, there is much less advertising for industrial goods than for certain consumer goods, irrespective of the market structure, because of the smaller number and greater knowledge of buyers. Other factors besides advertising, such as economies of scale, play an important role in market power. Advertising may create entry barriers but new entrants may actually use it to challenge market dominance. Even if advertising is a substantial barrier to small firms and new entrants, there still may be substantial competition within an industry. Despite these qualifications, it is clear that particular industries with a high degree of market power are characterized by large amounts of advertising, higher profit rates than normal and product stagnation.[26]

Certainly there is a case for a provision in the Fair Trading Act 1973 to limit advertising where it has the requisite anti-competitive effect. For some years the Labour Party advocated that 50 per cent of advertising expenditure be disallowed as a tax deduction. There are difficulties with such a measure which might push expenditure into other forms of promotion and might penalize the small firm or new entrant.[27] Another idea is to subsidize independent sources of information for consumers which would challenge the claims of advertisers and encourage a change in the character of advertising.

Legal controls

Present controls on advertising, both legal and voluntary, are primarily concerned with ensuring the truthfulness of the claims made. Untruthful advertising can lead consumers to misallocate resources and to lose confidence in the business community. Provisions such as the Trade Descriptions Act 1968 prohibit certain types of false and misleading advertisements about products and services. Advertisements have given rise to successful prosecutions under the Trade Descriptions Act 1968, but these have involved clear falsities about the quality of goods, their price or the existence of accommodation and facilities.[28] Legislation elsewhere, such as South Australia's Unfair Advertising Act 1970–1972, goes somewhat further and prohibits advertisements for products, services, land and credit which are inaccurate or untrue in a material particular, or likely to deceive or mislead in a material way. Provisions such as the Trade Descriptions Act 1968 and the Unfair Advertising Act 1970–1972 have little application to the great bulk of advertisements, for few are misleading to the degree necessary for a criminal prosecution.

Likewise, it is rare that consumers will have a civil claim in misrepresentation or deceit against the advertiser of something they have purchased: few advertisements are blatantly misleading and in civil law there is no duty of disclosure unless silence distorts a positive representation. An exception where a civil claim succeeded was *Smith* v. *Land and House Property Corporation*,[29] in which the defendant vendor had advertised property for sale saying that it had a 'very desirable tenant' when it knew that the tenant had been a bad payer. Another example is *Moorhouse* v. *Woolfe*,[30] where loans were advertised as being available 'on easy terms', and the interest rate for the particular consumer was about 125 per cent with security! The main reason that the courts do not give consumers a remedy in private law for advertising claims is that they do not regard most of them as being binding in law. *Esso Petroleum Ltd* v. *Commissioners of Customs and Excise*[31] should not be seen as heralding a change of attitude because the decision turned on the very definite nature of the advertising claim, which was quite unlike most claims to which critics of advertising take objection. There Esso offered a World Cup coin with every four gallons of petrol bought. A majority in the House of Lords held that there was an intention to create legal relations by the statement, which gave rise to a contract. The minority, however, thought that the statement was not intended to give rise to contractual relations because the offer was so trivial.

Advertising controls must be able to cope with instances of half-truth, ambiguity, undue emphasis and exaggeration as well as blatant dishonesty. They must be capable of examining the total impression created by an advertisement, not just the words, and should be able to require substantiation by advertisers of claims made and testimonials used. The legal measures mentioned above fail in these aims.[32]

Control of advertising in Britain is mainly through self-regulation. Other countries have varying mixes of self-regulation and legislation, with an emphasis on the latter. Britain may have to move in this direction, since the EEC favours legal control in its draft directive on misleading and unfair advertising (July 1979).[33] Misleading advertising is defined in the draft as false advertising or advertising which 'having regard to its total effect, including its presentation misleads or is likely to mislead persons addressed or reached thereby' unless it could not reasonably be foreseen that these persons would be reached. Unfair advertising includes advertising which abuses or unjustifiably arouses sentiments of fear, promotes discrimination on grounds of sex, race or religion or abuses the trust, credulity or lack of experience of a consumer, or influences or is likely to influence a consumer or the public in general in any other improper manner (art. 2). In deciding whether an advertisement is misleading or unfair, particular regard must be paid to representations concerning (i) the characteristics of the goods or services; (ii) the conditions of supply of goods or services; and (iii) the nature, attributes and rights of the advertiser (art. 3(1)). Moreover, advertising shall be regarded as misleading when it is not readily recognizable as an advertisement or when it omits material information and, by reason of that omission, gives a false impression or arouses reasonable expectations which the advertised goods or services cannot satisfy (art. 3(2)). Article 7 provides that where an advertiser makes a factual claim, the burden of proof that the claim is correct lies with it in civil and administrative proceedings.

Under the EEC draft directive member states are obliged to adopt adequate and effective laws against misleading and unfair advertising. Such laws are to provide persons affected by such advertising, as well as associations with a legitimate interest in the matter, with quick, effective and inexpensive facilities for either initiating appropriate legal proceedings or bringing the matter before an administrative authority with adequate powers. The courts or the administrative authority must have an injunctive power and a power to require corrective advertising (art. 5). The idea of a special administrative authority with these powers draws on the model provided by the Federal Trade Commission in the United States and the Market Court in Sweden.[34]

The advertising codes of practice

The self-regulatory system in Britain, for advertisements other
than those on television or radio, began in the early 1960s when the
Advertising Association drew up a Code of Advertising Practice and
constituted a Code of Advertising Practice (CAP) Committee and a
small secretariat to enforce it.[35] The action was taken under the threat
of statutory control as a result of the work of the Molony Committee.
The original code was clarified by a series of guidance notes but these
are now incorporated in the Code itself. To give self-regulation a
veneer of independence the Advertising Association also established
an Advertising Standards Authority (ASA), a company limited by
guarantee, to supervise the Code and its enforcement.

ASA's responsibilities in the present day are to investigate
complaints about advertisements, publish case reports giving the
results of its investigations and conduct a programme of monitoring
to check compliance with the Code. Its chairman is an individual
from outside the industry and two-thirds of its members must have no
connection with advertising. The advertising members are supposed
to sit as individuals and not as representatives of any sectional
interest. Coordinating the executive actions of the system is the CAP
Committee, which works under the general supervision of ASA. The
Committee consists of persons nominated by the various trade and
professional associations supporting the Code and is responsible for
ensuring that the Code is up-to-date and that industry is aware of and
abides by its provisions. The CAP Committee is solely responsible for
complaints by one advertiser against another – a point which should
be underlined because it has been mentioned how self-regulation can
be used to stifle competition. A copy panel gives pre-publication
guidance on copy and advises on post-publication problems. The
Code relies on adverse publicity as its main sanction, for ASA
publishes details of complaints – these are often reported in the press –
including whether they have been upheld and the names of the
advertisers involved. The ultimate sanction is that the media
adherents to the Code have undertaken not to publish any advertisements found to be in breach of the Code and not to accept
advertisements from agencies which defy the authority of ASA.

Following criticism in 1974 by the government and the Office of
Fair Trading of weaknesses in the self-regulatory system, several
changes were made. The size of the CAP–ASA secretariat was

increased; an advertising campaign was undertaken to familiarize consumers with the existence of the Code; independent ASA members now sit on CAP committees; ASA began publishing the names of advertisers against whom complaints were made (although for the first eleven years it refused on the grounds that it would undermine confidence); and to help emphasize the independence of ASA, it is no longer financed by the Advertising Association, but by a surcharge on display advertisements.

In an introduction the Code sets out its general principles. All advertisements should be 'legal, decent, honest and truthful'; be prepared 'with a sense of responsibility to the consumer and to society'; and 'conform to the principles of fair competition as generally accepted in business'.

Regarding interpretation, the Code says that it is to be applied in the spirit as well as in the letter, and that in assessing an advertisement's conformity to the terms of this Code, the primary test applied is that of its probable impact, as a whole, upon those who are likely to see or hear it. Under the heading 'General Principles', certain terms are spelt out, such as 'decency' – the standard is what in the light of generally prevailing standards of decency and propriety causes grave or widespread offence; 'honesty' – advertisements should not abuse the trust of consumers or exploit their lack of expertise; and 'fear' – advertisements should not without justifiable reason play on fear. The Code requires truthful presentation and all descriptions, claims and comparisons which relate to matters of objectively ascertainable fact should be capable of substantiation. Advertisers must hold such substantiation for immediate production to the CAP Committee or ASA. The paragraph on claims is quite wide:

> Advertisements should not contain any statement or visual presentation which, directly or by implication, omission, ambiguity, or exaggerated claim, is likely to mislead the consumer about the product advertised, the advertiser, or about any other product or advertiser.

Value judgements are permitted, even though they will fail to command universal acceptance, provided that there is no likelihood that consumers will be misled. Testimonials are allowed if they are genuine and related to the personal experience of the person giving them. Advertisements should be clearly distinguishable as such. In addition to such general sections, the Code makes provision for particular products, services and marketing practices.

The proponents of the Code claim that self-regulation has many advantages over legal control. Legal controls are said not to be adapted to identify advertisements which do not live up to the best professional standards. There is no absolute truth in many areas of advertising, and it is thus said there is no yardstick by which cases can be compared. The Code is said to maintain standards in areas like good manners and taste which defy legal definition. In the view of its supporters the Code can be applied speedily and flexibly and is enforced in spirit as well as in the letter. Finally the Code can foreshadow developments in the law, as with bargain offers.

The majority of complaints to ASA are not pursued because inadequate details are received; because there is no case to investigate; or because they are judged to be outside the scope of the Code. Complaints on subjective matters like decency account for a small percentage of those dealt with. Mail-order complaints, relating usually to service rather than copy claims, account for a substantial percentage of the total. ASA has expressed particular concern that a significant number of complaints upheld have resulted in claims not being satisfactorily substantiated on request. This is especially significant because of strong criticism of the substantiation provision, that it does not require that the substantiation be independent or made public.

There are a number of points to make about the Code's operation. First, most investigations arise from complaints by individual consumers or by other bodies. By themselves complaints are an inadequate way of detecting breaches of the Code. Organizations will only raise a matter when an advertisement touches on their area of interest and individual consumers are unlikely to complain to a great extent, proportionate to the number of breaches, because they do not know about the Code or its provisions or because they are not sufficiently affected to go to the trouble. ASA has now introduced a monitoring programme supposed to overcome these problems.

Secondly – and this is a related point – the number of breaches of the Code dealt with annually was relatively small in the early years. Independent surveys of advertisements by consumer groups before the reforms in 1974 detected as many breaches of the Code over a relatively short period as ASA handled in a year. After publicity campaigns for the Code there has been a substantial increase in complaints, which was particularly ironical because ASA had always trumpeted the smallness of their number as evidence that the self-regulatory system was working satisfactorily. ASA was quick to emphasize – and it was certainly true – that the increase was because more consumers were aware of the Code's operation.

Thirdly, the Code operates *ex post facto*, and an advertisement in breach can continue until ASA issues a ruling. While it may be impossible to operate a pre-vetting system for the millions of advertisements published annually, this is no reason for not requiring it for particular types of advertisements: those directed at vulnerable sections of the population, those where abuse is known to occur, those for products which are socially dangerous and those which play on fears of social and physical inadequacy. There is no provision for advertisers to compensate those who have suffered loss as a result of a contravention of the Code.

The fourth point to note is that in recent years over 50 per cent of complaints actually investigated have been substantiated. Breaches of the Code have been found not to be confined to those marginal or provincial journals which did not adhere to the Code. Misleading advertisements included some by leading manufacturers and re-tailers, inserted on their behalf by some of the leading advertising agencies. Even so, doubts have been raised in the past about how ASA has disposed of particular matters.[36] It has been said that ASA tended to throw the onus on consumers to substantiate their complaints rather than allowing them to raise a prima facie case which the advertiser must refute. Another criticism was that ASA regarded a matter as resolved if a business ceased to use a particular advertisement, although this practice deprived a case of any precedent value and allowed similar advertisements to be used in future. In addition, blame has been attached to the spirit in which the Code was enforced, which was thought to involve a wholesale and uncritical acceptance of commercial values. ASA has taken steps designed to overcome some of these criticisms.

Finally, there has been concern at the attitude of ASA to advertisements in breach of the law. ASA's general view is that it neither possesses nor seeks the sanctions available in the courts and that the Code is designed to complement and not to usurp legal controls. When the Price Marking (Bargain Offers) Order 1979[37] was introduced, the provision regarding price comparisons and worth and value claims in the Code was suspended on the basis that this permitted truthful price and value claims which had been made unlawful. Where there appeared to be a breach of the law it advised consumers complaining to it to approach their local consumer protection departments. The Director General of Fair Trading concluded, however, that ASA should review its policy towards breaches of the Order brought to its attention in the light of the general requirement of the Code that all advertisements should be legal, decent, honest and truthful.[38]

Television and radio advertising are also subject to self-regulation. The Broadcasting Act 1981 constitutes the Independent Broadcasting Authority (IBA) to have overall responsibility for the provision of commercial television and local radio. These can be provided by programme contractors or by the IBA itself in the absence of suitable companies offering themselves.[39] The Act imposes four broad obligations on the IBA regarding advertising. First, the IBA must appoint two committees – one comprising consumer and other interests, under an independent chairman, to give advice with a view to excluding misleading advertisements and otherwise as to the principles to be followed in connection with advertisements; and a Medical Advisory Panel to give specific advice as to advertisements for medicines, medical treatment and toilet products which make claims as to their therapeutic or prophylactic effects.[40] The committees are purely advisory but are the only formal channels for a consumer input into the control of radio and television advertising.

Secondly, the IBA must consult with the government from time to time about advertisements which may not be broadcast or methods of advertising which may not be used.[41] The government can give directives about these matters, along with rules about the programmes during which advertisements cannot occur and the minimum interval which must elapse between any two periods given over to advertisements.[42] In practice the government avoids issuing directives and approves the principles developed by the IBA.

Thirdly, the IBA must secure compliance with the provisions of the Second Schedule of the Act (it is clothed with a statutory duty to do this[43]) which requires in general terms that advertising should be recognizably separate from programmes and from each other, that they should not be excessively noisy or strident, that the amount of time given over to them should not be so great as to detract from the value of programmes, that they should only occur during programmes where there are natural breaks, that there should be no unreasonable discrimination either against or in favour of particular advertisers, and that no religious or political advertisements should be broadcast.

The IBA has drawn up rules to give effect to the provisions regarding the total amount of time given to advertising an hour and the nature of advertising intervals.[44] There is an argument that natural breaks are contrived, thus offending the principle that the insertion of advertisements must suit the programme rather than the reverse. The Annan Committee accepted that to ban advertisements during programmes would lead to shorter programmes, but thought that longer breaks between programmes might compensate for fewer breaks during them. Some critics have advocated block advertising to replace the present system of spot advertising so that advertisements would be banded together at one or two times in the evening. The Annan Committee supported the present system because the alternative would be less attractive to advertisers, who feared that many consumers would leave the room during the advertising period. Subliminal advertising and sponsoring of programmes are expressly prohibited by the Act.[45] The Annan Committee concluded that there should be greater control of sponsoring and other forms of indirect advertising – the use of television personalities, trackside banners and music companies buying their way on to pop programmes – because it could 'lead to the public being misled into watching programmes which in effect were elaborate advertisements for commercial interests'.[46]

Finally, the IBA has a duty to draw up and secure compliance with a code governing standards and practice in advertising and methods of advertising to be prohibited in particular circumstances. It has power to vet advertisements before broadcast and can withdraw or suspend a broadcaster's licence if it breaches the Code (or other contractual obligations) on more than three occasions.[47] The IBA Code is similar in content to the Code of Advertising Practice but is more succinct and also reproduces a number of the special statutory provisions. General rules (e.g. advertisements must be legal, decent, honest and truthful) are coupled with rules for particular types of advertising (e.g. medicines, children). Few of the provisions of the Code are peculiar to television advertising. An exception is a section on 'mock-ups', which are sometimes necessary because of the technical limitations of television in securing the faithful portrayal of a product. The Code permits the use of special techniques or substitute materials to overcome these difficulties but they must not be abused, and the resultant picture must present a fair and reasonable impression of the product and its effects. Unacceptable devices include the use of glass or plastic sheeting to simulate the effects of floor or furniture polishes. Mock-ups have been the subject of litigation in the United States and the Federal Trade Commission has obtained cease and desist orders against their use in particular cases on the grounds that they were deceptive within the terms of the Federal Trade Commission Act.[48]

It is in the enforcement of the IBA Code that self-regulation comes to the foreground. The IBA has an advertising control office to carry out its statutory obligations of implementing the Code, but this acts more in a supervisory capacity. In practice, a great deal of work is carried out by a secretariat of the copy committee of the Independent Television Companies Association (ITCA), which has obviously been established to pre-empt stricter statutory control. The ITCA committee acts as a sieve; it may reject certain advertisements, but the ones it passes are seen by the Authority. That the IBA, a public corporation, should surrender so much responsibility to an industry body seems extraordinary in the light of its statutory obligation. Doubts about the ITCA–IBA relationship are heightened when we are told that 'it is not an infrequent occurrence for the ITCA staff to argue an advertiser's case with the IBA and persuade them to accept what at first they were unwilling to.'[49]

Advertisers submit television scripts in advance and they are vetted by the ITCA committee for compliance with the Code. Medical and allied advertisers are referred to the Medical Advisory Panel of the IBA, and in other technical fields the services of appropriate specialists are retained. In due course members of the IBA's control office and the ITCA's copy clearing group join in a viewing of finished films. Procedures for radio commercials are similar, although only certain categories like medical and financial advertisements require central pre-clearance, with the rest being cleared by the stations themselves. Pre-vetting under the IBA code of advertising practice is theoretically more effective than the *ex post facto* operation of the Code of Advertising Practice, but critics maintain that misleading and undesirable commercials are still broadcast because of deficiencies in the Code. Criticism is also levelled at the spirit in which the Code is applied. Advertisements are judged at face value with only the superficial elements being scrutinized. Underlying the argument, as with criticism of the Code of Advertising Practice, is that the commercial view of advertising takes precedence in the implementation of the Code. This is not surprising when the Code is operated in many respects by those whom it is supposed to regulate.

Legal alternatives

Mention has already been made of legislation which prohibits misleading advertising by broad criminal provisions. There are other legal techniques, however, which might be adopted to supplement or replace the existing codes of advertising practice. A number of these have been pioneered by the Federal Trade Commission in the United States, under its statutory mandate to take action against unfair or deceptive acts or practices.[50] It is not suggested that the presence of these techniques on the statute book guarantees that advertisements will be any more legal, decent, honest and truthful than they are at present. There still needs to be an efficient enforcement procedure for detecting breaches of the standards established, including systematic monitoring and concentrating on known sources of wrongdoing and publicity to induce consumers to complain. A good deal also depends on the spirit in which any controls are operated. Enforcement bodies must be independent of those they are controlling. Consumer involvement in the enforcement process is one way of ensuring this, for example, on governing bodies of consumer protection agencies. Consideration must also be given to supplementing public enforcement by empowering private individuals or public interest groups to take legal action. Certain consumer organizations in West Germany have the right to seek injunctive relief against misleading advertising, but the provision is restrictive and has had only limited success.[51] In Australia any person can seek an injunction and/or damages (if they have suffered loss or damage) in relation to advertisements which contravene the Trade Practices Act 1974.[52]

A government working party has recommended that the Director General of Fair Trading should have an injunctive power, supplementing the existing self-regulatory system.[53] The recommendation is consistent with the EEC draft directive on misleading and unfair advertising. Of course an injunctive power is of limited usefulness unless combined with an interim injunctive power. Otherwise some advertisers will continue their deceptive advertisements and perhaps prolong litigation which they cannot possibly win until, by the time the matter is finally adjudicated, the advertising campaign has ended and a substantial number of consumers have been misled. The proposed injunctive power would be based on a new statutory duty not to publish advertisements likely to deceive, or mislead.[54] A wide definition is necessary to prevent the courts requiring strong evidence before an advertisement is regarded as deceptive or misleading. Legislation in British Columbia, the Trade Practice Act, tries to avoid a restrictive interpretation by spelling out what it regards as deception justifying injunctive action. Non-disclosure is included, as is the use in an oral or written representation

of exaggeration, innuendo, or ambiguity as to a material fact, or failure to state a material fact, if the representation is deceptive or misleading.[55]

Affirmative disclosure has been used by the Federal Trade Commission on several occasions to ensure that consumers are not misled. In one case a court upheld an FTC order that future advertisements about a purported cure for baldness should disclose that up to 95 per cent of all cases of baldness were not curable.[56] Affirmative disclosure can perform the additional function of ensuring that advertisements actually provide information to consumers to allow them to make intelligent choices. Modern advertising is often uninformative on precisely those matters like durability, performance and comparative value which consumers need to know. Chapter 9 discusses instances in which affirmative disclosure – not necessarily in advertising – is required. At this stage some of the difficulties of affirmative disclosure should be mentioned: there are finite limits to the amount of information consumers can absorb, consumers are selective in what they take in, some are less able to cope than others and information is more digestible if it is presented in a relatively simple form. Another point to be considered is that affirmative disclosure in advertising is likely to meet strong resistance because it goes against the grain of modern advertising and because in many respects it is directly against producers' interests to emphasize factors like utility and comparative value.

Claim substantiation can have two effects: it can give consumers useful information and it can act as a deterrent to prevent advertisers from making false claims. Neither result seems to occur with the claim substantiation provisions of the Code of Advertising Practice. Information made available is treated as confidential and producers cannot justify many of the claims they make about the attributes of products and services. A new policy of claim substantiation was

adopted in the United States in 1971.[57] A systematic programme has
been followed whereby manufacturers in various industries have been
called upon to provide complete documentation for advertising
claims. A case where a business could not substantiate its claim was
Firestone Tyre and Rubber Company v. *FTC*.[58] The company had
advertised its 'Super Sports Wide Oval' tyre 'stops 25 per cent
quicker'. Quite apart from the fact that it had only compared its own
inferior tyre, the court held that the claim was unsubstantiated
because the tests were carried out on only one type of surface. It
upheld a cease and desist order that prohibited the company from
making comparative claims without first making tests to assure their
accuracy.

Information under the Federal Trade Commission claim substantiation programme has been made available for public inspection, but this aspect proved disappointing because in many cases
the information was too technical for consumers to understand or out
of date. The FTC has adopted a revised programme seeking
substantiation for only major themes in advertisements and request-
ing the responses to include a summary in non-technical language.
Ideally, consumer groups should obtain the information and publish
it in simplified form. There are other difficulties with claim substantiation. First, it may induce advertisers to provide even less
information than at present. Secondly, it needs a substantial investment of administrative resources to enforce and access to independent
experts (perhaps in other government departments). Thirdly, it is
confined to claims which businesses choose to make. Finally, it needs
to be backed by strong criminal penalties against unsubstantiated
claims and not just by an injunctive power.[59]

Counter-advertising obliges the media to carry, free of charge,
advertising prepared by public interest groups which rebuts claims
made by commercial interests. Counter-advertising has been used in
the United States where public interest groups have taken advantage
of the 'fairness' doctrine applying to television and radio broadcasting
to get their views broadcast.[60] The doctrine has been applied to
cigarette advertising and commercials for large cars on the grounds
that such advertisements raise the requisite controversial issue of
public importance (health, pollution).[61] However, the courts have
said that the fairness doctrine does not invariably require counter-
commercials and that the Federal Communications Commission has
discretion not to apply it to a product advertisement (the policy it

adopted in 1974).[62]

An initial problem with counter-advertising is the width of coverage. Is it to be confined to matters of public controversy or will it extend to all commercials? Another issue is whether counter-advertisements must come immediately following an advertisement by a commercial interest. If 'equal time' is not to be given, what percentage of advertising space should be allocated to counter-advertising? One method of counter-advertising might be to conduct discussion programmes in which consumer organizations report on the tests they have conducted on products. It is said that counter-advertising on a broad basis would threaten the financial viability of the media. But before this occurs, and before counter-advertising becomes really effective, the government would have to subsidize public interest groups heavily, for few have the resources at present to launch a counter advertising campaign.

Corrective advertising might counteract the residual effects of deceptive advertising and deter businesses from using it in the first place. The first aspect is necessary because even after a deceptive advertisement has ceased it can continue to influence consumers, albeit subconsciously, if it has planted a factual claim in their minds or has generated goodwill which leads to later purchases. The deterrent aspect stems from the damage corrective advertising might do to the reputation of a business and to its financial position from a loss of sales. In the United States FTC orders for corrective advertising give an advertiser an option of ceasing to advertise for a year or of devoting 25 per cent of its advertising to corrective advertisements.[63] A notable example is an order directing the Warner-Lambert Co. to include the following statement in its advertisements for its mouthwash until it had spent an amount equal to its average annual advertising budget for 1962–72: 'Listerine will not help prevent colds or sore throats or lessen their severity.'[64]

The Trade Descriptions Act 1968 Review Committee in Britain recommended against corrective advertising. It thought that it might fail to reach those who were misled.[65] This argument loses most of its force if a corrected version must be run in the same sources and for the same period as the original. Equally specious is the argument that corrective advertising might reach those who were not originally misled, and in so doing cause damage to an advertiser out of all proportion to the original infraction. Two points can be made: at present penalties in law need not be equivalent to the damage occasioned to consumers or the gain accruing to a business. Secondly, the prime aim of corrective advertising is to introduce sufficient power in the law to deter misleading advertising. Advertisers which take preventive action from the outset need have no fear of disproportionate losses. It is interesting to note that the Federal Court of Australia can order corrective advertising under section 80A of the Trade Practices Act 1974 on the application of the Minister or the Trade Practices Commission.[66]

BUSINESS SELF-REGULATION IN PERSPECTIVE

Advocates of business self-regulation argue that it possesses a number of advantages over legislation. First, it is said that it conserves the public resources which would go into law-making and law enforcement. By encouraging businesses to police themselves, the costs to society are minimized. Secondly, it is said that self-regulation can be quicker and more flexible than introducing and enforcing legislation. Thirdly – and this is related to the previous point – voluntary standards are said to be well in advance of legal provisions and more favourable to consumers. A fourth advantage is said to be that the standards evolved for self-regulation can be applied in a practical and commonsense manner and not in the legalistic or rigid way of the courts. Finally, businesses are said to comply with voluntary standards in the spirit as well as the letter, whereas they might push the law to its limit and find loopholes. This more positive attitude to voluntary standards derives from businesses' interest in the proper implementation of something they have established and from their greater willingness to comply with peer-group pressure than when confronted with force.

The motivation for business self-regulation is sometimes far removed from the sense of social responsibility which we are led to believe underlies it. Companies with individual codes of ethics and social practice tend to be those subject to public criticism for polluting, using dangerous processes or consuming resources; those prone to difficult labour relations; and those with a high number of customers.[67] There can be no doubt that much self-regulation has been influenced by a fear of legislation in the event of business standards not being improved. Businesses have been aware that if they did not take the initiative to allay consumer dissatisfaction they would face more onerous government control. Businesses have also realized that self-regulation can lead to positive commercial advantage; for example, it can reduce costs by paving the way for more stringent quality control. Although the threat of statutory intervention has induced self-regulation, it would be unrealistic not to acknowledge the unwillingness of governments to intervene in certain areas for reasons such as ideology, cost and the practical difficulties of formulating legal controls.[68]

There is also a temptation for businesses to introduce self-regulation as a means of insulating themselves from competitive forces. An example is that the British Code of Advertising Practice allows comparative advertising, but subject to qualifications such as that it must not 'unfairly attack or discredit other products, advertisers or advertisements'. This has been interpreted by the Advertising Standards Authority to discourage knocking copy.[69] In one case, for example, a charity advertisement was judged to be in breach of the provision on the basis that it denigrated the flower industry by suggesting that donations be given instead of floral tributes. Law-makers have recognized that self-regulation can be for the protection of commercial rather than consumer interests. Self-regulation may be void as an unreasonable restraint of trade or action may be taken against it under the Restrictive Trade Practices Act 1976. An example of the former situation is *Pharmaceutical Society of Great Britain* v. *Dickson*,[70] where the Pharmaceutical Society purported to incorporate in its code of conduct provisions to control the trading activities of chemists. The number of pharmacies in large establishments (e.g. department stores) would be limited and pharmacies would be restricted in the non-pharmaceutical products they could sell. The Society justified the action on the basis of raising the status of the profession and of preventing it from being side-tracked from its main responsibility of selling pharmaceuticals. However, the House of Lords held that the policy was an unreasonable restraint of trade because it limited competition and rendered new pharmacies uneconomic; it was also not sufficiently related to the objects of the Society's charter.

Self-regulation also falls down in its implementation. Not all the businesses in a particular trade may adhere to the voluntary standards agreed on by the relevant trade associations. Experience suggests that the non-adherents are usually those most likely to be employing disreputable practices. Not only will they continue their prejudicial behaviour but they may even take advantage of whatever increased public confidence self-regulation engenders by misrepresenting themselves as adherents. Other difficulties with enforcing voluntary standards are that they may be mere window-dressing, that they may be so general as to be relatively useless or that the trade association involved may be too diverse.[71] An example of self-regulation failing for some of these reasons was the 1976 agreement covering pricing at garages. This was negotiated by the government, the oil companies and the relevant trade associations following strong public complaint that a price war for petrol had led to misleading road-side advertising about pricing as garages attempted to capture more trade. There was little improvement in the situation, however, and statutory regulations were eventually necessary because a considerable percentage of the garage trade did not comply.[72]

A further factor is that, by the very nature of things, a trade association will be slow to enforce voluntary standards against its members. It will generally share the values of its members as to what is acceptable or unacceptable under the standards; it will tend to allocate minimum resources to enforcement because its members will view any other course as wasteful; and it will wish to avoid disharmony in what is after all a voluntary grouping, particularly if its membership is small or the activity of an important member is at issue. Criticism of the Better Business Bureaux in North America – complaints bureaux run by local Chambers of Commerce – has been that their actions are hedged in by the desire not to alienate their source of funds, the business community.

Confidence in business self-regulation also can be weakened by the absence of a consumer voice in the formation and implementation of voluntary measures. Voluntary standards are usually drawn up by businesses without canvassing the viewpoint of consumers. Consequently, voluntary standards are based more often than not on the prevailing practices in an industry – admittedly not the least common denominator – and have a limited view of what is against the consumer interest and should be curtailed. This is certainly the case with the advertising codes where self-regulation is confined to matters of truth and decency and does not extend to the social consequences of advertising. Almost invariably business self-regulation lacks independent machinery for its implementation and the procedures which exist are likely to be shrouded in secrecy. Where independent representatives take part in the administration of voluntary standards, they are typically in the minority and seem to be chosen for their pro-business or at least 'neutral' attitude.

In summary, businesses support self-regulation and are prepared to allocate resources to it if it forestalls stricter legal control and reaps goodwill. Should it threaten to impinge on profits, however, many will ignore it. Where it is socially desirable that businesses cut back their operations (e.g. cigarette manufacturing), self-regulation must fail because business self-interest is diametrically opposed to it.[73] Self-regulation also fails in its enforcement. Rarely will it encompass all the members of a trade or industry. Moreover it is too optimistic to think that a trade association, wholly supported by the subscriptions of its members and imbued with their values, will assume the same independent stance in implementing controls as a government agency.

PART II
Private law

3
Private law in perspective

There is no area of 'consumer law' within the private law, and a consumer's legal rights derive primarily from the concepts of negligence and contract as modified by statute. There is a common assumption, in particular among lawyers, that private law is the best hope for consumer protection. Writing in 1969, Professor Jolowicz saw consumer protection as prevention on the one hand and financial redress for consumers when things go wrong on the other. He was sceptical about the extent to which law and lawyers could effectively contribute to consumer protection in the first sense.

> The criminal law can, no doubt, do something towards this end, but consumer- and producer-education seem to me to be more important. Consumer protection in its second sense, however, is something which the law, and in the ultimate result the law alone, can provide.[1]

One aim of this Part of the book is to demonstrate that the private law is an inadequate tool of consumer protection. The relevant legal principles are often biased against consumers, although in some cases legislation has been enacted because of judicial reluctance to bring the law into line with modern social conditions. The law of contract is based on the assumption of equal bargaining power between parties – quite inappropriate where consumers are bound to accept the terms dictated by businesses. Doctrines like privity of contract and negligence continue to impose fetters on the ability of consumers to sue businesses which are responsible in fact for their losses.

The doctrines of private law and their inadequacies are examined in the following chapters. The burden of the present chapter is to highlight the problem of standard form contracts and exemption clauses and the practical difficulties of implementing private law rights. These difficulties cast doubt on the effectiveness of private law to protect consumers.

STANDARD FORM CONTRACTS AND EXCLUSION CLAUSES

'Freedom of contract'

Writing in 1943, Friedrich Kessler concluded that while appearing to be non-authoritarian contract law protected the unequal distribution of power in society and in particular enabled 'powerful industrial and commercial overlords' to 'impose a new feudal order of their own making upon a vast host of vassals'.[2] It is still the case that consumers are bound to contracts, in the main standard form contracts, to which patently they do not agree but which they are obliged to accept if they want the products and services normally taken as an incidence of living in society. The underlying philosophy of the law is that all members of society are basically free to enter contracts, and that being the case, they must take care for their own interests. A Court of Appeal decision in 1975, *United Dominions Trust Ltd* v. *Western*,[3] is illustrative. A consumer signed a personal loan agreement in blank which he thought was a hire purchase agreement and which the dealer then fraudulently filled in as to the amounts. The Court of Appeal rejected the argument that there was no consensus *ad idem* between the consumer and the finance house to whom the dealer had sent the agreement. Scarman L.J., for example, said that there was no difference between signing 'blind' a completed document the contents of which had not been read, and signing a printed document with blanks which one authorized another person to complete. 'It seems to me that such a man does make the document that he is signing his document; he takes responsibility for it; and he takes the chance of a fraudulent filling in of the blanks.' The actual decision in *Western's Case*, that the consumer had to bear the loss, is no longer good law in the light of the Consumer Credit Act 1974, but the underlying approach of the court is typical and has changed little over the last hundred years.

Another aspect of contract law which is relevant to the discussion is the parol evidence rule, whereby verbal evidence is in general not allowed to derogate from the terms of a written contract. The

argument in favour of the rule is convenience, but there would not
seem to be any great difficulty in cases of dispute in deciding what was
actually said at the time the contract was made. Certainly in most
consumer transactions the natural tendency is to rely on what a
business's employees say without reading the written terms of any
agreement proffered, and there are cases where the former has been
given precedence when it was within the employee's ostensible
authority to make a promise.[4] In fact the rule has been significantly
undermined by such exceptions.

The doctrines of contract law have always been stated as applying
equally to all, but in practice it has been businesses who have taken
advantage of them. The law in effect protects the bargains of one
segment of society and so confirms the exercise of their power. Lord
Denning expressed the point this way:

> None of you nowadays will remember the trouble we had – when I was
> called to the Bar – with exemption clauses. They were printed in small print
> on the back of tickets and order forms and invoices. They were contained in
> catalogues or timetables. They were held to be binding on any person who
> took them without objection. No one ever did object. He never read them or
> knew what was in them. No matter how unreasonable they were, he was
> bound. All this was done in the name of 'freedom of contract.' But the freedom
> was all on the side of the big concern which had the use of the printing press.
> No freedom for the little man who took the ticket or order form or invoice. The
> big concern said, 'Take it or leave it.' The little man had no option but to take
> it. The big concern could and did exempt itself from liability in its own
> interest without regard to the little man. It got away with it time after time.
> When the courts said to the big concern, 'You must put it in clear words,' the
> big concern had no hesitation in doing so. It knew well that the little man
> would never read the exemption clauses or understand them.[5]

The extremities to which the law has been taken are well rehearsed in
the standard works on contract, although in most cases uncritically.
Exclusion clauses are the most common instance dealt with by the
English courts. *Thompson* v. *London, Midland and Scottish Railway Co.*[6] is
perhaps the most remarkable case, where an illiterate woman, injured
while descending from a train which had stopped short of the
platform, was bound by conditions, referred to on the ticket, which
her niece had obtained for her. To the court deciding the case in 1929,
the decision to enforce the conditions, in particular the exclusion
clause, was quite natural; to ordinary consumers it would have been
blatantly unjust, especially since the actual exclusion clause was

contained in a timetable which was only obtainable on an additional payment.

Some judges have seen the rules of English contract law as a means of minimizing disputes and providing a clear solution when disputes arise. Others no doubt have been motivated, perhaps in some cases unconsciously, by more fundamental policy aims, such as promoting self-reliance or supporting the operation of the market system. Ideologically, freedom of contract was a counterpart of free enterprise, a point well accepted in the writings of the nineteenth century.[7] Another factor which cannot be ignored is that the courts have been overly concerned with conceptual analysis and the application of precedent to the detriment of the social implications of their decisions. English contract law has focused on the formalities – offer/acceptance, consideration, etc. – rather than the substance of what the parties agreed. Too much should not be made of this point, however, for in other areas of the law the courts have displayed an ingenuity in developing new doctrine.

Nevertheless, standard form contracts are a necessity in modern business transactions. Bureaucracies want routine and certainty and they need to be able rationally to plan risks (e.g. fire, flood, accidents) if they are to operate efficiently. Moreover, standard form contracts perform other functions within large businesses: they standardize and formalize procedures; allow a corporation to control its agents, preventing them from compromising the corporation by generous deals with individual consumers; and act as a means of internal communication, for example indicating the extent of future payments.[8] One study found that finance and insurance companies used exclusion clauses in their consumer agreements as a form of psychological pressure to convince consumers to take the agreement seriously or to settle out of court in a dispute.[9] There can be little objection to standard form contracts in arms-length dealings between businesses of relatively equal bargaining power. There are even advantages for consumers because it is hardly possible to negotiate terms each time they enter contracts, and that is extremely frequent in everyday life. The objection to standard form contracts on the part of consumers is that frequently they are compelled to accept disadvantageous terms. In a way compulsion operates at two levels: in the first sense, about which little can be done, consumers have no option but to enter certain contracts if they are to act as ordinary members of society.[10] Secondly, and this is the real objection, there is compulsion in that the adverse terms are forced upon consumers and may subtract from or set at naught the rights which the law would otherwise give them.[11]

If it is accepted that standard form contracts are an inevitable feature of modern society, the need is to formulate criteria for identifying objectionable aspects. One line of argument, which derives very much from the classical model of contract, is to ask: what would consumers agree to if they could freely bargain? For those drafting the Uniform Commercial Code in the United States, the notions of surprise and oppression in bargaining became the bench-marks for identifying unconscionable contracts. In their view one asked: did consumers have access to expert advice, time to reflect on the terms, the experience to suggest alternatives, and so on. The whole notion of bargaining is rather unreal, for consumers are in no position to deliberate every time they enter a contract, even if enterprises were prepared to enter negotiations if they did. More importantly, however much consumers may be able to bargain, the end result will be that large businesses can use their power to force contract terms onto consumers. It is no use saying that consumers can deal with other businesses who would offer more favourable terms because the reality is that many enterprises offer identical, or nearly identical, terms.

Another way of dealing with standard form contracts, suggested by Slawson,[12] is generally to enforce only those terms to which consumers have explicitly or impliedly given consent. To give an example, a consumer handed a receipt which he signs without reading has only accepted a 'receipt'; i.e. what a receipt can reasonably be expected to contain, such as date and price. Slawson suggests that a business's behaviour has some role in determining what consumers can reasonably be regarded as having agreed; thus, exclusion clauses in standard form contracts would be disregarded if businesses do not publicize them. Slawson's argument has an appealing simplicity, but it seems rather difficult to apply it to the more complex standard form contracts. It is fairly easy to guess at what contracting parties have consented to or would consent to in relatively simple contracts, but what of the more complicated transactions like insurance, where some of the contingencies are so remote from ordinary experience that consumers will never appreci-ate them? Moreover, even if consumers expect exclusion clauses in particular types of contract, this is no argument for their continuation, because consumers might not appreciate that their deletion is possible.

The judicial and legislative response

The approach in Britain to objectionable features of standard form contracts and to exclusion clauses has been to proceed on a purely *ad hoc* and limited basis, depending on what terms have appeared to cause the greatest hardship and what have attracted the most publicity. Exclusion clauses relating to unsatisfactory products and services have been the main concern, but the courts have also been empowered to reopen extortionate credit bargains. In addition, we shall see in Chapter 7, the Consumer Credit Act 1974 provides that consumer credit agreements should be in writing and contain certain terms. The Unfair Contract Terms Act 1977 has various provisions designed to tackle the unfair terms in standard form contracts.

Despite the symbolic importance of freedom of contract the English courts, at the instigation of a few judicial mavericks, have conducted forays against exclusion clauses in standard form contracts.[13] In a number of cases the courts have found that the ordinary formalities of contracting have not been complied with because a consumer has not received notification of an exclusion clause before entering a contract or because a business has misrepresented, albeit innocently, the true nature of an exclusion clause.[14] Use of the *contra proferentem* rule has been possible in some circumstances to construe exclusion clauses narrowly; thus it has been held that to exempt itself from negligence, a business must state that quite categorically.[15] Interpretation has had only a limited effect, however, because businesses properly advised incorporate widely-drawn exclusion clauses in their contracts covering every contingency.

Another line of attack on exclusion clauses has been through the doctrine of fundamental breach. It is not proposed to examine this doctrine in detail – a field much-loved by lawyers who frequently concentrate on its technical aspects instead of on its role as a flexible instrument of public policy – except to say that the doctrine was enunciated in 1956, received a set-back in the House of Lords in 1966 which decided that it was simply a rule of construction, once again assumed the status of a rule of law in the Court of Appeal in 1970, but has now been reasserted by the House of Lords to be only a rule of construction.[16] Essentially, the doctrine of fundamental breach provided that a business could not exclude its liability for breaches of fundamental obligations or those which went to the root of a contract. In *Levison* v. *Patent Steam Carpet Cleaning Co. Ltd*,[17] for example, the plaintiff engaged a company to collect and clean a carpet and at the time of collection was obliged to sign a form which contained a number of printed conditions including that the carpet was 'expressly accepted at the owner's risk'. The carpet was never returned. The Court of Appeal held that the term gave exemption from liability for negligence but was not sufficient to cover fundamental breach of the contract. The company could not rely on it because it had not discharged the onus on it of showing what had happened to the carpet and that it was not guilty of fundamental breach. At least in consumer transactions the doctrine of fundamental breach has had little if any importance since the Unfair Contract Terms Act 1977.

There is no general doctrine in English law whereby a consumer can obtain relief because a contract is harsh.[18] Recent statements by some judges, that contracts can be set aside if there is an abuse by one side of a superior bargaining power, have not been widely applied.[19] Equity intervenes in cases of undue influence and there are a number of cases where courts have set aside unconscionable contracts because one party has taken advantage of its economic position and the weakness of the other (illiteracy, poverty, mental instability, etc.).[20] Such doctrines seem never to have been applied in consumer situations such as credit transactions, where persons were forced by circumstances to accept harsh and oppressive terms.

Following the Report of the Select Committee on Moneylending which documented many abuses by moneylenders, the courts were given the power to reopen harsh and unconscionable moneylending transactions. Despite an early decision it was soon accepted that this provision enabled the courts to reopen transactions merely because excessive charges made them harsh and unconscionable, irrespective of other factors.[21] The Moneylenders Act 1927 established the figure of 48 per cent as the interest which would be regarded prima facie as excessive. As with other aspects of private law, few consumers actually initiated actions under the provision, but in a number of instances it proved useful as a defence to claims by moneylenders for repayment of credit.[22]

The power to reopen extortionate credit bargains contained in the Moneylenders Act is continued in somewhat expanded form in the Consumer Credit Act 1974. The power extends to all credit bargains involving individuals – even those falling outside other provisions of the Act – and need not rest on an examination of the agreement alone. Section 138 defines a credit bargain as extortionate if it requires the debtor or a relation to make payments which are grossly exorbitant or if it otherwise grossly contravenes ordinary principles of fair dealing. The section then directs the courts to have regard to various matters in making this determination – the interest rate prevailing at the time the bargain was made; the age, experience, business capacity and state of health of the debtor; the degree to which at the time of making the credit bargain the debtor was under financial pressure; the degree of risk having regard to the security; the relationship to the debtor and whether the cash price for any item or service involved was colourable; other relevant considerations.[23] Unlike the Money-lenders Act there is no figure of 48 per cent as an interest rate which will be prima facie extortionate.[24] A court deciding that a bargain is extortionate may, for the purpose of relieving the debtor or surety from payment of any sum in excess of that fairly due and reasonable, set aside the whole or part of any obligation, require the creditor to repay the whole or part of the sum whether the sum was paid to it or someone else or alter the terms of the agreement.[25] For example, a court may decide that a lesser rate of interest is justified and order that the consumer pay this amount. Consumers can raise the issue that a credit bargain is extortionate on their own initiative, but by far the majority of cases are likely to arise where the creditor initiates proceedings and the consumer raises it as a defence to the claim. As soon as a debtor or surety alleges that a credit bargain is extortionate, the onus is then thrown onto the creditor to prove the contrary.[26]

Modern legislative attempts to deal with exclusion clauses began with the Hire Purchase Act 1938, which made the implied conditions of merchantability and fitness for purpose non-excludable. The Molony Committee recommended that a similar step be taken for sales transactions, and some twelve years later, following a Law Commission Report, the Supply of Goods (Implied Terms) Act 1973 rendered void terms in consumer sales and hire purchase trans-actions, purporting to exclude the implied terms as to title, compliance with description, merchantability and fitness for purpose. Steps were subsequently taken to prohibit certain statements rendered void by the Act; these are considered in Chapter 11. After further consumer pressure and another Law Commission Report, the Unfair Contract Terms Act, a Private Member's Bill, was enacted with government support in 1977.

The Unfair Contract Terms Act 1977 continues the provisions of the Supply of Goods (Implied Terms) Act 1973 in favour of a person dealing as consumer (s. 6).[27] Similarly, in other contracts under which goods are supplied (e.g. contracts of hire, contracts for work and materials) liability cannot be excluded in consumer transactions in respect of terms as to title, correspondence with description, quality and fitness for purpose (s. 7). In addition, contractual terms which exclude or restrict the liability of a party to a contract for a misrepresentation made by him before the contract was made, or any remedy available to another party to the contract by reason of such misrepresentation, are of no effect unless they satisfy the requirement of reasonableness (s. 8(1)).[28]

The main innovations of the Act are with respect to negligence and certain contractual terms. (The 'guarantee' provision, section 5, is discussed in Chapter 5.) Negligence is defined widely to include breach of any obligation arising from the express or implied terms of a contract to take reasonable care or exercise reasonable skill in the performance of a contract and of any common law duty to take reasonable care or exercise reasonable skill (but not any stricter duty) (s. 1(1)). The provisions are thus relevant to contracts for work and materials and contracts for the performance of a service. The Act provides that a business cannot by reference to any contract term or to a notice given to persons generally or to particular persons exclude or restrict its liability for death or personal injury resulting from negligence (s. 2(1)). Neither can a business so exclude or restrict its liability for negligence in the case of other loss or damage (e.g. property damage) except in so far as the term or notice satisfies the requirement of reasonableness (s. 2(2)). Because invalidity in section 2(2) turns on reasonableness, businesses have apparently continued to exclude or restrict liability for negligence claiming that the requirement is satisfied. Aggrieved consumers who challenge this exclusion or restriction – and there would be few of them – are no doubt often 'bought off' by the payment of compensation. Consequently the bulk of consumers continue to be misled as to their rights.

Section 3 of the Act contains what is potentially a wide power for the courts to render invalid terms in contracts where one party deals as consumer or on the other's written standard terms of business. As against that party a business cannot by reference to any contract term (a) when itself in breach of contract exclude or restrict its liability in respect of the breach, or (b) claim to be entitled to render a contractual performance substantially different from what is reasonably expected or to render no performance at all, except in so far as in any of these cases the contract term satisfies the requirement of reasonableness. An example covered by (b) might be a clause whereby a tour operator can substitute a different holiday from the one originally booked.[29] A claim providing for performance 'subject to strikes' would appear to be caught and would have to satisfy the requirement of reasonableness. Because the section only applies when a contract exists it is said that there is scope for evading its provisions by a business interposing a functionary between itself and the consumer. Even if this is legally possible it will be irrelevant in the great majority of consumer transactions: either it will not be a practical possibility, or the intermediary will be regarded as an agent so that contractual relations result between the business and consumers.

The Act is intended to have wide effect. To the extent that the Act prevents the exclusion or restriction of any liability it also prevents making the liability or its enforcement subject to restrictive or onerous conditions, excluding or restricting any right or remedy in respect of liability or subjecting a person to any prejudice in consequence of pursuing these, and excluding or restricting rules of evidence or procedure (s. 13(1)). Examples of such limitations are restricting liability to a certain sum for each article lost or damaged, or requiring that any complaints be made within three days.[30] To the extent that the Act prevents the exclusion or restriction of any liability the provisions relating to negligence, guarantees and the supply of products also prevent excluding or restricting liability by reference to terms and notices which exclude or restrict the relevant obligation or duty (s.13(1)). There is an argument that this does not prevent a business from avoiding liability by limiting its primary obligations. If no obligation or duty arises, it is said, section 13 cannot operate. Much will depend in practice, of course, on whether the courts will construe positively stated primary obligations as exclusions or restrictions of liability.[31] Indemnity clauses are also prevented if unreasonable, as is evasion by means of a secondary contract or a choice of law clause (ss. 4, 10, 27(2)). However, a written agreement to submit present or future differences to arbitration is not to be treated as excluding or restricting any liability (s. 13(2)).

As indicated certain exclusions and restrictions of liability are not prevented absolutely but only if a reasonableness requirement cannot be satisfied. In relation to a contract term the requirement of reasonableness is that the term shall have been a fair and reasonable one to have been included having regard to the circumstances which were, or ought reasonably to have been, known to or in contemplation of the parties when the contract was made (s. 11(1)). The obvious limitation here is that reasonableness is assessed at the time the contract was made, which is defended on the grounds of certainty and the undesirability of changing the rules of the game.

Yet clearly there are claims where unobjectionable contractual terms can be put to unfair use, and where what was reasonable originally transpires to be unreasonable in the context of later circumstances (as where the consumer would be left without any remedy). Reasonableness so confined cannot cope with these performance-related risks. One suggestion is that reasonableness ought to turn on whether the consumer is offered a choice of terms, with liability and without liability, varying with price.[32] This would be undesirable since there is a natural tendency for people to underestimate risk and to pay the lower price without taking out their own insurance. From the point of view of social policy it is frequently much better if businesses insure rather than expecting consumers to do so individually. (An exception might be for cars where consumers themselves ought to take out comprehensive insurance.) Moreover, as a practical matter, many businesses would find it impossible to operate a dual pricing system. In relation to a notice not having contractual effect, the requirement of reasonableness is that it should be fair and reasonable to allow reliance on it, having regard to all the circumstances obtaining when the liability arose or (but for the notice) would have arisen (s. 11(3)). Where by reference to a contract term or notice a business seeks to restrict liability to a specified sum of money and the question arises whether it satisfies the requirement of reasonableness, regard shall be had in particular to the resources which it could expect to be available to it for the purpose of meeting the liability should it arise and how far it was open to cover itself by insurance (s. 11(4)).

Critics have attacked the legislation as being badly drafted and as cutting short the flexible evolution of common law doctrine. Fortunately the courts have been sympathetic in the main in interpreting the Act and its predecessors. It is doubtful if they could have developed the common law to an extent comparable to the Act's provisions, if only because the lack of litigation would not have provided an opportunity to do so. Then the critics say that the Act reaches too far in denying parties the right to contract, that really it treats the law of contract as if it were an arm of public law. Such a view misconceives the whole thrust of modern legislative policy and its roots in developments such as standard form contracts where, as we have seen, freedom of contract is largely illusory. Indeed, the truth is that the Unfair Contract Terms Act 1977 is a misnomer, because given its scope and the specific exemptions to it many unfair terms caught in other jurisdictions fall outside its ambit.[33] Insurance contracts are excluded, for example, although standard clauses in these are grossly unfair to consumers who might well not see them until the policy begins. Insurance companies are in a dominant position because they operate in an oligopolistic market where most ordinary consumers do not understand the relative merits of different policies. There is also a need for reform in other areas of insurance law. For example, the common law enables insurance companies to disclaim liability because consumers have innocently misrepresented facts which are not relevant to the claim; because consumers have failed to disclose facts which the insurer claims are material even though at the time the policy was made the insurer would not have been influenced in offering cover and a reasonable consumer would not have regarded them as relevant; or because consumers have breached a provision of the policy, in which all terms have been declared to be 'the basis of the contract', even if the breach is immaterial to the claim.[34]

Alternative legal techniques

Legislation can exercise control over the imposed terms of standard form contracts along a number of lines. First, it can render invalid specific features of contracts which are considered objectionable. This has tended to be the approach in England. The advantage of specific legislative provisions is certainty. In practice there are various drawbacks. While the use of particular clauses might be rendered invalid, additional steps are necessary to prevent businesses continuing to incorporate them in their standard terms. There is the scope of the approach: it cannot operate with respect to the unique but must have provisions which are regularly incorporated as contractual terms. Another of the problems is the time involved in legislative steps being taken. For example, a decade elapsed before implementation of the Molony Committee's recommendation that the implied terms in sales transactions should be made non-excludable. Another obvious problem is that the clauses prohibited are not the only kinds which are unfair.[35] Conversely, it may be that the clauses prohibited are not always unfair, although policy-makers seem to have been more than justified so far in assuming that these instances are far outweighed by those where the clauses are unfair. A further danger is the complexity of the remedial legislation and the inflexibility which this entails. Inasmuch as this is the case it is largely a function of the narrow interpretation of statutes and the attempt by the drafters to minimize this by spelling out in detail what is to be covered.

A second approach to standard form contracts is along the lines of a general provision like that in section 3 of the Unfair Contract Terms Act 1977. The Uniform Commercial Code contains a general provision allowing a court to refuse to enforce an unconscionable clause or contract, which is wider than section 3 of the Unfair Contract Terms Act 1977.

Section 2–302. *Unconscionable Contract or Clause*

(1) If the court as a matter of law finds the contract or any clause of the contract to have been unconscionable at the time it was made the court may refuse to enforce the contract, or it may enforce the remainder of the contract without the unconscionable clause, or it may so limit the application of any unconscionable clause as to avoid any unconscionable result.

It is said that unconscionable means 'grossly unfair', and the Official Comment to the section says that the basic test is whether against the commercial background the clauses are too one-sided: 'The principle is one of the prevention of oppression and unfair surprise . . . and not of disturbance of allocation of risks because of superior bargaining power.' The unfair surprise aspect, for example, covers the situation where a business takes advantage of the ignorance or carelessness of consumers. Like the Consumer Credit Act 1974, the Uniform Consumer Credit Code has a specific provision – Section 5–108 – dealing with unconscionability in credit and similar contracts.[36] The one important difference is that by section 6–111 of the UCC there is a public remedy for unconscionable conduct in that a government agency may obtain an injunction against it.

Section 2–302 of the UCC has been put to considerable use,

although the facts in cases where relief has been granted are fairly extreme. An exorbitant price in relation to the value of a product has been held to be unconscionable, such as that in the contract between a 'home improvement' business and an 87-year-old woman, and that in a number of contracts negotiated by a firm selling door to door to low-income, poorly educated consumers.[37] Not all the decisions are as satisfactory, however, and some courts take the approach that although a price may be well above the value of an item, freedom of choice will render the agreement valid.[38] Apart from price, section 2–302 has been used to invalidate other aspects of consumer transactions such as exclusion clauses, and certain terms contained in consumer credit agreements. In *Williams* v. *Walker-Thomas Furniture Company*[39] the consumer had little education and was supporting seven children on social security payments when she purchased certain consumer durables on credit. By virtue of the credit agreement the payments were allocated *pro rata* among several items so that none was paid off and all could be repossessed. The District of Columbia Court of Appeals thought that in these circumstances the credit agreement appeared to be unconscionable. Parenthetically, it might be mentioned that the same problem as in *William's Case* could arise in Britain, for although under the Consumer Credit Act 1974 the consumer can decide to allocate payment to one of a number of agreements to discharge it at least, that can only be done at the time of payment, and not at a later stage when difficulties arise and the creditor is threatening to repossess all the items.[40]

The approach of section 2–302 of the UCC operates in some civil law countries and has recently been adopted in some common law jurisdictions.[41] The main justification for an unconscionability provision is that only a broad standard can cope with the unforeseen and perhaps marginal features of consumer transactions. The judiciary, it is said, is the most appropriate body to give substance to such a broad standard because of the wide range of fact situations which will be litigated and its capacity to generalize by analogy. An unconscionability provision, supporters argue, avoids judges having to do justice by stealth because a particular case falls outside the tight compartments available in specific legislation. The objection that an unconscionability clause introduces an uncertainty into the law is said to ignore the way courts have historically narrowed wide discretion, and the experience in the United States where the courts have built up an appropriate jurisprudence. Counter-arguments, however, caution against too great a faith being placed in a general unconscionability clause without the underpinning of specific provisions. Quite apart from the barriers to consumer litigation considered shortly, there is a question whether the judiciary possess the necessary breadth of vision for such a discretion to be entrusted to them.[42] While this is partly a matter of social values it is also a structural issue, that generalized decision-making is not always appropriate or possible in the context of particular cases. On one interpretation the American and West German courts have been cautious and conservative in exercising their powers under the unconscionability clause and have tended to avoid interference with transactions in ordinary terms.

It is possible to meet some of these criticisms by fleshing out an unconscionability provision on the basis of legislative and judicial experience in the area of unjust contracts. While entrusting the courts with a general discretion to consider whether a contract or a provision of a contract is unjust, having regard to the public interest and all the circumstances of the case, it is possible to direct them to give attention to factors such as any material inequality in bargaining power, prior negotiations, the practicability of the applicant negotiating an alteration or the rejection of any provisions of the contract, and conditions in the contract which are unreasonably difficult to comply with or not reasonably necessary for the protection of legitimate interests. Other relevant factors include the capacity of parties (or their representatives) to protect their interests given their age or physical or mental condition; the relative economic circumstances, educational background or literacy of the parties; the physical form and intelligibility of contractual language if in writing; the presence of independent legal or other expert advice; the extent of explanations of the legal and practical effect of a contract and whether these were understood; undue influence, unfair pressure or unfair tactics exerted or used; the conduct of the parties in similar contracts or courses of dealing; and the commercial or other setting, purpose and effect of the contract.[43] To be successful any unconscionability provision must focus not simply on the situation at the inception of a transaction but also on its subsequent performance, in other words on substantive as well as procedural unconscionability. In addition the courts' remedial power must extend beyond refusing to enforce, setting aside or varying the transaction to other aspects such as orders with respect to the disposition, sale or realisation of property, the payment of

money, compensation for third parties whose interests might otherwise be prejudiced, the supply/repair of goods and services, the
creation and enforcement of a charge on property, and the appointment of a receiver of property.[44]

A third approach to standard form contracts is that a public agency
is authorized to take legal action to have offending terms declared
void and their use prohibited. It might also be envisaged that the
agency will seek voluntary action by businesses by negotiation and by
drafting model contracts. Swedish legislation along these lines has
operated since 1971. Under the Act Prohibiting Improper Contract
Terms, the Consumer Ombudsman examines standard form
contracts and standardized terms except in matters such as banking
and insurance, and intervenes when he thinks that a clause is
improper, i.e. 'it gives entrepreneurs an advantage or deprives
consumers of a right and thereby causes such one-sided relations in
the parties' rights and obligations under the contract that a reasonable balance between the parties no longer exists.'[45] The Act
deliberately excludes any requirement that impropriety be manifest.
Terms can be referred to the Market Court which can issue an
injunction against their future use. Certain clauses are deemed to be
improper. Other clauses against which action has been taken include
those which enable a business more than three weeks to decide
whether to go through with a transaction and those which give a
business the categorical right to cancel a contract and forfeit a deposit
for delay in payment. Also subject to review and criticized in the
preparatory work for the Act are clauses which allow the contractual
price to be raised (except for changes in taxation).

Prior approval of standard form contracts is a fourth technique of
consumer protection. It has not been widely used, and at most a few
agreements like credit agreements must contain clauses presented in
a form which, it is assumed, will be understood by and visible to
consumers. Consumer groups have drawn up a number of model
standard form contracts, mainly for publicity purposes, and with the
hope that consumers would use them when they wanted work done,
but they have been given short shrift by businesses which regard them
as unfairly loaded against them.

Prior approval of standard form contracts could proceed on a broad
front as in Israel, where there is an administrative board to which
businesses can apply to have restrictive terms in standard form
contracts approved.[46] In carrying out its task the Board must

consider if, in the light of the surrounding circumstances, the clause is prejudicial to consumers or gives an unfair advantage to suppliers likely to prejudice consumers. Failure to approve renders the term(s) unenforceable, while approval prevents subsequent invalidation for a period of five years. Although certainty about the validity of their terms would seem an advantage, businesses have failed to obtain ratification, perhaps through fear that many clauses would be struck down. If the procedure is to be used some sort of mandatory provision must be introduced. In those few cases where standard form contracts have been submitted, and the Supreme Court has become involved, it has adopted a conservative interpretation and has been reluctant to invalidate restrictive terms in purely commercial contexts. The Israeli system would break down in the event that even a relatively small proportion of the standard form contracts in existence were submitted to it.

In the light of limited administrative resources, prior approval of standard form contracts is probably best concentrated in specific areas where the need for consumer protection is greatest. Insurance contracts would be an ideal place to start, for they are specifically excluded from the effects of section 3 of the Unfair Contract Terms Act 1977.[47] Pre-vetting on insurance contracts by public agencies is well-accepted.[48]

IMPLEMENTATION OF PRIVATE LAW RIGHTS

A general feature of private law is that it is not self-implementing. Consumers must take the initiative to enforce their legal rights. The assumption is that consumers know their rights and are sufficiently motivated to press them.[49] If they are harmed because a business infringes their rights, self-interest will impel them to take action, including court proceedings if a settlement cannot be achieved. Of course, consumers frequently fail to utilize their rights in this way. Consumers may not know of their rights to take advantage of them. For example, consumers frequently attribute responsibility for faulty products to manufacturers whereas the law imposes it on retailers.[50] A common way in which consumers take the initiative when they are dissatisfied is not by enforcing their rights through the legal system but by refusing to pay amounts which they do not believe are due. For example, they may stop paying credit instalments on the grounds that a product is defective. Such actions can have tragic consequences because the business involved may repossess the product, and/or obtain a default judgment and then an attachment order against the consumer's earnings if the judgment is not met.[51]

Consumers may not pursue their rights for various reasons. First, consumers may not perceive that there is a problem, for example, that the law obliged the business they dealt with to provide a written contract. Moreover, consumers may not realize that their problem is capable of remedy – they may simply accept a poor standard of service in ignorance of the fact that it falls below the legal standard. Again, they may accept competing interpretations of the problem, that, say, a defect in a product is temporary until it is 'broken in', or has manifested itself because the product is not being used properly.[52] Further, consumers may not think a problem is sufficiently serious to do anything about it – a particular item might not have cost very much, they may be more robust than other individuals and capable of tolerating inconvenience, they may also be philosophical about being 'ripped off' or reluctant to admit it, and they might themselves be able to fix sufficiently a defective item. Even if consumers know their rights there are reasons why they should not seek to enforce them. Some of the factors inhibiting consumers from upholding their legal rights are that they think the business involved will ignore them, that they feel helpless in the face of corporate power or that they simply do not know how to enforce them. As far as legal proceedings are concerned, the courts can appear remote and forbidding to individual consumers. By contrast legal action is less daunting to businesses, particularly if they handle it as a matter of routine.

An important factor in deterring consumers from pursuing their legal rights is the cost, including the opportunity cost of the time and effort. The Office of Fair Trading conducted some preliminary research in 1976 to calculate the cost to consumers of pursuing a complaint about a defective product or service. Taking a very conservative figure for the cost of a consumer's time (50p per hour) and costing telephone calls, visits and letters, it found that the mean aggregate cost was just under £8.[53] Consumers can quite rationally decide that the opportunity cost of attempting to secure redress is not justified if the amount involved is less than the cost of complaining. That consumers are influenced by cost considerations is evidenced by the pattern of their complaints. It has been confirmed in the United States that the unit price of products has a major effect on the rate of problems consumers perceive concerning their more substantial defects.[54] In terms of consumer complaints a nationwide survey in the United Kingdom in 1980 of complaints about durability gives a rough indication that consumers take more action with expensive items (Table 3.1).[55] Interviews with a small sample of consumers in Manchester came up with similar results. When asked whether they could recall any serious complaints, 55 per cent who did remembered items worth less than £5, while only 3 per cent of the claims lodged with a voluntary small claims scheme in the area were for less than that amount.[56]

Table 3.1   Relationship of Complaints About Durability and Cost

Product	Furni-ture	White goods	Vacuum cleaners	Foot-wear	Carpets & floor coverings	Clothes	Cars & motorcycles (serious problems generally)
Total number reporting problem	42	44	20	33	21	21	25
Per cent who complained	38%	<25%	20%	12%	14%	19%	60%

Likewise because many consumer problems involve a small amount it is not worth while for consumers to litigate them. Justice Brandeis of the United States Supreme Court noted:

> [A]lthough the aggregate of the loss entailed may be so serious and widespread as to make the matter one of public consequence, no private suit would be brought to stop the unfair conduct, since the loss to each of the individuals affected is too small to warrant it.[57]

The exception is that the value of litigation may be greater than the immediate sum at stake if a consumer is taking a test case and receives support from other sources.[58]

If social and economic factors do not inhibit consumers from complaining they still face barriers in enforcing their legal rights. An approach to the business involved will often lead to a satisfactory outcome,[59] but in the event that it fails there is a problem for consumers in obtaining assistance from those likely to know the law and how to implement it. Most lawyers have little interest in consumer problems or experience of consumer cases. If they have handled consumer matters this is at least as likely to be because they have represented a business in its dealings with a particular consumer or with consumers in general (e.g. in drafting standard form contracts). The reason lawyers do not encourage consumer problems is principally that they are a loss financially although it might also be that they fear a client's close interest in a case will be too great a nuisance.[60] Other possibilities are that lawyers recognize that they could lose work from businesses if they create difficulties on behalf of consumers or that they identify with businesses and regard complaints as illegitimate. Of course, lawyers do occasionally handle consumer matters for an established client (a 'loss-leader' service – clearly the wealthier benefit) or for friends, relatives or neighbours. But in this event they are likely to advise that it is not worth while pursuing the matter, to provide information on what the consumer ought to do on their own behalf, to refer the consumer to another source of assistance, or to act as an informal mediator with the business.[61] Few legal aid matters involve consumer problems. While there are many reasons for this, one might be that members of legal aid committees have a negative attitude to consumer problems. A Birmingham study discusses one instance where legal aid was refused on the grounds that although the consumer would obtain judgment if the case proceeded, he would probably not be successful in either locating the defendant or in recovering any compensation from him. The research team commented that consideration of the wider community interest might have been served by taking action against the defendant who appeared to be systematically deceiving consumers in the area.[62] Voluntary legal advice schemes receive varying numbers of inquiries about consumer matters and debt but tend to advise, refer or at most mediate. Neighbourhood law centres generally give low priority to consumer problems as a matter of policy. They have limited budgets and staff and are hard pressed by housing, welfare and employment problems, all of which they consider more important to the poor than the run-of-the-mill consumer complaint. Public interest law firms in the United States spend important efforts on consumer matters, but seem to concentrate on the larger aspects such as the dissemination of information, compelling agencies to enforce laws already on the books, and the mass media.[63]

The major burden of consumer advice and assistance falls on media 'action lines' (e.g. newspaper advice columnists), citizens advice bureaux and consumer protection departments. A study of media action lines in the United States concluded that the most disadvantaged complain infrequently and that forces within media organizations tend to push action lines in the direction of passive referral services, which simply transmit complaints to traditional public and private authorities. Adverse publicity by action lines can operate as a powerful weapon against recalcitrant businesses, but advertiser boycotts and threats of defamation have reportedly curtailed aggressive action in several cities.[64] Many consumer enquiries to citizens advice bureaux are solved by simple advice, but in the remainder CAB workers contact the business and negotiate on behalf of consumers, in most cases successfully. Citizens advice bureaux emphasize their impartiality and see themselves as mediators, so that if a business does not produce a positive response the tendency is for them to drop a case. The non-litigious approach of citizens advice bureaux is underlined in this quotation from one of its publications:

Citizens advice bureaux try, wherever possible, to bring about an amicable settlement between an enquirer and a retailer. As one bureau put it: 'A suit for recovery of damages which might be appropriate in a commercial transaction is seldom justified where a private person has a complaint about an article bought from a retailer. Our normal procedure is to try and obtain a replacement, either in whole or in part, an effective repair, or some financial adjustment. We would be reluctant to advise whether any case was one where a client might sue for damages and would refer the client to a solicitor for further advice, with the warning that litigation is expensive . . .'[65]

Quite apart from the fact that citizens advice bureaux retreat in the face of business resistance, there has been criticism that they are better suited to dealing with social problems. Because they are often staffed by volunteer, part-time workers it is said that they lack the knowledge and expertise for the more complicated consumer complaints. Certainly there is some patchiness in the quality of citizens advice bureaux around the country. The consumer side of citizens advice bureaux work has been greatly improved in recent years by government grants to the National Citizens Advice Bureaux to provide more training and information services to local bureaux.

High Street consumer advice centres are the most recent development in the delivery of advice and assistance to consumers. Services offered include pre-shopping advice about the comparative performance of consumer durables, local price surveys and advice and assistance on consumer complaints. In some cases the centres actually take up complaints and attempt to negotiate a settlement with businesses on behalf of consumers. Centres are usually prepared to advise consumers on bringing legal action where a business remains adamant, but few go so far as to send a consumer advice worker to court to assist a consumer present a claim.[66] The first consumer advice centre to give pre-purchase advice and help with complaints opened in Berlin in 1928 and there are now established centres elsewhere in Europe. Developments in Britain derive from the initiative of the Consumers' Association, which financed an experimental consumer advice centre in Kentish Town in North London in 1969. Initial moves were taken by the Conservative government in 1973, which sought the assistance of local authorities in building up a network of local advice centres to give help and information to consumers.[67] From twenty-five centres in March 1974, the number grew to over 130 by mid-1978. Whereas other local authority services were subject to financial cut-backs the expansion of consumer advice centres was fostered by the Labour government on the basis that they made a direct contribution to anti-inflation policy. However, the Conservative government withdrew central government grants to consumer advice centres in mid-1979 on the basis that they were not cost effective. All the evidence pointed the other way, estimates being that complainants received compensation or redress equivalent to many times the cost of the service. As a result of the government's action many consumer advice centres have closed.

Once consumers get to the stage of suing in court they still face difficulties in enforcing their rights. Court documents are complicated by the peculiarities of pleading. *Justice out of Reach* noted that a solicitor for the other side could confuse the lay litigant with various pre-trial notices like a notice for 'discovery of documents', to 'admit facts', or 'to inspect'. It commented: 'A layman can lose his case before it ever reaches hearing by admitting facts that he should not or by failing to demand to see important documents in the other side's possession.'[68] Procedure at a court hearing is quite foreign to consumers who are not used to the techniques of examination and cross-examination, and to whom hearsay is the most natural way of presenting evidence. An attempt to make the courts more accessible, particularly to consumers, is the procedure discussed below for dealing with small claims. The procedure is simplified, court staff assist in the completion of the relevant documents and consumers tend to handle their own case. Should a case fall outside the small claims jurisdiction, however, consumers face the possibility of an ordinary court hearing.

A particular obstacle to consumers in legal proceedings is the difficulty of proving their case. Some consumer transactions are more informal than commercial transactions and consumers are unlikely to keep a detailed record or to note carefully the circumstances of a transaction. Take as an example the problems facing consumers in proving misrepresentation. Salesmen will generally not commit a misrepresentation to paper, but a salesman's oral misrepresentations will normally be made in the absence of independent witnesses because it is not usual for consumers to take third parties with them for consumer transactions. Moreover, an oral misrepresentation which a consumer seeks to prove may be directly contradicted by the written contract which is ultimately signed. What is needed in cases where there are a number of complaints against one business is for consumer protection officials to pretend to be genuine consumers so that clear evidence is obtained of misrepresentation. Similar fact evidence of this nature should be admissible in civil proceedings.

Consumers may face similar problems in defending proceedings, for example, where a business claims that they owe money on a transaction. At one time receipts had to be given if requested for transactions over £2, bearing the requisite stamp duty.[69] Now there is no obligation on a business to issue a receipt unless it can be argued that it is customary in the type of transaction and thus a common law obligation. Persons who pay by cheque are at an advantage at present because production of a cheque cleared by a consumer's bank is evidence that the payee has received the money.[70] Legislation should make it a clear obligation for a business to issue a receipt – or at least a till-slip.

The Consumer Credit Act 1974 has improved the position of consumers as regards documentation of payment under regulated consumer credit transactions. A consumer is entitled on payment of 15p to a copy of a consumer credit or consumer hire agreement and to a statement as to what has been paid and what remains to be paid under it.[71] A business which fails to respond to the request cannot enforce the agreement until it does, and it also commits a criminal offence if it has not done so within a month. Similarly, consumers can request a business to issue a written statement acknowledging that the agreement has ceased and that the debt has been fully repaid.[72] The business must either comply with the request or issue a statement in which it disputes that the debt is extinguished. Statements of account and of termination are usually binding on the business.[73]

Many consumer cases turn on expert evidence, for example, about the exact quality of products or services. Experts are expensive to employ, particularly where small claims are involved. What is reasonable payment to an expert for his time will often seem to the consumer to be so great that it is better to abandon a claim. One solution is for small claims judges/adjudicators to build up an expertise in common sources of consumer complaint. Another possibility is that there should be schemes whereby consumers can obtain cheap, impartial opinions from experts about the true quality of products and services. It should not be too difficult for trade and professional associations to devise such schemes, and there have been some moves in this direction under the Codes of Practice approved by the Office of Fair Trading. For example, under the Voluntary Code of Practice for Footwear, an independent Footwear Testing Centre has been established to which consumers can forward shoes, mainly through retailers or consumer bodies, for an independent test of quality at a relatively low fee.

Small claims

Writing in 1913, Roscoe Pound advocated the establishment of small claims courts.[74] He chided lawyers for their concentration on the substantive principles of law and urged them to recognize the inadequacies and injustices obtaining for ordinary people. It was an injury to society that the will of individuals was subject to the arbitrary will of others because legal protection was too cumbrous and expensive to be available for the less well-off against aggressive opponents who had the means or inclination to resist. 'It is here that the great mass of urban population, whose experience of the law in the past has been too often experience only of the arbitrary discretions of police officials, might be made to feel that the law is a living force for securing their individual as well as their collective interests.'[75] Pound recognized that it was impossible to have lawyers for every person engaged in small claims litigation and instead advocated that claimants should be assisted by court officials and the judge, who could no longer be an umpire as in traditional legal settings.

Successive reformers have adopted Pound's rationale for small claims courts: to make the service of the courts more easily available to ordinary people; to simplify practice and procedure in such cases; to eliminate delay and reduce costs; and generally to promote public confidence in the administration of justice. Yet for sixty years Pound's call for a small claims procedure went unheeded in England and Wales. The legal establishment perpetuated the myth that the county courts were 'the poor man's civil courts'. That fallacy was rudely exposed in 1970 with the publication of the document *Justice out of Reach*.[76] Taking a sample of six county courts in England, the author found that nearly three-quarters of the summons were trader cases involving actions, usually for quite small amounts, against individuals for debt for goods or services. Plaintiffs were frequently the same large firms, and this could only lead to the conclusion that they were in the habit of giving credit without making proper inquiries about credit-worthiness.[77] There was not a single case of a consumer suing a business, except perhaps one for which details were not available. There were small numbers of instances, however, where consumers entered a defence, which usually led to an action being withdrawn.[78]

The upshot of *Justice out of Reach* was the introduction in England and Wales of a small claims procedure within the existing county court structure. The first innovation in 1972 was to introduce pre-trial review by the county court registrar and to simplify documentation with a view to helping unrepresented claimants prepare their cases adequately for the hearing.[79] The pre-trial review was designed to afford an opportunity for identifying the real issues, recording any agreement as to the amount of damages, dealing with the admissibility of evidence, estimating the length of hearing, and fixing a day for the hearing convenient to both parties. A study conducted by Applebey found that a considerable number of registrars did not always hold pre-trial reviews, and, of those who did, just over half claimed to give special help to the unrepresented. The remainder took the view that there were other sources of advice, that advice might appear to favour one side, and that it would be too burdensome. Some 40 per cent of the cases were settled at the pre-trial stage.[80]

Since 1981 a pre-trial review operates only for cases which are to proceed to trial. However, a similar procedure for users going to arbitration is for the arbitrator to appoint a date for preliminary consideration, at which a date for hearing can be fixed and directions given as to the steps which should be taken before the hearing. Preliminary consideration need not occur where the size or nature of the claim or other circumstances make such a course undesirable or unnecessary.[81] For example, in straightforward cases a preliminary hearing might be thought to be unnecessary, requiring two visits to the court. Where a preliminary hearing is held it can perform a useful function in affording arbitrators the opportunity to explain to litigants what is going on and in facilitating settlements. Indeed the filing of a small claim no doubt acts in general as a strong inducement to defendants to settle a dispute.[82]

The second innovation, introduced in 1973, is that either party can apply in county court proceedings for a matter to be referred to arbitration.[83] Matters will normally go to arbitration, as soon as a defence to a claim has been received, if not more than a certain amount is involved (the 'small claims limit'), whatever the views of the other party.[84] However, the registrar can rescind a referral to arbitration, on application of one of the parties, if satisfied that a difficult question of law or a question of fact of exceptional complexity is involved, that a charge of fraud is in issue, that the parties are agreed that the dispute should be tried in court, or that it would be unreasonable for the claim to proceed to arbitration having regard to the subject matter, the circumstances of the parties or the interests of any other person likely to be affected by the award.[85] Normally the registrar acts as arbitrator and is authorized to obtain expert evidence on a technical question with the consent of the parties.[86] Arbitration is coupled with a change in the rules to provide that in claims under the small claims limit no legal costs should be payable except those shown on the summons or incurred in enforcing the award, unless they are certified by the arbitrator to have resulted through the unreasonable conduct of the opposite party.[87] Beyond this amount the court can order an unsuccessful party to pay a successful party its costs in the ordinary way. In *Hobbs* v. *Marlowe*[88] the House of Lords held that the rule could not be evaded by artificially inflating a claim. The Lord Chancellor said of the rule:

> Its effect is to prevent a litigant being deterred from asserting what he regarded as a just claim or defence by the fear of being mulcted in relatively heavy legal costs if he loses. It is to be noted that the rule applies whether the successful party is the plaintiff or the defendant.[89]

Consumers are not prevented by the rule from taking along a friend or relative to help them present their case, and it is through this that a few consumer advice centres and citizens advice bureaux provide assistance to consumers making a claim.

Arbitration and the no costs rule are designed to simplify procedure and to encourage small claims, especially consumer claims. When arbitration was introduced it was anticipated that the strict rules of evidence would be dispensed with and that hearings would be in private so to ensure as much informality as was consistent with each party being given a fair and equal opportunity to present the case.[90] Over a third of consumers in the Consumer Council's survey thought that arbitration was not at all, or not very, informal.[91] The Applebey study found that although most registrars claimed to adopt an inquisitorial approach, about half still adopted basically adversary proceedings.[92] Proceedings were generally more informal than in court, but registrars still took the laws of evidence very seriously – for example, putting witnesses on oath.

Use of the small claims procedure has increased since it was established: in 1974 there were 3771 judgments by arbitration; in 1980, 13,945. However, a random survey of nearly 2000 people in 1980 found that none had used the small claims procedure against a shop or supplier.[93] In the Consumer Council's survey of the small claims procedure the outcome was as follows: settled before hearing (including judgments by default) (25); plaintiff won case in full (113); plaintiff won case in part (19); plaintiff lost case (13); defendant's counter-claim upheld/agreed (6); defendant ceased trading (3); incomplete (2); and not stated (7).[94] These findings suggest that justice was done in the great majority of cases where consumers were prepared to invoke the procedures.

The changes in 1971 and 1973 hardly parallel the establishment of separate small claims courts in other jurisdictions. The Lord Chancellor claimed that the introduction of separate small claims courts in England and Wales would 'neither be efficient nor just'.[95] Clearly governments in the United States, Australia and other countries disagree. One of the advantages of a separate small claims system is that it starts with a completely new image, which can encourage consumers to bring actions to enforce their legal rights. In addition, it is easier to adopt techniques to which objection would be taken if they were used within the framework by the ordinary courts. Thus some Australian small claims courts deliberately seek publicity with a view to having a salutary effect on business practices.[96] Some are also directed to proceed in a manner 'fair and equitable to all parties', which is a useful indication to adjudicators to ignore settled law if this is moulded on premises such as freedom of contract which are inappropriate to modern conditions.[97] The danger is that adjudicators might give compromise decisions, and consumers might be induced to settle for them, when a case demands that full judgment be given in a consumer's favour.[98] Similarly, some small claims courts have a wide order-making power – the payment of money, the performance of work, and the rectification of defects.[99]

A drawback to the small claims procedure in England and Wales is that to some extent old attitudes and principles associated with the county court still prevail. Consumers are probably still deterred and suspicious of a system which has been traditionally associated with debt-collecting. Steps have been taken to overcome this resistance and to publicize the possibility on consumers making claims. Forms have been revised to make them more intelligible, a guide has been prepared on how to make a claim and county court staff in some areas advise claimants about procedure and refer them to agencies like the citizens advice bureaux and the consumer advice centres if there are queries about the law.

There is nothing to prevent businesses using the small claims procedure in the county court. In the Applebey study over half the plaintiffs were companies and firms and these were defendants in less than a quarter of the cases.[100] The figures suggest that businesses are frequently using the arbitration procedure to bring claims against individuals when it was supposedly established to enable consumers to bring claims against businesses. Certainly this has been the experience in many United States jurisdictions, where small claims courts have been colonized by commercial interests, and the main function of the courts has turned out to be the collection of trade debts.[101] Businesses have found the courts are an efficient collection mechanism because they are often less costly than employing a collection agency. In addition, there is virtually no scrutiny of claims, which are simply rubber-stamped even when they are groundless in law. Default judgments are sometimes associated with 'sewer service', where court officials give perjured affidavits of service for summons which have never been served. Reform has been resisted in some United States jurisdictions mainly with the argument that it would be unfair to deprive businesses of the opportunity to use small claims courts, but gradually a consensus has developed that small claims courts are not the courts of the poor as originally intended. Reform of small claims courts in some jurisdictions has attempted to reduce business claims by limiting the number of suits which can be brought in any period. Suggestions have also been made that a small claims court should have two divisions, one for business and one for individuals and that their facility should be confined to businessmen not guilty of shady or unlawful practices.[102]

A number of United States jurisdictions, Quebec, and some Australian states have adopted the simplest and most practical solution: businesses have been barred from being claimants in small claims courts.[103] But this approach still has the difficulty that businesses can pursue judgments against consumers in other courts, although there may be some attrition of claims because of higher initial costs and closer scrutiny of claims. If a judgment is obtained the costs to an unsuccessful defendant consumer may be greater than if the case were heard in a small claims court. A solution would seem to be to devise some procedure whereby cases in which consumers have not paid for some valid reason are transferred into the small claims court. The most radical proposal is that businesses should be barred completely from pursuing through the courts any claim associated with products supplied on credit at the retail level.[104] Professor Ison justifies this reform on three main grounds: (1) by enforcing claims of credit grantors the courts are assisting businesses engaged in disreputable trading practices; (2) it is unfair that the legal system should allow retailers to pursue their claims when consumers have great difficulty in doing the same, and (3) businesses achieve satisfactory payment in the vast majority of cases. To ensure repayment, Ison argues, businesses would have a greater incentive to exclude the poorer risks from the outset and could also use sanctions such as an adverse credit report against non-payers.

The small claims procedure in the county court in England and Wales attempts to discourage legal representation through the rule that costs cannot normally be recovered from the other party where the amount at stake is less than the limit. It seems doubtful whether the cost sanction in claims for less than this deters those who have the money and think that they will be successful if they are represented.[105] Certainly, larger businesses have every reason to employ legal representation because it is a matter of routine and an ordinary business expense. There is no research about representation under the small claims procedure but the evidence suggests that businesses are represented and that this can have an effect on the outcome. A study of legal representation in the New York (Manhattan) small claims court found that defendants with legal representation had a clear advantage in terms of the outcome of a case where the consumer plaintiff was not represented.[106] There is no reason to think that the situation elsewhere is any different.

If representation is unnecessary in small claims there seems no reason why it should not be barred completely. The alternative of providing legal representation for consumers engaged in small claims would seem to be too costly. Most Australian jurisdictions bar legal representation in small claims courts.[107] Denying legal representation really only affects businesses, because at present, consumer claimants are rarely represented. In the Consumer Council's survey, of the ninety-one cases where a pre-trial review was held two people attended with their solicitor, and of the seventy-eight cases that went to trial or arbitration only two people said they were accompanied by a solicitor. Yet in fifty-six of the 188 cases the other side used a solicitor or barrister – it is unclear whether this was at the actual hearing or at other stages – although more than half the matters involved amounts under £100.[108]

There can clearly be an inequality of presentation in small claims cases where an inarticulate, unrepresented consumer is opposed by an experienced and knowledgeable businessman. In the absence of representation for the consumer it needs the adjudicator to break away from the adversary approach normally prevailing in English courts to redress the balance by taking an active inquisitorial role in the proceedings.

New mechanisms for implementing private law rights

What is needed if private law rights are to be adequately enforced is to ensure that worthwhile claims are initiated and ultimately get to court if necessary. Consumer education by bodies such as consumer advice centres is one way of ensuring that individual consumers are aware of their rights. But institutional reforms are required because even if consumers know their rights there is no guarantee that they will be acknowledged by businesses. Small claims courts are one such reform. This section looks at two other reforms for ensuring that consumers' private law rights are vindicated through legal process; these are (1) class actions and (2) legal proceedings by a public body on behalf of consumers.

Class actions enable a number of consumers to have similar complaints determined at one time instead of in separate proceedings. One or two consumers sue on behalf of all the other consumers similarly affected where a business is in breach of the civil law. A successful judgment binds the defendant business as regards all members of the class. The class action thus has an advantage over the test case, which may be ignored with reference to any consumers other than the successful plaintiff. Another advantage over the test case is that the class action limits the ability of a business to avoid an unfavourable precedent by settling with the plaintiff, for settlement of a class action should require court approval. Class actions obviously have advantages in terms of saving time and money over individuals instituting separate proceedings. A number of small claims can be aggregated into an action of some substance and it becomes easier to cover the legal costs.[109]

Class actions can also attract useful publicity because of the significance and number of people involved. For example, in a Californian case a consumer sued on behalf of all Standard Oil credit card purchasers of Chevron F–310 petrol in southern California, alleging that Standard's advertising for the petrol was false because it did not reduce exhaust emissions as claimed. The consumer alleged that she and the class had purchased some 300 million gallons of the petrol and she sued for $15 million in actual damages and for an equivalent amount in punitive damages. In the result, the action was ultimately dismissed because the plaintiff exceeded the limitation period.[110] A deterrent effect on businesses may also result from class actions when they find that their trade practices no longer pass unchallenged.

A dishonest trader might not be overly sensitive about adverse publicity surrounding litigation against him. But an action that poses a potential liability towards a class possibly numbering hundreds or even thousands is another matter. A threat of this magnitude may well provide the check that will stop the businessman with fraudulent intentions from carrying out his plans.[111]

Class actions can also have an important psychological effect on consumers and can provide an incentive for the formation or continuation of consumer groups. Possible examples of class actions in the consumer context are where a business continually supplies a sub-standard product to different consumers in breach of the implied terms of the Sale of Goods Act 1979, or where a number of consumers are misled by the same advertisement.

A new federal class action procedure was introduced in the United States in 1966.[112] For a class action to be instituted under the rule, the class must be so numerous that joinder of all members is impracticable; there must be questions of law and fact common to the class; the claims or defences of the representatives must be typical of the class; and the representatives must be able to fairly and adequately protect the interests of the class. In addition, a court must be satisfied that the questions of law or fact common to members of the class predominate over any questions affecting only individual members and that a class action is superior to other available methods of adjudication. The Supreme Court in *Eisen* v. *Carlisle & Jacquelin*[113] limited class actions under the federal rule by holding that plaintiffs must give individual notice at their own expense to all members of a class who can be identified with reasonable effort. The upshot of *Eisen* was thought to be that consumers would be deterred from taking class actions because of the initial costs required by notification.[114] The Supreme Court justified notice on due process grounds because a court could then be satisfied that a plaintiff was competent to represent the class. Yet consumers who would never have sued individually will not be prejudiced just because they are not notified before an action is begun. Furthermore, there are other ways of determining whether a plaintiff will adequately represent the interests of a class than by requiring that all members of the class be notified. For these reasons a Californian court has held that the *Eisen* ruling does not apply to consumer class actions under state law, and that consumers can proceed without individual notice to class members.[115] In determining what notice is required the court said that it depends on balancing the need to protect a business from future law suits and the economic feasibility of requiring a plaintiff to notify class members.

The 'fluid' class recovery procedure in the United States allows the class-wide assessment of damages, which then goes into a fund against which claims can be made. Beyond that there have been some novel remedies to overcome the unjust enrichment to a business if it is unlikely that consumers will claim their part of the damages recovered. The *Yellow Cab* case is an illustration of a cy-pres scheme; the defendant settled a class action brought against it for overcharging on the basis that it would apply an amount to lowering taxi fares for a period of time in the future.[116] Criticism of class actions in the United States include that they open the way to 'strike suits' (large claims simply in anticipation that they will be favourably settled), that they distort the substantive law, and that they impose enormous costs on business. There is no systematic evidence to support these claims and they neglect the controls which courts can exercise to prevent abuse. In many ways these claims are expressions of disquiet at the change in the balance of economic power which class actions potentially represent.[117] In fact there have been relatively few consumer class actions at the federal level, possibly because of the procedural impediments. At the state level there has been more activity especially in states where the procedural impediments are fewer and the substantive law more favourable to the type of claims made.[117a] However, certificates for class actions in relation to several notable products liability claims have been denied on the basis that while there are common questions about the existence and nature of the defect, these are outweighed by individual issues concerning conduct subsequent to purchase, proximate cause and contributory negligence.[117b]

In England and Commonwealth jurisdictions class actions have a limited scope although the basic procedure was long recognized in chancery as a matter of convenience to avoid multiple suits. The Rules of the Supreme Court and their interpretation by the courts now govern what English law calls the representative action. Order 15, rule 12 of the Rules provides:

(1) Where numerous persons have the same interest in any proceedings . . . the proceedings may be begun, and, unless the Court otherwise orders, continued, by or against any one or more of them as representing all or as representing all except one or more of them . . .

(3) A judgment or order given in proceedings under this Rule shall be binding on all the persons as representing whom the plaintiff sue . . . but shall not be enforced against any person not a party to the proceedings except with the leave of the Court . . .

The requirement of the 'same interest' has been interpreted narrowly: the accepted wisdom is that a representative action is not possible where the individual claims arise out of separate contacts with another person or where the relief claimed is damages (at least if the damages need separate calculation).[118] On this interpretation of the rule it would not apply to all the consumers who purchased a particular type of car with the same fault since each consumer would have a separate contract with a different retailer and would have a separate claim for damages although the contractual terms in each case might be identical. However, some Canadian courts seem sympathetic to the class action idea. For example, in *Naken* v. *General Motors of Canada Ltd*[119] four plaintiffs sued on behalf of all the persons who had purchased new 1971 or 1972 Firenzas, claiming $1000 for each on the basis that this was the amount by which each vehicle had depreciated in value. The cause of action they sought to establish was contractual, based on the warranties the manufacturers had made in its printed materials and advertisements. The Ontario Court of Appeal allowed the plaintiffs to proceed if they amended their statement of claim to confine it to purchasers who actually saw the material and as a result purchased a car, since only they could have a contract with the manufacturer of which such a warranty was part.

The Australian Law Reform Commission has considered the adoption of a class action procedure. 'If courts are to be able to continue to serve the public in a meaningful way when unlawful conduct has affected a large number of persons, new procedures are necessary. . . . Class actions have a unique capacity to overcome the barriers impeding access to courts and restore some equality to litigation.'[120] The Commission seeks to avoid some of the difficulties which have occurred in the United States; for example, it suggests that it may be sufficient to notify potential class members through the mass media and not by means of individual notice.[121] In the United States there is no great financial risk for someone initiating a class action since each party bears its own costs and lawyers work for contingency fees. This is not the case in Australia – or in England or Canada for that matter – where the general rule is that legal costs are paid by the unsuccessful party. Consequently, in many situations no plaintiff would have the financial incentive to institute a class action because of the possibility of having to pay the other party's costs as well if unsuccessful. Accordingly, the Commission suggests that each party should bear its own costs in class actions for damages or that a class action fund should be established to provide financial assistance to plaintiffs who satisfy the fund's administrators of their need and the merit of their claim.[122]

Class actions are not a universal panacea for consumers. They are only possible where there is a worthwhile claim in law and cannot be used to overcome problems of proof or deficiencies in private law doctrines. Class actions still require consumers to take the initiative, and too much should not be made of the United States experience where the society is more litigation-minded, the contingent fee system provides an incentive to lawyers to instigate legal actions, and consumer groups and consumer advocates are more established and more familiar with test case strategy. Much in class actions depends on the persons who take the initiative, and there is no guarantee that their interests coincide with those of the class or that they are competent to represent the class.

An amendment to the law in England and Wales in 1972 is designed to obviate the need for separate civil proceedings if a consumer is injured by a prejudicial trade practice for which a business is convicted under the criminal law.[123] Previously, a separate civil action had to be taken against the business in most consumer cases. Indeed, before 1968 it was impossible to use a conviction as a basis for a civil action,[124] although some consumer legislation provided that a breach of it was good grounds for civil proceedings.[125] Now under section 35 of the Powers of Criminal Courts Act 1973, courts can award compensation on conviction in criminal proceedings to persons suffering any personal injury, loss or damage as a result of an offence. No compensation can be made in respect of loss suffered by the dependants of a person in consequence of death; and in determining whether to make an order, and the amount to be paid under it, a court must have regard to the defendant's means.[126] The compensation to be paid must not exceed £1,000 in respect of each offence for which a person is convicted.[127] A claim for compensation must be proved in the normal way and the Court of Appeal has directed trial courts that the procedure should not be used where what is necessary is a complicated investigation and hearing of evidence after the criminal hearing has been concluded.[128] A compensation order does not foreclose subsequent civil proceedings, although civil damages will be reduced by the amount paid under any order.[129] However, if civil proceedings have been settled and the consumer is still out of pocket, it is not possible to claim the deficiency by way of a compensation order.[130]

Somewhat wider provisions than section 35 have been introduced directly into consumer legislation in other Commonwealth jurisdictions. Under the Australian Trade Practices Act 1974, the court can make such an order as it thinks appropriate to compensate persons for loss or damage caused by conduct constituting a contravention of the Act.[131] Orders include but are not confined to (a) declaring the whole or any part of a contract void; (b) varying a contract; (c) directing the refund of money; (d) ordering the payment of the loss or damage; (e) requiring repair or the provision of parts; and (f) requiring the supply of services. However widely couched, a compensation procedure for breach of criminal provisions suffers drawbacks. First, it only applies to malpractice which constitutes a criminal offence for which a conviction is obtained. These are a small percentage of the total number of breaches of civil and criminal law. Secondly, consumer protection departments must present con-sumers' claims for compensation if the procedure is to be a success. Yet many consumer protection departments take the view that it is up to individual consumers to present a claim despite the fact that the legislation in 1972 specifically dropped the requirement that applic-ation for compensation should be made by the aggrieved person.[132] Consumer protection departments could well emulate the practice in some police departments commended by the Court of Appeal of having victims instruct prosecuting counsel to make application for compensation on their behalf.[133]

What is really needed in Britain is a procedure along the lines of that in other jurisdictions whereby consumer protection agencies can take proceedings on behalf of consumers affected by a breach of civil law. The obvious advantage is that a procedure like this relieves consumers of the onerous and sometimes expensive task of instituting a civil action. Enabling consumer groups to institute action is well accepted in continental jurisdictions – for instance, consumer groups are authorized by statute in some countries to seek injunctive or declaratory relief against actual or threatened conduct harmful to the consumer.[134] There are certain difficulties with conferring such standing on private groups: for example, must they first be publicly approved, how representative must they be before approval, which cases will they choose to litigate, and is there to be a public subvention to cover their legal costs?

More in line with accepted methods in common law jurisdictions is the idea of a government body such as a consumer protection department suing on behalf of consumers. For example, in some Canadian and Australian jurisdictions consumer protection agencies have a power to institute or defend civil proceedings on behalf of a consumer if they are satisfied that a good cause of action exists and that it is in the public interest.[135] The consumer must specifically consent to the proceedings and the agency is then subrogated to his rights. Of course, there is the disadvantage that the public agency entrusted with such power might be the very agency whose failure to enforce the public law has led to calls for the new remedy.

The mass restitution suit goes one step further and allows a consumer protection department to bring a suit for damages or injunctive relief on behalf of all the consumers affected by 'multiple or persistent' breaches of the law.[136] There is no need for consumers to have complained before the action is commenced. The department bears the burden and the cost of instituting the proceedings although it can recover this amount in a successful action plus the costs of investigation leading to judgment. The advantage of mass restitution suits is obvious in that they can guarantee recovery to consumers who might not bring an action themselves. At the same time the possibility of a mass restitution suit would act as a deterrent to businesses which would ordinarily have to compensate only a few of the consumers adversely affected by a trade practice in breach of the law. Individual consumers need not be identified before a judgment is given, although the court might establish measures to notify potential recipients. To participate in any judgment consumers need only convince an officer of the consumer protection department of their entitlement.[137]

CONCLUSION

Private law works on the basis that individuals know their legal rights and will assert them. Neither assumption is justified. Surveys show that there is a widespread ignorance of legal rights and there are many reasons – notably the cost – why consumers do not pursue their rights even when they know them. Consumer advice centres and small claims procedures are two developments to encourage consumers to assert their private law rights. Neither is completely satisfactory although both are definite improvements. Consumer advice centres undoubtedly make people more aware of their rights as consumers, and as independent bodies can achieve many settlements with businesses on behalf of dissatisfied customers. Their existence sensitizes many businesses to consumer matters, so that many complaints can be solved without resort to legal measures. But consumer advice centres come to a dead-end when a business refuses to budge on a justified consumer claim. Few consumer advice centres have the inclination or expertise to shepherd consumers through the courts or have powers themselves to take legal action against businesses on behalf of consumers. The small claims procedure in the county court in England has made it easier for consumers to institute legal proceedings but it would have been better to establish separate small claims courts, as in the United States and Australia, to break away from the traditions of the existing county court. Businesses are using the small claims procedure to institute actions against consumers – it would seem the opposite of what was intended – and there is still the possibility than an unrepresented consumer will face a business with legal representation. Other jurisdictions have simply barred business claims and legal representation in their small claims courts.

The class action and the mass restitution suit are two mechanisms which go part of the way in overcoming the weaknesses of private law. Mass restitution suits, for example, where a public body can institute proceedings on behalf of all the consumers affected by a breach of consumer law, overcome the problem of consumers having to shoulder the onerous task of taking action individually to obtain compensation. At the same time, if the amount awarded to consumers is sufficiently high it will act as a deterrent to businesses. With some consumer offences, however, because few consumers are affected it can still be profitable for a business to pay compensation but not to take remedial action. This brings home the point that private law, even with improved procedures, is no substitute for public control as a tool of consumer protection.

4
Minimum quality standards for products and services: retailers' liability

One of the most important issues in consumer protection is the quality of products and services. Every year hundreds of thousands of consumers complain to retailers, manufacturers and consumer protection agencies that the products they have bought are defective or that the services they have contracted for are sub-standard. A small proportion of these complaints include consumers who have suffered personal injury as a result of a defective product or sub-standard service, although most complaints are about shoddy, as distinct from unsafe, products and services. This and the succeeding chapter examine those parts of the private law relating to the quality of products and services. There are aspects of the public law relevant to the issue – the Food and Drugs Act 1955 fixes the quality of food, the Medicines Act 1968 regulates the manufacture of drugs and under the Consumer Safety Act 1978 standards can be established for unduly hazardous products.[1] However, the main guarantee of the quality of products and services is the private law.

The previous chapter laid bare the procedural drawbacks to private law. This and the succeeding chapter discuss deficiencies in legal doctrine which relate to the quality of products and services. The greatest deficiencies derive from the doctrine of privity of contract and that of negligence. The first means that a manufacturer is not generally liable in contract for the quality of what it produces, since consumers buy from the retailer and not from the manufacturer ('vertical privity'). Consumers must sue the retailer for breach of contract, although it in turn may sue the manufacturer. If substantial loss is involved the situation is hardly satisfactory when the retailer has gone out of business or has few assets. Privity of contract also means that only purchasers can take legal action against a retailer in the absence of negligence ('horizontal privity'). In other words, if a consumer-purchaser has given what turns out to be a defective product to a third party – a member of the family, a friend, etc. –that third party consumer has no remedy in contract.

The doctrine of negligence means that consumers can only sue manufacturers where they suffer loss as a result of a defective product, if they can demonstrate 'fault' on its part – that it fell below the standard of care which the law requires. As we shall see, the children affected by Thalidomide would have had great difficulty in establishing this against the British manufacturer and may have ended up penniless if a settlement had not been reached.

This chapter examines the retailer's position, primarily that it is liable to compensate consumer-purchasers under the Sale of Goods Act 1979 where it supplies shoddy or sub-standard products. A retailer is also strictly liable under this provision where a consumer-purchaser is injured by a defective product. These remedies do not extend to third party consumers and may even prove illusory for consumer-purchasers where a retailer has gone out of business or has few assets. This chapter also examines liability for services: what is the responsibility of persons, like car repairers or medical practitioners, regarding the standard of work they perform? The next chapter on manufacturers' liability focuses primarily on products that give rise to personal injury. In English law manufacturers have a minimal responsibility for products which are simply shoddy or sub-standard, although in practice some issue guarantees or offer maintenance by which they undertake to repair products if faults develop. But the legal position is that the main burden for shoddy or sub-standard products falls on retailers.

Table 4.1 attempts to summarize the complicated pattern of the private law regarding responsibility for the quality of products.

BACKGROUND TO PRODUCT STANDARDS

There is no agreed definition of product quality despite the fact that it is regarded as a major factor in consumer transactions. At one end of the spectrum are the objective criteria of physical/chemical or microbiological standards; at the other is the marketing concept of a

Table 4.1   Legal Liability for Defective Products

Manufacturer
|
Retailer
|
Consumer – Third party consumer

| | Retailers' liability | | Manufacturers' liability | |
	Injurious products	Shoddy products	Injurious products	Shoddy products
Consumer-purchaser	Yes – Sale of Goods Act 1979[2]	Yes – Sale of Goods Act 1979[2]	Yes – if negligence	No[1]
Third party consumer	Yes – if negligence	No[3]	Yes – if negligence	No[1]

1   'Yes' if a manufacturer's guarantee is a contract.
2   Sometimes reluctantly in practice.
3   Usually 'yes' in practice although not in law.

consumer's 'subjective assessment' of quality.[2] The former governs the approach of the quality control departments of manufacturing concerns and the latter the approach of the marketing departments. Although the first book on quality control for industry was published in 1931, it was not until after the Second World War that widespread application of its techniques were made. This rise in interest is ascribed to competitive pressure and the requirement of high levels of precision within the manufacturing process itself.[3] However, uniform standards which were established (e.g. those of the British Standards Institution) met with some opposition on the grounds that they restricted innovation. Despite the rise in quality control, many manufacturers continued to market low-quality goods. As early as 1961 it was noted that falls in consumer product sales could be ascribed to consumer hostility to poor quality. Although the importance of good quality-control measures would seem established, in a 1963 survey of some two thousand British firms, only 14 per cent had good quality-control facilities.[4] It was estimated that British industry lost around £400 million a year through defective manufacture and that the gross national product could be increased by 5 per cent and wastage halved if correct quality procedures were observed.

What of the quality of consumer products today? Although there is a bias in complaints because consumers complain less about low-priced articles, in the absence of adequate monitoring procedures the 'consumer-complaint' method is one of the best available measures of product quality. The Office of Fair Trading collects statistics about the number of complaints to consumer protection departments, consumer advice centres and citizens advice bureaux. For 1978 it reported over 140,000 complaints about the quality of products.[5] Another way in which product quality may be assessed – particularly in regard to safety – is the extent of product recalls. These are fairly infrequent in Britain and there are no comprehensive statistics, but in the United States many million product units are recalled per annum by the largest consumer product manufacturers.[6] Product quality is also indicated by the number of lawsuits instigated against firms for defective products. There has been a rapid expansion of this type of litigation in the United States with approximately half a million product liability cases filed annually. In part this can be attributed to factors like increased consumer awareness, but it also reflects the scale to which faulty products continue to be marketed. Consumers elsewhere are less litigation-oriented; nevertheless, we noted in the last chapter that a considerable number of small claims actions are being taken. Of these, many concern faulty goods and sub-standard services. Surveys by bodies like the Consumers' Association are another indication of product quality and also throw light on the standard of servicing for consumer durables.[7] A comprehensive survey of domestic consumer durables in EEC countries showed that an average of 16 per cent of consumers bought products which were faulty on delivery and an average of 30 per cent had to have products repaired while under guarantee.[8] That Report also uncovered widespread deficiencies in servicing or faulty workmanship: it was unusual for a written estimate for repairs to be given and even if one was given it was rarely itemized in detail; there were delays, and few consumers were offered a replacement to use in the interim, and in many cases there were inadequate stocks of spare parts.

The present state of private law combined with the procedural difficulties of using it are inadequate to ensure satisfactory product quality. Perhaps this is not surprising because private law operates only to a limited extent as a means of social control. Its usual remedy of damages is to compensate an injured party, not to punish or correct the other side. A business responsible for defective products or sub-standard services can still be in a profitable position after paying compensatory damages and the calculation of other amounts such as opportunity costs. The amount of damages awarded to a successful consumer is unrelated to the purpose of deterrence and will only have that effect if it is less expensive for the business to alter its behaviour than to give relief to that consumer and others likely to take similar action in the future and succeed. As Leff notes: 'One cannot think of a more expensive and frustrating course than to seek to regulate goods or "contract" quality through repeated law-suits against inventive "wrongdoers".'[9]

How, then, can manufacturers be encouraged to improve design and to step up inspection of products as they come off the production line? How can they be induced to assess carefully the potential market, to test thoroughly prototypes, and to introduce a check-up system to find out consumer reactions and feed them back into the design and production process? Voluntary measures are one way, although they suffer drawbacks. The British Standards Institution, for example, which is financed by subscriptions from industry, government grant and the sale of standards, concerns itself with drafting standards of size, quality and performance in a number of industrial fields.[10] Draft standards are adopted by consensus in committees comprising manufacturers, distributors, technical experts and sometimes consumer representatives. Interest in consumer products has always been incidental to the main work of BSI. Even the 300-odd standards it identifies for consumer products are not of crucial importance to consumers.

Ultimately public regulation is necessary to improve product quality in addition to voluntary efforts and reform of the private law. Already the Director General of Fair Trading can obtain assurances, undertakings and orders against businesses which are consistently responsible for sub-standard products or poor services.[11] Perhaps this section offers the greatest chance for action to be taken to improve the quality of products and services. The Swedish Market Court has a similar power which it has used against manufacturers. Another technique to improve product quality is to require mandatory guarantees for consumer products, during which time consumers can have defects repaired without cost. This has been used in New South

Wales for motor cars where legislation deems that a mandatory warranty exists in every consumer transaction for the sale of a motor vehicle.[12] Dealers – not manufacturers – are obliged to repair any defect whether it existed at the time of sale or not, so as to place the vehicle in a reasonable condition having regard to its age.[13] For new cars the warranty is twelve months or 20,000 kilometres; for used cars it is on a sliding scale depending on the price, although it can be excluded completely by disclosure before sale. The dealer is still liable when a car is sold on hire purchase, and with new cars subsequent owners can take advantage of the warranty.[14] The warranty does not apply to defects in specific accessories (e.g. tyres) or to those attributable to an accident or consumer misuse.[15]

Consideration might also be given to enforcing minimum quality standards. A number have been enacted for safety reasons.[16] Something along these lines, for ordinary consumer durables, operated during the Second World War and the post-war period until 1952 under the Utility Schemes, which covered a wide range of consumer products.[17] The supply of materials to manufacturers was made dependent on the production of goods which conformed to certain broad descriptions and specifications. Admittedly there would be difficulties in introducing product standards today with the huge range of products currently on the market and the great variety of tastes. For these reasons clothing, for example, would generally be a poor candidate for product standards, but it might be possible to establish them for items like children's shoes where variety is not regarded as so important. Multi-level standards should overcome the objection that they lead to uniformity and the lowest common denominator. In 1977 the Minister of State for Prices and Consumer Protection floated the idea of a quality assurance scheme to combat shoddy products: the government might take power to ban the sales of products that fell below a standard or it might require manufacturers to label their products with an indication of quality.

PRODUCT QUALITY

In many cases consumers will obtain satisfaction from a retailer when they complain about a faulty product they have purchased. Some stores give an automatic refund or exchange. This sometimes extends to where consumers find that the size is wrong or the colour is not what they thought, or where they have simply changed their mind –

situations where there is no legal right to redress in the absence of misrepresentation. Consumers may still have to demonstrate proof of purchase, which is most easily done by producing the receipt or till-slip. In situations where retailers are not as obliging as this, the law provides two actions for the purchaser of a faulty product: an action for misrepresentation if it has been misdescribed, and an action for breach of the implied conditions of quality contained in the Sale of Goods Act 1979.

Misrepresentations about quality

Retailers can incur civil liability, as well as criminal liability under the Trade Descriptions Act 1968, when they misrepresent the quality of products and services either orally or in writing. For example, if they describe a product as being in excellent condition and it is not, a consumer may be able to rescind the contract or claim damages. It need not matter that the business did not know the statement was untrue. An oral statement might constitute an actionable mis-representation when it distorts a written representation. A clear case is *Curtis* v. *Chemical Cleaning & Dyeing Co.*,[18] where a shop assistant accepted a dress from a consumer for cleaning but innocently misrepresented that the exemption clause on the receipt covered things like beads and sequins, whereas it covered all damage. The Court of Appeal held that the consumer could claim damages when the dress was returned stained because the assistant's statement had created a false impression in the consumer's mind. The case also illustrates the point that retailers are in general vicariously liable for misrepresentation by their employees in the course of their employ-ment. Criminal liability for employees under the Trade Descriptions Act 1968 is much more limited. The following discussion focuses on representations about the quality of products, but the principles are general and consumers may have a remedy for misrepresentation about other matters like price or the identity of a seller (e.g. a misrepresentation by a doorstep seller that he is from an education authority). Generally speaking the law only gives relief for misrep-resentations of existing fact. A statement of opinion might be regarded as a statement of fact if, say, the facts on which it is based are peculiarly within the knowledge of the person making it. An action does not generally arise for misrepresentations about the law or about what a person promises to do (e.g. repair a car) unless the promise is contractual or unless the person has no intention of carrying out his promise.

Not all misrepresentations give rise to civil liability. The parol evidence rule makes it difficult for consumers to sue on an oral misrepresentation when it adds to or is inconsistent with the terms of a written contract. In an Australian case the court held that a consumer could not rely on an oral misrepresentation by a salesman that a car was in very good mechanical condition when the transaction was completed on the basis of an express 30-day or 1000-mile warranty.[19] In practice the courts are increasingly using the device of collateral contract to avoid the parol evidence rule and to regard a statement additional to or inconsistent with written terms as giving rise to a separate contract, consideration for which is entering the main contract. The courts have always allowed some latitude to sales 'puffs' or commendations, which will not give rise to an action for misrepresentation. Puffs, or commendations, are the laudatory statements businesses use in marketing products, the vacuous claims of modern advertising like 'whiter than white', which everyone is expected to take with a grain of salt. If this is the case, however, it is difficult to see why puffs are so widely used. There are no modern English cases in the consumer field deciding that a statement was a puff. In *Andrews* v. *Hopkinson*[20] the court had no doubt that a statement by a dealer that a car was 'a good little bus; I would stake my life on it' was not a puff. Some United States cases take a robust view of consumers' ability to see through advertising claims.[21]

Misrepresentations may give rise to a claim for damages or to rescission. Damages are payable if the misrepresentation is fraudulent, negligent or contractual.[22] The law says that a representation is a term of the contract if in the circumstances it can be said that this is what the parties intended. In practice the courts give substance to this rather unsatisfactory test by examining various factors such as the nature of the representation and the knowledge available to the parties. There is little difficulty in establishing that a representation is contractual if it is incorporated in a written contract.[23] Generally speaking representations by businesses in transactions with consumers are likely to be contractual because of the disparity in knowledge between the parties. The consumer in *Dick Bentley Productions Ltd* v. *Harold Smith (Motors) Ltd*[24] obtained damages for breach of contract when a car dealer innocently misrepresented that the car he bought had travelled a limited mileage. In the reverse situation, where a consumer was selling a car in part-exchange to a dealer and innocently misrepresented what model it was, this was not a term of the contract because the dealer was in a position to know whether or not the statement was true.[25]

The difference between a mere representation and a representation which is a term of the contract is less important than it was prior to the Misrepresentation Act 1967, because the Act imposes a statutory liability for damages where a person 'has entered into a contract after a misrepresentation made to him by another party thereto and as a result thereof he has suffered loss ... unless he [the representor] proves that he had reasonable grounds to believe and did believe up to the time the contract was made that the facts represented were true.'[26] It is a difficult matter for a person to show reasonable grounds.[27] The court also has a discretionary power to award damages in lieu of rescission in circumstances where a person has entered into a contract after a misrepresentation has been made to him and he would be entitled to rescind the contract.[28] Previously the consumer's only remedy for innocent misrepresentation was rescission.

Rescission for misrepresentation arises at law with fraudulent misrepresentation and in equity for innocent misrepresentation. Breach of a representation in a contract entitles a consumer to claim damages and might also give rise to a right to 'rescind' it. With serious breaches a right to treat the contract as having been repudiated is automatic for it arises by virtue of the breach rather than the misrepresentation.[29] The right to rescind a contract for misrepresentation can be lost on general equitable principles where a consumer has expressly affirmed the contract, where *restitutio in integrum* is impossible (e.g. the consumer has substantially modified the product or it has been seriously damaged through his fault), where an innocent third party would be prejudiced, or where a reasonable time has elapsed. The purchaser in *Leaf* v. *International Galleries*[30] purported to rescind on the basis that a painting was not a Constable, but the Court of Appeal regarded the five-year period since the sale as being too long. The justification was that the purchaser had ample opportunity to examine the painting in the first few years after he had bought it. Weighed against this, however, is the fact that the painting could have been returned quite easily in the same state as when it was sold. *Long* v. *Lloyd*[31] is an unsatisfactory case. There a lorry was described as being in exceptional condition but almost immediately the purchaser found that it was defective. A few days after the sale he complained to the dealer who agreed to pay half the cost of repairs. The purchaser then sent the lorry on a long journey during which it broke down. Six days after the sale, being thoroughly dissatisfied, the purchaser purported to rescind the contract for misrepresentation. The Court of Appeal held that the purchaser had lost his right to rescind, presumably because he had affirmed the contract by making the agreement about repairs or because the lapse of six days was too long. Pearce L. J. gives as a major reason for the decision that the purchaser could have had the lorry examined by an expert before or immediately after he bought it.[32] The Law Reform Committee concluded that the bar on rescission as applied in *Long* v. *Lloyd* was too rigid.[33]

The rules about misrepresentation are unduly complicated and inadequate. In part this derives from the drafting of the Misrepresentation Act 1967 which had the opportunity (but did not take it) of codifying the law on the subject. Another factor is that in misrepresentation cases the courts tend first to decide whether to give a remedy; they then have to force the misrepresentation into the appropriate legal category. The rules about misrepresentation are also limited in scope and do not apply to much misleading advertising or to statements used in sales techniques like 'bait and switch'. At the present time the best advice to consumers when there has been misrepresentation is probably to complain to a consumer protection department which may investigate the case for a breach of the Trade Descriptions Act 1968. Then the business may be more willing to give redress because of the threat of criminal proceedings. If the case comes to court and the prosecution is successful consumers can claim compensation under the procedure set out in section 35 of the Powers of Criminal Courts Act 1973.

There is a strong case for legislative reform of the law regarding misrepresentation. A business should be strictly liable for misrepresentations (including silence) if consumers are adversely affected. The New South Wales Law Reform Commission has suggested legislation along these lines.[34] Any representation would give rise to a civil action if the natural tendency was to induce a consumer to buy a product and if the consumer bought in reliance on it. The provision would apply to all misrepresentations including those in advertisements. Notice would be taken of to whom the misrepresentation was directed. Thus gullible sections of the population, like children, would be protected even if ordinary people would see through the misrepresentation. The Ontario Law Reform

Commission goes one step further and would apply such provisions to sales puffs and mere language of commendation in recognition of the importance of modern advertising techniques in influencing consumers' buying decisions.[35] As the New South Wales Commission points out, there is a clear moral basis for these reforms, which is recognized in the old cases like *Redgrave* v. *Hurd*,[36] where Jessel M. R. said that persons should not be allowed to profit from misstatements which they now admit are false or which are shown to be inaccurate or untrue.

Implied conditions in the Sale of Goods Act 1979

Prior to the Industrial Revolution most products were relatively simple in nature to evaluate, and purchases were mainly within fairly closed, stable groups.[37] Where trade with strangers was engaged in it was assumed that this was 'an arm's length proposition, with wits matched against skills'. Courts in the nineteenth century began developing implied terms in sales transactions in response to the commercial – not the consumer – problems thrown up by industrialization. As Karl Llewellyn noted:

Overseas trade in seaports introduces cargo-lot dealing, and dealing in goods at a distance, before they can be seen. Markets widen with improved transportation – internal water ways, railroads. This means reliance on distant sellers. Middlemen's dealings mean, sometimes, the postponement of inspection; always they mean some ignorance in the seller of the history of the goods. Industrialization grows out of and produces standardization, grading and sizing of lumber, grading and branding of flour or hardware, a certain predictability and reliability of goods. Contracts made by description, or by sample, which is a form of description, or by specification, which is an elaborate description, become the order of the day. Contracts come increasingly to precede production. Sellers begin to build for good will, in wide markets, to feel their standing behind goods to be no hardship, no outrage, no threat to their solvency from a thousand lurking claims, but the mark of business respectability and the road to future profit. The law of seller's obligation *must* change, to suit.[38]

As eventually settled, the courts decided that there was no general implied term as to the quality of goods.[39] But where a sale was by description and the buyers had no opportunity to inspect the goods – the typical commercial situation with goods on the high seas – there was an implied term that they should conform to their description and

be of merchantable quality.[40] Buyers were not protected in circumstances when it was possible to inspect the goods at the time of sale –
the typical consumer transaction. An exception was if they said
something to make known to the seller the purpose for which the
goods were wanted in order to demonstrate reliance on the latter's
skill and judgement, whereupon the courts implied a warranty that
the goods were reasonably fit for the purpose.[41] Clearly the doctrine of
implied terms was for the benefit of commercial interests; *caveat emptor*
was still the prevailing philosophy in sales to consumers.

The implied conditions in sections 13 and 14 of the Sale of Goods
Act 1893 were a codification, but in some respects an important
extension of the rules developed in the earlier part of the century. The
draftsman of the Act, Chalmers, justified the legislation on the
grounds that it was easier and cheaper to amend than the common
law and that certainty was of great importance in commercial
matters. He went on to note: 'Sale is a consensual contract, and the
Act does not seek to prevent the parties from making any bargain they
please.'[42] This philosophy led to unequal contracts between
businesses and consumers because the former were able to use
exclusion clauses to avoid the liability for defective products imposed
on them by sections 13 and 14. That was finally prevented by
legislation in 1973.[43] Nevertheless, the Sale of Goods Act 1893
afforded greater protection to consumers than the common law, for
they were no longer obliged to inspect goods for defects, and sellers
were liable even if they did so long as the inspection would not have
revealed the defects. The protection of the implied terms was
extended to hire purchase transactions in the Hire Purchase Act
1938.[44] The Supply of Goods and Services Act 1982 implies such
terms in other contracts for the transfer of property in goods and in
contracts for the hire of goods. However, there are still some
situations where there are no implied terms because there is no
contract. Consumers must then resort to non-legal remedies. An
example is faulty goods supplied by way of gift.[45] In the absence of
negligence, consumers will have no recourse against a retailer where
they are injured while taking a defective product off a supermarket
shelf because there is no contract until they reach the check-out
point.[46]

Patrick Atiyah characterizes the implied conditions now contained
in sections 13 and 14 of the Sale of Goods Act 1979 as establishing a
gradation in the standards required for products.[47] The lowest

standard is that a product must correspond with its description (section 13(1)). Then in section 14(2) there is the implied condition that a product be 'merchantable' – reasonably fit for its normal purposes. The highest standard a product must reach is fitness for a particular purpose specified by the consumer and agreed by the retailer (section 14(3)) – a standard which may be more demanding than fitness for normal purposes. Under the Unfair Contract Terms Act 1977 it is not possible for a business to exclude any of these implied conditions in consumer sales.

Section 13(1) provides that a product must correspond with its description where it is sold by description. Most sales are sales by description. Clearly where a product is a 'future good' (e.g. not yet made) and/or where the consumer does not see it before it is sold (as with mail order), there must be a sale by description. Legislation confirms that there can be a sale by description even where a product is selected by a consumer from those on display.[48] Thus a product selected by a consumer from the shelves of a supermarket must comply with the description on its label as to brand and contents. It seems that only where consumers buy a product as a specific thing on their own assessment of its value that there will not be a sale by description.[49]

In some cases the courts have taken a wider view of the implied condition in section 13 and regarded it as having relevance to the quality of a product. *Beale* v. *Taylor*[50] is an example, where a private motorist advertised his car for sale as a 'Herald convertible, white, 1961, twin carbs'. The buyer saw the car and drove in it with the seller, but unbeknown to either, the car was an amalgam of two parts, the front half being an earlier model. The Court of Appeal held that the buyer was entitled to succeed. In *Alton House Garages (Bromley) Ltd.* v. *Monk*[51] an advertisement for a second-hand Rolls-Royce indicated that the 'full history' was available. The service record of this type of car enhances its value and the buyer checked when he took delivery of the car that it was there. Later he found that it was the service record of another car. He successfully claimed that the contract was a sale by description and that by not supplying the record the car did not correspond with its description. However, the House of Lords has warned that the implied condition in section 13 really concerns descriptions which allow a product to be identified; in other words, which characterize it as belonging to a particular kind or class.[52] In the particular case the House of Lords held that an animal foodstuff still corresponded with its description despite contamination. Clear examples where a description relates to identity are a consumer who gets a second-hand car when he contracts for a new one, or a Ford when he contracts for a Chrysler.[53] The House of Lords has deprecated earlier cases which give buyers a remedy, however trivial the breach of description, and has said that the right approach is to ask whether a particular item in a description constitutes a substantial ingredient in the identity of the thing sold.[54] Nevertheless, it would still seem that extensive contamination or substantial defects may affect identity and give consumers a remedy because of the implied condition.[55] In other words a product of very bad quality may not come within the contractual description but be of a different kind from what the consumer agrees to buy. As the editors of Benjamin suggest: '[I]t is submitted that goods described by such terms as "baby food", "cough mixture", "cold cure" would not conform with description if they proved totally unsuitable to the purposes indicated by these words.'[56]

In most cases where a product is defective consumers will rely on the merchantability and fitness for purpose provisions of section 14 of the Sale of Goods Act 1979. These are the main instruments whereby the law ensures a minimum quality for both new and second-hand products. Subject to some qualifications the section implies conditions that a product will be merchantable and also fit for the purpose for which it is supplied. Under the Unfair Contract Terms Act 1977, sellers cannot exclude liability under it in consumer sales. With both conditions the retailer is strictly liable and whether it exercised reasonable care is irrelevant.[57] Liability extends to the container in which a product is supplied as well as to the product itself.[58] The onus of establishing that a product is not merchantable or fit for the purpose is on the consumer.

The merchantability and fitness for purpose provisions are confined to sales in the course of a business – unlike the implied condition that a product must correspond with its description. 'Business' includes a profession and the activities of any government department, or local or public authority.[59] Sales in the course of a business include those which are ancillary to the main trade of a seller, those by a seller who has not previously dealt with a particular line and those where the seller carries on the business on a modest part-time basis.[60] The major arguments for confining liability to business sales are that in private sales there is a substantial parity of bargaining power between the parties and that the courts should not be overburdened with disputes between private individuals which commonly involve items of comparatively low value. One would have thought, however, that in many cases private sellers will acquire considerable knowledge of something they own and later sell to put them at an advantage over buyers. At the same time there seems little reason to impose on private sellers liability for consequential losses, which can be very high in cases of personal injury.

The implied conditions of merchantable quality and fitness for purpose relate not only to the state of a product at the time of its delivery. There is now strong authority that a product should continue to be merchantable and fit for the purpose for a reasonable time after delivery, so long as it remains in the same apparent state as when delivered, normal wear and tear excepted. What is a reasonable time depends on the nature of the product.[61] Consequently, the courts allow recovery for latent defects which may not become manifest until after sale, and there is some authority that this liability even extends to defects which could not have been discovered in the light of scientific knowledge at the time of sale.[62] The mere fact that a defect develops a short while after being sold will be taken as strong evidence of breach of the implied conditions.[63] It should also be good evidence when a defect manifests itself within a guarantee period, which is an indication that in the manufacturer's opinion it should not have occurred. Where some time elapses, however, the possibility of misuse or interference by third parties increases and it becomes more difficult to establish a breach of condition. Where it becomes apparent that a product is defective and consequently is no longer in the same state as when it was delivered, the implied conditions of merchantability and fitness for purpose in relation to its safety may cease if a consumer has not taken the precaution of having it mended or at least finding out whether it is still safe to use.[64] So in *Lambert* v. *Lewis*[65] the implied condition that the coupling as fitted to a farmer's Land-Rover would be reasonably fit for towing trailers, in particular that it might be used on a public highway without danger to other users of the road, was brought to an end once it became apparent to the farmer that the locking mechanism was broken. Consequently the farmer failed when he sought an indemnity from the retailer for damages for which he was liable to the plaintiff who was injured, and whose husband and son were killed, when the trailer became detached from the Land-Rover and careered into their car.

'Merchantability' is a dated term. The Act contains a definition, which seems more than declaratory of pre-existing law.[66]

Goods of any kind are of merchantable quality . . . if they are as fit for the purpose or purposes for which goods of that kind are commonly bought as it is reasonable to expect having regard to any description applied to them, the price (if relevant) and all the other relevant circumstances.[67]

It is arguable that under this definition a product must be fit for all normal purposes, and that fitness for only one is insufficient.[68] Price seems to be relatively unimportant unless a substantial difference is involved.[69] Thus 'sale' goods must live up to the normal standard, although the consumer must expect slight damage or a degree of shop-soiling if the description 'seconds' is used. Given the need to consider what is it reasonable to expect and all relevant circumstances, it would seem that fitness for purpose means acceptability, rather than the lower standard of usability where minor defects are ignored. What is needed is a modern definition, which spells out the qualities goods must have to be merchantable (if that term is retained) – their fitness for all normal purposes, their freedom from minor defects (including finish), their durability and their safety – which it is reasonable to expect having regard to the circumstances. Merchantability is a question of fact, but some guidance can be derived from the relatively small number of consumer cases which have come before the courts. Toxic and dangerous products are clearly unmerchantable: beer containing arsenic; a catapult that breaks after three days' use; a soft drink bottle that disintegrates, etc.[70] At the same time the courts have held that products may not be merchantable if they have minor blemishes, for example in appearance, even though these can be repaired at trifling cost. Illustrative is a Canadian case where the court held that a calculator worth some $300 was not merchantable because it had a broken dial glass worth some 30 cents.[71] In *M. & T. Hurst Consultants Ltd* v. *Grange Motors Ltd and Rolls-Royce Motors Ltd*[72] a second-hand Rolls-Royce was sold with two defects, a ventilation fault in the petrol tank and a suspension fault, making it potentially dangerous and unroadworthy. Russell J. held that the car was unmerchantable although both defects were capable of being remedied at low cost.

In recent years motor cars have featured in a number of appeal cases, presumably because they are valuable enough to make ordinary legal proceedings worthwhile. In *Bartlett* v. *Sidney Marcus*

Ltd[73] the consumer was informed that there was something wrong
with the clutch but accepted a price reduction of £25 on the basis that
he would have the repairs completed elsewhere at his own expense.
The repairs ultimately cost £45 but the Court of Appeal held that the
car was merchantable and fit for the purpose. It was capable of being
driven along the road although like many second-hand cars it was far
from perfect. *McDonald* v. *Empire Garage (Blackburn) Ltd*[74] ultimately
turned on the state of the law prior to the Supply of Goods (Implied
Terms) Act 1973, but there was some disagreement in the Court of
Appeal as to whether a wrongly fitted brake tube, which ultimately
caused the brakes to fail, made the car unmerchantable. The
consumer faced expensive repairs in *Crowther* v. *Shannon Motor Co.*,[75]
where the engine of an eight-year-old Jaguar with 82,165 miles on the
milometer broke down completely after three weeks' use travelling
2300 miles. The previous owner, an engineer, gave evidence that the
engine was 'clapped out' when he sold it to the defendant, a second-
hand car dealer. The Court of Appeal thought that this was entirely
different from cases of minor repair and held that the car was not
reasonably fit for its normal purpose at the time of sale. Another
decision is *Lee* v. *York Coach and Marine.*[76] A consumer bought a
second-hand car for £355 which was found to be potentially dangerous
because of corrosion to the brake pipings and sub-frame, which
needed repairs worth about £100. The county court judge had decided
that the car was merchantable and fit for the purpose because the
consumer had driven it on several occasions. The Court of Appeal
allowed the consumer's appeal and gave emphasis to the new
definition of merchantability adopted in 1973. In its view the car was
not merchantable or fit for the purpose of being driven safely on the
roads even though no actual danger had yet arisen. The upshot of
these cases seems to be that second-hand cars must be capable of safe
and lawful use for a reasonable time after sale, depending on their age,
condition and price, but that consumers must expect some minor
defects to manifest themselves. Perhaps surprisingly, the courts have
held that even with new cars consumers must expect minor irritants
and defects.[77] It is arguable that it is not 'reasonable to expect' this,
within the terms of the definition of merchantability. From the
viewpoint of policy, it encourages slackness in manufacture.

The merchantability condition does not apply to defects specifically drawn to the consumer's attention before the sale.[78] The word
'specifically' requires that the precise defect be identified: general

statements by retailers that there may be defects are inadequate. Further, it does not apply if a consumer examines a product before the sale, as regards defects which that examination ought to reveal.[79] Signed statements on sale documents that a consumer has examined the product cannot substitute for a genuine examination and will also be void as an exemption clause. The proviso protects the lazy consumer who does not examine a product before purchase, although he may yet be denied recovery for any loss incurred on the grounds of not treating the product properly or of not mitigating losses.

Section 14(3) of the Sale of Goods Act 1979 provides:

Where the seller sells goods in the course of a business and the buyer, expressly or by implication, makes known –

(a) to the seller, or

(b) where the purchase price or part of it is payable by instalments and the goods were previously sold by a credit-broker to the seller, to that credit-broker,

any particular purpose for which the goods are being bought, there is an implied condition that the goods supplied under the contract are reasonably fit for that purpose, whether or not that is a purpose for which such goods are commonly supplied, except where the circumstances show that the buyer does not rely, or that it is unreasonable for him to rely, on the skill or judgement of the seller or credit-broker.

The section can frequently be used as an alternative to a claim that a product is not merchantable. The courts accept that there is no need for a consumer specifically to state the purpose of a product when it is obvious and they are prepared to infer a reliance on a retailer's skill and judgement in selecting stock unless there is evidence to the contrary.[80] The section can also be used to ensure a higher than normal standard in a product as long as the consumer informs the retailer about this. If a consumer buys a small car and on enquiry is told that it will pull a caravan although normally this would not be expected, he has a remedy if the retailer's assurances prove unfounded.[81] There will be a breach of the implied term if a consumer is assured that a particular cloth is suitable for making dresses although normally it would only be used for industrial purposes, like making bags.[82] A consumer with a peculiarly sensitive skin will have a remedy if he develops dermatitis as a result of wearing clothing, if he has been assured by the retailer that it is suitable for all skins.[83] As long as there is partial reliance by a consumer on the retailer's skill and judgement there will be a breach of the implied term even if the consumer has relied to a greater extent on his own judgement. Simply because a consumer selects products in a self-service store or inspects a product before buying does not exclude the section.[84] But if a consumer provides a retailer with a complete specification for a product and places no reliance on its judgement, the retailer is only responsible for sub-standard workmanship and not for the lack of suitability of the product for the purpose needed.

As we have seen, a product should remain merchantable and fit for the purpose for a reasonable period.[85] Perhaps the matter could be put on a statutory basis by expanding the definition of merchantability – to include a requirement that consumer products should be durable for a reasonable length of time, having regard to the circumstances.[86] Certainly surveys show that consumers frequently complain that products do not last as long as expected.[87] A more important reform is along the lines of Australian and North American legislation, whereby manufacturers of consumer durables are obliged to maintain sufficient spare parts and/or repair facilities to overcome the difficulty consumers experience in this regard.[88] The Law Commission sees problems in the nature of such an obligation: for example, should periods be laid down product-by-product? It objects to placing the obligation on retailers because of the hardship that might result for small shops and the associated costs. Moreover, as a matter of policy it believes that liability for safe but shoddy products should remain with retailers and not be extended to manufacturers.[89] Finally, it might be noted that Californian legislation provides that to be merchantable a product must be adequately contained, packaged and labelled.[90]

Remedies for breach of implied terms

The law provides two remedies for consumers who receive faulty products in breach of the implied terms of quality in sections 13–14 of the Sale of Goods Act 1979: the right to reject them and the right to money damages.[91] Frequently retailers offer a credit note, an allowance on future purchases, a replacement or a repair when consumers complain about faulty products. Acceptance of these may be the most practical means of settling a dispute. Once consumers have conclusively accepted a credit note or an allowance on future purchases they lose the right to reject or to damages. Accepting a repair or a replacement might foreclose the consumer's possibility of rejecting, but in any event he can still claim damages for a continuing or new defect.[92]

(a) Rejection

The immediate response of many consumers when they find a product is defective is to attempt to reject the product and to recover any money paid to the retailer. The implied terms of quality in sections 13–14 of the Sale of Goods Act 1979 are conditions, breach of which may entitle the consumer to reject.[93]

Consumers lose the right to reject a faulty product once they 'accept' it. This is the effect of section 11(4) of the Sale of Goods Act 1979:

> Where a contract of sale is not severable and the buyer has accepted the goods, or part of them, the breach of a condition to be fulfilled by the seller can only be treated as a breach of warranty, and not as a ground for rejecting the goods and treating the contract as repudiated, unless there is an express or implied term of the contract to that effect.

Section 61(1) provides that the remedy for breach of warranty is damages.

Acceptance is defined in sections 34–5 of the Act; their effect can be summarized as follows:

(a) Consumers are deemed to accept a product where they intimate to the retailer that they have accepted ('express acceptance'): section 35.
(b) Consumers are not deemed to accept if they have not previously examined a product delivered to them until they have had a reasonable opportunity to do so: section 34(1).
(c) Where consumers have examined a product, or have had a reasonable opportunity to do so, they are deemed to accept if (1) they do any act in relation to the product which is inconsistent with the retailer's ownership; (2) after a lapse of a reasonable time[94] they retain the product without intimating to the retailer that they have rejected it: section 35(1).

Express acceptance will be unusual in the consumer context. It mainly occurs in commercial dealings when a buyer tests a product and indicates satisfaction that it meets any requirements. It seems that a consumer who signs a receipt merely acknowledging delivery will not be accepting a product. Previously retailers could include clauses in written contracts excluding the right to reject or limiting the period within which rejection had to occur. Such clauses were not common in consumer transactions and in any event are now rendered void in consumer sales.[95]

Implied acceptance is more difficult: what is an examination or a reasonable opportunity to conduct one? what is an act inconsistent with the retailer's ownership? and what is the lapse of a reasonable period? If consumers fail to complain to a retailer about an obvious defect when they buy a product, or when it is delivered, they will lose the right to reject. *Milner* v. *Tucker*[96] is an old case but a useful illustration. A chandelier was incomplete when it was delivered to the consumer but nothing was done for six months. The court held that if the consumer had wanted to reject, he 'should have given the plaintiff notice immediately; and have returned it as soon as he could'.[97]

A typical situation these days is where a product has a latent defect which does not manifest itself until sometime after the consumer starts using it. The consumer complains and the retailer promises a repair. After attempts at repair prove abortive the consumer finally purports to reject. Now on one interpretation of the relevant sections it could be argued that the consumer loses the right to reject in these circumstances.[98] Use of a product could be said to be inconsistent with the retailer's ownership and might also mean that a reasonable period has elapsed.[99] The same points could be made if a consumer agrees to a product being repaired. In each case the underlying policy argument against allowing rejection would seem to be that sub-stantial use or having repairs done would prevent the consumer from returning the product in the same condition as when it was bought.

On the other hand there are strong arguments for allowing consumers to retain the right to reject in the circumstances outlined. Many defects in modern consumer durables are latent and not apparent until after considerable use.[100] Consumers cannot be expected to employ experts to examine every product they buy, even if it is prudent to do so for items like second-hand cars when organizations like the Automobile Association operate advisory services.[101] Moreover, consumers should not be prejudiced into postponing rejection just because they are misled by a retailer's assertion that a product can be repaired.[102] For these reasons it is desirable that the courts interpret the concept of acceptance in the Act as widely as possible. Consumers who use a product before a latent defect develops should be regarded as subjecting it to reasonable

examination, which is not inconsistent with the seller's ownership, as
long as the time period involved is not excessive. It should be
irrelevant that a product cannot be returned in the same state as when
the consumer purchased it.[103] Overall, the losses businesses consequently incur can be regarded as being counterbalanced by those
consumers suffer in terms of lost time, opportunity costs and mental
anguish.

The problem of acceptance with consumer products has never been
properly considered by the English courts, although several decisions
touch on it. A liberal approach has been adopted to the parallel issue
of affirmation in several hire purchase cases. The leading decision is
Farnsworth Finance Facilities Ltd v. *Attryde*,[104] where a consumer entered
a hire purchase agreement for a new motorcycle dated 24 July.
Subsequently he returned it to both the dealers and the manufacturers when he found that it was faulty. Although they had it for
substantial periods, not all the faults were remedied. Finally in
November, after paying four instalments, the consumer repudiated
the contract and the finance company repossessed the cycle. The
Court of Appeal found that its condition constituted a fundamental
breach of contract and that the consumer was entitled to repudiate
the contract.

Lord Denning said:

Counsel said that by using it all that time the first defendant had affirmed
the contract and it was too late for him to repudiate it. But as the argument
proceeded, I think that counsel for the first defendant gave the right answer.
He pointed out that affirmation is a matter of election. A man only affirms a
contract when he knows of the defects and by his conduct elects to go on with
the contract despite them. In this case the first defendant complained from
the beginning of the defects and sent the machine back for them to be
remedied. He did not elect to accept it unless they were remedied. But the
defects were never satisfactorily remedied.[105]

Similarly, in *Jackson* v. *Chrysler Acceptances Ltd*[106] there were a series of
repairs and replacements in the months after a car's purchase on hire
purchase. The consumer had indicated some time after purchase that
unless it were put right he would be seeking to return it and a refund of
what had been paid. The defendant claimed that the consumer had
affirmed the contract by paying instalments for some six months,
using the car for at least 6000 miles in that period, causing it to be
repaired free of charge by the dealer, and continuing to keep it and use
it despite the defects. The county court judge held that the car was not

merchantable or fit for the purpose but only awarded damages on the basis that the length of time since the contract ruled out rescission. The Court of Appeal was prepared to reopen the question of rescission although in the result the consumer was content to limit his claim to damages.[107] The decisions are not necessarily directly applicable to sale of goods cases. They could be distinguished either because a fundamental breach relates back to the time of delivery or because a hire purchase transaction involves a continuing breach of contract until the last instalment is paid.[108] Despite these legal distinctions there are no sound policy reasons for distinguishing between hire purchase and sale of goods cases.

The courts in sale of goods cases seem to be taking a less narrow view of acceptance. In *Lee* v. *York Coach and Marine*[109] the consumer had purchased a car on 7 March and immediately complained about its condition. The dealers made two attempts to put it right but refused to do anything after the third complaint. On 26 April and then again on 10 May the consumer's solicitor wrote to the dealer asking that the defects be remedied or a refund be given. The Court of Appeal decided that the consumer did not have the right to reject but only a right to damages. Their decision turned on the fact that the solicitor's letters did not constitute an unequivocal rejection and that it was too late to reject in the statement of claim.[110] It is arguable from the judgements that if the solicitor's letters had been more strongly worded, rejection would have been allowed. In an unreported decision, *M. & T. Hurst Consultants Ltd* v. *Grange Motors Ltd and Rolls-Royce Motors Ltd*,[111] rejection of the car was allowed nearly five months after sale; the buyer had returned on four occasions complaining about the car's condition.

The Canadian courts have said that consumers must not be regarded as accepting a defective consumer durable, even if they use it for many months, as long as they complain to the retailer and give it every reasonable opportunity to repair. The decisions are based on legislation almost identical to the Sale of Goods Act 1979 and give as the main legal justification that a retailer acquiesces in acceptance being delayed by asserting that repairs will remedy the defect. *Lightburn* v. *Belmont Sales Ltd*[112] is a useful illustration for it is so typical of the plight of many consumers. The consumer purchased a new car and took delivery. The first trouble was detected some three or four weeks later and involved a failure in starting and thereafter there was continuous trouble with the electrical system. Eight months after delivery the consumer wanted the purchase price returned. The dealer argued that the faults were promptly diagnosed and remedied, but the Supreme Court of British Columbia upheld the consumer's claim. Ruttan J. said:

> He was endeavouring to give it a reasonable chance to perform, and I do not agree that delay in finally repudiating this contract can be attributed to that period of time or the mileage that was covered. He was not acting as a capricious buyer who had repented the purchase and sought to get out of his contract at an early time on a frivolous basis.[113]

The Uniform Commercial Code provides for revocation of acceptance in certain circumstances where a product's non-conformity substantially impairs its value.[114] The United States courts have allowed consumers to invoke this section on finding some time after they buy a car that it suffers serious latent defects.[115] Note, however, that the approach of the UCC differs from that of the Sale of Goods Act.

If the courts interpret the Sale of Goods Act 1979 narrowly, to limit the circumstances in which consumers can reject for breach of the implied terms regarding quality, consumers will be confined to an action in damages. This may be fine in commercial transactions to prevent buyers seizing on a technical breach to avoid taking goods on a falling market, but the situation is entirely different in consumer transactions. As the New South Wales Law Reform Commission notes:

> What is commercially trivial may be of great moment to an ordinary citizen who purchases the goods for the personal use of his family or himself. The desire to maximize profits or minimize losses is not the motivating factor here in seeking rejection as a remedy. What the buyer wants is a chattel which will perform satisfactorily the task for which it was bought and if it will not do this he feels he is entitled to exchange it for a chattel which will be satisfactory.[116]

There would be a number of advantages if consumers had a broad right to reject in cases where they receive a product with a serious fault. First, it would bring the laws into line with consumers' expectations. Secondly, it would put a powerful weapon into the hands of consumers who might otherwise be fobbed off with a promise of eventual repair, or replacement if the trouble continued. Thirdly, it permits consumers to cut off contact with products and/ or retailers in whom they have lost confidence. Finally, it would

encourage retailers to improve the quality of their merchandise and/
or to handle complaints sympathetically, because the more rejec-
tions the more loss of profit on sales. Legislative reform is necessary.[117]

There seem to be good reasons for not making any deduction for use
where a product is rejected for a serious defect. None was made in
Farnsworth Finance Facilities Ltd v. *Attryde*,[118] nor in several Commonwealth decisions,[119] on the basis that consumers had been put to a
great deal of trouble and inconvenience because of a defective product
which cancelled out the benefit derived from use. Besides there is the
practical problem of calculating the exact benefit derived. If the right
of consumers to reject was widened, another consideration would be
how to deal with inflation. Consumers might find that when they
rejected they were no longer able to buy a substitute product for the
original price because it had risen. At present the problem would
probably not arise because rejection is confined within fairly narrow
time limits. If it did, there seems no reason why replacement value at
the time of rejection/judgement should not be the measure of
damages.[120] Since benefit to the consumer from use and loss through
inflation both increase with time, if there were no deduction for use,
this would roughly balance the disadvantage to consumers if the
courts made no allowance for inflation. From the point of view of law
reform, statute should make it clear that in the case of rejection, at the
very least consumers should be entitled to the replacement value of a
product.

(b) Damages

Consumers may claim damages for breach of the implied terms of
merchantability and fitness for purpose in section 14 of the Sale of
Goods Act 1979. Alternatively, if a retailer sues for the price,
consumers may set up a breach of the implied terms in diminution or
extinction of the claim. Three situations can be identified where
consumers will seek damages rather than rejection of the product.
First, it may be more advantageous to have a defect remedied than to
receive back the purchase price, as where supplies of a product are
short and it is relatively difficult to obtain. A second situation is where
consumers have suffered serious personal injury because of a defect
and need to sue for consequential damages to cover the losses
involved. Consumers can obtain substantial amounts in these

circumstances, out of all proportion to the cost of the product involved, which becomes largely irrelevant. In *Grant* v. *Australian Knitting Mills Ltd*[121] the plaintiff was awarded £2450 for dermatitis contracted from underwear, and in *Godley* v. *Perry*[122] a six-year-old boy obtained £2500 for the loss of an eye by a faulty catapult. Thirdly, there are those situations where consumers have no choice but to sue for damages because they have lost the right to reject, as discussed above, by accepting a product within the terms of the Act.

Under English law it is the consumer's responsibility to establish his damages. The measure of damages according to the first branch of the rule in *Hadley* v. *Baxendale*[123] is the loss flowing directly and naturally from breach of the implied terms. In the case of breach of warranty of quality, section 53(3) of the Act establishes a prima facie rule that the loss is the difference between the value that the product would have had without the defect and its actual value at the time of delivery. The prima facie rule would seem also to apply to products which do not conform to their description or which are not fit for their purpose. The value of a consumer product without a defect will generally be the contract price, so the prima facie rule means that damages are equivalent to the difference between the contract price and the value of the product with its defects. Frequently latent defects are not discoverable until some time after delivery and in these circumstances the prima facie rule is displaced and the difference in value is the contract price minus the value when the defect becomes manifest.[124] Delay on the part of the consumer in bringing a claim, however, may cause damages to be assessed at the time of delivery.[125]

If a defect renders a product completely useless the consumer should recover the full contract price under these rules. Some consumer products can be sold despite their defects, if only for their scrap value, and this is good evidence for calculating the value difference.[126] Many damaged products cannot be disposed of once they have defects, and in these circumstances a court has to do the best it can in determining their value. In practice the difference in value can often be calculated from the cost of repair. The cost of repair is of no assistance, however, in those cases where it costs more to repair a product than to purchase a new one. In applying these rules the Canadian courts favour consumers, by adopting the full purchase price as the prima facie measure of damages, and placing the onus on the retailer to demonstrate that a defective product retains some value.[127]

A consumer can also claim damages for consequential loss resulting from a defective product, as long as the loss is not too 'remote'. This is the second part of the rule in *Hadley* v. *Baxendale*, and the House of Lords has interpreted it to mean that there must be a 'serious possibility' or that it must be not unlikely that the consequential loss will occur.[128] Mention has been made of claims for losses incurred by personal injury, and damages in these cases are assessed on the same basis as similar claims in tort. Indeed, the circumstances may be such that the consumer can bring an action in negligence, but there is an obvious advantage of suing under the Sale of Goods Act 1979 because liability is strict. Even if the retailer has few assets it can usually claim an indemnity from its supplier, which will be joined in third party proceedings. The matter can be pursued in this way up the chain of supply to the manufacturer, provided there are no effective exemption clauses.[129] Since it is a serious possibility that consumer products will be used by members of the consumer's family, the consumer may recover damages for his pecuniary loss where a family member is injured. Thus in *Jackson* v. *Watson & Sons*[130] a husband obtained medical expenses and an amount for the loss of services of his wife who died from eating poisoned salmon.

Another example of consequential loss is where a defect in a product causes property damage, as where the brakes of a car fail and it is involved in a collision.[131] The transport costs of returning a defective product to a retailer can also be claimed under this head.[132] A number of interesting practical questions have never been considered by the courts. Launderette charges are no doubt recoverable if a washing machine develops a defect, and it seems that a consumer can claim an amount for bus and taxi fares or car hire when a car is off the road because of a fault.[133] A court in the United States has gone as far as awarding loss of wages incurred by a consumer in taking time off to try to negotiate a settlement with a retailer about a defective product.[134] It seems unlikely that an English court would reach a similar conclusion.

Consumers must mitigate their losses and may not recover damages in full if they fail to do so. Mitigation may involve the consumer in accepting an offer by a retailer if it is without prejudice to any rights he may have. The normal rule is that consumers should not use a defective product if they suspect that further damage will result, but there may be circumstances where a consumer who acts reasonably in seeking to mitigate may recover additional loss thereby incurred.[135] Mitigation is especially relevant to consequential losses; for example, the consumer who suffers personal injury must seek medical assistance. Similarly, the consumer who buys a defective car must use his second car if one is available, employ public transport if that is convenient, and if neither of these is feasible and he hires a substitute car he must do so at competitive rates.

Third party consumers

It remains to examine what action third party consumers have against a retailer. The doctrine of privity of contract means that they cannot sue for misrepresentation or breach of the implied terms in the Sale of Goods Act 1979. Few problems arise in practice because many retailers – and manufacturers for that matter – are prepared to exchange a shoddy product whether or not the particular complainant is the purchaser. If third party consumers are personally injured, however, the legal aspect assumes greater significance because even generous retailers will baulk at paying out substantial sums of money. The first possibility is that the purchaser was an agent for the third party so that direct contractual relations arise with the retailer.[136] It will be fairly easy to spell this out in family situations. Secondly, there are situations such as ordering food in a restaurant where unless the circumstances indicate otherwise each party is contracting with the retailer whatever the arrangements between them.[137] Thirdly, there is strong authority (although its legal basis is obscure) that a consumer may enforce particular types of contract made on behalf of a group, examples of which are persons contracting for family holidays, ordering meals in restaurants for a party, and hiring a taxi for a group.[138]

Fourthly, the third party consumer may attempt to claim from the retailer in negligence. The cause of action is clear if the retailer has been negligent in fitting or repairing the product. *Malfroot* v. *Noxal*[139] is a useful illustration, where the passenger in a side-car of a motorcycle successfully sued the sellers of it for negligently fitting the side-car so that it became detached from the motorcycle and over-turned. Another situation in which the third party consumer must attempt to sue a retailer is if a second-hand product is involved. *Hurley* v. *Dyke*[140] was an action in negligence against a garage proprietor for selling a second-hand car which was unroadworthy and dangerous. The car had gone out of control, killing the owner who was driving, and leaving the plaintiff-passenger a paraplegic. At the date of the accident third party liability insurance for passengers was not compulsory. The House of Lords held that since the defendant did not know that the car was actually dangerous, he had satisfied the duty of care by selling it at an auction at which the warning was given 'as seen and with all its faults and without warranty'. No clearer case could be advanced in support of a national compensation scheme, along the lines of that operating in New Zealand, for those injured in motor car accidents.

There is a category of cases, where the third party consumer will prefer to sue the manufacturer but must sue the retailer because the manufacturer has gone out of business or is a back-street firm without any assets. Mrs Fisher faced the latter problem in *Fisher* v. *Harrods Ltd.*[141] A friend had bought her a product for cleaning jewellery at Harrods and she was seriously injured when some of it sprayed in her eyes because of a faulty container. McNair J. held that she was entitled to damages because Harrods had fallen below the standard of care required: it had not vetted the manufacturer sufficiently and it had not carried out any investigation following complaints about faulty containers for the product prior to Mrs Fisher's accident.

There are good reasons for abandoning the privity doctrine in consumer transactions and allowing consumers to sue retailers whether or not they purchased a product or service. Privity is completely unrealistic in the consumer context. As Jolowicz remarks, it is an error to think that a normal consumer transaction simply involves the consumer. 'On the contrary, nothing is more common than for one member of a family or other social group to purchase goods for use or consumption by himself and the other members. . .'.[142] The Uniform Commercial Code provides in section 2–318 that the benefits of a seller's warranty shall extend to a purchaser's family, household and guests or alternatively to any person who may reasonably be expected to use, consume or be affected by a product. Courts in the United States have also held manufacturers to be liable for shoddy as well as unsafe products, irrespective of privity, on the grounds that the manufacturer makes the article and puts it in the channels of trade of sale to the public.[143] A similar result has been achieved in Australia under the Trade Practices Act 1974.[144]

SERVICES

Parliament has given much less attention to the standard of services than to the standard of products. Only recently have provisions for services been introduced comparable to the Sale of Goods Act 1979, with its implied conditions that products must comply with their description and be of merchantable quality and fit for the purpose. Presumably the absence of legislation is explained historically because services lacked the element of large volume trading at a distance which applied in the case of sales.[145] In the absence of commercial need there was no reason for Parliament to depart from the principle of not legislating extensively in the business area. Individuals were thus left to resort to the common law when they were dissatisfied with the quality of services. The absence of legislation did not have a great effect here, since the courts implied terms in contracts for services along the lines of those for products in the Sale of Goods Act 1893. But the absence of legislation has meant that reform in favour of consumers has lagged behind in the case of services. For example, exemption clauses are effective in excluding liability for the quality of services unless the Unfair Contract Terms Act 1977 applies. By contrast, exemption clauses were rendered completely void as regards the quality of products in 1973.

Consumers can often invoke general principles of law if they are dissatisfied with the quality of services. Negligence is one possibility. In addition to professional negligence,[146] there are other areas of liability in this regard. For example, builders who have been negligent in the construction of a house may be liable in relation to defects which affect the health and safety of occupiers or the disability of the building for the cost of repairing the defective structure, for the cost of damage to other property and for personal injuries.[147] Consumers might also argue that there has been a breach of contract. Several holiday cases are illustrative. Variations in the itinerary or accommodation because of over-booking by the travel agency or tour operator may constitute breach of contract for which damages can be claimed. In *Trackman* v. *New Vistas Ltd*[148] the contract specified accommodation in a hotel but the consumer was given a room in an annexe some 200 yards away. The Court of Appeal said that a hotel meant not only sleeping facilities but also other amenities – meals, sitting-rooms and the like – and that the consumer was entitled to move to another hotel nearby and charge the travel agency with the difference. Holidays which fall short of statements in a travel brochure might give rise to a successful action. The consumer in *Jarvis* v. *Swan Tours Ltd*[149] was awarded damages for the disappointment, upset and frustration when he found – contrary to statements in the brochure about his Swiss skiing trip – that there was no welcoming party, that several evenings the bar was not open, that there were no full-length skis or house-party arrangements, that a suitable yodler failed to appear and that he did not receive the delicious Swiss cakes promised for afternoon tea!

What of implied terms in contracts involving services? As regards the quality of any materials supplied, it was important at one time to distinguish a contract of sale from one for work and materials. The distinction is much less important now that legislation implies non-excludable conditions in contracts for work and materials similar to those in sale of goods transactions. The courts enunciated various tests as to how to draw the distinction. Is the substance of the contract to transfer property in a product? What is the relative importance of the product as opposed to the work involved (e.g. what degree of installation is required)? Is the production of an item crucial or is it incidental to the work or skill involved? The tests do not fully explain why making a set of dentures should be a sale of goods;[150] why a contract to paint a picture should be a contract for work and materials on one occasion but one of sale on another;[151] and why there should be any difference between laying carpets (sale of goods) and installing a swivelling cocktail cabinet (work and materials).[152] It is only when one examines the problem faced by the court that it becomes clear why a particular categorization was adopted. For example, at one time whether it was one or the other was of crucial importance, because sales contracts over £10 were not enforceable unless a written note or memorandum of the contract existed, or unless the buyer accepted and received part of the goods or gave something in earnest or in part payment. Many of the cases, and the sometimes artificial distinction they draw between contracts of sale and those for work and materials, are best understood against this historical background.

Once clear Sale of Goods Act cases are set to one side, the law identifies at least three types of contract involving services where terms are implied as to quality: contracts of hire, contracts for work and materials and contracts for services *simpliciter*. With contracts of hire legislation implies terms as to merchantability and fitness of the product hired which assimilates the supplier's obligations to those in contracts of sale or hire purchase.[153] This overcomes the position established in some decisions that at common law a hired product need be only as fit for the purpose as reasonable care and skill can make it.[154]

In contracts for work and materials legislation implies in relation to the materials conditions of merchantability and fitness for purpose comparable to those in section 14 of the Sale of Goods Act 1979.[155] Like them, the implied terms are strict, and a business is liable for latent defects in materials even though it has exercised reasonable care. Case law prior to the legislation is illustrative of the situations which can arise. For example, a car repairer was successfully sued when one of the new connecting rods it fitted turned out to have a latent defect which broke and caused extensive damage.[156] A hairdresser was held to be liable where a customer developed dermatitis because the hair-dye used – unbeknown to the hairdresser – contained excessive acid.[157] The leading case is *Young & Marten Ltd* v. *McManus Childs Ltd*,[158] where the House of Lords held that building contractors were liable for latent defects in the tiles they had used although they had purchased them from a nominated manufacturer. The implied term as to suitability for purpose was negated because the tiles came from a nominated source of supply, but that did not relieve the contractors from using materials of normal quality, even though the defects were latent and not apparent on reasonable examination. Reasons in favour of implying terms analogous to those in the Sale of Goods Act are first, a supplier of work and materials usually has recourse against its supplier; secondly, it usually charges customers more for the materials than they cost so there is no serious injustice in imposing the same liability as if he were a seller; thirdly, it is only logical that it should be under at least as high, if not a higher degree of obligation with regard to the materials it supplies than a seller who may be a mere middleman.

The work element in contracts for work and materials and contracts for services is generally provided for by section 13 of the Supply of Goods and Services Act 1982:

In a contract for the supply of a service where the supplier is acting in the course of a business, there is an implied term that the supplier will carry out the service with reasonable care and skill.

A contract for the supply of a service means a contract under which a person (the supplier) agrees to carry out a service but does not include a contract of service or apprenticeship. It also includes a contract where goods are transferred or hired, and whatever the nature of the consideration.[159] However, the Secretary of State may by Order exclude services. Where the time for the service to be performed is not fixed, left to be fixed in a manner agreed by the contract or determined by the course of dealing between the parties, there is an implied term that the supplier will carry out the service within a reasonable time – a question of fact.[160] Similarly, there is an implied term that the party contracting with the supplier will pay a reasonable charge where the consideration is not determined by the contract, left to be determined in a manner agreed by the contract or determined by the course of dealing between the parties.[161] Certainly disputes often arise over charges for services, for example, where consumers have products repaired. When the repair is finished the consumer is presented with a bill which he or she considers excessive. The consumer has no choice but to pay because the repairer has a lien over the product, i.e. the repairer can retain possession, although it cannot sell it, until the bill is paid.[162] Once the consumer has paid, he is of course in a much less favourable bargaining position. Quotations are one way of minimizing difficulties, for the consumer knows what he has to pay and the business knows that the consumer understands the price and has consented to it. The business cannot bind the consumer to pay for work additional to that specified in the original quotation.[163] If it finds that additional repairs are necessary it must approach the consumer to vary the original contract. While it is generally accepted that 'quotations' are a definite promise to do work at a fixed price, and 'estimates' are estimates of the total cost which may or may not be exceeded when the charge comes to be calculated, whether either is binding depends on the intention of the parties. In *Croshaw* v. *Pritchard & Renwick*[164] an owner of premises wanting alterations done contacted builders and invited them to tender for the work. They wrote a letter headed 'estimate' in which they gave £1230 as the cost of the alterations. The owner wrote telling them to go ahead with the work but some time later they contacted him to say that a mistake had been made and they must withdraw. The owner sued successfully for the difference between the estimate and what he paid other builders to do the work. The court rejected the argument that the word 'estimate' avoided a final and binding agreement and held that the letter was intended to give rise to such.

The most important implied term regarding work is the obligation to exercise reasonable skill and care. This is the common law standard which has been incorporated in legislation. The implied term at common law requires that a business must use the skill appropriate to a reasonably competent member of the relevant trade. For example, a lower standard of care is required from a jeweller piercing ears than from a medical practitioner.[165] In holding itself out as qualified to do certain work, however, a business warrants that it possesses those skills and so may be held to a higher standard.

There is a case for abandoning 'reasonableness' as the standard for workmanship and adopting strict liability as with the standard for products. Reasonableness is defended because of the variety of services to be covered (e.g. favours by neighbours), because those providing technical information services might be discouraged from supplying information and advice, and because many who provide services have small businesses and few fixed assets.[166] The first point can be met by confining liability to services provided in the course of a business. With regard to the second and third points it is difficult to see why the providers of services cannot insure against the cost of their potential liabilities. 'Reasonableness' is also defended as the appropriate standard on the basis that a person who has work performed frequently specifies its nature and extent – very often, for reasons of cost, the minimum necessary.

The person performing the service is not therefore in the same position as a seller in that he is controlled by the customer's instructions. He cannot require a customer to order a complete overhaul or even an adequate repair. Rules for servicing must therefore differ from rules governing the sale of goods and it would seem impracticable to require more than that the repair or service ordered by the customer should be competently performed and that it should not be defective or hazardous in itself, and that if it would in itself render the article's use more hazardous it should not be carried out.[167]

Whether consumers actually specify the standard of work they want done, particularly when it comes to professional services, is open to doubt. Sociologists have long pointed out that the professions are surrounded with a mystique which makes it unlikely that consumers understand what is being done. There seems every reason to believe that most consumers are equally as ignorant about repairs to consumer durables. The major arguments against the standard of reasonable skill and care for workmanship are those which suggest the abolition of negligence in tort: consumers might be denied a remedy because of the difficulties of making out a case, and it is fairer that an individual who has suffered loss should be compensated, with the cost being borne collectively, whether or not the business is at fault. In the absence of a national scheme to compensate those suffering misfortune, there is a case that businesses should be made strictly liable for the standard of their workmanship, the cost of which they can cover by making the appropriate insurance arrangements, when personal injury is involved. There would be difficulties, however, in defining the standard.

Reasonable care and skill as the standard for workmanship means that decisions turn on the nature of the trade and the particular circumstances involved. The expert carpet-layers in *Kimber* v. *William Willett Ltd*[168] were in breach of an implied term that their work would be done in a workmanlike and safe manner when they left a hall carpet in such a condition that it constituted a danger to anyone using the premises they knew to be occupied and exercising reasonable care. Motor repairers must provide good workmanship and are liable for defective work by sub-contractors, even if the consumer has consented to the work being done by a particular sub-contractor, unless the consumer does not place any reliance on the main contractor but choses a sub-contractor himself.[169] The implied term that a newly-constructed house must be finished in a workmanlike manner requires, for example, that fittings like water-taps and baths be properly installed and that walls be plastered.[170] Medical practitioners must bring to bear a reasonable degree of skill and knowledge, although the courts are quite lenient when compared with those in the United States. Apparently there is no requirement that medical practitioners be familiar with recent technical literature in journals like the *Lancet*.[171]

Firms which are entrusted with goods are liable for loss sustained if they have not exercised reasonable skill and care. In *Morris* v. *C. W. Martin & Sons Ltd*[172] the consumer sent a stole to be cleaned, but when in possession of the defendants it was stolen by an employee although there was no reason to suspect his loyalty. The Court of Appeal held that the defendants, as bailees for reward, had failed in their duty to exercise reasonable care and were responsible for the actions of the employee to whom they had delegated the job. If consumers park their car in an unattended car park adjacent, say, to a hotel or to shops, that would not ordinarily give rise to a contract or to a bailment. Consequently car park owners may avoid responsibility for theft when strangers take the car.[173] Comprehensive car insurance offers protection to consumers in these cases, although they may lose their 'no claims' bonus. Legislative provision enables airlines, for example, to limit their responsibility when consumers' luggage goes astray.[174]

There is evidence of a widespread dissatisfaction with services – their quality, delays in their performance (even when a time limit is agreed), and their cost.[175] A first step has been legislation incorporating implied terms as to the merchantability and fitness for purpose of goods in contracts of hire and contracts for work and materials, and as to the standard of reasonable care and skill in contracts for the supply of services.[176] Codification in this matter has clarified the law, meant ease of reference, and to an extent drawn public attention to the issue. The legislation could have gone further requiring, for example, that services be fit for the purpose for which they are customarily rendered and for any disclosed purpose communicated to the supplier before they are contracted for, that payment for services should be when they are completed unless the contrary is expressly provided for in writing signed by the consumer, and that the consumer should have a direct claim against subcontractors.[177] A deficiency at present is that a supplier can exclude or restrict the implied term as to reasonable care and skill unless this is in breach of the Unfair Contract Terms Act 1977.[178] For example, in the case of loss or damage (other than personal injury and death) caused through the negligent provision of a service, or in breach of contract with a consumer, a business can exclude or restrict its liability by a contract term satisfying the requirement of 'reasonableness'.[179]

Voluntary efforts are another approach, and the Office of Fair Trading has negotiated a number of codes of practice focusing on the servicing and repair of consumer durables. One suggestion is that a statutory duty be imposed on businesses to trade fairly, with codes of practice providing the detailed meaning of what such a duty specifically requires. The primary method of enforcement would be an obligation on the Director General to seek an undertaking or assurance from a business who persistently followed a course of conduct in breach of the general duty.[180] The success of this type of measure depends on the enthusiasm of the agency entrusted to enforce it and the willingness of the courts to back its decisions. Neither can be taken for granted. More specific government regulation would have a greater chance of success. Examples of experience elsewhere provide a guide. Michigan tackles the problem of below-standard workmanship in car repairs by establishing mandatory certification of car mechanics in addition to registration of repair facilities; it also obliges commercial repairers to employ at least one certified mechanic who must inspect all repair work.[181] Car repairers must give an itemized estimate for repairs, for which a charge can be imposed.[182] After a consumer approves the estimate any cost exceeding the stated figure requires his consent. Completed repairs must be accompanied by a signed, itemized invoice, and the consumer must be informed of the right to examine and receive back all replaced parts. Public regulation cannot solve all the problems, for example, there may be a shortage of skilled tradesmen in service industries, but it will go part of the way to eliminate abuses and to ensure the minimum standards required by the civil law.

5
Minimum quality standards for products: manufacturers' liability

In law manufacturers have a narrow legal responsibility for the quality of the products they produce. One, albeit limited, way that manufacturers may be legally liable to consumers is through their statements.[1] There have been several cases where the courts have held that an express representation by a manufacturer to a consumer as to the quality of its products gives rise to collateral contract.[2] The leading case of *Carlill* v. *Carbolic Smoke Ball Co.*[3] recognized that a statement in a manufacturer's advertisement could give rise to a collateral contract with a consumer who bought the product from a retailer.[4] The precedent is there; whether the courts will apply it to modern advertising depends on whether they are sufficiently attuned to its techniques and subtleties. The difficulty is that the courts do not regard most statements in advertisements as being intended to create contractual relations.[5] It seems that there must be an unambiguous promise, as there was in the *Carbolic Smoke Ball Co.* case, where the manufacturer promised £100 to a consumer who could disprove the claim.[6] The courts in the United States have had no difficulty in applying the doctrine of breach of express warranty where assertions in manufacturers' advertisements about product quality have proved untrue.[7] The same result is achieved in Australia by legislation, which provides that a consumer can sue a manufacturer for loss or damage by reason of the failure of a product to comply with an undertaking, assertion or statement in relation to its quality, performance or characteristics, the natural tendency of which is to induce persons to acquire it.[8]

In this chapter our concern is with the two major ways in which manufacturers are liable for defective products: manufacturers' guarantees and negligence. The former are by far the most important of the two in terms of the volume of matters dealt with, and there are literally tens of thousands of complaints under manufacturers' guarantees every year. But there has been an absence of judicial consideration of manufacturers' guarantees, because the law imposes liability for shoddy products on retailers, and in those instances where this has proved unsatisfactory because, for example, the retailer has gone out of business, the cost of litigation and the uncertainty of the manufacturer's position had deterred customers from instituting legal proceedings. Manufacturers' liability for products which cause personal injury or death is much less important numerically, but in the few cases when it is relevant, it is obviously vital to the consumer or his family to establish a claim.

To get some idea of consumer complaints to manufacturers, a sample of twenty-six manufacturers, mainly national companies, was contacted.[9] By far the major areas of complaint were servicing, failure of components (in domestic electrical appliances) and spoilage in the case of perishable products. Minor areas included early wear on parts and a poor supply of spare parts. One electrical manufacturer who cited service and parts as the main problem areas said that complaints about service 'can relate to speed of service and the cost of service, and as far as spares are concerned, it's usually the sending of incorrect parts or delays in their availability'. None of the manufacturers mentioned complaints about personal injury or death. The number of complaints received per annum in proportion to the total output of products ranged from 'infinitesimal' to 2 to 3 per cent. The figures were estimates and precise details were either not kept or were confidential.

Manufacturers thought that the great majority of complaints were justified. Only a small number among the twenty-six thought that consumer misuse was the major cause involved or that complainants were malicious. At the same time manufacturers did not think that they were always responsible for all the genuine complaints. Thus a number of food manufacturers pointed out that most genuine complaints were due to improper storage or handling by wholesalers or retailers after products had left their control. Even where complaints were unfounded, most manufacturers in the sample provided a remedy on the basis of good public relations. As one put it:

We deal with any complaint irrespective of its source at the highest possible level, as the ability to bring about customer satisfaction is the best way we can protect the brand image and ensure future sales of our products.

The exception was with manufacturers of domestic electrical appliances, who tended to reject unfounded complaints and to stick fairly closely to the terms of the guarantees they had issued. No doubt their attitude was determined because the cost of repairing or replacing items automatically would have been prohibitive.

It is against this background of how manufacturers actually deal with complaints that the present law must be viewed. That most manufacturers are generous with genuine consumer complaints, at least those involving claims about shoddy goods, is a good argument for bringing the law into line with the practice and making manufacturers jointly liable with retailers.

MANUFACTURERS' GUARANTEES AND SHODDY PRODUCTS

These days many manufacturers issue guarantees in which they undertake to replace unsatisfactory products (e.g. food) or to rectify manufacturing defects which become manifest within a specified period like six months or a year (e.g. cars, domestic electrical equipment). An example is

Your —— was carefully tested and inspected before leaving our factory. If, however, any defect in material or workmanship should develop within one year of purchase it will be rectified without charge.

Accidental damage, misuse or damage caused by repairs and adjustments made by any unauthorized person, is not covered by this Guarantee.

This guarantee does not replace or otherwise affect your rights regarding defective products . . .

Some manufacturers are even prepared to go beyond the precise terms of a guarantee; for example, a manufacturer of electrical products responded as follows to the survey on manufacturers' policies mentioned above.

We would replace or refund the purchase price of a rogue appliance under guarantee even though as manufacturers we are not legally bound to do this under the [law].

If the machine is shortly outside the guarantee period, we do office repairs at concessional prices dependent upon the age of the appliance; i.e., 13–18 months: labour charge only; 19–24 months: half of the material costs and labour charge.

Should we not be able to supply a spare within a reasonable time, we can offer to replace the appliance at a generous concessional price dependent on the age of the appliance.

Guarantees perform a promotional function for manufacturers, as well as acting as a system of quality control whereby information can be obtained about the performance of a product.[10] The advantage of a generous guarantee to consumers is that it gives them a remedy without the formality of establishing a legal claim. It can also mean that a product will be repaired by the manufacturer, who has the resources and expertise which the retailer lacks, although the latter is legally responsible. Retailers often try to avoid their legal reponsibility by pointing to a manufacturer's guarantee. Relying on the guarantee, then, may be the most practical means for consumers of settling a dispute. A possible disadvantage is that where manufacturers decide against giving redress, consumers may not be able to exercise the right to reject as against the retailer because of the delay and may be confined to an action for money damages.[11]

At one time the term 'guarantee' was a clear abuse of language because many manufacturers used a 'guarantee' to exclude their liability for negligence in situations where a consumer suffered personal injury from a defect. Guarantees of this type were disapproved of by bodies like the Advertising Standards Authority. The Law Commission recommended that consumers should have legal protection because they could not be expected before accepting a guarantee to evaluate precisely the risk involved.[12] Section 5 of the Unfair Contract Terms Act 1977 provides that liability for loss or damage cannot be excluded or restricted by reference to any contract term or notice contained in or operating by reference to a guarantee of a product, of a type ordinarily supplied for private use or consumption, where the loss or damage arises from the product proving defective while in consumer use and resulting from the negligence of a person covered in its manufacture or distribution. 'In consumer use' is defined widely to cover situations where a person is using a product, or has it in his possession for use, otherwise than exclusively for the purpose of a business. Anything in writing is a guarantee if it contains or purports to contain some promise or assurance that defects will be made good by complete or partial replacement, by repair, by monetary compensation or otherwise.[13] The upshot is that manufacturers' guarantees now give consumers additional remedies without subtracting from any of their legal rights.

Nevertheless, guarantees may not be as extensive as consumers expect. Consumers may still be liable for labour and transport charges where a product is repaired under guarantee. A guarantee may not extend to defective accessories and it may not apply at all if repairs have been attempted by the consumer. Then there are guarantees which, in addition to limitations like these, contain an additional clause which renders them virtually useless: 'In implementing this guarantee the Company and/or the Retailer may charge at their discretion for any service rendered.'[14] On one occasion Lord Denning spoke scathingly about guarantees of this nature which, in his view, could hardly be called 'guarantees' when the additional benefits they conferred were so restrictive:[15]

> We all know what happens. Be it a motor car, a refrigerator, or a washing machine, the supplier will 'guarantee' it for two, three or five years, as the case may be. It sounds splendid. It looks fine. It is often headed in ornamental lettering 'GUARANTEE', sometimes with a seal attached, as if to show it is of great value. The salesman asks the customer to sign an acknowledgment and return it to the supplier. It is in the customer's interest, he says, to do so. The customer does so, believing it is worth a great deal to him. He does not read it, of course. No one ever does. He takes it on trust that it is what the salesman says it is – a guarantee for those years. But when it comes to the pinch – when something goes wrong with the thing and he reads it – then he will discover that he would have done better without it. The guarantee gives him no more than the law would have done anyway. More often than not it cuts down the liability of the supplier. If the thing goes wrong, the supplier will not pay for the loss or damage which the customer sustains. He will only replace the defective part free of charge within the two years, three years, or five years, as the case may be. It is to my mind quite wrong that customers should be hoodwinked in this way. When a supplier says he gives a guarantee, he should be held to his word. He should not be allowed to limit it by clever clauses in small print – which, in 99 cases out of 100 the customer never reads. Certainly he should not be allowed to cut it down by phrases of doubtful or ambiguous import. If he wishes to excuse himself from liability, he should say so plainly. Instead of heading it boldly 'GUARANTEE' he should head it 'NON-GUARANTEE': for that is what it is.

The Office of Fair Trading has sought to improve the clarity, scope and presentation of guarantees on a voluntary basis. Its guide suggests that guarantees should embody a firm commitment to undertake to repair or replace specified or all defective parts for a stated period free of charge (including labour, carriage) and to extend the period if the product is out of action for a significant time. It suggests ways in which the clarity of guarantees can be improved and describes the kind of undesirable restrictions which it thinks shall be avoided.[16]

In the absence of steps to impose a mandatory guarantee on manufacturers, legislation can try to ensure that consumers clearly understand the undertakings set out in guarantees. So far the only action is a statutory order under Part II of the Fair Trading Act 1973, which requires a guarantee to make known to consumers that it does not affect their rights under the Sale of Goods Act 1979.[17] Legislation elsewhere is more far-reaching. The best known example is the Magnuson-Moss Warranty Act, which became law in the United States in 1975,[18] but there are similar provisions in several Commonwealth jurisdictions.[19] Basically the Magnuson-Moss Act requires that a business issuing a guarantee must clearly disclose certain basic information: its name and address; the identity of those to whom it extends; the parts covered; what the guarantors will do, at whose expense, for what period; what the consumer must do and what expenses he must bear; exceptions; the procedure to make the claim, and that there are additional legal remedies available to consumers. The guarantee must be available to consumers prior to a transaction and it becomes legally binding on a business and cannot be disclaimed or modified. In addition to the disclosure provisions, the Act requires that guarantees be clearly labelled as either 'full' or 'limited'. A 'full' guarantee must meet certain minimum standards. Basically it must provide that defects will be remedied without charge and within a reasonable period if it fails to comply to the warranty, and if this proves impossible consumers must be offered either a refund or a replacement. Maybe the two propositions which consumers will latch onto in guarantees under legislation like the Magnuson-Moss Act are the duration and the broad designation 'full' or 'limited'.[20] However, a later chapter views with scepticism the immediate impact of disclosure regulation like the Magnuson-Moss Act. The best approach, it is suggested, is direct regulation – in this context the introduction of mandatory manufacturers' guarantees.[21]

There is an absence of judicial authority on the legal status of manufacturers' guarantees. From basic principles of contract law, the major problem is consideration. When a consumer knows about a guarantee beforehand it seems that a collateral contract is formed with the manufacturer, the consideration for which is entering the main contract with the retailer.[22] There are difficulties if a consumer has no prior knowledge of a guarantee. One argument could be that manufacturers' guarantees are so common with some products that a consumer should be regarded as knowing of the practice and contracting on that basis. Another possibility is that the consideration is the benefit the manufacturer gets in goodwill, information, etc. when the consumer sends off a guarantee card to the manufacturer on finally discovering it.[23]

Should legislation introduce mandatory guarantees? In other words, should manufacturers be legally responsible for shoddy, as well as unsafe, products along the lines that retailers are under the Sale of Goods Act 1979? At first sight it seems extraordinary that manufacturers have a limited legal responsibility for the quality of what they produce. After all, manufacturers determine quality, and it is they who decide in many cases how products are advertised, what information is attached and what should be the availability of spare parts and servicing. As one consumer body remarked: 'If the manufacturer relies on the customer to be the final link in his quality-control system, he must take the responsibility for ensuring that the customer does not suffer as a result.'[24]

Certainly the law in this respect is out of line with consumers' expectations. Not surprisingly many think manufacturers are responsible for shoddy products and advertising and manufacturers' guarantees do nothing to disabuse them of this notion.[25]. The explanation for retailer's liability is that the courts decided the issue in the nineteenth century, before the age of mass-produced manufactured products, when retailers still played an important part in the quality of what consumers received. Now it is manufacturers who determine in the main the quality of what consumers receive, although a few large retailers do play a part by issuing detailed specifications to suppliers for own-brand products.

Unfortunately, the law has remained in the nineteenth century and seems unlikely to change. Official opinion remains wedded to the notion of privity of contract and that retailers and not manufacturers should continue to be responsible for shoddy products. The reason, says the Law Commission, is that much depends on the terms of the contract made with a retailer and the price paid.[26] Presumably, the Commission is thinking of cases where consumers know of defects before buying and this fact is reflected in the price. Yet these considerations are clearly irrelevant in the vast majority of cases where the complaint is about latent manufacturing defects. The Molony Committee raised the red herring that a change in the law would produce unjustified claims, although why this should occur against manufacturers and not retailers was never explained.[27] The Molony Committee also thought that it was unfair to make manufacturers liable when they made products to a retailer's design and specification for sale under the retailer's own brand name. The obvious reply to this point is that most complaints are about manufacturers' defects and not about design faults. In any event, it is unlikely that consumers claim against manufacturers in such circumstances because ostensibly the retailer is also the manufacturer.

In other jurisdictions manufacturers are made liable for shoddy as well as unsafe products. In New South Wales a court has power to add a manufacturer or importer as a party to any proceedings arising out of a consumer sale of a new product where it appears that it was defective when delivered.[28] The manufacturer can be ordered to repair the product or to pay an amount equivalent to the cost of doing this. Other legislation goes even further in imposing liability on manufacturers. California's Consumer Warranty Act creates implied warranties of merchantability, and where relevant fitness, on the part of manufacturers of consumer products which can only be excluded where the products are sold on an 'as is' or 'with all faults' basis.[29] Australia's Trade Practices Act 1974 is to similar effect and imposes a non-excludable requirement of merchantability on manufacturers in relation to products supplied to consumers of a kind ordinarily acquired for personal, domestic or household use or consumption.[30] Consumers or those who derive title to a product through or under them are entitled to compensation for loss or damage by reason of a product not being merchantable.[31] Manufacturers have an additional obligation reasonably to ensure that repair facilities and spare parts are available on a reasonable basis, unless they take reasonable action to ensure that consumers are notified at or before the time of acquisition that they give no such undertaking.[32]

NEGLIGENCE AND UNSAFE PRODUCTS

Negligence as it developed in the nineteenth century meant businesses were not responsible for industrial accidents or for injuries from defective products unless it could be established that they were at fault, and even then they could set up defences to bar a claim. To some extent the courts adopted this approach under the threat to infant industry of economic ruin posed by liability without fault. Friedman and Ladinsky remark with respect to negligence and industrial accidents:

[The courts] were anxious to see that the tort system of accident compensation did not add to the problems of new industry. Few people imagined that accidents would become so numerous as to create severe economic and social dislocations. On the contrary, rash extensions of certain principles of tort law to industrial accidents might upset social progress by imposing extreme costs on business in its economic infancy.[33]

At the same time liability for fault was in keeping with the individualistic moral philosophy of the nineteenth century: businesses should have freedom of action unless their behaviour was clearly unreasonable.[34]

Gradually there was a change in judicial philosophy towards negligence, particularly in the industrial sphere, and the defences to a successful claim were reduced as sections of society agitated against the miseries caused by the law not compensating injured persons and as economic growth meant that industry no longer needed the same protection. The manufacture of more complex and sophisticated products and the parliamentary attitude as reflected in legislation like the Food and Drugs Acts ensured that when the courts considered defective products they would be under pressure to compensate injured consumers and to try to encourage manufacturers to take steps to prevent defective products getting onto the market. This development occurred in the United States in 1916 in *Macpherson* v. *Buick Motor Co.*,[35] when the New York Court of Appeals held that a car manufacturer had to compensate a consumer who had been injured when one of the car wheels collapsed because of a defect. The court held that the manufacturer had been negligent because the defect could have been discovered by reasonable inspection. The breakthrough in Britain had to wait another sixteen years but it finally came in the leading case of *Donoghue* v. *Stevenson*,[36] where the consumer claimed to have suffered injury as a result of drinking from a bottle of ginger-beer containing a decomposed snail. Over a strong dissent the majority held that the manufacturer could be liable. The case did not herald strict liability but it facilitated more claims than were possible under the nineteenth-century approach. Lord Atkin enunciated the manufacturer's duty of care in the following words:

[A] manufacturer of products, which he sells in such a form as to show that he intends them to reach the ultimate consumer in the form in which they left him with no reasonable possibility of intermediate examination, and with the knowledge that the absence of reasonable care in the preparation or putting up of the products will result in an injury to the consumer's life or property, owes a duty to the consumer to take that reasonable care.[37]

Subsequent cases have considered further what the duty of reasonable care for manufacturers entails. First, reasonable care must be taken to ensure that products are designed in a way which ensures reasonable safety to consumers.[38] Secondly – and this is the most common source of complaint – manufacturers must have an adequate system of quality control to prevent the occasional defective in a product run from leaving the factory. Thirdly, manufacturers have a duty in marketing products to attach instructions or warnings when it is not obvious to consumers that there can be a danger.[39] Finally, manufacturers may be negligent if they fail to warn about, recall or cease marketing a product once they discover that it is dangerous.[40] In all four cases manufacturers as a minimum should adhere to current standards of practice in their particular industry, although adherence is by no means conclusive evidence that the duty of reasonable care is satisfied. Compliance with voluntary standards of bodies like those of the British Standards Institution might also be necessary to satisfy the duty of reasonable care. Manufacturers are not liable for design defects which could not have been foreseen given the state of scientific knowledge existing at the time (the so-called 'state of the art' defence).

In establishing that a manufacturer has breached the duty of reasonable care, consumers derive some assistance from the doctrine of *res ipsa loquitur*, whereby the very fact that a defect has occurred raises a rebuttable presumption of negligence on the part of the manufacturer. *Grant* v. *Australian Knitting Mills Ltd*[41] is a strong case, where a consumer contracted dermatitis after an excess of chemicals remained in woollen underclothes manufactured by the defendant. The Privy Council overturned the decision of the High Court of Australia and held that it was possible to draw an inference of negligence on the part of the manufacturer. It did not suffice for the manufacturer to show that it had a system of eliminating excess chemicals or that it had produced 4.5 million similar garments without complaint:[42]

According to the evidence, the method of manufacture was correct: the danger of excess sulphites being left was recognized and was guarded against: the process was intended to be fool proof. If excess sulphites were left in the garment, that could only be because some one was at fault. The appellant is not required to lay his finger on the exact person in all the chain who was responsible, or to specify what he did wrong. Negligence is found as a matter of inference from the existence of the defects taken in connection with all the known circumstances: even if the manufacturers could by apt evidence have rebutted that inference they have not done so.[43]

Similarly, in *Lockhart* v. *Barr*[44] a consumer bought a bottle of soft drink and was injured by drinking its contents, which were contaminated by phenol. The House of Lords had no doubt that they could draw the inference of negligence and that there was no need for the consumer to prove exactly how the presence of phenol had come about. The inference of negligence is clear in cases like those involving foreign matter in sealed containers or foreign substances in clothing.

Despite the *res ipsa* doctrine, consumers may still fail to establish that it was the manufacturer which was at fault. The defect may appear to be attributable to a faulty component made by a supplier. The consumer may discover this too late and be outside the limitation period to sue the supplier depending on the jurisdiction and type of damage. In such a case, if the manufacturer of the complete product is sued, it will only be held liable if the consumer can show that it failed to take reasonable care by not checking the reputation of the supplier or by failing to carry out random tests on the components supplied.[45] Other plausible explanations for a defect may be that it developed because of negligence on the part of the retailer.[46] The consumer will need expert evidence to establish who was to blame.[47] The difficulty of proving who in the manufacturing or distribution chain is at fault is illustrated by *Evans* v. *Triplex Safety Glass Co. Ltd*,[48] where a consumer bought a motorcar fitted with a Triplex toughened safety glass windscreen. About a year after purchase, when the car was being used, the screen suddenly broke for no apparent reason and the occupants were injured. The court held that the consumer had not discharged the onus of establishing that the glass broke because of negligence on the part of the component manufacturer. The disintegration was possibly due to the strain imposed on the windscreen in its fitting rather than to faulty manufacture.

Consumers can recover compensation in negligence for damage of two types. First, consumers can claim for personal injury or death resulting from a defective product; this may include the loss of wages as well as non-pecuniary losses (e.g. pain and suffering). Second, the defect may have caused property damage, as where a car crashes into another because of a negligently manufactured part.[49] Moreover, a manufacturer is generally liable for the cost of repair if a negligently manufactured product could injure someone or cause damage, but the defect is discovered in time.[50] In very special circumstances, where the relationship between the manufacturer and the consumer is sufficiently close, possibly where a product is made to order, consumers may recover for the defect in the product itself and for any pure economic loss which results.[51] However, in the ordinary case of manufacturers of products which are offered for sale to the public, the courts will not impose liability on manufacturers.[52] In other words, where a mass consumption good is simply shoddy through negligent manufacture, the consumer's only remedies are against the retailer under the Sale of Goods Act. The courts' refusal to impose liability on manufacturers in such cases derives from what they see as the legal problems of ascertaining the standard for defective products (apart from Sale of Goods standards), the satisfactory nature of existing Sale of Goods remedies, and the need for legislative action for major change.[53] What has already been said casts doubt on some aspects of this reasoning, for example, the nature of existing remedies. Several United States courts have allowed consumers to claim from manufacturers the cost of having a defective product repaired[54] and, as we have seen, legislation imposes liability on manufacturers in California and Australia.

Practical problems of factual proof can set up barriers to consumers making a successful claim in negligence. To establish negligence with complex products may require knowledge of the manufacturing process, the means of quality control or the system of supply and distribution. Manufacturers will not divulge such information freely, but the circumstances in which a consumer can obtain discovery are somewhat <u>limited</u>. In *Board* v. *Thomas Hedley & Co.*,[55] however, the consumer was able to obtain details of other complaints to the manufacturer which were relevant to the issue of whether the product was dangerous. Consumers may also find their claim defeated, or at least their damages reduced, by any one of the standard defences to negligence – that they voluntarily assumed the risk of the defect;[56] that they, too, were negligent; or that their claim is brought too late and falls outside the limitation period. Excluding or limiting liability

152   PRIVATE LAW

for negligence is restricted in accordance with the Unfair Contract Terms Act 1977.

The Thalidomide tragedy and the failure of negligence

The Thalidomide tragedy illustrates the deficiencies of negligence as a system of compensating consumers injured by defective products. Developed in Germany by the company Chemie Gruenethal, Thalidomide was manufactured in several countries under license and promoted widely as a safe tranquillizer without side-effects. Its marketing resulted in 8,000–10,000 children being born deformed. Quite apart from its other implications, the Thalidomide tragedy demonstrated the complete inadequacy in the law of most countries, either to prevent the marketing of an unsafe drug or to compensate those injured when it was marketed. The *Sunday Times* said in an editorial:

> The real lesson, so far unlearned, is that the ability of the citizen to resist corporate power is lamentable: that the law, Parliament and the Press all fail in varying degrees, but the law most. Death, injury and loss from manufacture is a commonplace of our society but compensation for it is pure roulette, only with lower rewards. There is no automatic benefit, no system of strict liability, as there is in some other countries. Negligence has to be proved, which is costly, cumbersome, and onerous for the individual and frequently beyond the capacities of the solicitors and barristers. The idea that somehow a negligence case is a contest of equals from which justice will emerge is a ludicrous illusion . . .[57]

The main difficulty facing the Thalidomide children in Britain in seeking compensation for their injuries was in grounding a good cause of action against the company marketing the drug, the Distillers Company (Biochemicals) Ltd. First there was the absence of clear authority on whether the common law provided a remedy for those suffering from a pre-natal injury caused by another's fault. The English Law Commission has said that a court would have decided the question favourably, but the matter was not clear.[58] More important was the necessity to establish negligence – that the company had fallen below the standard of care in marketing the drug and/or as to the withdrawing it once evidence of its effects became apparent.[59] As to the manufacture of Thalidomide, the German company had subjected the drug to only a small number of unsystematic clinical tests, most of which were conducted by doctors in a regular commercial relationship with the firm who lacked special training for the purpose. No proper evaluation of synergistic effects was made and certainly there was no testing for teratogenic effects. Early reports of adverse side-effects were suppressed by Gruenethal, who lied when doctors enquired whether such side-effects had been previously encountered; they also tried to suppress unfavourable reports and promoted favourable publicity, in some cases by dishonest means.[60]

What of the British distributors, Distillers? In their advertisements they claimed that the drug could be safely administered; a particular claim was that the drug could be given with complete safety to pregnant women and nursing mothers. Distillers carried out no scientific tests themselves before marketing the drug to establish the validity of this claim. The key question in any civil action, therefore, was whether Distillers were negligent in not doing so. Their argument was that tests for teratogenic effects were not customary at the time, although critics argued that they did not even follow the best testing procedures of the time. Almost all the legal authorities, including lawyers for the children, thought it unlikely that negligence would be established on this point, although there was greater hope for the time between when Distillers was first notified of suspected teratogenic effects by the Australian obstetrician, Dr William McBride, and before the drug was actually withdrawn from the market some months later.

The belief that the case was too weak for trial on the first point was based primarily on the assumption that at the time Thalidomide was marketed it was not accepted practice to test drugs for teratogenic effects. Scientific opinion then prevailing did not conceive that drugs would damage the developing foetus, especially if they caused little harm to the mother. This assumption about standards has been challenged, however, and the *Sunday Times* has alleged that in accepting it the lawyers for the children failed to mount as effective a case as possible in the circumstances. Certainly the issue was less clear cut elsewhere.[61]

The English High Court approved a settlement in a test case in 1969 for some of the children.[62] That settlement was quite inadequate in the eyes of many; and at one stage when Distillers made an offer for the remaining children conditional on all parents accepting it, the Court of Appeal upheld the refusal of a number of parents to agree. The Court held that, as best next friends of their children, the dissident parents were entitled to have regard to the interests of their children irrespective of the interests of the Thalidomide children as a whole.[63] Meanwhile public opinion from various quarters pressed Distillers to make a more favourable settlement: parliamentary opinion expressed disfavour at the company's proposals; shareholders of the company, including local authorities and institutional investors such as insurance companies, pledged their support for generous treatment; other large enterprises expressed displeasure at the tardy progress, including a major chain store which threatened to boycott Distillers' other products. Finally a settlement was reached which extended to those who had earlier compromised their claims.[64]

Procedural difficulties also faced the Thalidomide children. An overriding factor was the time delay; over a decade passed before compensation was finalized. The absence of class actions as compared with the United States meant the children had to issue separate proceedings alleging the individual circumstances of their injury.[65] A degree of consolidation of these actions was achieved in Britain where the legal aid authorities encouraged all claims to be processed by the same firm of solicitors. A further hitch was the limitation period, which required the institution of proceedings of this nature within three years of the cause of action arising. A large number of the children were outside the limitation period and it was necessary to obtain special leave under the extended time provisions of the Limitation Act 1963. The general point is that substantial periods can elapse before drugs are discovered to be dangerous and legal proceedings contemplated. A homely illustration is that the serious danger to human kidneys, caused by ingesting phenacetin in aspirin, is cumulative and only becomes apparent after a number of years. The difficulty is now overcome: the limitation period in the case of personal injury runs from when the prospective plaintiff first knows that an injury is significant and that it is the defendant which caused it.[66]

The weaknesses of the substantive and procedural law in compensating the Thalidomide children have been outlined. But this is not the end of the law's failings, for in Britain the law actually stepped in to hinder the children from benefiting from extra-legal tactics to further their claims. In effect it prevented the use of the one weapon the children had to pressure Distillers to increase the settlement offer – the force of public opinion – by granting an injunction to prevent publication of a critical article by the *Sunday Times*.[67] Six years later the European Court of Human Rights held this injunction to violate article 10 of the European Convention on Human Rights regarding freedom of expression.[68]

By contrast to the situation in many countries, the United States suffered comparatively little from Thalidomide. Because its safety was never satisfactorily demonstrated, the Food and Drugs Administration there never gave marketing approval for the drug. The legal provision used was introduced following a Thalidomide-type tragedy in the United States in 1937, where a liquid form of new sulpha drug caused nearly a hundred deaths. The Thalidomide tragedy led to controls similar to those in the United States, whereby drugs are not approved for marketing unless they are regarded as safe. These provisions are discussed elsewhere, but at this point it might be mentioned that the controls do not extend to dangerous substances such as tobacco and alcohol, and that governments have relied heavily on voluntary measures to reduce the risks to health from these commodities.

But the law is still unreformed concerning compensation for persons who suffer injury when a drug, quite unexpectedly, proves to be unsafe. Compensation still depends on proof of negligence. Thus persons seeking compensation for permanent damage from the heart drug Eraldin settled their claims for compensation after legal advice that the manufacturer, ICI, was not legally liable.[69] Current theories on the liability of drug manufacturers in the United States similarly offer uncertain prospects of recovery against manufacturers. If manufacturers have adequately warned physicians about a drug's foreseeable adverse effects, they will escape liability unless it can be shown that injury was caused by some impurity, or resulted from some unreasonably unsafe design.

Strict liability for manufacturers

The Thalidomide tragedy underlines the need for reform of negligence law as regards defective products. Although the number of injuries caused by products is relatively small, and the risk of death lower than for other categories of injury, there seems to be some 30,000–40,000 injuries a year caused by defective products including drugs, of which about only 5 per cent attract compensation through tort or contract.[70] Of course, there is a case for a compensation scheme to cover all those affected by misfortune, including accidents from defective products. Until such a scheme is introduced, however, the best approach in this area may be to introduce strict liability for manufacturers. Strict liability already exists under the Consumer Protection Act 1961 and the Consumer Safety Act 1978, since breach of the regulations and orders under these is actionable as breach of statutory duty owed to any person affected, not simply the buyer.[71]

In the United States the courts have adopted a stricter liability for defective products.[72] Doctrinally, United States courts developed this liability from the old English law notion of warranty, as an action in tort – not in contract – for a false affirmation of fact, whether or not the person making it knew it was false. The advantage of this approach conceptually was that there could be a breach of warranty without a contract of sale. The United States courts built on the idea and implied a warranty on the part of manufacturers that products were free from defects. Now the development is only of historical interest, for it is accepted as law that manufacturers and distributors are liable to any person who is injured by a 'defective' product. Leading cases are *Henningsen* v. *Blomfield Motors Inc.*[73] and *Greenman* v. *Yuba Power Products Inc.*[74] The doctrine is now in section 402A of the Second Restatement on Torts, which provides liability for products which are in a defective condition, unreasonably dangerous to individuals or their property, even if a business has exercised all possible care and there is no privity of contract. Jurisdictions like California allow recovery in the absence of an unreasonable danger, as long as there is damage resulting from the defect.[75] Obvious as well as hidden dangers are covered and misuse by the consumer will not necessarily absolve a business from liability.[76] In *Vandermark* v. *Ford Motor Co.*,[77] liability for retailers of defective products was justified on the basis that they were an integral part in the marketing process, and in some cases were the only defendant reasonably available to an injured person. The latest development is the possibility of imposing 'market-share' liability on an industry as a whole to overcome the difficulty or impossibility of consumers' proving the identity of the manufacturer or seller responsible.[78] But the scope of products liability in the United States rests on the notion of 'defect'. In the case of manufacturing errors, this is not difficult and liability is established much as it would be in negligence. Considerably more difficulty attaches to design defects, and most American courts have in practice eschewed genuine strict liability here, applying a negligence-like cost-benefit analysis.[79]

There are now strong pressures for legislation to introduce stricter liability for the manufacturers of defective products which cause personal injury or property damage. An EEC draft directive, a Convention of the Council of Europe, a Law Commission Report, and the Pearson Commission all support the move.[80] The existing system of negligence is accepted as a failure because it creates procedural and evidential difficulties which impede the course of justice. The policy considerations underlying the groundswell of opinion in favour of strict liability are outlined in the Law Commission Report.[81] First, there is the moral argument: losses associated with a defective product should be borne by the manufacturer who creates the risk by putting it into circulation for commercial gain. Secondly, there is the consideration of equity: the easiest way of spreading the loss fairly is to place it on the manufacturer who can recover the cost of insuring against the risk in the price charged for a product. Thirdly, there are matters of efficiency: it is desirable to impose liability on manufacturers because they are in the best position to exercise control over the quality and safety of products, and they can most conveniently insure against the risk, rather than leave it to individual consumers to arrange their own first-party insurance.[82] Finally, there is the political argument: it is desirable to bring the law into line with consumers' expectations, who are led to believe by advertising and promotional material that manufacturers are liable.

These factors in favour of stricter liability outweigh the disadvantages of the change. Any tendency of this liability to discourage innovation is more than counterbalanced by the need to compensate adequately those injured by defective products. Despite stricter liability, it seems that companies will be impelled to develop new products for their continued existence, possibly with a greater emphasis on safety to avoid legal actions. The small number of spurious claims should not be affected, because consumers will have to establish that their injury is attributable to a defect as at present. Further, there is little reason to think that the change to stricter liability will make consumers more careless because their claims will no longer be defeated, or at best reduced, on the basis of contributory negligence. It is unrealistic to think that at present consumers know the law, appreciate the risks they face from defective products or take steps to avoid them. Most consumers undervalue the likelihood of their own involvement in accidents.

It is unlikely that consumers acquire much information about product-related risks from personal experience, since they are unlikely to experience multiple incidents of product-related accidents. Nor are they likely to learn from other consumers because of the unorganized nature of consumers in society. Of course manufacturers have no real incentive to provide the information. But even if consumers knew the risks, there is no reason to think that they could take preventive action to avoid every possible accident. The conclusion is obvious: negligence has no deterrent effect on consumers and there will be no change in their behaviour if strict liability is adopted.

The most serious objection to stricter liability is the cost. Experience in the United States is that the cost argument is exaggerated. Insurance cover in the United States adds only a small amount to manufacturing costs.[83] More importantly, it seems clear that factors in the United States creating pressures for a large number of high value product claims are not present elsewhere. There is nothing like the contingency fee system which encourages American lawyers to seek personal injury litigation in return for a percentage of any amount recovered. In addition, the National Health Service contrasts with the high cost of medical care in the United States, which is a large component of personal injury awards there.[84]

The EEC draft directive, the Council of Europe treaty and the Law Commission's Report are basically similar in recommending stricter liability for manufacturers for defects for which they are responsible. Consumers would have to prove that the product was defective, that their injury was caused by the defect, and that the defendant was the producer. Each proposal applies to unsafe but not shoddy products. Mention has already been made of how the courts in some American jurisdictions and legislation in Australia make manufacturers liable for both. Each proposal regards a product as unsafe if it does not comply with the standard of safety that a person is entitled to expect.[85] Generally such a standard does not impose liability when a consumer has a particular subjective tendency to suffer injury, such as allergies to a product which is objectively harmless.[86] It can be argued that manufacturers should be liable in such circumstances because individual consumers very often do not know of their allergy; manufacturers can spread the risk; and many adverse reactions would be prevented if producers did more than at present in the way of further testing or providing consumers with more accurate information.

All three proposals would normally limit liability to producers.[87] Extending liability to those such as retailers is rejected as too costly because each member in the chain of distribution would have to insure. What happens, however, if the producer is insolvent or uninsured? The consumer's chances of having a claim satisfied increase as the number of persons liable is extended. Enterprise liability – where all in the chain of production and distribution are liable – needs to be coupled with a provision enabling a business in the chain which is sued to claim an indemnity from the culprit. Yet even enterprise liability cannot cope with a situation where companies typically arrange their affairs (e.g. dummy companies, insolvency) so as to avoid substantial product liability claims. Legislation needs to enable claims to be made against the assets of a business, wherever in law they might be and whatever priorities of claim would otherwise obtain. Alternatively, it might be necessary to require compulsory insurance against product liability claims.

Each proposal makes a producer liable to pay compensation for death or personal injury.[88] The EEC draft directive would impose an aggregate financial limit on the amount recoverable in product liability suits for identical articles having the same defect.[89] But such a limitation creates difficulties as to how the amount should be applied between various claimants: do latecomers get nothing, or is the amount to be divided rateably among all? It would also mean delays as producers would think it unsafe to meet any individual claims until all were known. All three proposals make provision for the defences of assumption of the risk and contributory negligence.[90] But they do not spell out in detail what assumption of the risk entails; for example, will smokers have an action against cigarette manufacturers when it is public knowledge that they can be afflicted by lung cancer?[91] The answer would seem to be in the negative if the current approach to assumption of the risk is continued. Unlike the approach of American courts, the proposals do not accept a 'state of the art' defence.

6
Title, risk and performance

The present chapter examines a number of ancillary rules associated with sales to consumers apart from those already considered regarding the quality of items. The most important complaint that consumers have is about defects in products and sub-standard services, but there are also complaints about matters like delivery. Three topics are isolated for discussion in this chapter: (1) Title: what happens when the consumer buys from a seller who does not have title? (2) Risk: does the consumer have a remedy if an item is lost or destroyed after it is paid for but before it is delivered? and (3) Performance: what can the consumer do if the retailer is late in filling an order, and to what extent is the consumer liable who wants to pull out of a contract of sale? At the outset it should be understood that the rules on these matters are rather technical and in many respects highly prejudicial to consumers.

To get some idea of what happens in practice regarding these matters, two small surveys were conducted in which retailers were interviewed about their trade practices.[1] In the first, called the Shops Survey, forty-three retailers were interviewed in the West Midlands area, including seventeen furniture stores, twelve stores selling mainly domestic electrical items, nine dealing mainly in carpets and the rest being a miscellaneous group. Only four of the retailers were small businesses (defined as having only one retail outlet), the great majority being either regional or national firms. In addition thirty-seven car dealers were contacted in the London and Manchester areas (the cars survey); all sold both new and second-hand cars, and on average their stock was between twenty to forty cars.

THE SELLER WITHOUT TITLE

On rare occasions a consumer may obtain an item from a seller who does not have title or any authority to sell: the item may be stolen, on hire purchase, etc. In such circumstances the law gives the consumer a remedy against the seller, but in many cases this person may be fraudulent and will have disappeared, be in jail, or not have any assets. The dispute will be with the owner, who in some cases will be a retailer or a finance house. As between the rights of the owner and those of the third party the law is in an entirely unsatisfactory state. Instead of adopting the simple approach in consumer sales of generally favouring the innocent third party consumer, the law contains some highly technical and in some cases unjust rules. The origin of these rules in some cases derives from historical considerations quite out of touch with modern conditions.

The seller's liability

An action against the seller is in many cases quite illusory because he will either have disappeared or have no assets. Nevertheless, section 12(1) of the Sale of Goods Act 1979 implies a non-excludable condition in contracts of sale that the seller has a right to sell an item or, in the case of an agreement to sell, will have that right when property is to pass.[2] The implied condition does not apply when it appears from the contract or can be inferred from its circumstances that the seller is only transferring such title as it or a third party has. In such a case, however, there is an implied warranty that all charges or encumbrances known to the seller and not known to the consumer have been disclosed to the latter before the contract is made.[3] *Rowland* v. *Divall*[4] is the leading case, where several months after the sale it was discovered that the car was stolen. The Court of Appeal held that the consumer was entitled to get back the full purchase price, without any amount taken into account for use, since there had been a total failure of consideration. Commentators say that the rule in *Rowland* v. *Divall* is too rigid because it fails to take account of the consumer's use of an item and makes the seller bear the full loss. On the other hand consumers have every right to be compensated for the bother caused and in any event, because of price rises, may find it difficult to buy a substitute without further expenditure.

Owner v. *consumer – the* nemo dat *rule*

In many cases where title is defective the real contest will be between the owner and the third party consumer. The basic rule of English law is that a person cannot give a better title to an item than he possesses (the *nemo dat* rule), but because of the obvious injustices there are a number of exceptions where third parties are favoured at the expense of owners.[5] The exceptions are dealt with at length in standard texts, but in summary they are:

Agency: Agents at law selling within the actual scope of their authority pass good title to third parties even where the existence of a principal is undisclosed. The same applies to cases of ostensible authority where a person sells an item in circumstances where the power to do this normally attaches, or where the owner does something which allows the agent to represent that he has the power to do so (estoppel). Several decisions establish that merely to put a person in possession of a car and its registration book does not constitute ostensible authority, nor does it give rise to an estoppel even if it was being negligent because, it is said, there is no duty to the public in general, including the innocent consumer.[6] The decisions are questionable: surely owners should not entrust a relative stranger – even a personable one – with the possession of their car and the means without which it is highly difficult to sell (the registration book), and then expect to upset the very reasonable assumption of a third party consumer that the stranger had a right to sell?[7] More importantly, car owners might be able to protect themselves from such loss by taking out insurance.

Mercantile agent: The original Factors Act 1823 was enacted because, according to its preamble, 'the law [is] highly injurious to the interests of commerce in general.'[8] Now section 2(1) of the Factors Act 1889 provides:

> Where a mercantile agent is, with the consent of the owner, in possession of goods or of the documents of title to goods, any sale, pledge, or other disposition of the goods, made by him when acting in the ordinary course of business of a mercantile agent, shall, subject to the provisions of this Act, be as valid as if he were expressly authorized by the owner of the goods to make the same; provided that the person taking under the disposition acts in good faith and has not at the time of the disposition notice that the person making the disposition has not authority to make the same.

The definition of a mercantile agent is quite wide, covering those who in the customary course of business have authority to buy or sell items.[9] It seems that a business both selling and repairing cars does not fall within the Factors Act if it quite fraudulently purports to sell a car entrusted to it for repair, but title might pass to a third party consumer because of apparent authority. Under the Factors Act, a mercantile agent must act in the ordinary course of business in selling or otherwise disposing of an item. This is a question of fact; it has been held in the circumstances that it was in the ordinary course of business for a mercantile agent to sell a car for cash in a street market.[10] However, the courts have not been especially solicitous of consumers who buy second-hand cars where fraudulent dealers have obtained the registration book from a private owner in an un-authorized manner. It has been held in these circumstances that a dealer does not pass good title because it has not acted in the ordinary course of business – a fact about which the consumer has no means of knowing.[11] The result is unsatisfactory and the solution would seem to be to protect the innocent consumer and to ensure that insurance policies for theft are wide enough to protect owners in the event of such loss.

Finally, the Factors Act requires the consumer to act in good faith and without notice or constructive notice of the seller's lack of authority. It has been suggested that a consumer should be put on notice when the purchase price is well below the market price, although the most obvious reaction of consumers in such circumstances would be that they have got a bargain, not that the seller is a crook.[12] It has also been said that a consumer being sold a second-hand car is put on notice if the registration book is not handed over at the time, however plausible the excuse for its absence.[13]

Market overt: A consumer gets good title, whatever the seller's, if an item is bought in an open market, constituted by custom or by statute, according to the usage of the market.[14] Blackburn J. in an old case said that the rule was originally established by the law 'in consequence of its policy of encouraging markets and commerce'. Cockburn C. J. said:

[T]he law in question was established for the protection of buyers, that, if a man did not pursue his goods to market in which such goods were openly sold, he ought not to interfere with the right of the honest and bona fide purchaser.[15]

An early case was in 1291, when Mathilda Frances was allowed to keep stolen malt on proving that she bought it in good faith in the precincts of a fair. Decisions like this were incorporated in the law merchant, then recognized by the common law as an exception to the *nemo dat* rule, and finally preserved for posterity by the Sale of Goods Act 1893.[16] The rigidity of the common law meant that the market overt rule was never extended to the new forms of retail sale which developed after the Middle Ages. The exception is that the rule covers consumers buying from any retailer within the precincts of the City of London. Fletcher Moulton L.J. suggested that London was so protected because of its political strength, and certainly in the *Market Overt Case* (1596) we read that the City, by their town clerk, argued for a wide application of the rule.[17] As if to highlight the anachronistic nature of the market overt rule, in 1973 the Court of Appeal held that it only applied to sales between sunrise and sunset, and not to a sale in a market which began at 7 a.m. when it was only half-light.[18] Instead of abolishing the rule, however, it should be extended to all retail sales as explained below.

Sellers and buyers in possession: A fraudulent retailer who has sold an item but remains in possession can pass good title to a subsequent consumer who buys it in good faith and without notice of the defect in title.[19]

The typical case of the buyer in possession is a person buying an item on credit sale; he can pass good title to a third party consumer.[20] By statutory enactment a buyer on conditional sale is not a buyer in possession, and by judicial decision neither is a person acquiring an item on hire purchase.[21] Legislation is necessary to remove the distinctions between the different forms of selling on credit.

Hire purchase: After support from the Molony Committee, Parliament passed Part III of the Hire Purchase Act 1964 which protects ordinary consumers,[22] acting *bona fide*, who acquire a motor vehicle from a person in possession under a hire purchase or conditional sale agreement.[23] Part III of the Hire Purchase Act 1964 seems to be working reasonably well and has not involved those engaged in hire purchase in significant loss.[24]

Seller with voidable title: The typical case is where a person fraudulently induces an owner to part with an item, by misrepresenting his identity and then sells to a consumer.[25]

Law reform

Consideration of these rules leads to a number of suggestions for reform with a view to simplifying the law, and to some extent offering a greater protection to ordinary consumers. Legislation reversing the protection which court decisions have extended to owners at the expense of consumers will not be new in this area.

First, consumers buying from a retailer or obtaining an item on hire purchase through a retailer should get good title as long as they are acting *bona fide* and without notice of any defect in title. Such a reform was suggested by the English Law Reform Committee in 1966.[26] Such a change will extend the law little and its main justification is that it will make it simpler. Secondly, by extension of the principle in Part III of the Hire Purchase Act 1964, consumers should get good title in all cases where they buy from persons who are acquiring an item on credit. There is no means whereby ordinary consumers can ascertain whether an item is being bought on credit – trade purchasers can do so through organizations like HP Information Ltd[27] – and finance houses are obviously in a better position to bear any loss.[28] When South Australia's Consumer Transactions Act 1972–1982 introduced reform along these lines, a system of title insurance was established to cover losses from fraudulent sales because it was thought to be more efficient than the cost of a registration system.[29] Despite the fears of the credit industry in South Australia, actual claims on the insurance fund have been relatively slight.

Apart from these two reforms, it is difficult to formulate general rules; the plain fact is that when a crook is involved both the owner and the third party consumer suffer. In *Ingram* v. *Little*,[30] Devlin L. J. suggested that in such circumstances the loss should be shared. A more satisfactory reform is to impose the loss on the party most likely to be insured. Take motor vehicles: it seems that the great majority of vehicle owners are insured for theft (as opposed to the number of householders insured for burglary), so that whenever a motor vehicle is involved the courts should favour the third party. Insurance premiums are unlikely to be affected by this policy: first, instances of disputes in motor vehicle theft between owners and third parties are very rare, at least according to the police;[31] and secondly, theft claims represent only a fraction of the losses of motor vehicle insurers, so that to increase the number by offering greater protection to third party consumers would not have a great impact.

THE RISK OF LOSS

This section is concerned with the question of who bears the loss if a product is lost or destroyed, without the fault of either party, before it is unequivocally the consumer's, or if the retailer becomes insolvent. Take the simple example of a consumer buying a washing machine which is stolen or destroyed by fire before the retailer delivers it. Is the risk with the retailer or must the consumer bear the loss? The law in this area is highly technical, prejudicial to consumers, and out of touch with what happens in practice. The rule in section 20 of the Sale of Goods Act 1979 is that risk passes to a consumer when property passes unless there is an agreement to the contrary. Rarely do consumer transactions contain a specific term about risk, so that generally risk is associated with the passing of property. A proviso in section 20 is that the risk falls on the party responsible for any delay as regards any loss which otherwise would not have occurred.

Risk thus turns on the question: when does property pass?[32] In English law a consumer can have property in a product even though it has not been delivered. The Sale of Goods Act 1979 says that property passes when the parties intend it to pass, having regard to their conduct, the terms of the contract, and the circumstances of the case.[33] Unless a different intention is apparent, section 18 of the Act lays down a number of arbitrary rules for determining the intention of the parties as to when property passes. Rule 1 provides that when there is an unconditional contract of sale of a specific product in a deliverable state, property passes when the contract is made and it is immaterial that payment or delivery is postponed. The rule is blatantly unsatisfactory because it means that a consumer becomes responsible for loss as soon as a contract to which the rule applies is made. The effects of the rule are mitigated first, if delivery has been delayed through fault of the seller as regards loss which might not otherwise have occurred and, second, by the law of bailment.[34] As regards the latter, if the product is still in the possession of a retailer the retailer as bailee bears responsibility for any loss occurring through its failure to exercise reasonable care. But a bailee is not responsible, for example, for fire damage occurring through no act of negligence on its part, and in circumstances like this the law thrusts the full burden of the loss onto the consumer.

It is not surprising that the courts have attempted to avoid the effects of section 18, rule 1, by finding a contrary intention in contracts of sale. Despite the rule, a consumer who has yet to pay for a product or take delivery of it is generally not treated as having any property in it.[35] Similarly, a retailer who retains some control over a product until clearance of a cheque is not regarded as having parted with property in it, and thus bears the risk.[36] Section 18, rule 1, only applies to contracts for a *specific* product – one identified and agreed upon at the time of sale. The arbitrary effect of the rule in this respect is obvious because risk varies with the market techniques and types of product involved. For example, the rule does not apply to sales which are based on consumers' seeing a demonstration model, so that the particular product the consumer is to receive is not identified and agreed upon at the time of sale because it has to be fetched from stock or ordered from the manufacturer. Further, section 18, rule 1, only applies if the product is in a deliverable state.[37] Rule 2 provides that where a contract is the sale of a specific product and the retailer is bound to do something to it to put it in a deliverable state, property does not pass until that is done. The Canadian case of *McDill* v. *Hilson*[38] is a useful illustration. A retailer agreed to polish certain furniture the consumer had bought before delivering it. The consumer paid the price but before the furniture could be polished or delivered it was destroyed by fire. The court held that the furniture was not in a deliverable state and thus property had not passed to the consumer who could recover the price paid. It rejected the retailer's contention that the deal should be looked at as a contract of sale and a separate contract to polish.

Where a contract is for an *unascertained* or a *future* product by description, property passes to the consumer under rule 5(1) where a product of that description, and in a deliverable state, is unconditionally appropriated to the contract by the retailer with the assent of the consumer or vice versa. An *unascertained* product is one that is not *specific*, that is, one which is not identified or agreed upon at the time of sale; while a *future* product is one which has yet to be manufactured or acquired by the retailer.[39] Situations covered by rule 5(1) include where a retailer makes a product to order or where it uses a demonstration model and fills particular contracts by taking from stock or ordering from its suppliers. *Re London Wine Company (Shippers) Ltd*[40] involved a firm which had bought a considerable amount of claret and burgundy which it sold to consumers as an investment or for later enjoyment. Each consumer paid in full and was given a detailed certificate of title by the company, but the company kept the wine in storage and consumers paid rent and an insurance premium. The firm became insolvent and the receiver appointed by the major creditor, National Westminster Bank, claimed the wine. Oliver J. held that the bank was entitled to succeed because property had not passed to individual consumers within the terms of the Sale of Goods Act 1893.

For property to pass under section 18, rule 5(1), the product must be in a deliverable state. In *Philip Head & Sons Ltd* v. *Showfronts Ltd*[41] carpets were ordered from house furnishers who were also to lay them. The carpets were delivered, but before they could be laid they were stolen. The court held that the house furnishers must bear the loss since the carpet had not been unconditionally appropriated to the contract in a deliverable state, and thus property in it had not been passed to the buyer. Mocatta J. commented:

I think one is entitled to apply everyday common sense to the matter; a householder, for example, purchasing carpeting under a contract of sale providing that it should be delivered and laid in his house would be very surprised to be told that carpeting, which was in bales which he could hardly move deposited by his contractor in his garage, was then in a deliverable state and his property.[42]

Usually an unascertained or a future product will not be unconditionally appropriated to a consumer contract within the meaning of the rule until it is actually delivered. It is not sufficient for the retailer simply to select or identify it, to do an act such as packing it or labelling it with the consumer's name, or to inform the consumer that it can be collected.[43] Delivery to an independent carrier may be sufficient[44] unless the retailer has contracted specifically to deliver the product to the consumer's residence.[45] It has been said that when a consumer orders a product by post, delivery occurs when the retailer posts it, so that the consumer bears the loss if it goes astray.[46] The contrary argument is that with products sent by post the intention is that they should be delivered at the consumer's residence.

Final mention will be made of the special rule for items sent on approval or on sale or return or other similar terms, of which mail order might be an example. Where a consumer is in possession of a product for a trial period pending sale, property, and hence risk, do not pass until the consumer signifies approval or until this is implied, for example by excessive use or by retention of the product for an unreasonable period.[47] Where a consumer signed a document by a mail order company providing for him to have books on 'free approval', the books to be returned in seven days, unmarked, if he were not satisfied, a New South Wales court held that property passed at the end of the seven days.[48] With some mail order, however, it may be that property does not pass automatically at the end of the period, but only when the mail order company writes to the consumer requiring it to pay for the item or to return it immediately.[49] A consumer in possession of an item on approval is a bailee and hence liable for any damage caused to it through his negligence. An example from mail order might be a consumer's negligence in packing an item for return to the company. Unsolicited goods are a special case of sale on approval, and at common law there is no liability as bailee in the absence of wilful default.[50] Legislation now provides that the recipient of unsolicited goods becomes the owner after six months, or a shorter period of thirty days if the seller is contacted but does not collect them.[51]

The rules as to risk are highly artificial because they turn on the ambiguous concept of 'property', and at the same time are highly unjust to consumers in some aspects of their application. Professor Grant Gilmore points out that rules like these derive from the nineteenth century when the courts developed rules highly favourable to sellers with a view to fostering business enterprises.[52] The modern approach in the Uniform Commercial Code of the United States is to get away from the arbitrary shifting of risk with property. Generally speaking, the Code provides that consumers bear the risk only when the product is delivered, and merchants cannot transfer the risk of loss even though full payment has been made and the consumer has been notified that a product is at his disposal.[53] Making a retailer in possession bear the risk is obviously the most sensible course because it can insure for any loss, whereas it is most unlikely that consumers will carry insurance for a product not yet in their possession.[54]

Certainly in practice retailers ignore the rules about risk for reasons of consumer goodwill. In the shops survey mentioned above, all the retailers assumed that items had to reach the consumer 'in merchantable quality', and that they were liable for any damage or loss before delivery, even where they had agreed to store an item as a favour to a consumer who for some reason could not take immediate delivery.[55] No doubt in many cases the assumption coincided with the legal position. A contract to supply fitted carpet, for example, would not be completed until the carpet were laid. Moreover, unascertained goods are generally not matched to particular consumers until just before collection or delivery (for example, in the sale of new cars the period is about twenty-four hours), thus lessening the chance of the loss falling on the consumer. But even in cases where by law the risk would have passed to the consumer, retailers were quite clear that they would bear the loss. The same attitude prevailed in the car surveys, and there the practice is confirmed to some extent by the voluntary Code of Practice for the motor industry.

Most retailers in the surveys carried insurance for theft, fire and other loss. Inquiries at some half dozen insurance firms in London in 1976 revealed that in their experience it was rare for an insured retail business to agree to sell a specific product to a consumer or to put a product aside for a consumer and then to find that it was stolen or destroyed by fire, flood, etc. Apparently, retailers often wish to insure all the products on their premises, irrespective of the legal position regarding individual consumers and whether property in particular products has passed to them. Most insurers accept this type of business provided it is made clear at the outset what they are being asked to cover. A common wording in insurance policies for retailers covers stock 'the property of the insured or held by them in trust or on commission for which they are responsible'. Presumably the wording is interpreted to extend to the type of situation being discussed on the basis that a retailer holds 'on trust' for consumers to whom property has passed. Most of the companies indicated that they would pay the retailer under an insurance policy, provided the sum assured was adequate, without inquiry as to the legal position regarding particular products. In turn they expected that when the claim was settled, consumers affected would receive similar products in substitution. Two companies said that if cover under an insurance policy was not as broad as indicated, the legal position would be examined and the matter dealt with on the merits. But in practice it seems that even they will pay such claims when the value of the property in question is small in relation to the total loss. Only one of the six respondents, a firm of chartered loss adjusters, said that they would treat an item which had become the property of a consumer as something for which they were not responsible and thus not covered by the retailer's policy unless the loss resulted from the retailer's negligence.

PERFORMANCE OF THE CONTRACT

Delivery

Delivery is usually effected in consumer sales by physical transfer of an item or by transferring the means of control over it (e.g. car keys). As a general rule, retailers need not deliver an item to a consumer's home unless there is an express or implied undertaking to this effect in the transaction.[56] In such circumstances the business, its servants and agents are obliged to exercise reasonable care; for example, it will not be sufficient if, finding no one at home, they leave the item on the pavement where it can be stolen, but it is enough if they hand it to someone who appears at the door and seems to live there.[57] When an independent carrier is engaged, the Sale of Goods Act 1979 provides that delivery to it is prima facie delivery to the consumer, but this is subject to the obligation on the part of the retailer unless otherwise authorized by the consumer to make 'such contract with the carrier on behalf of the buyer as may be reasonable having regard to the nature of the goods and the other circumstances of the case.'[58] There seems to be a good argument that under this provision a seller should check that a carrier is insured for any loss and, if not, to take out insurance with it.

All the firms in the shops survey were prepared to deliver, and the majority used their own carriers. Some charged extra for delivery but others thought that it was implied in the contract when items were such that consumers could not carry them home. As the manager of a furniture store put it: 'Where a customer buys furniture there's an implied agreement that they should not be merely moved out of the shop onto the pavement, but delivered in good order to their home.' Experience of items being damaged during delivery was very rare, but all the businesses accepted responsibility once they were satisfied that the damage was not a result of a consumer's misuse or desire to renege on a transaction. Where outside carriers were involved, retailers obliged them to accept liability for any loss. The decision to compensate consumers was made easier because about half the retailers were insured for this type of loss (although not all bothered to call on insurers for minor defects like scratches), and a number of others had sufficient market power to force the manufacturer to accept liability although the latter had nothing to do with the loss.

A consumer is bound to accept delivery, but need not accept part only of the goods (e.g. one part of a three-piece suite) unless that was agreed.[59] As Bramwell L. J. suggested in an early case, that a person ordering a suit of clothes cannot be made to take the coat only, or the trousers and waistcoat first.[60] An additional obligation on a consumer when an item is delivered is to pay for it, unless credit is given, and hence the term 'cash on delivery' (COD).[61] The Sale of Goods Act 1979 gives the unpaid seller a lien over an item, which means the right to retain it until payment unless there are arrangements for credit in existence.[62] The lien comes to an end if the seller gives credit, delivers the item or waives the lien.

Non-performance or late performance by the retailer

Consumers not receiving an item can generally recover any money paid in an action for total failure of consideration. Where there is an available market in an item, section 51(3) of the Sale of Goods Act 1979 says that prima facie the consumer can also claim as damages the difference between the contract and the market or current price. Usually the consumer can obtain a substitute from another retailer and damages under the section are nominal; an exception is if the consumer has obtained a 'bargain' whereupon the retailer is liable for the difference in prices. Where there is no available market (e.g. the consumer ordered a special article or contracted to buy a second-hand item), the measure of damages will be the difference between the contract price and the price paid for the nearest and most satisfactory, if slightly more expensive substitute.[63] Where the retailer still has an item in its possession the consumer might seek a decree of specific performance ordering the seller to perform the contract, but the item must be unique and specific performance will not be ordered, for example, merely because there is a short supply of the item.[64] The consumer in all cases where the seller does not perform its side of the sale is allowed special damages where these are within the contemplation of the parties at the time of the contract; for example, if a retailer knows that a consumer wants a car for a holiday and undertakes to deliver it by then, it is liable for damages for the spoiled holiday.[65]

What of *late* performance, as opposed to non-performance? As regards payment time is not of the essence in a contract for the sale of goods, unless a different intention appears from its terms.[66] Whether any other stipulation as to time is of the essence depends on the terms of the contract.[67] The courts are prepared to imply that time is of the essence in commercial transactions, but the matter is unclear in consumer dealings.[68] Certainly if the consumer is able to have a definite time inserted in the contract, late delivery is in breach of contract.[69] Much more likely in consumer transactions is the reverse: a condition in a standard form contract that the retailer is not to be liable for any delay.[70] Should no time be fixed by the contract, the retailer is obliged to perform within a reasonable time.[71] But the rules about time cut both ways: thus delay on the part of the consumer in paying – if, for example, he is having temporary financial difficulties –does not constitute a breach of contract entitling the seller to repudiate. However, an unpaid seller can give notice to the consumer of its intention to resell, and if the consumer does not pay within a reasonable time the seller can go ahead with its threat and sue for any loss.[72]

There is a clear need for spelling out the consumer's right to cancel in the case of delay. In its report *Shopping* (1982), based on a national survey, the National Consumer Council reveals a not inconsiderable number of complaints about delays in delivery, ranging from under 6 per cent of those who had bought floor coverings in the previous twelve months to 10 per cent of the purchasers of a new car. Sweden's Consumer Sales Act 1973[73] provides that a consumer can rescind a contract in cases of delay, unless the delay is of minor importance, after making a specific request for delivery to take place within a reasonable time. A specific request is unnecessary if it must be apparent to the retailer that delay is of some significance to the consumer. Exceptions to this right to rescind are for specifically manufactured items, or items which can not be sold elsewhere unless it is apparent that the consumer's whole purpose in concluding the contract will fail through delay.

The shops survey revealed that most retailers took preventive measures to avoid difficulties with consumers over delays. Carpet retailers, for example, had efficient stock lists – in some cases daily lists from head office – and thus could give consumers highly reliable delivery dates. Other retailers had a very good idea of the time period involved in getting stock from suppliers and would inform consumers accordingly. Those retailers unsure about times avoided giving firm delivery dates and usually 'played safe' by adding a week or two to what suppliers told them. In cases of unexpected delay retailers urged their suppliers to deliver and kept consumers informed either by telephone or in writing. A few retailers loaned items to consumers in the meantime, but others accepted cancellation. Many consumers appeared to accept delays presumably because it would have been just as difficult to obtain the item elsewhere.

The consumer is not liable for any increase in price arising from delay if price was agreed upon at the time of sale. In the shops survey, of the twenty-eight retailers commonly experiencing delays and not selling from stock, twenty-one claimed to absorb any price increase because they felt obliged having quoted the price, although five wanted a deposit or full payment to fix the price. Interestingly, at least one of them absorbed price increases in practice, although the order form placed the obligation squarely on consumers. Of the seven stores which insisted that consumers should bear any price increase, one avoided aggravating consumers by never quoting prices, and another had consumers sign an order form like that just described.

The consumer's non-acceptance

Consumers who refuse to go through with a transaction expose themselves to legal action by retailers for breach (or anticipatory breach) of the contract. In summary, retailers have three remedies against the consumer. They can:

Retain the deposit: The retailer may choose not to sue but to retain the deposit, including an item given in part-exchange in lieu of a monetary deposit.[74] The authorities suggest that equity may intervene to relieve a consumer if the result is unconscionable, and that in any event forfeiture should generally only occur with genuine deposits (i.e. payments given by way of security for completion) and not with advance payments.[75] In practice the scope of equitable relief is uncertain, and there have been important decisions which suggest that even payments other than by way of deposit are irrecoverable.[76] The present rules are quite arbitrary, for the consumer's loss depends on the size of the deposit or advance payment. Moreover, if a retailer sues in court for its losses for non-acceptance (see below) it might be entitled to far less than the amount of the deposit or payment.

Sue for the price: Section 49(1) of the Sale of Goods Act 1979 entitles the retailer to sue for the full price (less any deposit already received) if property has passed to the consumer. The rule is thoroughly unsatisfactory in the consumer context and should be abolished. Fortunately in many consumer transactions, the passing of property does not occur until the consumer takes delivery – thus the retailer cannot maintain an action for the price. Another limitation on suing for the price is that a retailer must still be ready and willing to perform its part of the contract, that is, it must have the item ready for delivery.[77] Retailers will prefer in practice to resell an item if possible.

Sue for damages for non-acceptance: The consumer's liability under this head varies quite arbitrarily depending on the state of the market and the nature of the item involved (e.g. whether it is new or second-hand). The law, not uncharacteristically, looks at the matter from the point of view of the retailer and aims to compensate it for the loss of profit if it has made one less sale.[78] Section 50(3) of the Sale of Goods Act 1979 provides that where there is an available market, the retailer is prima facie entitled to the difference between the contract price and the market or current price when the consumer should have accepted delivery. Otherwise the damages are equivalent to the loss flowing directly and naturally in the ordinary course from the consumer's action.[79] Two contrasting decisions illustrate the point: in *Charter* v. *Sullivan*[80] the court held that since the retailer could sell every new Hillman it could obtain, it was only entitled to nominal damages. Contrast *W. L. Thompson Ltd* v. *Robinson (Gunmakers) Ltd,*[81] where demand was not sufficient to absorb all the new Vanguard cars coming onto the market at that time; the court held that there was not an available market and hence the retailer was entitled to its loss of profit. There is no available market for an item made specially to a consumer's order or, it is said, for second-hand items because each is different.[82] In such cases the loss flowing directly and naturally from a consumer's refusal is not necessarily the loss of profit, because it might reasonably be expected that the item would be sold to someone else. At most the loss contemplated would be the difference if the price obtained on resale were lower than the original price; of course if it is higher there is no loss. Whether or not there is an available market the retailer can claim for incidental losses, such as the cost of readvertising, but must account for any deposit already received.

Retailers' remedies for consumer cancellation are quite arbitrary and need revision. From the viewpoint of consumers there seems a good case for limiting a retailer's remedy to losses incurred excluding the loss of profit. If any deposit exceeded this amount it would be refundable to the consumer. Were this change to be adopted, an obligation would have to be placed on retailers to obtain the best possible price if any resale were involved to avoid retailers' selling through the trade in the knowledge that they could sue the consumer for any deficiency. Support for the reform is derived from the actual practices of retailers. The majority (26) of retailers in the shops survey accepted cancellation and repaid any deposit, although they tried to persuade consumers to go through with transactions, perhaps as an inducement allowing them to change their minds on details like colour. The main reason given for this policy was to retain goodwill, and in a few cases it was taken to extremes. For example, one retailer accepted cancellation even if it had cut carpet to a customer's specification. A minority of retailers imposed some penalty on consumers' cancelling, although with relatively cheap items like clothing this took the form of giving a credit note. With more expensive items, deposits were usually retained or cancellation charges imposed. A carpet store, for example, retained the deposit unless it thought it had a good chance of selling a piece of cut carpet to another consumer. One factor involved in cancellation was the relationship with suppliers; if a retailer could return an item to a supplier without penalty, it treated consumers leniently.

In the cars survey, about three-quarters of the dealers automatically returned any deposit on cancellation. Of the remainder some credited the deposit to consumers if they bought another car from them in the next few months while others retained the deposit if they had begun work on the car to the customer's specification. All the dealers accepted that it was a hazard of the business that consumers might change their minds. A few dealers were quite sympathetic, although some of these recognized that if credit were involved a consumer in financial difficulties was not a good proposition to pass on to a finance house. As far as loss of profit was concerned, only four out of the thirty-seven considered suing for it, and only one did so automatically. The great majority could not be bothered with the fuss of legal action, particularly if the consumer was in financial difficulty (judgement would probably not be satisfied), and some mentioned that legal action would adversely affect their reputation.

7
Consumer credit

THE DEVELOPMENT OF CONSUMER CREDIT

Credit is one of the essential features of modern capitalism for it enables businesses to sell goods and services to consumers which their current income or wealth would not otherwise enable them to buy.[1] As Galbraith puts it: 'The process of persuading people to incur debt, and the arrangements for them to do so, are as much a part of modern production as the making of the goods and the nurturing of wants.'[2] Tradesmen credit, in which consumers were presented with a periodical bill to be paid in full, had developed in the seventeenth and eighteenth centuries, and pawnbroking had been regulated by legislation as early as 1603 because of the abuses practised against the many ordinary consumers who obtained credit in this way.[3] It is not surprising that the development of modern forms of consumer credit coincided with the production of mass-produced consumer durables, for credit enabled businesses readily to market their goods and at the same time gave them a tidy profit. At first sewing machines, pianos and furniture were the subject of these new forms of credit, and then in the twentieth century they were extended to cars, radios, televisions, etc. so that now consumers can obtain most products and most services through credit.

Initially credit was provided by manufacturers and retailers, but by the 1920s separate finance houses had been established which specialized in advancing credit to enable consumers to finance the purchase of products from retailers which did not give credit themselves, either as a matter of policy or because their financial assets were insufficient or directed to other purposes. Finance houses obtained finance from banks and the deposits of investors and institutions. One judge described the development in 1920:

Table 7.1 New Credit Extended by FHA Members (excluding finance charges)

| Quarters ended | 1982 | | 1981 | | | | | | | |
| Not seasonally adjusted | Sept. | | June 30 | | March 31 | | Dec. 31 | | Sept. 30 | |
	£m.	%	£m.	%	£m.	%	£m.	%	£m.	%
1. Total	1864	100.0	1734	100.0	1635	100.0	1781	100.0	1596	100.0
2. To Consumers	866	46.4	675	39.0	583	35.7	596	33.5	685	42.9
3. To business customers (excluding leasing)	502	27.0	608	35.0	522	31.9	484	27.2	457	28.6
4. Leasing (original cost of assets purchased for lease)	496	26.6	451	26.0	530	32.4	701	39.3	454	28.5

Note: These figures include all advances whether payable by instalment or not.
Source: Finance Houses Association.

There were, of course, many cases in which a person or firm had a motor car which they wished to sell and in which a customer was found who desired to purchase but had not the money to pay for it in a lump sum; and on the other hand the owner did not want the bother of a hire-purchase agreement. That this was a common situation was shown by the fact that there had sprung up all over the country a system of calling in the assistance of business firms which existed largely, if not solely, for the purpose of giving assistance to both classes of persons by carrying out negotiations of the following nature. The company or firm not infrequently called itself a finance company. They bought the car and then proceeded to let it out on a hire-purchase agreement to the person who was desirous of acquiring it.[4]

Finance houses never captured the whole market and retailers continue to play a vital role. Manufacturers never came to provide credit to the same extent as in some other countries.

From the consumer's viewpoint buying on credit has its advantages. It may simply be convenient either at the point of sale or in enabling payment to be made for something over a period. With major purchases consumers can obtain the present enjoyment of products and services without the need for immediate payment; there is an argument that the use of credit in this way is a desirable form of forced saving for some people. Any doubts about the integral role that consumer credit has in the economy is belied by the enormous amounts currently being extended (see Table 7.1).[5]

The effects of consumer credit are not uniformly advantageous. Some economists condemn it for fuelling inflation, while others think that it dampens desirable investment either directly because consumers no longer save, or indirectly because it ingrains the consumption ethic.[6] Of more immediate interest, consumer credit also causes untold hardship for many consumers who are induced to over-commit themselves by the blandishments of sales or promotional techniques or the pressures of their social milieu, and who find that they default on their repayments when unexpected events like sickness or unemployment occur. It is these casualties of the credit system who feature prominently in the courts and about whom a large part of this chapter is concerned.

Forms of consumer credit

After the 1890s hire purchase was adopted as the preferred method of instalment credit. In law, hire purchase involves the consumer in hiring an item, either from a retailer or from a finance house to whom the retailer has sold it, with an option to purchase it at the end of a period if all the instalments are paid. Apparently hire purchase had developed in the early nineteenth century in France and in the United States, where furniture was leased for periodic payments to the wealthy who after a period could buy it if they wished. There was no inherent reason why hire purchase should have become the norm in England – conditional sale, in which consumers agree to buy an item, but do not acquire property in it until all payments are made, has been widely used in the United States and Canada – and indeed until the late nineteenth century the differences between hire purchase and conditional sale were hardly important. The reason for the change in popularity of hire purchase in England was that alternative forms of instalment selling became less desirable. The technicalities of the Bills of Sale Acts meant that the chattel mortgage never really took root, in which the consumer buys an item but gives security over it for the credit extended. More importantly, as the result of the Factors Act 1889, consumers purchasing a product on conditional sale could, in certain circumstances, pass good title to an innocent third party and thus defeat the rights of the seller.[7] Hire purchase on the other hand secured the seller's rights against third parties on the basis, estab-lished by the House of Lords in *Helby* v. *Matthews*,[8] that the consumer under hire purchase was simply hiring an item and not committed to buying it. That conceptualization of the transaction was artificial, for it ignored the fact that almost all consumers entered hire purchase with the intention of acquiring ownership.

Gradually hire purchase was subject to greater control both by Parliament and the courts as abuses by particular businesses became apparent. The first major step was the Hire Purchase Act 1938, which introduced documentary formalities for hire purchase contracts and imposed restrictions on businesses' remedies, for example, a court order was needed for an item to be repossessed after a third of the purchase price had been paid. Some twenty years later the courts accepted the artificiality of hire purchase and began attacking the unequal terms in hire purchase agreements with traditional con-tractual doctrines like the rule against penalty clauses.[9] A persuasive argument is that the larger finance houses accepted these restrictions without great objection because they legitimized credit-buying in the eyes of the public and also made trade difficult for the smaller finance companies, 'which were giving hire purchase a bad name, and were cutting into the profits of the larger companies.'[10]

By the 1960s hire purchase had fallen out of favour with some of the larger finance houses. Hire purchase was subject to legal restrictions, including terms controls (e.g. minimum deposits were required) imposed as a matter of economic policy to dampen consumer demand. It was not thought as essential to have a security interest in items being sold on credit because their resale value when repossessed was sometimes quite low (although not for items like cars) and because it was possible with the increase in personal wealth and the establishment of credit reference agencies to be assured initially about the credit worthiness of the great bulk of consumers. Moreover, consumers began needing finance for what the law categorized as services, like the installation of central heating and home improvements, for which hire purchase (which deals with goods) was not really appropriate.[11] The outcome of these various factors was that a number of finance houses began providing personal loans to consumers to be used for the purchase of products and services from retailers with whom they had arrangements.[12] Legally, the consumer buys products and services from an independent retailer in a transaction quite distinct from that in which the loan is obtained from the finance house. Table 7.2 highlights the differences where a finance house is involved between hire purchase and a personal loan agreement made to finance a purchase.

Table 7.2

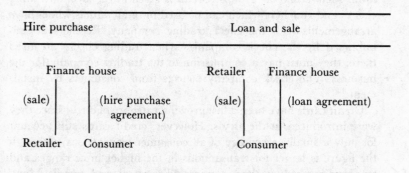

Hire purchase		Loan and sale	
	Finance house	Retailer	Finance house
(sale)	(hire purchase agreement)	(sale)	(loan agreement)
Retailer	Consumer		Consumer

One of the benefits which the loan and sale arrangement gave to finance houses was that, unlike in hire purchase transactions, they had no responsibility for the quality of the merchandise supplied. The

Consumer Credit Act 1974 overturns this result by making finance houses liable for the quality of the products and services obtained with its credit pursuant to or in contemplation of arrangements with its retailers.[13] Consumers, of course, have no inkling of the difference when they approach a retailer to obtain something on credit and are asked to complete a personal loan agreement, rather than a hire purchase agreement, which is then forwarded to the finance house for approval.[14]

Retailers, as we saw, still provide directly to consumers a large amount of credit for the purchase of products and services. Hire purchase may be used but credit sale, in which property passes to the consumer immediately, is the more common method used by large department stores. Some department stores have budget account schemes, a form of revolving credit in which a consumer periodically pays a fixed sum into an account and in return receives revolving credit for up to six to twelve times that amount. The cost to consumers of a budget account is the 'service' charge imposed, for example, on the monthly balance. Mail order firms also use credit sale and many offer interest-free credit for some time, although the cost of the credit may be hidden in the prices charged.

Many other forms of credit are available to consumers. Banks, of course, provide credit to consumers to purchase goods and services, although the facility is usually only available to those with accounts. Check trading has a long history in Britain, mainly for those in the lower socio-economic groups. Credit is given in the form of trading checks and vouchers which can be used in retail outlets which have arrangements with the check trading company. Retailers are reimbursed by the check companies when trading checks are used there; they must pay a commission to the trading company for the business. The check company collects from consumers by instalment.[15]

Credit cards have been a fast growing category of credit since they were introduced in the 1950s. However, credit cards still account for only a small percentage of all consumer transactions, although the figure is larger for transactions in the higher price ranges and for certain products and services like petrol and travel. Many consumers apparently use credit cards not to obtain credit but for convenience. Terms between credit cards vary. Bank credit cards generally offer a system of revolving credit, whereby consumers are issued monthly accounts, part of which must be paid within twenty-five days with interest being charged on the balance. 'Travel and entertainment' or 'charge cards' charge an amount per annum for use of the card and usually demand immediate settlement of a monthly account, otherwise charging so much interest per month. 'In house' cards are issued to regular customers by or on behalf of department stores, garages, hotels, and so on; they may involve extended credit. The different methods of operation are of direct legal significance: bank credit cards are regulated consumer credit agreements within the Consumer Credit Act 1974, but travel and entertainment cards are exempt agreements if, for one, they demand repayment immediately of a monthly account in one instalment. Issuers of the latter are not jointly liable with the retailer when a consumer receives a defective product or substandard service.[16]

There has been criticism that credit cards result in discrimination against those paying cash. It is said that credit cards have a direct effect in pushing up prices because retailers have to recoup the 'commission' which they pay to credit card companies and because they must employ extra staff to handle credit card transactions. Defenders of credit cards say that they increase the turnover of stores, and this has a dampening effect on prices. Moreover, there is not the same need for security arrangements as with cash. Consumers also benefit because they can be assured that a retailer who accepts credit cards has been vetted by the credit card company for the quality of its merchandise and/or service. At present any effect on prices is small because credit cards account for only a small number of consumer transactions. The credit card companies generally insist that credit card customers should not have to pay higher prices than cash customers. Consumers Union in the United States objected to the practice on grounds including the elimination of price competition. It is now unlawful there for credit card issuers to prohibit sellers from offering discounts to cardholders who pay by cash, cheque or similar means, although little advantage seems to have been taken of this provision because retailers fear it would alienate credit card holders.[17] For similar reasons the Monopolies and Mergers Commission has concluded that the practice should be made unlawful in Britain, and has suggested that where retailers take advantage of its termination it might be desirable to oblige them to give adequate notice to consumers of any difference between what will be charged against presentation of a particular credit card and what will be charged for other means of payment.[18]

The Consumer Credit Act 1974 contains provisions which apply specifically to credit cards and similar forms of credit.[19] The mass mailing of unsolicited credit cards, which was used in the early years to attract custom, is forbidden.[20] A consumer is not liable if a credit card is lost and used fraudulently before it is signed (or a receipt for it signed) or before it is first used. A consumer might have to pay up to a maximum of £30 if a credit card is lost and used fraudulently after that, unless the company is notified of the loss before the card is used whereupon there is no liability.[21] Limiting liability in this way is justified because the credit card companies can spread the risk among many consumers and are also in the best position to take preventive steps against fraud through card design or the way they can be used.[22] That the consumer can be liable for up to £30 provides an incentive to ensure that the card is kept safely.

The law of consumer credit

The relevant legal principles relating to consumer credit are drawn widely from common law principles, the Consumer Credit Act 1974, and other statutory law from the Bills of Sale Acts to the Bankruptcy Act 1914. The core of consumer credit law is contained in the Consumer Credit Act 1974. The Act is derived from the work of the Crowther Committee which was established in 1968 to review existing and alternative arrangements for consumer credit. The main thrust of the Committee's exhaustive analysis was directed to improving consumers' rights and to rationalizing the law into a new coherent framework. As far as consumers were concerned, the Committee proceeded on the basis that credit contributes to the well-being of consumers as a whole and that only a small number of people, who, as it put it, for some reason or another are incapable of managing their own affairs or who are unable to cope with sudden sickness or unemployment, have repayment difficulties. Since the problem of default as the Committee saw it was not inherent in credit transactions, the Committee concluded that the best policy was to interfere as little as possible.[23]

Rationalization, according to the Committee, should proceed along various lines: credit transactions should be regulated according to their substance, not their form; consumer transactions should be given separate treatment from commercial transactions; and credit when provided in loan form should be assimilated with that provided in a hire purchase or similar instalment sale contract.[24] Two pieces of legislation were recommended: a Lending and Security Act to rationalize the treatment of security interests and the conflict between secured parties, primarily along the lines of article 9 of the American Uniform Commercial Code,[25] and a Consumer Sale and Loan Act which would license those in the consumer credit market and extend protection currently applying to hire purchase to all forms of consumer credit agreement. The Lending and Security Act has never been implemented on the grounds of its complexity and unnecessary cost, but the proposals for a Consumer Sale and Loan Act became in effect the Consumer Credit Act 1974.[26]

The Consumer Credit Act 1974 has been widely hailed as a great advance in consumer protection, and certainly the licensing scheme for all engaged in consumer credit (considered in Chapter 12) seems to have improved standards. But given the philosophy behind the Act it is not surprising that some of its provisions relating to consumers' rights and obligations are less protective than the law elsewhere. Certainly the larger finance houses had nothing to fear from the Act because it did not impose undue restrictions and in the main confirmed their existing practices. A director of one member firm of the Finance Houses Association, in welcoming the Act, commented:

There are two aspects of competition to which attention should be drawn. The impact of government controls over banks and finance houses in the past twenty years has consistently led to the promotion and growth of smaller fringe companies who have contrived to 'escape the net' and in many cases to remain unaffected by the controls imposed on the larger and more reputable companies – to the extent that this will no longer be possible (as a result of the licensing system) the Bill is to be welcomed.[27]

The Consumer Credit Act 1974 is rather complex, partly because existing forms of credit like hire purchase, conditional sale and personal loan agreements continue in existence, and partly because a great deal of the law is contained in regulations made under the Act. Professor Lindgren comments, 'A shortcoming of the Act is that some of its provisions are so technical as to be unintelligible to the average citizen. . . . This is particularly unfortunate in a consumer protection measure.'[28] Neverthelesss, it is necessary to appreciate the coverage of the Act to understand the substantive provisions.[29] Most of the protections in the Act are confined to consumer credit agreements, which are in effect agreements in which creditors provide individuals with credit not exceeding £5000.[30] Credit includes a cash loan and any other form of financial accommodation such as allowing a consumer time to pay.[31] Interest and certain ancillary charges are excluded when calculating the £5000 limit in fixed sum credit agreements, while in running account credit agreements (like bank overdrafts, budget accounts and some credit cards) the £5000 figure is the credit limit, or probable credit limit, when the agreement was entered.[32] Hire purchase agreements are regarded as credit agreements and credit is regarded as being provided to the extent of the total price of an item less the aggregate of any deposit and credit charges.[33] Because of their similarity to credit agreements, many provisions in the Act apply to consumer hire agreements, which are defined as bailments capable of subsisting for more than three months which do not require the hirer to make payments exceeding £5000.[34]

A further definition to be appreciated is of the debtor-creditor-supplier agreement.[35] A debtor-creditor-supplier agreement can involve two parties, the consumer and the creditor-supplier, as with hire purchase where the finance house is the creditor and supplier. The other type of debtor-creditor-supplier agreement is the tripartite agreement. This is a restricted use credit agreement where the agreement is made by a creditor under existing or contemplated arrangements with a supplier, or where a creditor advances un-restricted-use credit in the knowledge that it will be used with a supplier with whom it has pre-existing arrangements. A simple example is where a finance house provides a personal loan for a consumer to purchase a motor car from a retailer who has an arrangement whereby it introduces consumers to the finance house for credit. A debtor-creditor agreement is a regulated consumer credit agreement other than a debtor-creditor-supplier agreement. Basically, it is an agreement for the lending of money with no supplier involved such as a bank loan.[36]

Most provisions of the Act – the advertising and extortionate credit bargain provisions are exceptions – apply only to *regulated* consumer credit agreements and *regulated* consumer hire agreements, meaning those which are not exempt. Exempt consumer credit agreements include mortgages given on land by building societies and local authorities; fixed sum debtor-creditor-supplier agreements (not being hire purchase or conditional sale agreements) where the number of payments does not exceed four; and debtor-creditor-supplier agreements where the rate of total charge for credit does not exceed the higher of 13 per cent or the rate of 1 per cent above the minimum lending rate in operation twenty-eight days before the date of the agreement.[37] Further limitations in the Act are that some provisions do not apply to non-commercial agreements (e.g. between friends) and to small agreements, where the credit or hire charge does not exceed £30, not being hire purchase or conditional sale agreements or secured transactions.[38]

OBTAINING CREDIT

A right to credit?

Like other businesses creditors have wide freedom to grant or deny their facilities to whom they choose. But there are limitations. Creditors are now forbidden to discriminate on the grounds of sex or race.[39] In *Quinn* v. *Williams Furniture Ltd*[40] the Court of Appeal held that a retailer was in breach of the former provision in insisting on a married woman having her husband guarantee a hire purchase agreement, when it would not have imposed a similar requirement on a married man whose circumstances were in all material respects similar. In addition the Director General of Fair Trading in exercising its licensing powers must have regard to whether a creditor has practised discrimination on the grounds of sex, colour, race or ethnic origins.[41]

Evidence of discrimination in the granting of credit has been well established, even among those women who are employed or who are the heads of families. Discrimination has been based on the belief that women are not as creditworthy as men, because they do not remain long in employment but marry and become pregnant. Studies elsewhere have shown that women are just as good credit risks as men. In the United States, the Equal Credit Opportunity Act and legislation at the state level deal specifically with a number of objectionable practices which may not fall within the sweep of the Sex Discrimination Act 1975; for example, sending application forms directed in their wording to men which would discourage women applicants, excluding a woman's earnings when a couple apply for joint credit, asking a woman for information about her husband's assets and liabilities when she applies for credit and refusing to grant credit to a married woman in her own name.[42] Moreover, women in Britain may be hard-pressed to obtain sufficient evidence of discrimination, for creditors may simply say that they have an inadequate credit rating. The Equal Opportunities Commission may be of some assistance in collecting information about a business's systematic discrimination.

If there is some protection against creditors discriminating on sexual or racial grounds, what of other types of discrimination? Reference has been made on several occasions to the problems which the less affluent have in obtaining credit. In some instances there is clear discrimination against them and they are denied credit even though they are creditworthy. For example, some creditors will refuse to grant credit to all those living on a particular street or council housing estate, whatever the merits of an individual applicant, because in the past they have had a disproportionate number of defaulters from the area.[43] As a matter of economics it is easier to deny credit to all those living in the area than to take the matter further and to investigate the creditworthiness of those inhabitants who apply.

Amendments to the Equal Credit Opportunity Act in the United States in 1976 provide some protection against discriminatory practices used in relation to the poor. The Act makes it unlawful to discriminate against a consumer because of age or 'because all or part of the applicant's income derives from any public assistance program'.[44] It does not constitute discrimination for a creditor to make inquiry about the applicant's age or whether his income derives from any public assistance program 'if such inquiry is for the purpose of determining the amount and probable continuance of income levels, credit history or other persistent element of credit-worthiness as provided in regulations.'[45] Further, it is not unlawful to use an approved empirically-derived credit system which is age based, nor is it a violation of the Act to refuse credit under any credit scheme specially operated for the economically disadvantaged. To enable consumers to take action if they feel they have been discriminated against, creditors must give specific reasons for denying or altering the terms of credit, and there is a wide discovery power so that consumers can obtain evidence as to a business's credit-granting standards. The main sanction in the Act is that a creditor can be liable to a consumer for up to $10,000 in punitive damages, in addition to any actual damage suffered. The possibility of class actions is recognized in the Act, although damages cannot exceed the lesser of £500,000 or 1 per cent of the net worth of the creditor.

Creditworthiness and credit reference agencies

Credit reference agencies are businesses which provide information about the financial standing of consumers. Some are profit-making bodies, but others are trade protection associations operated as a service to members. The largest credit reference agencies have files covering millions of consumers.[46] Credit reference agencies draw on a number of sources of information. An important source is the county court judgment register, which lists every judgment for not less than £10 which remains unsatisfied for a month.[47] Other sources of information are public records like the reports of bankruptcy proceedings or the electoral register, and trade members who supply items for the files such as information about bad debts and repossessions. Credit reference agencies record the enquiries which they receive about a consumer, and if the record shows a number of enquiries over a period with no derogatory information reported, the consumer is likely to be regarded as very creditworthy. Status reports, in which local enquiries are made from neighbours and traders, are relatively rare in the case of individual consumers, although more common with business concerns.[48] The Younger Committee on Privacy concluded that checking creditworthiness prevented reckless or dishonest people from obtaining credit, kept down overheads and prices by reducing bad debts and stimulated trade by facilitating the ready granting of credit in appropriate cases.[49] In the survey of public attitudes carried out for the Committee, about half the consumers interviewed said that they would not regard it as an invasion of privacy if a creditor contacted a credit reference agency when they intended to buy on credit. While 37 per cent said that the practice should be prohibited by law, 62 per cent disagreed. The great majority, however, objected to the information being freely available.[50]

Despite the value of credit reference agencies in determining the creditworthiness of consumers, there has been cause for concern. The Younger Committee commented on complaints it had received from the public:

In some cases people suspected that they were 'blacklisted' because of the similarity of their name to that of a relative, because of a failure on the part of an agency to appreciate that an earlier undischarged debt was the result of a dispute with a retailer over the quality of goods or services supplied, or because an earlier debt had been discharged but not noted by the agency.[51]

Situations such as this are personally damaging to consumers and also lead to inefficiency in the provision of credit. The Consumer Credit Act 1974 goes part of the way to ensure that information in the files of credit reference agencies is accurate. Consumers can now contact a credit reference agency at any time and request a copy of the information held about them.[52] If they consider that the file is inaccurate they can ask the agency to correct it, and if it fails to remove the entry they can require the agency to add to the file a notice of correction (not exceeding 200 words) which they draw up, and a copy of which must be included whenever information is furnished based on that entry. Disputes can be referred to the Director General of Fair Trading for resolution. A major omission in the Act is a provision enabling consumers to sue for any loss suffered because inaccurate information has been distributed. Whenever consumers negotiate with a creditor or with a retailer with a view to purchasing on credit, they can also demand to know the name and address of any credit reference agency from which information about their financial standing has been sought.[53] This information must be provided whether or not credit was refused, but there is no need for the creditor or retailer to reveal what the credit reference agency said or whether it affected any decision about the application for credit. Once the consumer knows the name of the credit reference agency, however, he can then obtain a copy of the information on file.

The Consumer Credit Act 1974 and its attendant regulations tackle the major problem with the information collected by credit reference agencies – that it may be inaccurate. But there are other undesirable practices which can occur and which legislation in other jurisdictions covers.[54] Fears have been expressed that information could be collected by some credit reference agencies on matters like the personal behaviour of consumers, which is really quite irrelevant to their creditworthiness. Status information of this sort is unusual but to ensure that this remains the case it would be appropriate to introduce legislation along the lines of that in South Australia, which actually restricts the type of information that can be stored.[55] Should steps be taken to ensure that information collected by credit reference agencies is only used for legitimate trade inquiries, and not for other perhaps improper purposes? At present consumers might have a private law remedy in these circumstances for breach of confidence or defamation, but the exact boundaries of the former have not been adequately delineated by the courts, and in a defamation action the consumer may be defeated if the credit reference agency can claim qualified privilege.[56] There is a clear need for greater control over the collection and disclosure of information. Stale information is usually weeded out of the files of credit reference agencies because of the costs of storage, for example, but it would still seem desirable to have a provision which requires agencies to eliminate information after, say, five years.[57]

The right to copies and to cancel

Consumers entering regulated agreements under the Consumer Credit Act 1974 are entitled to receive at least one, and in many cases, two copies of an agreement with the aim of informing them of their rights and obligations and of making it more difficult for retailers to engage in fraud. In the common situation where the consumer signs an agreement and it does not become an executed agreement immediately (e.g. the consumer's creditworthiness must first be checked or a finance house must decide on the proposal submitted through the retailer), the consumer must be supplied with a copy of the unexecuted agreement.[58] Moreover, when the agreement becomes executed (i.e. the creditor approves the credit) the consumer must be supplied with a copy of the executed agreement, and any other document referred to in it, within seven days of its being made, unless the agreement is actually sent to the consumer for signature and thereupon becomes an executed agreement.[59] In the special case where an unexecuted agreement is personally presented to the consumer and it becomes executed when he signs it, the consumer must receive a copy of the executed agreement there and then and must also be sent a notice of his right to cancel within seven days.[60]

Failure to supply the copies makes the agreement non-enforceable without a court order, so that in theory a consumer can keep possession of an item without having to pay for it, but may be liable for conversion if he parts with it to a third party.[61] As a matter of practice the courts will be lenient in granting orders to creditors to enforce agreements, despite a failure to send copies within the time limits required, so long as the consumer is not, in their view, irreparably prejudiced, and is given a copy of the executed agreement before legal proceedings are commenced.[62] In other words, the non-enforceability provision is not regarded as a sanction – perhaps severe in its effects – on creditors to induce compliance with the Act, so that clearly criminal penalties are needed, as in legislation elsewhere, to achieve this result.

The cancellation ('cooling off') provisions apply to regulated agreements in which the antecedent negotiations included oral representations made in the presence of the consumer unless the unexecuted agreement was signed by the consumer at business premises.[63] The cancellation provisions thus apply mainly to door-step transactions, although there are other situations which can be envisaged as being covered; for example, an agreement signed at a trade display or a fair. Unscrupulous businesses operating door to door can avoid the effects of the cancellation period quite simply by conning the consumer at home and then bundling him off to business premises to sign the agreement. The limitation of the cancellation provisions to mainly doorstep transactions also completely ignores the point that pressure can be applied to consumers at business premises. Thus, as a matter of policy, it is desirable to allow consumers some time for reflection with major credit agreements because of their onerous and complicated nature. There should be no prejudice to businesses in making this the law; they need simply to hold off delivering goods or providing services or advancing credit until the cooling-off period has elapsed.

A cooling-off period is of little value if consumers are not fully informed of their right to cancel within the time set for its exercise. The Consumer Credit Act 1974 fails to achieve this. With cancellable agreements there must be included in every copy of the unexecuted and executed agreement mentioned above a notice of the consumer's right to cancel, how and when that right is exercisable, and the name and address of the person to whom it may be given. A separate notice of cancellation is required in the special case where the agreement becomes executed when the consumer signs it.[64] There seems to be no reason why the Act should not provide for a separate notice of cancellation to be sent in all cases to notify consumers of their rights, for it is clear that consumers cannot be expected to, and in fact do not, read complicated agreements like those covered by the Act, and thus remain ignorant of the right to cancel. The Crowther Committee recommended that consumers should be provided with a notice of cancellation which could simply be signed and posted within the period created, because 'many consumers find it difficult to write even the simplest letter, and it is possible that for this reason many consumers who would like to exercise a right to cancel do not do so.'[65]

The limited application of the cancellation provisions and the infrequency with which they are invoked is inversely related to their complexity. The actual period in which cancellation can take place begins when the consumer signs the unexecuted agreement and finishes on the end of the fifth day following the day on which the consumer receives a copy of the executed agreement or the requisite notice about cancellation.[66] Consumers sending a notice of cancellation by post are deemed to exercise their right at the time of posting, even if it is never received, and notice of cancellation can be served not only on the creditor or owner, but also on a person it has specified, any agents, a credit broker or supplier who was a negotiator in antecedent negotiations, and any person who in the course of a business acted on behalf of the consumer in any negotiations for the agreement.[67]

The effect of cancellation is to render void the agreement, a separate sale transaction (in the event of a debtor-creditor-supplier agreement for restricted use credit) and other 'linked transactions' (e.g. a contract of insurance). The consumer is released from further liability for payment and is entitled to recover payments made.[68] The consumer must be ready to return any goods received except if goods have been incorporated into land or other goods, whereupon liability arises for the cash price, but with perishable goods, or those consumed by use which have been consumed, the consumer is under no obligation either to return or to pay the cash price.[69] Specific provision is made for cancellation where part-exchange goods are involved, and consumers are entitled to recover a sum equivalent to the part-exchange agreed (otherwise a reasonable allowance) if the goods are not returned within ten days of cancellation.[70]

CONSUMER CREDIT AGREEMENTS

The contents and form of an agreement

The Hire Purchase Acts traditionally empowered the executive to control the form and content of the contractual documents. The Consumer Credit Act 1974 continues the provision so that basic information can be provided to consumers as to the terms of the regulated agreements upon which they are embarking. Non-commercial agreements (e.g. between friends) and small debtor-creditor-supplier agreements for restricted use credit are not covered.[71] Contractual documents will furnish consumers with essential information on matters such as the cash price of a product or the amount of the loan; the interest and other compulsory charges expressed both absolutely and as an annual percentage rate; details of the instalments; the security interest of the business; and the protections and remedies available to consumers (e.g. the right to cancel or to accelerate payment). Requirements can also be promulgated regarding the location and size of these matters.[72]

Parliament rejected the course of actually mandating a statutory form for credit contracts, with a standard set of terms laid out in uniform manner, on the basis that this would inhibit the evolution of new forms of credit and be an unnecessary burden on businesses.[73] The result is that agreements will contain not only the statutory information but much else besides, and in language which ordinary consumers might not understand. Judge White, then Chairman of the South Australian Credit Tribunal, commented that the Tribunal has found that much consumer credit documentation there is quite unacceptable, and the Tribunal is using its licensing powers to ensure that the often erroneous and misleading documentation is ended. He argues the case for standard forms on the basis that existing documentation is concerned less with consumer understanding than industry advantage, and that the industry should welcome shorter, clearer contracts to 'save time, paper and anxiety about compliance with the legislation'.[74] Certainly, there seems no reason why the task of facilitating changes in a standard form should be as exacting as policy makers seem to think. In any event there is a clear case for requiring greater simplification of the language in which contractual documents are drafted, for only the most sophisticated consumers can readily comprehend them.[75]

Contractual documents are not the most appropriate means of conveying information to consumers. Consumers will never engage in comparative shopping if it is only then that they first become aware of credit terms and charges. Consumers commonly sign credit documents without knowing what they contain, so that they may be in complete ignorance of the terms until the possibility of withdrawal or cancellation has passed. The Consumer Credit Act 1974 tries to get around this to some extent, and contains a regulatory power to oblige disclosure to consumers of specified information before a regulated agreement is consummated.[76]

The wide potential of provisions about content and form is illustrated by *Mourning* v. *Family Publications Service, Inc.*,[77] a case decided by the United States Supreme Court. A Mrs Mourning purchased a five-year subscription to four magazines and agreed to pay $3.95 monthly. It was successfully argued that the contract involved the provision of credit and that consequently the transaction violated provisions like those in the Consumer Credit Act 1974 concerning the content and form of credit documentation, since the seller omitted to state the total purchase price and the relevant service and finance charges. Under the Consumer Credit Act 1974 non-compliance with the provisions about the form and content of regulated agreements makes a credit transaction unenforceable without a court order.[78] A court in making an enforcement order must have regard to the prejudice caused and the degree of culpability for non-compliance.[79] Where essential information is omitted by reason of fraud on the part of a dealer – for example, the dealer has the consumer sign the proposal form in blank – a court clearly could not enforce the agreement as later completed.[80]

Control over credit terms

Considerable criticism has been made that consumers are often forced into transactions on credit by sales pressure when they cannot really undertake the repayment responsibilities. Their budgets are so tightly committed that the least interruption by illness or un-employment will produce default. The Crowther Committee commented:

> It would appear that responsibility for the majority of court cases rests with a small number of credit-granting bodies which habitually grant credit without making any enquiries about creditworthiness of the debtor. Some-times the same creditor is issuing judgment summonses against a debtor while through its agents it is persuading that debtor to accept extra credit.[81]

The Committee concluded that the best policy was not to restrict the granting of credit, but to ensure that creditors were more careful in assessing creditworthiness and to assist those who defaulted.[82] It recommended that the body administering licensing under the Consumer Credit Act 1974 should be empowered to receive infor-mation on default rates and overdue accounts from creditors and to take appropriate action (it was not clear what this would entail) if it appeared that creditors were extending credit unwisely and that they were still able to operate successfully despite high rates of bad debt.[83] The Director General of Fair Trading could take such considerations into account in exercising his licensing powers under the Act.

The too-ready extension of credit by businesses can be tackled in a number of ways. It might be made unlawful to pressure consumers into credit transactions, but such a provision would probably only catch the most blatant cases.[84] Restrictions could be imposed on the remedies which creditors can enforce in the event of default, along the lines considered in the final section of this chapter, to induce them to be more careful in extending credit. Retailers' commission on business which they introduce to creditors could be controlled on the basis that it encourages retailers to push credit onto consumers who are in no real position to repay it. Another mischief with retailers' commission is that consumers may think that they are obtaining an objective evaluation about the comparative advantages of a particular type of credit when in reality a retailer's advice is self-interested and determined by which credit institution provides the highest commission. Retailers' commission has been strongly condemned in Australia by committees investigating consumer credit,[85] and were controlled by the uniform hire purchase legislation in the various states.[86] Apparently evasion of these provisions was common: finance charges were reduced to enable the retailer to increase the cash price or the part-exchange allowance and retailers were given other benefits as inducements, such as assistance with the financing of stocks. Laxity of enforcement is of course no argument that the prohibition is unworkable.

Controlling the terms of credit (requiring minimum deposits, limiting the repayment period, etc.) is another way of encouraging consumers not to undertake transactions when there may be a risk of getting into difficulties. Terms control was first introduced in Britain during the Second World War, but with the purpose of supporting price control by preventing excessive prices being hidden in credit charges. After that terms control was utilized as an instrument of macro-economic policy but was abandoned in 1982.[87] Changes in terms control are made depending on how the government wishes to regulate consumer expenditure. Its advantages as an economic regulator are that it takes effect immediately and that it is one of the few instruments that acts solely on consumer expenditure and not on business investment, in contrast, say, to controls over the commercial banks' lending policy. Terms control is rather discriminatory, applying only to certain forms of consumer credit and to certain products. For this reason its overall economic bite may not be startling, although it may have a drastic impact on the consumer durable industries which are the mainstay of transactions subject to its effects.

No doubt terms control had some effect in curbing consumer default, although its aim in Britain had an economic character. In countries like Sweden and Australia, consumer protection policy has been the motivating factor. The fact that a consumer can pay a large deposit is no guarantee in itself that he can repay the instalments, and thus terms control is no substitute for a creditor properly assessing credit-worthiness.[88] Terms control has been frequently evaded in practice; for example, by inflating the trade-in price of an item given in part-exchange. It is not inevitable that terms control will be difficult to enforce, and the poor record in Britain was because enforcement had not been delegated from central government to consumer protection departments. A more far-reaching and better-enforced system would overcome drawbacks from both the economic and consumer protection viewpoints.

Rate regulation

Rate regulation has a long history deriving from the suspicion with which moneylending has always been regarded. In England the common law held that it was unlawful if a Christian took any kind of usury; and thus if a person were found to have committed usury, after his death all his chattels were forfeited to the king and his lands escheated to the lord of the fee.[89] Methods were found of evading the prohibition; raising loans on mortgage was one way, for the profit made by the creditor was not regarded as reducing his debt. Eventually the statute 37 Hen. VIII, c. 9, while making usury unlawful, recognized the realities and fixed a legal rate of interest for commercial and real transactions at 10 per cent, subsequently reduced to 5 per cent by 12 Anne, c. 16. Writers like Adam Smith, Bentham and J. S. Mill in the eighteenth and nineteenth centuries declared that the rate of interest was fixed by market forces and to restrict it was harmful.[90] A Select Committee of the House of Commons agreed in 1818: restrictions on usury were being evaded, it concluded, but by methods which impeded commercial transactions and only caused litigation. Finally, the laws against usury were repealed in 1854. The consequence was that abuses multiplied, as demonstrated in the report of the Select Committee of thè House of Commons which considered the matter in 1898. As a result of the report the Moneylenders Act 1900 required moneylenders to register and provided that the courts could reopen transactions where the interest was excessive. The Moneylenders Act 1927 substituted licensing for registration and introduced the figure of 48 per cent as prima facie excessive.

Rate regulation has been suggested in modern times as a means to encourage creditors to lend more prudently, because no longer would they have the same latitude to cover the cost of default by high credit charges, and to prevent the exploitation of more vulnerable consumers by excessive credit charges. Implicit in both arguments is that existing measures, like information disclosure and the power of the courts to open extortionate credit bargains, are inadequate in protecting consumers. Consumers themselves have mixed views about credit charges, although often they have little choice in the credit they can use and thus the rates they pay. In a survey for the National Consumer Council in 1979, consumers thought that the type of credit determined whether it was 'expensive'. Hire purchase was generally thought to be the most costly common form of credit. In general, most people reckoned that the cost of credit they had been using was more or less as they had planned, and over three-quarters of credit users reckoned that its cost had been reasonable.[91] People tended to use particular forms of credit for reasons of habit, convenience, ignorance and indifference to alternatives. Those without bank accounts, poorer and older people, had a narrower choice of credit – for example, credit cards, bank loans and bank overdrafts were virtually ruled out. Charges for the credit sources open to them were usually higher.[92]

A form of rate regulation existed under the Moneylenders Acts, for on a loan covered by the Acts, it was noted above, a true interest charge of greater than 48 per cent per annum was regarded as prima facie excessive and the transaction harsh and unconscionable, enabling the courts to reduce it. Now there is the power in the Consumer Credit Act 1974 to reopen extortionate credit bargains if the payments required are grossly exorbitant.[93] The wide discretion given to the courts in considering bargains for their extortionate character, and the fact that so much can depend on the individual circumstances of a credit transaction, suggest that little control of credit charges will result from the enactment of this provision. Another disadvantage is that the provision only becomes operative when court proceedings are taken. Almost invariably this means that it will be used as a shield when consumers are sued and not as a sword to challenge a wide range of interest rates, for consumers who enter extortionate credit agreements are those least likely to invoke the provisions of private law.

More specific control of credit charges has been imposed in other jurisdictions. Rate regulation existed in hire purchase transactions in New South Wales until 1974 and flat rate ceilings of 7, 9 and 10 per cent were imposed depending on the nature of the deal.[94] In Canada it is a criminal offence to enter an agreement or arrangement to receive interest at a criminal rate or to receive a payment or partial payment of interest at a criminal rate. A criminal rate of interest means an effective annual rate of interest that exceeds 60 per cent on the credit advanced.[95] The United States has a heritage of state governments fixing rate ceilings, usually at market level, designed to prevent loan sharking. Under the Uniform Consumer Credit Code, which has been adopted in some of the states, there is a ceiling rate of 18 per cent per annum calculated on unpaid balances.[96]

Rate regulation is generally regarded as undesirable by those who accept the conventional wisdom that it is better to leave matters to the market.[97] The first argument against rate regulation is that it causes distortion, as businesses inflate the cash price of items and services to enable them to charge the same price as would be payable without a regime of control. Whether such distortion would occur on a wide scale depends on a number of factors, such as the proportion of transactions of a particular type involving credit. If this was relatively small, inflated cash prices in credit transactions would be obvious and it would simply be a matter of allocating adequate enforcement resources to prevent it. Secondly, it is said that there would be a large administrative burden to imposing rate regulation because different credit institutions charge widely differing amounts and credit charges vary according to consumers' individual circumstances. The argument is hardly as strong as the critics make out because credit institutions tend to charge a uniform rate to consumers once they decide that they are creditworthy.

Finally, it is said that if rate regulation were introduced certain forms of credit would disappear, to the disadvantage of consumers.

Whether this is undesirable depends on the value of the type of credit, who is affected, and whether alternative institutional arrangements are possible. For example, opponents of rate regulation argue that low income consumers have an inelastic demand for credit which will force them into the arms of loan sharks if rates are fixed. One answer to this is that the poor use credit far less often than the rest of the population, conventional wisdom notwithstanding.[98] Another is that credit unions and government-supported loan schemes can be developed to provide a better service to low-income consumers than at present. The greater competition in the credit market which would result might also have a beneficial effect on credit rates for consumers other than those who would be the immediate beneficiaries. Perhaps the most practicable means of rate regulation is to foster these institutional reforms, which could be supplemented by other measures. There could be a fairly high ceiling for credit charges to prevent loan sharks, and consumer protection agencies could be empowered to issue court challenges on behalf of consumers against rates below these if the circumstances suggested that they were extortionate.

Creditors' liability for retailers' breach

For a considerable time there has been concern that finance houses had not exercised sufficient care in the choice of retailers through whom they provide credit to consumers. Fraudulent, and in some cases criminal, second-hand car dealers flourished, for example, because finance houses were so eager to acquire their business that they failed to investigate their records or references.[99] A limited step was taken in the Hire Purchase Act 1964 to make finance houses liable for the misrepresentations of retailers, but the provision was confined to hire purchase and associated transactions.[100] Finance houses have been liable for some time for title to products taken on hire purchase, and for their correspondence with description, merchantability and fitness for purpose. From the early 1960s, finance houses provided credit through personal loans to consumers for the installation of central heating and home improvements. Some contractors canvassed for this type of work door to door, and induced consumers to sign documents by high pressure salesmanship, including the application for a loan from a finance house. The work was often inadequate – in some cases not even begun – yet the finance houses showed little concern on the grounds that they were not legally liable and quite ignorant of the contractors' malpractices.

The upshot of practices like these was a recommendation by the Crowther Committee that a creditor providing credit for consumers for specific deals with a retailer with whom it had connections should be responsible for misrepresentation by that retailer and for defects in the goods.[101] Over the objections of finance houses, check traders and credit card companies, the recommendation was embodied in the Consumer Credit Act 1974. A justification for the move is that it induces creditors to exercise their economic power over retailers to discourage malpractices. Moreover, retailers which make misrepresentations or supply defective products or services can only continue in business with the support of creditors.

The means by which the law now achieves joint and several liability on the part of creditors and retailers is not straightforward. Tripartite debtor-creditor-supplier agreements are dealt with by section 75(1) of the Consumer Credit Act 1974. It provides that if a debtor under certain debtor-creditor-supplier agreements has, in relation to a transaction financed by the agreement, a claim against a supplier in respect of misrepresentation or breach of contract, he 'shall have a like claim against the creditor, who, with the supplier, shall accordingly be jointly and severally liable to the debtor.'[102] The debtor-creditor-supplier agreements are those where the agreement is a restricted-use credit agreement and the loan is made by a creditor under pre-existing arrangements or in contemplation of future arrangements between the creditor and the dealer, or is an unrestricted-use credit agreement made by the creditor under pre-existing arrangements between itself and the supplier in the knowledge that the credit is to be used to finance a transaction between the debtor and the supplier. The section does not apply to non-commercial agreements or where the claim relates to any single item to which the supplier has attached a cash price not exceeding £30 or more than £10,000.[103] However, it applies notwithstanding that the debtor, in entering into the transaction, exceeded the credit limit or otherwise contravened any term of the agreement.[104] Section 75(1) applies to a finance house which advances a loan to a consumer to acquire a product from a supplier with which it has existing arrangements or with which it contemplates future arrangements. It also applies to a check trader or a credit card company as regards retailers with whom consumers are entitled to use the facility.[105]

Consumers in situations like this who, say, have a misrepresentation made to them or who receive a defective product have a 'like claim' against the finance house, check trader or credit-card company as they have against the supplier.

Where the retailer itself is the creditor or hirer, liability is direct as regards title to products and their correspondence with description, merchantability and fitness for purpose.[106] Similarly in hire purchase transactions the finance house has a direct responsibility in an almost identical manner by virtue of the Supply of Goods (Implied Terms) Act 1973.[107] A slight difference in the provisions, taking into account the nature of the transaction, is that to benefit from the implied condition of fitness for purpose it is sufficient for the consumer to make that purpose known to the retailer.[108] Retailers in hire purchase transactions may be liable for a misrepresentation on a collateral contract, the consideration for which is the consumer entering the main contract with the finance house.[109] What of the finance house's responsibility for the retailer's misrepresentation? Section 56(2) of Consumer Credit Act 1974 means that the negotiations with a debtor conducted by a retailer in relation to a product sold or to be sold on hire purchase are deemed to be conducted by the retailer in its capacity of agent of the finance house as well as in its own capacity. Consequently, any misrepresentation by a retailer in these circumstances, including a misrepresentation in an advertisement, is attributable to the finance house and is actionable by the consumer.[110] By virtue of section 56, finance houses might also be liable for retailer fraud such as where a retailer misappropriates a deposit.[111]

Can finance houses avoid this liability for the behaviour of retailers? In the United States – and to some extent in Britain[112] – retailers have provided credit themselves by getting consumers to give a promissory note or bill of exchange payable by instalments, but then discounting these to a finance house. In law the finance house as holder in due course of the promissory note or bill of exchange could avoid responsibility for any misrepresentation or breach of contract on the part of the retailer.[113] In Britain the Consumer Credit Act 1974, section 123, now prevents creditors and owners from taking a negotiable instrument like a bill of exchange or a promissory note from a consumer in relation to a regulated agreement. If a negotiable instrument is taken in contravention of the section, the agreement is only enforceable by court order, and the person who takes it is not to be regarded as a holder in due course and capable of enforcing the instrument.[114] The section does not apply to cheques but these must only be negotiated to a banker.[115]

In Britain block discounting has been used to some extent, whereby retailers have written credit agreements themselves but sell them to finance houses at a discount on the value of the contract rights on the face of the agreements.[116] The finance houses have usually retained the retailer as the agent for collection and have not bothered to call for formal assignment of the agreements. Finance houses could not by block discounting avoid their liability for retailers' actions under section 75 because a creditor is defined in the Consumer Credit Act 1974 to include those to whom rights and duties under an agreement have passed by assignment or operation of law.[117]

TERMINATION OF A CONSUMER CREDIT AGREEMENT

Most consumer credit agreements terminate with the consumer repaying the credit in the manner anticipated by the agreement. Occasionally consumers wish to pay out the creditor what is owing before the agreement is due to expire – they have won the pools, a wealthy aunt has died, they have received redundancy money, or some other reason. The Consumer Credit Act 1974 gives consumers the right to do this, and provides that they should receive a rebate for early payment on the charges outstanding.[118] The rebate is not a simple reduction in the total credit charge related to the time the agreement has to run because this would not compensate the creditor for the cost of setting up the transaction. The Crowther Committee therefore recommended that a mathematical calculation, known as the 'rule of 78', be made mandatory to calculate the rebate. Some commentators argue that the 'rule of 78' becomes increasingly inaccurate as the interest rate and the term of a transaction increase, and constitutes an implicit penalty on consumers when they wish to repay credit before time.[119]

Although most consumer credit agreements terminate as contemplated – or in some cases before then – we shall concentrate in this section on situations where consumers experience serious difficulties in meeting their repayments.[120] For convenience these situations are called default situations. Concentrating on default is clearly justified because the courts are primarily concerned with this type of problem case; as the Crowther Committee remarked, if all debtors repaid on time the law would be quite simple.

The nature of default

The incidence of default among consumers is relatively small. A survey for the National Consumer Council in 1979 found that only 3 per cent (nine people) of the credit-buying sample had had a problem over some aspect of the credit arrangement after purchase. Of these apparently only 1 per cent (four people) had found difficulty in making payments.[121] An NOP survey in 1969 found that 10 per cent (seventy-eight consumers) had had difficulty in meeting repayments at some time, a somewhat greater proportion of these being among the lower socio-economic groups. Of the twenty-eight consumers who failed to meet several consecutive repayments, no action was taken by the creditor in four cases, reminders and letters threatening court action were sent in eighteen cases, and in only eight instances were legal proceedings actually instituted.[122] Earlier research by Rock had found that of eighty-five consumers in London who had taken credit at one time or another, only four had problems in repaying on their current transactions and seven on transactions in the past.[123] While lenders told the National Consumer Council that about 1 per cent of credit transactions turned into bad debts, the evidence of trade associations to the Crowther Committee was that bad debts constituted only 0·5 per cent of the consumer credit extended.[124]

The nineteenth-century view that defaulters are the authors of their own misfortune still finds expression in authoritative sources. The Crowther Committee recognized that consumers often experienced difficulties with credit because of matters beyond their control, like sickness and unemployment, but it still saw their irresponsibility as an important cause.

> There are many, particularly in the low-income group, who are not reckless so much as improvident. They lack the ability to budget or to manage their income. They have little or no sense of values and are not motivated by rational considerations in selecting their purchases. Such people will, for example, spend a slice of their income not on articles they really need but on other less important items; and they will spend regardless of whether they are getting value for money.[125]

Creditors have stereotypes of defaulters: there are cases of genuine misfortune but equally strong numbers of feckless defaulters who enter credit transactions irresponsibly, and professional defaulters who from the outset never have any intention of repaying.[126] Their views draw some support from community attitudes. The small sample of 119 Londoners interviewed by Rock thought that the causes of consumers' troubles in repaying credit were primarily their own responsibility. Lack of self-control, etc. (61) and drunkenness and gambling (11) far outweighed factors such as the ease of getting credit (20), poverty (9), illness and unemployment (7) or high pressure salesmanship (6).[127]

The reality of repayment difficulties from the point of view of those involved is radically different from the common stereotypes. In the National Consumer Council survey, the four persons experiencing difficulty in making payments had been subject to changes in personal circumstances (one became unemployed, one suffered illness and two had other unforeseen financial demands).[128] In the NOP survey, the seventy-eight consumers experiencing difficulties gave illness, unemployment or labour disputes as the major explanations, while only 6 per cent mentioned over-commitment on credit buying. The findings are set out in Table 7.3 and parallel those of similar studies elsewhere.[129]

Table 7.3   Reasons given by Consumers as Cause of their Default

Illness	20%
Unemployment	15%
Over-commitment on credit buying	6%
Marital difficulties	5%
Defective goods and subsequent dispute with vendor	5%
Industrial labour disputes	4%
National financial situation	3%
Miscellaneous causes	3%
Unforeseen debts arising	1%
Reasons unknown or not remembered	37%

N = 78

There may be some underestimate by consumers of their own behaviour in contributing to repayment difficulties, because for some consumers it would be embarrassing to admit bad management. But if this is a 'hidden figure' in the replies, it can be argued with equal conviction that the findings underestimate the amount of business error or fraud, of which consumers are unaware, in causing repayment difficulties. And it is difficult not to feel sympathy for some of those who knew they were over-committing themselves; for example, for those who did it as an escape from a low standard of living.[130] Of the eight persons in the NOP survey against whom legal proceedings were taken, six were cases of unemployment, illness or marital difficulty, one was the result of fraud on the part of the retailer, and one involved a consumer who insisted that the vehicle being acquired was defective.[131] Another point which the NOP survey uncovered was that a disproportionate number of consumers from the lower social classes had repayment difficulties – 5 per cent in social grades A and B; 6 per cent in social grade C1; 11 per cent in social grade C2 and 15 per cent in social grades D and E.[132] This finding lends support to the hypothesis that some consumers are caught in a circle of poverty – consumers who are least able to afford it are seduced into credit transactions which further undermine their economic position.[133]

If the primary reasons for default are unemployment and illness and not irresponsibility or fraud, there seems no need for creditors to use harsh collection methods. As Caplovitz notes:

> Perhaps the most impressive finding is that substantial numbers of debtors resume payments regardless of the reason for their default and the type of credit threat. We have repeatedly made this observation in order to question the basic premise of the credit industry – that harsh collection devices are needed to control the credit system.[134]

A finance house, if it is sensible, will accept that in the great majority of cases the best approach is to treat consumers leniently if they are in temporary difficulties, for there is the assurance that ultimately they will be paid without having to incur the cost of collection procedures. Indeed a good number of consumers in difficulty said that their creditor behaved in a sympathetic manner when contacted. A real problem, however, is that consumers in difficulty frequently feel inhibited from approaching the creditor to explain their plight and before long action is being taken against them.[135]

Initially creditors use extra-judicial methods to induce defaulters to pay. Typically creditors rely on sending letters to consumers which become increasingly threatening if default continues.[136] There are isolated instances of creditors using harassment where letters fail to prompt payment, but it seems that these are less frequent than formerly. The Payne Committee collected evidence of the different types of harassment used; for example, frequent calls at the home of the debtor leaving threatening cards, informing neighbours of the debtor about his indebtedness under the guise of seeking information, and writing to the employer under the guise of avoiding the need for the debtor to absent himself from work to attend court.[137]

The Committee condemned these methods and pointed out that consumers defaulting because of misfortune were peculiarly vulnerable to them.[138] Paul Rock's study of debt collection provides some clues as to why harsh methods are sometimes adopted. Debts are sometimes enforced, although economically the time and effort cannot be justified, as a retributive act because the creditor believes that it is dealing with a fraudulent debtor or that otherwise it would gain the reputation of being too lenient and thus attract a number of bad accounts.[139] Another factor is that large creditors like finance houses sometimes sell bad debts to a small collection firm instead of simply employing it as an agent, so that there is every incentive for the latter to collect the debt.

The private law contains remedies for trespass, assault and the wilful infliction of mental injury, which may be used against certain types of collection harassment.[140] To say falsely that a person refuses to pay his debts, is deliberately delaying payment of them, or is unable to pay them may be defamatory.[141] Needless to say, the typical defaulter is not a person who will utilize his private law rights. Criminal law offers some protection, although a major problem is lack of enforcement. As a result of the Payne Committee Report, section 40 of the Administration of Justice Act 1970 was enacted which makes it an offence if, with the object of coercing another to pay a debt, a person (a) falsely represents that criminal proceedings will lie for failure to pay; (b) falsely represents that he has official authorization to enforce payment; (c) wrongly uses a document which appears to be official, and (d) unreasonably harasses '. . . with demands for payment which, in respect of their frequency or the manner or occasion of making any such demand, or of any threat or publicity by which any demand is accompanied, are calculated to subject him or members of his family or household to alarm, distress or humiliation.'[142] Canadian legislation is somewhat wider and prohibits other

practices, such as conducting inquiries at a person's place of
employment, with a view that he will then pay because of the fear of
being dismissed if the matter becomes public knowledge.[143] The
biggest restraint on undesirable collection methods in Britain is that
businesses collecting debts must obtain a license under the Consumer
Credit Act 1974, and to do so they must be able to demonstrate that
they do not engage in undesirable trade practices.[144] The Director
General of Fair Trading has said that he will refuse a license to any
debt collector who persists in using such methods as the threat or use
of physical violence; the parking of vans outside debtors' houses with
the name and business of the debt collector prominently displayed;
visiting people at their place of employment; and using letters
couched in terms suggesting it is a legal summons (sometimes
referred to as a 'blue frightener'). He has issued four 'minded to
refuse' notices – the preliminary to actually refusing a license – to debt
collectors who had charged debtors for collecting their debts. In all
four cases the licenses were eventually issued because the debt
collectors dropped the practice.[145]

The NOP survey found that most consumers in repayment
difficulties consulted with their family, friends or even their creditor,
but that none of them mentioned citizens advice bureaux, and that
there was 'a disinclination to be involved with the legal profession'.[146]
None the less, a small number of consumers with debt problems
consult bodies like the citizens advice bureaux, legal advice centres
and charitable organizations which engage in debt counselling, like
the Birmingham Settlement. These bodies can often negotiate short-
term accommodation with creditors on behalf of debtors and
occasionally they may be able to achieve something on a long-term
basis; for example, they may serve as a conduit through which regular
payments can be made reducing indebtedness.[147] They may also be
able to advise on legal procedures like an administration order.

Warnings have been issued in the past against business enterprises
using titles like 'credit counsellor', who claim to assist consumers with
their financial problems.[148] The activities of similar firms in the
United States were so notorious that they were banned in more than
twenty states. The worst excesses in Britain should now be curbed
because debt counsellors must be licensed under the Consumer
Credit Act 1974.[149] The case law illustrates the pitfalls of consumers'
entering refinancing agreements through the offices of credit
counsellors. In *Snook* v. *London and West Riding Investments Ltd*,[150] the

consumer was paying off a car on hire purchase – he had paid nearly the full amount cash down – with Totley Investments (T.I.), when he saw an advertisement by Auto Finance (A.F.) which offered to assist consumers by refinancing hire purchase debts enabling them to pay off an amount over a longer period. The consumer approached A.F. who prepared documents which he signed, clearly without appreciating their full import. One was a letter saying that he had sold his rights in the car to A.F., and the other was a new hire purchase agreement with the London and West Riding Investments Ltd (L. & W.). L. & W. accepted the hire purchase agreement, paid £300 to A.F., which paid out T.I. and gave £125 to the consumer, keeping £15 itself. When the consumer fell behind with his repayments through unemployment, the car was repossessed by A.F. (acting as agents for L. & W.), who refused the consumer's offer to pay off the arrears. The car was sold for £575; A.F. paid L. & W. £280 and kept the balance of £295. In other words, the consumer found himself without a car on which he had paid some £800 for falling behind in two instalments worth under £30. The majority of the Court of Appeal upheld the result – Lord Denning saw the injustice and dissented – because the consumer by his conduct had allowed A.F. to represent that it was the owner, and thus title passed to L. & W.[151] The transaction between the consumer and A.F. could not be said to be a sham, said Diplock and Russell L. JJ., because L. & W. were not aware of it. The upshot of the decision is that the law preferred an ignorant finance house to an ignorant consumer, although the former was undoubtedly in a better position to uncover the realities of the transaction and to bear any loss.

The creditors' remedies

Where a consumer is in default with repayments under a regulated agreement, a creditor will have at least one of a number of remedies. Before it can become entitled, by reason of the breach, to terminate the agreement, to demand earlier payment of any sum, to recover possession, to treat any right conferred on the consumer by the agreement as terminated, restricted or deferred, or to enforce any security, it must serve a default notice on the consumer specifying the nature of the alleged breach, if it is capable of remedy and the remedial action required or, if none is possible, the payment required as compensation.[152] If the consumer can remedy the breach within seven days it is treated as not having occurred.[153] The idea is that consumers should be given an opportunity to make the payments owing or to apply to a court for an extension of time. In addition, preparation of a default notice has the advantage that it might lead the creditor to discover a mistake in its claim. Once a period of seven days expires from service of the notice, the creditor can then proceed to enforce its remedies. Default notices by themselves are far from satisfactory because they assume that a consumer in default can correct it within a relatively short period, or if not will seek a court order. The typical defaulter, previously described, is hardly likely to be in a position to do either and in general the only effect of a default notice will be to postpone the creditor's remedies for seven days.

A creditor or owner under a credit or hire agreement is entitled to claim the instalments as they become due. Should a consumer be in default under a regulated consumer credit agreement, legislation provides that the creditor cannot charge a higher rate of interest (default interest) than in the agreement.[154] An acceleration clause may provide that a consumer in default becomes liable for the full outstanding balance. Acceleration clauses are said to be justified because otherwise creditors would have to bring a series of actions as each instalment becomes due, or wait for the agreement to run its course when the chances of recovery will be increasingly remote.[155] The injustice of acceleration clauses to consumers is obvious because the agreement may provide that they can be invoked in the event of a single default – incidentally defeating the whole purpose of purchasing on credit. The validity of an acceleration clause has been upheld, as being a genuine pre-estimate of the creditor's loss and non-penal in effect, under which the consumer had to pay the outstanding balance, but only a proportion of the charges in accordance with the rule of 78.[156] Their existence is recognized in the Consumer Credit Act 1974.[157] But acceleration clauses will not be given unlimited effect by the courts and will be construed strictly because of their nature.[158] Indeed it seems an acceleration clause is unenforceable as a penalty if, under it, in addition to the principal, the consumer has to pay the whole of the charges, without any rebate, although credit is no longer outstanding.[159] Another possible attack on an acceleration clause now is that its operation contravenes the extortionate bargain provisions of the Consumer Credit Act 1974 because it requires payments which are grossly exorbitant or because it grossly contravenes the ordinary principles of fair dealing.[160] Whether the extortionate bargain power can be brought to bear against acceleration clauses depends very much on how widely the courts are prepared to interpret it.

Repossession is perhaps the strongest weapon a creditor can have because of its immediacy. The Finance Houses Association informed the Crowther Committee that its members repossessed about one in forty of the cars being purchased on hire purchase.[161] Repossession is less useful when utilized against some household domestic appliances because their resale value hardly justifies the effort. Nevertheless, the threat of repossession can still be used as a tactic by creditors against consumers in default. Swedish proposals would deny creditors the right to repossess, except for expensive items like cars, in order to prevent empty threats of repossession which cause consumers unnecessary distress.[162]

Legally a consumer does not become the owner of an item being acquired on hire purchase until all the instalments are paid and the option to purchase is exercised. Businesses thus have the right at common law to repossess an item on hire purchase if a consumer is in breach of the agreement.[163] The courts held that relief against forfeiture was not possible in the case of hire purchase – a result which would have gone part of the way to mitigating the harshness for consumers.[164] Public concern about how some businesses used their rights to 'snatch back' items led to reform in the Hire Purchase Act 1938.[165] In introducing this part of the legislation – a Private Members Bill – the M.P. responsible, Ellen Wilkinson, referred to the 'snatch back' as the 'cancer' afflicting hire purchase. She gave an example of how the 'snatch back' operated.

For instance, a poor woman got furniture for which she was to pay a total of £27 1s 6d. With some difficulty, she paid £25 16s 9d, and then she got behind in her payments and was prosecuted, the court ordering £6 8s 9d for costs. While she was out charing, a van called, took away all the goods and what was considered to be £5 worth of other goods for the court costs.[166]

The protection is now embodied in the Consumer Credit Act 1974 and provides that a creditor in a regulated hire purchase or conditional sale agreement must obtain a court order to repossess an item when more than one-third of the total purchase price has been paid.[167] The Act provides that the protection ceases if the consumer terminates the agreement.[168]

Under the Hire Purchase Acts, the Court of Appeal in *Mercantile Credit Ltd* v. *Cross*[169] held that a consumer who gives up possession of an item voluntarily to a creditor loses the protection of the one-third rule. The decision turned on the wording of the hire purchase legislation – an owner could not *enforce* a right to recover possession of protected goods, and merely passively to accept was not to enforce. The Consumer Credit Act 1974 provision is much wider and prohibits the creditor from *recovering* possession without a court order. But it has been argued that creditors can now take advantage of section 173(3) of the Act, which provides that an act which can only be done by court order can also be done with the person's consent given at the time.[170] It is submitted that the courts should be reluctant to use a general provision like section 173(3) to reduce consumers' rights in other parts of the Act.[171] In any event, the actual decision in *Mercantile Credit Ltd* v. *Cross* is quite unacceptable on its facts in the light of later Court of Appeal authorities.[172] The consumer was in default and received a notice requiring him to give up possession of the car, which he thought he was obliged to do. Quite unrealistically the Court held that the consumer must be regarded as being aware of the legal consequences of what he was doing, since he had only to read the agreement.[173] It is suggested that nowadays the courts will require a much more informed decision on the part of consumers before they lose the protection of the one-third rule. However, if a consumer abandons an item the creditor can repossess it, even if more than one-third the total price has been paid.[174]

The one-third rule is not the only limitation on repossession. The Consumer Credit Act 1974 prohibits creditors from entering a consumer's home without his consent, given at the time, to repossess an item under a regulated hire purchase, conditional sale or hire agreement unless they have obtained a court order.[175] Breach of this provision gives the consumer a remedy in damages but does not of itself constitute a criminal offence.[176] There are of course provisions in the criminal law which prohibit the forceful entry of premises.[177]

The limitations on repossession in the Consumer Credit Act 1974 apply to regulated hire purchase and conditional sale agreements. No provision is made for other types of consumer credit and hiring agreements, a sad omission when one of the stated aims of the Act was said to be to place consumers in all types of consumer credit agreement on the same footing. For example, a consumer who just happens to acquire an item on credit through a finance house who uses loan agreements rather than hire purchase may find that the creditor is able to repossess the item, however much has been paid, by entering the consumer's home. The creditor will be able to do this where there is a written agreement giving it these rights, which is in proper form and registered as a bill of sale under the Bills of Sales Acts.[178] A repossession clause in a credit sale agreement or loan agreement associated with a sale would convert the agreement into a bill of sale if in terms of the Acts it would enable the creditor to seize the item as security for the credit. It would be void unless it complied with the formalities laid down in the Act. Seeking to exercise repossession if the agreement was void would constitute trespass and breach of the criminal law.

In practice no bill of sale may be registered in credit sale transactions or loan transactions associated with a sale. Creditors using these forms of credit may rely on the creditworthiness of the consumer and not desire a security interest in their favour. Nevertheless, a substantial number of bills of sale are registered involving consumer transactions for domestic furniture, other household consumer durables and an increasing number of cars.[179] If these are in proper form, the Bills of Sale Acts empower creditors to seize the security. To do this they have wide power to enter premises subject only to the restraints of the criminal law.[180]

There has been much criticism of the way finance houses sell items which they repossess. Empirical studies elsewhere have shown that repossessed items are sold at a considerable undervalue unless they are sold by retailers rather than finance houses.[181] Finance houses have no retail outlets themselves, so the items must be disposed of in private contracts with retailers or at auctions at which retailers predominate.[182] But as Shuchman comments, there seems to be a real discrepancy between the efficiency with which creditors sell repossessed items and that present in their other business transactions.[183] The law at present provides no incentive to creditors to obtain the best possible price because they can always sue consumers for the deficiency of any loss that still results on the deal. The only incentives to creditors to obtain a good price on a resale are the value of getting their money now and not in the future, and that if a surplus is obtained over the loss the consumer may not claim it. On one occasion Lord Denning seemed prepared to refer to *Glass's Guide*, which is a trade publication giving the expected retail prices of different types and models of second-hand cars, in preference to the price which a repossessed car actually realized in the trade.[184] Certainly if repossession is to continue, along with the creditor's right to sue for any deficiency, there needs to be a clear obligation imposed on finance houses to obtain the best retail price possible where repossessed items are resold.[185]

Even if a creditor repossesses a product being bought on credit, its sale might not realize an amount sufficient to cover the loss of profit on the transaction. The first point to note is that a minimum payment clause in a credit agreement, by which the consumer must pay a specific amount to the finance house, will probably be invalid. The courts tend to regard minimum payment clauses as a penalty and not as a genuine pre-estimate of the losses experienced because they mean a consumer will be liable for a substantial percentage of the total purchase price, however little use has been derived from the product.[186] *Bridge* v. *Campbell Discount Co. Ltd*[187] is the leading case in hire purchase law, where the House of Lords held that a hire purchase company could not enforce a minimum payment clause obliging the consumer, who had already returned the car, to make payments equal to two-thirds of the purchase price. It seems that it will be difficult to frame a minimum payment clause which the courts will not regard as a penalty clause.[188] In *Capital Finance Co.* v. *Donati*,[189] a minimum payment clause provided that the consumer should pay the finance house for the actual losses suffered, but the clause was regarded as a penalty because it did not differentiate between trivial default and repudiatory breach. Now minimum payment clauses may also be invalid because they constitute a grossly exorbitant payment or grossly violate the ordinary principles of fair dealing in breach of section 138 of the Consumer Credit Act 1974.

What can a creditor claim if a minimum payment clause is invalid? It is fair to say that the law is anomalous. Except in the specific cases mentioned, resort must be had to the agreement and to common law principles. Depending on its nature, the agreement will usually contain provisions such as an acceleration clause, a provision for the creditor to terminate the agreement in specified events, a power for the creditor to remedy breaches itself and charge the consumer with the cost, and a power for the creditor to repossess and sell the items covered by the agreement or security.[190] So in the case of a credit sale or loan, the creditor will be entitled to sue for the price or the outstanding balance, respectively, both of which will become payable immediately if an acceleration clause can be invoked. The creditor might also be entitled to claim against any security taken. With hire purchase and conditional sale, as well as repossessing the item the losses for which a creditor can claim lie along a graduated scale.

(a) if the creditor terminates the agreement – the instalments then in arrear only;

(b) if the consumer terminates a regulated hire purchase or conditional sale agreement – the amounts specified in section 99 of the Consumer Credit Act 1974;

(c) if the consumer repudiates – the creditor's loss of profit (with some minor reductions).

(a) arises if the consumer fails to pay an instalment and the finance house exercises its rights to terminate the agreement. In practice this will not usually occur because consumers are likely to do acts which constitute either termination or repudiation, and finance houses will protect their position by invoking an acceleration clause in an agreement. As a matter of public policy there is strong justification for legislation to limit finance houses from claiming arrears in instalments in these circumstances, which is to restrain finance houses from ending agreements simply because a consumer is in temporary difficulties although he intends to complete. *Financings Ltd* v. *Baldock*[191] is a good example of this policy at work. The consumer defaulted on his first two instalments and some ten days after the second instalment became due the finance house repossessed the vehicle, although the consumer said that he might be able to pay within three days. The finance house then sought damages of some £538 – the unpaid balance of the hire purchase price – when the consumer had only had the vehicle ten weeks and had paid an initial instalment of £100! The Court of Appeal held that the consumer's conduct did not constitute repudiation, that the losses of the finance house were due to its own conduct and that consequently all it could claim were the two instalments owing plus interest thereon.

Sections 99 and 100 of the Consumer Credit Act, which apply generally and not simply to default situations, give consumers the right to terminate a regulated hire purchase or conditional sale agreement by returning the item to the creditor. Unless the agreement provides for a smaller amount they must make up their payments to one-half the total purchase price (if they have not already paid that amount).[192] However, if the court is satisfied that the creditor's losses are a lower amount, it may order payment of that amount instead. Consumers using this right to terminate are liable for an additional payment if they have breached an obligation to take reasonable care of the item.[193] The right to terminate must be exercised before the final payment falls due; consequently, it seems to be defeated if a creditor invokes an acceleration clause.[194] The right to terminate under the '50 per cent rule' only applies to regulated hire purchase and conditional sale agreements, presumably because in other credit agreements the law regards consumers as having committed themselves to buy. Needless to say the distinction perpetuates the artificial – and to consumers incomprehensible –distinction between hire purchase and other forms of sale on credit.

What sort of behaviour on the part of the consumer will be regarded as repudiation, enabling the finance house to claim damages for its loss of profit? Mere non-payment of a few instalments is not sufficient –*Financings Ltd* v. *Baldock* cited above established that – and a finance company cannot assume that a consumer has repudiated when he does not respond to a default notice.[195] But persistent non-payment, whatever the reason, will probably constitute repudiation. It is anomalous that the creditor might be able to claim more on the same facts if consumers terminate in ignorance by repudiation than by exercising their rights under section 99.

For a consumer simply to write to a finance house saying that he can continue no longer and wishes to terminate probably will be interpreted as repudiation.[196] For a consumer's repudiation to be effective, of course, the finance house must accept it. Where a consumer repudiates a hire purchase agreement and the repudiation is accepted, the finance house can claim virtually the whole of what it would have received if the deal had gone through – the difference between the total purchase price and what the consumer has paid, *less* the proceeds of sale of the repossessed item, the fee for exercising the option to purchase and a rebate on the interest charges because the agreement does not run its full life.[197]

Where creditors get back possession of an item, they may try to claim damages for the cost of repair on the basis that the consumer has breached an obligation to take reasonable care of it. Consumers should resist the common attempt by finance houses to charge them for the cost of bringing the item up to the standard necessary for resale.[198] The Court of Appeal has said that the consumer's obligation in a hire purchase agreement to keep an item in good order and repair only imposes a duty to keep the car in the condition in which it might reasonably be expected to be if he had looked after it properly. He need not put it in a better condition than it was when he hired it. He need only keep it in the condition in which a reasonably minded hirer would keep it. Thus he would repair it if there was an accident, and he would do the immediate repairs in the course of running the car, but no more.[199]

The Consumer Credit Act 1974 considerably limits the remedies of businesses under regulated consumer hire agreements from the position obtaining at common law. In *Galbraith* v. *Mitchenhall Estates Ltd*,[200] a consumer signed a contract of hire for a caravan without reading the agreement, but assuming that it was a contract of hire purchase. The initial payment was £550, followed by sixty rentals of £12.50. The retail value of the caravan was £1050. The caravan was repossessed when the consumer did not pay any instalments, and the court held that the company was entitled to keep the initial payment and the value realized on resale as provided for in the contract. Sachs J. said that the only possible method of attack on the contractual result was if there was fraudulent or unconscionable conduct at the time it was made, but there was no evidence of this. The upshot was that the consumer paid £550.15 for some four months' use of a caravan and the company made more than was contemplated in the original transaction. Under section 101 of the Consumer Credit Act 1974 the hirer under a regulated hire agreement is entitled to terminate after eighteen months. Also section 132 of the Consumer Credit Act 1974 provides that in a regulated consumer hire agreement, if the business recovers possession of an item, a court can give relief to the consumer by ordering that he need not pay any more under the agreement, or that the business must actually repay an amount. In making an order the court must have regard to the amount of enjoyment of the item by the consumer.

The consumer's position

This section discusses some aspects of the consumer's position when faced with repayment difficulties. It is worth saying at the outset that in the main their rights and the procedures mentioned suffer from the basic deficiency of private law as an instrument of consumer protection – they require the initiative of consumers to invoke them.

Consumers in difficulty with a regulated hire purchase or conditional sale agreement, who have no chance of making repayments in the foreseeable future and who are quite clear that they would rather be free of future involvement, might consider terminating the agreement pursuant to section 99 of the Consumer Credit Act 1974. Unfortunately, a decision might have to be made quickly, for a finance house might invoke an acceleration clause which, as we have seen, seems to exclude the possibility of using the termination provision. Whether exercise of the right to terminate is a wise move depends on the circumstances. Consumers who terminate early on in an agreement are at an obvious disadvantage unless it provides for the payment of an amount lower than the 50 per cent figure. Otherwise they must be prepared to go to court for an order that the creditor's losses are less than this amount. Creditors are likely to claim substantial losses if a consumer terminates an agreement early, because they will have recouped little of their profit, even taking into account the resale value of the item. And there is the problem mentioned previously that the values creditors obtain when reselling items are relatively low. On the other hand, consumers terminating an agreement after some time may not be at a great disadvantage in paying the 50 per cent figure: they may already have paid it, especially if the item is one subject to fairly rapid depreciation.

Many default situations will result in a court making a time order under section 129 of the Consumer Credit Act 1974, which gives a consumer additional time to pay instalments and/or reduces their individual (but not total) amount. The court is given wide discretion as to the nature of a time order, but one factor to be considered is the consumer's means. The power to make a time order in the case of consumer hire purchase or conditional sale agreements extends to future instalments, but in other agreements it only applies to payments in arrear unless an acceleration clause has come into operation whereby all remaining instalments are due immediately.[201] In addition to a time order, section 135 of the Act empowers a court to make a suspension order; for example, it might suspend a creditor's power to repossess an item on condition that the consumer keeps up the payments required. A time order can be made on application of a consumer who has received a default notice, as well as when a creditor brings an action in court against the consumer.[202] Because consumers are unlikely to seek a time order themselves they will be at a disadvantage in some situations, as when creditors are entitled to repossess items being acquired on credit without a court order.

South Australian legislation solves the problem of consumer inertia to some extent by empowering a public agency to seek relief on behalf of consumers experiencing repayment problems. The legislation provides for relief against the consequences of a breach where, by reason of any circumstances which were not reasonably foreseeable at the time of entering into the consumer credit transaction, like illness or unemployment, a consumer is temporarily unable to discharge his obligations.[203] The consumer applies in the first instance to the Commissioner, who must negotiate with the creditor if he is satisfied that there are proper grounds. If the finance house refuses to give the consumer a moratorium, the Commissioner can apply to the Credit Tribunal on behalf of the consumer, for example, for a compulsory extension of the time for repayment.[204] The advantages of the procedure are illustrated in *Davies* v. *Kobi Finance Co. Pty Ltd*[205] where the Credit Tribunal considered the case of a husband and wife whose weekly income was quite low. They had purchased a house for their family and two cheap cars because they lived far from work and shops. At the time they were paying off two temporary mortgages but expected permanent finance and lower repayments in a few months. The Credit Tribunal approved their repayment plan: their difficulties were temporary and they had not been improvident initially. The possibility of long delay in permanent finance and refinancing fees did not occur to them, although they might have occurred to better-educated consumers. The Credit Tribunal commented that little hardship would result to the creditor because it had security for the debt and had received a return of 37 per cent per annum nominal interest rate for the first year of the loan. Moreover, it took the risk of delay by not making any inquiries as to creditworthiness.

An orderly payment of debts has the dual advantage of reducing consumer anxiety and at the same time of guaranteeing payment to creditors. One possibility for the orderly repayment of a number of creditors where they might prove resistant in negotiation is to obtain an administration order in the county court, whereby all debts are consolidated and the debtor makes regular payments to the court which distributes them to the creditors.[206] Administration orders are not used extensively – there were 1653 applications in 1980, of which 1252 were granted, the great bulk involving payment in full of debts over £500[207] – because jurisdiction is limited to a total indebtedness of about £5000 and to situations where at least one judgment debt is outstanding, and because they require either an application by a debtor or for the court to take the initiative when an attachment of earnings order is being considered. An administration order has the advantage of staying all proceedings by creditors to whom it applies, and courts are apparently fairly benevolent in suspending orders when consumers are in temporary difficulties. For amounts greater than £5000, a consolidated attachment of earnings order may be appropriate.[208] Court-administered debt consolidation like the administration order and the consolidated attachment of earnings is to be preferred to the private enterprise system of debt pooling which operates in some parts of North America. Debt pooling has given rise to various abuses and legislation has been enacted in a number of jurisdictions to control it.[209]

Bankruptcy is the obvious course for defaulters in the more serious cases because it offers the prospect of a fresh start when the order is finally discharged. Present bankruptcy law, however, has a number of disadvantages from the point of view of consumers.[210] There is the obvious effect on a consumer's reputation, coupled with the limitation on his ability to obtain credit because of the legal obligation to inform potential creditors of his bankrupt status.[211] Hardship also arises because a bankrupt has to contribute to his creditors from after-acquired property.[212] Delay in obtaining a formal discharge can also disadvantage consumers. The Australian Law Reform Commission has suggested comprehensive legislation involving a moratorium on debt recovery actions for consumers, as long as they use the procedures under it for an orderly repayment of creditors. The procedures would be available outside bankruptcy, and would include arrangements where payment in full was not expected. The procedures would not involve meetings of creditors, but instead creditors would be informed by post and they would signify approval in the same way. The legislation would be coupled with a scheme to train persons in the art of debt counselling.[213]

Enforcement of the judgment debt

A creditor who obtains a money judgment against a consumer in the event of a default – for arrears in instalments, for the full amount outstanding (less a rebate) if an acceleration clause is valid, for the losses incurred if the consumer has repudiated a hire purchase agreement, etc. – can seek to enforce it in a number of ways if, as is likely, the consumer cannot satisfy it. A county court judgment may be followed by a warrant of execution whereby personal property of the consumer can be seized (with the exception of the family's clothing and bedding, and the debtor's tools of trade below a certain amount) and sold at a public auction to satisfy the judgment.[214] Execution in this way is not always satisfactory from the point of view of creditors: one study of the first returns on 115 warrants of execution issued by a London county court found that in forty-three there were problems of obtaining access to the property and in another fifty-one the warrant could not be satisfied because the property was the subject of hire purchase agreements – and hence not available for execution – or not worth the cost of removal and sale.[215] Consumers can be driven to borrow at high interest rates to stave off execution – in this sense the immediate creditor may be satisfied, but from the point of view of the consumer the situation has hardly improved. Other grave drawbacks to execution for the consumers are the wide powers the bailiffs have in using force to levy execution,[216] the limited categories of items which are exempt and the low resale that items fetch when sold. However, a current study into the enforcement of county court judgments for debt under the direction of Professor R. M. Goode has found that for one court only 0.8 per cent of the total warrants issued were enforced by sale. Difficulties from the point of view of creditors are also associated with other methods of satisfying a judgment such as a charging order on the consumer's home – the Court of Appeal has warned courts against issuing a charging order when a debtor is likely to be insolvent and the order would give an advantage to the creditor applying for it[217] – or initiating bankruptcy, whereupon other creditors will be able to put in rival claims.

A popular form of enforcing judgment now is an attachment of earnings order, a procedure which was introduced in 1971 following the report of the Payne Committee.[218] Attachment of earnings was the *quid pro quo* for abolition of imprisonment, which had existed for centuries as the ultimate method of enforcing debts. Imprisonment for debt still exists in other jurisdictions like Australia, where it is often imposed without regard to ordinary standards of due process.[219] Imprisonment for debt is, of course, largely futile in getting consumers to pay because most default arises not from recalcitrance but from misfortune, and because imprisonment cuts off debtors from the capacity to repay. An attachment order directs the debtor's employer to deduct certain amounts from the debtor's earnings and periodically to pay these to the court which distributes them to creditors. The court fixes a rate of earnings so that they will not fall below a certain minimum – the protected earnings rate – usually fixed at the supplementary benefits level.[220]

A creditor can be awarded costs on applying for an attachment order, which can constitute a substantial additional burden for the consumer. Much concern has been expressed that an attachment order can jeopardize a consumer's employment because the employer might object to the burdens of collection; if this occurred it would defeat the very purpose of the attachment order, because debtors would no longer be in regular employment to pay the order. The Attachment of Earnings Act 1971 tries to avoid this by allowing employers to deduct an amount from the earnings attached for administration.[221] In addition, an employer who dismisses an employee because of an attachment order will probably be liable to pay compensation for unfair dismissal. Nevertheless, one study of county court registrars found that some had experienced cases of dismissal of employees with attachment orders, and for this reason they operated a system of 'suspended' attachment of earnings orders, which were not enforced if the debtor paid the creditor regularly.[222] There seems no reason for not adopting a provision similar to that in other jurisdictions which prohibit an employer from discharging an employee with an attachment of earnings order.[223]

A Canadian study showed that attachment orders undermine the incentive to work because consumers can obtain as much in welfare payments, which are not subject to attachment, as when they are working.[224] For these reasons the courts should not impose attachment of earnings orders as freely as they can at present. Attachment of earnings orders should be a last resort for debtors who will not pay voluntarily after receiving suitable counselling and an adequate period of time to pay. As long as the law continues to allow creditors to use its processes to enforce debts, however, attachment of earnings orders seem a more satisfactory method of enforcing judgments against debtors than imprisonment or a rigorous execution against their real or personal property.[225]

Reform of the law

A number of disturbing features associated with creditors' remedies have been discussed; for example, even though a creditor may obtain a low value for an item which it has repossessed compared with its retail value, it still has the right to sue for its losses ('deficiency'). One of the reforms in the Crowther Credit Act 1974 is that a creditor cannot enforce any security taken in relation to a regulated agreement (e.g. over the consumer's other property) so as to benefit to an extent greater than would be the case under the agreement itself.[226] Reform in other jurisdictions has taken the course of closing off to creditors one of their two remedies: repossession (proceeding against the security), or the personal action in damages. Several jurisdictions oblige creditors to elect between the two remedies when consumers default ('seize or sue' provisions).[227] Saskatchewan goes further and limits the right of creditors to proceeding against the security; creditors cannot sue for any part of the purchase price.[228] From the point of view of creditors this is probably the least satisfactory course because they say that, except for cars, boats, etc., the resale value of most items sold on credit is very low. The great virtue of the Saskatchewan approach is that creditors have every incentive to obtain the best price possible on selling an item which has been repossessed. The alternative of abolishing security in consumer credit transactions seems to have growing support, because it would curb the abuses associated with repossession and the problem of items being resold at a substantial undervalue. Certainly, it would confirm a trend in modern forms of credit, such as retailers' credit sales and credit cards, towards giving credit without security. Even some finance houses have abandoned the idea of security by moving away from hire purchase to personal loans without taking a bill of sale. Mr Justice White, then Chairman of the South Australian Credit Tribunal, suggested:

Industry reliance upon security . . . does not appear to be based so much on present favourable levels of consumer dishonesty and collection efficiency as on lending habits acquired from another age . . . and on industry's preference for the well-trodden path of volume (secured) sales to that of making proper inquiries as to creditworthiness. Why go to the trouble and expense of proper inquiries when they might prejudice a possible sale?[229]

A fundamental question is whether creditors should be entitled to any remedies at law. Why should the state lend its support to enforcement of consumer debt? Why should the law become the collection arm of business? The great bulk of consumers – some 95 per cent – repay the credit advanced to them without difficulty, and consumers who strike problems are mainly those on lower incomes who experience illness or unemployment. It is inaccurate to say that consumers freely contract credit agreements, and therefore the state should help creditors enforce them, because many consumers are pressed into credit agreements at both a personal and societal level. There will be a small number of consumers who will practise fraud, but they can be dealt with by the criminal law.[230] If creditors were denied the law's assistance, the incentive to consumers to repay credit would not derive from the threat of legal processes at present, but from the fear of an adverse credit rating. To be balanced against this of course is that a greater invasion of privacy might be entailed.

Abolition of creditors' rights to enforce consumer credit transactions might lead to extra-judicial methods of collection, but the criminal law and licensing could do much to curb this. Another consequence of abolishing creditors' legal remedies might be an increase in the cost of credit to cover bad debts.[231] Just how severe this would be is the subject of some doubt, but it does not deter adherents to market economic theory from concluding that an important number of consumers, especially the poor, would be excluded from the credit market. One study which has some bearing on the matter was conducted in Wisconsin after the law there placed curbs on self-help repossession and required notice to be given to debtors and an opportuntiy for a judicial hearing. It concluded that there had not been a substantial decline in motorcar loans after the change, although there was a marginal impact in restricting credit availability because retailers required larger down-payments.[232] Were the law's assistance to be denied to creditors, alternative institutions, like credit unions, could be encouraged to assist those consumers adversely affected by restrictions on availability.

INSTITUTIONAL CHANGES IN CONSUMER CREDIT

Reforms have already been suggested in a number of areas of consumer credit law further to protect consumers. Credit counselling has been mentioned as a development to assist consumers who get into difficulty. Should creditors still be entitled to enforce credit agreements at law, moratorium periods are necessary, longer than those provided by the present provisions for a default notice, to give consumers time to get out of difficulties. Consumer education is a solution suggested by a number of writers, and although its benefits in familiarizing consumers with the nature of credit and credit transactions should not be downgraded, it is a little facile to think it will have much effect on the level of default so long as such strong pressures bear on consumers to purchase on credit. If the desirability of credit is accepted then it seems that institutional reforms are one way of ensuring that consumers can obtain credit on reasonable terms with a reasonable prospect of repaying it.

Credit unions are a development which has attracted favourable comment in consumer circles. Credit unions began in Europe in the nineteenth century as mutual aid organizations, spread to North America in the early twentieth century, and have taken root in many developing countries since then. The idea of a credit union is the common pooling of financial resources by those having a common bond – occupational, religious, professional, etc. – which can then be used to provide loans to its members. Credit unions in their literature draw on the Rochdale principles, drafted by the first consumer cooperative in Rochdale in 1844, and emphasize values such as democratic control in which each member has one vote in the annual meeting of the organization.[233]

The rate of interest charged by the credit unions is uniform for all borrowers and relatively low. Loans seldom extend over more than three or four years, because otherwise capital is tied up by only a few members. Credit unions usually vet the purpose for which a loan is needed and the standard manual for credit union lenders states, rather paternistically,

> The Credit Committee is concerned with the applicant's welfare. It is not enough for the loan to be safe. It must be for a worthwhile purpose that will prove helpful to the borrower. . . . [M]any loans are made for the purpose of self or family improvement or to enable members to acquire things which result in a better living for them.[234]

Loans normally only cover the purchase of consumer durables and are not large enough for house purchase, for example. Borrowers obtain protection insurance so that the loan can be repaid in the event of death or disability of the borrower. The shares of a borrower in the credit union also act as a form of security. In its formative years a credit union usually relies heavily on the voluntary effort of members in running the organization, but this can have the advantage that annual dividends and interest refunds to borrowers are possible.

Credit unions are strongest in the United States, where they are big business: $12.2 billion of credit was provided in 1970, 12 per cent of the total instalments credit in the United States, and a twentyfold increase over the previous twenty years. State and national organizations supply services to local credit unions, stabilize the funds of member groups and generally promote credit unions by advertising, and so on. American credit unions are now using share drafts, which resemble bank cheques, over strenuous objections from banking circles. Occupational credit unions are the largest category, associations come next (religious, professional, etc.) and residential last. The early credit unions in the United States were directed to productive purposes – mainly loans for small businesses and farmers. The early driving forces behind the credit unions there saw them not as anti-capitalist but as a basically conservative force to make employees more content and efficient and thus less likely to adhere to radical principles.[235] Similarly, American credit unions' leaders in the 1950s promoted credit unions in developing countries because they conceived them as 'bulwarks against Communism'. In the 1960s, those involved in the War on Poverty thought that credit unions might be the answer to the problems which the American poor experienced with credit, as well as providing an example of community action. The old principle of the gradual accumulation of savings was abandoned and the Office of Economic Opportunity subsidized management, office space and other overhead costs. Generally the movement was a failure: the default rate was high, poor consumers without employment were hardly in a position to contribute to credit unions' funds and, most importantly, the Republicans cut off federal funding in 1970.[236]

Credit unions in Britain have had a very slow growth.[237] The majority owe their origin to immigrants, who brought the idea with them. One factor inhibiting the growth of credit unions in Britain has been the existence of alternative sources of credit like hire purchase and check trading. Another explanation has been the lack of a modern legislative framework. However, the Credit Unions Act 1979 creates a legislative framework for the operation and supervision of credit unions.[238] A society which meets the requirements of the Credit Unions Act 1979 may be registered as a credit union under the Industrial and Provident Societies Act 1965 (s. 1(1)(2)). Admission to membership of the society must be restricted to those having a common bond (ss. 1(2), (5)). The rules must provide that the qualifications for admission to membership is following a particular occupation, residing in a particular locality, being employed in a particular locality or by a particular employer, being a member of a *bona fide* organization or otherwise associated, or such other quali- fication as the registrar approves (s. 1(4)). Only registered credit unions can use that description (s. 3). Savings must be in £1 shares, and no member can hold generally more than £2000 in shares (ss. 5, 7). Credit unions must have a minimum of twenty-one members and generally not more than 5000 members (ss. 6(1)–(2)). Loans may be made 'for a provident or productive purpose' but cannot be more than £2000 in excess of a member's total paid-up shareholding, must be repaid with a maximum of five years (if secured) or two years (if unsecured), and generally cannot involve interest in excess of 1 per cent per month on the amount outstanding (s. 11). The Chief Registrar can prescribe the manner in which credit union funds may be invested, and credit unions must establish a general reserve (ss. 13, 14). With approval, credit unions can make insurance arrangements to protect members against loss (s. 16). The Chief Registrar is empowered to appoint inspectors to investigate the affairs of a credit union, to suspend certain of its operations and to cancel or suspend its registration (ss. 18–20).

The National Consumer Council has been encouraging the establishment of bulk-buying associations based on a place of work or in a community. Products are bought in bulk at a discount and then sold to consumers at a lower rate than that obtained in ordinary retail outlets. One difficulty with bulk buying is that in the present state of the law a consumer receiving a defective product may not have an action against the business from which it was obtained. The buyer in law might be the association organizer, unless he or she can be regarded as an agent for group members. So far bulk buying has been mainly confined to food, but bulk-buying associations in other countries enable members to obtain a fairly wide range of products on credit of up to a month.

Insurance is one means of reducing the risk for commercial institutions when they extend credit to low-income consumers who subsequently fall into difficulties through illness, etc. One possibility would be a government-supported system of insurance. Creditors would still be obliged to vet a customer before extending credit, and a high rate of claims against it would lead to its exclusion from the scheme. Government-subsidized loans for low-income consumers are another reform. Strangely enough, these existed in a form during the Middle Ages in Europe. Florence set up a municipal pawnshop to combat high interest rates in 1472 and the idea spread, although an attempt along similar lines in London apparently floundered.[239] Jurisdictions with government-owned banks should be able to institute such a scheme relatively easily although there would undoubtedly be opposition from existing financial institutions. Another move is that social welfare offices should be encouraged to use existing statutory powers more readily to provide loans to those in temporary difficulties through unemployment or illness.[240] Special funds for this purpose would be one way of furthering the practice. Government-run institutions providing credit to low-income consumers, however, seem the best method of eliminating, or at least reducing, many of the problems which presently arise in the consumer credit area.

PART III
Public control

8
Broad statutory standards

The simplest form of public regulation is where legislation announces a standard of behaviour in broad terms and imposes penalties on any deviation from it. In some cases the standard may be taken from the private law, so that it is simply the remedial law that is changed. Broad statutory standards usually operate so that official action is deferred until wrong-doing occurs. The individual has the choice of complying with the standard or of violating it and incurring a penalty.[1] The assumption is that the majority of those being regulated will choose to comply with the standard. So many laws are enacted that if the majority did not obey, law enforcement agencies could not cope.[2] Public compliance with broad statutory standards is assisted if they correspond with societal values and if they are precise and well known so that individuals can bring their behaviour into line without much official guidance. The major difference between broad statutory standards and other forms of public regulation is usually that the former need fewer resources for enforcement. The drain on enforcement resources increases, however, if specific exemptions from the standard can be made, or if breaches are difficult to detect or to prove.

Broad statutory standards, backed by criminal sanctions, are generally an unsophisticated instrument of regulation and not always a satisfactory method of controlling undesirable features such as business acts prejudicial to consumers. First, their edge is blunted because they compete with each other for enforcement. A method of counteracting this tendency is to entrust the enforcement of a particular type of standard to a specialized agency, the success of which is then identified with its vigorous application.[3] Thus consumer laws ought to be enforced by separate consumer protection departments and not by the police. Secondly, if there is some uncertainty as to the application of a broad standard, there is a temptation for enforcement authorities to refrain from taking any action because of the possibility of not being successful. Thirdly, broad criminal standards are not interpreted liberally because, as a matter of course, courts construe criminal statutes narrowly. While this may be justified where individual liberty is at stake, it is different with matters like consumer offences and imprisonment is hardly ever involved. Fourthly, criminal procedure is inappropriate when applied to intricate consumer offences.[4] Existing criminal procedure evolved for discovering truth in straightforward crimes like murder or theft, where evidence is relatively simple and is capable of being assessed by ordinary citizens comprising a jury or a bench of lay magistrates. By contrast, some consumer offences are relatively complex and in some cases can only be understood by experts. Detailed regulatory control greatly reduces the difficulty in such cases because it narrows the issues and usually results in expert witnesses having a larger role in appraising the evidence.

The burden of enforcing broad statutory standards in consumer matters is somewhat eased because the great bulk are strict liability offences. Penalties can be incurred for their unintentional or in-advertent breach.[5] The crucial question is whether the elements of the prohibited act (the *actus reus*) have been committed, and it is irrelevant whether there is *mens rea*. In law there is a presumption that offences require *mens rea* in the absence of a clear legislative indication to the contrary.[6] Quite early, however, it was accepted that consumer protection offences are generally among those regulatory offences where the presumption is displaced.[7] With some consumer protection statutes the courts have been assisted in this interpretation by the need for there to be intention in certain, but not all, of the offences in a particular statute; by the fact that imprisonment is not a necessary penalty; and perhaps most importantly, by the insertion of specific defences which would have little role in the absence of strict liability.[8]

The major policy reason for making consumer offences strict liability offences is the overriding need to protect the public from social harm. When an offence occurs consumers are concerned that they have been harmed, and whether the business involved has a guilty mind is irrelevant to them. The assumption is that businesses are never completely innocent, for they can always reorder their affairs to avoid breaches of statutory standards. Indeed, this is true as a matter of law because, as we shall see below, the statutory defences in consumer legislation enable a business to avoid liability where, to put it in general terms, it is not at fault. In other words strict liability in consumer protection matters does not involve punishing the 'morally blameless'.[9] Strict liability also makes for convenience in law enforcement. It would be virtually impossible to penalize undesirable business behaviour if it were necessary to establish *mens rea* in each case. A survey of consumer protection departments and environmental health departments found that the overwhelming view was that strict liability was crucial to the process of investigation and prosecution.[10] An argument of some commentators is that strict liability offences are shielded from the process of being regarded as criminal. In other words, because they dispense with the requirement of *mens rea* they are not regarded as morally reprehensible, and hence their effectiveness is weakened.[11] The fact is, however, that there are other more important reasons why the impact of the law in areas like consumer protection is diluted. The high status of businessmen – an outcome, in part, of their association with production – is one reason that those who commit offences are not condemned by the community.[12] A further argument against strict liability is that it makes it difficult for courts to distinguish between the unscrupulous and the less serious offender, and that there is a tendency to impose uniformly low penalties which are not a burden to the former.[13] In practice enforcement bodies can use the general reputation of a business as an element in exercising discretion to prosecute, and courts might also be able to identify unscrupulous businesses after conviction from the antecedents made known for sentencing.

An important correlate of broad statutory standards is that a fairly wide discretion will repose in the relevant enforcement agency. Some discretion is always present with law enforcement, partly because of the vagueness of language and the need to apply legal categories to specific circumstances, but generally speaking an enforcement body will possess less discretion if standards are detailed and specific. Discretion involves flexibility, and it may be that Parliament chooses a general standard in preference to other forms of regulation which can be adapted according to changing social conditions. In other words Parliament feels incapable of dealing with the details of regulation and deliberately entrusts the task to an enforcement body which, it assumes, will have the advantages of flexibility and accumulated expertise. Of course, broad and vague standards may also result from a failure of legislative draftmanship or because a statute incorporates competing and inconsistent values.

This chapter deals with three types of broad statutory standards in the consumer protection area: those relating to misdescriptions, quality and quantity. It then turns to the complexities of corporate criminal liability as they affect prosecutions for the breach of such standards.

TRADE DESCRIPTIONS

Consumers' buying decisions can be influenced by the manner in which products and services are described. If this is inaccurate, consumers can easily be misled and suffer financial loss. Legislation prohibiting false or misleading descriptions goes part of the way to protecting consumers in such circumstances. In Britain the Trade Descriptions Act 1968 is the most important legislation in the area. There is comparable legislation in other jurisdictions. The predecessor of the Trade Descriptions Act 1968, the Merchandise Marks Act 1887, had its origins in attempts by certain businesses to protect themselves from what they regarded as the threat of unfair competition.[14] As originally conceived, the legislation was directed against businesses which falsely portrayed their products by copying the marks and names of others. Later, it penalized businesses which incorrectly indicated that imported items were manufactured in the United Kingdom. The basic prohibition against the application of false, and later misleading, written descriptions was somewhat unclear, had a limited scope and was rarely enforced.[15]

The Trade Descriptions Act 1968, originally entitled the Protection of Consumers (Trade Descriptions) Bill, is an outcome of the report of the Molony Committee on Consumer Protection.[16] Unlike its predecessor, the Trade Descriptions Act 1968 is clearly a consumer protection measure. The Trade Descriptions Act 1968 extended the ambit of the previous law by clearly including oral misdescriptions and false statements about prices and services, by clarifying the law relating to advertisements, and by imposing an obligation on consumer protection departments to enforce the legislation.

Descriptions dealt with by legislation such as the Trade Descriptions Act 1968 fall conveniently under four main headings: descriptions of products, prices, services and property. From the point of view of enforcement this order seems to reflect the relative importance of the different aspects. In Britain, between 30 November 1968 (when the Trade Descriptions Act 1968 came into force) and 31 March 1975, 8489 cases were brought to court, in 7477 of which the defendants were convicted on one or more counts (another 706 cases were pending.) Products accounted for 4443 convictions; prices for 2260 and services for 774. (The Act is without a specific provision for misdescriptions of property.) The categories of products and services involved in these cases are set out in Table 8.1.[17]

Table 8.1   Convictions under the Trade Descriptions Act 1968: Products, Prices and Services

	Misdescribed products	False price claims	Misdescribed services, etc.
Motor vehicles & accessories	2533	86	Accommodation, holiday & travel 167
Food and drink	390	697	
Soap, detergents & toilet requisites	29	985	Repairs & servicing 288
Solid & liquid fuels	298	64	Laundering & dry-cleaning 15
Clothing & textiles	281	113	Others 304
Others	912	315	
Total	4443	2260	774

Misdescribed products

Section 1(1) of the Trade Descriptions Act 1968 prohibits persons in the course of trade or business from applying a false trade description to products and from supplying (or offering to supply) any falsely described products. The requirement that an offender be in the course of trade or business clearly excludes transactions involving private persons. However, the section encompasses ancillary business dealings, as where a car hire firm sells its cars after using them.[18] A trade description covered by the statute is 'an indication, direct or indirect, and by whatever means given', of the matters mentioned in section 2(1):

(a) quantity, size or gauge;
(b) method of manufacture, production, processing or reconditioning;
(c) composition;
(d) fitness for purpose, strength, performance, behaviour or accuracy;
(e) any physical characteristics not included in the preceding paragraphs;
(f) testing by any person and results thereof;
(g) approval by any person or conformity with a type approved by any person;
(h) place or date of manufacture, production, processing or reconditioning;
(i) person by whom manufactured, produced, processed or reconditioned;
(j) other history, including previous ownership or use.

Omitted from the list are matters such as the identity and standing of businesses and the contents and authorship of books, films and records. In addition the results and the fact of testing might not be covered if standing alone and not in combination. It has also been said that the section needs widening, for it leaves untouched businesses which create false impressions that consumers are paying trade prices by describing themselves as 'discount stores' or as 'wholesale supplies'.[19] Reference is made to the German Law on Unfair Competition 1909, under which it has been held that a business must not portray itself to a consumer as a wholesaler if its consumer prices are higher than those charged to other businesses, even if the larger part of its sales are to the latter.

The ambit of a false trade description of a product is defined in sections 3–5. Trade descriptions, to be caught by the statute, must be false to a material degree (s. 3(1)), but the prohibition extends to trade descriptions which, although not false, are misleading (s. 3(2)). Anything which, although not a trade description, is likely to be taken as such is covered (s. 3(3)), along with situations where a purchaser uses a trade description in ordering and products are supplied pursuant to the order (s. 4(3)). A false trade description can be annexed to a product, made orally, or contained in an advertisement (ss. 4–5). An offer to supply a product extends to where a business exposes for supply (to cover invitations to treat) or has it in its possession for supply (s. 6). Use of the term 'supply' covers hire purchase, hiring and giving away as part of a promotion, as well as ordinary sales.

A wide range of situations have been handled under section 1.[20] Table 8.1 shows, however, that the rather mundane misdescriptions of cars and accessories predominate in prosecutions. The prevalence of these in the offences that come to official attention is attributed to the malpractices of second-hand car dealers and to the willingness of consumers to complain (perhaps because, apart from a house, cars are likely to be the most expensive items they ever purchase). Prosecutions have been successfully directed against the sales techniques of second-hand car dealers, in particular the language employed in effecting sales. For example the phrase 'beautiful' when applied to a car has been held to refer to both the appearance and running of a vehicle and to constitute a false trade description if the car is unroadworthy.[21]

The largest number of detected offences has been in relation to the purported mileage of vehicles. An incorrect odometer is capable of being a false trade description in that it is an indication of the history or use of a vehicle (s. 2(1) (j)), even though the seller does not know about the falsity.[22] However, second-hand car dealers can protect themselves by disclaimers, which are discussed below. Jurisdictions such as those in the United States and Australia have felt the need for specific prohibitions against making false statements about, or tampering with, odometers.[23] Under this legislation, car dealers must also provide consumers with a written statement of the mileage, and if no statement is given, or if it is knowingly false, the consumer can obtain damages. Because of his conclusion that the practice of 'clocking' cars has reached the level of widespread fraud in the United Kingdom, the Director General of Fair Trading has recommended various measures: that the vehicle registration document be re-designed and expanded to list the names and addresses of as many previous keepers as possible to make it easier to check the history of the car; that urgent consideration be given to the introduction of legislation to require the installation of tamper-proof odometers in all new cars sold; and that legislation be introduced requiring the provision of a written statement to accompany used cars, including a statement of whether or not the mileage reading has been verified.[24] The vehicle registration document has been changed, although a full listing of previous owners can apparently still be avoided by 'losing' the document and using fictitious names, and the so-called tamper-proof odometers being voluntarily introduced by some manufacturers can be clocked without too much difficulty.[25]

In considering whether there is a trade description, whether it is false, and whether it is false to a material degree, the courts use the test: what is the impression likely to be made on the minds of ordinary consumers to whom it is directed?[26] From this follows a number of subsidiary conclusions. First, even if experts or more experienced consumers are likely to discount a description does not make it any the less false or misleading.[27] Secondly, the issue is not whether a false description actually affected the consumer whose complaint gives rise to a prosecution, it is whether it is likely to affect ordinary consumers. The fact that the particular consumer was not deceived is immaterial although it may be a mitigating factor in fixing the penalty.[28] Conversely, evidence that a consumer or that consumers have been misled is not conclusive. Thirdly, a statement of opinion might constitute a direct or indirect indication of the matters constituting a trade description, and in any event is likely to be taken as such.[29] Fourthly some, but not a great deal of, latitude is allowed for 'puff', which consumers discount as meaningless.[30] Finally, it is also irrelevant that a particular transaction is on the whole fair to the consumer involved.[31] In determining the effect of a description on ordinary consumers the judges use hunch, and their knowledge and experience of the world (such as it is). Unlike business executives, they do not have access to empirical research about the actual impact on consumer behaviour of descriptions applied to particular products.

In relation to these matters, is it necessary for a significant section of the public to be misled? To put it differently, when assessing the impression likely to be made on the minds of ordinary consumers, are ordinary consumers reasonable consumers or do they encompass, as some decisions in the United States and Australia suggest, 'the ignorant, the unthinking and the credulous, who, in making purchases, do not stop to analyze, but are governed by appearances and general impressions'?[32] In *Parkdale Custom Built Furniture Pty Ltd* v. *Puxu Pty Ltd*,[33] where the High Court of Australia held that it was not engaging in misleading conduct to market a lounge suite almost identical to that made by another manufacturer, if properly labelled, Murphy J. endorsed the latter approach. Gibbs C.J., however, adopted the test of the reasonable consumer.

Although it is true, as has often been said, that ordinarily a class of consumers may include the inexperienced as well as the experienced, and the gullible as well as the astute, the section must in my opinion be regarded as contemplating the effect of the conduct on reasonable members of the class. The heavy burdens which the section creates cannot have been intended to be imposed for the benefit of persons who fail to take reasonable care of their own interests. (pp. 717–18)

Mason J. took a middle path: the class to be protected by the particular section varied according to the facts of the case. With relatively expensive items one would in the ordinary course expect consumers, within the admittedly wide range of potential purchasers, to exercise somewhat more vigilance than with less expensive items or those with less aesthetic importance in the home.[34] Quite apart from its apparent inconsistency with legislative purpose to protect all consumers including the inexperienced, the ignorant and the un-educated, the Gibbs-Mason approach can be faulted because it turns on the judges determining whether a description or conduct is misleading. Thus in *Parkdale* Gibbs C.J. and Mason J. held that consumers ought to have looked for and detected a label, only 2½ inch square, which could be tucked under the upholstery, when buying a suite of the type mentioned.

Despite the wide wording of the prohibition contained in section 1(1)(a) of the Trade Descriptions Act 1968, the English courts have held that to fall within it a false trade description must be connected with the supply of a product. In *Wickens Motors (Gloucester) Ltd* v. *Hall*,[35] forty days after a consumer purchased a second-hand car he returned to the defendant car dealers to complain. An employee told him: 'There is nothing wrong with the car,' whereas it was unroadworthy then and at the time of sale. The Divisional Court held that no offence had been committed because any false trade description applied had not been associated with the sale of the car. The justification for this conclusion was that a broad application had never previously been suggested during eighty years of the Merchandise Marks Acts – strange reasoning when the Act was hardly ever enforced and when it is the nature of appellate litigation to raise points never previously suggested. On the other hand the courts have said that there is no need for a person who applies a false trade description to be a contracting party to the transaction.[36]

Under the civil law the sale of many products is regarded as being by description even if consumers select a product themselves.[37] In addition, where the purpose of a product is obvious, consumers benefit from the condition of fitness implied by law, although they do not specify the purpose for which they require it.[38] Are implied trade descriptions similarly covered by the criminal law? For example, can the mere appearance of a product be held to constitute a trade description about its fitness for purpose under section 2(1)(d)? If these questions are answered in the affirmative, the effect would be to impose criminal liability for products that are below the standard normally expected and the obligations about quality implied in the sale of products by the Sale of Goods Act would be transformed into criminal obligations. Many consumers would support such a move because when they receive shoddy products their remedies in civil law sometimes prove illusory and the criminal law might be a good way of deterring businesses from selling such products.[39] Further, the criminal law applies if consumers ask the right questions and a trade description is used. Why should there be a distinction between a shoddy product sold without being described and the same product sold when falsely described? Commentators point out that the two situations are different because false descriptions may induce consumers to buy when otherwise they would not do so. They also regard the introduction of implied descriptions into the criminal law as undesirable because of the uncertainty it would engender. For example, the purpose of articles is not always self-evident – it is not always clear whether they are bought for design or performance.[40] But the policy question still remains: would not the criminal law be the best means of ensuring that shoddy products are not marketed?

It is clear that there is no need for an express trade description before the Trade Descriptions Act 1968 can be invoked (s. 3(3)). It is also clear that an omission may render a description misleading.[41] In addition a trade description is regarded as being applied if used in any manner likely to be taken as referring to a product (s. 4(1)(c)). But can the analysis be taken one step further, that the mere appearance of a product might sometimes be such that a trade description can be implied?[42] R. v. Ford Co. Ltd[43] has now established that as a general rule there is no scope for implied trade descriptions. That case involved a consumer purchasing a Ford motor car which he thought was new and which was so described in an invoice. The car had been damaged while it was in a compound awaiting retail delivery, but repairs had been effected. The documentation between Ford and the retailer did not contain the word 'new' but the Court of Appeal (Criminal Division) held that the order form was such that it gave an indirect indication that the trade description 'new' was being applied. In considering the matter the court rejected the proposition that whenever there is an implied term of a contract of sale relating to a matter covered by the Act, there is a corresponding application of a trade description.

This seems to us to go much too far; it would be very startling if, for instance, the effect of the 1968 Act were to make a criminal of every seller of goods by description who delivers goods in breach of the condition of merchantable quality which is implied by s. 14(2) of the Sale of Goods Act 1893.[44]

The court then developed three criteria for identifying a new car: it should not have been previously sold by retail, nor travelled miles significantly in excess of what may be expected for delivery to a retailer, nor have been repaired unless the damage, although extensive, is either superficial or limited in area and is repaired to a satisfactory condition that it can be said that it is as good as new.[45]

Businesses can circumvent the consequences of their false trade descriptions by the use of disclaimers.[46] Their legal efficacy derives from the fact that whether or not there is a false trade description applied to a product depends on the whole description, and that includes the presence of any disclaimer. Analytically, an effective disclaimer prevents a false trade description arising in the first place. If a disclaimer is not effective in this way it might still constitute a defence under section 24.[47] The policy justification for disclaimers is to enable retailers to negate a description, already applied to a product by a supplier, the truth of which they doubt but which cannot easily be altered. A similar situation arises when a description originally true becomes false but is difficult to change (as in a mail order catalogue). There is the danger that disclaimers can undermine the protection afforded by the legislation. The courts have said that disclaimers must be as bold, precise and compelling as the description. For example, the use of a general disclaimer in one part of a shop cannot negate descriptions on particular products.[48] Another example is that disclaimers of odometer readings generally cannot be effected by casual remarks during negotiations, by small print clauses in contractual documents, or by a notice inside a dealer's office.[49] Moreover, the words of a disclaimer must be unambiguous and render a description meaningless; if not, the disclaimer itself might constitute a false trade description. In *Corfield* v. *Starr*[50] the disclaimer in relation to an odometer read: 'With deep regret due to the Customers Protection Act we can no longer verify that the mileage shown on this vehicle is correct.' The Divisional Court held that the reference to a non-existent Act and the actual phraseology was misleading since it suggested that the mileage was correct, but that this could not be said.

What of unscrupulous businesses applying false descriptions, and then using disclaimers to avoid liability in the hope that the disclaimer will not entirely neutralize the impact of the description? An example is a second-hand car dealer who turns back odometers but uses prominent disclaimers. The courts have held that they will not permit disclaimers in situations where the charge is of applying a false trade description and the circumstances indicate that this was done intentionally.[51] Another problem which disclaimers raise is that businesses might cease to make checks but might use disclaimers to repudiate liability. The extent to which they do this is limited, however, because they may be reluctant to create apprehension among prospective customers about the quality of their merchandise by widespread use of disclaimers.

Mispricing

Legislation prohibiting false statements of price is quite distinct from price control. The present concern is not with selling at an unduly high price, but with false representations about price. British law in this area is limited when compared with that of other countries. Section 11 of the Trade Descriptions Act 1968 creates three specific offences: it is an offence to give a false indication that a price is equal to or less than the recommended price (11(1)(a)); to give a false indication about a price previously charged (11(1)(b)); or to give an indication that a price is less than that actually being charged (11(2)). Section 11 only applies to persons offering to supply goods – services are not covered.

Many prosecutions for false statements regarding recommended prices are for 'flash offers' – the '3p off'-type claim – which are especially prevalent in the marketing of detergents, washing powders and similar products, but not limited to them. Flash offers fall within the section by virtue of s. 11(3)(c) – they are 'likely to be taken as an indication as to a recommended price'. These offences are easy to prove and consumer protection departments justify prosecution because of their prevalence and the way they mislead customers. Indeed, flash offers confuse consumers even when they are correctly marked. A survey in 1975 showed only 55 per cent of respondents approved the practice and only one-half understood that the reduction was incorporated in the retailers' price markings and was not deducted at the check-out. Two years later a similar survey found that less than half the respondents thought such price reductions to be genuine. More recently, of a random national sample of nearly a thousand, while some three-quarters thought it was useful to know a manufacturer's recommended price, only 54 per cent thought the comparison 'Manufacturer's recommended price £x – Our price £y' was good, and a quarter thought it was likely to mislead.[52] Should recommended prices be allowed at all? Among arguments in favour of recommended prices is that they are necessary to guarantee the margins of distributors and to avoid excessive price-cutting and other unethical practices.[53] Administrative convenience for retailers in pricing their goods – calculating, negotiating and marking prices – is another factor mentioned, although this is not as compelling a reason where competition means widespread divergence from recommended prices or where retailers handle a small range of products.[54] Recommended prices are also said to assist consumers: they can see whether they are obtaining a bargain and competition between manufacturers is promoted.

On the other hand the Monopolies Commission concluded that recommended prices may reduce price competition by inducing retailers to charge the one price and that the government should have power to prohibit them.[55] Such a power was contained in the Price Commission Act 1977. The Monopolies Commission and the Office of Fair Trading have concluded that recommended prices, when they are well above the actual selling price, can mislead those consumers who regard them as the normal selling price.[56] The discrepancy occurs in areas of trade where competition is vigorous but also where manufacturers deliberately set recommended prices at a high level to enable retailers to show large price cuts and where several levels of recommended prices exist so that retailers can select those which they will discount. Another reason recommended prices can be misleading is that unless consumers know the particular recommended price they cannot assess whether the reduction has been made by the retailer. Thus it falls to enforcement bodies, who have this information, continually to check the products which are subject to recommended price claims.[57]

In 1978 the Director General of Fair Trading recommended that all bargain offer claims which indicate that the seller's price is less than a recommended, suggested or maximum retail price should be prohibited because they were unhelpful or even positively misleading. However, the Price Marking (Bargain Offers) Order (as amended)[58] permits the comparison with recommended prices or charges except in relation to scheduled items – namely, beds, electrically-powered and similar domestic appliances, consumer electronic goods, carpets and furniture. The sectoral approach to banning recommended prices has been criticized as leading to confusion and anomalies, and to traders establishing their own list prices as a basis for price comparison advertising, regardless of whether they ever intend to charge those prices. It has also been suggested that in a number of sectors where they are permitted, some recommended prices are unrealistically high. The Director General of Fair Trading has reiterated his call for a complete ban on the use of recommended prices, but if the sectoral approach is continued has suggested additional sectors be included, that any recommended retail prices should be stated in cash terms or the difference be calculable, and that retailers be prohibited from establishing their own recommended prices.[59]

The attempt in section 11(1)(b) of the Trade Descriptions Act 1968 to strike at fictitious references by a business to a previous price it has charged produces the most bizarre results. This is because it must be read in conjunction with the statutory presumption that a reference to a previous price shall be taken as an indication of the price charged for any period of twenty-eight consecutive days in the preceding six months.[60] A completely misleading impression can therefore be given about how prices have changed. An apparent price reduction can mask a real price increase. For example, a claim 'Normally £12 – Special Offer £11' is within the law if the price was £12 in month 1, fell to £9 in months 2–5 and then increased to £11 in month 6. Further, there is an intolerable burden of enforcement placed on consumer protection departments to demonstrate that a business has not charged the higher price in the previous six months. Resources are not available to monitor continually a wide range of prices over a long period, and consequently prosecutions do not occur for this offence unless consumers complain. To overcome these difficulties proposals have been advanced to stipulate that the minimum twenty-eight day period during which the higher price has been charged should immediately precede the change in price. An alternative suggestion is that the present section should remain but that the onus of proving that a product was offered at a higher price be placed on the business making the claim.[61]

Supplementing s. 11(1)(b) is the Price Marking (Bargain Offers) Order (as amended), which prohibits references to a business's previous price unless this was charged in the ordinary course of business on the same or on other identified premises at least once (art. 3(2)(a)(i), 7(2(b)). An important aim of the provision is to avoid businesses charging a higher price on an item in one branch and then claiming in all branches that their price on that item is less than what they had previously charged at those branches. However, the provisions relating to previous prices are still deficient: it is not clear under the Orders whether the previous price has to be stated – 'particular price' in art. 3(2)(a) probably means that it does; the terms 'normal', 'usual' and 'regular' used in relation to prices do not refer unambiguously to a business's previous prices but can refer to prices charged elsewhere; a previous price has only to be charged once; and relatively meaningless claims are possible, for example, 'Normally £10 at our X store – special offer £5', when X store is at the other end of the country. The Director General of Fair Trading has recommended that the first issue be clarified, that the terms 'normal', etc. be defined as indications of a previous price, that previous price be defined as one which has been offered for a period of twenty-eight consecutive days in the previous six months (but with a reversed onus); and that comparisons should only be allowed with other identified premises in the area where the goods are offered.[62]

General 'sale' notices are misleading if the great majority of items are being sold at normal prices or if the sale items are specially made for the sale. Provided the sale items themselves are properly marked to comply with section 11 and the Price Marking (Bargain Offers) Orders, general sale notices are permissible.[63] The matter is discussed further under 'Other Misstatements'. It is sufficient to note at this point that some European countries have very tight control over sales; for example in West Germany they can only be held at certain times of the year.[64] A closely related problem to sales is dealt with in New Zealand legislation, which creates offences where a product is sold at 'cost price' but the price is higher than the amount the retailer paid to obtain it.[65]

False indications of prices at which a person is offering to supply goods are covered by section 11(2) of the Trade Descriptions Act

1968. Offences often occur with supermarket pricing; for example, items may be advertised as being at a special price although the existing prices marked on the products or shelves are not changed. The following comment of a consumer protection department is pertinent in considering whether supermarkets can avoid mistakes:

> Whilst there is no reason to believe that the traders' efforts are caused by any deliberate or intentional act, it is perhaps surprising to note that rarely do officers find prices marked below the advertised price. It is that latter feature which prompts the comments that if traders can exercise care to ensure that no trading loss is made, then they ought to be equally careful to see that no excessive charge is also made.[66]

The courts have held that the maxim *de minimis* has no relevance to supermarket mispricing of this nature, however small the discrepancy.[67] Their approach can be justified because although an individual consumer may suffer little, unfair profits accrue to businesses.

Overcharging might be caught by section 11(2) if the prices supposedly being charged are displayed. An illustration is *Whitehead* v. *Collett*,[68] where 24p was charged for two bottles of a particular brand of beer when it was 10½p a bottle on the price list. If there is to be an offence in this way, prices must somehow be displayed. Under the Prices Act 1974 the government has statutory power to require businesses to mark prices and several orders have been made, but we shall see in the next chapter that there is a hesitant approach to obliging businesses to mark prices in Britain compared with other European countries. Not all overcharging is caught by section 11(2). The Divisional Court has held that when a price has been quoted, and a contract entered into on that basis, no offence is committed if, when the item is later supplied, a higher price is demanded.[69] The legal justification given is that section 11(2) applies only to offers to supply, not to cases of supply, and that while section 1(1)(b) covers the latter it does not apply to prices. While this is the straightforward interpretation of section 11(2), an expansive approach would have been to accept that since offering to supply covers instances where persons have goods in their possession for supply (s. 6), an offence is committed under it when goods are appropriated to the contract and a higher price placed on them before delivery. The Divisional Court ignores social realities when it says, with apparent satisfaction at the result of its interpretation of section 11(2), that the consumer is not under any obligation in civil law to pay the later, higher price. Many ordinary consumers do not know that they can oblige a business to adhere to the price quoted in a contract. Even if they do they are at a disadvantage with an intransigent business if they have paid a deposit or they want that particular item since they are virtually forced to pay the higher price unless they are prepared to incur legal costs.[70]

Where there is no indication of the limits of an offer at a reduced price, an offence is generally committed if a qualification is imposed. In *Read Bros Cycles (Leyton) Ltd* v. *Waltham Forest L.B.C.*[71] a business unconditionally offered to sell a motorcycle listed at £580 for £540. It agreed to accept £90 as part-exchange on a trade-in, but only on the full price of £580. The Divisional Court held that an offence was committed under section 11(2). The section, it held, is concerned with offers, rather than with the legal analysis of contracts which result. An offence may be committed when an advertisement appears, before any consumer arrives on the scene. In reaching this conclusion the court confined an earlier decision to its own special facts, in which it had been held that a business which offers goods at a special cash price, even when it holds itself out in a general way to accept particular forms of credit cards, need not indicate specifically that those credit cards cannot be used for such special offers.[72] Certainly there seems little if any policy justification for not requiring a person to insert any qualification regarding a reduced price in the advertisement pertaining to it, whether it be that the reduced price does not apply with trade-ins, that only certain types of item are available at that price, or that cash must be paid if advantage is to be taken of it.

An incidental aspect of the subject is whether prices quoted should be inclusive of tax payable on a retail sale (e.g. VAT). It has been held that an offence might be committed if such tax is not included and there is no indication that it will be included.[73]

The Trade Descriptions Act 1968 does not deal with every type of untrue statement about prices. *Cadbury Ltd* v. *Halliday*[74] establishes that 'worth' and 'value' claims are generally not controlled by the legislation. The court pointed to the indefinite nature of the comparison implied by use of the term extra value; it could be to other similar articles presently or previously on sale, made by that or another manufacturer and sold by that or another retailer. The court held that it was impossible to say that the terms referred unequivocally either to weight or to price previously charged so as to constitute the requisite indication under either section 2(1) or

11(1)(b).

Worth and value claims, and a variety of other price claims, are now regulated by the Price Marking (Bargain Offers) Order (as amended).[75] Subject to certain exceptions where it is thought that comparisons of prices and charges are clear, the Order prohibits indications of prices and charges in relation to goods for sale by retail and services for consumers which include any statement, however framed and whether express or implied, that a price or charge indicated is lower than (a) the value ascribed to goods or services; or (b) the price or charge for goods or services of the same description (whether or not that price or charge is specified, quantified or has been made, indicated or proposed by another person) (arts. 2, 3(1), 4(1)). Among the exceptions to these prohibitions, as we have seen, are recommended prices for items not listed in the Schedule to the Order, and references to a particular price or charge the person has previously imposed in the ordinary course of business on the same or other identified premises (arts. 5, 3(2)(a)(i), 4(2)(a)(i)). Other exceptions are references to a particular price or charge which the person intends to charge in the future (but the date from which this is to be done must be specified: art. 7(2)(a)); which another identified business has charged; which is applicable to the sale or provision of goods or services of the same description but upon specified different terms, in specified different circumstances, in a specified different condition or quantity, or to persons not in a class or description to whom the indicated price applies; or which applies where goods or services are sold or provided with other specified goods or services (arts. 3(2), 4(2)).[76]

The aim of the Order is to confine bargain offer claims to where they are not misleading but useful to consumers and capable of easy verification because they are clear and understandable. While the Order seems to have reduced certain misleading price claims – for example, worth and value claims – there are still a considerable number of misleading price claims in use. Some take advantage of the widely-drafted exceptions provided for in the Order.[77] Others fall outside the Order altogether because they do not refer directly to a specific price or charge.[77a] The Director General of Fair Trading has recommended regulation of these latter claims.[78]

Should the Trade Descriptions Act 1968 incorporate a general prohibition on false descriptions of price in order to cover false price claims presently unregulated? A general provision is said to be too imprecise to be enforceable whatever its problematical deterrent effect. Besides, it is said that a general provision would create uncertainties because of its dependence on subjective judgements when a basic object of the criminal law is certainty. Doubts would remain, it is said, until the courts resolved them. A number of points can be made to rebut these arguments. First, regulation in this area needs flexibility to cope with the constant flow of claims which those involved in marketing can generate. Second, it is not suggested that the specific provisions already in force be repealed, only that they be supplemented by a general provision. Third, it is important to distinguish between ordinary criminal offences where certainty is desirable because the liberty of the subject is at stake, and consumer offences where imprisonment very rarely occurs either because courts regard these offences as less serious or because corporate bodies are mainly prosecuted and not individuals.

General mispricing provisions have been successful in other countries such as Australia and Canada, which have a comparable legal tradition. For example, section 53(e) of the Australian Trade Practices Act 1974 provides that a corporation shall not, in trade or commerce, in connection with the supply or possible supply of goods or services, or in connection with the promotion by any means of their supply or use, make a false or misleading statement with respect to their price. In addition, section 53A(1)(b) provides that a corporation shall not, in trade or commerce, in connection with the sale or grant, or the possible sale or grant, of an interest in land, or in connection with the promotion by any means of the sale or grant of an interest in land, make a false or misleading statement concerning its price. Price in the definition section of the Act includes a charge of any description (s. 4(1)). These sections go beyond the ambit of the Trade Descriptions Act 1968 and the Price Marking (Bargain Offers) Order.[79] For example, section 53(e) has been applied to advertisements that prices would be reduced in the future when this was not eventually done.[80] Moreover, in *Henderson* v. *Pioneer Homes Pty Ltd*,[81] the Full Court of the Federal Court rejected the argument that misleading advertisements referring to deposits and weekly payments in relation to houses were about finance and the repayment of mortgages and not about price. The court also held that in prescribing the manner and time in which the obligation to satisfy the payment of price might be discharged, the advertisements were with respect to price although not with respect to the amount of the price.

Misdescribed services

False statements about services or facilities made knowingly or recklessly in the course of any trade or business are prohibited by section 14 of the Trade Descriptions Act 1968. Section 14(1) provides as follows:

14.—(1) It shall be an offence for any person in the course of any trade or business—
    (a) to make a statement which he knows to be false; or
    (b) recklessly to make a statement which is false;
as to any of the following matters, that is to say,—
     (i) the provision in the course of any trade or business of any services, accommodation or facilities;
    (ii) the nature of any services, accommodation or facilities provided in the course of any trade or business;
   (iii) the time at which, manner in which or persons by whom any services, accommodation or facilities are so provided;
   (iv) the examination, approval or evaluation by any person of any services, accommodation or facilities so provided; or
    (v) the location or amenities of any accommodation so provided.

Unlike other consumer protection provisions including those relating to the misdescription or mispricing of goods, the offence is not one of strict liability and it is necessary to prove *mens rea*. Recklessness, however, has a broad meaning and covers situations where businesses simply ignore the truth or falsity of their statements. There is no need to establish dishonesty or that a business has deliberately closed its eyes to the truth.[82]

The *mens rea* requirement means that consumer protection departments prosecute proportionately fewer section 14 offences of which they become aware because of the difficulties of proof. The departure from strict liability was originally justified because of the novelty of the section. The present justification of *mens rea* is that it acts as a safeguard because the description of services is likely to be more subjective than of products, and because an indefinite range of matters can be caught by the section. The former argument is now without any basis after fifteen years of operation of the legislation. The other arguments must be juxtaposed with the illogicality of treating the description of products and services differently when their supply is often closely linked. The Review Committee on the

Trade Descriptions Act 1968 concluded that liability for the mis-description of products and of services should be assimilated on the same strict liability basis.[83] Strict liability obtains in relation to misdescribed services in other jurisdictions.

Although section 14 applies to anything likely to be taken for a statement as to any of the matters specified in the section, it is somewhat narrowed by use of the term 'false' (despite the side-heading to the section) and the omission of specific reference to statements which are simply misleading. The term 'facilities' is wide enough to cover ancillary aspects of consumer transactions, such as guarantees or the offer of products on approval or with free carriage.[84] The location of services and facilities would seem to fall outside the Act, as well as statements about the need for them.[85] False statements about the price of services or facilities are not covered by the Act unless price relates to the 'provision' or 'nature' of these or the 'manner' in which they are provided.[86] The courts have confined section 14 to statements of fact of which it can be said at the time they are made that they are either true or false. Statements about the future – assurances, promises or predictions – are not caught unless they imply a statement of present fact; for example, about the intention of a business or about its capacity to realize its intentions. The approach is in keeping with the civil law of deceit where the plaintiff must prove that there is a false representation of fact as distinct from the failure to fulfil a promise. However, in thus interpreting the section the courts have robbed it of a protection it was originally thought to have.

A well known case is *Beckett* v. *Cohen*[87] where a builder undertook to complete a garage in ten days and to build it 'as the existing [garage]' but did not finish it within the period nor construct it similar to the one already standing. The Divisional Court held that no offence was committed because the undertaking was a promise, unrelated to existing fact. Lord Widgery C.J. said of section 14 that Parliament never contemplated for a moment that the Act should be used to make a criminal offence out of what was really a breach of warranty. The decision would have been different, however, if the defendant had never intended to complete the work as contracted or was clearly unable to do so. It has been suggested that legislation should overturn judicial interpretation of section 14, to make it an offence to supply services or facilities which do not correspond with the description by reference to which they are supplied.[88] A defence would be necessary for persons who, discovering they are unable to supply the service or facility as described, take steps to inform intending recipients.

Most of the cases about future services in Britain have concerned statements in the advertisements of travel agents or tour operators which prove to be untrue when consumers take their holidays. Consumer protection departments have received thousands of complaints from consumers aggrieved about poor value for money, inferior hotels, inadequate food or poor facilities.[89] The Code of the Association of British Travel Agents purports to regulate some of these matters. Convictions have been obtained where advertisements have been interpreted as describing an existing state of affairs. In one, a business issued a brochure purportedly describing a hotel which was not completed, while in another a trip continued to be advertised although it had been cancelled.[90] Contrast *R.* v. *Sunair Holidays Ltd*[91] where convictions were quashed because a statement in a brochure as to a swimming pool could be interpreted as a simple promise, unrelated to existing fact, and it was not disputed that the other statements related to the future. In the judgment of the Court of Appeal (Criminal Division), MacKenna J. said:

We come now to the construction of section 14. The section deals with 'statements' of which it can be said that they were, at the time when they were made, 'false'. That may be the case with a statement of fact, whether past or present. A statement that a fact exists now, or that it existed in the past, is either true or false at the time when the statement is made. But that is not the case with a promise or a prediction about the future. A prediction may come true or it may not. A promise to do something in the future may be kept or it may be broken. But neither the prediction nor the promise can be said to have been true or false at the time when it was made. We conclude that section 14 does not deal with forecasts or promises as such. We put in the qualifying words 'as such' for this reason. A promise or forecast may contain by implication a statement of present fact. The person who makes the promise may be implying that his present intention is to keep it or that he has at present the power to perform it. The person who makes the forecast may be implying that he now believes that his prediction will come true or that he has the means of bringing it to pass. Such implied statements of present intention, means or belief, when they are made, may well be within section 14 and therefore punishable if they were false and were made knowingly or recklessly.[92]

British Airways Board v. *Taylor*[93] is now the leading case on statements about the future; it concerned airline overbooking. All major airlines operate a policy of overbooking to counteract 'no-shows', that is, passengers who make reservations on flights but do not appear. No-shows are usually far higher on the main business air routes because some businessmen who intend to travel on a certain day book every flight in the timetable and then take whichever is most convenient. Airlines could discourage no-shows by suing for breach of contract, but accept them as part of commercial life. The practice inevitably results in the occasional off-loading ('bumping') of passengers who have booked (about two passengers in 10,000) but these are inconsiderable when compared with the number of no shows (up to 20 per cent on some routes).

The decision in the case of *Taylor* ultimately turned on the point that the British Airways Board was not liable for the criminal acts of BOAC, which was the airline involved. But the House of Lords accepted that a breach of section 14 of the Trade Descriptions Act 1968 had occurred, since BOAC had written to the consumer confirming his flight without qualification. The confirmation involved BOAC in knowingly making a false statement about its intention as to the provision or timing of a service, since it implied that there was a seat reserved for the consumer when there was always the intention of 'bumping' if more passengers arrived than there were seats available. Three Lords expressly approved MacKenna J.'s judgment in *R* v. *Sunair Holidays*.[94]

In the course of the argument in *Taylor*'s case, the policy of overbooking flights was mentioned. The House of Lords refused to countenance whether the policy was commercially sound, fair to passengers, or operated conscientiously. Such questions, it held, were primarily within the control of administrative authorities. One approach would be to ensure that it was made clear to consumers that they might be 'bumped'. Another would be a scheme under which the airlines must recompense passengers who find themselves off-loaded – payment varying on the length of the flight, and on how long passengers have to wait for another seat. Prohibiting overbooking in the absence of effective measures against no-shows would be uneconomical because airlines would operate at less than their potential capacity. Fares would increase, contrary to the interests of most passengers. On the other hand it is difficult to control no-shows except by imposing reconfirmation requirements, or by obliging prospective customers to place a deposit which would be forfeited if they failed to appear.

Property

Many statements in relation to property are excluded from the ambit of the Trade Descriptions Act 1968. Although section 14 covers services, *accommodation* and facilities, 'accommodation' does not appear to extend to dispositions of substantial interests like long leases; rather it applies to short-term leases like those associated with holiday lettings.[95] However, descriptions of houses and property may fall within other heads of the Act, such as section 1. In *Breed* v. *Cluett*,[96] twenty days after the exchange of contracts for the sale of a bungalow the builder wrongly stated it was covered by the National House-builders' Registration Council ten-year guarantee. The Divisional Court held, first, that statements covered by section 14 are not confined to those inducing the entering into of a contract. 'There may well be statements made after a contract is completed – a contract for repairs to my motorcar, a contract for repair to my roof, stating the effect of what has been done by way of repair which may constitute an offence if made recklessly – even though the contract has been completed and the payment has been made.'[97] Secondly, the Court accepted that the builder's statement could be about the provision of services, viz. performance of an obligation during the ten-year guarantee period.

Because the Trade Descriptions Act 1968 does not appear to apply to descriptions of the size, position or other characteristics of houses or land, many business practices associated with their sale presently escape regulation, except by the general criminal law. The licensing of estate agents offers some protection for consumers.[98] Even if consumers are normally prevented from major blunders by the expert advice of surveyors or solicitors, there is no reason why they should incur an unnecessary waste of time and expense in viewing property and perhaps arranging for surveyors when this would never have been done if it had not been misdescribed. An especially serious abuse involving fraud is as follows. A property company purchases land in a remote area, sub-divides it into plots and advertises it in urban areas as suitable for retirement, holidays or investment. The advertisement may state, quite wrongly, that planning permission has been granted and that services like roads, gas and electricity will be available. Purchasers buy the land primarily on the basis of the advertisement, which shows photographs or drawings of local beauty spots and perhaps contains hints about soaring land values or a local boom. Consumers finally discover that it is difficult to build on, a considerable distance from the nearest road, and clearly without the services promised. Land sales along these lines have been a thriving business in many countries. To tackle such unscrupulous practices the United States Congress instituted detailed regulation of interstate land sales.[99]

Given the uncertainty as to the meaning of the term 'accommodation' in section 14, and the abuses which are possible, there is a definite need for an express provision covering misstatements about property. A precedent is provided by section 53A(1) of the Australian Trade Practices Act 1974, which reads as follows:

53A. (1) A corporation shall not, in trade or commerce, in connexion with the sale or grant, or the possible sale or grant, of an interest in land or in connexion with the promotion by any means of the sale or grant of an interest in land—

  (a) represent that the corporation has a sponsorship, approval or affiliation it does not have;
  (b) make a false or misleading statement concerning the nature of the interest in the land, the price payable for the land, the location of the land, the characteristics of the land, the use to which the land is capable of being put or may lawfully be put or the existence or availability of facilities associated with the land; or
  (c) offer gifts, prizes or other free items with the intention of not providing them or of not providing them as offered.

Interest in land is defined widely (s. 53A(3)). *Pryor* v. *Given*[100] is typical of the cases to which section 53A(1) is directed. There informations were laid against the defendant for being knowingly concerned in a contravention by a company of section 53A(1)(b). The company placed an advertisement on television for the sale of land which contained the words 'A wonderful place to live', 'Watch it grow', and various pictures of the land, including some showing houses. In fact, the land was zoned non-urban and houses could not be built without satisfying onerous conditions. The defendant was convicted: the pictorial representations formed part of the statement, and although the land was physically capable of supporting houses, the advertisement would lead persons to conclude that houses could lawfully be built there.

Whether statements about property prices should be controlled along the lines of section 11 of the Trade Descriptions Act 1968 is a matter on which some commentators have expressed doubt. A particular aspect which both the Law Commission and the Review Committee on the Trade Descriptions Act 1968 think unsuitable for regulation is 'gazumping', whereby those selling property agree to sell at a price 'subject to contract' but later withdraw or threaten to do so in expectation of a higher price.[101] The prospective purchaser who has been gazumped is then put in the position of having to pay the higher price or losing the house. Arguments against regulation were that the problem only arises when houses are in short supply, that it is unfair to invoke the criminal law against sellers while leaving consumers free not to continue in order to pay less, and that if sellers ceased to use 'subject to contract' agreements, buyers would be subject to uncertainty as to price until contracts were exchanged. Even if these arguments are accepted, there is no reason why gazumping would not be satisfactorily handled within a general prohibition on false statements about prices. The term 'subject to contract' might be regarded as a disclaimer neutralizing a price which is later gazumped.

Other misstatements

Misstatements other than those mentioned can cause consumer loss, but are not always covered by the Trade Descriptions Act 1968. False statements by persons about their qualifications have given rise to difficulty in the past, but in some cases the courts have been able to bring these under the Act.[102]

Misstatements about availability are particularly worrisome. Non-availability of an advertised product can cause consumers loss in time and money if they go to the trouble of visiting the retailer but discover that it is unavailable. Businesses can benefit unjustifiably. The problem is most acute with the 'specials' supermarkets advertise. Once consumers enter a supermarket because its advertisements suggest that it has the best 'specials' for the week, they will usually complete their shopping even if some of the 'specials' are not available because of the inconvenience of going elsewhere. A number of studies in the United States have concluded that supermarkets have for many years abused the practice of advertising 'specials'. For example, a Federal Trade Commission study revealed significant discrepancies between supermarket promise and performance. Fourteen per cent of the items advertised by all supermarket chain stores surveyed in Washington D.C. were unavailable and 6 per cent in San Francisco, and only eight of the 137 stores surveyed in the two cities had every item available for potential customers. The range in the average number of items unavailable for the various chains was between 3 and 19 per cent in Washington and between 3 and 8 per cent in San Francisco.[103] Supermarkets argued to the Commission that staff errors (in marking stock, in writing advertising copy, and so on) led to an unavoidable margin of error in advertising 'specials'. However, the Commission's surveys demonstrated a considerable deviation in pricing practices between stores, indicating that some stores were capable of a far better performance.

In its most extreme form non-availability of products constitutes the fraudulent practice of 'bait and switch'. 'Bait and switch' has been described as follows:

Basically, a seller seeks to attract customers by advertising a product, which he does not intend to sell, at an extremely low price. When a customer responds to the ad, the seller discourages him from purchasing the 'bait' and instead tries to 'switch' him to a higher priced, more profitable item. To qualify as a bait and switch scheme, an advertisement might create a false impression about the size, the model, or the general condition of the product so that upon disclosure of the true facts, the customer would switch to another product. Or the seller might discourage a sale by refusing to demonstrate a product or to sell it, by disparaging it through words or acts, or by discrediting its guarantee, its credit terms, and the availability of service, repairs, or parts. . . . Since customers are psychologically prepared to spend their money once they're inside a store, it is merely another step for the salesman to convince them to purchase a 'better' product than the one advertised, but at a higher price.[104]

In the United States studies have demonstrated that 'bait and switch' advertising is used by ghetto merchants to the detriment of con-sumers. A closely related practice with services is 'lo-balling', a term developed to cover situations where companies advertise repairs at low prices as an enticement to obtain possession of products so that the owner can be charged for additional unnecessary repairs.

Can it be argued that the availability of goods is a facility and hence any false statement is actionable under section 14 of the Trade

Descriptions Act 1968? In *Westminster C.C.* v. *Ray Alan (Manshops) Ltd*,[105] the Divisional Court held that there was no infringement of section 14 of the Trade Descriptions Act 1968 when a retailer advertised a 'Closing Down Sale', although in fact it continued to trade. The prosecution had unsuccessfully argued before the magistrates that the advertisement constituted a recklessly false statement within section 14(1)(ii) as to the nature of facilities provided in the course of a trade or business. On appeal Ormrod L. J. held that the word 'facilities' in section 14 should be construed *ejusdem generis* with the preceding words 'services' and 'accommodation'. Although 'facilities' had a very wide meaning, and was increasingly popular in commercial circles, it had to be construed strictly in a penal statute such as the Trade Descriptions Act 1968. Woolf J. agreed, but he conceded that if 'facilities' had appeared by itself it could cover shopping facilities. The omission of any reference to goods in section 14 was counterbalanced by the reference to 'any trade or business', which was clearly wide enough to cover a shopping or retail trade. However, looking at the mischief aimed at by the offence, and its penal nature, Woolf J. considered that facilities must be considered as 'something close to services and accommodation and not covering shopping facilities'. With regard to use of the *ejusdem generis* rule, it can hardly be said that 'services' and 'accommodation' are of the same kind or nature to qualify the meaning of 'facilities'.[106] Moreover, weighed against the penal nature of section 14 is the desirability, in Woolf J.'s words, 'for there to be some protection for the public which prevented persons advertising something as a closing down sale if it is not such a sale' (p. 775).

Australia, Canada and New Zealand have specific legislation for non-availability of advertised sale items. For example, under section 56(1) of the Australian Trade Practices Act 1974[107] a corporation commits an offence if it advertises goods or services for supply at a special price but does not intend to offer them for supply at that price for a period that is, and in quantities that are, reasonable having regard to the nature of the market and advertisement. To avoid the difficulties of the prosecution having to prove intention, the section also creates an offence if a corporation, having advertised goods or services for supply at a special price, fails to offer such goods or services for supply at that price for a period that is, and in quantities that are, reasonable, having regard to the nature of the market and the nature of the advertisement (s. 56(2)). The qualifications in this offence ensure that a genuine selling campaign is not placed at risk. Moreover, the section provides for a corporation facing genuine difficulties in giving it a defence if it establishes that it offered to supply or procure the goods or services advertised within a reasonable time or that it offered to supply or procure equivalent goods or services within a reasonable time (s. 56(3)). In *Reardon* v. *Morley Ford Pty Ltd*[108] a motorcar trader was convicted of offences under both sections 56(1) and (2) for advertising a particular model Ford Falcon for sale at $6600 plus on-road costs and delivery fees. On two separate occasions individuals enquired about purchasing such a model for $6600 but the salesmen stated that none was available, that the car on display had already been sold, and that if the consumers insisted on buying a car at that price the matter would have to be referred to a higher authority. Smithers J. was satisfied beyond reasonable doubt on the circumstantial evidence that the ultimate controlling mind of the company, namely the managing director, did not intend when the advertisements were published to honour them. In relation to section 56(2) the judge said that there is no obligation for a business to encourage consumers to accept an offer and there is no objection to it explaining the benefit of entering into some other deal. However, a business has to continue, genuinely at all times, to offer to supply the goods on the terms advertised. In the instant case the steps taken in displaying one of the vehicles with its price markings did not constitute an offer to satisfy the section because there was no intention that it would become binding when a consumer purported to accept it.

In the United States the Federal Trade Commission has ruled that it is a violation of the Federal Trade Commission Act for any food retailer to offer any product for sale by advertisement if a store does not have it in stock and readily available to consumers.[109] The regulation specifically states that one defence will be records that show that an advertiser ordered sufficient quantities to meet reasonable demands. Certain disclaimers concerning availability can appear in advertisements. Despite provisions elsewhere, a committee reviewing the Trade Descriptions Act took the insular view that legislation was unnecessary. It regarded the problem as minor, and accepted that firms would face cash flow problems by having to acquire stock.[110] Whether such assertions are true is a matter for research, but they certainly fly in the face of experience in other countries.

THE QUALITY OF FOOD

Quality is primarily a matter for private law. Products, for example, must be merchantable and fit for the purpose, but if they are not it is the consumer who must institute legal action against the business involved. Chapter 10 examines a number of products, potentially dangerous to humans, for which detailed safety standards have been set. A limited number of provisions also exist which incorporate quality standards into the criminal law. Reference can be made, for example, to sections 60 and 60A of the Road Traffic Act 1972, which makes it illegal to sell, supply, offer to sell or to supply, or to expose for sale unroadworthy vehicles or to fit or sell etc. defective or unsuitable parts. The most important of these broad criminal provisions, and the concern of this section, are those directed at sub-standard food and drink.

Legislation in 1860 laid the foundation for the general framework of control of food quality.[111] Until then the quality of food depended on a combination of the common law and specific enactment. The former was concerned with those serious cases where food was potentially injurious to health. It was an offence knowingly to sell someone food injurious to health or to mix noxious ingredients with a food.[112] If someone died as a result of eating unwholesome food the seller could be indicted for manslaughter if he had sold the food knowingly or negligently.[113] In addition, a common law nuisance arose whenever diseased or unwholesome food was exposed for sale.[114] Specific enactments were designed mainly to prevent the adulteration of products on which excise duty was payable. The preambles to legislation on tea, coffee and beer in the eighteenth and early nineteenth centuries recited that adulteration threatened public health, ruined fair trade and diminished the revenue.[115] The latter consideration was apparently paramount. Thus, when a duty was imposed on chicory comparable to that on coffee, the Board of Revenue no longer interfered with the mixture of these substances since its previous concern had been simply to prevent the evasion of excise duty on the latter.[116] Earlier legislation was motivated by a more general concern with public health: bread was regulated from 1266 by the Assize of Bread and Ale,[117] and support was given to guilds in their attempts to suppress food adulteration.

Writers like Hassall described in the nineteenth century how milk was watered, alum added to flour and lead acetate used to sweeten beer. The aim was to lower the price of foods by mixing in other, cheaper substances to improve the appearance of adulterated articles.[118] In some cases the adulterants were of an innocuous character but others were actually injurious to health as well as being a fraud on the public. In the 'Bradford Incident' in 1858, 200 people were poisoned eating adulterated lozenges, seventeen fatally. Finally Parliament was impelled to act. Not without some opposition,[119] the view was abandoned that the forces of competition and the knowledge of the consumer were sufficient to guarantee the sale of unadulterated foodstuffs of adequate quality.[120]

Instead of forbidding the use of particular substances or processes, or of directing that food be treated in specified ways,[121] the 1860 legislation contained a broad and simple provision making it unlawful for a person knowingly to sell food which contained injurious substances or which was adulterated or impure. Offenders were subject to a fine and – a sanction not included in later legislation but still incorporated in the food and drugs legislation of some of the Australian states[122] – a court could publicize that a trader had been convicted of a particular offence, perhaps by a newspaper advertisement. In practice, the Act proved a failure because Parliament did not create the machinery for its enforcement,[123] but it represented a major blow to the principle of *laissez-faire* and established the important principle 'that it was within the proper role of the State to protect the consumer against injury to his pocket and his health.'[124]

The law was strengthened in the Sale of Food and Drugs Act 1875 which prohibited the admixture with food and drugs of ingredients injurious to health, and which made it an offence to abstract an ingredient so as to injuriously affect quality.[125] Most importantly, the Act made it unlawful to sell to the prejudice of a purchaser any article not of the nature, substance and quality demanded.[126] Taken in conjunction with the Public Health Act 1875, which contained provision to deal with the sale of unsound food, the aim was to safeguard the public against hazards to health and to protect it economically. In those early years the latter aim went no further than attempting to guarantee that consumers received what they ordered; but later its scope was enlarged to encompass protection from false descriptions and labelling.

The substance of this early legislation has been re-enacted in subsequent statutes both in Britain and other Commonwealth countries. Safety, and ensuring that consumers obtain what would reasonably be expected, remain the basic aims of the law.[127] Current legislation creates three broad offences in relation to the sale of food. It is an offence to sell food (a) which is injurious to health because of its preparation or processing; (b) which is not of the nature, substance or quality demanded; or (c) which is unfit for human consumption.[128] Some Australian jurisdictions and Canada have another provision prohibiting 'adulteration' which is additional to, or partly in substitution for, these provisions.[129] 'Adulteration' is defined to include the addition of a substance to food which diminishes its beneficial property or which is of lower commercial value. The approach in other countries such as the United States is different in that greater emphasis is placed on requirements for particular foods.[130]

The broad provisions in Britain and other countries which have adopted its lead remain basic in controlling the quality of food despite regulations, discussed in a later chapter, which control food additives, compositional standards of food and food hygiene. Except for those jurisdictions with an adulteration provision, the 'nature, substance or quality' section quickly became the most important of the provisions in the administration of the legislation,[131] and today the majority of prosecutions are brought under it. As an illustration, Table 8.2 lists the number of prosecutions reported in the *Annual Report of the Director General of Fair Trading*, 1981.[132]

Table 8.2   Prosecutions under Food and Drugs Act 1955

Not of nature, substance or quality demanded	988
Unfit food	256
Labelling regulations and others	635
Total	1879

The prominence of the 'nature, substance or quality' section is partly because it is an offence of strict liability, whereas the section dealing with food injurious to health requires proof of intention.[133] Additionally, it is unnecessary to prove that a consumer has sustained actual injury in a 'nature, substance or quality' prosecution. Courts assume that a consumer who receives an article inferior to that expected or contracted for is automatically prejudiced within the meaning of the section.[134] Even if it can be shown that a consumer is not prejudiced economically, because a better quality product would cost more, there might still be prejudice within the meaning of the section. However there will be no prejudice if a consumer is notified at the time of sale that an article is not of the accepted or usual standard.[135] In *Smedleys Ltd* v. *Breed*[136] the House of Lords accepted (Viscount Dilhorne *dubitante*) that the presence of a caterpillar rendered a tin of peas not of the substance demanded by the consumer, although it was quite harmless through sterilization in the manufacturing process. Lord Diplock said that the section

is not concerned with health or hygiene but with breaches of contracts for the sale of food or drugs. . . . So if the purchaser gets what he contracted to buy there is no contravention of this section, though if the food is injurious to health there may be an offence under some other section even though there is no breach of the contract of sale. . . . [I]n determining what was 'the food or drug demanded by the purchaser', the words by which the goods that he purchased were described must be understood in their popular sense.[137]

Likewise, the prohibition on 'adulteration' looms large in prosecutions in jurisdictions which have it because it is an offence of strict liability, and there is no need to establish harmfulness or for scientific or expert evidence to determine its presence.[138]

Over the last decades there has been a remarkable reduction in prosecutions for deliberately altering food (e.g. adding cheaper substances to a genuine article) or for compositional deficiency. Whereas packaging and preparation of foods by individual merchants gave every opportunity for such practices, precisely the opposite is the case with large-scale food manufacturers marketing prepacked products throughout the country under their brand names. Today the greatest concern of enforcement bodies in prosecuting food offences is the presence in food of foreign bodies and mould. Many such prosecutions arise from complaint from dissatisfied consumers rather than from the detection activities of enforcement bodies. This follows because prepacked foods cannot be thoroughly examined until after they have been opened.

Insects and pieces of metal are common foreign bodies and result mainly from the mass production of food. Insects enter inadequately screened factories and metals find their way into food from insufficiently maintained machines. Poor stock rotation, especially in small shops, and inadequate storage conditions explain the incidence of many cases of mould. The importance of foreign bodies and mould in British food prosecutions is obvious from Table 8.3, which is taken from a survey by the *British Food Journal*.[139]

Table 8.3   Average Percentage of Prosecutions for Food Offences Involving Foreign Bodies or Mould, 1978–81

	Foreign bodies	Mould	Hygiene
1978	53.1%	14.5%	22.2%
1979	51.6%	11.7%	27.1%
1980	44.1%	14.8%	31.8%
1981	42.1%	15.6%	27%

The wide ambit of the broad prohibitions in food legislation means that prosecutions are relatively straightforward once the presence of a foreign body or of mould has been established. One qualification is that sometimes the presence of a sterile and harmless foreign body will not constitute an offence.[140] It is impossible to devise a test for when this happens because the judges react to the particular facts before them. On one side of the line is the extra bottle top floating in a bottle of milk; on the other, the presence of a small sliver of glass or an object like a caterpillar.[141] Another minor problem in enforcement is that there is no necessary overlap between food which is not of the nature, substance or quality demanded, and food which is unfit for human consumption. A number of prosecutions have failed because they have chosen the wrong offence for the particular facts. The 'unfit for human consumption' offence occurs where food has decomposed or is putrid, but does not cover other situations such as where food contains non-toxic extraneous matter and the character of the food has not changed.[142] Generally the cases are clear-cut: food is prima facie unfit if mould or maggots are present or if, in ordinary terminology, it is 'bad'.[143]

The major sanction supporting food legislation is the fine. Fines operate *ex post facto*, however, and enforcement authorities need power to act quickly where food is in breach of the legislation and already on the market. At present they do not have this power except where food is unfit for human consumption when it may be seized and destroyed. That power is used commonly against substantial quantities of unfit food. The Food and Drugs Administration in the United States exercises a recall power which is not confined to unfit food only. Although there is no legal power as such, recalls are possible because the FDA has the threat that if businesses fail to comply a court can be requested to issue an injunction or to order a seizure.[144] The recall procedure is not limited to situations where a hazard to health had been found in a product. Chapter 11 will explain the 'cease and desist' order under the Fair Trading Act 1973 which can be obtained against businesses in persistent breach of consumer law, including food legislation. In the case of the latter the Office of Fair Trading has obtained assurances from a number of bakers, dairies and restaurants involving convictions for foreign bodies in bread and milk and breaches of hygiene regulations and similar complaints.[145] The power should be used more widely; the present level of fines and the fines being imposed by magistrates courts are quite inadequate to deter some businesses from breaching the Food and Drugs Act 1955 because they can simply treat fines as a minor business expense.[146]

QUANTITY

The broad prohibition against incorrect quantity in force in many countries is illustrated by section 24 of the Weights and Measures Act 1963.

[A]ny person who, in selling or purporting to sell any goods by weight or other measurement or by number, delivers or causes to be delivered to the buyer a lesser quantity than that purported to be sold or than corresponds with the price charged shall be guilty of an offence.

The legislation also contains a prohibition on misrepresenting or misleading consumers about quantity. These provisions are supplemented by others to enable consumers properly to evaluate quantity. A wide range of items must be sold by weight; for many items it is incumbent on sellers to inform consumers about the weight at the time of sale; and a number of commodities must be marketed in prescribed quantities.

A uniform system of weights and measures is obviously essential to commerce and industry. Legislation established the present imperial standards in the early nineteenth century, although attempts can be traced back to Magna Carta.[147] All transactions in trade must be conducted by reference to the imperial or metric units required in the legislation. Control of weighing and measuring equipment began some time earlier in 1795–7, when statutes were passed to suppress the use of defective weights and of false and unequal balances. The principles of this earlier legislation remain in the Weights and Measures Act 1963 ensuring that weighing and measuring equipment conforms to the standardized units, is kept in accurate condition and is constructed so as not to facilitate fraud. Weighing and measuring equipment, as prescribed, must be verified as fit for use, but since the Weights and Measures Act 1979 regulations can permit this to be done by means of batch testing. Enforcement authorities regularly inspect business premises to ensure that the equipment remains in good working condition. In order to ensure their suitability for use in trade, the government approves patterns of new weighing and measuring appliances, both as to the material of which they are constructed and the principles on which they are designed.

Legislation to ensure that the quantities actually sold were what they purported to be originated much more recently. It was long rejected on the grounds that it would constitute an unacceptable intrusion into commerce by the State.[148] Bread and coal were commodities specifically regulated. Both products had to be sold in specified quantities and traders could be punished for short measure.[149] The Weights and Measures Act 1878 imposed a penalty on the fraudulent use of weighing and measuring equipment, but this was ineffectual because of the difficulty of proving fraud and because of the advent of prepackaging.[150] Attention was frequently drawn to the anomaly of controlling weighing and measuring equipment, but of not prohibiting the giving of short weight or measure.[151] Particular concern was expressed that the poor suffered in the absence of such a prohibition.

Finally in 1914 a parliamentary committee accepted the need for a strict liability offence of giving incorrect quantity. While pointing out that the state should interfere with relations between buyers and sellers in only exceptional circumstances, the committee justified legislation because consumers, especially the poor, were vulnerable to business malpractice.[152] After some delay, the Sale of Food (Weights and Measures) Act 1926 penalized short weight and measure in the sale of food and compelled traders to sell a number of foods by quantity. The latter provision was gradually expanded and the Weights and Measures Act 1963 extends it to a wide range of consumer commodities. Enforcement of the short weight prohibition, although it receives little publicity, is of continued importance to ordinary people.

CORPORATE CRIMINAL LIABILITY AND THE STATUTORY DEFENCES

This section is concerned primarily with consumer offences committed by companies. Who is to be punished in these circumstances; the employee whose immediate mistake gave rise to the offence, the senior executives whose promotional practices inevitably led to such mistakes being committed, or the company itself? Imposing sanctions on the company confiscates any illegal profits accruing from the offence.[153] Further, prosecuting the company may lead its top management to police observance of legal requirements by those in the organization.[154] Sometimes there is no alternative to proceeding against a company if a prosecution is to be instituted. Decision-making is diffuse in a large organization and it may be impossible to locate an individual responsible for a particular occurrence. The same happens if an offence is the accretion of decisions by many individuals.

There are equally cogent reasons for proceeding against the senior executives of a company whose promotional practices are responsible for an offence.[155] If only the company is prosecuted the effect on these individuals is indirect. Assuming that the stigma of a conviction attaches to the company, it is highly unlikely to filter through to the relevant company executives. Similarly, when a company is fined this will rarely affect the senior executives financially. On the other hand there is little value to be gained in prosecuting junior employees unless they have committed consumer offences for their own benefit. They are the captives of promotional practices adopted by their employers and it is quite unfair to lay the blame at their feet.

In the light of these considerations, what does the law say about offences committed by companies? The subject is best considered under different headings.

Liability of individual officers

Top management: Consumer legislation generally provides that if a company is liable for an offence, its top management can also be prosecuted if it is directly responsible or should have taken steps to prevent its occurrence. For example, section 20 of the Trade Descriptions Act 1968 provides that top management such as directors, managers or company secretaries (or those acting in such capacities) can be prosecuted along with their company if the offence has been committed with their consent and connivance, or is attributable to any neglect on their part. Neglect involves failure to perform a duty about which a person knows or ought to know. Consent requires knowledge, but mere suspicion, coupled with acquiescence, may be sufficient for connivance.

A decision of the United States Supreme Court, *United States* v. *Park*,[156] is a useful illustration of these points, although the case may not be directly applicable in other jurisdictions. The president and chief executive officer of a large national food chain (Park) was held liable for unsanitary storage conditions in one of the company's warehouses. The enforcement authority had inspected the warehouse, found conditions in violation of the Food, Drug and Cosmetic Act, and notified Park by letter. On receipt of the letter, Park had conferred with his vice-president of legal matters, who informed him that the divisional vice-president would take corrective action. Park argued that he could not have taken more constructive action. The United States Supreme Court disagreed and ruled that under the Act Park had responsibility and authority either to prevent violations in the first instance or promptly to take steps to seek out and correct them once they were discovered. Liability was not predicated on Park's position, title, or on his closeness to the violation, said the Court, but because all officers who have power and authority, regardless of how extended and indirect, to secure compliance with the law have an affirmative duty to do so. Objective impossibility of preventing a violation, however, would have been a defence. The decision in Park's case is to be welcomed as an indication that company executives should bear a responsibility for violations of the law arising from the way their organizations operate. We shall see shortly that the law elsewhere, as interpreted by the courts, has the opposite effect: that liability falls on junior employees.

Employees: If employees are responsible for all the elements of an offence, they can be prosecuted directly.[157] They may also be prosecuted under general provisions such as section 23 of the Trade Descriptions Act 1968, which make it possible to prosecute a person whose act or default has given rise to an offence.[158] As a matter of practice consumer protection departments will rarely prosecute employees.

Corporate liability

Since a company is incapable of performing acts itself, a basis must be found for imputing to it acts performed by individuals. The law approaches this problem in two ways.

Personal liability of company: The law regards certain individuals working for a company as being so closely identified with it that their acts can be treated as its acts. Those in respect of whose actions liability may be ascribed occupy the top management positions in the organization. They may be those strictly allowed by the Articles of Association of a company to exercise its powers or those defined in statutory provisions like section 20 of the Trade Descriptions Act 1968.[159] They are the 'directing minds' of the company, characterized by Denning L.J. in a well-known passage:

A company may in many ways be likened to a human body. It has a brain and nerve centre which controls what it does. It also has hands which hold the tools and act in accordance with directions from the centre. Some of the people in the company are mere servants and agents who are nothing more than hands to do the work and cannot be said to represent the mind or will. Others are directors and managers who represent the directing mind and will of the company, and control what it does. The state of mind of those managers is the state of mind of the company and is treated by the law as such.[160]

Vicarious liability of company: The general rule is that a company is not *criminally* liable, as opposed to being liable under the civil law, for the acts of its employees, but this can arise:

(a) in the exceptional cases where top management delegates their full discretion to those at lower levels who can act independently of instructions from them.[161] It has been held that the delegation of duties to a branch manager or sales manager, however, does not fall within this head.[162]

(b) Where the courts regard a statute, and this is the case with consumer protection statutes, as creating vicarious criminal liability. A company will therefore be liable for the acts of even junior employees, even if it is quite unaware of those acts, when they are committed in the course of their employment.[163] The justification for such extensive liability is that substantial authority is delegated to the lower echelons of modern business organizations. Lower officials can endanger the public and profit a business by unlawful acts to the same extent as top management. Vicarious liability also encourages the top management of businesses to supervise closely the activities of their lower officials. A limitation on vicarious liability is that the courts are reluctant to infer a parliamentary intention to impose it in cases where consumer offences require *mens rea*. This follows from the difficulty of attributing the mental state of one person to another.[164] However this is not a major problem with consumer legislation since offences are generally of a strict liability nature.

Statutory defences: the employer (company)

To mitigate the harshness of strict liability, Parliament provides certain statutory defences in consumer legislation.[165] The most important defence, exemplified in section 24(1) of the Trade Descriptions Act 1968, is if a person can show: (a) that the contravention was due to a mistake, to reliance on information supplied, or to the act or default of another person, an accident or some other cause beyond its control; and (b) that it has taken reasonable precautions and exercised all due diligence to avoid the commission of such contravention. Defences of this nature vary slightly. Where the allegation is that someone else is to blame most legislation simply requires the defendant to give the prosecution beforehand information identifying or assisting to identify that other person.

The leading case on defences is *Tesco Supermarkets Ltd* v. *Nattrass*.[166] There a national supermarket was prosecuted for mispricing and successfully raised the defence, under section 24(1) of the Trade Descriptions Act 1968, that it was the fault of its branch manager. The House of Lords held that a branch manager could be 'another person' under the section. He was not at sufficiently high a level to be regarded as a directing mind of the company (instead he was one of the directed), and neither was he a delegate of the directing minds because they always retained control through their chain of command. It had already been accepted that the company had taken reasonable precautions and exercised due diligence instructing its branch managers and other staff on how to avoid mispricing, by its method of selecting branch managers, by providing adequate staff and conditions, and by its system of area inspectors.

The underlying rationale of the decision in *Tesco*'s case is to avoid making companies criminally liable when they are regarded as not being to blame for a criminal offence. The justification for this approach in Lord Reid's words is: 'But if he has done all he can how can he do more?' But this argument misses several points. First, it is the business that makes any profit when an employee commits an offence.[167] In general terms, the result of a prosecution is simply to deprive the business of this wrongly acquired profit, although in particular cases the business may be fined an amount greater than the profit made or the publicity surrounding the prosecution may cause financial loss in excess of the profit. Secondly, the employees identified by a company as being responsible for an offence are open to prosecution. Yet it is socially undesirable for employees to be punished for such offences which they commit not for their benefit but in the course of their employment. Why should they be blamed? They are locked into a system where they have to carry out a company's marketing scheme; in the case of junior employees, for low wages in an uncreative environment. Consumer protection departments may not prosecute them as a matter of practice, but should companies be able to escape liability in such circumstances and transfer it to them?

The most telling point, however, is that some firms are able to operate without committing consumer offences. Comparable businesses have completely different conviction records, and these seem to vary with a company's marketing policies and the way it treats its employees. Businesses with low conviction rates eschew promotional schemes which give rise to offences and create an atmosphere, in terms of the way they treat their staff and the conditions under which they employ them, where the risk of infringement is minimized. What more can a business do, asks Lord Reid? Some businesses can emulate their competitors by abandoning certain marketing techniques and can improve the position of their staff so that they have an incentive to avoid mistakes. But obviously certain businesses will not do this until the cost of doing so, in terms of the penalties involved, is a sufficient deterrent. Vicarious liability for offences committed by employees in the course of their employment would seem to be the only solution.

Another criticism of the approach in *Tesco*'s case is that it is all too easy for a company to appear to have taken reasonable precautions and to have exercised due diligence. *Tesco*'s case contains warnings against ready acceptance of paper schemes for preventing offences and perfunctory efforts to implement them. Despite these warnings, courts sometimes adopt a lenient view of what has to be done to prevent offences. The company's standing orders at issue in *Nattrass* v. *Timpson Shops Ltd*[168] did not expressly require a check after repricing and made no provision for supervision of branch managers. Nevertheless, the Divisional Court concluded that the standing orders could be held by a reasonable bench of justices to be adequate for the purpose of a defence under section 24(1) of the Trade Descriptions Act 1968. It went on to hold that, on the facts, the manager of the store in question could not claim to have taken all reasonable precautions to enable him to push the responsibility further down the line onto his shop assistants, because there was no evidence that he had checked whether repricing had been done properly. The latter seems sound enough when the incorrect price ticket was displayed on the product over a fortnight after repricing had rendered it obsolete.

In *McGuire* v. *Sittingbourne Co-operative Society Ltd*[169] a magistrates' court accepted that a retailer had satisfied the defence although it could not identify the manager or other persons whose act or default caused the mispricing. The prosecutor's appeal was allowed because the retailer had not proved that the act or default was due to another, even if reasonable precautions had been taken and due diligence exercised. Watkins J. (with whom Lord Widgery C.J. and Kilner Brown J. agreed) said:

> No inquiry had been made by the justices as to how the act or default occurred. The justices had contented themselves with the bare acceptance of the admission that the offences were committed as a result of a shop assistant mispricing the goods. The justices could not be satisfied that the defendants had established a defence under section 24 unless they had established, on the balance of probabilities, that they had done all that could reasonably be expected in the way of inquiry and investigation as to who was responsible for the default. The justices ought to have asked what steps the defendants had taken, but in fact they were left with no evidence as to how the offence occurred or who was in default.

Lord Widgery C.J. added that unless care was taken the administration of the Act might become slipshod. 'The onus on a defendant was not so easily satisfied. He must have done his best to show how and why the offence was committed.'

Statutory defences: suppliers

In addition to blaming employees, companies can use defences such as section 24(1) of the Trade Descriptions Act 1968 to push liability onto their suppliers. Retailers would seem to have a heavy job in establishing a section 24 defence following the decision in *Sherrat* v. *Gerald's The American Jewellers Ltd.*[170] That case involved a watch engraved 'water-proof', a claim which the consumer demonstrated to be untrue when he dipped the watch in a bowl of water. The retailer attempted to invoke the section 24 defence when prosecuted under section 1 of the Trade Descriptions Act 1968 on the basis that the watch had been obtained from a responsible company and that no previous complaints had been received. The Divisional Court rejected the argument: no precautions had been taken, although the retailer could have done quite easily what the consumer did.

Irrespective of a section 24 type defence, however, retailers cannot be liable if it is the supplier which has actually committed the offence. The retailer in *Feiner* v. *Barnes*[171] had been named as a stockist of a product in an advertisement inserted in a national newspaper by the supplier. The Divisional Court held that the retailer could not be regarded as having given a false indication of price contained in the advertisement and that the mere fact that they were named as stockist imposed no obligation to obtain a copy of the advertisement and check it.

The steps that second-hand car dealers must take to satisfy the statutory defences to blame their suppliers have tightened considerably over the years, which reflects the courts' attitude to the continuing need for second-hand car dealers to be prosecuted for trade description offences. For example, second-hand car dealers must generally contact the previous owner and use disclaimers if they are to show reasonable precautions and due diligence in relation to odometer readings.[172]

An additional defence for retailers under the Food and Drugs Act 1955 is if they can prove that they purchased an item from their suppliers as being one which could lawfully be sold, etc. under the name and description or for the purpose under or for which they sold it, and with a written warranty to that effect.

But they must have no reason to believe otherwise at the time of the alleged offence and the product must be in the same state as when purchased.[173] The entry in the invoice of a brand name can amount to a written warranty.[174] A warranty might not have to be given on each occasion a product is supplied but might be able to apply to a course of dealings between a retailer and a supplier.[175] An example of the use of the defence is *Watford Corporation* v. *Maypole Ltd*.[176] In this case the retailer successfully invoked a warranty when prosecuted for selling a mouldy article of food. Because the manufacturer had not provided an adequate guide as to the article's shelf-life, the retailer had no reason to believe there was non-compliance with the law. Even though the article would not have been mouldy when sold to the retailer, it was in the 'same state' for the purpose of the defence because that requirement is limited to whether articles had been tampered with by the retailer. The decision illustrates the main drawback to the warranty defence. Instead of focusing on whether a retailer has taken all reasonable precautions and exercised all due diligence, its focus is on the artificial issue of whether a food is in the same state as when purchased.[177]

Statutory defences: machinery

Defences comparable to section 24 of the Trade Descriptions Act 1968 may be applicable where an offence can be attributed to a fault in the manufacturing process and the manufacturer has taken reasonable precautions and exercised due diligence. *Bibby-Cheshire* v. *Golden Wonder Ltd*[178] involved a prosecution for short weight crisps, but the court was satisfied that the manufacturer had a defence when it demonstrated that if the machines were functioning normally the error was equivalent to 0.0006 per cent of weekly output, that it was economically impossible to weigh manually the 20 million bags produced weekly, that the filling machine was the most modern available and was adequately maintained, and that various check weighing procedures were in operation.

There are also a number of special defences where a fault arises from manufacturing processes. The best example is under the Food and Drugs Act 1955, where a food manufacturer has a defence to a section 2 prosecution it if can establish that the presence of extraneous matter is 'an unavoidable consequence of the process of collection or preparation.'[179] The House or Lords considered the matter in *Smedleys Ltd* v. *Breed*,[180] when a caterpillar was found in a can of peas.

The evidence was that the caterpillar had escaped the manufacturer's mechanical screening process which eliminated waste matter of markedly higher or lower specific gravity than the peas, as well as the further process of visual inspection whereby a team of sorters removed any foreign matter they saw. Since the situation could have been avoided by the sorters seeing the caterpillar, the House of Lords held that the defence did not apply, even if it could be said that the manufacturer had taken all reasonable care to avoid such an accident. In addition, some of the judges expressed doubt about whether the presence of the caterpillar was a consequence of the processes of collection, because the caterpillar occurred despite the processes rather than because of them. In this view the defence is directed more to situations where the foreign matter is used in the process of preparation (e.g. in this case brine and salt).[181]

CONCLUSION

The broad statutory standards considered in this chapter are those most frequently used by consumer protection departments in ensuring acceptable standards of business behaviour.[182] By no means are the existing provisions entirely satisfactory and a number of suggestions have been made for reform. For example, the law is quite inadequate with regard to false statements about services and there is a need for a broad provision making it unlawful to represent that services are of a particular standard, or to mislead consumers as to the nature, characteristics and suitability for purpose or quality of any service. Moreover, there is an urgent need to overturn the *Tesco* decision, which emasculated the liability of corporations for breaches of consumer protection law. Something along the lines of section 84(2) of the Australian Trade Practices Act 1974 provides a model: it deems conduct engaged in on behalf of a company by an employee to be also engaged in by the company if committed 'at the direction or with the consent or agreement (whether express or implied) of a director, agent or servant of the body corporate'.[183] On this basis the branch manager in *Tesco* would not have been 'another person' for the purposes of the section 24(1) defence.

Enforcement is crucial with broad statutory standards because it is only by constantly bringing prosecutions in the courts that consumer protection departments can bring home to businesses the need to ensure compliance with consumer law. Moreover, judicial decisions are often necessary to establish the parameters of an enactment incorporating broad standards. In *Regulating Business*[184] I criticized the operation of some consumer protection departments which too readily adopt an advisory role on the basis that they can ensure compliance with the law simply by informing businesses of its provisions, at the expense of giving businesses sharp reminders through prosecution about the need to prevent violations. At the next level, the 'secondary enforcers' – in the main the magistrates courts – fail to appreciate the nature and seriousness of consumer offences. Too often businesses can breach statutory standards in the consumer protection area without incurring a great cost in monetary penalties or in stigmatization. One solution is the establishment of a special court for consumer protection matters, like the Market Court in Sweden.

Making breaches of criminal law automatically give rise to civil liability is one way of strengthening the broad statutory standards. In 1856 a select committee recommended that 'a cheap and easy remedy, by summary charge before a magistrate', should be afforded 'to consumers who received adulterated or falsely described food'.[185] The suggestion was taken up not in the food and drugs legislation but in the Merchandise Marks Act 1887. Section 17 of that Act provided that a person applying a trade description to a product was deemed to warrant that it was true, so that a false trade description constituted a breach of both the criminal and civil law. The section was deliberately omitted from the Trade Descriptions Act 1968, which contains a specific provision that a contract for the supply of a product is not void or unenforceable by reason only of a contravention of the Act.[186] Unlike with industrial safety legislation, the courts have rejected an attempt to ground a civil action on breach of a criminal statute in the consumer protection area. In *Square* v. *Model Farm Dairies (Bournemouth) Ltd*[187] the Court of Appeal justified the result because a purchaser could already in most cases bring an action under the Sale of Goods Act, but to give other consumers a civil action on the basis of a criminal offence would undermine the doctrine of privity of contract. At present only breach of the Consumer Protection Act 1961 and the Consumer Safety Act 1978 automatically gives the consumer an action in civil law.[188] These also provide that any term of an agreement is void so far as it has the effect of excluding or restricting such liability. Wide use of such a provision in consumer legislation would have the advantage that consumers would readily obtain compensation in the event of a business committing a criminal offence. More importantly, it would act as some deterrent to wrongdoing if enforcement authorities instituted mass restitution suits on behalf of consumers adversely affected, as discussed in Chapter 3.

9
The provision of information

The Consumer Protection Charter of the Council of Europe espouses the principle of making information available to the consumer 'to enable him to make a rational choice between competing products and services.'[1] Actually forcing businesses to divulge information about their products, practices and processes, under threat of criminal sanction, is now a popular technique of modern consumer legislation.[2] The assumption is that once information is disclosed, consumers will use it to protect themselves. Government's enthusiasm for disclosure regulation is based partly on the fact that it is relatively inexpensive when compared with other forms of regulatory control. Compliance can be readily checked where it is simply a matter of determining whether advertisements, contracts in standardized form, or the like contain the requisite information.

The economic justification for disclosure regulation is that it facilitates competition, one of the necessary conditions for which is that consumers possess a high degree of knowledge about products and services in the market. This is recognized explicitly in the Fair Packaging and Labeling Act of the United States, which says by way of preamble: 'Informed consumers are essential to the fair and efficient functioning of a free market economy.'[3] At present there is widespread consumer ignorance because of the vast array of complex products, which are frequently concealed by prepacking. Businesses are deterred from providing information voluntarily because of the cost, and also because of self-interest, since consumer ignorance furthers oligopoly power by impeding the market.[4] Disclosure regulation forces businesses to place greater emphasis on price and quality factors and less on advertising and promotion. This furthers competition and limits the ability of businesses to acquire monopoly power. An illustration is that information about the comparative advantages of products and services made available through *Which?*, *Choice*, *Test* or *Consumer Reports* makes consumers less vulnerable to advertisements. Even a relatively small change in consumer behaviour brought about by such information can have a magnified impact on business behaviour because it may not take much to render particular products or services unprofitable. By enabling consumers to spend their income more rationally, information of this sort leads to a more optimal allocation of society's resources.

Disclosure regulation as the major tool of consumer protection law is espoused particularly by those with political philosophies seeking to minimize the intervention of the state in the economy. The non-interventionalists say that regulatory control can never replace *caveat emptor* or substitute for informed decisions by individual consumers. Their view is that regulatory control is necessary in only isolated instances, involving safety and health, or for consumers who are particularly susceptible to exploitation because of their dependence or vulnerability. Instead, the non-interventionalists argue that the combination of informed consumers and competition among businesses best serve the cause of consumer protection. In their view ordinary consumers command little sympathy if they lay out appreciable sums of money without first informing themselves. With less expensive items, the argument runs, consumers can easily acquire information from experience. It is conceded that this is less practicable with hazardous or expensive purchases, and for this reason non-interventionalists concede government a limited role in compelling businesses to make sufficient information available to consumers for rational choice. What is said does not mean that those with different political philosophies, like socialists, never advocate disclosure regulation, or that it is inconsistent with their politics, only that they do not see it as the main tool of consumer protection. They are more inclined to advocate other more direct forms of regulation, for they see a number of drawbacks associated with disclosure regulation, some of which are considered later in this chapter.

Disclosure regulation goes one step further than laws controlling trade descriptions, which are simply concerned with the accuracy of information which businesses elect to make available. Disclosure regulation actually mandates the provision of certain types of information. Potentially its ambit is very wide, covering the quality of products and services, their price, including the cost of credit, and the actual terms of consumer transactions. Traditionally legislation obliging businesses to disclose information was confined almost entirely to product labelling. More recently legislation has concerned itself with information about prices and the cost of credit. Indicative of the narrow use of disclosure regulation – despite the political and economic arguments in support – is the history of sections 8–10 of the Trade Descriptions Act 1968. These sections clothe the executive with wide power to compel the marking or accompanying of their products with, or the insertion in advertisements of, information of value to consumers. Yet to date few orders have been made along these lines.[5] At least two reasons are advanced to excuse the dearth of such orders. It is said that there is an absence of reliable, objective standards to express such information and to measure its use. Then there is the legal opinion that the sections are drafted narrowly, and that within these terms information must be about 'goods' and not about business-consumer transactions.[6] These reasons do not bear close examination as an excuse for inaction, for organizations like the British Standards Institution have drafted numerous objective standards concerning products, which could form the basis of such orders.

CHANNELS OF INFORMATION DISCLOSURE

A possible means of analysing laws requiring business to disclose information is to proceed in terms of the way information must be presented under them. The following categories suggest themselves:

Product labelling

Product labelling has been an important method of protecting consumers for some time. As well as ensuring market transparency, product labelling sometimes has the more direct role of ensuring physical protection by warning consumers about product hazards. The Molony Committee concluded strongly in favour of product labelling because it ensured rational choice by permitting consumers to assess and compare the suitability of items for their individual requirements.[7] It also assisted after consumers had purchased an article if there were instructions on matters like care or use. The criteria which the Committee identified for introducing product labelling were whether its absence was creating difficulties for consumers, whether its presence was important for initial choice or subsequent use, whether important facts about a product or service were identifiable by observation and whether the requisite information was describable within the limits of a label.[8] In the main governments have confined compulsory product labelling to cases involving consumers' health or safety or involving a statement of relatively simple matters of fact as distinct from value judgements.[9]

Advertisements

Corrective advertising has already been considered. Another possibility is to require advertisements to contain particular information, which is something that the Swedish Market Court can do.[10] An example in Britain is that the government can require tests on the fuel consumption of cars and require the results to be published.[11] A further step involves the state in actually issuing advertisements about the quality of products and services offered by private businesses (e.g. best buys). Most Australian jurisdictions have the power – apparently never used – to conduct tests on a food or a drug and to publish the results.[12] On the whole governments eschew the course of evaluating products and services because objections would be raised that they were favouring one business over another. West Germany, for example, avoids this difficulty by subsidizing an independent comparative testing organization similar to Britain's Consumers' Association.[13]

Terms of sale

Consumers' ability to compare prices is impaired by the large number of items available, their range of sizes and the variations in the way they are promoted. In an oft-quoted study, college-educated women in the United States were instructed to select the most economic package for each of twenty products. The women erred on 43 per cent of their selections, although the results differed between products according in part to the nature of the packaging.[14] Standardized quantities are an illustration of how regulating the terms of sale can inform consumers and overcome some of the confusion in purchase decisions. The requirement is an alternative to unit pricing, and like that practice depends for its effectiveness on whether consumers use the information.

The idea of standardized quantities for products is to reduce the proliferation of sizes at present on the market. Thus the law might compel manufacturers to sell a prepacked product in quantities of two, four, eight and twelve ounces, a pound and multiples of a pound. The aim is to enable consumers to choose more rationally because of the simpler relationships involved. Standardized quantities facilitate comparisons between different sizes and between the same size for different brands. At present as little as a quarter of an ounce separates pack sizes and different sizes proliferate. Another advantage is that standardized quantities make it more difficult for manufacturers to disguise price increases by a marginal reduction in the quantity of the product.

An EEC Directive requires this change from the confusing array of existing sizes to standardized ones for foods and other consumer products such as cosmetics, detergents and aerosols.[15] In Britain some twenty classes of products (in general basic foodstuffs like bread, butter and milk, but more recently biscuits and toothpaste) must be sold in standardized quantities when prepacked.[16] Prescribed quantities by no means remove consumer confusion if the units chosen are not easily identified. Consumer groups have also said that too many standardized quantities are allowable for some products. This defeats the object of standardized quantities because consumers cannot distinguish standard sizes which are too closely bunched. Manufacturers have successfully opposed the extension of standardized quantities. A major objection is that standardized quantities will discourage standardized containers, because the same weight of different brands of a product can occupy a different volume because of a variation in density.[17] It is also said that standardized quantities place too great an emphasis on price to the detriment of quality. Both objections cannot bear close scrutiny; even if the first is true it can be solved by varying fills of different brands, and the second is in direct contravention of the consumer's right to know comparative prices.

TYPES OF INFORMATION DISCLOSURE

Another means of exposition is to focus on the particular concerns of disclosure regulation laws.[18] Information about credit rates and price are dealt with separately; here, we shall consider the following categories.

Safety

Safety is a major consideration of many laws obliging the provision of information. The labelling of drugs is a good example and is dealt with in Chapter 12.[19] In some jurisdictions there are far-reaching provisions for the compulsory labelling of dangerous consumer products. The Canadian regulations, for example, require the labels of prescribed products to contain information such as the nature of any hazard (e.g. 'flammable', 'corrosive'), a signal word such as 'danger' or 'caution', instructions for first-aid treatment (e.g. the names of antidotes) and a hazard symbol.[20] Domestic cleansers are a major product covered by the legislation. Compulsory labelling is justified for these products because of their widespread use, diversity and often technically complex nature. A large number of accidental poisonings from household cleaning products are reported and the vast majority occur with children under five years of age. In Britain poisons legislation might apply to some hazardous consumer substances, and some might come under the labelling requirements for dangerous substances introduced in compliance with EEC requirements.[21] This is hardly the comprehensive approach demanded by the nature of the hazard.

The United States was first in the field of safety labelling for cigarettes. The Federal Cigarette Labeling and Advertising Act 1965 made it unlawful to market cigarettes without a prominent statement on the packet that smoking was dangerous to health.[22] Countries such as Australia followed suit; cigarette packets have to be labelled and warnings have also to accompany advertisements.[23] In 1972 a Private Member's Bill in Britain to similar effect failed to obtain a second reading. Voluntary agreements have subsequently been reached between the government and the tobacco manufacturing industry that warnings would appear on cigarette packets and in poster and press advertisements and would be such that they were easily seen by consumers. The warnings by themselves have not greatly affected the per capita consumption of cigarettes – a reminder that simply obliging businesses to provide information to the public is frequently ineffective as a means of consumer protection. In 1967 a Federal Trade Commission Report in the United States concluded that the warnings could not overcome the prevalent attitude maintained by the barrage of advertising on television and radio, particularly persuasive to the young, that smoking was a harmless and enjoyable social activity.[24] Consequently the Public Health Cigarette Smoking Act 1969 was passed by Congress, which made it unlawful to broadcast cigarette advertisements on radio and television.[25] The voluntary codes for advertising practice in Britain were subsequently amended to prevent cigarette advertising on radio and television.

Despite these moves, cigarette smoking still takes a terrible toll. There are difficulties in trying to give up the habit voluntarily because of the social pressures and because nicotine is addictive. In other words, comparatively few individuals will act on the information readily available to them about the dangers of smoking. The anti-smoking lobby has campaigned for more drastic laws, such as a total ban on all forms of advertising (e.g. on hoardings, in newspapers and in the cinema); prominent mention of tar levels on cigarette packets; a significant increase in taxation to make excessive consumption of cigarettes prohibitive, and ultimately a ban on sales.

Quality

Grading is a direct means of indicating quality if there is agreement on how to set the grades, and providing consumers appreciate the difference between products of different grades. About thirty fruits and vegetables, eggs and wine are subject to grading regulations in EEC countries.[26] The grading is primarily to encourage growers to improve quality and marketing, but it also benefits consumers by informing them about the quality of their purchases. Under the grading regulations for fresh fruit and vegetables, products offered for sale at both wholesale and retail outlets must clearly show the origin; the quality class (Extra, I, II, and III); and the variety. It is sufficient for retailers to sell products direct from a container with the requisite information attached if the details are clearly visible to consumers. Otherwise there must be a display card or the information must be on the packet if there is prepacking. The EEC grading is not concerned directly with eating quality but with size and condition. Within a class a particular fruit or vegetable must be of a minimum size and within a batch the particular fruit or vegetable must not vary in size by more than a specified tolerance. There are difficulties in enforcing the regulations with the multifarious retail outlets for fruit and vegetables, and surveys have shown that some retailers fail to display the requisite information.

Grade labelling is more difficult with complex consumer durables than with natural products like fresh fruit and vegetables. Performance characteristics are one way of conveying information about the quality of consumer durables; for example, light bulbs and car tyres might be marked to indicate their average life.[27] The most common method of disclosing quality information, however, is through compositional labelling. Traditionally, compositional labelling was confined to processed food, but in recent years has been extended to products like textiles. Textiles are said to be a suitable area for compulsory labelling because consumers face difficulties in distinguishing and in appreciating the characteristics of the many synthetic fibres. EEC countries, the United States, Canada and Australia compel fibre content labelling for textiles.[28] A broad statement of the EEC Directive is that the names of fibres must be specified on a garment or in advertisements, together with the percentage of the different fibres used. Further, the limited number of generic names mentioned in the Directive must be used to describe fibres, and restrictions are placed on the use of words such as 'pure' when referring to fibre content.

One aspect of quality labelling in some countries has been to encourage voluntary action on the part of businesses. Quality marks convey a guarantee of a certain quality without normally providing details of use, composition or performance.[29] The marks usually take the form of a symbol, which indicates compliance with a standard fixed by a body like the British Standards Institution. Its 'Kitemark' symbol tells consumers that a product complies with a BSI standard, and that the manufacturer's production process is regularly inspected, its quality control methods checked and a specified number of sample items ready for retail sale tested. Surveys indicate that there is considerable public ignorance of such quality marks and that consumers, especially those in the lower socio-economic groups, are quite unsure about the properties to which the marks refer.

Quantity

One of the first pieces of information the law obliged businesses to provide to consumers was a statement of the quantity of products being sold. Legislation obliges manufacturers to mark many prepacked goods with a statement of their weight or other appropriate quantity. If goods are not prepacked, weight may still have to be made known to consumers; one course is to require weighing or counting in the presence of purchasers.[30] A less satisfactory alternative is to allow retailers to have a self-indicating type of scale available for use by consumers with a notice drawing attention to the facility.[31] Observation suggests that few consumers use the facility. Quantity marking must sometimes be done in a manner which facilitates inter-product comparisons by consumers. For example, packets may have to be marked in complete ounces, and not in pounds and ounces, to avoid confusion through a mixture of units. The United States Fair Packaging and Labeling Act makes necessary a statement of the net quantity of a serving if representations are made concerning servings.[32]

For marketing executives, the package is often more important than the product it contains. This attitude has led to a situation where packaging often misleads consumers about the nature – in particular the amount – of an enclosed product. Modern packaging is frequently a waste of economic resources and a cause of environmental pollution. It results in consumers spending substantial amounts on what may be discarded as soon as a product is opened. Containers may be necessary for reasons of hygiene and freshness, and to store the product, but promotional considerations frequently dictate an unnecessary extravagance in design. Bulk-buying might achieve considerable savings because the packaging content of products is equivalent to a not insignificant part of the retail price.

Legislation directed at deceptive practices, such as the Trade Practices Act 1968, is only a partial answer to misleading packaging. As a result of the Weights and Measures etc. Act 1976 regulations may be made obliging containers to be filled to specified levels (e.g. in percentage terms). South Australian legislation actually lays down percentage levels for the amount of slack – 25 per cent in normal cases and 35 per cent where there is an inner container.[33] New Zealand law attempts to suppress spurious advertising about sizes (e.g. 'economy size') by making it unlawful to suggest that there is a price advantage associated with a particular size when this is not the case.[34]

Origin

Marking of goods with their country of origin is criticized as an unreliable indication of the quality and properties of products, and a hindrance to free trade among countries and thus to consumer welfare. One of its justifications is that it permits consumers to discriminate against imported goods on patriotic, political or personal grounds and that it may inform them about quality. Origin marking can take various forms. It can be limited to ensuring that foreign products are not passed off as national products.[35] Alternatively, it can require that products be marked with or accompanied by an indication of origin, which might also have to be included in certain advertisements.[36]

Use

Use marking is mainly voluntary; where compulsory it is almost solely concerned with safety (e.g. 'Keep out of reach of children' for poisons and drugs). However, care instructions are an aspect of use marking of growing importance. Consumer advocates justify care instructions for textiles because fibre content alone is insufficient to inform consumers exactly what cleaning processes may be used. Without care labelling, appreciable numbers of garments can be rendered useless, causing consumer dissatisfaction and wasting economic resources. In many countries care labelling depends on the voluntary efforts of trade associations.

The objection to compulsory care labelling has been mainly that the variety of factors determining how textiles respond to treatment is too great – and includes behaviour solely within the province of consumers – for manufacturers to be threatened with criminal sanctions. The Federal Trade Commission in the United States proposes to make care labelling compulsory for textile products and leather clothing by adopting a rule that not to label in specified circumstances constitutes an unfair or deceptive act or practice.[37] The rationale of the rule is that technological advance in the apparel and cleaning industries and the host of textiles on the market, each with different characteristics, made it impossible for consumers to inform themselves or to determine care information by the traditional means of trial and error.

Contractual terms

Chapter 7 contained a discussion of how regulated agreements under the Consumer Credit Act 1974 must contain information about important contractual terms. The Federal Trade Commission in the

United States has gone one step further than such a provision. It has ordered particular businesses to disclose *orally*, in dealings with consumers, information already required to be set down in written form. In *Tashof* v. *Federal Trade Commission*,[38] a Federal Trade Commission order was upheld obliging a businessman located in an area inhabited by low-income consumers, who employed 'bait and switch' (see Chapter 8) with respect to sales, adequately to disclose his charges, both orally and in writing. Critics argue that to require oral disclosure of important terms of sale would face insuperable barriers of enforcement. Perhaps a more pertinent point to make is that other forms of regulation (like banning particular modes of sale) are a more efficient method of protecting consumers.

Consumers need an effective means of identifying those behind a business to further their complaints, to sue, or to enforce any judgment. If a business is incorporated it might be possible to trace the controllers of the company through the companies' office. The Registration of Business Names Act 1916 provided a central registry of business names for those carrying on a business under a name different from their real name or for a company carrying on a business under a name which was different from its corporate name. That Act has been repealed by the Companies Act 1981. Instead of a central registry, the Companies Act 1981 introduced a system of disclosure by businesses themselves of their proprietors' names. Disclosure is required in business documents, at business premises and immediately on request in writing to a person with whom anything is done or discussed in the course of a business (ss. 28–9). Disclosure is not required in advertisements. Breach of the disclosure requirements constitutes a criminal offence. Moreover, a court must dismiss any action brought by a person who is in breach of the provisions, arising out of a contract made in the course of the business, if the breach was in existence at the time the contract was made, and if the defendant shows that he has been unable to pursue a claim arising out of that contract or has suffered financial loss by reason of the breach (s. 30). A court can permit the proceedings to continue if satisfied that it is just and equitable (s. 30). The deterrent effect of this provision is undermined considerably by the difficulties of establishing an inability to pursue a claim or financial loss.

At one time in Britain – it is still the law in some circumstances in Australia but never used in practice[39] – the courts could publicize the fact that a business had been convicted of a consumer protection offence. The nature and outcome of, and the businesses involved in, small claims adjudications are prominently published in local newspapers in some Australian jurisdictions. In addition, some state consumer affairs commissioners publish annual lists of businesses whose methods are open to question or who have given rise to consumer complaints which have not been resolved satisfactorily. The Office of Fair Trading in Britain has deliberately publicized the names of businesses against whom it has obtained undertakings for breaches of the civil and criminal law under Part III of the Fair Trading Act 1973. These are some examples of how the law requires that information about business behaviour must be publicized. Such action is not to be disparaged because it can have a powerful deterrent effect on those businesses which are mindful of their responsibilities. The deterrent effect is lessened, however, to the extent that larger firms are prepared to counteract a bad reputation by conducting an advertising campaign, and that smaller firms simply change their name and carry on in the same way. Generally speaking, governments are reluctant to countenance laws which would lead to the more efficient dissemination of information about the reputation of individual businesses, such as the publication of blacklists. They are dissuaded from this action because of the strong opposition such a move would engender.

Post-contractual rights

An underrated aspect of disclosure regulation is providing consumers with information about their legal rights if something goes wrong with a consumer transaction. With cancellable agreements under the Consumer Credit Act 1974, consumers must be notified about their rights to cancel an agreement, but few read the obtuse language and even fewer readily comprehend it.[40] The Consumer Transactions (Restrictions on Statements) Order 1976 requires signs in shops, advertisements, containers and documents issued with products such as manufacturers' guarantees, not to be worded so as purportedly to deprive consumers of their rights when goods are sold without title, do not correspond with their description, or are unmerchantable or not fit for the purpose.[41] In *Hughes* v. *Hall*[42] second-hand car dealers included the phrase 'sold as seen and inspected' in their documentation. The magistrates dismissed informations for breach of the Order on the grounds that the phrase was too vague and would not enable the dealers to avoid their civil liability. The Divisional Court allowed the prosecutor's appeal: prima facie, and subject to what else might be expressly said in the contract, the phrase would negate a sale by description and therefore be in breach of the Order.

These are limited steps: concise and understandable information attached to products, set out in written documents or displayed at retail premises should benefit many consumers. Another approach is for the government to promote the establishment of consumer advice centres in major shopping areas where consumers can obtain advice about their post-contractual legal rights.

FOOD LABELLING

A broad prohibition in food legislation seeks to prevent food labelling and advertising which falsely describes a food or which is likely to mislead consumers as to the true character of a food.[43] The EEC Directive on food labelling contains an additional prohibition, against suggestions that a food will produce effects which have not been proved scientifically.[44] Despite the law, manufacturers still use descriptions and pictorial designs on food labels which represent food as something it is not, for example, using names like 'farm', 'country' and 'traditional' for products that were invented by technicians and produced in factories.

In addition to the broad prohibition on misleading labelling, the law requires manufacturers to disclose specific information on all food labels. When this aspect of food labelling was first introduced in Britain in 1944 it was simply assumed that it would protect consumers to the same extent as compositional standards.[45] Developments in the technology, processing and marketing of food over the last thirty years have strengthened the importance of food labelling as the most effective form of overall control, supported by compositional requirements for staple foods. The Food Standards Committee says that consumers are now more dependent on food labelling because an increasing proportion of foods is sold prepacked, which partially or wholly prevents visual assessment, and because there is an increasing diversity of foods, the result of factors such as modern processing techniques and the popularity of foreign cuisines.[46]

In the nineteenth century it was thought sufficient to inform the consumer when an article of food was a mixture and not a pure product. The assumption was that consumers were sufficiently protected as long as they were not misled. They were benefiting by purchasing a mixed and therefore a cheaper article, and they would not be safeguarded further by knowing the actual ingredients.[47] A similar attitude was adopted to the labelling of drugs. A select committee which considered the matter in 1914 concluded that labelling would not protect the public since, to the majority of purchasers, a statement of composition or contents would afford no information because of its technical language. Indeed, said the committee, the simplest substances might acquire distinction from being described in complicated chemical terms.[48]

Under section 4 of the Sale of Food (Weights and Measures) Act 1926, a number of prepacked foods had to be labelled with an indication of quantity. Restrictions on the use of preservatives under the Public Health (Preservatives, etc., in Food) Regulations 1925 were accompanied by a requirement that certain foods containing permitted preservatives had to be labelled to that effect, not so much to benefit ordinary consumers, who were protected by the general limitations on their use, but to benefit children, invalids and other particularly vulnerable persons who, in the absence of any declaration, would if necessary be unable to avoid their use.[49] Wartime conditions provided the impetus for wide-ranging mandatory food labelling. Under the Labelling of Food Order (No. 2) 1944, prepacked articles of food had to bear a label indicating the name and address of the business, the common name of the food, its quantity and a list of ingredients in descending order of amounts (although the fact that the ingredients were listed in descending order of amounts did not have to be stated).

The basic requirements have been substantially re-enacted in subsequent regulations where modification has tended to extend labelling requirements. Quantity markings for prepared foods are now governed by the Weights and Measures Acts 1963 and 1979 and Regulations.[50] The Food Labelling Regulations 1980[51] apply to most food which is ready for delivery to the ultimate consumer or to a catering establishment. Food has to be marked or labelled with the name of the food, a list of ingredients, an indication of minimum durability, any special storage conditions or conditions of use, the name or business name and an address or registered office of the manufacturer or packer or of a seller established within the EEC, particulars of the place of origin of the food if failure to give such particulars might mislead a purchaser to a material degree as to the true origin of the food, and instructions for use if it would be difficult to make appropriate use of the food in the absence of such instructions (r. 5).

Generally speaking, ingredients must be listed in descending order by weight determined as at the time of their use in the preparation of the food (r. 13(1)). But consumers are not always aware that ingredients are listed in this manner and it has been suggested that an explanation should be added to this effect. The Consumers' Association has recommended that with certain foods – meat products, jams and soft drinks are examples – the principal ingredient should be declared in percentage terms (in these cases, meat or fruit).[52] At present percentage declarations of ingredients are only necessary if a food is characterized by the presence, or conversely the low content, of a particular ingredient and the labelling of the food places special emphasis on this: minimum and maximum percentages are necessary respectively (r. 19(1)–(2)).

Simply listing ingredients in descending order by weight will not always enlighten consumers as to the composition of foods. By using two substances with similar functions in a food instead of one, it may appear that the principal ingredient is present in greater amounts than is really the case. An example is two jams, labelled in accordance with present legal requirements, but also showing their undeclared percentages besides the respective ingredients. The fruit content remains the same, but by substituting more glucose syrup for sugar it may appear that one jam contains more fruit than the other.[53]

Jam 1		Jam 2	
Sugar	45%	Fruit	35%
Fruit	35%	Sugar	31%
Glucose syrup	15%	Glucose syrup	29%
Pectin, etc.	5%	Pectin, etc.	5%

The regulations require that ordinary consumers should be able to understand the nature of the ingredients listed. In some situations where generic names are permitted, the description of an ingredient is so general as to be unenlightening. In the case of certain additives it is sufficient simply to use a category name without naming the particular additive.[54] Objection has been taken to this leniency because consumers may, as a matter of choice, wish to avoid ingesting particular types of additives, which are presently permitted although there is evidence of their danger to humans.

Another criticism of the present regulations is that the list of ingredients need not state that a food contains water unless water has been added as an ingredient, whereupon it must be declared in the list of ingredients.[55] But even in the latter case no declaration is necessary if water is used for rehydration, if it is used as, or as part of, a medium which is not normally consumed, if added water does not exceed 5 per cent of the finished product, or, in the case of water added to frozen or deep-frozen poultry, if EEC standards are met.[56] Two foods with different amounts of undeclared water can have identical declarations of ingredients. One suggestion is that the presence of water be indicated, together with the drained weight of the contents (i.e. the weight of the solids after any liquid is drained). On the other hand, the Hodgson Committee, which reported in the early 1950s, recommended in favour of minimum filled weights for tinned products (i.e. the weight of solid products originally used).[57] Drained weight differs from minimum filled weight because osmosis occurs with water moving to and from the solid. Minimum filled weight has the advantage that inspection for it can be more easily carried out at food factories than any form of subsequent testing on the basis of drained weight.

For the period between 1940 and 1952, regulations were in force requiring minimum filled weights for tinned fruit and vegetables and a standard type of syrup in tinned fruit.[58] The regulations were succeeded by a voluntary code of practice by which manufacturers agreed to maintain the minimum filled weights previously laid down although there was no requirement that these agreed weights would be marked on the tin.[59] The code was approved by most manufacturers and under it tinned food manufacturers agreed to permit enforcement bodies to visit factories to check filled weight. Evidence suggests that the code is no longer being complied with by all manufacturers, and that enforcement bodies fail to monitor its implementation. Until now the government has taken the view that the adoption of the concept of drained weight is too difficult to implement, for there is no accepted method of determining it. This reason cannot be given much longer: the EEC Directive on food labelling includes a provision for the declaration of drained weight and lays down a procedure for establishing it.[60]

Broad standards for food are ineffective in dealing with the sale of stale food or food which might otherwise have deteriorated to an unacceptable degree. Food needs to be mouldy or 'bad' (in ordinary parlance) rather than simply stale before it is caught by the present unfit food provisions. Open-date marking of food is an important solution to the problem. It recognizes the consumer's right to know the freshness of food being purchased as well as providing an incentive for retailers to institute a workable system of stock rotation and to ensure that food is in as fresh a condition as is technically possible.[61]

Opponents of open-date marking have raised arguments against its technical feasibility as well as its cost. It is said that poor stock rotation by retailers can render a manufacturer's date marking completely inaccurate as an indication of freshness. Yet date marking raises the possibility of consumer pressure on retailers and can thus actually encourage more efficiency in handling stock. Opponents have also raised the possibility of selective consumer purchases of foods with later dates, with the consequent wastage of other foods which are still perfectly fresh. Experience tends to refute this possibility, although it takes some time to educate consumers fully about the implications of date marking for their shopping. Open-date marking is mandatory in many European countries, but not all foods are covered: both the Food Standards Committee and the Steering Group on the Freshness of Food favoured a 'sell by' date for prepacked short-life food, with long-life foods being marked with the month and year of manufacture, packing or of removal from a cold store.[62]

As a result partly of the EEC food labelling Directive an indication of minimum durability is required for many foods by the words 'best before' followed by the date up to and including which the food can reasonably be expected to retain its specific properties if properly stored, and any storage conditions which need to be observed if the food is to retain its specific properties until that date.[63] In the case of a perishable food which is intended for consumption within six weeks of being packed, the minimum durability of the food may be indicated by a 'sell by' date, an indication of the period from the date of purchase for which the food can reasonably be expected to retain its specific properties if properly stored, and any storage conditions which need to be observed if the food is to retain its specific properties for that period.[64] The 'best before' date informs the consumer most directly, but the rationale for a 'sell by' date is that as an instruction to the shopkeeper it ensures proper stock rotation. There is the argument against 'best before' dates that they lead to unnecessary wastage because of the implication that to eat a food any time later than the 'best before' date is dangerous. Another problem is that consumers store foods differently and 'best before' dates may have to be set to take account of the worst possible storage conditions. It is not an offence to sell food beyond the 'best before' or 'sell by' date, although an offence under the legislation would occur if food was not of the nature, substance or quality demanded or was unfit for human consumption. Date marking is not the complete answer for food freshness for there are other matters such as stock control, temperature control and further food labelling (e.g. setting out storage conditions). There is legislation in other countries relating to food storage, setting minimum storage temperatures for certain foods (e.g. frozen foods).[65]

Special provisions govern the labelling and advertising of certain foods, and the way particular claims about food are made. For example, there are additional labelling requirements for food sold from vending machines and for alcoholic drinks.[66] Certain nutritional claims are prohibited on labels or in advertisements unless the food is capable of fulfilling the claim and the particular nutritional characteristics are identified.[67] Food specially made for nutritional requirements must also have a detailed energy statement. Claims that a food is capable of preventing, treating or curing a human disease shall not be made unless it is licensed under the Medicines Act 1968.[68] Disease is defined widely to include any injury, ailment or adverse condition of body and mind.

PRICE INFORMATION

Price information is crucial to consumers, especially in times of severe inflation. It is essential for comparative shopping, in which an increasing proportion of consumers seem to engage.[69] Unless prices are displayed, however, the opportunity cost of comparative shopping increases since more time and effort must be expended. Price information also avoids the situation of consumers entering transactions, despite misgivings, because once they have made personal contact with a business through a price enquiry they may feel embarrassed at not going further.

Despite the importance of price information to the economic interests of consumers, compulsory price marking is a relatively recent and as yet limited development. French and German law now requires businesses, including those providing services like credit houses, restaurateurs and car repairers, to display their prices at their place of business.[70] Developments elsewhere, however, are much less advanced, although many businesses display prices voluntarily.

Section 4(1) of the Prices Act 1974[71] now provides that

(1) The Secretary of State may by order make provision for securing:
  (a) that prices are indicated on or in relation to goods which a person indicates are or may be for sale by retail, whether or not the goods are in existence when he does so;
  (b) that charges are indicated for services which a person indicates are or may be provided, except services which he indicates are or may be provided only for the purposes of businesses carried on by other persons;
  (c) that prices of such goods or charges for such services are not indicated in a manner which the Secretary of State considers inappropriate and that no part of a penny except one half-penny is specified in the amount of an indicated price or charge.

Section 4(2) goes on to provide that the regulations can specify how the prices are to be indicated, which includes requiring unit pricing. In addition, the government under the Act can oblige retailers to display information about the range of prices within which particular goods are being commonly sold by retail, in the country as a whole or in particular areas. This provision is limited to food and to necessities which are important to poorer families and are normally the subject of recurrent expenditure by them.[72]

Regulations have been made obliging the display of the total selling price of various products and services on sale. Various orders have been made covering food for retail sale.[73] In addition premises such as public houses, restaurants and hotels must display in a clear and legible manner the price of food and drinks intended to be consumed on the premises.[74] Another order requires the display of petrol prices at garages on each pump; and in the case where there is a price display legible to a person in a motor vehicle on the highway, that price display must clearly contain certain information.[75]

The other area where tentative steps have been taken in price marking is with unit pricing. Unit pricing, which requires goods to be marked with their price per unit quantity is a means of assisting consumers to compare values. At present, competing products are not made up in equal or simply related quantities, and any comparison involves a complex calculation which the average consumer is unable or unwilling to make. Legislation in Europe and a number of United States jurisdictions has introduced unit pricing but it differs as to the products controlled and as to how markings are to be displayed. Standardized packings are often exempt in European jurisdictions on the basis that standardization equally meets the requirements of consumer protection.[77]

Businesses claim that there are difficulties associated with wide-spread unit pricing. First, it is said that there are the costs and administrative problems in determining the unit price of products and then ensuring the display of that information. A fluctuation in price necessitates an alteration in the marking, which may discourage 'reduced' offers. But unit pricing might have compensating advantages – tighter inventory control, better space management, fewer price-marking errors, and showing their own-brand labels to advantage. The second argument used by opponents of unit pricing is that, unsupported by other information, it is misleading for it may bear little relationship to product quality. In reply it can be said that unit pricing would at least inform consumers how much they are paying, even if other factors such as quality determine their decisions. Finally, there is the contention that only a minority of consumers will use unit pricing: faced with additional information the majority will ignore it. Even if this is true, it is not an argument against unit pricing, but one in favour of further consumer education about the value of comparative shopping. Indeed, evidence suggests that unit pricing is used by consumers when available. In one laboratory experiment in the United States, 200 women were shown a display of the most popular brands of detergents and soft drinks and asked to identify which they normally purchased. Initially they did not have a clear idea of relative values, but when specifically informed of the unit prices, a dramatic switch in their choices occurred.[78] Perhaps the fear of such a significant change in purchasing decisions is the major, if unpublicized, objection that businesses have to unit pricing.

Unit pricing is in operation at the retail level, but is mainly for food. There are specific requirements for fish, fresh fruit and vegetables (except when prepacked or when a total selling price is required), for vending-machine milk in quantities less than half a pint, for cheese which is not prepacked, and for certain prepacked cheeses, and for meat.[79] Food not covered by these specific requirements has to be unit priced if sold by reference to quantity or to a unit of measurement.[80] Unit pricing for petrol is required to be marked on the pumps and on roadside price displays.[81]

Unit price orders require the marking to be clear, legible and easily recognized by consumers. But the unit price need not be adjacent to a product and may be grouped with other unit prices in a comprehensive list as long as it is readily discernible by intending purchasers from where they will normally order goods in a shop. The unit of measurement used in unit pricing is crucial, for the higher the unit the more the price differences between products will be accentuated. So far unit pricing mainly uses pounds, pints and gallons (litres) which are suitable measures for demonstrating the price differences of the products covered.

A final aspect of price disclosure is comparative price information. Assuming that it is not practical for business to provide this directly themselves, an independent or government body has to do so. Consumer journals such as *Which?* contain comparative price information, but this dates quickly and is usually limited to relatively expensive items. At one time central government subsidized local consumer groups and consumer advice centres to undertake local price comparison surveys with a view to increasing consumers' purchasing power and stimulating retail competition.[82] Some 300 weekly surveys operated under this scheme covering commonly purchased items in a variety of shops. Monthly and quarterly surveys of non-food products such as fuel and petrol were also common. The information was disseminated by display on notice boards in consumer advice centres, on leaflets distributed by consumer advice centres, citizens advice bureaux and public libraries, and in a few areas through newspaper advertisements. One study concluded that the savings for a consumer in using a price comparison survey was typically in the range of 2½ to 5 per cent, but suggested that the usage rates might not justify the public expenditure.[83]

CREDIT DISCLOSURE

One approach would be to ban credit advertisements on the basis that they can never convey enough relevant information about credit transactions and can only be misleading. Law-makers have rejected this approach on the grounds that advertising is an inescapable feature of society and can perform a valuable service in making members of the public aware of credit facilities of which they might otherwise be ignorant.[84] Under the Consumer Credit Act 1974 there is a general prohibition on the credit advertisements covered conveying a false or misleading impression to consumers.[85] More importantly, credit advertisements and advertisements regarding the bailment of goods must disclose detailed information to give a fair and reasonably comprehensive indication of the nature of the credit or hire facilities offered and of their true cost.[86] Advertisements are defined to include display cards and catalogues.[87] Failure to comply with the credit advertising requirements is a criminal offence,[88] and it may be that a consumer can also obtain a compensation order against a defendant convicted in criminal proceedings for any loss suffered due to the omission of the requisite information.[89]

The main aim of credit disclosure is to redress part of the inequality of bargaining power between consumers and those offering credit by making it easier for consumers to discover the advantages and disadvantages of the alternative credit available. Credit disclosure ('truth in lending') permits the consumer to obtain an accurate description of the total credit charge, to allow easy comparison of different lenders' credit terms, and to help consumers decide whether a purchase should be financed by credit or by other means. An ancillary aim is to sharpen competition between credit institutions – assuming consumers engage in comparative shopping – which may improve the terms on which credit is offered.

The application of this credit disclosure part of the Act is quite wide and applies to advertisements by anyone carrying on a consumer credit business or a consumer hire business or a business which involves providing credit to individuals secured on land (e.g. building societies and others financing house purchases on mortgage), whether or not the particular agreements are otherwise regulated by the Act. Exceptions include advertisements which indicate that the credit is only available to corporations, or that the credit must exceed £5000 and that no security is required, or that the security is to consist of property other than land.[90] Advertisements by credit brokers are also covered.[91]

The Consumer Credit (Advertisements) Regulations 1980[92] confine advertisements for credit and bailment to three types, 'simple', 'intermediate' and 'full'. 'Simple' credit advertisements must only give the name and occupation of the business but nothing else indicating a willingness to provide credit (r. 6). Certain information is obligatory in an 'intermediate' advertisement – the name and address (or telephone number); the security, deposit or insurance ordinarily required; the cash price of any goods, services, land, etc. specified; the rate of the total charge for credit and related information; and an indication that written quotations may be obtained on request. Optional information in 'intermediate' credit advertisements includes restrictions of credit to particular groups, the extent to which cash and credit consumers are treated differently, the maximum and minimum credit, and in some cases the total amount payable (r. 7, Schedules 1–2). 'Full' credit advertisements must contain all the compulsory information in intermediate advertisements (with slight modifications), restrictions to a particular group, and the extent to which cash and credit consumers are treated differently. In certain circumstances it is also obligatory to give information on advance payments, liabilities which cannot be ascertained when the advertisement is published, the frequency of payments, and the amount of each repayment. With fixed-sum credit additional information is required in 'full' advertisements – the cash price, the total amount payable, and either the number of repayments or the period over which they are to be made (r. 8, Schedules 1–2). Comparative advertising suggesting better terms or conditions are forbidden except in 'full' credit advertisements when those terms or conditions are set out and the business making them is identified (r. 12(b)). The requirements for hire advertisements are along similar lines (rr. 13–16, Schedules 1, 4).

Obligatory information, and optional information in the case of 'intermediate' credit advertisements, must be presented clearly and together as a whole (r. 17). An exception to the latter requirement is that credit advertisements on the premises of a dealer can be split so that certain information (e.g. the cash price) is displayed on or near products or when consumers enquire about services, with an indication that other information relating to their supply or credit is displayed or available elsewhere on the premises (r. 9). When a statement of the rate of the total charge for credit is included, it must be afforded greater prominence than a statement relating to any other rate of charge and no less prominence than a statement relating to any period, advance payment, or the amount, number or frequency of any other payment or charge (except the cash price) or of any repayments

(r. 20). Representative terms can be disclosed in certain credit and hire advertisements where an item of information in relation to one transaction differs from that which applies in relation to another transaction of the same class (e.g. credit terms vary with the subject matter of the transaction or the status of the consumer).

What are the rates of the total charges for credit and the total amount payable by a debtor to be stated in advertisements? Calculations in accordance with the Consumer Credit (Total Charge for Credit) Regulations 1980[93] are subject to permissible tolerances in advertisements.[94] The total charge for credit is defined in these regulations as (a) the total interest, and (b) other charges payable under the transaction by or on behalf of the debtor or a relative whether to the creditor or another (r. 4). Examples of such other charges are set-up fees, insurance premiums, documentation charges and maintenance agreement charges.[95] The rate of the total charge for credit is then the total charge for credit expressed as an annual percentage rate. This is the rate determined according to specified formulae or to consumer credit tables when they are exactly applicable (rr. 6–10).[96] Certain assumptions are necessary in making these calculations, mainly because relevant factors are uncertain at the time the calculations have to be made (rr. 2, 12–18). For example, with running account (revolving) credit the actual rate of charge cannot be calculated in advance if it depends on how individual consumers use the facility (the time of purchase, the time and frequency of payments, and so on). For example, in one survey in the United States a department store charged 1½ cents in the dollar per month on its revolving credit accounts, which amounted to a nominal annual percentage rate of 18 per cent. A survey of its credit customers found that the annual rate for customers ranged from 0.8 per cent to 17.1 per cent, the rate on average being 10.5 per cent.[97] To avoid this difficulty the Regulations ignore how consumers use running account credit or the repayments they make where a constant period rate of charge is imposed in respect of periods of equal or of nearly equal length. The calculation of the rate of the total charge for credit is made on the assumption that the amount of credit at the beginning of the period remains outstanding throughout (r. 2(2)(b)). The credit limit is taken as the amount of credit, but if there is no credit limit and the amount of credit cannot be ascertained the amount is taken as £100 (r. 13).[98]

Without the obligation to disclose credit charges and terms

businesses could state the cost of an item on credit or the cost of a loan without specific reference to interest, to other charges or to significant features of any agreement. Advertisements for credit could be in terms of instalments at so much per month or of a global sum to be repaid over a specified period. Interest, if stated, could be in terms of a confusion of rates – flat rates, reducible rates, compound rates, add-on rates, effective annual rates and nominal rates (i.e. they might be reduced by bargaining). Flat rate interest (i) is calculated by dividing a hundred times the credit charges (C) by the credit originally extended (P; with purchases this is the cash price less the deposit) and the duration of the agreement in years (T). Thus the formula $i = 100C/PT$. As an indication of the cost of credit in instalment transactions, flat rate interest is quite misleading if consumers repay the original credit extended over the period of the agreement and not in a lump sum at its termination. The true rate of interest in such cases is much greater than the flat rate, because in effect consumers are paying interest on money which they have already repaid.[99]

Problems arise where an advertiser of products or services purports to have no credit charge or a modest credit charge but will not sell for cash. With no cash price there is no base to calculate the cost of credit and the advertiser could be charging a substantial amount for it. The Consumer Credit Act 1974 makes it an offence to advertise products or services for sale on credit if they are not available at the same time for cash.[100] Since the section fails to specify the level of the cash price, there is still the possibility of the real cost of credit being hidden by an inflated cash price. United States law overcomes the problem by making it a violation if a creditor represents as part of the 'cash price' any amount charged in excess of the amount at which a cash sale would be effected.[101] In other words, it makes equivalent the 'cash price' in a credit transaction and the price at which products and services are sold in cash. Yet even here there is the possibility that the price at which cash sales are effected may be inflated and consumers may not realize this because they do not engage in comparative shopping or because it is uncommon to pay cash in such a transaction.

What is the effect of credit disclosure on consumers' knowledge and behaviour? Studies in the United States indicate that after the introduction of credit disclosure, customers were more aware of the general level of interest rates being charged, especially those in higher socio-economic groups. Consumers actually committed to credit transactions were also more knowledgeable about what they were being charged. This says very little, however, because there was still an abysmal ignorance of credit charges, particularly among poorer consumers. In one survey after credit disclosure legislation began operating, only 10 per cent of borrowers could estimate what interest they were paying with a 10 per cent margin of error, and nearly half missed the amount by 50 per cent or more.[102] Very few consumers compare sources of credit before committing themselves to particular transactions, and in this regard credit disclosure had virtually no impact. A survey in California, for example, found that not even a fifth of those noting information about credit charges indicated that it had any effect on past or anticipated behaviour.[103] These surveys are not conclusive, however, particularly since they were conducted soon after credit disclosure was introduced. The effect of credit disclosure is likely to be indirect as consumers gradually become aware that certain sources of credit are cheaper (just as they gradually became aware that some prices at discount houses were lower).[104]

To be effective, credit disclosure must be associated with a concerted campaign of educating consumers about credit. There is an overriding need for teaching school children to appreciate the nature of credit transactions and the associated costs and pitfalls. Further, the scope of credit disclosure might need to be widened. Consumers have little appreciation of the extent to which credit transactions limit their ability to adapt to new needs or unforeseen problems like sickness or unemployment. One suggestion is that charts should be developed which would show how much of a budget under different conditions can safely be committed to credit transactions.[105]

Does credit disclosure achieve the subsidiary aim of furthering competition between credit institutions? A detailed survey of the impact of credit disclosure on the major credit companies in the United States discovered that few companies had lost customers. Only 6 per cent of those companies making consumer finance loans and only 5 per cent of the ones purchasing sales finance contracts found it necessary to reduce their annual percentage rate of charge.[106] One of the reasons that most were not seriously injured was that they were able to move into the more profitable areas of consumer credit.[107] However, the total number of finance companies in the United States fell, and it seems that some were forced out of business perhaps as a result of increased competition arising from the obligation to disclose cost of credit.

DISCLOSURE REGULATION IN PERSPECTIVE

The evidence suggests that many consumers are not greatly assisted by laws which require businesses to disclose information. The major problem with disclosure regulation is not in securing business compliance, but rather that consumers are unaware of the information disclosed, do not appreciate its significance or simply do not employ the information provided in the market-place. Those who theoretically are likely to benefit most from the information, poorer consumers, may face different market conditions from others, which information disclosure is unable to equalize.[108] The evidence from the United States is that credit disclosure, at least initially, had only a minor impact on consumer behaviour. Surveys of knowledge about detailed food labelling reveal that consumers are often misinformed about statutory standards of food composition and that although they might study the lists of ingredients when first purchasing a product, they do not really understand them (particularly the technical terms), nor do they know that the ingredients are listed in order of amounts.[109]

A number of reasons can be suggested for the ineffectiveness of disclosure regulation. First, consumers may not have a strong desire for information. This derives partly from habit and partly from a deficiency in consumer education; it is no surprise that it is the middle class who reads consumer publications like *Which?*, *Test*, *Choice* and *Consumer Reports*. Consumers may also overlook crucial information. For this reason the food compositional standards might be better than food labelling although the latter has the advantages of simplicity, of avoiding the difficulty of definition and of not inhibiting the development of new products. Another factor is that consumers may not regard as important much of the information presently the subject of disclosure laws. They may respond differently to an obligation on businesses to inform consumers about crucial characteristics of consumer products like performance and durability.

Next, certain types of disclosure are more effective than others. Information on food labels or in contractual documents may be incomprehensible to ordinary consumers, but non-technical information can have a greater impact. Examples are the display of prices on supermarket shelves or the dissemination of specific information about businesses (e.g. public blacklists). There is a dilemma in communicating technical information to a non-technical audience.[110] Information must be capable of being understood by consumers, but at the same time it must be accurate – and that can mean use of technical expressions. Even simply understood information may not have an impact on consumers, depending on its manner of presentation. When bold and simple warnings are set out in contract documents, for instance, consumers are no longer psychologically disposed to take them into account because in most cases they have already committed themselves to go ahead with a transaction.[111] Even if the barrier is overcome there remains the complexity of choosing despite adequate and clear information. As Leff notes: 'Anyone who has tried to use *Consumer Reports* has experienced the frustration of deciding between a superb Frammis with a shock hazard and a not-so-fine Wudgis without.'[112]

Another factor in the relative ineffectiveness of disclosure regulation is that consumers may have no choice but to enter certain transactions whatever their state of knowledge. Thus many poor consumers have no realistic alternative to paying high interest rates for credit because they are regarded as bad credit risks by established finance houses. Of course other factors are involved in the poor seeking credit.[113] Even if they know of cheaper prices they may prefer to do business with familiar, if more expensive, institutions. In the Californian credit disclosure survey mentioned above, low-income and minority (black) consumers believed their attempts to borrow from low-cost sources of credit would be frustrated, even though this was not always strictly true.[114] A related point is that the impact of information disclosed can be counteracted by other aspects of a consumer transaction. Advertising is a force so strongly influencing choice that it offsets detailed, objective information available to consumers. Pressures existing at the point of sale – such as the manipulative ploys of salespersons – can override the knowledge which consumers have obtained. In other words, the problem is sometimes misleading or fraudulent marketing practices and not ignorance on the part of consumers.

Finally, consumers may make a rational choice in disregarding available information. It is quite common for consumers to ignore price information because other factors – quality, the desire to possess a product, and so on – make price a minor consideration. When seeking credit, poor consumers may be more concerned with the size of a deposit and of the monthly repayments than with the interest rate charged. Opportunity costs (the time and effort) associated with using information may not be worth while, especially if small amounts of money are at stake. Thus a survey of consumers obtaining credit for new cars concluded that lack of knowledge was by no means the principal deterrent to their seeking the lowest-cost loan for which they were qualified.[115] There were a variety of other reasons: inconvenience, legitimate impossibility, belief that the low-cost lender was tougher in other respects (larger deposit, more references, etc.), too much trouble to join a credit union, and so on.

Because disclosure regulation has these drawbacks, other forms of regulatory control will often be the preferred course for legislative action. Even so, disclosure regulation can perform a useful if supplementary role in consumer protection. Its continued and more extensive use, together with rising levels of consumer education, will render it more worth while with time. For these reasons it is misguided to adopt the attitude that because consumers at present will not use information there is no need for it. Another point which has not yet been mentioned is that disclosure regulation is an invaluable aid for those charged with implementing consumer law, for discrepancies between the substance of business claims and their performance are immediately apparent or subject to investigation. Disclosure regulation can also be justified on other than utilitarian grounds: there is the consumer's basic right in a democratic society to be informed about products and services on the market so that they can have control over their daily decisions.[116]

Product standards

The civil law requires products to meet certain minimum, but very general, standards of merchantability and fitness for purpose. There are no counterparts in the criminal law which outlaw inferior products in broad terms, but certain criminal statutes fix general standards for particular products. For example, there are the general standards for food quality considered in Chapter 8. Generally speaking, however, there are few general criminal standards compelling businesses to manufacture or market products to attain specific standards of quality, composition, performance or durability.[1] In addition to these few general standards, there are a number of detailed standards for particular products. These differ from general criminal standards in that legislation actually sets out the details of what is mandated. Businesses need simply to comply with the specifications in the legislation and have no need to guess at what is required. This chapter examines the detailed product standards for (a) unusually hazardous products, and (b) for two particular products, motor vehicles and food. These are the main examples of detailed product standards.[2]

The major reason that policy-makers use to explain why there is not more use of detailed product standards is that it would be impracticable. There is the initial difficulty in fixing them. Consumer requirements, it is claimed, are diverse and variable, and it is impossible to reconcile them and devise standards which are generally satisfactory.[3] Different consumers attach widely varying importance to the characteristics of products. For example, some have an overriding interest in aesthetic factors such as appearance, while others desire value for money. Standards are also said to produce uniformity and to reduce the variety of types and styles of products available.

Technical difficulties are said to stand in the way of formulating worthwhile standards. Not only do a variety of production techniques have to be regulated, but it is also not easy to foresee the type of use to which products will be put. The complexity of the task may be reduced by performance standards, which a manufacturer must meet in whatever way it can, as opposed to standards which actually specify the way a product is to be manufactured. Performance standards, in transferring the burden of product design to manufacturers, lessen the degree of regulatory control, minimize possible adverse effects on competition and provide businesses with flexibility as well as the opportunity to participate in developing standards. On the other hand, more specific standards mandating modes of manufacture may be more easily enforceable, in that a particular product can be readily identified as in breach of legal requirements.

There may be practical difficulties as well in fixing product standards. If a standard is too high it may prevent the sale of products which are satisfactory in relation to the possible incidence of risk. Unrealistic standards in this sense are detrimental in that they raise the cost of products without providing any corresponding benefits to consumers. On the other hand, a standard set at too low a level will achieve little. It may actually operate as an inducement to a manufacturer to degrade the quality of its products to or near to the standard if the market is non-competitive and better quality articles do not command a significantly higher price.

Although governments have been reluctant to fix detailed product standards, this has been done for motor vehicles, for certain foods, for drugs and for some items which are unusually hazardous. Policy-makers have been impelled to legislate in these areas because physical harm and not just economic detriment may occur. Experience demonstrates that competition, information and even the broad prohibitions of the civil and criminal law are inadequate in preventing physical harm to consumers. Consumers do not have the opportunity to protect themselves because frequently they are unable to assess whether a product is unsafe. Unsafe products have repercussions on innocent bystanders or on vulnerable sections of the population, such as children, who are not in a position to protect themselves. The setting of standards in such circumstances is facilitated because of the central aim of preventing harm to consumers. The variables in fixing any particular standard are reduced, for other factors are subordinated to this major consideration.

Except for drugs, product standards have not gone as far as a system of prior approval. In other words, there is no stipulation that products – or at least those potentially unsafe or used by vulnerable segments of the population such as children – should be approved by a government body before being marketed. Individualized control of this nature has been rejected because of inherent difficulties in foreseeing all the hazards associated with the use of a product.[4] A government would also be faced with the repercussions of having to withdraw its imprimatur from a product because experience demonstrated that it was unsafe for consumers. Moreover, such control would involve elaborate and expensive administrative machinery and would be impracticable because of the volume and variety of products marketed.

Compromise is inherent in any particular decision about standards for potentially harmful products. Factors to be taken into account include the cost of preventing harm by introducing a standard as opposed to the loss which might occur without it, the tolerable incidence of injury, how serious injuries are likely to be without a standard and so on. Little can be said about the outcome as opposed to the factors involved in decision-making, for disagreement will inevitably arise over the weights to be attached to different factors. In some situations injury to persons will be taken extremely seriously and its prevention will become the paramount consideration.

UNUSUALLY HAZARDOUS PRODUCTS

Of the many injuries people suffer every year, it seems that about a third occur at work or on the road, and that the remainder fall in the categories of injuries occurring through the manufacture, supply or use of goods or services, on premises belonging to or occupied by another, or in miscellaneous ways (at school, through games or sport, in the street, at home, and so on).[5] Unusually hazardous products such as electrical appliances are thus an explanation for a number of injuries. Of course few consider making a private law claim for damages and even fewer obtain legal advice or pursue legal action.[6]

The law regulating unusually hazardous products could be in terms of a broad directive prohibiting outright dangerous items or those at risk to health.[7] A closely related approach would be to impose a duty on businesses to ensure so far as was reasonably feasible that products marketed were safe and without risk to health when properly used for their intended purpose.[8] The obligation in both cases would be on businesses to develop the appropriate standards for their products. Enforcement agencies would institute proceedings if they thought that this had not been accomplished and the burden of deciding the matter would rest on the courts.

Law-makers have rejected a broad prohibition for unusually hazardous products in favour of detailed product standards specifying the methods by which compliance can be ascertained. The argument is that there would be considerable doubt as to how a broad provision would be interpreted in relation to particular products. Manufacturers must know what is required of them and enforcement authorities must be able to identify examples of wrongdoing. Safety requirements must also take into consideration that with some products it is impossible to attain absolute freedom from risk. It is also said there are practical difficulties where the law eschews detailed safety standards and relies on flat prohibitions, as with reference to the presence of lead in particular products. Critics argue that such provisions have little meaning because of the present technical ability to find trace quantities of lead in everything. As two scientists complain: 'To deny that these elements are in beer, toys, wallpaper, etc., is impossible. What is important is legally to define limits in which these amounts are considered toxic. Therefore, in drafting laws and regulations statements like "X must not contain Y" should be replaced by "X must not contain more than a certain amount of Y".'[9] The objection that in practice a broad prohibition would not be sufficiently precise overlooks the fact that other broad provisions operate satisfactorily. Businesses, enforcement bodies and the courts have no major difficulties in identifying statements which are false or misleading, or food which is not of the nature, substance or quality demanded by the purchaser. There seems no inherent reason why flesh could not be given to the concept of an unusually hazardous product along similar lines.

What is an unusually hazardous product for which standards should be set? Initially there is the difficulty in distinguishing the unusually hazardous product from the product which, by its very nature, is potentially dangerous if mishandled or used without proper care. Knives and staircases are two examples of the latter. There are a number of factors which may distinguish the two categories, one being consumer knowledge of a potential danger. Consumers often do not know that a danger exists with unduly hazardous products, and if they are aware of it they are frequently unable to estimate its nature or severity, or they do not know how to cope with it. But the dividing line is far from clear-cut. Another problem is that many product-related accidents are attributable not simply to faulty design or manufacture but at least in part to carelessness, misuse, failure to comply with instructions, or lack of proper maintenance by the consumer. Individuals differ in their accident-proneness: some are clumsy and reckless and engage in hazardous activities. It is well known that some individuals remove safety guards from power tools, use ladders propped on boxes, remove grass from the blades of motor mowers with their bare hands.[10] Proper design can reduce or eliminate many risks, even for the careless or foolhardy. Cars and power mowers are examples, for although they are patently dangerous, design features can reduce the hazards. If the risks associated with a product can in fact be reduced or eliminated by better design there is a strong argument for saying that it is candidate for a product standard. An illustration is that 'dead man's controls' can be fitted to motor mowers to reduce the incidence of injuries.

The practice adopted with unusually hazardous products in Britain, then, has been to introduce detailed measures for particular products. In the past this was by separate statutory enactment,[11] but then the Consumer Protection Act 1961 clothed the executive with regulatory power to set product standards if expedient to reduce the risk of personal injury.[12] The power to promulgate regulations is more flexible than legislation and permits prompt action when hazards appear in new products or in those already on the market. The Consumer Safety Act 1978 empowers the Secretary of State to make 'safety' regulations for the purpose of securing that products are safe or that appropriate information is provided and inappropriate information prohibited. Safety regulations may contain provisions with respect to the composition, design, construction, finish or packing of products; requiring products to comply with the standards or to obtain the approval of a body; standards for products; approvals for products; testing; warnings, instructions or other information; and prohibiting unsafe products and those in breach of the regulations (s. 1). It then is an offence to act in contravention of the regulations (s. 2). Table 10.1 lists the products for which standards have been fixed and their respective year of issue.

Table 10.1   Product Standards for Unusually Hazardous Items

Stands for carry-cots (1966)	Children's clothing (hood cords) (1976
Nightdresses (1967)	Oil heaters (1977)
Electrical appliances (colour code) (1969; 1970)	Aerosol dispensers (1977, 1980[13])
	Babies' dummies (1978)
Electric blankets (1971)	Cosmetic products (1978)
Cooking utensils (1972)	Perambulators & pushchairs (1978)
Heating appliances (1973)	Oil lamps (1979)
Pencils and graphic instruments (1974)	Novelties (1980)
	Upholstered furniture & fabrics (1980)
Toys (1974)	Ornamental objects (1980)[13]
Glazed ceramic ware (1975)	Textile products (1980)[13]
Electrical equipment (1975)	

Whereas the United States leans towards performance standards leaving manufacturers to reach the requisite level of safety by methods of their own choosing, Britain tends to specify particular modes of manufacture. An exception is the Electrical Equipment (Safety) Regulations 1975, which make some reference to standards but in the main prescribe safety requirements in very general terms to cover a wide range of domestic electrical equipment. Manufacturers of electrical equipment are free to meet the basic statutory safety requirements in any way they choose, but to assist them and to help enforcement authorities, the government has issued an Administrative Guidance (which is kept up-to-date by periodic amendment) showing the standards which are considered to afford the degree of safety required by the regulations.[14]

In specifying modes of manufacture for unusually hazardous products, regulations take two forms: some set out product specifications in detail, which has the advantage of completeness, while others simply make reference to standards developed by the British Standards Institution, where these are sufficiently precise for enforcement. Making reference to BSI standards in effect delegates law-making power to this body. In certain respects bodies like the British Standards Institution are not always suitable to rely on for safety standards since safety is not *necessarily* a consideration in its deliberations and many consumer goods are not covered by its standards. Formulation of standards by the BSI is a lengthy process and since its standards rest on consensus within committees, comprising mainly business representatives, the outcome can be seen as not in the interests of consumers.

Law-makers have discharged their function of formulating standards in an *ad hoc* fashion, reacting when unusually hazardous products have been brought to their attention by publicity or consumer complaint. They contend that this approach is necessary, for the hazardous nature of many products can only be determined with the benefit of hindsight. Even if this were true, the United States experience demonstrates that the task can be undertaken in a more sophisticated manner than at present. In 1972 Congress entrusted a newly-established Consumer Product Safety Commission with the job of formulating consumer product safety standards.[15] The Commission has proceeded systematically to collate information about hazardous products before drafting standards. It received reports from hospital emergency units across the country about injuries sustained in relation to consumer products as well as more detailed reports about selected cases.

An upshot of the Consumer Product Safety Commission's activity is the publication of an index ranking the most dangerous consumer products in the United States. Criticism has been levelled at the index because it glosses over the causes of product-related injuries and because it does not identify the specifics of the products involved (age, design, manufacturer, and so on). The establishment of a Home Accident Surveillance Scheme in Britain in 1976 whereby information on accidents is collated from some twenty hospital accident and emergency departments, promises that product standards will evolve more rationally. However, the British government has rejected the idea of a body comparable to the Consumer Product Safety Commission as bureaucratically unnecessary.[16]

Even where the authorities have their attention drawn to an unusually hazardous product, there is no guarantee that a product standard will be made. Regulations have usually only been considered when the problem is quite serious and voluntary methods are unworkable. In assessing seriousness, the government must be convinced of the presence of an unacceptable risk due to a defect in the design or construction of a product. It must be clear that the hazard is caused by the failure of a manufacturer to meet adequate safety standards and not through the carelessness or misuse of consumers. It is assumed that legislation can do little to protect adults from becoming victims of their own negligence, although education and publicity may make them more careful. The incidence of accidents and how widely a product is used are other factors taken into account, although there is no definite policy of requiring an impressive total of serious accidents before considering the need for statutory regulations.

Critics rightly say that few product safety standards have been made and then only after a long period of gestation. A way of accelerating the process, and at the same time of introducing a consumer input into standard-setting, is through a procedure similar to that which existed under the Consumer Product Safety Act in the United States, where the Commission had to consider petitions from consumers advocating particular safety standards.[17]

It was anticipated at the time when the Consumer Protection Act 1961 was passed that voluntary action by businesses would frequently obviate the need for regulations. The power to promulgate standards was thought to have a salutary effect in ensuring high standards and in guaranteeing voluntary compliance with government requests. Since enactment of the legislation the government took the view that regulations were unnecessary in many cases because it was able to secure the cooperation of businesses.[18] Voluntary labelling has been introduced warning consumers of specific hazards, distributors have withdrawn unsatisfactory items from sale, and manufacturers have undertaken to vary the materials used in their products to eliminate hazards. The non-regulatory approach is said to be useful if prompt action is needed or if practical difficulties are associated with drafting a legal standard, as when a variety of component parts and materials need be considered or if a hazard is associated with only one use to which a product can be put. However, voluntary agreements have not always been successful.

Precisely because voluntary action was not always satisfactory in securing a prompt withdrawal of unsafe products from the market, and because there was no power to prohibit outright any class of products which was inherently unsafe and not capable of being made safe by modification in design or construction, the Consumer Safety Act 1978 empowers the Secretary of State to make prohibition orders, prohibition notices and notices to warn in respect of unsafe products (s. 3).[19] Prohibition orders apply in general in relation to particular products while prohibition notices are served on particular businesses. A prohibition order cannot last for more than twelve months but a further order can be made. Time-lapses are built into the making of prohibition orders and notices to enable representations to be made and considered, unless the measures contain a statement that the Secretary of State is of the opinion that the risk of danger is such that they must come into force without delay.[20] The 'banning' power of the Consumer Safety Act 1978 does not encompass recalls of unsafe products which are already in consumers' hands; at most consumers benefit if a notice to warn is required. The prospect of a prohibition order can even be an incentive to business to speed up sales before it is issued. The United States Consumer Product Safety Commission has a power to demand corrective action in the event of a 'substantial product hazard', including dissemination of public warnings, recalls and refunds to consumers.[21] This is supplemented by a clause obliging businesses to report to the Commission immediately the existence of any substantial product hazard. Once alerted, the Commission can demand corrective action.

MOTOR VEHICLES

Some discussion of standards for motor vehicles is in order since it was publication of Ralph Nader's *Unsafe at any Speed* about the unsafe design of modern motor cars, which was a catalyst for the consumer movement in the mid-1960s.[22] Road accidents are ranked among the major causes of death in developed countries. They still occur despite the attempt in recent decades to modify driver behaviour through road safety education. Even if the overwhelming majority of drivers were careful at all times, accidents would still occur because of the actions of a careless minority or through chance. These considerations have led many to conclude that there is a case for obliging manufacturers to design safer cars to reduce the severity of accidents. As Nader and Page argue: '[I]t is easier to change the design of future vehicles than to redesign and rebuild the thousands of miles of poor existing highways or to alter the habits of millions of individuals.'[23] Improved vehicle design, however, does not render redundant alternative strategies to minimize injuries from car accidents. Road safety education must be continued and there is scope for tighter controls over other aspects of driving.[24] Sterner penalties are needed, including the mandatory loss of a licence for drink-driving offences, together with random breathalyser or blood tests. Driving tests could be stiffened in a number of ways.

Passage of the National Traffic and Motor Vehicle Safety Act 1966 in the United States accorded great publicity to the formulation of vehicle standards and has meant that that country has been a leader in safer vehicle design. The Act in effect establishes four categories of motor vehicle safety for which standards are to be issued: to reduce the risk of accidents, to reduce the risk of injury when accidents occur, to provide greater tolerances for pedestrians on impact[25] and to protect persons from injury while vehicles are not in operation.[26] The procedure is that manufacturers certify the incorporation of a standard and the authorities then conduct spot-checks and also purchase cars to be tested in independent laboratories. Problems have arisen in the formulation and administration of federal safety standards because of the opposition of the politically-powerful car manufacturers. Standards have been delayed by their sometimes questionable arguments that there is no proof that they are needed or would serve any purpose, that their terms and requirements are vague, that changes cannot be put into effect by the stipulated date or that more research is needed before a proper proposal can be written.[27] However, since 1966 manufacturers in the United States have recalled millions of vehicles under their statutory obligation to notify owners of any defect relating to safety which comes to their knowledge.[28] In most cases manufacturers must repair, replace or refund in the event of any such defect; of course, only a few of the total number of cars recalled have actually needed repair.

Provision has long existed in Britain demanding adequate lighting and braking on motor vehicles. Proper maintenance of these aspects of car design are assured after purchase by the regular inspection which motor vehicles must undergo.[29] Recent years have seen the development of other detailed controls over construction. Collapsible steering columns, burst-proof locks and seat belts with suitable anchorage points are examples of installations now required by law.[30] Design features along these lines are confined to new cars, which reduces the cost, in that it is less expensive to fit them on the assembly line than to add them later. Further design features have been suggested on the basis of experience elsewhere, such as hazard flashers, heated rear windows to maintain clear vision, head restraints to minimize whip-lash effects and modified bumper bars to protect pedestrians. Type approval requires approval of a particular

model of motor vehicle or component by a state agency. Until a
certificate is obtained from the appropriate agency that the design
characteristics are in accordance with relevant construction standards, marketing cannot commence. The general method of enforcement is that a motor vehicle for which type approval has not been
given cannot obtain the necessary license plates and/or road tax
certificates.[31] Britain has moved towards type approval in accordance with Continental practice.

As well as the structural aspects of car design, additional safety
features have been suggested for motor vehicles and in some cases
their use mandated. Compulsory seat-belt wearing was first introduced in Victoria, Australia, in 1970,[32] spread to other state
jurisdictions, and has been adopted in some European countries.
Regulations can be made under an amendment to the Road Traffic
Act 1972, introduced in 1981, requiring the compulsory wearing of
seat belts for particular vehicles, drivers, passengers and circumstances (s. 33A). Only the person failing to wear the seat belt commits
an offence although the driver is liable if a child under the age of
fourteen is in the front seat not wearing a seat belt in conformity to the
regulations (ss. 33A(3), 33B). Evidence shows that compulsory seat-
belt wearing has effectively reduced the number of deaths and injuries
for car occupants involved in motor vehicle crashes whilst those for
the unprotected pedestrian and pedal- and motorcyclist have continued to increase.[33] The United States has failed to implement
compulsory seat belt wearing, primarily on the grounds that it is an
infringement of civil liberties. The civil liberties argument overlooks
that other considerations are paramount in this situation, such as the
costs to the community of motor accident victims. The courts have
attempted to get people to wear seat belts by reducing the damages of
those injured persons who were not wearing them at the time of an
accident on the grounds that such behaviour is contributory negligence.[34] It is unlikely that this has had any effect on the incidence of
seat-belt wearing, simply because ordinary people are not abreast of
the niceties of tort law. Alternatives to seat belts in the United States –
for example, seat belt buzzer interlock devices – have failed to gain
support.

FOOD

In many cases the standard of food is sufficiently safeguarded by the general provisions of the Food and Drugs Act 1955. Industry can be left to ensure that food is of the nature, substance and quality expected by consumers and is neither injurious to health nor unfit for human consumption. In recent years, however, there has been a tendency for more detailed control because of potential hazards to health. The radical change in food technology, in particular the use of chemical substances, means that consumers are often unable to tell whether food products are safe. Neither do they know whether the price of food bears a reasonable relationship to quality, a marginal deficiency which can rarely be detected by taste. The assumption of law-makers has been that these new circumstances require something more than the general provisions which involve awaiting a decision of a court that, in a specific instance, an offence has been committed.

Therefore in conjunction with the broad provisions of the Food Act, provisions have been felt necessary to control the composition, quality and handling of various foods in specific ways.[35] The Act enables government to promulgate regulations on these matters.[36] Compositional standards have been fixed in some instances. In others, regulations list permitted additives and contaminants, fix maximum levels for their use either generally or for particular foods, and in some instances determine the foods in which they may be used. Finally, there are detailed provisions covering food hygiene.

The formulation of these controls rests on the work of expert committees.[37] The procedure when a topic is reviewed is that evidence is invited from interested parties and a report published. Comments are invited on the report before the government announces its proposed regulations and further views are solicited once the regulations are drafted. The procedure is thus laborious and time-consuming; recommendations may be rejected or there may be a substantial delay before the government takes any action. Criticism has been voiced that consumers do not have adequate opportunity to comment on the work of the committees and, in contrast to the business community, lack the resources to make meaningful representations.

Food additives and contaminants

Food additives have a number of useful functions: they inhibit food spoilage and reduce the danger of microbial disease, they enable food to be transported long distances and to be stored for considerable periods on grocery shelves and they meet the demand for 'convenience food'. The major food additives are preservatives (which limit food spoilage by inhibiting microbe growth or combating specific reactions), antioxidants (which retard oxidation of fats), colourants (designed to make food more appealing to consumers), emulsifiers (to delay separation of the ingredients of prepared food, such as to prevent less dense liquids floating to the top, solids settling, or gas being lost), thickeners, sweeteners (the emphasis on weight control has led to the replacement of sugar) and other flavouring agents such as monosodium glutamate. If food additives have advantages, there is also the possibility that they may cause harm to consumers, if not immediately, then by accumulation over long periods.[38] Thus in the interests of safety legal controls have been imposed on their use. However, the aim of these controls is not absolute safety, which can never be guaranteed, but a level of safety in keeping with the scientific evidence and the utility of using a particular additive.

Rather than simply to protect the public, early control of food additives was also designed to prevent revenue evasion.[39] Then in the early years of the present century a government committee reported on preservatives and colourants. While agreeing that their use might be necessary for the distribution of food in an urban society, the committee drew attention to the danger from the cumulative effect of small amounts of these substances. It advocated the proscription of any preservative or colouring matter which, after inquiry and experimentation, might be regarded as dangerous to the public health and specifically recommended that preservatives be disallowed in milk and all dietetic preparations intended for consumption by invalids or infants.[40] The outcome of the report was the Public Health (Regulations as to Food) Act 1907, which gave the government authority to make regulations authorizing measures to prevent danger arising to public health from the preparation of food or drink. Few steps were taken to implement these legislative powers before 1924, when another official committee urged the government to emulate other countries in controlling the preservatives and colourants permissible in the preparation of food. The committee reiterated the point made previously: the effects of preservatives and colourants may not be immediately obvious, but could be harmful over prolonged periods, yet unlike drugs they were not subject to direct medical or other supervision. The committee noted that preservatives were being used haphazardly, and even in ignorance, with frequently no effort being made to do without them. After reviewing the use of preservatives in various foods, the committee proposed a number of foodstuffs in which limited and declared amounts of chosen preservatives should be tolerated.[41] The following year the Public Health (Preservatives etc., in Food) Regulations 1925[42] made unlawful the manufacture of any food containing any added preservative, except for named foods where the use of specified amounts of specified preservatives was sanctioned.

Thus before 1925 the technique for controlling food additives was to ban those demonstrated or suspected to be a danger to health. That was a form of negative control because the use of other additives remained legal. The 1925 Regulations initiated the system of positive control by specifying which chemicals could be used as preservatives, in which foods and in which amounts. This continues to be the approach in Britain.[43] Positive control is justified by the Food Additives and Contaminants Committee as the only practicable and enforceable method, because 'enforcement is possible by analysis, and good manufacturers know which substance may be used as ingredients.'[44] It can be further supported on the grounds of reasonable prudence and that an additive which has not been proved safe may cause harm to human beings.[45] Of course manufacturers favour negative lists because the inclusion of a new substance in a list of approved additives requires long scientific investigation to establish its harmlessness.[46]

The technique of positive control has been extended to other additives, besides preservatives.[47] For example, provisions stipulate the colouring matters that may be used and forbid them completely for particular foods. Antioxidants must be of a particular type and are permitted only in certain foods in specified quantities. Regulations forbid artificial sweeteners which have not been approved. The drafting technique in the Regulations is to define preservatives, antioxidants, artificial sweeteners, and so on in wide terms, and then to prohibit such substances in food unless they are specifically permitted. Although new regulations must be introduced with the discovery of each new group of additives, the present approach avoids the difficulty of formulating a definition of a food additive in a general prohibition and distinguishing it from a natural food substance. The respective expert committees are moving towards a situation where all additives will be controlled by permitted lists and the use of others rendered unlawful. There are a number of gaps at present, for there are no controls for a group of miscellaneous substances such as enzymes.

To be permitted as an additive a compound must be such that it does not constitute a hazard to health, that there is a distinct technological advantage to the consumer and that satisfactory specifications exist for its use in food.[48] Considerations of public health are overriding and the Food Additives and Contaminants Committee would claim to err on the side of caution. An absence of apparent ill-effects over a period is not acceptable evidence that a substance is harmless, for although it may not be acutely toxic in the amounts customarily ingested, there may be possible chronic effects. Safety is assessed mainly on the basis of toxicological tests on animals. Experimental results are then extrapolated to humans by use of an appropriate conversion figure, which varies according to the toxic potential of the compound and the extent of knowledge of its direct effect on humans.[49]

Indirect effects on health are also considered by the Food Additives and Contaminants Committee. Preservatives, for example, might be used as a substitute for process control in manufacture, masking incipient putrefaction by destroying its obvious warning signals. Whether there is an advantage to the consumer depends on whether there is a real need for an additive as opposed to a minor commercial advantage. The consumer, it is said, might be benefited to the same degree as from food additives as by improved methods of production, by more satisfactory ways of distributing or packaging a food or by more informative labelling.

Environmental contaminants, such as lead, pesticides and chemicals from wrapping materials find their way into food in various ways. It is recognized that environmental contaminants cannot be completely eliminated, because of limitations of technology and resources. For example, it is impossible to test exhaustively for every compound likely to become an environmental contaminant of food. The aim is to restrict the amount of contamination to the smallest levels commercially practicable. The controls over such contaminants are relatively simple and in the main maximum limits have been made compulsory for their presence in food. For example, lead may not be present in excess of specified amounts.[50] Unlike other countries, Britain has not adopted tolerances for pesticides in food, although there is a voluntary scheme for their use in agriculture.[51] There need to be controls on the migration of chemicals from packaging materials into food which balance dangers to health from the cumulative effect of contaminants on the one hand, and the alternative that food might be handled less satisfactorily from the viewpoint of health, for example, with germ-laden bare hands. To implement an EEC Directive, the Materials and Articles in Contact with Food Regulations 1978[52] provide that materials which will come into contact with food should be manufactured in accordance with good manufacturing practice, that is, in such a way that under normal conditions they will not transfer their constituents to food in quantities which would endanger human health or bring about a deterioration in the organoleptic characteristics of food or an unacceptable change in its nature, substance or quality.

By contrast, United States legislation regulating food additives is in one respect much blunter. With carcinogens there can generally be no trade-off between the relative toxicity of a particular food and benefits; the so-called Delaney clause of the Food Drug and Cosmetic Act prohibits any additive in food which causes cancer in man or animals.[53] The courts have accepted that the clause proscribes any additive which can be used in experiments to augment, ever so slightly, the incidence of cancer in animals.[54] Those favouring the Delaney clause point out how prevalent cancer is and claim that at present science cannot establish a threshold beneath which doses of known carcinogens can be allowed without danger. They defend the method whereby an additive is banned if carcinogenic effects are detected by giving animals inordinately large doses of it over a short period. The argument is that chemical carcinogens act more strongly when administered in small amounts over time, and that scientists are limited to the lifetime of test animals whereas humans are exposed for a much longer period. On the other hand, critics of the Delaney clause draw attention to the need for food additives with the growing market for convenience foods.[55] They point out that the growing sophistication of analytical chemistry has attained sensitivities in detecting small amounts of contamination, thus increasing the number of products or processes which could come under the absolute prohibition. Moreover, it is far from certain that there exists any substance which cannot increase the incidence of cancer in animals if used in sufficiently high concentrations. To give support to the critics' cause, the Food and Drugs Administration itself has interpreted the law to allow administrative discretion in many cases in setting permissible tolerance levels for constituents of food, rather than banning them if they satisfy the criterion of the Delaney clause.

Critics argue that control over food additives is difficult to justify since there are more imminent threats to public health. Should not the consumption of sugar be minimized because of its harm to dental health? Should we not pay more attention to hazards that affect the largest number of people – smoking, alcohol and poor diet? One aspect of diet would be to encourage persons to reduce the intake of fat (especially polysaturated fat from both animal and vegetable sources). Law has some relevance here: for example, there are legal restrictions on the marketing of margarine.

Compositional standards

Present compositional standards vary: some define identity, some prescribe a method of preparation, and some relate to the minimum quality of a food. Identity compositional standards are in effect a definition of a common name of a food with a list of its ingredients and their requisite proportion. The United States adopted identity compositional standards under the Food Drug and Cosmetic Act; standards were prescribed setting out in detail every ingredient for certain foods. Generally these 'recipes' began not only to specify mandatory ingredients but to allow certain optional ingredients as well.[56]

Britain has few compositional standards prescribing identity or a method of preparation – the definition of butter, and the necessity for certain procedures in the manufacture of ice-cream are exceptions[57] –and has concentrated on fixing minimum compositional standards for certain foods. To take one example: marmalade in England and Wales must be prepared with a minimum of 200 grams of citrus fruit for every kilogram of finished product, of which at least 75 grams must be from the endocarp (inner pulp), and the soluble solids content of the finished product must be a minimum of 60 per cent.[58] Nutritional quality is directly regulated for only a few foods: for example, bread must be made from flour which contains nutrients sufficient to ensure certain specified minimums.[59]

The main reason advanced for compositional standards is that consumers would otherwise be prejudiced in health by consuming poor quality food and economically by being deceived as to the true quality of food. Consumers are said to be particularly vulnerable to deception about the quality of modern food products. Taste and price are some, but by no means an infallible, guide to consumers as to the value for money of a food. Without compositional standards, the argument continues, unscrupulous manufacturers would market products of low nutritional value, or would lower existing standards, for economic motives, which would elude detection by consumers.

Compositional standards have been attacked in the United States on the ground that their objectives can be achieved through less costly forms of regulation.[60] An aspect of the criticism is that compositional standards inevitably restrict the variety of formulations marketed and thus deprive consumers of the choice they would otherwise have of buying less expensive foods. The poor are said to be especially prejudiced. However, the criticism rests on the questionable assumptions that compositional standards will increase prices (even accepting that they increase costs), and that certain sections of the population, notably the most vulnerable, should constitute a market for less wholesome foods. The suggested alternative, to provide consumers with more information, has already been shown to have drawbacks.

The critics also say that compositional standards lead to monopoly practices on the part of food producers. Innovation is discouraged because particular products must comply with the standards set by law. Compositional standards render products substantially homo-geneous and thus minimize the possibilities of competition between food producers as to quality. Compositional standards also establish a baseline for costs and thus limit the amount of price competition. Food producers must focus on advertising to improve their market position, but this in turn establishes barriers for new entrants.[61] To what extent, if any, compositional standards promote monopoly practices is difficult to gauge – a fact which even the critics concede. But it should be emphasized that even accepting that there is a tendency for monopoly practices to develop the problem is by no means as significant if compositional standards are minimum standards of quality rather than identity standards, because the former provide flexibility for competitors to vary quality above the minimum fixed by law.

Early compositional standards were confined to staple items like bread, milk and butter. The universal use of these articles and their importance in the national diet mean that they have been long accorded special treatment and subject to restrictions. Under the Bread Acts of the early nineteenth century, bread had to comprise specified ingredients and it was illegal to adulterate wheat flour with other cereals.[62] At the turn of the present century a uniform presumptive standard was prescribed for milk, not as an indication of nutritive value but as a method of identifying milks which reasonably might be presumed to be genuine. Milk not sold as skimmed, separated or condensed was to be presumed not genuine if it contained less than 3 per cent of milk fat and 8.5 per cent of milk solids other than milk fat.[63] To curb the addition of excess water to butter, butter with more than a certain percentage of water was presumed to be not genuine.[64] A departmental committee observed that the matter could not be left to public taste through the operation of supply and demand and that prosecutions could be more successfully brought if regulations were promulgated.[65] Restrictions were imposed on the sale and composition of margarine, which were designed to prevent its fraudulent sale as butter.[66] Restrictions on margarine went much further in countries like Australia because of the political power of dairy farmers: manufacturers had to be licensed and the quantity of margarine produced was limited by the imposition of quotas.[67]

Apart from these three commodities, compositional standards were not fixed in Britain until during the Second World War. The prevailing view was that the consumer was afforded sufficient protection by the high standards of food manufacturers, coupled with the general provisions of the Food and Drugs Acts. Furthermore, it was believed that compositional standards might stifle innovation in manufacture, that the varying tastes and requirements of consumers made it unlikely that any one standard would be satisfactory and that the average purchaser was fully capable of judging for himself the nature of the article he was buying.[68] Only where the public health or a particularly vulnerable group of consumers was endangered were standards or declarations of composition believed to be necessary.

Wartime conditions gave the necessary impetus for the establishment of compositional standards in Britain. The shortage of supplies, and the consequent danger to the national diet, accentuated the need to control the sale of inferior articles for which exaggerated claims

were made.[69] In 1941 an attempt was made to exclude from the
market worthless preparations claiming to replace foodstuffs which
were in shortage. Manufacturers were forbidden to prepare any food
substitute, except under license.[70] Two years later, the Minister of
Food was authorized to make regulations on the composition of food if
it appeared necessary for the prosecution of the war or the maintenance of supplies or services essential to the life of the community.[71]
The government continued to exercise this power until the mid 1950s
when it was placed on a firm legislative basis in the Food and Drugs
Act 1955.

In recommending that a compositional standard be fixed for a food,
the Food Standards Committee takes into account the food's
nutritional importance, its value in the diet or in the market place, the
possibility of adulteration, and more generally the need to prevent
inferior and debased products from being marketed.[72] The low-meat
content of meat pies, which form a not negligible part of the diet of
many people, and the difficulties of giving consumers an indication of
what they are buying in respect of meat content, established the need
for a standard for this food.[73] A compositional standard for yogurts
has been recommended because consumers are unaware of what they
are buying with the substantial variations in yogurts currently
marketed under identical or similar descriptions.[74] The existence of
legislation and legislative proposals in other jurisdictions, the
generally held view that the composition of infant formulae should
approximate to that of human milk, and the hazards to health
associated with artificial feeding, led to the recommendation that the
law require an expert panel to give prior approval to any infant food
intended as a sole source of nourishment.[75]

Compositional standards are thus recommended in the interests of
public health, economic protection and nutrition. Yet control seems
to have proceeded in a rather *ad hoc* manner. A number of commonly
consumed foods such as breakfast cereals, infant foods and beer which
satisfy the committee's yardsticks, have no standards, while some
minor commodities such as salad cream and essences which are of
little or no nutritional or economic significance, are subject to
regulation. The Food Standards Committee recognizes this and is
attempting to stimulate a more rational system of food standards.
Present deficiencies are certainly no argument against compositional
standards, particularly with the effects on nutrition of the increasing
proportion of manufactured foods in people's diet. While national

food surveys show that overall there is a substantial surplus of protein over recommended intake, the surplus for large low-income families is not great. There are the new techniques which modify the physical properties of food, especially texture, to allow its use in new ways (for example, the use of soya products in substitution for meat).[76] With minor foods, however, it seems sufficient simply to require manufacturers to label their product.

As well as statutory compositional standards, there have been some compositional standards in Britain resulting from voluntary agreement on the part of food manufacturers. In the 1930s, at the initiative of manufacturers disturbed by competition from low-standard goods, standards of quality were reached for jams and vinegar. During the war voluntary agreements (Codes of Practice) were concluded between the Ministry of Food and manufacturers on the standard, labelling and advertising of food. This work was continued by the Local Authorities Joint Advisory Committee on Food Standards (LAJAC), comprising representatives of local authorities and public analysts. The codes – six of which have been agreed to – were said to be drawn up when standards could not be defined with sufficient precision for the purposes of statutory regulation, when the ingredients of a food could not be ascertained by chemical analysis so that a legislative standard could not be adequately enforced and when the government declined to use its statutory power.[77]

The existence of compositional standards, either statutory or voluntary, makes the task of implementing food law much easier. A food manufacturer knows what is expected and can be sure that products complying with the detailed requirements will not be subjected to official action. Few manufacturers are prosecuted for infringing compositional standards; most food prosecutions are for foreign bodies and mould. Although this reflects in part the extent to which enforcement agencies detect and prosecute breaches of the regulations, independent evidence by consumer organizations seems to confirm that most manufacturers comply with the law. Exceptions of any significance are confined to a few particular products.

Compositional standards relieve enforcement agencies of much of the burden of enforcing the law. In the absence of a standard, an enforcement agency must prosecute under the general provisions of the Food and Drugs Act if it believes that a food product falls below what consumers would generally expect. A qualified analyst will express an opinion on what constitutes a fair and reasonable minimum standard for the food, taking into account its composition both now and in the past. Preparing such an opinion is a time-consuming task and a manufacturer may well challenge it by adducing expert testimony to the contrary. Conflicting evidence by experts may lead a magistrates' court to dismiss a case. Moreover, where no standard has been prescribed by statute or regulation, a court may conclude that it should not be given effect to under the general provisions of the Act, despite the fact that it is favoured by analysts. That magistrates' courts can determine a compositional standard, in the absence of a regulation, opens the possibility of standards varying between areas.

Some of the problems came to the surface in *Goldup* v. *John Manson Ltd*.[78] There the owner and manager of a butcher's shop were charged under section 2 of the Food and Drugs Act 1955 with selling minced beef not of the quality demanded by the purchaser in that it contained not less than 33 per cent fat. It was being sold at 58p per pound. Higher quality minced beef was also on sale, but was less popular at 74p per pound. A notice displayed in the shop stated that minced beef contained up to 30 per cent fat. Expert evidence was that the fat content of minced beef should not exceed 25 per cent. The justices dismissed the information. On appeal by the prosecution, the Divisional Court upheld their decision. The standard required by section 2 was defined in terms of the purchaser's demand, it held, which was a question of fact depending on the express terms of the contract, on all the surrounding circumstances, or in the absence of specific circumstances on what is normally sold in the trade. Where an article is sold by description a purchaser impliedly demands a product which is of merchantable quality. Where no standard is set by statute or regulation a court is not bound to accept the uncontradicted opinions of analysts as to what the standard should be, because they by themselves are not evidence of the quality demanded by the purchaser. Here the justices were entitled to hold that the prosecution had not established that the purchaser of minced beef at 58p per pound was demanding minced beef of a quality containing significantly less than 33 per cent fat, especially given the notice about fat content.

The *Goldup* decision proceeds on the fallacious assumption that simply because consumers, even in significant numbers, buy a food this indicates that it corresponds with the quality being demanded by them within the meaning of section 2. The whole thrust of the foregoing discussion has been that consumers do know the quality of many food products quite apart from what quality is desirable – even if they are actually told that, say, it contains 30 per cent fat. (In parentheses it might be remarked that information is hardly adequately conveyed when, as in the instant case, all that existed was a 10-inch by 4-inch sign displayed in the shop.) The decision opens the way to fraud because it enables food to be sold, the content of which falls significantly below what is its usual quality. By enabling lower courts to ignore the uncontradicted evidence of analysts in determining the quality of food demanded by a consumer, the Divisional Court lays the ground for more extensive compositional standards.

Merely to establish a compositional standard for a named food is insufficient, for a product which does not use the same name or have the requisite composition may nevertheless be believed to be the same by ordinary consumers. To obviate the problem American law binds manufacturers to a compositional standard if a food purports to be, or is represented as being, a standardized product.[79] Britain adopts a different approach to legal drafting and closely defines standardized products by reference to their origin, mode of manufacture and/or use. Compositional standards are then enumerated for these products, often in the form of a schedule to the regulations. Restrictions are then placed on the use of the names of the particular standardized products.

Hygiene requirements

Failings in food hygiene and the consequent contamination of food by micro-organisms are a more direct threat to health than chemical contamination of food or food sub-standard in composition. Food poisoning incidents are by no means rare. National figures in England show that thousands of cases of food poisoning are notified annually (Table 10.2). The causes of food poisoning are various: for example, handling of food by persons bearing disease; inadequate cooking and storing of food, thus providing a good medium for growth of pathogenic organisms; and neglect to apply normal cleaning routines to premises involved in food preparation. An extreme case of food poisoning was the appearance of over 400 cases of typhoid fever in Aberdeen in 1964. The explanation most consistent with the evidence examined by a committee of inquiry was that typhoid bacillus gained entry to a large tin of corned beef after it had been sterilized, most probably from the unchlorinated river water used for cooling the cans in their manufacture in Argentina.[80] The contents of the infected cans were sold in a supermarket in Aberdeen and the disease spread. Conditions within the supermarket, although by ordinary standards it was well managed and clean, were such as to favour the extension of the bacteriological contamination because cold cooked meats were sold from an unrefrigerated counter after being displayed in a warm window or on an unrefrigerated shelf.

Table 10.2   Food Poisoning in England 1975–9

	General (incidents)	Family (incidents)	Sporadic cases	Total cases
1975	230	765	4144	10,936
1976	497	852	3634	11,912
1977	284	1071	3206	10,365
1978	329	1096	4877	11,326
1979	444	855	5892	14,597

To curtail the incidence of food poisoning the law prescribes particular methods of manufacture for a small number of foods. Closely related are the controls exercised over the processing of primary products; thus dairies must generally be registered and must meet certain standards as to their facilities and design. Food Hygiene Regulations in conjunction with the relevant legislation are the main instruments in limiting food poisoning, however, and set up machinery for the enforcement of standards of hygiene in food handling.[81]

The standards set by the Food Hygiene Regulations take the form of detailed rules on matters such as the cleanliness of food premises and of equipment used, the hygienic handling of food, the cleanliness of persons engaged in handling food and of their clothing, the construction of food premises, the provision of water supply and washing facilities, the proper disposal of waste material and the temperature at which certain foods must be kept. Thus regulation 10 of the Food Hygiene (General) Regulations 1970 provides:

Personal cleanliness

10. A person who engages in the handling of food, shall while so engaged

   (a) keep as clean as may be reasonably practicable all parts of his person which are liable to come into contact with the food

   (b) keep as clean as may be reasonably practicable all parts of his clothing or overclothing which are liable to come into contact with the food

   (c) keep any open cut or abrasion on any exposed part of his person covered with a suitable waterproof dressing

   (d) refrain from spitting

   (e) refrain from the use of tobacco or any other smoking mixture or snuff while he is handling any open food or is in any food room in which there is open food.

Complementing the Food Hygiene Regulations are codes of practice which contain additional standards to which commerce and government have agreed. The codes deal with those aspects of food hygiene which are unsuitable for statutory regulations. For example, the codes have details which would perhaps be unmanageable in legislation or regulations. Thus a code for the bakery trade has some 124 paragraphs about matters such as the structure and conditions of bakeries and delivery vans and the handling and storage of bread. The codes of practice are without legal force but are apparently accepted by magistrates courts as evidence of good commercial practice.

The Food Hygiene Regulations are designed to act preventively by setting standards to which businesses engaged in food manufacture or marketing will comply. Another aspect of prevention is that enforcement bodies engage in publicity and advice about the value of good hygiene in avoiding food poisoning. For example, some examine building plans in connection with the alteration or construction of food premises, while others carry out in-depth inspections of food premises with a view not to prosecuting, but to preparing a report which the business can use to improve its practices. Education is directed towards the general population as well as those engaged in producing food commercially. Despite these efforts, there are still significant breaches of the Food Hygiene Regulations.

Significant malpractices in handling food were discovered in a survey of 461 food shops by thirty-seven voluntary consumer groups in 1975. In over 35 per cent of cases shop assistants were without any protective covering over long hair (in some cases the hair was seen touching unprotected food); over 30 per cent of the shops infringed requirements as to the handling of cooked or uncooked foods, mainly meat; and in a number of cases live animals, mainly dogs, were seen inside shops.[82] To improve the situation, the National Federation of Consumer Groups proposed *inter alia* that Food Hygiene Regulations be drafted in terms even more specific than at present. 'We feel that the effect of the introduction of detailed specific offences will be to improve the education of shop managers and to encourage them to train their staff in good hygiene practices.'[83] On the other hand, the committee investigating the Aberdeen typhoid outbreak concluded that it was impossible to lay down requirements more specific than in the Food Hygiene Regulations, presumably in part because it would be more difficult to get these across to people.[84] A particular difficulty of enforcement at present is that while some food hygiene violations are clear-cut, like cockroaches in food premises or food staff with cigarettes,[85] others require detailed scientific measure.

One area where provisions furthering food hygiene can be more effective is in controlling the opening and continuation of food premises. Legislation in some countries requires food premises (including eating houses) to register with the enforcement authorities and contains power for enforcement bodies to close unclean or insanitary food premises.[86] British legislation is less forceful. Commercial opposition in the 1950s emasculated proposed food hygiene regulations which would have made registration of food premises compulsory. The Association of Environmental Health Officers still claims that registration is necessary in view of the growing number of restaurants and take-away establishments, the difficulty of explaining hygiene regulations to foreign restaurant staff, and the shortage of enforcement officers to carry out regular inspections.[87]

Recent legislation goes some way to controlling whether food premises operate. The Food and Drugs (Control of Food Premises) Act 1976 empowers the courts to close food premises which pose a danger to health. On a conviction for a food hygiene offence, if a court is satisfied that there is still a danger to health by reason of the condition of the premises, the infestation of vermin or the accumulation of refuse, it may issue a closure order as well as impose a fine.[88] In situations of imminent risk of danger to health, a closure order can be granted on three days of notice being given to the other party (who need not be present at the hearing) with the main prosecution to be heard at a later date.[89] However, a serious inhibition on local authorities seeking emergency orders is that they can be liable for substantial compensation if later the court determines that there was no imminent risk of danger to health.[90] In addition, there are powers under public health legislation enabling enforcement authorities to remedy the filthy or unwholesome condition of food premises and to recover the expense incurred from the business, or to request staff to absent themselves from work in the case of certain infectious diseases.[91]

CONCLUSION

Product standards are a powerful tool of consumer protection and there are good arguments considered in Chapter 4 for extending them well beyond their present limited role to deal with the problem of 'shoddy goods'. The proper formulation of product standards depends on policy-makers having firm criteria for guiding their decisions. One of the overriding factors in deciding whether to fix a compositional standard for a foodstuff should be its importance in the national diet, but the point was made that some of the present standards cannot be justified on this basis whereas other important foodstuffs are unregulated. Firm views may not be possible, however, and a product may not be amenable to control because standards against which it can be evaluated are non-existent; for example, product standards may be impracticable in many aspects of taste or design because of wide divergences in public opinion about these matters. Information is also vital in the formulation of product standards; for this reason the collection of data on product-related accidents is the first step in the making of safety regulations.

A point to make about the formulation of product standards is that the process has been far too long-winded. In part this derives from a reluctance to interfere with industry and commerce and to regulate the manner in which products can be marketed. Another reason is that consultation with trade interests is taken to extreme lengths, which creates the impression that they have a veto over the standards that are made. The lack of a consumer input into the formulation of product standards has been commented upon and it need only be reiterated that reform in this area, if properly implemented, would overcome many of the problems like delay and the apparent bias in favour of the trade viewpoint.

Without enforcement product standards are to little effect because there are always businesses who will not comply with the law. Enforcement agencies may not possess the requisite human resources or technology to assess whether businesses are complying with product standards. For example, the readily available techniques of chemical analysis cannot easily determine with reasonable certainty the presence and concentration of some of the restricted food additives. The problem may be partially overcome by requiring businesses to devise methods of attaining the prescribed standards and of monitoring their own compliance with them. Enforcement would also be much more effective at manufacturers' premises in overcoming, for example, the limitations on the chemical analysis of foods. At present, however, enforcement under the Food and Drugs Act 1955 occurs mainly at the retail level and there is no general power to enter manufacturing premises to ensure, say, that the ingredients a product is said to contain actually go into it. Moreover, the enforcement authorities need additional powers in the product standard area, such as the power to issue recall notices where unsafe products have already been distributed. The prosecution process is quite deficient in these circumstances because the damage will be done before a matter gets to court.

Control of trade practices

In the past governments were reluctant to control trade practices
other than by private law or by broad criminal prohibitions if this
would interfere with the substance of consumer transactions. Apart
from the administrative costs of further legal requirements, it was said
that trade practices were so varied that widespread control was
impracticable. A major objection advanced was that the great
majority of consumers were sensible enough to protect themselves
and that their range of choice would be restricted if controls were
introduced for the benefit of the minority. It was said that on the rare
occasions when difficulties arose, consumers had certain rights at civil
law and there might even be a criminal offence involved. The great
majority of businesses were assumed to be reputable, one piece of
evidence being that many had agreed to codes of practice setting high
standards of behaviour.

Recent years have witnessed some change in this attitude and a
growth in public control. Consumers have failed to institute civil
proceedings against businesses under the private law to secure
redress for their grievances and many prejudicial trade practices are
not caught by the broad criminal prohibitions on the statute book
penalizing fraud or false trade descriptions. The very complexity and
range of trade practices and the need for considerable resources of
investigation and detection are now seen as positive arguments for
preferring public control in particular instances to other methods like
voluntary codes of practice.[1] While voluntary codes are observed by
many businessmen, it is recognized that others ignore them so that
overall effect might be patchy and that areas of trade most in need of
reform are usually the least likely to subscribe to them.[2] It has even
been said that public control stimulates efficiency and removes

enterprises from the market which survive only through prejudicial practices.[3] The costs incurred by government and business in enforcing and complying with additional legal requirements are now balanced against the economic advantages which accrue to consumers as a result. In some cases policy-makers conclude that such costs are small in relation to turnover and in any event can be minimized by businesses if they adopt better procedures.

The major features of the public control of trade practices are the subject matter of this chapter. A major preoccupation of the early part is with the Fair Trading Act 1973, which introduced a new procedure for formulating controls and a new technique for disciplining businesses whose behaviour fails to match suitable standards. A final section of the chapter takes the special case of what businesses charge for their products and services and examines the various techniques of price control.

THE FORMULATION OF CONTROLS

Over the years a limited number of statutes were enacted to control specific marketing and promotional practices which were particularly obnoxious from the point of view of consumers. Controlling prejudicial trade practices through legislation has the self-evident disadvantage that trade practices change and new ones develop, yet legislative time is precious and the legislative machinery ponderous, so that measures may be delayed or in some cases never enacted. With this in mind procedures have been introduced in several countries supposedly designed to permit more frequent and flexible regulatory action to be taken against particular trade practices prejudicial to consumers. However, the experience in both the United States and Britain has been disappointing, an important reason being that the procedures have proved to be too inflexible.[4]

The justification for the Fair Trading Act 1973 was that new machinery was needed in the face of rapidly changing trade practices. The Act established a new institution, the Office of Fair Trading, to exercise continual surveillance of commercial activities. The Office of Fair Trading is intended to act quickly and effectively against practices prejudicial to consumers as their effects become manifest, to collate information on matters affecting consumer interests, and to inform and educate consumers about their legal rights. The regulatory powers under the Fair Trading Act 1973 are what one writer on public administration has categorized as modern legislative scheme-making:

It involves a number of stages, covering broadly the general determination by the legislature of the subjects that the schemes are to cover and the limits within which they are to work, the issue of information by the administration for the general guidance of the scheme-making authority, the making of the scheme by that authority, its submission to and criticism by interested persons and bodies, and its examination, modification where necessary, and approval by the administration, which may be called to submit approved schemes to the legislature.[5]

In the event of a prejudicial trade practice becoming evident, the government has powers under Part II of the Fair Trading Act 1973 to prohibit or regulate it to protect consumers. The procedure is that the Director General of Fair Trading makes a recommendation to the Consumer Protection Advisory Committee that action be taken against a practice. The Consumer Protection Advisory Committee comprises independent persons appointed by the government, drawn from those with a variety of experience.[6] In considering the proposal, the Committee receives representations from interested parties and can either agree with the recommendations of the Director General, suggest modifications or disagree entirely. The government can then promulgate a statutory order unless the Committee adopts the last of these three courses.[7] Breach of an order is an offence; however, a contract is not void or unenforceable by reasons only of a contravention of an order, and no civil cause of action arises for breach of statutory duty.[8] In general terms, the ambit of Part II of the Act extends to trade practices which relate to the terms and conditions on which goods and services are marketed, the manner in which those terms and conditions are communicated to consumers and the methods of promoting, selling and paying for the sale of goods and services.[9] Many provisions of existing consumer protection legislation fall within these heads. Under the legislation, objectionable trade practices may be completely prohibited or permitted subject to modification. The full range of control techniques available is contained in Schedule 6 of the Act.

1. Prohibition of the specified consumer trade practice either generally or in relation to specified consumer transactions.
2. Prohibition of specified consumer transactions unless carried out at specified times or at a place of a specified description.

3. Prohibition of the inclusion in specified consumer transactions of terms or conditions purporting to exclude or limit the liability of a party to such a transaction in respect of specified matters.

4. A requirement that contracts relating to specified consumer transactions shall include specified terms or conditions.

5. A requirement that contracts or other documents relating to specified consumer transactions shall comply with specified provisions as to lettering (whether as to size, type, colouring or otherwise).

6. A requirement that specified information shall be given to parties to specified consumer transactions.

To be considered for a statutory order under Part II of the Act, a business practice must have certain specified undesirable effects on consumers. First, it must adversely affect their *economic* interests as distinct from their other interests, such as in safety or health.[10] In addition, a practice must have one or more of the effects mentioned in section 17(2), which refers to matters such as whether a practice misleads consumers, pressurizes them into transactions, or involves them in contracts which include inequitable terms. These requirements, especially economic detriment, are difficult to satisfy even though once the effects are demonstrated there is no need to examine whether or not they are intended. In addition, the procedures have proved time-consuming and inflexible. The Consumer Protection Advisory Committee has shown by its deliberations that it will closely and systematically scrutinize a proposal from the Office of Fair Trading to determine whether all the necessary effects are produced and whether the proposals for control are requisite for the purpose of preventing a practice. While the various points at which representations can be made about proposed controls ensure that there are consultative processes comparable to those operating in the legislative sphere, they do prolong the law-making process considerably. More importantly, following the Committee's report the government's discretion is confined for it must implement either the original proposal of the Director General as agreed to by the Committee or the proposal as modified.

For these reasons, the order-making power of the Fair Trading Act 1973 has not proved as effective as was expected. Only four trade practices have been referred to the Consumer Protection Advisory Committee for possible regulation.

Statements as to consumers' rights: The first reference concerned two practices related to the passage of the Supply of Goods (Implied

Terms) Act 1973. That Act rendered void exemption clauses purporting to deprive consumers of the benefit of the statutory terms implied in contracts of sale and hire purchase regarding title, correspondence with description, merchantable quality and fitness for purpose. (The Act's provisions in this regard have been replaced by section 6 of the Unfair Contract Terms Act 1977.) After passage of the 1973 legislation businesses continued to display notices in shops or to give documents such as receipts which purported to restrict certain rights of consumers (e.g. statements like 'No money refunded': 'No articles exchanged': 'Money will not be refunded, credit notes will be given'). Moreover, consumers continued to receive documents such as guarantees which referred to rights and liabilities in connection with goods being sold, but which did not make clear the existence of inalienable rights against the retailer. The Office of Fair Trading took the view that these practices adversely affected consumers' economic interests. For example, they misled consumers as to their rights under a transaction so that they did not press a claim for redress in a situation where this was justified.[11] The Consumer Protection Advisory Committee agreed, but concluded that the proposed regulation by the Office of Fair Trading to ban the use in notices and documents of wording *likely* to suggest that the consumer's inalienable rights were restricted, went further than the practice.[12] Thus a notice 'No money refunded', while void in relation to a complaint about faulty goods, is perfectly valid regarding consumers who desire a refund simply because they have changed their minds. The government accepted the qualification suggested by the Consumer Protection Advisory Committee. The Consumer Transactions (Restrictions on Statements) Order 1976[13] prohibits certain statements which would be void by virtue of the Unfair Contract Terms Act 1977, or be inconsistent with a warranty implied by the Trading Stamps Act 1964 (r. 3).[14] Thus there is now the unsatisfactory situation where statements such as 'No money refunded except as required by the Unfair Contract Terms Act 1977' are legal, although quite unintelligible to many consumers. The Consumer Protection Advisory Committee agreed to the second proposal of the Office of Fair Trading regarding retailers' and manufacturers' guarantees, and the Order requires them to include a clear and conspicuous statement that they have no effect upon consumers' statutory rights (rr. 4–5). The Order does not apply to terms and notices made void by the Unfair Contract Terms Act 1977, sections 2 and 7, which purport to exclude or restrict liability for death or personal injury resulting from negligence, or for the fitness of goods hired, exchanged or supplied as part of a service. The Office of Fair Trading has taken steps to eliminate the use of these terms in the course of its consumer credit licensing activities and in evaluating agreements under restrictive trade practices legislation but is considering whether their use ought to be made a criminal offence.[15]

The identity of mail order advertisers: The second reference of the Office of Fair Trading covered the practice of businesses taking prepayment for goods without any undertaking to return the money if the goods were not delivered in reasonable time. Associated with this in the case of some mail order transactions was another practice of not identifying the business's real name or giving its proper address. The argument was that these practices adversely affected consumers' economic interests, because once they had parted with their money they were largely at the mercy of such traders.[16] Evidence was available that some mail order companies, from which consumers had ordered goods and paid in advance, had gone into liquidation leaving consumers without a remedy. An Order has been promulgated that mail order advertisements directed at consumers which suggest that prepayment has to be made should state the name and address of the business.[17] The Order is much more limited than that proposed by the Director General, who thought that mail order companies should also state a delivery date in their advertisements and should be obliged to refund the payment if the specified date were not met. Following the Order complaints by consumers who experienced delayed deliveries or the loss of their money because of fraud or insolvency continued at high levels. The Office of Fair Trading issued a Consultative Paper in 1979 proposing that traders (other than mail order advertisers) who accepted prepayments from consumers should provide information about delivery times in a standard, written form. As a result of opposition to the proposal, the Office of Fair Trading has abandoned its intention to seek changes in the law and has instead sought a solution in amendments to codes of practice.[18] The National Consumer Council believes that debts due in respect of payments made in advance by private consumers should have a form of preferential status in the event of insolvency. It also has under study the merits of a rule (perhaps only applying in particular sectors) that pre-payments should be placed in a trust account.

Disclosure of business character: In 1975 the Office recommended, and the Consumer Protection Advisory Committee concurred, that it be made an offence for a trader to advertise goods for sale to the public without making it reasonably obvious that the goods were being sold in the course of a business.[19] Concern was expressed that consumers were prejudiced by advertisements in the classified columns of newspapers offering goods, creating the impression a private seller was involved, whereas they were being sold by a trader. An Order has now been made.[20]

VAT exclusive prices: The Director General referred to the practice of businesses advertising prices not including the amount of VAT payable. The practice was to the economic detriment of consumers, he argued, because it misled them into thinking that the amount payable was less than it really was. The Consumer Protection Advisory Committee agreed, but with qualifications.[21] So far little has been done. The Price Marking (Food and Drink on Premises) Order 1979[22] has limited application as its name suggests; it requires that in the case of food, or of a service relating to the supply of food, the price or charge indicated should be inclusive of VAT.

Other matters: At one time the Office of Fair Trading was considering for possible Orders under Part II of the Fair Trading Act 1973 door-to-door selling, one-day sales and party-plan selling (where persons invite friends and neighbours to their home so that a representative from a selling company may demonstrate to the group and take orders for items for future delivery). Nothing has resulted. However, because of the difficulties associated with Order making under Part II, recommendations of the Director General regarding bargain offer pricing were effected by statutory instrument under the Prices Act 1974.[23]

TECHNIQUES OF CONTROL

Certain trade practices prejudicial to consumers have a long pedigree while others demonstrate the ingenuity of unscrupulous businessmen in uncovering loopholes in new law in order to fleece customers. A major concern in regulating prejudicial trade practices has been to prevent consumers being precipitated into transactions which they may regret on reflection. Since manipulation sometimes takes the form of subtle psychological pressure the freedom to choose is effectively reduced. Policy-makers have found difficulties in devising appropriate legal machinery to control prejudicial practices. One difficulty has been to eliminate consumer manipulation without infringing on the useful side, if there is any, of a trade practice. Another problem is that some trade practices are quite complex and it is not easy to devise forms of legislative drafting to encompass them. To some extent this simply illustrates the general difficulty of expressing the complex aspects of modern society in simple language. The following discussion focuses on several prejudicial trade practices and the legal techniques adopted to deal with them.

Banning or severely limiting a prejudicial practice

It would be of great benefit on the grounds of convenience and public enlightenment if the provisions scattered through legislation which ban or severely limit trade practices prejudicial to consumers were gathered together into an omnibus consumer protection statute, like those enacted in other Commonwealth jurisdictions. For example, the Australian Trade Practices Act 1974 prohibits outright a number of prejudicial trade practices including false representations (not all of which are dealt with in the Trade Descriptions Act 1968); free gimmick promotions (offering gifts, etc. with no intention of providing them as offered); referral selling (inducing consumers to acquire goods and services by representing that they will receive a benefit *after* a contract in return for introducing other consumers to the corporation); accepting payment without intending to supply as ordered; and using coercion at a consumer's place of residence.[24] In the absence of such a measure, it requires a careful consideration of a wide range of statutory materials to determine the relevant provisions in Britain.

Trading stamps are severely restricted in some jurisdictions.[25] The main justification is that they hamper consumers from comparing values and establish artificial ties with particular retailers which make it difficult for consumers to transfer their custom without loss to take advantage of superior service and value offered by others.[26] The legislation in Australia is widely drafted to extend to other forms of promotions where consumers receive some sort of coupon, etc. which entitles them to receive a product free or at a reduced rate. Thus it has covered an advertisement offering anyone buying a washing machine an additional unit such as a television set for a small payment, and also where consumers received – along with thousands of others – an individualized letter promising that if they returned one of the 'savings cheques' they would receive a year's subscription to a magazine at a reduced rate.[27]

In Britain trading stamps are subject to regulation to assist consumers to know what advantages, if any, they are obtaining when they receive trading stamps. The Trading Stamps Act 1964 requires trading stamps to be marked with their cash value, makes stamps redeemable for cash at the customer's option, prohibits misleading advertising as to their value, and obliges retailers to display information enabling consumers to calculate the number of stamps to which they are entitled. Trading stamp companies claimed that many adults collect stamps, that retailers increase their turnover when they offer stamps and that few books are redeemed for cash.[28] The claim that trading stamps do not affect prices seems somewhat belied by the decision of one national supermarket chain in 1977 to give up stamps and instead to offer price reductions.

Mock auctions (sometimes known as one-day sales) are normally conducted on premises not associated with retail trade, such as a public hall or hotel. The nature of a mock auction has been described as follows:

A mock auction may be described as a sale conducted by a person . . . whose ultimate aim is to sell goods to the gullible purchasers at highly inflated prices. Usually, the entrepreneur first attracts attention by distributing free or selling at 'give-away' prices small articles of low intrinsic value. This is followed by an offer of a moderately priced article which is sold to the highest bidder, who, however, received an unexpected refund from the 'auctioneer' of most of the purchase price he has paid for the article. Having thus gained the confidence of those present, the salesman then offers unopened parcels for sale at set prices . . . well above their true value.[29]

Complaints about mock auctions are usually that the trader has left the district and that consumers are unable to obtain redress for shoddy merchandise. Items are stated to be worth far more than the price at which they could be purchased in retail shops; they are presented in lavish boxes and packaging more in keeping with goods of higher value; and consumers are generally unable to inspect them prior to sale. Objection is also taken to the psychological techniques used in running mock auctions, whereby an artificial atmosphere of excitement is created and to the strategic placement of colleagues of the auctioneer (unidentified as such) around the hall to bid.

Legislation in Britain makes it unlawful to conduct a mock auction. A mock auction is defined as the sale of goods by way of competitive bidding if, during the course of the sale, (a) items are sold to persons at a price lower than the amount of his highest bid or part of the price is repaid or credited; (b) the right to bid is restricted to persons who have previously purchased articles; or (c) articles are given away or offered as gifts.[30] Competitive bidding is defined widely and includes any mode of sale in which prospective purchasers are enabled to compete for the purchase of articles in any way. Thus it covers situations where purchasers are asked who will pay a specified amount for a particular item and a number raise their hand to be first or to be chosen by the auctioneer, even though there is no competitive bidding as to price.[31] The mock auctions legislation is enforced spasmodically and is not wide enough to cover all types of one-day sales. The legislation is confined to sales involving a limited number of prescribed items including crockery, linen, furniture, jewellery and musical or scientific instruments. Certain techniques would appear not to be caught by the legislation such as secret bidding, the use of mystery boxes and the creation of a general atmosphere of frenzy and excitement to encourage spending. Moreover, the Court of Appeal seems to have taken an unduly lenient view of mock auctions, comparing them to a form of entertainment where consumers must expect to be caught.[32]

Pyramid selling, which takes a number of forms, has caused untold hardship to consumers in many countries. One writer describes a typical pyramid selling scheme:

The typical multi-level distributorship plan involves the manufacture or sale by a company, under its own trade name, of a line of products through 'franchises' which appear to be regular franchise distributorships. These plans may include three to five levels of nonexclusive distributorships, and individuals may become 'franchisees' at any level by paying the company an initial fee based on the level of entry. Once a member of the plan, the individual earns commissions by selling the company's products and attracting new members. Each distributor pays less for the product than the price he receives from the public and from those at lower levels in the distribution chain to whom he sells. Since one profits merely by being a link in the product distribution chain, the emphasis is on recruiting more investor-distributors rather than on retailing products.[33]

Another less common type of pyramid scheme is the founder-member plan or customer referral agreement, where an investor becomes a founder-member by buying an item of merchandise at several times its retail value.[34] The combined investment of founder-members finances a local discount store which founders induce others to visit. Pyramid selling is inherently unstable with its emphasis on selling distributorships rather than the product or service. Eventually growth must come to a halt as the market is saturated with participants. A scheme yields quick profits for promoters, who recruit members by high pressure salesmanship at 'opportunity' meetings or parties where false enthusiasm is generated. A technique used at one pyramid scheme was that the audience, which was liberally sprinkled with existing participants, started humming. 'The hum would rise to a crescendo and then everyone would shout: "Money!".'[35] Pyramid selling schemes are aimed at individuals with little business experience and those most susceptible to the lure of get-rich-quick schemes. To participate, many owner-occupiers have been persuaded to take out second mortgages on their homes.

When the abuses associated with pyramid selling became apparent in the early seventies, it was clear that existing laws were inadequate. Fraudulent misstatement was generally avoided and there was doubt whether pyramid selling fell within laws such as those prohibiting lotteries.[36] Statutory provisions were thus enacted in various countries to make illegal certain pyramid selling schemes.[37] The Fair Trading Act 1973, sections 120(3)–(4), create the offences of promoters or participants receiving or soliciting payment from participants in a pyramid scheme, if the payment is induced by the prospect of benefiting from the recruitment of further participants. It seems that payments made for a participant to become a higher level distributor, on the prospect of receiving part of the payments made by the other participants seeking promotion, would not be an offence.[38]

A weakness in the British legislation is that it is restricted to pyramid selling schemes where most of the participants' transactions occur away from business premises (which means, in the main, by doorstep selling).[39] Yet it appears that most transactions between promoters and participants, or between participants at different levels of distributorship, take place at meetings conducted at the promoter's regular place of business or at a regularly used convention hall. The Fair Trading Act 1973 also contains regulation-making power to create new offences in respect of the issue of invitations to potential participants and of the operation of pyramid schemes.[40]

The Pyramid Selling Scheme Regulations 1973[41] require advertisements and literature about these pyramid-type schemes to include certain information, such as the identity of the promoters and a description of the scheme's operation. Advertisements and circulars must not suggest that recruitment of further participants or general success is easy, or set out hypothetical profits which may accrue. Participants must be provided with written contracts and there is a cooling-off period of seven days within which they can withdraw without loss. Commitments of participants must not exceed £25, unless in writing, and if at any time participants withdraw, promoters are obliged to take back goods purchased under the scheme for not less than 90 per cent of the original price.

A number of persons setting up schemes have been successfully prosecuted and the courts have imposed jail sentences.[42] Moreover, several companies engaging in pyramid selling under the guise of marketing retail products have been wound up by court order on petition of the government under the Companies Act 1967 that they were operating against the public interest.[43] The legislation, however, is preventive and no provision is made for compensating those who have been ensnared by a pyramid scheme. The government has refused to compensate victims, apparently because this would introduce a new principle of assisting those who lose money in business ventures.

Creating new consumer remedies

Another method of discouraging an objectionable trade practice, or the objectionable aspects of a trade practice, has been to create certain rights for consumers which are such that abuse becomes unprofitable.

An example is the action taken against inertia selling, whereby businesses send or provide *unsolicited goods and services* to consumers in the hope that they will feel obliged to buy them or at least do something to create a contractual obligation. The legislative technique in Britain has not been to prohibit the practice outright, perhaps because it might be difficult to draft a statute which distinguishes between inertia selling and the provision of unsolicited goods and services in other situations; e.g. a doctor giving assistance in an emergency.[44] Instead, consumers who receive unsolicited goods are made the unconditional owners of them after expiration of six months if the business has not reclaimed them.[45] The period can be shortened to thirty days if the business fails to collect the goods after being notified that they are unsolicited and the address where they can be collected. Further, unless a business has reasonable cause to believe that it has a right to payment for unsolicited goods, it is an offence for it to demand payment, to threaten any legal proceedings or to invoke any collection procedure such as placing the name of a consumer on a list of defaulters.[46] In *Readers' Digest Assoc. Ltd* v. *Pirie*[47] a former subscriber was sent copies of a magazine and requests for payment. This was done at the direction of the company computer, which junior officials had failed to reprogramme on notice of cancellation. The court held – on the basis of *Tesco Supermarkets Ltd* v. *Nattrass*[48] – that the knowledge of the junior officials could not be imputed to the company and that it could not be said that the company did not have reasonable cause to believe it had a right to payment. Associated with the provisions on unsolicited goods are controls designed to protect businesses from the practice engaged in by a few unscrupulous firms of demanding a substantial payment for unsolicited entries in business directories which they publish.

Doorstep selling provides a service for a number of consumers who, for a variety of reasons such as age, illness or geographic location, cannot shop in the ordinary way. Credit trading done at home has been engaged in by some householders for generations. But doorstep selling has led to considerable abuse since it has been used to unload products and services which would not be sold at such high prices in shops and to induce consumers to sign contracts committing them to substantial payments for things which, on reflection, they do not want. Unlike shops, which rely to varying extents on consumer goodwill, doorstep sellers can ignore consumer dissatisfaction if they are geographically mobile, and some have taken advantage of this to make quick profits. Quite apart from other factors, the presence of a seller in the home makes consumers particularly vulnerable to a sales pitch. Doorstep sellers are notorious for utilizing deceptive ploys of various kinds; these are by no means new[49] and are fairly well known because of the considerable adverse publicity they have attracted. Claims that a seller is engaged in educational research, is a student working to win a travel scholarship, or represents a company which has chosen the consumer's house to be a showhouse, have all been exposed time and again as blatantly untrue. The Molony Report commented on the more extreme psychological and other pressures used in some doorstep selling:

> We have received numerous and lurid accounts of the lengths to which some of these men are prepared to go in order to secure an order. We are told that they are known literally to force their way over the doorstep, to remain in the house for as long as six hours at a time – sometimes until midnight or later – keeping up a hypnotic flow of persuasive sales talk. It is alleged that their attitude and behaviour is sometimes such as to reduce households – in particular women – to a state of acute physical fear. . . . By whatever proportion of door-to-door salesmen such practices are followed, and with whatever frequency, a considerable volume of evidence insisted that they are widespread (and successful) enough to amount to a serious social evil; resulting in homes labouring under an excessive burden of debt and sometimes torn by consequential domestic disharmony.[50]

In a number of cases doorstep sellers have been prosecuted for fraud. *Potger*[51] was a prosecution of a doorstep seller for obtaining money by deception, by falsely claiming that he was a student taking part in a competition. Interestingly, the defence was partly the contention that any lies told were not dishonest, it being common for fellow sellers to tell lies of this nature! But fraud is absent in most cases where consumers are prejudiced because unscrupulous doorstep sellers know an overt lie is too risky and that a highly developed sales pitch is just as effective.[52]

Legislation has been enacted in many jurisdictions in an attempt to curb abuses by doorstep sellers. Section 2(1) of the Danish Consumer Contracts Act (No. 139, 29 March 1978) prohibits the practice unless there is a prior request by the consumer.[53] In some jurisdictions doorstep sellers are obliged to reveal their purpose on arrival by means of an identification card.[54] Elsewhere doorstep sellers, as in Italy, require a license.[55] Hawkers and pedlars have long needed licenses in Britain but the requirements are confined to doorstep sellers actually carrying goods with them.[56] In some United States jurisdictions doorstep sellers must not only obtain a license, but in a few areas must deposit a bond with enforcement authorities. Examples of supplementary restrictions in these jurisdictions are limited selling hours and a prohibition on calling on residences displaying signs such as 'No Hawkers'.[57] The Molony Report rejected a general scheme of licensing for doorstep selling on the grounds that it would create a considerable administrative burden and that there were doubts about its effect on unscrupulous sellers who moved rapidly throughout the country, often under aliases.[58] Now under the

Consumer Credit Act 1974 doorstep sellers selling on credit must obtain a license.[59]

The major legislative technique to control malpractices in doorstep selling has been to create a 'cooling-off' period within which consumers may cancel a transaction resulting from a doorstep sale. In countries adopting it, it was anticipated that a cooling-off period would operate at two levels. First, it would provide individual consumers with a remedy if they felt they had been prejudiced by a doorstep transaction. Secondly, it was hoped that doorstep salesmen would take a greater interest in consumer satisfaction, and be less concerned with making a sale by whatever methods could be deployed, if they knew that consumers could rescind a transaction. The main cooling-off provision in Britain is that for regulated agreements under the Consumer Credit Act 1974.[60] The provision was discussed in Chapter 7 and it will be remembered that not all consumer credit agreements are covered; for example, a doorstep trader selling on credit sale is only affected if the agreements involve an amount greater than £30. A proposal by the EEC is that *all* contracts over a certain amount arrived at away from commercial premises must be in writing, that the consumer must receive a copy and a separate cancellation form and that a cooling-off period of seven days should apply.[61]

The period for cancellation under the Consumer Credit Act 1974 is relatively short on the assumption that consumers can quickly assess the wisdom of a transaction since 'decompression' normally occurs once the salesman departs. The assumption is questionable, however, where the complaint is about faulty goods or about sub-standard services like, say, poor installation, for it will only be much later that the inadequacies are discovered. The effectiveness of written notice of cancellation under the Consumer Credit Act 1974 must also be questioned: even if consumers read and understand their right they may be reluctant to invoke it against a source of much-needed credit.

The right to cancel has no doubt curbed the incidence of abuse among doorstep salesmen, yet consumer protection bodies still receive a substantial number of justified complaints about their activities and this raises the question of whether more drastic action is warranted. A former director of the law enforcement division of the New York City Department of Consumer Affairs argues for a complete ban on doorstep selling:

I believe that the frequency of fraud in door-to-door credit sales not initiated by the customer suggests that this type of business, at least, if not all door-to-door selling, should be abolished altogether. Its utility is slight; although there are some Americans who rarely leave their homes, most door-to-door selling is forced upon people who are quite capable of shopping for their genuine needs in stores, in mail-order catalogues or at least by telephoning a seller.[62]

Against this it is said that some consumers would be prejudiced because in less prosperous areas doorstep selling is associated with collecting credit. To ban the former would be to withdraw credit from poor consumers, to increase its cost or to encourage alternative collection pressures of equivalent or greater severity.[63] In considering whether all doorstep selling should be prohibited, further investigation is needed as to how essential it is in certain geographic regions and for certain sections of the population, and as to whether alternative sources of goods, services and credit are adequate or could be devised. Certainly countries like Denmark do not seem to have suffered greatly by severely restricting doorstep selling.

A limited prohibition on doorstep selling is that the Consumer Credit Act 1974 forbids doorstep canvassing by those offering money loans not associated with the purchase of goods or services.[64] This should avoid the situation where agents have been engaged to peddle loans door-to-door, in particular on council-housing estates, but of course it does not prevent unscrupulous salesmen going door-to-door offering to install central heating on credit terms. Legislation also makes it unlawful for anyone except a local authority or charities, etc. employing the blind or disabled to represent that such persons are employed in the making of a product or benefit from its sale.[65] The legislation covers a not uncommon situation where doorstep salesmen make representations along these lines and blind or disabled persons, if involved at all, are employed at a minimal wage on insignificant tasks.[66]

Sales pressure can be exercised just as much in a shop or showroom as on the doorstep. The Molony Report recommended against extending any cooling-off provision to shops because abusive practices are not as prevalent there, and because in the case of shops it is more a 'self-inspired interest' in the articles on display and not sales pressure that motivates consumers.[67] Another objection raised is that the finality of consumer transactions would be continually threatened and business would be placed under severe strain if consumers could change their mind 'simply because they found a shop a little further down the road offering more attractive terms.'[68] But the proposal to universalize the cooling-off period is not as radical as it seems at first, since the current practice of many retailers is to offer a refund without question if goods are returned unused within a reasonable time after purchase. The methods of selling of those businesses which do not give a refund are thus called into question. Their response might be that it is the larger businesses, with a high turnover, which can afford to refund. Extending cooling-off to general retail sales would provide consumers with a simple, inexpensive and speedy remedy in all cases when they have been victimized by defective products, dilatory delivery, deception, high pressure sales practices or even by their own stupidity.[69] In other words, it would act as a useful supplement to existing remedies in the private law which, as we have seen, are deficient in many respects.

'Cease and desist' orders

A concern that existing legislation was inadequate in deterring business malpractices has led various jurisdictions to emulate the United States by introducing a 'cease and desist' power whereby orders can be obtained against businesses to prevent them engaging in conduct detrimental to consumers. Particularly with respect to breaches of the private law it is recognized that consumers fail to institute legal proceedings even when they have a good case. When criminal convictions are obtained or favourable civil judgments rendered, some businesses are observed to continue their objectionable behaviour because it is more profitable simply to pay the fine or the damages awarded than to change their modes of behaviour. The technique of the 'cease and desist' order is designed to avoid this situation by ordering a business to desist from certain practices on pain of substantial penalties, including imprisonment. In this way the 'cease and desist' power is a supplement in securing compliance with existing legal provisions. An alternative mechanism for their enforcement is provided and the sanctions underlying them are strengthened.

In the United States the Federal Trade Commission is empowered to act against unfair or deceptive trade practices. As a quasi-judicial body it can issue 'cease and desist' orders itself against businesses engaging in such practices, and if the orders are not obeyed civil penalties can be imposed.[70] 'Cease and desist' orders have prospective force and the Commission has rarely incorporated in its orders restitution to compensate those injured by an offender.[71] Critics of the operation of the 'cease and desist' power point out that an order can be postponed for substantial periods by the delaying tactics of businesses. Violation of the order has to be proved in new and separate proceedings. Apparently the Federal Trade Commission monitored 'cease and desist' orders on a haphazard basis in the past, and in many cases has been unaware whether its orders were obeyed.[72] In some cases the Federal Trade Commission did not react sufficiently speedily to halt unscrupulous businesses before they had victimized consumers and accumulated substantial profits.[73]

Under Part III of the Fair Trading Act 1973, the Director General of Fair Trading is empowered to obtain 'cease and desist' orders against businesses which engage in a persistent course of conduct detrimental to consumers which is in breach of criminal or civil law. The interests of consumers which must be jeopardized before the Office of Fair Trading can act include economic, health and safety interests.[74] The ambit of the legislation is very wide, for the breaches of law need not have been the subject of court proceedings. Thus action could be taken against a business if complaints from consumers established that it was constantly in breach of contract, even though no civil judgments to this effect had been obtained against it. The procedure for obtaining a 'cease and desist' order is that initially the Office of Fair Trading must seek a written assurance from a business that it will refrain from its objectionable or similar conduct. Only if an assurance is refused or broken can the Office of Fair Trading seek a 'cease and desist' order from a court. A court may accept an undertaking from the business, but if it refuses, or if the court thinks an undertaking is unacceptable, it can issue a 'cease and desist' order forbidding the business to engage in the objectionable or a similar practice.[75] An assurance, undertaking or order has prospective force only and neither punishes a business for past behaviour nor expropriates any illegal profits that it has accrued. Moreover, disadvantaged consumers are not compensated as a result of an undertaking or order and they must bring individual civil claims. 'Cease and desist' orders are therefore oriented towards the general public interest rather than the individual interests of consumers in transactions. To prevent the possibility that businessmen will evade the legislation by, for example, changing the corporate form of their business or by engaging in a different sphere of commercial activity, changes are necessary in sections 34 and 37 which refer to an assurance, undertaking or order in relation to 'that course of conduct' or 'any similar course of conduct in the course of that (or his) business'.

Undertakings or orders may be obtained directly against traders and not just against their businesses. Directors, managers, secretaries, etc., who can be shown to have consented to or connived at the detrimental course of conduct of a company, might be required to give a threefold assurance that they will refrain: (a) from continuing to consent to or connive at the course of conduct in question; (b) from carrying on any similar course of conduct in the course of any business which may at any time be carried on by them; and (c) from consenting to or conniving at the carrying on of any such course of conduct by any other body corporate in relation to which they are a director or similar officer.[76] There is also power to proceed against persons controlling more than 50 per cent of the voting shares in a particular company. The courts can act against interconnected companies, including companies formed after the making of the original order, which prevents evasion by creation of a new subsidiary.[77] Breach of a court order constitutes contempt of court and exposes a business to an unlimited fine or a businessman to imprisonment.

The Office of Fair Trading necessarily relies on the work of consumer protection departments to obtain information relevant to the exercise of its power. A central registry of convictions is maintained which has enabled the Office to identify a number of businesses for possible action. Other sources of information have been solicited for details of relevant convictions or complaints including consumer organizations, the mass media and the courts. A difficulty in relying on the past record of a business, as contained in the register of convictions or in the complaints received by the Office, is that some current perpetrators of prejudicial trade practices will not have a record. Thus they may be able to avoid undertakings or an order, unless by fortuitous circumstances the Office of Fair Trading hears about them and takes action despite the fact that they have no record.

The Office of Fair Trading has investigated a considerable number of companies, a number of which have subsequently gone into liquidation. At the end of December 1981, 291 assurances, undertakings or orders had been obtained. The Office of Fair Trading regards the legislation as effective in that few traders appear to have acted unfairly to consumers once they have given assurances and only in seven cases has it been necessary to bring an action for breach of an assurance.[78] Over the period 1974–80 there was a rough correspondence between the pattern of complaints and the areas in which assurances were obtained. The status of the person giving the assurances is shown in Table 11.1.

Table 11.1   Assurances Obtained Classified by Status of Person Giving the Assurance

| Year | Company | Section 34 | | Section 38 | Total |
		Individual trader	Partners	Director or other officer	
1974–80	52	60	27	103	242

The businesses against which assurances, undertakings and orders have been obtained have been mainly small or middle-sized traders. Quite apart from the comparatively large number of such businesses, another factor might be the difficulty of relating the record of a large business to size: are ten convictions for a national business equivalent to two convictions for a local firm? Businesses have given assurances to comply with the terms of the contracts they enter, to supply goods which are merchantable and fit for the purpose, to perform work in a proper and workmanlike manner, to carry out work in a safe manner, not to make false statements about the products or services they market, and not to be in breach of duty in failing to return money paid in advance. Assurances can thus be finely tuned to the details of the particular products or services involved. The policy of the Office of Fair Trading has been to release the text of all assurances and some background information to the press. The power to publicize has been upheld by the Divisional Court as an essential monitoring device, ensuring that breaches of assurances, undertakings or orders are reported.[79]

The 'cease and desist' power in the Fair Trading Act 1973 is a most important legal technique in furthering consumer protection, but it could be further improved by legislative amendment. The ambit of the 'cease and desist' power could be widened beyond the requirement that there be a breach of civil or criminal law. The Swedish Market Court, for example, can issue a prohibition order against a business or those associated with it if they advertise or take any action 'which, by conflicting with good commercial standards or otherwise, adversely affects consumers or tradesmen.'[80] The immediate objection to a similar provision will be that the law has always demanded clear standards of behaviour before imposing sanctions, but this overlooks a number of points: first, there are widely-accepted standards among businesses for dealing with consumers, many of which are embodied in codes of practice but not necessarily in law; second, the 'cease and desist' power does not constitute the imposition of criminal sanctions, although these may follow if an order is breached; third, there is a fundamental difference between provisions which can lead to the loss of liberty on the part of a subject and those where any sanction will almost invariably be the imposition of a monetary penalty.

Another idea drawn from the Swedish experience is that there should be a separate court for dealing with consumer protection matters, in particular 'cease and desist' orders. At present the Office of Fair Trading can proceed in the Restrictive Practices Court and, in less important cases in the county courts or the sheriffs' courts.[81] None of these bodies seems to be appropriate for hearing 'cease and desist' applications, and any delays in the county courts and sheriffs' courts make them quite unacceptable as forums in situations where speed is often essential. A final reform would be to enable the Office of Fair Trading to obtain redress on behalf of consumers from those from whom it obtains an undertaking or a 'cease and desist' order. Under the Australian Trade Practices Act 1974, the Trade Practices Commission can obtain an injunction against conduct which breaches the consumer provisions of the Act and at the same time the court can grant an order of redress for consumers.[82] In Canada a written undertaking or assurance can contain a clause relating to consumer reimbursement.[83]

PRICE RESTRAINT

The government can influence the level of prices in various ways.[84] Monetary and fiscal policy are important tools of economic policy which can be used within limits to affect the general level of prices. Another possibility is that the government can vary the price of resources under its control by manipulating their supply; for example, it might alter the rate at which minerals are extracted, thus raising or lowering their price.[85] The government also buys commodities and may be able to determine their price through its powerful bargaining position; an example considered in the next chapter is the purchase of drugs. Marketing schemes for primary products may be made compulsory by legislation to ensure price stabilization and adequate returns to producers. Competition law can be used against monopoly conditions and restrictive practices and this can affect prices. The present section discusses in a rudimentary manner three direct methods by which the government can restrain prices as an anti-inflation measure:[86] subsidies (a fiscal measure), moral suasion and price control.

Economists are divided about the origins of inflation. Monetarists consider inflation to be caused by an excess of money in proportion to goods and services available, leading to a situation where there is too much money chasing too few goods and services.[87] The excess in the money, they say, arises because government is too inclined to increase the supply as a matter of policy to boost consumer-demand and hence output and employment. If this theory of inflation is accepted the general remedy for excessive price increases is not to introduce controls over businesses but properly to regulate the money supply. For some monetarists wage-price controls might be acceptable, however, to demonstrate in a dramatic way government's determination not to use monetary policy to stimulate the economy and to prevent wage and price increases motivated solely by an anticipation of continued inflation.[88] The second theory in vogue is that inflation results from excessive wage demands (cost-push inflation) and that the remedy lies in limiting wage increases to improvements in productivity. In this view price increases would not be necessary if wages rose in line with productivity because average labour costs would remain the same. Direct government control of prices might be necessary, however, as a means of inducing workers to accept wage restraint.

Adherents to the theories generally dislike direct government measures to restrain prices and say that they are ineffective in curbing inflation because they are irrelevant to its causes. To the extent that direct government measures have an impact, adherents of the monetarist and cost-push theories say that they are positively harmful. The argument sometimes derives from theory; for example, the monetarists conclude that lower prices will simply generate more inflation since its cause is excessive demand. At a practical level it is said that direct government measures against prices misallocate resources and create a downturn in economic activity. An example of this line of reasoning is as follows. Price control presses on company profits, but businesses may attempt to maintain profit levels by reducing quality, producing fewer lines or cutting down on service (shorter hours, fewer deliveries, etc.) To the extent that profits fall there are not the retained earnings to plough back into investment and there is a disincentive for the stock market to purchase new equity. As investment falls, the adverse consequences for productivity, employment and consumer welfare become clear.

There are counter-arguments to those just presented. It can be argued that profits need not fall as a result of price control if a business increases sales or improves productivity. Indeed, systems of price control usually make provision for firms to pass on the cost of new investment in higher prices. The argument that prices legislation has led in the past to a fall in investment ignores the other more significant factors relevant to this phenomenon. Moreover, an important obstacle to investment is inflation because of the uncertainty it causes, and price control may have an effect in reducing this.

Economic arguments favouring direct price control are few since the majority of economists are wedded to market analysis, but there is a good economic argument that inflation is caused because powerful business enterprises are 'price-setters' rather than 'price-takers'; they can, within limits, determine the prices which consumers pay for their products and services and are not affected by market forces.[89] These corporations derive power from their size, the concentration of modern industry and the difficulties of entry for new competitors. Government-backed price restraint commends itself if it is accepted that corporate power is the explanation for inflation, for it seems to be a direct way of reducing it and at the same time of controlling an unacceptable concentration of power in society. Prices legislation thus makes businesses socially accountable: companies must make important financial information available for scrutiny by a public body, they are sensitized to the public interest when making pricing decisions and their behaviour is subject to at least some government control. Moreover, price control can have some effect on redistributing wealth in society – from the owners and controllers of corporate power to others in the community like workers and consumers. If private investment falls as the result of price control, government can fill the gap by providing finance, at the same time acquiring a stake in private industry.

Subsidies

Subsidies are one way of limiting the cost of living. An example of a policy of subsidies were the Prices Acts 1974 and 1975 which authorized up to £1000 million for subsidies for milk, butter, cheese, flour and other foods specified by statutory order. The government had power to recoup money paid in respect of exports. It could also impose conditions on the payment of subsidies (e.g. to avoid double payment) and require businesses receiving subsidies to keep relevant records.[90] In some cases the subsidies were administered through existing marketing schemes. The value of these subsidies to consumers at one stage was estimated to be significant for larger families; the lower-income groups benefited most as a proportion of their disposable income.[91]

Economists generally dislike subsidies because they interfere with market mechanisms. It is said that they can be self-defeating in making food cheaper because consumers respond to price cuts in subsidized products by buying more of them, which in the short run forces up prices or has adverse effects on the balance of payments. Whether these results follow, however, depends on the price elasticity of demand for the subsidized products and whether local output can be rapidly increased, perhaps difficult with agricultural products, to obviate the need for imports. Subsidies are criticized for not sufficiently assisting poorer consumers since everyone benefits from them. Income transfers are preferred, for they go directly to those in greatest need. One estimate is that during 1974–5 about 63 per cent of the government's expenditure on food subsidies went to families on above-average incomes because they bought more of the subsidized products. In addition, some threshold wage rises were frustrated because food subsidies kept the Retail Price Index from rising sufficiently. Through this indirect effect of wages, it is said, subsidies in some months withheld from poorer families almost as much as they gained in cheaper food.[92]

Food subsidies can be useful, however, as a way of helping poorer consumers in addition to dampening price rises in certain products. They do not involve a means test, which some object to as humiliating and undesirable. Food subsidies have most effect for poorer consumers if they are paid on the staple products which are of greatest significance in their diets. Moreover, subsidies have other aims besides assisting poorer consumers. They can keep down the cost of living, something income transfers cannot achieve because the latter simply add to a household's spending capacity. Food subsidies can encourage wage restraint on the part of the trade unions. Wartime food subsidies were used to induce greater food production and to encourage consumers to buy particular foods for nutritional reasons.[93]

Moral suasion

Moral suasion is said to be 'the attempt to coerce private economic activity *via* governmental exhortation in directions not already defined or dictated by existing statute law'.[94] To back up its exhortations, government may threaten to introduce legal measures or it may publicize a business's unsatisfactory behaviour so that consumers will take retaliatory action. Because the public's response is important, moral suasion is at its most effective when the businesses at which it is directed are few in number, dependent on consumer goodwill and are highly 'visible' so that non-compliers are readily identifiable. Moral suasion is an important technique of price restraint when political philosophy dictates against tighter control. Moral suasion has its detractors. They say it is inequitable because non-complying businesses may benefit by ignoring a government plea for price restraint. It also constitutes extra-legal and *ad hoc* coercion by government without judicial review and may entail the danger of an over-familiar relationship between government and business. Whatever the merit of these arguments, the most forceful criticism is that moral suasion can be used as an excuse for government's failing to take more definite action.

Moral suasion was a major factor in the operation of the National Board for Prices and Incomes between 1965 and 1971.[95] Under the legislation, certain businesses had to notify the Board of price increases, which the latter could report upon. The government could also charge the Board with investigating particular prices or with keeping certain prices under continuous review.[96] The government had no power to take action to implement the Board's reports. But a study of the Board's workings suggests that its reports deterred some businesses from increasing prices, and also that fear of investigation led some businesses to avoid price increases.[97] A countervailing tendency, however, might have been for other businesses to increase their prices inordinately in anticipation of a Board inquiry. Certainly it seems that the Board, through its investigations, brought home to industry the need to curtail costs and modernize plant.

Related to moral suasion are voluntary agreements whereby businesses agree to limit price increases. The advantage to government is that voluntary agreements may not arouse the same opposition from businesses as legal controls.[98] At the same time voluntary agreements on prices can have drawbacks: lack of definiteness, not all businesses may adhere and no provision for effective enforcement. There have been a number of voluntary agreements on prices in Britain in recent years. In 1971–2 the Confederation of British Industry, in an effort to forestall legal controls, undertook to limit price increases to 5 per cent per annum.[99] 'Price Check' operated in 1976 as the immediate *quid pro quo* to the trades unions for further wage restraint. Under it, businesses agreed to hold price increases to a ceiling of 5p in the pound on some forty-seven product categories of importance to consumers.[100] 'Price Check' differed from previous agreements in the massive publicity the government accorded it. The Price Commission concluded that items in the scheme remained well within the 5 per cent limit.[101] Critics were quick to point out that businesses originally nominated items that would fall within the limit and that there was nothing to prevent them making substantial price increases when it terminated.

Price control

In recent decades many industrialized countries have tried a temporary (usually ninety-day) wage and/or price freeze[102] to fix wages and prices at the levels they are when it is announced.[103] The experience of such freezes suggests that they can limit inflation if they are followed by more permanent measures. Overall, a freeze seems to have a greater impact on wages than prices because wage increases are more easily identified and controlled. Another factor is that wage increases take place on a fixed-cycle across-the-board basis, while price increases are continual and involve differential increases for different commodities; consequently, once a freeze terminates workers are less quickly able to make up lost ground.[104] It is difficult to sustain a rigid wage-price freeze for a considerable length of time because it inevitably leads to resource misallocation as well as political strains. These effects can be mitigated by incorporating flexibility into a freeze but this raises problems of unequal treatment and undermines two of its main advantages – certainty and simplicity.

There are various problems of legislating for the prices part of a freeze.[105] Are the ceiling prices those which were quoted immediately before the freeze becomes effective, or can businesses obtain the highest price previously charged? How are adjustments to be made when a business has not previously supplied a strictly comparable product or service? What of unique goods or services, or goods sold by auction? Should there be a price increase when it was arranged before the freeze to take place during the freeze? What about products and services, the supply of which extends beyond the freeze period? Should a promotion, discount or other allowance (like trading stamps) be included in calculating the ceiling? Is an increase in a hire purchase/conditional sale deposit in violation of a freeze? Must a business absorb cost increases beyond its control, such as on imported materials or those which arise from changes in supply for seasonal or for other reasons? Should appropriate reductions in prices be made in view of factors like substantially lower costs? Will the freeze extend to export prices?

Fixed maximum prices operated during the second world war and the immediate post-war period. For example, the Goods and Services (Price Control) Act 1941 enabled the government to fix prices or to direct that they be fixed in a specified manner (e.g. with reference to cost prices and margins of profit), and the government could also require steps to be taken to bring controlled prices to the notice of consumers.[106] It became an offence to offer to sell at a price greater than a controlled price and bartering to avoid the controls was forbidden. Wartime controls were generally successful, despite evasions, because of wide public acceptance.[107] Even so, the task was administratively burdensome and involved the issue of a great number of general price regulations, together with an even greater number of individual regulations for particular products, services and businesses.

It is uncommon in peacetime for maximum prices to operate on a longer term basis than a ninety-day freeze. The general view is that fixing maximum prices leads to severe dislocations in the economy and is difficult administratively, even with a considerable bureaucracy.

The administering agency would eventually find it necessary to review applications for price adjustments of nearly every price in the economy, and there are billions of such prices. The process, once begun, would snowball; each price adjusted ordinarily changes costs or demands elsewhere and so becomes the occasion for many more applications.[108]

Even if these points are accepted, they do not mean that a limited system of fixed maximum prices is unworkable. A number of Australian jurisdictions have quite successfully fixed maximum prices for commodities like bread, milk and petrol for several decades.[109] At various times the controls have extended to other products (e.g. to footwear), to professional services and to land.[110] While having little effect on inflation, such controls have proved a means of assisting poorer consumers and of preventing excessive profits being made on important commodities.

Enforcement of fixed maximum prices is facilitated because it is possible for consumers to know when excessive prices are being charged and to complain to enforcement agencies. Maximum price legislation might render a transaction invalid for that part of the consideration in excess of the limit, and enable the consumer to recover this amount. Alternatively, it may allow the consumer to render the whole transaction invalid if restitution is possible, not much time has elapsed, and the rights of third parties will not be prejudiced. Express provision is necessary in either case because the courts do not regard prices legislation as giving individual consumers a right of civil action.[111] The deterrent effect of such provisions in the future would be strengthened by allowing class actions or empowering enforcement bodies to institute mass restitution suits.

An indirect means of price control compared with fixed minimum prices is to limit businesses from increasing their prices except to the extent that costs have risen.[112] The difficulty is that such controls can become over-complicated and inflexible, and arbitrary and outdated in their application to particular products. Some firms come to regard the controls as an entitlement to price increases when otherwise these would not have occurred, and the controls might adversely affect efficiency and employment. An example might be that some businesses are encouraged to cut output to justify a price increase through higher unit costs rather than to boost sales by keeping prices low.

Another indirect technique of price control is to control the profit margins of businesses.[113] There are obvious problems of definition; for example, there needs to be detailed rules for calculating net margins in the light of matters like depreciation, changes in corporate structure and the depreciation and appreciation of assets. Margins are regulated on an historic basis, by tying businesses to their past profits. In choosing the reference period – how far back it would extend and its length – the government has to balance the consequence of a short period, that it might be unrepresentative, with that of a longer period, that it might include 'stale' margins. This method represents a more sophisticated means of price control than fixed maximum prices, although there is the danger that its detailed rules can lead to company calculations which make profits highly artificial, bearing little resemblance to profits as calculated on accepted accounting principles.[114] A real difficulty is enforcement. Without a highly trained team of investigators, the control is meaningless, for it is not difficult to conceive of ways in which unscrupulous companies can juggle their figures to misrepresent their true financial position. Individual consumers are simply not in a position to know whether excessive prices are being charged, for this requires a detailed knowledge of a company's records and financial state.[115] The one area where consumers can have an impact is with the practice of retailers in repricing stock already on the shelves. The practice can damage consumer confidence and undermine a policy of price and wage restraint. Consequently, repricing for products on display might be forbidden, even when it is otherwise justified.[116]

CONCLUSION

The control of trade practices overlaps with that involving broad criminal prohibitions, with the difference that it is more preventive because it is more selective in its field of application. Businesses know what is expected of them with greater certainty because they are specifically directed as to the nature of their trade practices. But whereas violations of these laws simply give rise to the imposition of criminal penalties, we shall see in the next chapter that under a regime of licensing businesses may actually be denied the right to operate unless they meet certain standards.

Despite the advantages of closely controlling objectionable behaviour, critics argue that there are a number of limitations which
attach to the control of trade practices as described in this chapter.
One argument is that once a business attains a standard required by
law, it may have little incentive to go beyond it. It is said that control
may actually operate as an inducement to a business to degrade the
standard of its trade practices when they are superior to those
required by law if they do not command a higher price. Whether this
result actually occurs is open to doubt: it may occasionally occur with
product standards but it is difficult to conceive it happening with the
controls over trade practices considered. Another objection is that the
control of trade practices calls for a disproportionate amount of scarce
resources in drafting and then in enforcement. Certainly the enforcement of controls over trade practices requires resources, but as
Summers puts it, the technique proceeds on the assumption that 'an
ounce of prevention is worth tons of cure.'[117] A technique which has
been adopted in some jurisdictions is for the law to contain a broad
prohibition against misleading and deceptive practices. For example,
section 5 of the Federal Trade Commission Act as amended provides:
'Unfair methods of competition in or affecting commerce, and unfair
or deceptive acts or practices in or affecting commerce, are declared
unlawful.'[118] The authorities are then empowered to take action
against businesses which in their view violate this standard, not by
prosecution, but by seeking a 'cease and desist' order or injunction.
Damages might also be obtainable. The advantage of such a
provision over the Fair Trading Act 1973 is its flexibility as compared
with the lengthy and inflexible process of drafting a statutory order
under Part II. The provision also has a wider ambit than Part III of
the Fair Trading Act 1973, which is confined to behaviour which
breaches existing criminal or civil law.

Moreover, as a supplement to public enforcement, some jurisdictions enable consumers and other businesses, either individually
or in class suits, to sue where they are affected by deceptive acts or
practices. This is one counterbalance to public authorities identifying
too closely with the regulated although the full potential of this
provision cannot be realised without financial assistance going to
consumers and procedural reforms to facilitate their bringing
actions.[119] Britain would be well advised to consider whether a
provision along the lines of that just described should be incorporated
into the Fair Trading Act 1973.

Prior approval by licensing

The hallmark of prior approval by licensing is that businesses must satisfy certain prerequisites before engaging in specified commercial activity. The theory is that licensing permits beneficial activity but at the same time prevents its harmful consequences. Licensing varies in the ambit of its control. Approval may have to be sought if a business is to engage in trade, but it may also be needed for more specific activity, for example, for each product marketed.[1] The former is far more common, but the case study on drugs demonstrates that licensing of products has a role.

The present chapter opens with some general remarks on licensing, examines occupational licensing and consumer credit licensing and concludes with a case study of prior approval for drugs and drug manufacturing. At the outset it should be emphasized that the focus of the chapter is on licensing, whose primary purpose is the definite control of business behaviour in the public interest. Governments also use licensing to develop natural resources (e.g. oil and petroleum licensing) or to allocate scarce resources (e.g. airline routes, television transmission bands). This type of licensing has repercussions for consumers – it impinges on competition and involves the government in distributing wealth to particular groups in the community – but these are rather indirect and not necessarily adverse to their interests.

THE TECHNIQUE OF LICENSING

Licensing is a powerful tool of control. Instead of the occasional private law proceeding or prosecution if it breaches the law, a business is faced with the possibility of being denied the right to continue an activity altogether. The Crowther Committee advanced this as a leading argument for licensing institutions granting consumer credit:

> The protective measures [in existence] are all concerned with individual transactions. . . [T]he more unscrupulous type of credit grantor may well take the view that the occasional check on his malpractices by a determined consumer in an isolated transaction is not a serious deterrent, and is outweighed by the financial advantages he may derive from evading the law. There is thus a need for an agency entrusted with the continuing supervision of consumer credit grantors, with power to investigate trading practices, require production of accounts and records and, in the case of serious malpractices, suspend or revoke the offender's licence.[3]

Licensing can also give a state agency wide access to knowledge about an area of business through ancillary requirements relating to the supply of information. It may also be useful where a business engages in objectionable behaviour which does not fall exactly within any criminal prohibition – the business can be threatened with the loss of its license if it does not desist.

The scope for controlling businesses through licensing can be limited because of the cost of administering it. If individual businesses or particular activities have to be approved, a substantial bureaucracy may be necessary. Should insufficient resources be allocated to the administrative side of licensing, experience suggests either that there will be a delay in issuing licences or that the vetting procedure will be perfunctory with only a cursory check of applications.[4] Likewise, licensing can become futile where it is not supported by adequate enforcement machinery to ensure that businesses adhere to the standards set. However, licensing can be self-supporting financially if the fees charged for licenses are high enough to cover the administrative costs, and in this event any objection must be to the size of the bureaucracy rather than to its cost.

When first introduced licensing can have a powerful weeding-out effect on businesses. After the consumer protection administration in New South Wales refused several hundred early applications for car-dealer licences, apparently almost half the 8000 dealers then operating in the state went out of business because they realized that they would not obtain a licence. The same weeding-out occurred, although comparatively on a less extensive scale, when consumer credit licensing was introduced in Britain.[5] A similar effect may operate to deter businessmen from entering fields where licensing obtains, if it is unlikely that they will qualify for a licence and if heavy penalties can be imposed on unlicensed trading.

Once established, a licensing system is deficient if it does not contain a gradation of sanctions ranging from the mild to the severe. This illustrates a general point about sanctions, that enforcement agencies are handicapped if there is a discrepancy between the sanctions they can initiate and the objectionable behaviour they are charged with eliminating.[6] If a sanction is too mild it will not deter, an illustration being a low fine; while if a sanction is too severe the agency will be reluctant to have it imposed. If variation, suspension or revocation are the only penalties for non-compliance with a licence, it seems that licensees can commit minor transgressions with impunity because such severe sanctions cannot be justified.[7] Suspension or revocation are especially out of the question with larger firms because innocent employees would be out of a job. In cases such as this the hope of policy-makers must be that there will be a deterrent effect because of the possibility, albeit remote, that the licence can be suspended or revoked. In addition it might be thought that the threat that a licence can be suspended or cancelled will encourage informal resolution of disputes to the satisfaction of consumers. Much more sensible than simply having the sanctions of suspension or revocation are varied disciplinary powers: for example, Australian Credit Tribunals can reprimand licensees, impose fines or suspend or cancel a licence in the event of major abuses.[8]

OCCUPATIONAL LICENSING

Countries vary in their use of occupational licensing. Some European countries retain the wide restrictions of the medieval guild system. West German law, for example, establishes a comprehensive classification of skilled trades for which tests of competence are required and only those persons registered with the Registrar of Crafts can use the title 'master' and exercise their trade.[9] In addition, West German law requires persons wishing to engage in retail trade to obtain a license demonstrating that they are both competent and reliable to do so. Reliability is applied with reference to the particular business involved and so, for example, a travel agent in poor financial condition will be treated as unreliable because monies which consumers entrust to it may be seized by creditors.[10]

Some eighty occupations are licensed in the United States, ranging from tree surgeons, guide-dog trainers and pest controllers on the one hand, to cosmetologists, funeral directors and barbers on the other. Pressure for licensing has come mainly from the members of these occupations and almost invariably licensing is administered by the occupations themselves. Consumer support has been minimal except in a few instances like car repairs where licensing has been seen as a means of raising standards.[11] The strange occupations to which licensing applies, its tenuous connection with consumer welfare, and the fact that business has advocated its adoption, lead strongly to the inference that sometimes it acts against the public interest by restricting entry and raising prices.[12]

Occupational licensing in Britain has been far less frequent, and the general rule has been that businesses can be established without prior government approval. A long-standing exception has been retail outlets for intoxicating liquor, and prior approval has also been required for doctors, pharmacists and others connected with the public health. Nationalization of certain industries means that businesses cannot engage in those areas of trade without a licence.[13] Otherwise licensing encompasses a rag-bag of businesses such as taxis, market trading, and employment agencies.

The main consumer justification of occupational licensing is to ensure adequate knowledge and standards on the part of those engaged in an occupation by defining the conditions of admission to and continuance in them. Persons are held to high standards through the threat that their license will be revoked. Government action is necessary since sometimes consumers cannot readily identify the incompetent, either because specialized knowledge is involved (e.g. health matters) or because they would first have to spend substantial sums of money by engaging in a transaction. The cost of error in such cases can be high. An added reason for licensing in the case of some professional services is to limit conflicts of interest because the professionals are in a position to generate unnecessary demand (e.g. over-servicing by doctors and lawyers). While it is more a benefit of, rather than a justification for, licensing, licensing can furnish consumers with a simple and inexpensive avenue for redress of their complaints. For example, under the system of builders' licensing in New South Wales, dissatisfied consumers can complain to the licensing authority, which can make a rectification order or order that redress be paid out of a compensation scheme.[14] Other justifications for occupational licensing are to suppress fraudulent and deceptive practices and to suppress a public nuisance (e.g. hawking). Perhaps the best example of the former is licensing for the used-car trade. It will be recalled that the car trade is a major source of consumer problems, and that dealers who misdescribe cars have been prosecuted frequently under the Trade Descriptions Act 1968. Australian states such as New South Wales have grasped the nettle and have introduced licensing for car dealers whereby they must show that they are fit persons to engage in the trade (having regard to their character, police reports and other matters), and that they have sufficient resources to meet their obligations under the legislation (e.g. they are obliged to give warranties).[15] In Britain many used-car dealers must be licensed under the Consumer Credit Act 1974, and as well action can be taken against them under Part III of the Fair Trading Act 1973. The Director General of Fair Trading has concluded that the resources are not available for a special licensing or registration regime for used-car traders. Instead, he has recommended that legislation shall require the provision of a written statement about a car's condition and of a mileage information notice where a trader cannot verify its accuracy.[16] However, an empirical study of the effects of 1974 Wisconsin legislation along these lines concluded that although pre-1974 buyers paid relatively more than post-1974 buyers, the disadvantage of poorer consumers remained constant across time and also in relation to two neighbouring states which did not have such legislation. Moreover, although after the 1974 law Wisconsin dealers might have sold used cars in better condition, there was no difference between pre- and post-law buyers as to the defects of which they were aware before purchase.[17]

Monopoly effects

Critics have argued that occupational licensing frequently acts against the consumer interest because it restricts competition and inhibits innovation. Sometimes the attack is by anti-collectivists who believe that individuals can decide matters for themselves and that the market offers the best guarantee for consumer protection. Occupational licensing, they say, simply means higher prices. The view taken in this book is that the consumer frequently needs government protection, but the point must be conceded that some licensing has monopoly effects and operates as a cartel in the interests of the members of an occupation. For example, it is said that the licensing of taxis has degenerated from its primary purpose of control into a self-perpetuating system of excluding competition, where taxi licenses which cost little when issued change hands for substantial sums of money.[18] The judgement is too harsh, for where public authorities operate taxi licensing as it is intended by statute, consumers can be assured that the vehicles they travel in are safe and that the fare meters used register uniform rates and have not been tampered with.[19] Moreover, consumers can always choose to travel in unlicensed mini-cabs although these have been subjected to statutory restrictions, for example, on the use of descriptions like 'taxi' or 'cab'.[20]

In 1970 the Monopolies Commission tried to characterize situations where occupational licensing of the professions perpetuated undesirable monopoly practices.[21] It accepted that sometimes licensing was necessary to protect consumers because of the special nature of the skills required for professional practice or the peculiar fiduciary or personal character of the services involved. Risks to health and safety lent support to licensing, particularly where consumers were bad judges of their own interests. Rather than identifying particular occupations where collective restrictions on competition were against the public interest, the Commission concluded that the best approach was to examine particular criteria for licensing. It concluded that education and training prerequisites were generally unobjectionable, although they could increase the cost of entry and thus benefit those already in a profession. Certain character tests could usually be justified, because the public interest was endangered if the whole structure or machinery of a profession was brought into disrepute. By contrast, the Commission thought collective restrictions on price competition were most likely undesirable, because they raised prices unnecessarily. It also said that complete freedom to advertise might involve the danger of consumers falling into the trap of the incompetent, but to prevent dissemination of price information was almost invariably adverse to consumers' welfare.

The adverse monopoly effects of occupational licensing are most pronounced where the state hands over its administration to the occupation itself. Particular reasons may dictate this decision, such as the government's lack of expertise or resources, or that state administration would meet strong political resistance.[22] Clear examples of state-backed self-regulation are law and medicine.

The monopoly effects of occupational licensing are not inevitable and guidelines like those drawn up by the Monopolies Commission can do much to ensure that restrictions are only employed when the benefit to consumers outweighs the cost. Another important factor in preventing consumers being disadvantaged by occupational licensing is to ensure that they are adequately represented on licensing boards, a step which may require government funds but which will guarantee that licensing does not degenerate into a successful effort by the established members of an occupation, acting with the knowledge of government officials, to exclude competition.

Certification

Friedman draws the distinction between registration, certification and licensing proper.[23] Registration is where individuals simply must list their names in an official register. Certification goes one step further, for an individual must demonstrate that he has reached a certain standard, but the government does not prevent the practice of skills by those who have not obtained a certificate. Licensing proper is much more restrictive, for once individuals meet certain criteria they are given the exclusive right to engage in a particular occupation. Certification is said to have the advantages that it does not prevent persons from working in a particular trade or profession, while allowing consumers to choose between the uncertified at (presumably) a lower price and a (presumably) higher quality service at a higher price.

An example of certification is the regulation of insurance brokers. Considerable criticism has surrounded their activities. It was felt that some were incompetent or dishonest and that others were not acting as the independent advisers which consumers assumed them to be because many were really agents of insurance companies. The insolvency of some insurance brokers has also resulted in consumer loss.[24]

It has been an offence for some time to make misleading statements knowingly or recklessly, or dishonestly to conceal material facts which induce or are an attempt to induce consumers to enter contracts of insurance.[25] There is a provision for a cooling-off period to enable consumers to cancel certain insurance contracts if they feel, for example, that a contract is not as advantageous as a broker has suggested.[26] Insurance brokers who work exclusively for an insurance company must also inform prospective consumers in writing of their links, so that consumers will not be misled into thinking that they are obtaining unbiased advice about the relative merits of different policies.[27] Regulations will also be made to improve the standard of insurance agents by making the companies employing them responsible for their actions.[28] The rule at common law is that in filling out a proposal insurance agents are acting on behalf of an insured and that consequently consumers bear the loss if brokers make misstatements or omissions, even if these are deliberate.[29] The policy behind the change is that making companies liable for the acts of their agents gives them an incentive to select responsible and trained agents and that consumers are also in a better position to obtain redress. So far legislation has left brokers' commission untouched, despite criticism that it leads them to promote policies which may not be to the best advantage of particular consumers.[30]

The government rejected state licensing for insurance brokers –which operates in some European countries like Holland[31] – because of the cost and because it did not have civil servants with the requisite expertise.[32] Instead, it opted for a scheme of certification, administered mainly by registered insurance brokers. Brokers have to meet certain standards of good character and either experience or professional qualifications or both, and must comply with rules as to solvency and independence. Legislation reserves the title 'insurance broker' to those certified.[33]

The chief disadvantage of certification is its limited operation. There is no guarantee that consumers will know the distinction between the certified and uncertified and what that entails. Take the insurance broker example. People will still be able to set themselves up as insurance intermediaries without any guarantee as to their training, impartiality or financial probity as long as they use a style which does not suggest that they are certified insurance brokers. Many consumers will fail to make the distinction, so there is little incentive for the non-certified to become certified. At present there are tens of thousands of part-time insurance intermediaries such as solicitors and accountants who place insurance business on behalf of clients, property companies, estate agents, motor traders and travel agents. These intermediaries will continue to place insurance business, whatever their training in or knowledge of insurance matters.

The standards required of licensees

Schemes of occupational licensing vary in the standards which they require of potential business licensees, depending on what reasons underlie the decision to adopt this particular method of legal control. In many cases the unacceptable incidence of malpractice in a trade is the major reason for introducing occupational licensing, and consequently good character will be given pride of place in the factors which potential licensees must demonstrate. Certainly the need for high standards of probity is an important factor behind moves to license estate agents, since consumers engage estate agents for probably the biggest single financial transaction of their lives and thus undertake a considerable risk that all will proceed smoothly. Experience has demonstrated that a number of unscrupulous persons have been attracted into estate agency and there have been a number of instances where consumers have lost deposits due to misappropriation by an agent. An example is *Sorrell* v. *Finch*,[34] where the House of Lords held that a vendor is not liable in ordinary cases where an estate agent misappropriates a deposit received from a prospective purchaser at the stage where negotiations are still subject to contract. The case involved an undischarged bankrupt who set himself up as an estate agent, and when finally found and prosecuted by the police pleaded guilty to thirteen cases of theft of deposits. In the Court of Appeal Lord Denning commented on 'how undesirable it is for young men with no proper training, not only to be able to set themselves up in business as estate agents, but to be in a position to accept large sums of money from the public.'[35]

There have also been complaints about estate agents engaging in 'sharp' practices involving conflict of interest (like selling their own property), disreputable mortgage-broking activities, misdescription of property and failure to give essential information about it, and persuading clients to use their services on the basis of terms or conditions which are unfair (such as demanding commission for merely introducing a purchaser, however unsuitable).[36] The professional associations have codes of conduct on these matters but their membership does not cover all estate agents in the country.

The Estate Agents Act 1979 has introduced *negative* licensing[37] – the Director General of Fair Trading is empowered to prohibit estate agents from engaging in 'estate agency work' generally or specifically if he is satisfied that they are unfit to do so. Unfitness is determined by reason of an agent's conviction for certain offences; discrimination committed in the course of estate agency work; failure to comply with certain obligations imposed under the Act; engaging in practices declared by Order to be undesirable; and engaging in any practice which involves breach of any material legal duty.[38] Because of the definition of estate agency work, the Act does not generally cover lettings or estate agents or developers selling land or houses direct to the public. While negative licensing has cost advantages both to business and government, it still requires that a monitoring system be established to collect information for its effective implementation.

Sometimes financial solvency is the most crucial factor in licensing. Not only must a business be run by persons who are competent and of good character, but it must also have sufficient financial backing to compensate consumers if, despite this, things go wrong. A simple way of ensuring this is to make a licence conditional on a business taking out a bond with a bank or insurance company so that, in the event of financial failure, a specified sum will become available.

Air travel operators and organizers must hold a licence from the Civil Aviation Authority, which may refuse to grant it or revoke it unless a business is financially sound.[39] To provide further protection, licensed organizers must take out a bond related to turnover, the amount depending on its bond either with the Association of British Travel Agents or another approved body.[40] Unfortunately, bonding proved insufficient when Britain's largest air travel organizer, Courtline, collapsed in the summer of 1974, leaving some 49,000 holiday-makers stranded abroad and a further 150,000, who had paid their deposits or the balance, without their holidays. The Civil Aviation Authority had renewed Courtline's licence four months previously without increasing the bonding requirement, saying that it was sufficiently satisfied about its future.[41] The fault lay not with the regulatory mechanism, however, but with Courtline's operation and the economic climate.[42] The very magnitude of the crash meant the bond was insufficient, after bringing back stranded holiday-makers, to reimburse fully the consumers who had paid money without getting a holiday. The government established an Air Travel Reserve Fund to compensate Courtline customers and to act as a future back-up where bonding and similar securities proved insufficient. The Fund is made up of compulsory contributions from licensed air travel organizers.[43] While bonds operate in relation to particular licensees, the Fund is a central fund available generally. A major defect of the legislation is that the air travel organizer must have had the licence at the time of the booking. Problems have arisen when a particular air travel organizer did not need a licence under the terms of the legislation and could arise where a licence is revoked unbeknown to consumers who subsequently make a booking.[44]

Legislation in Britain and elsewhere has made licensing of insurance companies turn on financial solvency. The Life Assurance Companies Act 1870 was the outcome of the collapse of two large insurance companies.[45] It introduced the safeguard that life assurance companies had to deposit a sum in court by way of security for its policyholders until it could prove that it had accumulated a fund of £40,000. Amalgamations and transfers of insurance businesses were also subject to court approval. These controls were gradually extended to other forms of insurance. The next major step in regulatory control took place in 1967 after a series of insurance company insolvencies.[46] Since nine companies were involved, most of which were motor vehicle insurers, there was strong public pressure for legislative action. Under the system of licensing the government controls insurance companies by reference to their business plans, financial forecasts, etc., and whether their top management (or those controlling them) are fit and proper persons.[47]

The insurance example illustrates that to work properly licensing must be supplemented by other provisions where large corporations are involved. In the case of insurance these controls have been strengthened since 1967 following further insurance company failures. In broad outline, insurance companies must prepare accounts and balance sheets in the prescribed form, undergo regular auditing and actuarial investigations and handle their assets in the required manner (e.g. separate those attributable to long-term business).[48] Further provision in the Policyholders Protection Act 1975 is the creation of a Board, financed by levies on insurance companies, to secure payment of the liability of insolvent companies to individual policy-holders. It may perform its functions by making arrangements for the transfer of a company's business to other firms. Otherwise it pays consumers 90 per cent (100 per cent in the case of compulsory insurance) of the value of their policies in liquidation.[49]

CONSUMER CREDIT LICENSING

A major area of licensing in Britain is of businesses involved with consumer credit. Over 100,000 licenses have been issued from retailers selling on credit at the one extreme to debt collectors at the other. The scheme is administered by the Office of Fair Trading although it draws on assistance from a number of sources including local consumer protection departments. Consumer credit licensing in Britain is perhaps the most extensive in the world.

Licensing in the consumer credit area took modern shape in the Moneylenders Acts 1900 to 1927 and the Pawnbrokers Act 1872, which required those engaged in these activities to hold a licence. The impetus for licensing was that many moneylenders and pawnbrokers were guilty of manifest abuses, including fraudulent misrepresent-ation, and it was thought licensing would raise standards by excluding the unscrupulous.[50] Applicants for licenses were required to demonstrate that they were of good character and suitable to carry on business and the licences could be lost if the trader was convicted of certain offences. The Moneylenders Acts extended to commercial as well as consumer transactions, but important categories of lenders, notably banks and certain finance companies, were exempt. Besides their limited application, the provisions were never adequately enforced.

The rationale of the Consumer Credit Act 1974 is to protect the consumer across the whole spectrum of credit transactions and to release the credit industry from outdated restrictions which varied according to the legal form of a transaction rather than its underlying nature. On this basis, licensing is extended to the whole credit industry so that all businesses are subject to the same licensing requirements.[51] The justification for selecting consumer credit for special treatment over other areas of consumer protection is said to be that it is particularly prone to abuses from which consumers can do little to protect themselves.

Licences are required to carry on a consumer credit or consumer hire business as well as by those acting as intermediaries or debt adjusters, debt counsellors, debt collectors and credit reference agencies.[52] Businesses must obtain separate authorization for each activity. Generally speaking, all those holding a particular type of licence are subject to the same restrictions. However, there is power for the Office of Fair Trading to circumscribe the scope of individual licenses, for example, by authorizing a consumer credit business to enter into only certain types of agreements.[53] Specific authorization is needed in a licence if a business is to canvass debtor-creditor-supplier agreements or regulated consumer hire agreements off trade premises.[54] Group licences (as opposed to standard licenses) can be issued covering those in a particular field if the public interest is better served than by requiring each to apply separately.[55] The Law Societies, the Institutes of Chartered Accountants and the National Association of Citizens Advice Bureaux are three categories for which group licences have been granted; in the main their members are debt adjusters or debt counsellors under the Act. An analysis of the standard licences issued by category of business is contained in Table 12.1.[56]

Table 12.1   Analysis of all Standard Licences Issued by Category of Business[1]

(a) Consumer credit	45,665
(b) Consumer hire	23,873
(c) Credit brokerage	87,524
(d) Debt adjusting & debt counselling	33,104
(e) Debt collecting	12,505
(f) Credit reference agency	2,918
With the right to canvass, off trade premises, debtor-creditor-supplier agreements or regulated consumer hire agreements	32,358

[1] The total number of categories covered by licence is greater than the total numbers of licences issued, as one licence can cover more than one category of business.

The wide ambit of licensing is illustrated by reference to retailers. Many retailers need a licence as a consumer credit business (if they provide credit themselves), as a credit broker (if they introduce their customers to independent finance houses to provide credit), as a debt collector (if they collect instalments and follow up arrears either on their own account or on behalf of a finance company) or as a debt adjuster (if they accept goods in part exchange, where the goods are on hire purchase and negotiate a settlement figure from the finance company). Businesses commit a criminal offence if they engage in activities for which a licence is required without a licence. In addition, a credit or hire agreement regulated by the Act cannot be enforced against the consumer without an order of the Director General of Fair Trading if it was made by an unlicensed business or if an unlicensed credit broker was involved.[57] The latter is some inducement to creditors to exercise control over the credit brokers they use.

To obtain or renew a licence, a tender has to demonstrate to the Director General of Fair Trading that it is fit to carry on the licensed activities and that its name is not misleading or undesirable.[58] Factors which are taken into account are whether the tender or persons associated with it have committed any offence involving fraud, dishonesty, violence or a breach of consumer law; practised discrimination on sex, colour, racial, ethnic or national grounds; or engaged in deceitful, oppressive, unfair or improper business practices (whether lawful or not). Examples of the first category range from contraventions of the Consumer Credit Act 1974 itself, through breaches of the Trade Descriptions Act 1968, to supplying items which are not of merchantable quality or do not meet the seller's description or the buyer's stated requirements, and failing to carry out repairs properly. The Director General has given as illustrations of unfair or improper business practices: charging interest on the full loan when only part was advanced initially; variation of the interest rate stated in the agreement; failure to check other consumers' accounts when one consumer has successfully challenged a settlement figure as too high; failure to give satisfactory information to consumers because agents were completing parts of the application forms after they were signed; circulars from television rental firms implying wrongly that consumer agreements enabled the rent to be increased simply by giving notice; failure to settle outstanding debts on cars taken in part-exchange; and pressuring consumers into purchases by inducing anxiety about their health.[59]

Unless the Director General determines to issue a licence in accordance with an application, he must inform the applicant that he is 'minded to refuse' it, give his reasons and invite representations.[60] The Director General has indicated the difficulties of constructing a 'minded to refuse' notice on the basis of complaints alone.

It is in the nature of complaints, even where these take the form of formal witness statements, that they comprise only one side of the story and are in a form where the applicant or his legal representatives are often unable to test their veracity and accuracy during the course of representations. . . . [C]ounter-statements designed to show that the complaint is misconceived may raise sufficient questions about the validity of the complaint that we are unable to make a finding of fact on the issues raised. In short, it is very difficult for me to arrive at a decision which is *not* favourable to the applicant in those cases which are comprised solely of complaints. Such cases are, however, very rare indeed, for we would try to obtain other supportive evidence to lend weight to the proposed case.[61]

Table 12.2   Consumer Credit Act 1974 – Statistics of Licences Refused, Revoked, etc., 1979–81[1]

	1979		1980		1981	
Notice that the Director General is minded to refuse or revoke a licence, etc.						
Notices	216		178		107	
Not determined in previous year	20	236	73	251	92	199
Cases concluded as follows:						
Favourable determination	111		111		74	
Adverse determination	52		48		57	
Application withdrawn	—		—		9	
Still under consideration	73	236	92	251	59	199
Appeals to the Secretary of State						
Lodged	10		12		14	
Brought forward from previous year	9	19	6	18	9	23
Disposed of as follows:						
Upheld	1		3		4	
Dismissed	10		4		5	
Abandoned	2		1		—	
Terminated	—		1		1	
Still under consideration	6	19	9	18	13	23
Appeals to the High Court						
Lodged	5		1		—	
Brought forward from previous year	—	5	5	6	1	1
Disposed of as follows:						
Dismissed	—		5		—	
Withdrawn	—		—		1	
Still under consideration	5	5	1	6	—	1

[1] As well as the refusal and revocation of licences, the statistics cover notices and decisions to refuse a variation in a licence, to grant a licence in different terms, or compulsorily to vary it.

Statistics relating to the 'minded to refuse' procedure – and to the parallel procedure in the case of the variation, suspension or revocation of a licence – are contained in Table 12.2.[62] Representations by the applicant may convince the Director General to issue a licence, for example, if an undertaking is given to improve trading practices. The Director General must take into account any representation, but if he is still minded to refuse, the applicant can appeal to the Secretary of State, or to the High Court on a point of law.[63]

In deciding whether to grant a licence, the Office of Fair Trading places heavy emphasis on information provided by the applicant, supplemented by that received from other sources, such as consumer protection departments. The form to accompany a standard licence application asks whether an applicant has been involved in a bankruptcy, scheme of arrangement or liquidation, has been convicted on certain types of criminal offence, has been adjudged in breach of the Race Relations Act 1976 or the Sex Discrimination Act 1976, or has been refused a licence under other legislation. In the case of a company, information on these matters must also be supplied for its directors, company secretary, chief executive and controlling shareholders, and for other persons in a position to control the company. Information about the spouse and other close relatives of each of these persons is also required if relevant.

Licensing in Britain is a social and not an economic tool. Licences cannot be refused on grounds of economic policy, for example to regulate competition, or because of the financial instability of a firm. This contrasts somewhat with Australia, where credit providers are licensed on the basis of whether they (or their controllers) are fit and proper persons *and* whether they have sufficient financial resources to carry on business in a proper manner.[64] There is a public register of licence applications and licences granted, but the public has no right to be heard when a business is licensed (except with the approval of the Director General of Fair Trading), or to challenge the Director General's decision to grant or continue a licence. These are serious deficiencies in the legislation.

Initially consumer credit licenses were to run for three years, but in 1979 the period was extended to ten years on the grounds that the burdens which the licensing provisions placed on traders, especially small firms, could be considerably reduced without diminishing the benefits to consumers.[65] The latter assumption can only be justified if there are sufficient enforcement resources to monitor the performance of licensees, with a view to varying, suspending or revoking a licence in the event of significant wrongdoing being detected. Power resides in the Director General of Fair Trading to vary, suspend or revoke a licence, or to exclude a person from a group licence.[66] Flexibility is limited, however, for there are no additional sanctions such as the imposition of monetary penalties if a licensee engages in objectionable activities which are not serious enough to justify varying, etc. the licence. As mentioned, the Australian Credit Tribunals can exercise a variety of disciplinary powers. However, the Director General has had some success in persuading businesses to desist from certain practices, in compensating consumers, in issuing firmer instructions to employees, and in tightening up their procedures, agreements and publicity material. The legal basis is that since he can have regard to unfair or improper business practices, *whether unlawful or not*, he can 'use the licensing system either to compel a course of conduct which the applicant or licensee may not be legally obliged to adopt at present or to require him to refrain from activities which he is at present legally entitled to pursue.'[67] Those who have their licence varied, suspended or revoked can appeal to the Secretary of State or, on a point of law, to the High Court,[68] but the wide discretion conferred by the legislation means that the chances of challenging an adverse decision are small (as evidenced in Table 12.2).

A CASE STUDY: DRUGS

As early as 1747 a select committee of the House of Commons heard evidence about abuses in the preparation of drugs, their poor quality, the incompetence of many pharmacists and the insufficiency of powers given to the authorities to authorize the destruction of adulterated drugs.[69] Letters of patent of James I had incorporated the apothecaries of London because 'The ignorant were preparing drugs to the peril of the King's subjects', but the letters patent were never confirmed by Parliament. In 1856 another select committee remarked of patent medicines that 'there can be no doubt that the public health is endangered by the use of several of these compounds', and it recommended the registration of chemists and druggists.[70] Pharmaceutical chemists were already registered under the Pharmacy Act 1852, which provided for examinations for those wishing to register and prohibited persons who were not duly registered from assuming the title of pharmaceutical chemist. Legislation in 1868 extended the examination and registration requirements to those who compounded the prescriptions of medical practitioners but called themselves 'chemists and druggists' to avoid the earlier statute.[71]

Apart from these requirements there were few restrictions on the sale of drugs.[72] There were the broad provisions of the Food and Drugs Acts that drugs were not to be injurious to health and were to be of the nature, substance and quality expected by the normal consumer. Drug samples were taken for testing under the Acts on an extremely haphazard and uncoordinated basis and the chemical analysis was performed by public analysts who had neither the knowledge nor equipment to examine other than simple patent medicines. The Pharmacy and Medicines Act 1941 required non-prescription drugs to bear their name (the appropriate designation) or the name of each ingredient on the assumption that doctors and pharmacists could use the information to advise their patients or customers. The only other control was with a limited range of obviously dangerous substances.[73] The Dangerous Drugs Act 1920 and attendant regulations implemented the Hague Convention of 1912 and prohibited the manufacture, trading in and possession of certain narcotics without authority. Control over a few therapeutic substances went as far as a system of licensing and inspection to ensure that manufacturers had the proper staff and facilities.[74] Interference of this nature was justified on the basis that these substances were especially liable to contamination in the process of preparation, that they were administered by injections which entailed great risk if the highest purity were not reached, and that they could not be properly tested for purity or potency by chemical analysis of samples on the market.[75]

The unrestricted sale of scheduled poisons was also limited by various Acts which obliged such substances to be labelled as 'poison' or 'poisonous', set up licensing for non-pharmacists qualified to vend poisons and enacted general formalities on their sale, specifically, an entry of the sale in a 'Poisons Book' kept by the vendor.[76] Similar requirements still operate for poisons in Britain and other countries; some poisons can only be sold retail by pharmacists, but others which are commonly used for purposes not involving the treatment of human ailments (such as weed-killers) are more freely available.[77] The Poison Rules 1978 contain detailed provisions regarding the restrictions on sales, the colouring of certain poisons, the labelling and form of containers, and the storage and transport of poisons.[78]

For example, a poison must be in a stout container to prevent leakage resulting from ordinary handling, the outer surface of some containers must be fluted vertically with ribs/grooves recognizable by touch, labels should contain the warning 'Poison', or in some cases other words of warning, and certain poisons must be kept in a special place reserved solely for poisons. The legal restrictions are potentially far-reaching and it is thus a question of whether they are adequately implemented. Criticism has been levelled at the dual enforcement of the legislation between the Pharmaceutical Society and the local authorities. Further, the process of scheduling a poison has received adverse comment.

With reference to drugs apart from narcotics and poisons, the general view was that the Pharmacy and Medicines Act 1941 and the Food and Drugs Acts were sufficient. There was some support for the idea that the British Pharmacopoeia should be legally constituted as the standard for drugs.[79] Commonwealth countries like Australia did this: the Therapeutic Substances Acts 1953–9 provided that any drug imported, used in inter-state trade or provided under the Pharmaceutical Benefits Scheme should conform to BP standards unless modified by regulation.[80] Britain had to wait for the Medicines Act 1968 to grant official recognition to the British Pharmacopoeia as containing the standards with which drugs should comply.[81]

The unsatisfactory position regarding most drugs was highlighted by a House of Commons Select Committee on Patent Medicines which, shortly before the First World War, investigated the widespread fraud in and the potential danger associated with the unregulated sale of patent drugs. No government department was officially concerned with the sale or advertisement of these articles, which meant that products were marketed with fraudulent claims, sometimes causing injury by leading sick persons to delay proper treatment. Few prosecutions were instituted for fraud in connection with the sale of such products for no government department was charged with this responsibility, combined with the difficulty of showing the requisite *mens rea* on the part of the vendor. The Committee characterized the lack of adequate legal controls as follows:

For all practical purposes British law is powerless to prevent any person from procuring any drug, or making any mixture, whether potent or without any therapeutical activity whatever (so long as it does not contain a scheduled poison), advertising it in any decent terms as a cure for any disease or ailment, recommending it by bogus testimonials and the invented opinions and facsimile signatures of fictitious physicians, and selling it under any name he chooses, on payment of a small stamp duty, for any price he can persuade a credulous public to pay.[82]

The Committee recommended that a special commission should be empowered to authorize the marketing of patent drugs. Drug manufacturers should be registered and required to submit a statement of the composition and therapeutical claims of their products to a government chemist for verification. For fifty years such suggestions went unheeded, and it required the Thalidomide tragedy to galvanize the government into action.

The aftermath of Thalidomide: prior approval for drugs

The Thalidomide tragedy focused attention on the absence of legal safeguards for drugs in all countries except perhaps the United States. New drugs were marketed without any official inquiry into their safety, their unrevealed dangerous properties or their harmful side-effects. Consumers relied entirely on the reputations of the drug manufacturers and of their prescribing doctors. As was said in the House of Commons at the time: 'The House and the public suddenly woke up to the fact that any drug manufacturer could market any product, however inadequately tested, however dangerous, without having to satisfy any independent body as to its efficiency or its safety. . . .'[83]

A government-appointed committee (the Cohen Committee) accepted that the pharmaceutical industry as a whole discharged its responsibilities under the Food and Drugs Act 1955 of ensuring that drugs were safe, but concluded that no matter how meticulous the preparatory work, ultimately there was no substitute for the pro-longed experience of the use of a drug in practice. The Committee felt that public and professional opinion demanded formal machinery, independent of drug manufacturers, to assess the safety of drugs.[84] Following the Committee's report and pending legislation, the Committee on the Safety of Drugs was constituted, which operated between 1963 and 1971. The drug industry voluntarily agreed to submit details of new drugs to the scrutiny of the Committee before they were released for clinical trials or placed on the market.

The Medicines Act 1968 firmly rejected the premise 'that drugs are ordinary commodities whose sale can take place anywhere and be left to the ordinary commercial pressures of the market.'[85] Reliance on broad criminal provisions has been greatly curtailed, although it remains an offence to supply a drug which is not of the nature or quality the ordinary consumer would expect.[86] Retention of this provision means checks will continue to be made by sampling to ensure that drugs actually conform to recognized standards of purity and potency. The general framework for controlling safety, efficacy and quality, however, is a system of statutory licensing, administered by an independent expert body, the Committee on the Safety of Medicines.

Although the voluntary system was supplanted, the hope of the government was that licensing would not operate in a rigid manner and that legal proceedings would be exceptional. The latter has proved to be the case. The justification for singling out drugs for licensing was that special care was needed with the revolutionary changes in modern drugs because of the possibility, made real in the Thalidomide tragedy, that they could have dangerous properties or dangerous side effects.[87] An additional factor of course is that consumers are in the very vulnerable position of having no choice to exercise when it comes to prescribed drugs, for they simply rely on their medical practitioners. The government has regulatory power to bring within the scope of the Act articles or substances which are not medicinal products but which can be put to medicinal use.[88] Substances which are in wide domestic use covered by regulations are contact lenses, cleaners, etc. and intra-uterine contraceptive devices.[89]

The Medicines Commission was established in accordance with section 2 of the Medicines Act 1968 with the general duty to advise the government on matters relating to the execution of the legislation or otherwise relating to drugs. In particular the Commission supervises the other committees which administer the details of the legislation, advises the government regarding licensing where there is an appeal against the advice of the Committee on the Safety of Medicines, considers representations against a proposed order prohibiting the sale of a drug, and supervises the body which draws up the British Pharmacopoeia, responsibility for the preparation of which has now been assumed by the government. The Committee on the Safety of Medicines advises on the safety, quality and efficacy of medicines, as well as promoting the collection and investigation of information relating to adverse reactions to drugs in use.

The licensing scheme of the Medicines Act 1968 operates at three different levels. First, manufacturers, assemblers and wholesalers of drugs must obtain a licence by demonstrating that their facilities are suitable. For instance, a manufacturer has to show that he has the capacity, equipment, staff and arrangements as to quality control to carry out the drug manufacturing operations specified in its licence.[90] Secondly, to guarantee that appropriate toxicity testing has taken place on animals, a new drug cannot generally be clinically tested on humans unless a certificate has been obtained.[91] Thirdly, a manufacturer must obtain a product licence before marketing any particular drug; considerations are the safety, efficacy and quality of a drug and the proposed methods for securing its specified quality.[92] Manufacturing and product licences are normally issued for five years but they may be renewed.[93] The operation of product licensing is summarized in Table 12.3, which sets out the results of licence applications for new drugs.[94] An obvious conclusion from the table is that had there not been a licensing system, a number of drugs would have been marketed which the Committee on the Safety of Medicines at least initially regarded as unsafe.

Table 12.3   Applications for Product Licences 1979–81

		1979	1980	1981
(i)	Grant advised	81	63	70
(ii)	Variation determined	9	3	15
(iii)	Applications withdrawn	5	0	0
(iv)	No. of provisional adverse recommendations	85	101	74

The Medicines Act 1968 directs the licensing authority, in considering an application for a product license, to leave out of account whether other drugs are more efficacious unless they may also be as safe or safer.[95] In implementing the statutory mandate, the Committee on the Safety of Medicines initially adopted the criteria of its predecessor. In 1972 the Committee changed its policy and with respect to products which are of doubtful efficacy, although harmless, it will not now grant a product licence unless some positive evidence of efficacy is forthcoming.[96] This policy can be justified in terms of the statutory language on the basis that an inefficacious drug, although harmless in one sense, may still have adverse results. For example, it may fail to cure a disease, albeit minor, for which a remedy is available, or it may relieve a symptom, the natural danger-signal, without affecting the disease which causes it. The change in policy by the Committee brings the practice into line with the law in the United States, where the 1962 Kefauver-Harris amendments to the Food, Drug and Cosmetic Act added proof of efficacy to proof of safety as a prerequisite for drug marketing.[97] Critics have said that not only should safety and efficacy be taken into account, but that consideration should also be given as to whether a drug is a therapeutic advance. The concern is with drugs which are simply variations of those already on the market, but which are developed to avoid patent restrictions or to improve the sales position of a manufacturer which can promote them with suggestions that they are newly formulated.

Decisions about licences are made by the licensing authority on the basis of information submitted by the drug companies. The Committee on the Safety of Medicines neither conducts research nor specifies designs for either toxicity or clinical trials. Regulations require that an application for a product licence set out, *inter alia*, the name of the drug, its constituents and their chemical formulae, certain details about the method of manufacture and the way the drug is to be used, and any experimental and biological results which 'in the view of the proposed licensee', are relevant to the assessment of the product.[98] It seems unlikely that the Committee will adopt a more active stance. It has been suggested that the government actually regulates the way clinical trials are conducted to eliminate unethical practices. Another reform suggested is that information submitted by the drug companies in their licence applications should be available to the public for critical evaluation, subject to a protection for trade secrets.

It seems accepted that complete safety in drugs cannot be guaranteed before they have been used on a widespread basis for a substantial period. Neither may it always be desirable that drugs be absolutely safe; for example, a considerable degree of toxicity might be tolerated in a drug which stayed the progress of cancer, although not in one used for the treatment of trivial conditions. To monitor the safety of drugs after they have received a product licence and are on the market standard cards are issued on which doctors can report adverse reactions. Additional to this voluntary scheme is the statutory obligation on drug companies to keep records of adverse reports they learn about, to include warnings in advertisements if directed and to institute suitable procedures in case a drug must be recalled from the market.[99] When the evidence warrants it, the Committee on the Safety of Medicines communicates information on adverse reactions to the profession at large, for example, warning them about the prescription or dispensing of particular drugs in certain circumstances.

The Medicines Act 1968 actually empowers the suspension, revocation or variation of a licence, *inter alia*, where a drug fails to a material extent to correspond to its characteristics as licensed, where it can no longer be safely administered for the purposes indicated in the licence, or where the specification to which it is manufactured can no longer be regarded as satisfactory.[100] In practice the Committee has convinced manufacturers to withdraw drugs where serious adverse reactions have been reported without legal moves being necessary. A particular problem has been to induce the medical profession to report adverse reactions. Following publicity of the matter the number of reports has increased but many adverse reactions are unreported. One reason is that an individual doctor may not realize the connection between a symptom and the use of a particular drug. There are pilot studies in which patients using a new drug are being monitored over a period of years so that correlations between adverse effects and a drug's use can be identified.

Restrictions on sales and promotions

The Medicines Act 1968 marked a change in the status of drugs in relation to retail sales, for until then they could be sold from any shop unless specifically restricted as poisons, narcotics or therapeutic substances. Under Part III of the Act, drugs may be divided into categories: those which may be sold only from registered pharmacies or upon the prescription of a medical practitioner, and those on a general sale list which may 'with reasonable safety' be sold otherwise.

The General Sale Lists Committee examined the composition of approximately 7000 products and gave effect to the statutory criterion of 'reasonable safety' by selecting products for general sale 'where the hazards to health, the risk of misuse, or the need to take special precautions in handling is small and where wider sale would be a convenience to the purchaser.'[101] In the absence of any reference to efficacy or quality in the statutory provision, section 51, the Committee ignored these factors so that inclusion in the General Sale Lists in no way implies that the product is regarded as having the therapeutic value or that harm will never come from its use. However, pharmacists have argued that it is dangerous to sell some drugs over the counter (e.g. in a supermarket). The Committee also recommended that it was unnecessary to restrict pack sizes – except for a few products like aspirin – because these are already limited by commercial considerations and a determined customer will simply purchase several packs.

Advertising for drugs occurs at two levels: the ordinary consumer is a target of advertising for over-the-counter drugs, but with prescription-only drugs it is to medical practitioners that the drug companies must direct their attention. Drug companies obviously find advertising useful in selling a product. Indeed the community benefits if there is no time-lag in doctors' prescribing disease-curing innovations. Many regard the amount spent on promotion and advertising as too high; it represents substantial amounts of sales revenues.[102] One solution is to reduce the amount of spending on drug promotion that would be set against profits for the purposes of the price regulation scheme considered below.

The Medicines Act 1968 prohibits false and misleading advertisements, and provides wide regulatory power to control the form and content of drug advertisements in the interests of securing adequate information, preventing misleading claims and promoting safety.[103] Regulations prohibit the advertising altogether of medicines available on prescription only and certain representations made by commercially interested parties.[104] Other regulations provide for prescribed information to be shown in advertisements direct to medical and dental practitioners (e.g. active ingredients, contraindications, warnings and precautions).[105] Voluntary advertising codes of the Advertising Standards Authority and the Association of the British Pharmaceutical Industry (ABPI) purport to regulate drug advertisements. A wide-ranging survey in 1974 judged more than half the advertisements for over-the-counter drugs as misleading.[106] Besides blatant cases, consumers are also misled if a drug gives the appearance of relief, as claimed by an advertisement, although any relief is the result of natural processes or would have been achieved just as effectively by a less costly substitute.

With prescription drugs the pharmaceutical industry has to direct its advertisements at medical practitioners. Promotion of a drug is achieved in three main ways: by advertisements and articles in medical journals, by mailed promotional literature and by sales representatives and samples. The Royal Commission on the National Health Service criticized the massive pressure from the drug companies in promotion.[107] Other critics point to examples of objectionable advertisements in the promotional literature and also argue that doctors cannot properly evaluate a drug unless they receive more information than that included, primarily about its comparative merits in relation to other drugs on the market. Medical representatives are usually employed as a follow-up after advertising. A survey for the Sainsbury Committee found that doctors identified sales representatives most frequently as the source of knowledge of new drugs, although they were more inclined to rely on independent journals when it came to evaluating their efficacy.[108] The Committee itself detected a tendency of some sales representatives to overstate both uses and merits of products and to make light of side-effects.[109] It recommended that sales representatives be obliged to place the data sheet for a drug before a doctor with whom they discussed it. The false advertisement prohibition already mentioned normally applies to oral statements by representatives, but there would seem to be acute difficulties of enforcement.

Regulations along the lines of those in other jurisdictions[110] now require drugs to be labelled with certain information in a clear and legible manner.[111] Standard requirements are that they should contain the particulars such as: the name of the drug; its pharmaceutical form; appropriate quantitative particulars; the quantity; directions for use; contraindications, warnings and precautions; storage conditions if applicable; expiry date if within three years; details of the product licensee and the batch reference, manufacturer's licence number and product licence number. Different provisions apply to dispensed drugs.

The current policy on containers is that it would be 'inopportune' to introduce a statutory scheme whereby particular drugs had to be placed in containers of a particular shape, colour or marking.[112] However, the Medicines (Child Safety) Regulations 1975 prohibit the sale of aspirin and paracetamol products other than in child-resistant containers.[113] The regulations were promulgated following evidence that more than 16,000 children under five were admitted to British hospitals each year for suspected drug poisoning (half due to aspirin) of whom some twenty died. Following the introduction of similar legislation in the United States the number of child poisonings fell by almost half. A further step to minimize child poisoning might be to insist in building regulations that all new houses have a child- proof medicine cabinet.

An evaluation of present controls

The controls in Britain are comparable in their form to those of the United States, yet they are less strict in their operation. A commentator highlighted the difference:

[There is] a growing split between the US and Britain on regulatory action. Because many suspected carcinogens and teratogens affect only a small percentage of the population, the data will rarely be highly statistically significant. The US continues to ban food and drug additives or require strong labels when the data are only suggestive of a hazard. It then puts the onus on the manufacturer to prove safety – which is both very difficult and expensive. Thus the US has banned several food colours and chloroform in medicines, both of which continue in use here. Like most other countries, Britain waits for stronger evidence of a hazard on the ground that by acting too soon the US is needlessly forcing off the market many useful products. The US response is that often they are not needed.[114]

If this is the case, there is cause for public disquiet. This is particularly so because consumer organizations in the United States, such as the Public Citizens Health Research Group, argue controls there are still not strong enough and have documented cases where the Food and Drugs Administration has approved drugs for marketing when research has raised questions of safety.

A criticism of the existing system of control, which comes not only from the drug industry, is that it inhibits the development of new drugs. It has been said that the cost of testing new drugs is so high and the time taken to introduce them to the market so long – now an average of eight to ten years – that the number of products available to treat diseases has declined rapidly. The costs of existing regulations cannot really be justified, it is said, by the benefits.[115] Statistical evidence indicates that the tightening of the Food Drug and Cosmetic Act in the United States in 1962 led to a decline in approvals for new drugs but not for clinical trials.[116] In

Britain in the decade 1962–71 (i.e. until licensing restrictions were introduced), nearly four times as many new drugs became exclusively available as in the United States, and where differences occurred in the dates drugs were marketed, twice as many were introduced first in Britain as in the United States.[117] Licensing in Britain soon affected the position and there was a downturn in the number of applications and approvals.

Without further evidence, however, it is not possible to draw adverse conclusions from the figures, as some do. Applications for new drugs have obviously fallen – the approval rate has not fluctuated greatly – but it may be that licensing deterred drugs of questionable value, inefficacious drugs, or drugs which were simply variations of those already on the market. In other words the community might not have benefited at all if these drugs, which it is said would have otherwise been developed, had been marketed. There might also be an increasing scientific difficulty in discovering new drugs.[118] There are also benefits from licensing associated with the reduction in the amount of drug toxicity. A number of drugs once available in Europe, but not marketed in the United States because of the strict operation of licensing, have later proved to be unsafe: Thalidomide and certain aerosol sprays for asthmatics are two examples.[119] This is not to say that the existing regulatory framework is sacrosanct; for example, earlier clinical trials on humans might well be justified, if closely monitored.

A constant concern over the years has been the price of drugs, an issue related to the profits enjoyed by the drug companies. Drug manufacturing is said to justify above-average profits because it is a speculative business with a tiny percentage of new developments actually reaching the market. Yet even if expenditure incurred on unsuccessful research has to be compensated for in the pricing of the successes, disproportionately high overall profits are not justified. Moreover, the high price levels of drugs derives partly from a lack of price competition. The order of the day between drug companies is product competition, rather than price competition, and thus different brand-named drugs are promoted which are therapeutically similar. With product competition there is little incentive for companies to reduce their prices and, carried to extremes, it may increase the cost of drugs by encouraging the search for unnecessary variations of existing products. Drug research seems to have a bias to alleviating common but minor problems because this is profitable, rather than to solving serious if relatively rare diseases.[120]

The legislative controls exclude price from being considered when new drugs are being approved. The government is a large purchaser of drugs – those dispensed and used in connection with the National Health Service. Since 1958, voluntary price regulation schemes have been negotiated with the drug companies regarding the price of these drugs.[121] Excess profits of up to £500,000 have apparently been claimed by the Department of Health and Social Security, although the number of firms involved and the total amount reclaimed is confidential. How effective the Voluntary Price Regulation Scheme has been in limiting prices is difficult to judge. The pharmaceutical industry argues that the prices of drugs are no cheaper in other comparable countries. Yet it still seems that the profits of drug companies are inordinately high and that even these may be understated because multinational drug companies engage in artificial transfer pricing.

The government rejected a suggestion of the Sainsbury Committee that the scheme should ensure that drug companies did not make excessive profits on individual products, as well as overall. It was thought that additional bureaucracy would be necessary to carry out the requisite monitoring. Omitting to take profits on individual products into account, however, led to the Hoffman La Roche affair. The company held a patent for two very widely used tranquilizers, Librium and Valium. Following a reference from the government, the Monopolies Commission reported that profits on the drugs were too high.[122] Acting on the Monopolies Commission's report, the government fixed maximum prices for the two drugs under what is now the Fair Trading Act 1973.[123] The government was obliged to seek an interim injunction against Hoffman La Roche – which was unsuccessfully challenged in the House of Lords[124] – when the company stated that it would disregard the maximum prices because the Monopolies Commission had failed to observe the principles of natural justice. The final outcome was that the company agreed to reduce its prices and to pay a rebate of £3.7 million to the British government. Subsequent to these events in Britain, proceedings were instituted against the company by West Germany, Holland and the European Economic Community.

A satisfactory solution regarding the pricing of drugs has not yet been devised. Voluntary approaches are deficient because governments negotiate with drug companies on the basis of less than full knowledge about their operations. Apart from direct price control, another avenue for lowering drug prices is through the patent system. For example, section 55 of the Patents Act 1977 enables the government to grant a license to someone other than the patent holder 'for the services of the Crown'. The provision was invoked in the early 1960s to permit the importation of tetracycline for hospitals from countries such as Italy which did not grant drug patents. The House of Lords upheld its use and the outcome was a drastic fall in the price of the drug – from £60 per 1000 tablets to £6 10s.[125] A possible long-term solution to drug prices is a government-owned drug company to compete with the existing firms. This is the basis for proposals that the government enter into the commercial production of drugs by buying out an existing manufacturer.

Prior approval through licensing may secure safer drugs but it has little influence on the way drugs are actually used. Even if drugs cannot be sold without a prescription, there is still the problem of over- or needless prescribing by doctors. Pressure on doctors to do this, such as the expectations of patients or their relatives, together with the difficulty of providing a sound training to doctors in a field as rapidly changing as pharmacology, can undermine the safeguards provided by prior approval. Another aspect of this is that prescriptions are written by receptionists or other staff employed by family doctors. There is also a great variety in prescribing habits. Asked by the Sainsbury Committee what they would prescribe for five common illnesses, a representative sample of medical practitioners named thirty to forty different drugs for each illness, the cost of which ranged from a few pence to several pounds.[126] Pharmacists could act as a brake on doctors' prescribing habits, but the evidence suggests that they are to some extent ill-equipped and in any event reluctant to challenge prescriptions.

To promote more rational prescribing it has been suggested that doctors should use generic and not brand names. At present, one drug can appear under different names within the same country, which can make it difficult to determine precisely which drug is being taken. For example, doctors continued to prescribe Thalidomide in Sweden after adverse reports in Germany, for an intensive study of the literature failed to identify the different brand-names in the two countries with Thalidomide.[127] The drug companies strongly resist the suggestion to eliminate brand-names on the basis that unbranded drugs are often of lower quality and that where a patient is on a delicately balanced maintenance therapy, changes caused by the switch from one manufacturer's product to another could be harmful.[128] These objections could be overcome by use of the generic name, combined with that of the brand-name favoured by the physician. There is the additional but unstated objection of the drug companies that replacing the many brand-names with one generic name for each drug might induce greater price competition.[129] The traditional reluctance of government to interfere with doctors' prescribing habits means that the present position is likely to continue. One approach is to specify an official name for each drug, which is the only name other than the chemical name by which the drug can be designated, and to require that the generic name always appear near the brand-name.

PART IV
Conclusion

13
Conclusion

One theme that runs through this book is that government controls are the best protection for consumers and that other techniques like the free operation of market forces, business self-regulation and the private law are of only limited effect. It is futile to think that businesses will introduce self-regulatory measures which are adverse to their interests, and it is not surprising that self-regulation has only been practised against the background of threatened legal action should standards not be improved. Competition between producers can assist consumers, for example, in terms of the level of prices, and for this reason steps taken against monopoly practices and restrictive trade practices are valuable. But there are severe limits on the degree to which consumers will support measures like tariff cuts to further competition which conflict with their interests as producers. Moreover, no amount of action to further competition can affect the fact that economic concentration is endemic in modern economies or that there will always be an inequality in the market-place between business and consumers.[1]

It is difficult to take seriously the argument that the market will further consumer protection. It leads to a 'do nothing' attitude, and in some cases is based on the idea that there can be a return to a mythical age of *laissez-faire*. Apologists for the market often argue against government regulation because it excludes poorer consumers from particular benefits like credit by increasing costs, and they conclude that the real answer lies in making the poor less poor. Yet their concern for the poor is false. Suggest any reform which makes the poor less poor – except perhaps a negative income tax, which has no effect on structural inequalities – and they object violently.

A hallmark of the views which society has about consumer

protection is that it is still seen largely as a collection of individual problems which individual consumers must attempt to solve by taking individual action. Consumers who receive a faulty product or sub-standard service, for example – the most common consumer complaints – must seek redress on their own, and if a business should refuse a reasonable settlement, consumers are expected to enforce their private law remedies by taking court action. Professor John Western has contrasted this perception with that towards similar issues in society:

> [Consumer] problems are still seen as very much an individual affair which the citizen must attempt to solve on his own. The contrast was made with other situations he might confront: a burglary, a major breakdown in services such as a massive power failure or interruption to the water supply. In these situations societal resources would immediately be called upon to assist.[2]

Much of consumer protection law is private law, which consumers must initiate by themselves if they are to benefit. Part II highlighted the inadequacies of private law remedies. To start with, many consumers fail to complain, and those who do and face business resistance rarely have the knowledge or incentive to take the matter further. The problem is especially acute with poorer consumers, a fact which reflects their general inequality in society. Poorer consumers are more likely to pay higher prices for what they buy and to be exposed to unscrupulous marketing techniques and shoddy goods. The mass restitution suit, in which consumer protection agencies or consumer protection organizations can seek redress on behalf of the many consumers adversely affected by an unlawful trade practice, even if they have not complained, was suggested in Chapter 3 as the main way of overcoming the drawbacks to the private law as an instrument of consumer protection.

Apart from the procedural deficiencies of the private law, we saw the doctrinal inadequacies as well. The notion of freedom of contract, for example, explains many of the defects of the private law in practice, because it has been used by the more powerful party in the market-place, business, to the detriment of the less powerful, the consumer. Some legal doctrines directly protect business from consumer claims. Sometimes the courts are to blame: for example, a manufacturer is relatively insulated from direct legal action, as compared with the United States, when a consumer suffers harm as a result of a defective product. Other times Parliament has failed to keep pace with business practices; for example, finance houses can evade restrictions on repossession in the Consumer Credit Act 1974 by the simple expedient of using a personal loan coupled with a bill of sale instead of hire purchase. Philip Schrag, in summing up his experience of bringing test case litigation in the New York courts, remarked that he found the courts 'to be so insensitive – not only to the need for substantive law reform but even to the need for a semblance of expeditious justice'.[3] To an extent the same applies elsewhere: for every *Farnworth Finance Facilities Ltd* v. *Attryde*,[4] there is a *United Dominions Trust Ltd* v. *Western*;[5] for every *Donoghue* v. *Stevenson*,[6] a *Daniels and Daniels* v. *White & Sons Ltd*;[7] and for every *Financings Ltd* v. *Baldock*,[8] a *Galbraith* v. *Mitchenhall Estates Ltd*.[9] These examples could be multiplied. Yet there are those who argue that the courts are beginning to appreciate their critical, if modest, role in developing common law doctrines of benefit to consumers. Reference is made to instances where the courts have overridden established and inappropriate common law 'principles' and indicated a willingness to develop notions such as unreasonableness and unconscionability.[10] Despite this optimism, however, the evidence seems only to suggest that doctrinal developments will be a mixed bag from the viewpoint of consumers.

Another defect of private law is that it operates to only a limited extent as a means of compelling a change in business behaviour. First, there is the problem already mentioned that an enterprise may cause harm to many consumers but the cost of their instituting legal proceedings may outweigh the harm they suffer. The outcome in such a case is that the enterprise will continue committing the harm, despite the fact that there will be an inefficient utilization of resources, if the value of the harm to the enterprise is less than its total cost to individuals. Rosenfield gives this example of 10,000 individuals illegally harmed by a large enterprise.

Let the economic harm to each be relatively small – say $1,000. Assume also that by causing the harm, the enterprise benefits by $8,000,000. Then if the cost of joining the claims of the harmed individuals is great, and if the cost of bringing an individual action for damages is greater than $1,000, it will pay no one to litigate the issue. The enterprise will have an incentive to commit the harm, and the result will be an inefficient utilization of scarce resources (the harm is worth $8,000,000 to the firm but imposes costs of $10,000,000 on the harmed individuals) and a clandestine redistribution of wealth from the harmed individuals to the firm.[11]

Class actions and mass restitution suits have been suggested as ways in which consumers can be assisted in making claims and, in economic terms, of moving a situation towards a more efficient point.

The usual remedy in private law is damages, which is primarily concerned with compensating individuals who have been harmed rather than with operating in a preventive way against wrongdoing. Businesses can still be in a better position and can profit by wrongdoing after paying damages to the few consumers who complain and incurring other amounts such as opportunity costs. Damages will only have a deterrent effect if it is less expensive for a business to alter its behaviour than to give relief to consumers who complain or who are likely to complain in the future.[12] The award of punitive damages might have a deterrent effect, but the courts are reluctant to award them because, it is said, they involve a windfall for plaintiffs and a punishment of defendants without the protection of the criminal law. If private law has a modifying effect on business behaviour, this should be evident following the huge volume of product liability litigation in the United Sates, yet it does not seem that this has affected the safety of consumer products in that country.

There is the separate issue of whether the courts are competent consciously to give judgment with a view to improving consumer standards. One line of thought is that it is beyond the limits of adjudication, because the courts can only manage separable issues, which can be isolated analytically at one time, as opposed to 'polycentric' questions, where a litigant's argument relating to any matter changes depending on how the court reacts to any other issue.[13] In this view courts which attempt to set standards are engaged in polycentric balancing – they have to place values on factors such as functional ability, aesthetics and safety – but they have neither the knowledge nor expertise to do this. In rebuttal, other commentators argue that standard setting is not necessarily highly polycentric and that courts are capable of investigating, understanding and evaluating evidence of a scientific or technical nature if the adversary process is improved with more sophisticated trial methods. The debate seems peculiarly American, for there the courts take an active role in standard setting in the consumer area. Elsewhere in the common law world there seems little possibility that the courts will be bold enough to engage in setting consumer standards, and in any event the matter can be more efficiently dealt with by government regulation.

Perhaps the fundamental problem of private law, at least as a means of influencing the behaviour of businesses, is that its impact is interstitial rather than comprehensive.[14] Courts are primarily concerned with settling concrete disputes on a case-by-case basis rather than with the long-term social implications of their decisions. Judicial decision-making is incremental, and an overall policy must be derived inductively from a succession of separate decisions, each based on its own facts. The nature of a seminal case can influence the entire trend of the law, but in many cases the courts will not be aware of the drift of legal change. The courts are subject to procedural and evidentiary limitations which make a full examination of the relevant facts impossible, with judicial notice expanding the scope of the investigation only slightly. Courts cannot enforce their decisions, oversee the consequences or make adjustments in the event that these are unforeseen.

Public regulation in the area of consumer protection became important in the nineteenth century when it was realized that the courts were not a suitable vehicle for consumer protection measures. Reformers quite rightly recognized that the costs of litigation meant that change through the courts would come slowly, if at all; as Hurst notes of developments in the United States:[15]

> Slowest to develop was a third great field of public responsibility for the social environment – the protection of the ultimate consumer, now reduced to individual insignificance in the mass markets the law had helped to form. One set of problems had to do with sales of goods. Here common law remedies by actions for damage negligently inflicted or for fraud and deceit or breach of warranty were expensive; the complaining party carried a difficult burden of proof against remote sellers or manufacturers, and the law was liberal in defenses offered the entrepreneur; the loss in the particular instance often was not big enough to warrant the trouble and cost of suit, though the aggregate of individual losses might represent a substantial total waste or oppression. From about 1881 the states began to legislate to protect consumers of food.

At the same time reformers also had a healthy suspicion of the political philosophy underlying judicial doctrines. It is clear from the courts' decisions earlier in the century that the adoption of negligence assisted industrial growth by insulating businesses from liability and imposing the social cost on workers and consumers.[16]

This is not to say that judicial doctrines were unaffected by the dominant morality and the notions of individual responsibility prevalent at the time, or that the doctrines, in the interests of consistency, did not apply equally to all. But the reality of formal equality was substantive inequality in practice, because businesses were responsible for the great bulk of the activities causing harm to others, in particular in the industrial sphere. Likewise, 'freedom of contract' meant that entrepreneurs could use their power to force contracts onto consumers to the latter's disadvantage.[17] A true concern on the part of the courts with equality in practice would have seen them develop further the notions of unconscionability and contracting in good faith. Doctrinally, the courts have taken some steps to further consumer protection in the twentieth century, but the main advances have passed the courts by; for example, there is still no doctrine of strict products' liability and statute has been necessary to overturn some of the worst excesses of standard form contracts.

It has been against this background – the lamentable inadequacy of private law remedies – that public law has assumed such an importance in the field of consumer protection. The general favour with which the present work views public law is not, however, a completely uncritical acceptance. One of the reasons for the categorization of public law adopted above was to bring out the advantages and disadvantages of the different techniques. For example, broad criminal prohibitions are relatively simple to formulate and, in the main, to enforce. On the other hand, they are not always diligently enforced in practice, and when legal proceedings are taken the courts tend to impose minor penalties which businesses can treat as an ordinary expense. Professor Philip G. Schrag, who was for a time head of the enforcement division of the New York City Department of Consumer Affairs, tells how initially under his leadership the division began with a 'judicial model' of action: it interviewed witnesses, gathered facts and then went to court to prosecute.[18] But in doing so it encountered numerous frustrations, in particular delays and an unsympathetic judiciary who regarded crime in the streets as much more important than consumer fraud. As a reaction, the Department evolved what Schrag calls a 'direct action' model: in addition to prosecution, it sought out non-litigious methods of pressuring disreputable companies into changing their practices. Among techniques used were publicity, mass restitution suits, revocation of licences, taking advantage of technical breaches of legislation and putting pressure on reputable financial institutions and suppliers to withdraw support.

One suggestion to improve the threat of the criminal law is that civil consequences should attach to violations of criminal provisions. For example, contracts could be automatically unenforceable when criminal provisions have been breached. Coupled with the power of consumer protection agencies to seek compensation for individual consumers adversely affected through mass restitution suits, this would greatly increase the deterrent effect of criminal provisions. There seems no reason whatever, apart from the political power of organized business, for a provision such as section 35 of the Trade Descriptions Act 1968, which provides that contracts are not void or unenforceable simply by reason of breach of the Act.

Another suggestion is for a 'middle system' of law, distinct from the existing civil and criminal law, in which criminal penalties are converted into civil penalties. One justification for the 'middle system' is that present legislation subjects businesses to criminal penalties for offences which are 'technical' and not criminal in any real sense. Of course this justification turns on how consumer offences are perceived. A mispricing offence might appear 'technical', and cause trivial loss to individual consumers, but mean a substantial loss to consumers as a whole and an unjustified accrual to business profits. Moreover, many consumer protection offences are far from 'technical' by whatever standards they are measured – for example, the marketing of dangerous products and the harassment of debtors. A second argument for the 'middle system' argument is that the courts would be more prepared to impose civil penalties because of the lower standard of proof and because offenders would not be stigmatized.[19] Clearly if civil penalties imposed are equal to or greater than any profits accruing as a result of unlawful activity, they would affect the behaviour of rational businesses. But courts are in no position to know this under present judicial procedures, and consequently it seems premature to abandon the uncertain but real stigmatization associated with the imposition of criminal penalties.

What is really needed is a completely different approach by the courts to criminal offences such as violations of consumer law. One possible way of achieving this is the establishment of a separate court for considering consumer protection offences, like the Market Court in Sweden. Such a body could be expected to treat consumer offences with greater severity, because it would get to know their adverse consequences for ordinary citizens, and at the same time have a bureaucratic desire to demonstrate output. The establishment of a consumer court is only a first step, however, and there needs to be a much more fundamental reshaping of opinion in the community towards violations of consumer law.

Public control has the difficulty that the vigour of its implementation is often compromised by the paucity of resources allocated to enforcement. Enforcement agencies are thus limited in what they can do, and tend to rely on public complaint or public outcry to determine their priorities. As a result objectionable behaviour, whose adverse effects are not immediately obvious to ordinary consumers, may be overlooked.

Another major defect with public control is that enforcement agencies may become closely identified with those they are supposed to regulate. It has been observed how enforcement agencies go through a degenerative life-cycle, starting it as vigorous protagonists of the public interest, then gradually becoming bureaucratized and more increasingly solicitous of those they are regulating. To the Marxist, this is a logical development of monopoly capitalism: economic power is in the hands of private capital and subject only to nominal control by a government, which itself is in the hands of private capital. As Marx put it in the *Communist Manifesto*: 'The executive power of the . . . state is simply a committee for managing the common affairs of the entire bourgeois class.' In other words, the Marxist argues that government regulation is a sham to assuage public opinion, while in fact it leaves quite undisturbed the real locus of power. Baran and Sweezy, two Marxist economists, argue that the main reason for government regulation is to ensure that industries are neither too profitable nor too unprofitable, for extra large profits are gained at the expense of both consumers and other capitalists, while extra low profits damage elements of the capitalist class.

It therefore becomes a State responsibility under monopoly capitalism to ensure, as far as possible, that prices and profit margins in the deviant industries are brought within the range prevailing among the general run of giant corporations. . . . In each course some worthy purpose is supposed to be served – to protect consumers, to conserve natural resources, to save the family-size farm – but only the naive believe that these fine-sounding aims have any more to do with the case than the flowers that bloom in the spring.[20]

My own view is that this type of analysis is too fatalistic and that social engineering is possible. One immediate way in which enforcement agencies can be reinvigorated is by greater participation by consumers, and a more powerful National Consumer Council is one way of ensuring that the consumer voice is heard when government policies affecting consumers are made and implemented. Mere participation of consumers in decision-making is not enough, however, for it does not guarantee that a particular type of decision will be made. Moreover, there is always a temptation for consumer advocacy bodies like the National Consumer Council to take on the easy issues which will gain wide publicity and acclaim in the mass media. Other drawbacks are that such bodies may not represent all aspects of the consumer interest, for example, poorer consumers, and that they may be co-opted by the bodies to which they make representations.[21]

Ultimately, the question of whether enforcement agencies can exercise sufficient control over businesses is a question of whether these agencies have political support for their tasks. Political support at the level of party politics is of obvious importance, for while an enforcement agency can attain a degree of autonomy from its political masters, that will be fairly short-lived if its behaviour is diametrically opposed to their interests. Direct political support from the community on a day-to-day basis gives a clout to enforcement agencies enabling them to ignore to some extent political forces. An unfortunate feature is that, on the whole, community perceptions have not advanced to a stage where consumer protection offences are equated with the petty criminal offences which are an everyday feature of magistrates courts. Consumer groups and the enforcement agencies themselves have a role here in changing perceptions, although the realities of political power impose limits to what can be done.

Notes

PREFACE

1 cf. Mark V. Nadel, 'Consumerism: A Coalition in Flux', (1975) 4 *Policy Studies J.* 31.

2 Economist Intelligence Unit, *Pilot Study of the Additional Costs to the British Consumer of Compliance by Industry with Consumer Legislation*, November 1979.

3 For example, P. S. Atiyah, 'Consumer Protection – Time to Take Stock', (1979) 1 *Liverpool L.R.* 20.

4 For example, Robert B. Reich, 'Toward a New Consumer Protection', (1979) 128 *U. Pennsylvania L.R.* 1.

5 'Consumer Protection and Economic Theory', in A. J. Duggan and L. W. Darvall (eds), *Consumer Protection Law and Theory* (Sydney: Law Book, 1980).

6 See M. Green and N. Waitzman, 'Cost, Benefit and Class', (1980) May–June *Working Papers for a New Society* 39.

7 One small step of consumer protection reform to assist the unemployed would be a prohibition on false representations about employment. cf. Trade Practices Act 1974 (Australia), s. 53B; *Wilde* v. *Menville Pty Ltd* (1981) 50 F.L.R. 380.

8 'Regulation and Deregulation: General Issues', (1982) 5 *U.N.S.W.L.J.* 1, 25. See also *Regulating Business* (London: Macmillan, 1979). cf. Edward P. Belobaba, 'Unfair Trade Practices Legislation: Symbolism and Substance in Consumer Protection', (1977) 15 *Osgoode Hall L.J.* 327.

9 Preface to 1st edition.

10 See Howard Reben, 'Organizing Consumers', (1972) 30 *NLADA Briefcase* 127.

11 See Richard H. S. Tur, 'Litigation and the Consumer Interest: The Class Action and Beyond', (1982) 2 *Legal Stud.* 135; Iain D. C. Ramsay, 'Consumer Redress Mechanisms for Poor Quality and Defective Products', (1981) 31 *U.Tor. L.J.* 117.

12 [1982] A.C. 225.

13 [1982] 3 All E.R. 201; [1982] 3 W.L.R. 477.

14 (1982) 56 A.L.J.R. 715; 42 A.L.R. 1.
15 S.I. 1979, No. 364; S.I. 1979, No. 633; S.I. 1979, No. 1124.

CHAPTER 1

1 D. S. Ironmonger, *New Commodities and Consumer Behaviour* (Cambridge University Press, 1972), pp. 133–6.
2 Jeremy Mitchell, 'The Consumer Movement and Technological Change', (1972) 25 *Int. Soc. Sci. J.* 358.
3 Mark J. Green, 'Appropriateness and Responsiveness: Can the Government Protect the Consumer?', (1974) 8 *J. Econ. Issues* 309–10.
4 For example, C. Y. Lee, 'EFTS – Implications for the Consumer', (1982) 10 *Austn. Bus. L.R.* 289.
5 See, generally, Robert Millar, *The Affluent Sheep* (London: Longman, 1963).
6 Terje Assum and Rolf Dahl, 'Technical Development of Household Appliances – For the Benefit of Consumers or Producers?', (1979) 3 *J. Cons. Studies and Home Econ.* 289.
7 Chris Pond, 'Inflation', in Frances Williams (ed.), *Why the Poor Pay More* (London: Macmillan, 1977).
8 See Colin Adamson, *Consumers in Business* (London: National Consumer Council, 1982).
9 Ralph Nader, 'The Great American Gyp', *N.Y. Rev. of Books*, vol. 11, 21 November 1968, p. 28. Note, for example, the marketing of the Pinto by Ford: Michael A. Schmitt and William W. May, 'Beyond Products Liability: The Legal, Social and Ethical Problems Facing the Automobile Industry in Producing Safe Products', (1979) 56 *J. Urban L.* 1021.
10 Consumer Council, *Final Annual Report* (London: HMSO, 1971), p. 1.
11 See Chapter 3.
12 David Caplovitz, *The Poor Pay More* (New York: Free Press, 1963).
13 National Consumer Council, *For Richer, For Poorer* (London: 1975), pp. 9–14; David Piachaud, *Do the Poor Pay More?*, Poverty Research Series 3 (London: Child Poverty Action Group, 1974), p. 5. Alisdair Aird, 'Goods and Services', in Frances Williams (ed.), op. cit., pp. 14–15. See generally Alan R. Andreasen, *The Disadvantaged Consumer* (New York: Free Press, 1975); Ronald Sackville, *Law and Poverty in Australia* (Canberra: AGPS, 1975), Chapter 4.
14 R. C. Mussehl, 'Neighbourhood Consumer Centre: Relief for the Consumer at the Grass-Roots Level', (1972) 47 *Nôtre Dame L.* 1093, 1121.
15 See further, p. 188 below.
16 National Consumer Council, op. cit., p. 17.
17 David Caplovitz, op. cit., p. 17.

18 Ibid., pp. 1130–1.

19 Op. cit., pp. 16–17.

20 Ibid., pp. 18–19. See also John Baker, *The Neighbourhood Advice Centre. A Community Project in Camden* (London: Routledge & Kegan Paul, 1978), p. 125.

21 Eric H. Steele, 'Fraud, Dispute and the Consumer: Responding to Consumer Complaints', (1975) 123 *Penn. L. Rev.* 1107, 1123–5; National Consumer Council, *The Fourth Right of Citizenship* (London: 1977), p. 26.

22 'Consumerism', *Political, Social, Economic Review*, 2 July 1975, p. 9.

23 Barry Elliot, 'Consumer Activism in Australia', (1975), 10 *Politics* (Sydney), 188, 191–2.

24 See Kenneth McNeil *et al.*, 'Market Discrimination Against the Poor and the Impact of Consumer Disclosure Laws: The Used Car Industry', (1979) 13 *Law & Soc. Rev.* 695.

25 Sale of Goods Act 1979, s. 61(1).

26 For example, Fair Trading Act 1973, s. 137(3); Supply of Goods and Services Act 1982, s.12. cf, Trade Practices Act 1974 (Aust.), ss. 4(1), 74(3).

27 Unfair Contract Terms Act 1977, ss. 6(2)–(3).

28 Fair Trading Act 1973, s. 137(2).

29 'Introduction: A Guide to Consumerism', David A. Aaaker and George S. Day, *Consumerism*, 2nd edn (New York: Free Press, 1974), p. xvii.

30 *Council Housing* (Welsh Consumer Council, 1976); *New Tenancy Agreements* (London: 1981); *Behind with the Rent* (London: 1976); *Soonest Mended* (London: 1979).

31 Ivan Illich, *Tools for Conviviality* (London: Calder & Boyars, 1973), p. 56.

32 Law Reform Commission of Papua New Guinea, *Consumer Protection*, Working Paper No. 17, 1981, pp. 9, 11.

33 J. De Moerloose, *Foods for Infants and Young Children: A Survey of Relevant National Legislation* (World Health Organisation), noted in (1981) 7 *Commonwealth Law Bull.* 813.

34 For example, Charles Medawar, *Insult or Injury? An Enquiry into the Marketing and Advertising of British Food and Drug Products in the Third World* (London: Social Audit, 1979).

35 cf. Medicines Act 1968, ss. 48, 49.

36 Ivan R. Feltham, 'The New Regulatory State: Economic and Business Regulation Tomorrow', (1973) 51 *Can. Bar. R.* 207, 209.

37 Ralph Winter, 'Economic Regulation vs. Competition: Ralph Nader and Creeping Capitalism' (1973) 82 *Yale L.J.* 890, 901.

38 Anthony Downs, *An Economic Theory of Democracy* (New York: Harper & Row, 1957), pp. 254–5.

39 Mancur Olson, *The Logic of Collective Action* (Cambridge, Mass.: Harvard Univ. Press, 1965), p. 166.

412 *Notes to pages 13–17*

Leonard Tivey, 'The Politics of the Consumer', (1968) 39 *Pol. Q.* 181, 192.

41 Previously consumers were regarded as having little influence; e.g. S. E. Finer, *Anonymous Empire* (London: Pall Mall, 1958), p. 122.

42 S. Beer, *Modern British Politics* (London: Faber, 1965), p. 349.

43 William Roberts, 'The Formation of Consumer Protection Policy in Britain 1945–1973' (Kent, Ph.D. Thesis, 1975), p. 15.

44 Solomon Parkin, 'Trade Unions and Consumerism', (1973) 7 *J. of Econ. Issues* 317. Andrew Hopkins, *Crime Law and Business* (Canberra: Australian Institute of Criminology, 1978), p. 92.

45 T. F. Carbery, *Consumers in Politics* (Manchester University Press, 1969), p. 187. See also Christopher S. Axworthy, 'Consumer Co-operatives and the Rochdale Principles Today', (1977) 15 *Osgoode Hall L.J.* 137, 144.

46 The European organizations are outlined in Norbert Reich and H.-W. Micklitz, *Consumer Legislation in the EC Countries* (Wokingham, Berks.: Van Nostrand Reinhold, 1980), pp. 3–4. And see ibid., pp. 36–8 on the civil liability which can arise through publication of information regarding comparative testing. For Canada: D. Fox, *Public Participation in the Administrative Process* (Ottawa: Law Reform Commission of Canada, 1979), Chapter 5.

47 Ursula Wassermann, 'Comparative Testing of Consumer Goods', (1973) 7 *J. Wld. Trade L.* 247, 250.

48 Mark V. Nadel, *The Politics of Consumer Protection* (New York: Bobbs-Merrill, 1971), pp. 233–4.

49 Department of Prices and Consumer Protection, *National Consumers' Agency* (1974), Cmnd 5726, pp. 4–5.

50 *The Bulk Buy Book* (London: National Consumer Council, 1977). See also Colin Hines, *Food Co-ops* (London: Friends of the Earth, 1976).

51 For example, Consumer Safety Act, 1978, s. 1(4).

52 s. 3(5)(c).

53 Broadcasting Act 1981, ss. 16–18; for example, Gas Act 1972, ss. 9(2)(b) (4)(b). See Justice, *The Citizen and the Public Agencies* (London: 1976); Department of Trade, *Consumers' Interests and the Nationalised Industries – A Consultative Document* (London: 1981); L. A. Rutherford, 'The Consumer Voice in Nationalised Industry', (1980) 130 *N.L.J.* 620; Charles Medawar, *Consumers of Power* (London: Social Audit, 1980), pp. 52–62.

54 Trade Union and Labour Relations Act 1974, ss. 13–15, as amended by Employment Act 1980, ss. 16–18.

55 [1976] Q.B. 142. The matter never came to trial, but of course the interlocutory injunction had the desired effect.

56 *The Times*, 5 February 1975. See also *Bestobell Paints Ltd* v. *Bigg* [1975] F.S.R. 421; (1975) 119 Sol. J. 678.

57 *Temperton* v. *Russell* [1893] 1 Q.B. 715. In the United States courts have held picketing of business premises lawful where it was designed to

induce consumers to boycott stores practising racial discrimination in employment or charging unacceptable prices: Ina Leonard, 'The Consumer Boycott', (1971) 42 *Mississippi L.J.* 226, 235. France's Union Fédérale des Consommateurs and other European consumer groups have used boycotts successfully on a number of occasions: Robin Young, 'Continental Consumers Who Vote With Their Feet', *The Times*, 22 October 1980.

58 See generally Roger A. Bowles, 'The Contribution of Modern Economic Theory' in David Morris (ed.), *Economics of Consumer Protection* (London: Heinemann, 1980).

59 Peter Jay, 'The Biter Bit: or the Apotheosis of Corporatism', *The Times*, 25 March 1976, p. 23.

60 *Report from the Select Committee on Adulteration of Food etc.* (1855), Parl. Pap. 1854–5, viii, p. 73.

61 *Parkdale Custom Built Furniture Pty Ltd* v. *Puxu Pty Ltd* (1982) 56 A.L.J.R. 715, 720; (1982) 42 A.L.R. 1, 11.

62 See, for example, Valentine Korah, *Competition Law of Britain and the Common Market*, 3rd edn (The Hague: Martinus Nijhoff, 1982).

63 ss. 11, 12.

64 T. T. Jones and J. F. Pickering, 'The Consumer's Interest in Competition Policy', (1979) 3 *J. Cons. Stud. & Home Econ.* 85.

65 cf. Lee Benham, 'The Effect of Advertising on the Price of Eyeglasses', (1972) 15 *J.L. & Econ.* 337.

66 Thomas Sharpe, 'Refusal to Supply', (1983) 99 *L.Q.R.* 36, 50.

67 See Dennis Swann, *Competition and Consumer Protection* (Harmondsworth: Penguin, 1979), Ch. 8; Peter Smith and Dennis Swann, *Protecting the Consumer – An Economic and Legal Analysis* (Oxford: Martin Robertson, 1979).

68 Richard A. Posner, 'The Federal Trade Commission', (1969) 37 *U. Chi. L. Rev.* 47, 62.

69 Richard A. Posner, *Economic Analysis of Law*, 2nd edn (Boston: Little, Brown, 1977), p. 85.

70 Ibid., pp. 404–7. Another argument is that government intervention is less effective because government employees are corruptible and appointments are on a patronage basis.

71 Ronald N. McKean, 'Products Liability: Trends and Implications', (1970) 38 *U. Chi. L. Rev.* 3, 44, 52.

72 For a thorough critique see A. J. Duggan, *The Economics of Consumer Protection* (Adelaide: Adelaide Law Review Research Paper No. 2, 1982). See also Ross Cranston, 'Consumer Protection and Economic Theory', op. cit.

73 Mark Kelman, 'Choice and Utility', [1979] *Wisc. L.R.* 769.

74 James Buchanan, 'In Defence of Caveat Emptor', (1970) 38 *U. Chi. L. Rev.* 64, 67.

75 Cf. Phillip Nelson, 'Information and Consumer Behaviour', (1970) 78 *J. Pol. Econ.* 311.

76 Cf. Walter Y. Oi, 'The Economics of Product Safety', (1973) 4 *Bell J. of Econ.* 3, 7.

77 Ellen R. Jordan and Paul H. Rubin, 'An Economic Analysis of the Law of False Advertising', (1979) 8 *J. of Legal Stud.* 527.

78 Mark Green and Beverly Moore, 'Winter's Discontent: Market Failure and Consumer Welfare' (1973) 82 *Yale L.J.* 903, 907.

79 A. J. Duggan, op. cit., pp. 134–6.

80 Richard A. Posner, 'A Theory of Negligence', (1972) 1 *J. of Legal Stud.*, 29, 48.

81 Richard A. Posner, *Economic Analysis of Law*, p. 449; cf. George J. Stigler, 'The Law and Economics of Public Policy', (1972) 1 *J. of Leg. Stud.*, 1, 9.

82 Ibid., p. 272.

83 Harold Demesetz, 'The Exchange and Enforcement of Property Rights' (1964) 7 *J. Law & Econ.*, 11, 13.

84 Guido Calabresi, 'Transaction Costs, Resource Allocation and Liability Rules – A Comment', (1968) 11 *J. of Law & Econ.* 67, 69.

85 See Robert B. Seidman, 'Contract Law, The Free Market and State Intervention: A Jurisprudential Perspective', (1970) 7 *J. of Econ. Issues* 553, 571; Warren J. Samuels, 'In Defence of a Positive Approach to Government as an Economic Variable', (1972) 15 *J. of Law & Econ.* 453; Ronald M. Dworkin, 'Is Wealth a Value', (1980) 9 *J. Legal Stud.* 191.

86 A. J. Duggan, op. cit., pp. 60–88. cf. M. J. Trebilcock and D. N. Dewees, 'Judicial Control of Standard Form Contracts' in Paul Burrows and Cento G. Veljanovski (eds), *The Economic Approach to Law* (London: Butterworths, 1981).

87 E. J. Mishin, 'Pareto Optimality and the Law', (1967) 19 *Oxford Econ. Papers* 255, 278.

CHAPTER 2

1 J. A. C. Hetherington, 'Fact and Legal Theory: Shareholders, Managers, and Corporate Social Responsibility', (1969) 21 *Stan. L. Rev.* 248, 274–92.

2 Peter Blood, 'Good Manners for Marketing', *Marketing*, April 1976, p. 24.

3 Milton Friedman, *Capitalism and Freedom* (Univ. of Chicago Press, 1962), p. 133.

4 J. Melrose-Woodman and I. Kverndal, *Towards Social Responsibility*, Report No. 28 (London: British Institute of Management, 1976), pp. 10, 12.

5 Ibid., p. 6.
6 Note also the National House-Building Council scheme, which guarantees against defects and shoddy workmanship in new homes (see *Barnsley's Conveyancing Law and Practice* (London: Butterworths, 1982), pp. 177–81) and the Insurance Ombudsman Bureau, supported by various insurance companies, which attempts settlement of complaints, disputes and claims arising out of insurance policies (see Insurance Ombudsman Bureau, *Annual Report 1981*).
7 ss. 8, 16.
8 ss. 1, 2.
9 s. 21(2). See Appendices to the Director General's Annual Report.
10 M. J. Methven, 'The Role of the Office of Fair Trading', *City of London L. Rev.*, Lent 1975, p. 10.
11 *Annual Report of the Director General of Fair Trading, November 1973–December 1974* (London: HMSO, 1975), p. 9.
12 Instead of arbitration some refer technical complaints to independent test centres.
13 The Office of Fair Trading has made recommendations regarding some of the criticisms. *Redress Procedures Under Codes of Practice* (London: Office of Fair Trading, 1981). cf. Thomas L. Eovaldi and Joan E. Gestrin, 'Justice for Consumers: The Mechanisms of Redress', (1971) 66 *N.W.U.L. Rev.* 281, 305.
14 Arbitration Act 1979.
15 Such 'fines' were upheld in *Thorne* v. *Motor Trade Association* [1937] A. C. 797.
16 *Annual Report of the Director General of Fair Trading 1980* (London: HMSO, 1981), p. 73.
17 As reported in the Office of Fair Trading publication, *Bee Line*.
18 *Bakers Franchise Corp.* v. *FTC*, 302 F.2d 258 (1962). An exceptional case, where a prosecution was successful for a literally true statement which was false by reason of omission, is *R* v. *Kylsant (Lord)* [1932] 1 K.B. 442.
19 Frederick A. Laux, 'Deceptive Advertising, the Law and the Canadian Consumer', in G. H. L. Fridman, *Studies in Canadian Business Law* (Toronto: Butterworths, 1971), p. 157. A case where it was recognized that an ambiguous statement can be false, even though one of its meanings is accurate, is *Doble* v. *David Greig Ltd* [1972] 1 W.L.R. 703, 710; [1972] 2 All E.R. 195, 201.
20 Bureau Européen des Unions de Consommateurs, *A Study of Advertising in the United Kingdom and the Federal Republic of Germany* (London: Consumers' Association, 1974), p. 26.
21 *Public Attitudes to Advertising* (London: Advertising Association, 1976). But in a nation-wide survey in 1979–80 only four per cent said that *they* had been misled in the previous twelve months: *Consumer Concerns Survey*

(London: National Consumer Council, 1981), p. 97.

22 *European Consumers* (Brussels: Commission of European Communities, 1976), pp. 57–8.

23 *Report of the Committee on Broadcasting*, Cmnd 1753 (London: HMSO, 1962), p. 80.

24 Home Office, *Report of the Commission on the Future of Broadcasting*, Cmnd 6753, 1977, p. 171.

25 For example, C. J. Sutton, 'Advertising, Concentration and Competition', (1974) 84 *Econ. J.* 56; W. Duncan Reekie, 'Advertising and Market Share Mobility', (1974) 21 *Scot. J. of Pol. Econ.* 143; T. T. Nagle, 'Do Advertising-Profitability Studies Really show that Advertising Creates a Barrier to Entry?', (1981) 24 *J. Law & Econ.* 333.

26 See A. J. Duggan, 'The Great Soap Opera', (1978) 11 *Melbourne U.L.R.* 467.

27 W. Duncan Reekie, *Advertising* (London: Macmillan, 1974), pp. 119–24.

28 For example, *Chidwick* v. *Beer* [1974] R.T.R. 415; [1974] Crim. L.R. 267 (car, 'excellent condition'); *R.* v. *Clarksons Holidays Ltd* (1972) 57 CAR 38 (travel brochure, newly-built hotel); *Sweeting* v. *Northern Upholstery Ltd*, *The Times*, 28 June 1982 (advertisements silent as to colour, but only one colour suite available at the lower price).

29 (1884) 28 Ch. D. 7.

30 (1882) 46 L.T. 374; cf. *Richardson* v. *Silvester* (1873) L.R. 9 Q.B. 34.

31 [1976] 1 W.L.R. 1; [1976] 1 All E.R. 117. See also the classic *Carlill* v. *Carbolic Smoke Ball Co.* [1893] 1 Q.B. 256.

32 Advertisers like to point to the many statutes affecting advertising, but most are of marginal importance for the problems mentioned. Some advertising is banned or strictly regulated because it is indecent, creates medical risks, leads to socially undesirable practices (e.g. massage parlours), misleads as to credit, encourages discrimination or affects social amenities (e.g. billboards). See R. G. Lawson, *Advertising Law* (Plymouth: Macdonald & Evans, 1978).

33 The draft directive is set out in R. G. Lawson, *Advertising and Labelling Laws in the Common Market*, 2nd edn. (Bristol: Jordan, 1981). See also R. G. Lawson, 'Unfair and Misleading Advertising', (1982) 1 *Tr. L.* 71.

34 For example, Robert Pitofsky, 'Beyond Nader: Consumer Protection and the Regulation of Advertising', (1977) 90 *Harv. L. Rev.* 661.

35 See Lord Drumalbyn, 'Advertising Control: The Evolution of the Self-Regulatory System', *Advertising Q.*, No. 41, Autumn 1974, p. 4; J. C. Braun, 'Voluntary Control within the Profession', Alexander Wilson (ed.), *Advertising and the Community* (Manchester Univ. Press, 1968); Peter Thompson, 'Informal Resolution of Disputes in Advertising –The Role of the Code of Advertising Practice Committee', (1982) 1 *Tr. L.* 233.

36 For example, Lucy Hodges and Charles Medawar, 'Advertising: The

Art of the Permissible', *Social Audit*, vol. 2 (1974), p. 21; Charles Medawar and Lucy Hodges, 'The Social Cost of Advertising', *Social Audit*, vol. 2 (1974), p. 48; Bureau Européen des Unions de Consommateurs, op. cit.; Office of Fair Trading, *Review of the United Kingdom Self-regulatory System of Advertising Control* (London; Office of Fair Trading, 1978); National Consumer Council, *Advertising Legislate or Persuade?* (London: National Consumer Council [n.d.]); Lindsey Morison, 'An Investigation into Advertising Accountability', (1979) 3 *J. Consumer Studies & Home Econ.* 59.

37 S.I. 1979 No. 364, as amended by S.I. 1979, No. 633; S.I. 1979, No. 1124.

38 Director General of Fair Trading, *Review of the Price Marking (Bargain Offers) Orders 1979* (London: Office of Fair Trading, 1981), para. 2.13.

39 ss. 1–2.

40 ss. 16(2)(b), (4)–(5).

41 s. 8(5).

42 Ibid., Schedule 2, para. 5.

43 s. 8(3).

44 s. 9(4)–(5); *Advertising Control* (London: IBA, 1981), p. 4.

45 ss. 4(3), 8(6)–(9).

46 Annan Committee, p. 169.

47 s. 21. The Television Act 1954 had an additional sanction – a gradation of monetary penalties of £500 could be imposed for the initial breach, £1000 for second and £1500 for subsequent breaches: ss. 6(2)–(3).

48 *F.T.C.* v. *Colgate-Palmolive Co.* 380 U.S. 374 (1965); see also Libbey-Owens-Ford Glass Co. v. *FTC* 352 F. 2d 415 (1965).

49 Harry Turner, 'The ITCA/AIRC Copy Clearance System', *Admap*, vol. 12, March 1976, p. 126.

50 15 U.S.C. §45.

51 Act Prohibiting Unfair Competition 1909, ss. 1, 3, 13. See Warren S. Grimes, 'Control of Advertising in the United States and Germany: Volkswagen Has a Better Idea', (1971) 84 *Harv. L. Rev.* 1769, 1781–6; Norbert Reich and H. W. Micklitz, *Consumer Legislation in the Federal Republic of Germany* (New York: Van Nostrand Reinhold, 1981), pp. 112–3.

52 ss. 80, 82.

53 *The Self-regulatory System of Advertising Control – Report of the Working Party* (London: Department of Trade, 1980).

54 *Ibid.*, p. 9.

55 ss. 3(1), 3(3) (r).

56 *Ward Laboratories Inc.* v. *FTC* (1960), 276 F. 2d 952, cert. den. (1960) 364 U.S. 827. See also *J. B. Williams Co.* v. *FTC* 381 F. 2d 884 (1967).

57 Note, 'The FTC Ad Substantiation Programme' (1973), 61 *Georgetown L.J.* 1427; Lee M. Weiner, 'The Ad Substantiation Programme', (1981)

30 *Am. U.L. Rev.* 429.

58 481 F. 2d. 246 (1973): cert. denied 414 U.S. 1112 (1973). See also *National Commission on Egg Nutrition* v. *F.T.C.* 570 F. 2d 157 (1977), cert. denied, 439 U.S. 821 (1978).

59 The objection that it 'reverses the onus of proof' is misconceived; so do many other aspects of consumer law (e.g. licensing). See *Review of the Trade Descriptions Act 1968*, Cmnd 6628 (London: HMSO, 1976), pp. 55–6.

60 Comment, 'And Now a Word Against Our Sponsor: Extending the FCC's Fairness Doctrine to Advertising' (1972) 60 *Calif. L. Rev.* 1416. Note, 'Application of the Fairness Doctrine to Ordinary Product Advertisements', (1979) 20 *Boston Coll. L.R.* 425.

61 *Friends of the Earth* v. *FCC* 449 F.2d 1164 (1971); *Banzhaf* v. *FCC* 405 F. 2d. 1082 (1968), cert. den. 396 U.S. 842 (1969).

62 *National Citizens Committee for Broadcasting* v. *F.C.C.*, 567 F.2d 1095 (1977), cert. denied, 439 U.S. 926 (1978).

63 Richard S. Cornfeld, 'A New Approach to an Old Remedy: Corrective Advertising and the Federal Trade Commission', (1976) 61 *Iowa L. Rev.* 693; Note, 'Corrective Advertising and the Limits of *Virginia Pharmacy*' (1979) 32 *Stan. L.R.*, 121.

64 *Warner-Lambert Co.* v. *F.T.C.*, 562 F.2d 749 (1977), cert. denied 435 U.S. 950 (1978).

65 op. cit., pp. 58–9.

66 See *Annand and Thompson Pty Ltd* v. *T.P.C.* (1979) 25 A.L.R. 91.

67 Melrose-Woodman and Kverndall, op. cit., p. 6.

68 A. C. Page, 'Self-Regulation and Codes of Practice' [1980] *J. Bus. L.* 24, 26–7.

69 Legal restrictions are outlined in R. G. Lawson, 'Advertising Law', op. cit., pp. 253–61; Norbert Reich and H. W. Micklitz, *Consumer Legislation in the EC Countries* (Wokingham, Berks.: Van Nostrand Reinhold, 1980), p. 53.

70 [1970] A.C. 403; cf. *Thorne* v. *Motor Trade Association* [1937] A.C. 797.

71 James R. Krum and Richard H. Greenhill, 'The Extent of Industry Self-Regulation through Trade Association Codes of Ethics', (1972) 17 *Antitrust Bull.* 379, 389.

72 *Annual Report of the Director General of Fair Trading 1977*, p. 13.

73 Harper W. Boyd and Henry Claycamp, 'Industrial Self-Regulation and the Public Interest', (1966) 64 *Mich. L. Rev.* 1239.

CHAPTER 3

1 J. A. Jolowicz, 'The Protection of the Consumer and the Purchaser of

Goods under English Law', (1969) 32 *Mod. L. Rev.* 1, 2.

2 'Contracts of Adhesion – Some Thoughts about Freedom of Contract', (1943) 43 *Col. L. Rev.* 629, 640.

3 [1976] Q.B. 513.

4 For example, *Mendelssohn* v. *Normand Ltd* [1970] 1 Q.B. 177.

5 *George Mitchell (Chesterhall) Ltd.* v. *Finney Lock Seeds* [1982] 3 W.L.R. 1036, 1043. cf. Grant Gilmore, 'Products Liability: A Commentary', (1970) 38 *U. Chi. L. Rev.* 103, 113.

6 [1930] 1 K.B. 41; see I. W. Duncanson, 'Contract as a Remedy', (1976) 5 *Anglo-Am. L. Rev.* 7.

7 See P. S. Atiyah, *The Rise and Fall of Freedom of Contract* (Oxford: Clarendon, 1979).

8 Stewart Macauley, 'Private Legislation and the Duty to Read', (1966) 19 *Vand. L. Rev.* 1051, 1059.

9 David Yates, *Exclusion Clauses in Contracts*, 2nd edn (London: Sweet & Maxwell, 1982), pp. 20, 29.

10 cf. Max Radin, 'Contract Obligation and the Human Will', (1943) 43 *Col. L. Rev.* 575, 578–9.

11 See Francis Reynolds, 'Formulation of Standard Terms and their Incorporation in Contracts', in *Standard Terms in Contracts* (Strasbourg: Council of Europe, 1979), pp. 18–19.

12 W. David Slawson, 'Standard Form Contracts and Democratic Control of Lawmaking Power', (1971) 84 *Harv. L. Rev.* 529. Standard form contracts might be enforced in the absence of private consent if they comply with standards in the public interest.

13 For reviews, see George Gluck, 'Standard Form Contracts: The Contract Theory Reconsidered', (1979) 28 *I.C.L.Q.* 72; David Yates, op. cit., Chapters 2, 4, 6.

14 For example, *Daly* v. *General Steam Navigation Co. Ltd* [1979] 1 Lloyd's Rep. 257, on appeal at [1981] 1 W.L.R. 120; [1980] 3 All E.R. 696; *Mendelssohn* v. *Normand Ltd* [1970] 1 Q.B. 177. See also *Tilden Rent-A-Car Co.* v. *Clendenning* [1978] 18 O.R. 2d 601 (consumer's reasonable expectations).

15 *White* v. *John Warwick & Co. Ltd* [1953] 1 W.L.R. 1285; [1953] 2 All E.R. 1021. Exemption clauses which provide for a limitation, as opposed to a total exclusion, of liability are more likely to be construed to protect the party in default: *Ailsa Craig Fishing Co. Ltd* v. *Malvern Fishing Co. Ltd* [1982] S.L.T. 377.

16 See *Photo Production Ltd* v. *Securicor Transport Ltd* [1980] A.C. 827.

17 [1978] Q.B. 69.

18 *Bridge* v. *Campbell Discount Co. Ltd* [1962] A.C. 600, 614, 626.

19 *Lloyds Bank Ltd* v. *Bundy* [1975] Q.B. 326; *A. Schroeder Music Publishing Co. Ltd* v. *Macaulay* [1974] 1 W.L.R. 1308; [1974] 3 All E.R. 616; *Pao On* v.

Lau Yiu Long [1980] A.C. 614; *McKenzie* v. *Bank of Montreal* (1976) 70 D.L.R. (3d) 113. See also *Harrison* v. *National Bank of Australasia Ltd* (1928) 23 Tas. L.R. 1.

20 See K. L. Fletcher, 'Review of Unconscionable Transactions', (1973) 8 *U. Qld. L. Rev.* 45; P. D. Finn, *Fiduciary Obligations* (Sydney: Law Book, 1977), pp. 82–8; S. M. Waddams, 'Unconscionability in Contracts' (1976) 39 *Mod. L.R.* 369.

21 *Samuel* v. *Newbold* [1906] A.C. 461.

22 See Meston, *The Law Relating to Money-lenders*, 5th edn (London: Oyez, 1968), Chapter 12.

23 s. 138(2)–(5).

24 In *A. Ketley Ltd* v. *Scott* [1981] I.C.R. 241, Foster J. held that the credit bargain was not extortionate although the rate was 48 per cent. But the peculiar facts of that case provide no definite guide for the application of the provisions in more typical consumer transactions. See also *Popjak* v. *Finance and General Corporation Ltd* [1964] A.L.R. 340.

25 s. 139(2). The court has a discretion: in *A. Ketley Ltd* v. *Scott* it was exercised against the debtor because of his deceitful acts in failing to make full disclosure in the application form for the loan.

26 s. 171(7).

27 A party to a contract deals as consumer if he neither makes the contract in the course of a business nor holds himself out as doing so, the other party makes the contract in the course of a business, and any goods involved are of a type ordinarily supplied for private use or consumption (s. 12(1)). See *Peter Symmons & Co.* v. *Cook* (1981) 131 N.L.J. 758. But on a sale by auction or by competitive tender the buyer is not in any circumstances to be regarded as dealing as consumer (s.12(2)).

The provisions discussed here (except of sale of goods; hire purchase; misrepresentation) apply only to business liability, i.e. liability arising in the course of a business or from the occupation of business premises: ss. 1(3), 6(4). General examinations of the Act include G. H. Treitel, *The Law of Contract*, 5th edn (London: Stevens, 1979), pp. 180–93; David Yates, *Exclusion Clauses in Contracts*, 2nd edn (London: Sweet & Maxwell, 1982), pp. 73–109; Richard Lawson, *Exclusion Clauses after the Unfair Contract Terms Act* (London: Oyez, 1978), pp. 81–105.

For criminal liability for using certain terms invalidated by the Act, see p. 339 below.

28 *Walker* v. *Boyle* [1982] 1 W.L.R. 495; [1982] 1 All E.R. 634 and *Southwestern General Property Co. Ltd.* v. *Marton* (1982) 263 E.G. 1090 are applications of the section.

29 cf. *Anglo-Continental Holidays Ltd* v. *Typaldos Lines (London) Ltd* [1967] 2 Lloyd's Rep. 61.

30 *Lally and Weller* v. *George Bird* (1980), unreported, noted in W. H.

Thomas, *Encyclopedia of Consumer Law* (London: Sweet & Maxwell, looseleaf) ss. 3–208/1.

31 Critics have said that the provision goes too far because it might require the deletion of a primary obligation which is an essential characteristic of the transaction and which the parties knowingly and willingly concluded: Norman Palmer and David Yates, 'The Future of the Unfair Contract Terms Act 1977', (1981) 40 *Cambridge L.J.* 108, 127; cf. Brian Coote, 'Unfair Contract Terms Act 1977', (1978) 41 *M.L.R.* 312. *Contra* John N. Adams, 'An Optimistic Look at the Contract Provisions of Unfair Contract Terms Act 1977', (1978) 41 *M.L.R.* 703.

32 A county court judge has found the idea persuasive. In *Woodman* v. *Photo-Trade Processing Ltd* (1981) unreported, noted in Thomas, op. cit., ss. 3–318/1, a business sought to limit its liability to the replacement of film where it lost photographic exposures it had accepted for developing and printing. The judge held that the clause was unreasonable because it excluded liability for negligence as well as mere accident; the trade all offered the same terms so consumers had no choice, and no insurance facility was offered. On reasonableness, see also *Waldron-Kelly* v. *British Railways Board* [1981] *C.L.Y.* §. 303 (county court); *Southwestern General Property Co. Ltd* v. *Marton, The Times,* 11 May 1982; *Rasbora Ltd* v. *J.C.L. Marine Ltd* [1977] 1 Lloyd's Rep. 645.

33 An incisive critique is Francis Reynolds, 'Unfair Contract Terms: A Comment', in Alan C. Neal (ed.), *Law and the Weaker Party* (Abingdon, Oxon.: Professional Books, 1981), vol. 1.

34 See Law Commission, *Insurance Law: Non-disclosure and Breach of Warranty,* Law Comm. No. 104, 1980; Leon E. Trakman, 'The Unharnessed Insurer: A Foreboding Presence', (1981) 31 *U.Tor. L.J.* 318; Law Reform Commission (Australia), *Insurance Contracts,* Report No. 20, 1982.

35 S. M. Waddams, 'Legislation and Contract Law', (1979) 17 *W. Ontario L.R.* 185, 194.

36 For example, Arthur Leff, 'Unconscionability and the Code – The Emperor's New Clause', (1967) 115 *U. Penn. L. Rev.* 485; Sinai Deutch, *Unfair Contracts* (Lexington, Mass.: D. C. Heath, 1977).

37 *F. N. Roberts Pest Control Co.* v. *McDonald* 208 S.E. 2d. 13 (1974); *Kugler* v. *Romain* 279 A. 2d. 640 (1971).

38 *Morris* v. *Capitol Furniture and Appliance Co.* 280 A. 2d. 775 (1971).

39 350 F.2d. 445, (1965).

40 s. 81.

41 See A. H. Angelo and E. P. Ellinger, 'Unconscionable Contracts – A Comparative Study', (1979) 4 *Otago L.R.* 300; John P. Dawson, 'Unconscionable Coercion: The German Version', (1976) 89 *Harv. L. R.* 1041; John R. Peden, *The Law of Unjust Contracts* (Sydney: Butterworths, 1982); Reich and Micklitz, 'Consumer Legislation in the EC Countries',

op. cit., pp. 161–3. Wolfgang Freiherr von Marschall, 'The New German Law on Standard Contract Terms', [1979] 3 L.M.C.L.Q. 278.

42 For example, Michael J. Trebilcock, 'An Economic Approach to the Doctrine of Unconscionability', in Barry J. Reiter and John Swan (eds), *Studies in Contract Law* (Toronto: Butterworths, 1980), pp. 389–90, 396–404.

43 cf. Contracts Review Act 1980 (New South Wales), s. 9. See also Unfair Contract Terms Act 1977, Schedule 2.

44 Ibid., ss. 7–8, Schedule 1.

45 See Ulf Bernitz, 'Consumer Protection and Standard Contracts', (1973) 17 *Scandinavian Studies in Law* 11; James E. Sheldon, 'Consumer Protection and Standard Contracts: The Swedish Experiment in Administrative Control', (1974) 22 *Am. J. Comp. L.* 17. A somewhat similar, but much more limited, system operates in Britain in that the Office of Fair Trading vets recommendations of trade associations on standard terms and conditions for their effect on competition:

> [T]o ensure there is no likely detriment [to competition] the terms should be fair and reasonable to all concerned, not likely to mislead those who will use them, and not unnecessarily exclude variation to meet special circumstances and requirements. The benefit to customers of having standard conditions must be balanced against any detriment to them of being deprived of the freedom to secure more favourable terms than those likely to result from the restrictions imposed by them. In general mandatory standard terms and conditions are not regarded as suitable. . . .
>
> Agreements with contractual clauses void under the Unfair Contract Terms Act are not acceptable. . . .
>
> In considering whether the limitation of liability recommended by an association to its members is acceptable depends very much on individual circumstances. For instance, it may be more economical for the customer to provide insurance cover, for the supplier to accept less liability, and for this to be reflected in the charge. In some cases, notably in respect of carriage and storage services, some customers are already covered by their own insurance at all stages. It might be reasonable for the association to recommend standard terms and conditions which offer several options as to acceptance of liability, depending on the insurance required by the customer and the charge to be made for the service.
>
> A further question that sometimes arises in liability clauses, in particular in the services field, is whether it would be appropriate to include a recommended level of compensation for small claims, or for the contractor to accept liability up to a declared value, to be proved in the event of a claim. Proposals of this sort are still under discussion with the Office.

Another feature of some standard terms and conditions is provision for surcharges on overdue accounts. Where specific rates of interest are provided, it is often difficult to assess what is reasonable. What is appropriate depends on the varying circumstances of the trade or industry and would need to be justified by the association as a genuine pre-estimate of loss. The Office would not be able to make a representation on any surcharge which included an element of penalty.

Standard terms and conditions have in many cases recently been supplemented by formulae for contract price adjustment to cover costs where delivery is not effected until some time after the contract is made and costs have varied in the meantime. These formulae are regarded as desirable in certain trades, as they provide the customer with some indication of the extra amount which he will have to pay. Provided that there is freedom for negotiation of fixed prices or alternative formulae, and that the terms of the formulae are fair and reasonable, there does not appear to be any obstacle. . . .

Annual Report of the Director General of Fair Trading 1980 (London: Office of Fair Trading, 1981), pp. 51–2. Under West Germany's Standard Terms Act 1976, certain organizations of consumers can apply to the courts for an injunction against unlawful standard form clauses. Reich and Micklitz, 'Consumer Legislation in the Federal Republic of Germany', op. cit., pp. 295–305; Otto Sandrock, 'The Standard Terms Act 1976 of West Germany', (1978) 26 *Am. J. Comp. L.* 551, 567.

46 Comment, 'Administrative Regulation of Adhesion Contracts in Israel', (1966) 66 *Col. L. Rev.* 1340; Kenneth F. Berg, 'The Israeli Standard Contracts Law 1964: Judicial Controls of Standard Form Contracts', (1979) 28 *I.C.L.Q.* 560. The Attorney-General and the Israel Consumer Council with the approval of the Attorney-General, can apply for cancellation of a restrictive term of a standard contract, but not once over the period 1969–79 did the Attorney-General bring a case.

47 Schedule 1, para.1(a).

48 S. L. Kimball and W. Pfennigstorf, 'Administrative Control of the Terms of Insurance Contracts', (1965) 40 *Ind. L.J.* 143.

49 H. C. Bredemeier, 'Law as an Integrative Mechanism', in W. M. Evan (ed.), *Law and Sociology* (New York: Free Press, 1962), p. 82.

50 See p. 146.

51 In theory consumers may have a right to a set-off, but only for the amount of damages they can claim under the general law. See Robin C. A. White, 'Self-Help: When to Withhold Payment', [1981] *LAG Bull.* 158.

52 Jack Ladinsky, Stewart Macaulay and Jill Anderson, *The Milwaukee Dispute Mapping Project: A Preliminary Report*, Working Paper 1979–3, (Dispute Processing Program, University of Wisconsin-Madison Law School, 1979). See generally Arthur Best and Alan R. Andreasen, 'Consumer Response to Unsatisfactory Purchases: A Survey of Perceiving Defects, Voicing Complaints, and Obtaining Redress', (1977) 11 *Law & Soc. Rev.* 701.

53 *Annual Report of the Director General of Fair Trading 1976*, p. 18.

54 William R. Thomas *et al.*, 'The Plight of the Discontented Consumer', (1979) 3 *J. Cons. Stud. & Home Econ.* 161, 164.

55 Drawn from National Consumer Council, *Faulty Goods*, Occasional Paper No. 1, June 1981.

56 K. Foster, 'Problems with Small Claims', (1975) 2 *Brit. J. of Law and Soc'y.* 75, 77.

57 *F.T.C.* v. *Klesner* (1929) 280 U.S. 19, 28.

58 V. Aubert, 'Courts and Conflict Resolution', (1967) 11 *J. of Conflict Resolution* 40, 44.

59 For example, H. Laurence Ross and Neil O. Littlefield, 'Complaint as a Problem-Solving Mechanism', (1978) 12 *Law & Soc. Rev.* 199.

60 Consumer Council, *Justice out of Reach* (London: HMSO, 1970), p. 10.

61 Stewart Macaulay, 'Lawyers and Consumer Protection Laws', (1979) 14 *Law and Society Rev.* 115, 124–7. A survey for the Royal Commission on Legal Services (England and Wales) found that only 2 per cent of matters about which lawyers were consulted in 1977 concerned problems about the purchase of goods or services and faulty goods. When respondents were asked about matters where a lawyer's assistance might have been useful but was not consulted, however, problems about faulty goods or services constituted 10 per cent: Cmnd 7648, 1979, vol. 2, pp. 198–9, 258–9.

62 L. Bridges *et al.*, *Legal Services in Birmingham* (Birmingham: Institute of Judicial Administration, 1975), p. 158.

63 Joel F. Handler, 'Public Interest Law Firms in the United States', in Mauro Cappelletti and Bryant Garth (eds), *Access to Justice* (Milan: Guiffre, 1979), vol. 3, p. 437.

64 Frank S. Palen, 'Media Ombudsmen: A Critical Review', (1979) 13 *Law & Soc. Rev.* 799.

65 National Citizens Advice Bureaux Council, *Memorandum for the Law Commission . . . in Relation to Products Liability*, 10 November 1972, p. 1. See, generally, Michael H. Whincup, *Consumer Legislation in the United Kingdom and the Republic Of Ireland* (Wokingham, Berks: Van Nostrand Reinhold, 1980), pp. 156–9.

66 See Ross Cranston, *Regulating Business* (London: Macmillan, 1979), pp. 20–1, 61–9, 82–98; *The Fourth Right of Citizenship: A Review of Local Advice*

Services (London: National Consumer Council, 1977) pp. 17–26. For elsewhere see Ladinsky *et al.*, op. cit., pp. 14–69; Martin Eisenstein, 'The Swedish Public Complaints Board: Its Vital Role in a System of Consumer Protection', in Cappelletti and Weisner, *Access to Justice*, op. cit., vol. 2.

67 Department of Trade and Industry, *Consumer Advice Centres*, Discussion Document, 1973.
68 *Justice out of Reach*, (London: HMSO, 1970), p. 19.
69 Stamp Act 1891, s. 103 r. Finance Act 1970, s. 36(8). Of course a receipt does not close the matter: oral evidence might contradict that it accurately states the transaction which took place, and there is nothing to prevent a creditor going back on his word to accept a lesser sum in what the receipt says was 'in full settlement': See Ronald Irving, 'Right to Receipt', (1980) 124 *Sol. J.* 423.
70 Cheques Act 1957, s. 3.
71 ss. 77–9.
72 s. 103.
73 s. 172.
74 Roscoe Pound, 'The Administration of Justice in the Modern City', (1913) 26 *Harv. L.R.* 302.
75 See p. 315.
76 (London: HMSO, 1970).
77 Ibid., p. 14.
78 Ibid., pp. 14–15.
79 Now County Court Rules: O.17, r. 1.
80 George Applebey, 'Small Claims in England and Wales', in Cappelletti and Weisner (eds), *Access to Justice*, op. cit., pp. 697–8, 707–9.
81 0.19, r. 1(10).
82 Austin Sarat, 'Alternatives in Dispute Processing: Litigation in a Small Claims Court', (1976) 10 *Law & Soc. Rev.* 339, 345–8.
83 0.19, r. 1(2)–(3).
84 0.19, r. 1(4). At the time of writing the small claims limit is £1,000.
85 0.19, r. 1(5). cf. *Pepper* v. *Healey, The Times*, 9 March 1982, where the Court of Appeal held that the registrar was right to rescind a reference to arbitration because justice might be frustrated since the defendant was backed by her insurers while the plaintiff was not in a similar position. Presumably the reasoning was that if the matter went to trial the plaintiff would be legally aided and would therefore be on the same footing as the defendant with legal representation.
86 0.19, r. 1(10).
87 0.19, r. 1(11). Costs other than solicitors' charges – court fees, travel expenses, the reasonable costs of preparing the case, and so on –remain in the discretion of the arbitrator.

88 [1978] A.C. 16.

89 At p. 32. See also p. 40, *per* Lord Diplock.

90 Practice Direction [1973] 1 W.L.R. 1178. See now O.19, r. 1(10).

91 *Simple Justice. A Consumer View of Small Claims Procedures in England and Wales* (London and Cardiff: National and Welsh Consumer Councils, 1979), p. 52.

92 op. cit., pp. 719–20.

93 National Consumer Council, *Shopping*, Occasional Paper No. 4 (London: National Consumer Council, 1981), p. 23.

94 *Simple Justice*, op. cit., p. 28.

95 'Small Claims Courts – The Lord Chancellor Elucidates' (1973) 123 *N.L.J.* 215. See also Lord Chancellor's Department, *Simple Justice Proposals for Amending the County Court Rules* (1980), p. 2, where the Consumer Council's idea of a small claims division in the county court was rejected as 'unnecessary and undesirable'. The National Consumer Council has proposed a small claims division with a separate code of procedure. It has prepared a model code which is designed to be understood by all participants. See Richard Thomas, 'The Code of Procedure for Small Claims', (1982) 1 *Civil Justice Q.* 52.

96 In Queensland newspaper space is taken regularly in the press to publicize details of the cases (including the names of the parties).

97 Consumer Claims Tribunals Act 1974 (New South Wales), s. 23(2); Small Claims Tribunals Act 1973–1978 (Queensland), s. 10(2). *Contra Walsh* v. *Palladium Car Park Pty Ltd* [1975] V.R. 949.

98 Maurice Rosenberg and Myra Schubin, 'Trial by Lawyer: Compulsory Arbitration of Small Claims in Pennsylvania', (1961) 74 *Harv. L.R.* 448, 457. Kim Economides, 'Small Claims and Procedural Justice', (1980) 7 *Brit. J. Law and Society* 111, 118.

99 For example, Consumer Claims Tribunals Act 1974 (New South Wales), s. 23(1). A manufacturer might be ordered to rectify defects even though not in direct contractual relations with the consumer: *Fairey Australasia Pty Ltd* v. *Joyce* [1980] ACSCLR 55–091.

100 op. cit., p. 736.

101 See Barbara Yngvesson and Patricia Hennessey, 'Small Claims, Complex Disputes: A Review of the Small Claims Literature', (1975) 9 *Law & Soc. R.* 219.

102 See Comment, 'Small Claims Courts as Collection Agencies', (1952) 4 *Stan. L.R.* 237.

103 For example, Quebec C.C.P., s. 953(d); N.S.W.: Consumer Claims Tribunals Act 1974, s. 4; see Christopher S. Axworthy, 'Controlling the Abuse of Small Claims Courts', (1976) 22 *McGill L.J.* 480, 486.

104 T. G. Ison, 'Small Claims', (1972) 35 *Mod. L. Rev.* 18, 24–6; T. G. Ison, *Credit Marketing and Consumer Protection* (London: Croom Helm, 1979),

pp. 284–9.

105 In the Applebey Study, two in five plaintiffs were represented: op. cit., p. 732.

106 Sarat, op. cit., p. 350.

107 For example, Consumer Claims Tribunals Act 1974 (New South Wales), s. 30(4). Quebec bars lawyers from small claims courts: Christopher S. Axworthy, 'A Small Claims Court of Nova Scotia – Role of the Lawyer and the Judge', (1978) 4 *Dalhousie L.J.* 311, 315.

108 *Simple Justice*, op. cit., p. 67.

109 Richard F. Dale, 'Consumer Class Actions Under the Uniform Deceptive Trade Practices Act', (1968) *Duke L.J.* 1101, 1102–3.

110 *Standard Oil Co. of California* v. *Superior Court*, 132 Cal Reptr. 761 (1975), discussed in 'Notice and Consumer Class Actions in California', (1976) 64 *Calif. L. Rev.* 1222.

111 Neil J. Williams, 'Consumer Class Actions in Canada – Some Proposals for Reform', (1975) *13 Osgoode L.J.* 1, 50.

112 Federal Rules of Civil Procedure, r. 23. See 'Class Actions for Consumer Protection', (1972) 7 *Harv. Civil Rights – Civil Lib. L.R.* 601. 'Developments in the Law – Class Actions', (1976) 89 *Harv. L.R.* 1318; Patricia L. Wells, 'Reforming Federal Class Action Procedure: An Analysis of the Justice Department Proposal', (1979) 16 *Harv. J. Legis.* 543. The Supreme Court in several other cases has adopted a restrictive approach to the 1966 rule. In *Snyder* v. *Harris*, 394 U.S. 319 (1969), it held that the different claims of those in a class could not be aggregated to satisfy the jurisdictional amount for a case to be heard. *Zahn* v. *International Paper Co.*, 414 U.S. 291 (1974), determined that each plaintiff must satisfy the jurisdictional amount.

113 417 U.S. 156 (1974).

114 James Andrew Hinds, 'To Right Mass Wrongs: A Federal Consumer Class Action Act', (1976) 13 *Harv. J. Leg.* 776, 790–2.

115 *Cartt* v. *Superior Court*, 124 Cal. Reptr. 376 (1975).

116 *Daar* v. *Yellow Cab Co.*, 433 P.2d 732 (1967). See also *West Virginia* v. *Charles Pfizer & Co.*, 314 F.Supp. 710 (1970), affirmed 440 F.2d. 1079, cert. denied 404 U.S. 871 (1971).

117 See Arthur R. Miller, 'Of Frankenstein Monsters and Shining Knights: Myth, Reality, and the "Class Action" Problem', (1979), 92 *Harv. L. Rev.* 664.

117a Ontario Law Reform Commission, *Report on Class Actions*, (Toronto: Ministry of the Attorney General, 1982), vol. I, pp. 250–4.

117b For example, *Rosenfeld* v. *A. H. Robins Co., Inc.*, 407 N.Y.S. 2d 196; 385 N.E. 2d 1301 (1978); *Rose* v. *Medtronics, Inc.*, 166 Cal. Rptr. 16 (1980). cf. *Payton* v. *Abbott Labs*, 83 F.R.D. 382 (1979).

118 *Markt & Co. Ltd* v. *Knight Steamship Co. Ltd* [1910] 2 K.B. 1021 is the

leading authority, although it is only a majority decision and only Fletcher Moulton L.J. decided that damages alone could not be claimed in a representative action. cf. *Duke of Bedford* v. *Ellis* [1901] A.C. 1; *EMI Records Ltd* v. *Riley* [1981] 1 W.L.R. 923; [1981] 2 All E.R. 838; *H. P. Bulmer Ltd and Showerings Ltd.* v. *J. Bollinger S.A. and Champagne Lanson Père et Fils* [1978] R.P.C. 79; *Payne* v. *Young* (1980) 30 A.L.R. 577. See Richard H. S. Tur, 'Litigation and the Consumer Interest: The Class Action and Beyond', (1982) 2 *Legal Studies* 135, 154–60.

119 (1979) 21 O.R.(2d) 780. See also *Chastain* v. *B.C. Hydro Power Authority* (1972) 32 D.L.R. (3d) 443. cf. *Murphy* v. *Webbwood Mobile Home Estates Ltd* (1978) 19 O.R. (2d) 300; *Cobbold* v. *Time Canada Ltd* (1980) 28 O.R. (2d) 326.

120 *Access to the Courts – II. Class Actions*, Discussion Paper No. 11 (1979), pp. 10–11. See also Ontario Law Reform Commission, *Report on Class Actions* (Toronto: Ministry of the Attorney General, 1982), esp. vol. 1, chapter 4.

121 Ibid., pp. 23–4.

122 Ibid., p. 26.

123 Criminal Justice Act 1972, s. 1. This is now Powers of Criminal Courts Act 1973, s. 35.

124 Civil Evidence Act 1968, s. 11.

125 Merchandise Marks Act 1887, s. 17.

126 ss. 35(3)–(4). Courts should refrain from making an order which involves a weekly payment over a period of years: *R.* v. *Inwood* (1974) 60 C.A.R. 70. Where a court considers that it would be appropriate both to impose a fine and to make a compensation order but the offender has insufficient means to pay both, it shall give preference to compensation: s. 4A.

127 Magistrates Courts Act 1980, s. 40(1). Even if other offences are taken into account, the total amount of compensation cannot exceed £1000 for each offence of which the defendant is convicted. Thus if the defendant is convicted of two charges and three others are taken into account, the total amount of compensation that can be awarded is £2000 even if consumer loss in the five cases exceeds this.

128 For example, *R.* v. *Kneeshaw* [1975] 1 Q.B. 57; *R.* v. *Vivian* [1979] 1 W.L.R. 291; [1979] 1 All E.R. 48.

129 s. 38(2).

130 *Hammertons Cars Ltd* v. *Redbridge L.B.C.* [1974] 1 W.L.R. 484; [1974] 2 All E.R. 216.

131 s. 87. See also Consumer Protection Act 1969 (New South Wales), s. 33A; Trade Practices Act 1974 (British Columbia), s. 22. Note also South Australia's Second-Hand Motor Vehicles Act 1971, s. 35(3)(4), where a consumer can claim *three* times the difference in value between the sale price and a fair value in the case of the dealer committing certain

trade description offences.

132 cf. Forfeiture Act 1870, s. 4.

133 *R. v. Salem Mohammed Monsoor Ali* (1972) 56 C.A.R. 301.

134 Tur, op. cit., pp. 161–8; Mauro Cappelletti, 'Government and Private Advocates for the Public Interest in Civil Litigation', in Cappelletti and Weisner (eds), op. cit., pp. 840–6.

135 Trade Practices Act 1974 (British Columbia), s.24; Consumer Affairs Act 1972 (Victoria), ss.9A-C.

136 cf. Allan D. Jergesen, 'New York City's Alternative to the Consumer Class Action: The Government as Robin Hood', (1972) 9 *Harv. J. Leg.* 301. David M. Trubek, 'Public Advocacy: Administrative Government and the Representation of Diffuse Interests', in Cappelletti and Garth, *Access to Justice*, op. cit., vol. 3, pp. 451, 472–3; Susan E. Nash, 'Collecting Overcharges from the Oil Companies: The Department of Energy's Restitutionary Obligation', (1980) 32 *Stanford L. Rev.* 1039.

137 Professor Maurice Rosenburg has suggested that dissatisfied consumers should be compensated automatically from a state fund where small losses are involved. The fund would attempt to recoup those monies, possibly by mass restitution suits; abuse could be curbed by spot checks. See 'Devising Procedures that are Civil to Promote Justice that is Civilized', (1971), 69 *Mich. L. Rev.* 797, 813–15.

CHAPTER 4

1 s. 6(1) of the Consumer Safety Act 1978 establishes a form of strict liability where a person is injured because of non-compliance with obligations created under the Act. See Peter Cane, 'Civil Liability Under the Consumer Safety Act 1978 (UK)' (1979), 3, *J. Products Liability* 215.

2 R. S. Mason, 'Price and Produce Quality Assessment' (1974), *Eur. J. Mar.*, vol. 8, Spring, p. 29.

3 A. W. Willsmore, *Modern Product Control*, 3rd edn (London: Pitman, 1963), p. 187. See also Malcolm Dewis *et al.*, *Product Liability* (London: Heinemann, 1980), Part III.

4 Sidney Weinberg, *Profit Through Quality* (London: Gower Press, 1969), p. 8.

5 *Annual Report of the Director General of Fair Trading 1978*, p. 56. Figures have not been reported since 1978.

6 Information is kept under the voluntary code between the Department of Transport and the Society of Motor Manufacturers and Traders governing the recall of motor cars: over a million have been recalled since the Code began in July 1979. See 'Safety Recalls' (1982), *Which?* April, p. 231.

7 As well as testing products, The Consumers' Association draws on surveys of members' experience: for example, 'Reliability Make-By-Make [of Cars]' (1982) *Which?* January, p. 25; 'Cameras and Projectors: Servicing and Reliability' (1981) *Which?* May, p. 263.

8 Bureau Européen des Unions de Consommateurs, *After-Sales Service in the EEC* (London: 1976).

9 Arthur A. Leff, 'Unconscionability and the Crowd-Consumers and the Common Law Tradition', (1970) 31, *U. Pitt. L. Rev.* 349, 356.

10 Note also the Design Council.

11 See pp. 351–5 below.

12 Motor Dealers Act 1974, s. 27.

13 Disclosure involves estimating the cost of repair; the consumer can recover if it is inaccurate, s. 29(4).

14 With vehicles costing less than $1500, dealers can exempt themselves from liability if they use a prescribed notice: s. 28(5).

15 s. 28(1). See also s. 28(2)–(3).

16 See p. 312 below.

17 *Final Report of the Committee on Consumer Protection*, Cmnd 1781 (1962), pp. 76–89.

18 [1951] 1 K.B. 805.

19 *Lough* v. *Moran Motors Pty Ltd*, [1962] Q.S.R. 466.

20 *Andrews* v. *Hopkinson* [1957] 1 Q.B. 229; cf. *Esso Petroleum Co. Ltd* v. *Mardon* [1976] 1 Q.B. 801. *Marks* v. *Hunt Bros. (Sydney) Pty Ltd* (1958) 58 S.R. (New South Wales) 380; *J. J. Savage and Sons Pty Ltd* v. *Blakney* (1970) 119 C.L.R. 435.

21 *Carpenter* v. *Alberto Culver Co.* 184 N.W. 2d 547 (1970); see *Williston on Sales*, 4th edn (1974),§. 17–6; Bruce G. Donald and J. D. Heydon, *Trade Practices Law* (Sydney: Law Book, 1978), pp. 538–42 and Supplement.

22 See, for example, G. H. Treitel, *The Law of Contract*, 5th edn (London: Stevens, 1979), pp. 253 ff.

23 *Liverpool & County Discount Co. Ltd* v. *A. B. Motor Co. (Kilburn) Ltd* [1963] 1 W.L.R. 611; [1963] 2 All E.R. 396; *Academy of Health & Fitness Pty Ltd* v. *Power* [1973] V.R. 254.

24 [1965] 1 W.L.R. 623; [1965] 2 All E.R. 65.

25 *Oscar Chess Ltd* v. *Williams* [1957] 1 W.L.R. 370; [1957] 1 All E.R. 325.

26 s. 2(1).

27 *Howard Marine and Dredging Co. Ltd* v. *A. Ogden & Sons (Excavations) Ltd* [1978] Q.B. 574.

28 s. 2(2).

29 For example, *Porter* v. *General Guarantee Corporation Ltd* [1982] R.T.R. 384.

30 [1950] 2 K.B. 86.

31 [1958] 1 W.L.R. 753; [1958] 2 All E.R. 402.

32 [1958] 1 W.L.R. 753, 760; [1958] 2 All E.R. 402, 407.

33 Law Reform Committee, *Tenth Report (Innocent Misrepresentation)*, Cmnd 1782 (1962) p. 4.

34 *Working Paper on the Sale of Goods* (Sydney: 1975), pp. 34–5, 38–40, 44–5.

35 *Report on Consumer Warranties and Guarantees in the Sale of Goods* (Toronto: 1972), p. 29; *Report on Sale of Goods* (Toronto: Ministry of the Attorney General, 1979), p. 140.

36 (1881), 20 Ch. D. 1, 13.

37 See W. N. Hamilton, 'The Ancient Maxim Caveat Emptor', (1931) 40 *Yale L. J.* 1133, 1138, 1143; P. S. Atiyah, *The Rise and Fall of Freedom of Contract* (Oxford: Clarendon, 1979), p. 545.

38 Karl N. Llewellyn, *Cases and Materials on the Law of Sales* (Chicago: Callaghan & Co., 1930), p. 204.

39 *Barr* v. *Gibson* (1838) 150 E.R. 1196, 1200.

40 *Gardiner* v. *Gray* (1815) 171 E.R. 46; *Jones* v. *Just* (1868) L.R. 3 Q.B. 197.

41 *Gray* v. *Cox* (1825) 107 E.R. 999, *Randall* v. *Newson* (1877) 2 Q.B. D. 102.

42 *Chalmers Sale of Goods*, 18th edn (London: Butterworths, 1981), Introduction to 1st edn, p. viii.

43 Supply of Goods (Implied Terms) Act 1973, s. 4. Now Unfair Contract Terms Act 1977, s. 6.

44 s. 8. Now Supply of Goods (Implied Terms) Act 1973, ss. 9, 10; Consumer Credit Act 1974, Schedule 4, s. 35.

45 See *Esso Petroleum Co Ltd* v. *Customs & Excise Commissioners* [1976] 1 W.L.R. 1; [1976] 1 All E.R. 117; cf. *Chappell & Co. Ltd* v. *Nestlé Co. Ltd* [1960] A.C. 87; *Buckley* v. *Lever Bros Ltd* (1953) 4 D.L.R. 16.

46 *Pharmaceutical Society of Great Britain* v. *Boots Cash Chemists (Southern) Ltd*, [1953] 1 Q.B. 401.

47 P. S. Atiyah, *The Sale of Goods*, 6th edn (London: Pitman, 1980), p. 85.

48 Sale of Goods Act 1979, s. 13(3).

49 See *Benjamin's Sale of Goods*, 2nd edn, §. 779.

50 [1967] 1 W.L.R. 1193; [1967] 3 All E.R. 253; see also *Hall* v. *Queensland Truck Centre Pty Ltd* (1970) Qd. R. 231 (truck described as CBEW type, in fact CADY type). Cases under the Trade Descriptions Act 1968 may be relevant: see pp. 235–42.

51 (1981), unreported, noted in W. H. Thomas, *Encyclopedia of Consumer Law* (London: Sweet & Maxwell, looseleaf), §. 1–1067.

52 *Ashington Piggeries Ltd* v. *Christopher Hill Ltd* [1972] A.C. 441. The approach diminishes the rights of consumers: see Brian Coote, 'Correspondence with Description in the Law of Sale of Goods', (1976) 50 *A.L.J.* 17.

53 *Andrews Bros (Bournemouth) Ltd* v. *Singer & Co. Ltd* [1934] 1 K.B. 17; *Clarke* v. *McMahon* [1939] S.A.S.R. 64, 67.

54 *Reardon Smith Line Ltd* v. *Hansen-Tangen* [1976] 1 W.L.R. 989, 998; [1976] 3 All E.R. 570, 576.

55 *Osborn* v. *Hart* (1871) 23 L.T. 851 (undrinkable wine described as superior old port); *Wilson* v. *Rickett Cockerell & Co. Ltd* [1954] 1 Q.B. 598, 608 (coalite containing explosive).

56 *Benjamin's Sale of Goods*, 2nd edn (London: Sweet & Maxwell, 1981), p. 374.

57 *Frost* v. *Aylesbury Dairy Co. Ltd* [1905] 1 K.B. 608.

58 *Wilson* v. *Rickett Cockerell & Co. Ltd* [1954] 1 Q.B. 598.

59 s. 61(1). A sale by a private individual who sells through an agent acting in the course of a business is covered unless the consumer knows that fact or reasonable steps are taken to bring it to the notice of the consumer before the contract is made: s. 14(5).

60 *Stevenson* v. *Beverley Bentinck Ltd* [1976] 1 W.L.R. 483; [1976] 2 All E.R. 606; *Blakemore* v. *Bellamy* (1982) 90 M.R. 235.

61 *Lambert* v. *Lewis* [1982] A.C. 225.

62 *Henry Kendall & Sons* v. *William Lillico & Sons Ltd* [1969] 2 A.C. 31, 75–6, 108–9.

63 *Crowther* v. *Shannon Motor Co.* [1975] 1 W.L.R. 30; [1975] 1 All E.R. 139; *Rasbora* v. *J.C.L. Marine* [1977] 1 Lloyd's Rep. 645.

64 It is said that the implied conditions will not cease if their continuation would be reasonably supposed to have been contemplated by the parties despite the obvious defect. The test is obviously artificial; so stated it will be unusual for a court to find that the implied conditions continue indefinitely.

65 [1982] A.C. 225. See also *Hunnerup* v. *Goodyear Tyre & Rubber Co. Australia Ltd* (1974) 7 S.A.S.R. 215; *Heil* v. *Hedges* [1951] 1 T.L.R. 512; *Erdman* v. *Johnson Bros Radio & Television Co. Inc.*271 A. 2d 744(1970). See also J. K. Macleod, 'Instructions as to the Use of Consumer Goods' (1981) 97 *L.Q.R.* 550, 566–73.

66 *McDonald* v. *Empire Garage (Blackburn) Ltd, The Times,* 8 October 1975, *per* James and Bridge L.JJ. cf. *Cehave N.V.* v. *Bremer Handelsgessellschaft m.b.H.* (The Hansa Nord) [1976] Q.B. 44, 62 *per* Lord Denning M.R.

67 s. 14(6). cf. U.C.C. § 2–314(2).

68 Despite the statutory language commentators have said that this view is too extreme: for example, *Benjamin's Sale of Goods*, 2nd edn (London: Sweet & Maxwell, 1981), p. 387. cf. G. Q. Taperell, R. B. Vermeesch and D. J. Harland, *Trade Practices and Consumer Protection,* 2nd edn (Sydney: Butterworths, 1978), p. 665; Ontario Law Reform Commission, *Report on Sale of Goods* (Toronto: Ministry of the Attorney General), p. 214.

69 *B. S. Brown & Son Ltd* v. *Craiks Ltd* [1970] 1 W.L.R. 752; [1970] 1 All E.R. 823. Studies in the United States based on *Consumer Reports* show that the relationship between price and quality is problematical.

70 *Wren* v. *Holt* [1903] 1 K.B. 610; *Godley* v. *Perry* [1960] 1 W.L.R. 9; [1960] 1

All E.R. 36; *Morelli* v. *Fitch & Gibbons* [1928] 2 K.B. 636; *Daniels & Daniels* v. *R. White and Sons Ltd* [1938] 4 All E.R. 258.

71 *International Business Machines Co. Ltd* v. *Shcherban* [1925] 1 D.L.R. 864; cf. *Jackson* v. *Rotax Motor and Cycle Co.* [1910] 2 K.B. 937.

72 1981, unreported, noted in W. H. Thomas, *Encyclopaedia of Consumer Law* (London: Sweet & Maxwell, looseleaf) §. 1–1070, 3–194/2. cf. *Millars of Falkirk Ltd.* v. *Turpie* [1976] S.L.T. 66 (Notes).

73 [1965] 1 W.L.R. 1013; [1965] 2 All E.R. 753.

74 *The Times*, 8 October 1975. Prior to 1973 the merchantability condition only applied if there was a sale by description.

75 [1975] 1 W.L.R. 30; [1975] 1 All E.R. 139.

76 [1977] R.T.R. 35. See also *Peter Symmons & Co.* v. *Cook* (1981) 131 N.L.J. 758.

77 For example, *Leaves* v. *Wadham Stringer (Cliftons) Ltd* [1980] R.T.R. 308; *Millars of Falkirk Ltd* v. *Turpie* [1976] S.L.T. 66 (Notes); *Spencer* v. *Claud Rye (Vehicles) Ltd*, unreported, cited in M. Whincup, 'Reasonable Fitness of Cars' (1975), 38 Mod. L.R. 660, 661–2. cf. *Jackson* v. *Chrysler Acceptances Ltd* [1978] R.T.R. 474.

78 s. 14(2)(a).

79 s. 14(2)(b).

80 *Grant* v. *Australian Knitting Mills Ltd* [1936] A.C. 85; *Godley* v. *Perry* [1960] 1 W.L.R. 9; [1960] 1 All E.R. 36; cf. *Henry Kendall & Sons* v. *William Lillico & Sons Ltd* [1969] A.C. 31, at 84, 106–7, 124–5.

81 cf. *Baldry* v. *Marshall* [1925] 1 K.B. 260.

82 cf. *B. S. Brown & Sons* v. *Craiks* [1970] 1 W.L.R. 752; [1970] 1 All E.R. 823.

83 *Griffiths* v. *Peter Conway Ltd* [1939] 1 All E.R. 685. See also *Ashington Piggeries Ltd* v. *Christopher Hill Ltd* [1972] A.C. 441.

84 For example, *Priest* v. *Last* [1903] 2 K.B. 148.

85 *Lambert* v. *Lewis* [1982] A.C. 225.

86 Law Commission, *Implied Terms in Contracts for the Supply of Goods*, Law Comm. No. 95, 1979, pp. 32–6. See also Ontario Law Reform Commission, *Report on Sale of Goods* (Toronto: Ministry of Attorney-General, 1979), pp. 215–16.

87 National Consumer Council, *Faulty Goods*, Occasional Paper 1, 1981.

88 For example, Trade Practices Act 1974 (Australia), s. 74 F; Consumer Products Warranties Act (Saskatchewan), §. 11(8), 13(2). cf. Californian Civil Code, ss. 1793.2.

89 Law Commission, *Implied Terms in Contracts for the Supply of Goods*, Law Comm. No. 95, 1979, pp. 38–41.

90 Californian Civil Code, §. 1791.1(a) (3).

91 In New South Wales the courts can order an actual repair. Sale of Goods Act 1923, s. 64(5) (inserted by Commercial Transactions (Miscl.

Provisions) Act 1974).

92 Implied terms of merchantability and fitness for purpose arise on the exchange in relation to the replacement product. Supply of Goods and Services Act 1982, s. 4. It seems that the replacement operates as a recision of the first contract and the consumer can no longer rely on the implied terms in that contract. Cf. *Robinson* v. *Motor Mart Ltd* (1955) 2 D.L.R. 427.

93 See also Sale of Goods Act 1979, s. 36 (consumers' duty on rejection).

94 By s. 59 what constitutes a reasonable time is a question of fact.

95 Unfair Contract Terms Act 1977, s. 13. But clauses in 'acceptance notes' might not be caught if they are not contract terms, the linchpin of many sections of the Act.

96 (1823) 171 E.R. 1082.

97 See p. 1083.

98 K. T. C. Sutton, *Sales and Consumer Law* (Sydney: Law Book, 1983), p. 375.

99 cf. *Armaghdown Motors Ltd* v. *Gray Motors Ltd* [1963] N.Z.L.R. 5 (registration of car in own name inconsistent with seller's ownership).

100 See Brett J.'s judgment in *Heilbut* v. *Hickson* (1872) L.R. 7 C.P. 438.

101 *Long* v. *Lloyd (supra)* and *Leaf* v. *International Galleries (supra)* can be distinguished on these grounds; they involve products where expert examination was practical.

102 *Shofield* v. *Emerson Brantingham Implements Co.* (1918) 43 D.L.R. 509; *Freeman* v. *Consolidated Motors Ltd* (1968) 69 D.L.R. (2d) 581.

103 cf. the principle that examination can involve partial consumption of the goods: Benjamin's Sale of Goods, §. 905.

104 [1970] 1 W.L.R. 1053; [1970] 2 All E.R. 774.

105 [1970] 1 W.L.R. 1053, 1059; [1970] 2 All E.R. 774, 778. Fenton Atkinson and Megaw L.JJ. agreed.

106 [1978] R.T.R. 474.

107 at pp. 480-1. See also the commercial case, *Manifatture Tessile Laniera Wooltex* v. *J. B. Ashley Ltd* [1979] 2 Lloyd's Rep. 28, where the Court of Appeal held that the buyer did not lose the right to reject despite a lapse of three months, for during that time the scope of the defects was being explored.

108 *Yeoman Credit Ltd* v. *Apps* [1962] 2 Q.B. 508, 522; *Guarantee Trust of Jersey* v. *Gardner* [1973] 117 S.J. 564.

109 [1977] R.T.R. 35.

110 Contrast the more liberal interpretation of letters: *Hammer & Barrow* v. *Coca-Cola* [1962] N.Z.L.R. 723, 733-4.

111 See note 72 above.

112 (1969), 6 D.L.R. (3d) 692; (1969), 69 W.W.R. 734. See also *Barber* v. *Inland Truck Sales Ltd* (1970) 11 D.L.R. (3d) 469; *Rafuse Motors Co.* v.

Mardo Const. Ltd (1963) 41 D.L.R. (2d) 340; *Cain* v. *Bird Chevrolet – Oldsmobile Ltd* (1976) 12 O.R. (2d) 532; *Finlay* v. *Metro Toyota Ltd* (1977) 82 D.L.R. (3d) 440.

113 (1969) 6 D.L.R. (3d) 692, 699; (1969) 69 W.W.R. 734, 741.

114 U.C.C., §. 2–608.

115 For example, *Pavesi* v. *Ford Motor Co.*, 382 A. 2d 954 (1978).

116 op. cit., pp. 215–16.

117 cf. Trade Practices Act 1974 (Australia), s. 75A. At the time of writing the Law Commission is preparing a working paper on the subject.

118 [1970] 1 W.L.R. 1953; [1970] 2 All E.R. 774. Nor in *M. & J. Hurst Consultants Ltd* v. *Grange Motors Ltd and Rolls Royce Motors Ltd*, note 72 above.

119 *Vella* v. *Eagers Retail* [1973] Q.L. 236; *O'Flaherty* v. *McKinlay* (1953) 2 D.L.R. 514. cf. Law Commission, *Exemption Clauses: First Report*, Law Comm. No. 24, 1969, pp. 4–5.

120 See I. N. Duncan Wallace, 'Cost of Repair and Inflation', (1980) 96 *L.Q.R.* 101; 'Inflation and Assessment of Construction Cost Damages', (1982) 98 *L.Q.R.* 406.

121 [1936] A.C. 85.

122 [1960] 1 W.L.R. 9; [1960] 1 All E.R. 36.

122 (1854), 9 Ex. 341.

124 *Ashworth* v. *Wells* (1898) 78 L.T. 136.

125 *Robert Holt & Sons Ltd* v. *Lay* (1972) 7 Recent Law (N.Z.) 226.

126 *Vella* v. *Eagers Retail* [1973] 1 Q.L. 236 (Unroadworthy car = contract price – worth for spare parts.)

127 *Ford Motor Co. of Canada Ltd* v. *Haley* (1967) 62 D.L.R. (2d) 329.

128 *Koufos* v. *C. Czarnikow Ltd* [1969], 1 A.C. 350.

129 *Kasler & Cohen* v. *Slavouski* [1928] 1 K.B. 78.

130 [1909] 2 K.B. 193.

131 cf. *McDonald* v. *Empire Garages (Blackburn) Ltd, The Times*, 8 October 1975. See also *Junior Books Ltd* v. *Veitchi Co. Ltd* [1982] 3 W.L.R. 477; [1982] 3 All E.R. 201.

132 cf. *Molling & Co.* v. *Dean & Son Ltd* (1901) 18 T.L.R. 217.

133 *Gascoigne* v. *British Credit Trust* [1978] C.L.Y. 711 (County Court). cf. *Jackson* v. *Chrysler Acceptances Ltd* [1978] R.T.R., 474 (damages for spoilt holiday – but this known about and so foreseeable); *Daily Office Cleaning Contractors Ltd* v. *Shefford* [1977] R.T.R. 361; *Hobbs* v. *Marlowe* [1978] A.C. 16 (hire charges – but both were negligence cases for which damages need only be reasonably foreseeable, and not a substantial possibility as in contract).

134 *Zoss* v. *Royal Chevrolet Inc.* 11 U.C.C. Rep. Serv. 527 (1972).

135 *McGregor on Damages*, 14th edn 1980, pp. 174–6.

136 *Wallis* v. *Russell* (1902) 2 I.R. 585; *Cockerton* v. *Navier Aznar S.A.* [1960] 2

Lloyds L.R. 450.

137 *Lockett* v. *A. & M. Charles Ltd* [1938] 4 All E.R. 170.

138 *Woodar Investment Development Ltd* v. *Wimpey Construction U.K. Ltd* [1980] 1 W.L.R. 277, 283; [1980] 1 All E.R. 571, 576.

139 (1935) 51 T.L.R. 551. See also *Stennett* v. *Hancock and Peters* [1939] 2 All E.R. 578; *Burfitt* v. *A. & E. Kille* [1939] 2 K.B. 743.

140 [1979] R.T.R. 265.

141 [1966] 1 Lloyd's Rep. 500.

142 Jolowicz, op. cit., p. 3. See also S. M. Waddams, 'The Strict Liability of Suppliers of Goods' (1974) 37 *Mod. L. Rev.* 154.

143 For example *Santor* v. *A. & M. Karagheusian Inc.* 207 A 2d 305 (1965). The retailer had gone out of business.

144 ss. 74, B, D.

145 Jon Chait, 'Continuing the Common Law Response to the New Industrial State: The Extension of Enterprise Liability to Consumer Services', (1974) 22 *UCLA L. Rev.* 401, 405.

146 See A. M. Dugdale and K. M. Stanton, *Professional Negligence* (London: Butterworths, 1982).

147 *Anns* v. *Merton London Borough Council* [1978] A.C. 728; *Batty* v. *Metropolitan Property Realisations Ltd* [1978] Q.B. 554; *Junior Books Ltd* v. *Veitchi Co. Ltd* [1982] 3 W.L.R. 477; [1982] 3 All E.R. 201. See *Salmond and Heuston on the Law of Torts*, 18th edn (London: Sweet & Maxwell, 1981), pp. 277–9.

148 [1959] C.L.Y. 527. See also *Stedman* v. *Swan's Tours* (1951) 95 Sol. J. 727; *Cook* v. *Spanish Holiday Tours (London) Ltd* (1959) 103 Sol. J. 873; *Anglo-Continental Holidays Ltd* v. *Typaldos (London) Ltd* [1967] 2 Lloyds R. 61.

149 [1973] 1 Q.B. 233. See also *Jackson* v. *Horizon Holidays Ltd* [1975] 1 W.L.R. 1468; [1975] 3 All E.R. 92. Two county court cases are *Askew* v. *Intasun North* (1980) 88 M.R. 120; *Levene* v. *Metropolitan Travel* (1981) 89 M.R. 51.

150 *Lee* v. *Griffin* (1861) 30 L.J.Q.B. 252.

151 *Robinson* v. *Graves* [1935] 1 K.B. 579; *Issacs* v. *Hardy* (1884), Cab. & El. 287.

152 *Philip Head & Sons Ltd* v. *Showfronts Ltd* [1970] 1 Lloyds Rep. 140; *Brooks Robinson Pty Ltd* v. *Rothfield* [1951] V.L.R. 405. A more convincing case is *Collins Trading Co. Pty Ltd* v. *Maher* [1969] V.R. 20 (domestic heater; sale).

153 Supply of Goods and Services Act 1982, s. 9.

154 *Reed* v. *Dean* [1949] 1 K.B. 188. See also *White* v. *John Warwick Co. Ltd* [1953] 1 W.L.R. 1285; 2 All E.R. 1021; *Astley Industrial Trust Ltd* v. *Grimley* [1963] 1 W.L.R. 584; [1963] 2 All E.R. 33.

155 Supply of Goods and Services Act 1982, s. 4.

156 *G. H. Myers & Co.* v. *Brent Cross Service Co.* [1934] 1 K.B. 46.

157 *Watson* v. *Buckley Osborne, Garrett & Co. Ltd* [1940] 1 All E.R. 174; cf. *Ingham* v. *Emes* [1955] 2 Q.B. 366 when the customer knew she was allergic to a hair dye but did not disclose the fact.

158 [1969] 1 A.C. 454. See also *Reg Glass Pty Ltd* v. *Rivers Locking Systems Pty Ltd* (1968) 120 C.L.R. 516. *Laminated Structures & Holdings Ltd* v. *Eastern Woodworkers Ltd* (1962) 32 D.L.R. (2d) 1.

159 Supply of Goods and Services Act 1982, s. 12.

160 s. 14. See *Charnock* v. *Liverpool Corporation* [1968] 1 W.L.R. 1498; [1968] 3 All E.R. 473; *McDougall* v. *Aeromarine of Emsworth Ltd* [1958] 1 W.L.R. 1126; [1958] 3 All E.R. 431.

161 s. 15.

162 *Green* v. *All Motors Ltd* [1917] 1 K.B. 625; *Albemarle Supply Co. Ltd* v. *Hind & Co.* [1928] 1 K.B. 307. But there is no lien in the case of a maintenance agreement. *Hatton* v. *Car Maintenance Co. Ltd* [1915] 1 Ch. 621. Regarding the power of sale, see Torts (Interference with Goods) Act 1977, s. 12(3).

163 *Forman & Co. Pty Ltd* v. *The Ship 'Liddesdale'* [1900] A.C. 190.

164 (1889) 16 T.L.R. 45.

165 *Philips* v. *William Whiteley Ltd* [1938] 1 All 566.

166 *Royal Commission on Civil Liability and Compensation for Personal Injury,* Cmnd 7054, 1978, p. 278. The British Insurance Association proposed a form of strict liability for services to the Commission. Strict liability might already exist at common law for some professional services: *Independent Broadcasting Authority* v. *E.M.I. Electronics Ltd and BICC Construction Ltd* [1980] 14 Build. L.R. 1. This is not affected by the Supply of Goods and Services Act 1982, which preserves existing rules about the standard of services: s. 16(3)(a).

167 Department of Prices and Consumer Protection, *Consumer Safety, A Consultative Document,* Cmnd 6398 (London: HMSO, 1976), p. 22.

168 [1947] 1 All E.R. 361.

169 *Stewart* v. *Reavell's Garage* [1952] 2 Q.B. 545.

170 *Perry* v. *Sharon Development Co. Ltd* [1937] 4 All E.R. 390; cf. *McKone* v. *Johnson* [1966] 2 N.S.W.R. 471. It must also be fit for habitation. cf. *Batty* v. *Metropolitan Property Realisations Ltd* [1978] Q.B. 554. Section 1 of the Defective Premises Act 1972 confirms these common law obligations: a person taking on work for or in connection with the provision of a dwelling (erection or renovation) owes a duty to the person ordering the work and to subsequent persons who acquire a legal or equitable interest in the dwelling to see that the work is done in a workmanlike or professional manner with proper materials and so that the dwelling will be fit for habitation when completed. The duty is non-excludable (s. 6(3)).

171 *Crawford* v. *Board of Governors of Charing Cross Hospital* [1953] C.L.Y. 2518. See generally *Whitehouse* v. *Jordan* [1981] 1 W.L.R. 246; [1981] 1 All E.R. 267.

172 [1966] 1 Q.B. 716. See also *Houghland* v. *R. R. Low (Luxury) Coaches Ltd*
[1962] 1 Q.B. 694; *Levison* v. *Patent Steam Carpet Cleaning Co. Ltd* [1978]
Q.B. 69.

173 *Ashby* v. *Tolhurst* [1937] 2 K.B. 242; cf. *Mendelssohn* v. *Normand Ltd* [1970]
1 Q.B. 177 (consumer had to leave his keys); *Sydney Corporation* v. *West*
(1965) 114 C.L.R. 481; N. E. Palmer, *Bailment* (Sydney: Law Book,
1979), pp. 195–213.

174 For example, *Fothergill* v. *Monarch Airlines Ltd* [1981] A.C. 251; Thomas
A. Dickerson, 'Travel Law: Baggage Claims', (1980) 5 *Air Law* 130.

175 See Barbara Lantin and Geoffrey Woodroffe, *Service Please. Services and the
Law: A Consumer View* (London: National Consumer Council, 1981), pp.
5–21; *Home Improvements* (London: Office of Fair Trading, 1982).

176. Supply of Goods and Services Act 1982, ss. 4, 9, 13.

177 See Jeremy Phillips, 'Contracts for the Provision of Consumer Services:
A Case for Reform?', (1981) 131 *N.L.J.* 916.

178 Supply of Goods and Services Act 1982, ss. 11–16.

179 Unfair Contract Terms Act 1977, ss. 2(2), 3(2)(a). See also Geoffrey
Woodroffe, *Goods and Services – The New Law* (London: Sweet & Maxwell,
1982), pp. 123–9. cf. Trade Practices Act 1974 (Australia), s. 68.

180 *Home Improvements*, op. cit., pp. 33–4.

181 A. Russell Localio, 'Michigan Motor Vehicle Service and Repair Act of
1974', (1975) 8 *U. Mich. J. L. Ref.* 402, 409–10.

182 Similarly in California and New York. Ibid., pp. 411, 415–16. See also
Vic.: Consumer Affairs Act 1972, s. 61C.

CHAPTER 5

1 The developing area of negligent misstatement might be invoked in this
regard: *Shaddock (L) & Associates Pty Ltd* v. *Parramatta City Council* (1981)
36 A.L.R. 385. cf. *Lambert* v. *Lewis* [1982] A.C. 225, 263–4 (Court of
Appeal).

2 *Shanklin Pier Ltd* v. *Detel Products Ltd* [1951] 2 K.B. 854. cf. *Wells
(Merstham) Ltd* v. *Buckland Sand and Silica Co. Ltd* [1965], 2 Q.B. 170. In
Canada one decision held that the manufacturer in these circumstances
could be regarded as a seller within the Sale of Goods Act: *Traders Finance
Corp. Ltd* v. *Haley* (1966) 57 D.L.R. 2d 15; cf. *Johnson* v. *Relland Motors*
[1955] 2 D.L.R. 418. Incidentally there is little possibility of arguing that
the retailer is the agent of the manufacturer. *International Harvester
Company of Australia Pty Ltd* v. *Carrigan's Hazeldene Pastoral Co.* (1958) 100
C.L.R. 644.

3 [1893] 1 Q.B. 256.

4 Similarly *Wood* v. *Lectrik Ltd, The Times,* 13 January 1932 (£500
guarantee); *Goldthorpe* v. *Logan* [1943] 2 D.L.R. 519 (results guaranteed);

Murray v. *Sperry Rand Corp.* (1979) 23 O.R. (2d) 456.

5 For example, *Lambert* v. *Lewis* [1982] A.C. 225, 262–3 (Court of Appeal).

6 Gordon Borrie and Aubrey L. Diamond, *The Consumer Society and the Law*, 4th edn (Harmondsworth: Penguin, 1981), pp. 104–9.

7 *Baxter* v. *Ford Motor Co.* 12 P. 2d 409 (1932); *Greenman* v. *Yuba Power Products Inc.* 377 P. 2d 897 (1962).

8 Trade Practices Act 1974, s. 74G. The limitation 'in relation to the quality, performance or characteristics' of a product excludes, for example, a manufacturer's promises in relation to servicing.

9 The survey was conducted in Spring 1976 and Spring 1977 by a postal questionnaire.

10 The promotional function is prominent in the sale of new cars. In the survey of twenty-six manufacturers mentioned above, nearly all manufacturers referred to a feed-back system in which information regarding complaints was passed to the production (or relevant) stage. In some firms the collection of complaint data was formalized into monthly reports which were circulated throughout the company, even reaching in one case the desk of the chief executive. The role of guarantees is discussed in George L. Priest, 'A Theory of the Consumer Product Warranty', (1981) 90 *Yale L.J.* 1297.

11 See pp. 122–5 above.

12 *Exemption Clauses*, Law Comm., No. 69, 1975, p. 40ff.

13 See Douglas J. Cusine, 'Manufacturers' Guarantees and the Unfair Contract Terms Act', [1980], *Juridicial R.* 185.

14 'Guarantees, (1976) *Which?*, April p. 79.

15 *Adams* v. *Richardson & Starling Ltd* [1969] 1 W.L.R. 1645, 1648–9; [1969] 2 All E.R. 1221, 1224.

16 *Guarantees: A Guide for Manufacturers* (London: Office of Fair Trading, 1979).

17 Consumer Transactions (Restrictions on Statements) Order 1976, S.I. 1976 No. 1813, r. 5.

18 15 U.S.C. ss. 2301–12. Regulations under the Act are at 16 C.F.R. ss. 701 *et seq.* See Stephen W. Lee, 'The Magnuson-Moss Warranty Act: Consumer Information and Warranty Regulation', (1976) 51 *Indiana L.J.* 397.

19 For example, Consumer Affairs Act 1970–82 (Qld), ss. 36 A-G.

20 M. J. Trebilcock, 'Manufacturers' Guarantees', (1972) 18 *McGill L.J.* 1, 30.

21 cf. Michael J. Wisdom, 'An Empirical Study of the Magnuson-Moss Warranty Act', (1979) 31 *Stan L.R.* 1117, who found that although the Act increased the information available to consumers, there was little evidence that it had stimulated warranty competition or substantially affected the substance of written warranty policies.

22 cf. *Shanklin Pier Ltd* v. *Detel Products* [1951] 2 K.B. 854; *Carlill* v. *Carbolic Smoke Ball Co.* [1893] 1 Q.B. 256; *R.* v. *Small Claims Tribunal and Munro ex p. Escor Industries Pty Ltd (No. 2)* [1979] V.L.R. 635.

23 Kenneth Rees, 'Legal Effect of Manufacturers' Guarantees' (1960) 104 *Sol. J.* 879; *Benjamin's Sale of Goods*, 2nd edn, 1981, pp. 519–23. Before the Unfair Contract Terms Act 1977 there was a more definite benefit to manufacturers – they could avoid any liability for negligence.

24 Editorial, 'Car Buyers Warrant a New Deal', *Focus*, vol. 2, September 1967, p. 1. See also Saul Schwartz, 'The Manufacturer's Liability to the Purchaser of a "Lemon" ', (1979) 11 *Ottawa L.R.* 583, 584–90.

25 'Product Liability' (1975) *Which?*, January p. 5; 'Simple Justice', op. cit. p. 15.

26 'Liability for Defective Products', op. cit., p. 16.

27 *Molony Report*, p. 133.

28 Sale of Goods Act 1923 (New South Wales), s. 64(5) (inserted Commercial Transactions (Miscl). Provisions Act, 1974).

29 Civil Code, s. 1790, *et seq.*

30 s. 74D. See also Consumer Products Warranties Act (Saskatchewan), ss. 11, 13; Quebec Civil Code, art. 1522; *General Motors Products of Canada Ltd.* v. *Kravitz* (1979) 93 D.L.R. (3d) 481.

31 s. 74D (1). A greater incursion on horizontal privity would have been to allow borrowers and third parties to seek compensation.

32 s. 74F.

33 Lawrence M. Friedman and Jack Ladinsky, 'Social Change and the Law of Industrial Accidents' (1967) 67 *Col. L. Rev.* 50, 58. See Richard L. Abel, 'A Critique of American Tort Law', (1981) 8 *Brit. J. Law & Soc.* 199. cf. Gary T. Schwartz, 'Tort Law and the Economy in Nineteenth-Century America: A Reinterpretation', (1981) 90 *Yale L.J.* 1717.

34 Robert L. Rabin, 'Some Thoughts on Tort Law from a Socio-Political Perspective' [1969] *Wisc. L.R.* 51, 58.

35 217 N.Y. 382, 111 N.E. 1050 (1916).

36 [1932] A.C. 562. See C. J. Miller and P. A. Lovell, *Product Liability* (London: Butterworths, 1977); C. J. Miller, *Product Liability and Safety Encyclopaedia* (London: Butterworths, looseleaf); S. M. Waddams, *Products Liability*, 2nd edn (Toronto: Carswell, 1980).

37 [1932] A.C. 562, 599.

38 *Goodchild* v. *Vaclight, The Times*, 22 May 1965; [1965] C.L.Y. 2669; cf. *Hindustan S.S. Co.* v. *Siemens* [1955] 1 Lloyds L.R. 167, 177; *Wyngrove's Executrix* v. *Scottish Omnibuses Ltd* [1966] S.C. (H.L.) 47; *Hill* v. *Crowe (James) Cases Ltd* [1978] 1 All E.R. 812; *Lambert* v. *Lewis* [1978] 1 Lloyd's Rep. 610; [1979] R.T.R. 61 (on appeal [1982] A.C. 225).

39 *Devilez* v. *Boots Pure Drug Co. Ltd* (1962) 106 *Sol. J.* 552; *Clarke* v. *Army & Navy Coop. Society* [1903] 1 K.B. 155; *Fisher* v. *Harrods Ltd* [1966] 1 Lloyd's

Rep. 500; *O'Dwyer* v. *Leo Buring Pty Ltd* [1966] W.A.R. 67.

40 *Wright* v. *Dunlop Rubber Co.* (1972) 13 K.I.R. 255; *Walton* v. *British Leyland (UK) Ltd* (1978) [1980] *Product Liability International*, 156. See Bernard W. Bell, 'The Manufacturer's Duty to Notify of Subsequent Safety Improvements', (1981) 33 *Stan. L.R.* 1087.

41 [1936] A.C. 85.

42 [1936] A.C. 85, 94–5.

43 [1936] A.C. 85, 101. See also *Mayne* v. *Silvermere Cleaners* [1939] 1 All E.R. 693. Other strong *res ipsa* cases are *Chaproniere* v. *Mason* (1905) 21 T.L.R. 633; *Shandloff* v. *City Dairy* [1936] 4 D.L.R. 712; *Martin* v. *Thorn Lighting Industries Pty Ltd* [1978] W.A.R. 10.

44 [1943] S.C. (H.L.) 1. The case implicitly overrules the appallingly bad decision in *Daniels and Daniels* v. *White and Sons Ltd* [1938] 4 All E.R. 258. McKenna J. refused to follow the latter decision in *Hill* v. *J. Crowe (Cases) Ltd, supra.*

45 *Taylor* v. *Rover Co Ltd* [1966] 1 W.L.R. 1491; [1966] 2 All E.R. 181, 186; cf. liability in the U.S.: *Ford Motor Co.* v. *Mathis* 322 F. 2d. 267 (1963).

46 *Godfrey's Ltd* v. *Ryles* [1962] S.A.S.R. 33.

47 For example, *Phillips* v. *E. W. Lundberg & Son* (1968) 88 W.N. (N.S.W.) 166.

48 [1936] 1 All E.R. 283. See also *Smith* v. *Inglis Co.* (1978) 83 D.L.R. (3d) 215.

49 cf. *Vacwell Engineering Co. Ltd* v. *B.D.H. Chemicals Ltd* [1971] 1 Q.B. 88; *Anns* v. *Merton London Borough Council* [1978] A.C. 728.

50 *Anns* v. *Merton London Borough Council* [1978] A.C. 728, 759. See Peter F. Cane, 'Physical Loss, Economic Loss and Products Liability', (1979) 95 *L.Q.R.* 117, 123–4, 126, 134.

51 *Junior Books Ltd* v. *Veitchi Ltd* [1982] 3 W.L.R. 477; [1982] 3 All E.R. 201. See also *Caltex Oil (Australia) Pty Ltd* v. *The Dredge 'Willemstad'* (1976) 136 C.L.R. 529. A simple example of pure economic loss would be where parents buy a typewriter for their child and explain that it is needed for copy typing at home. The typewriter has a defect and the child is unable to earn money as a copy typist. The lost wages are pure economic loss. Law Commission, *Liability for Defective Products*, Working Paper No. 64, 1975, p. 10.

52 Ibid.

53 *Junior Books Ltd* v. *Veitchi Co. Ltd* [1982] 3 W.L.R. 477, 483, 486, 500; [1982] 3 All E.R. 201, 204, 207, 218.

54 *Lang* v. *General Motors Corp.* 136 N.W. 2d 805 (1965); cf. *Inglis* v. *American Motors Corp.* 209 N.E. 2d 583 (1965).

55 [1951] 2 All E.R. 431. See also *Hales* v. *Kerr* [1908] 2 K.B. 601; *Lambert* v. *Lewis* [1978] 1 Lloyd's Rep. 610, 615–17; [1979] R.T.R. 61, 71–4 (on appeal at [1982] A.C. 225).

56 For example, *Daley* v. *Gypsy Caravans* [1966] 2 N.S.W.R. 22 (negligently manufactured caravan with electrical fault; plaintiff deemed to assume risk as qualified electrician).

57 'The Vulnerable Citizen and the Unlearned Lessons', *Sunday Times*, 27 June 1976, p. 15. See Harvey Teff and Colin Munro, *Thalidomide – The Legal Aftermath* (Saxon House, 1976); 'Insight Team' of the *Sunday Times*, *Suffer the Children* (London: Futura, 1979).

58 Law Commission, *Injuries to Unborn Children*, Report No. 60, 1974, pp. 2–3. See now Congenital Disabilities (Civil Liability) Act 1976 and *Williams* v. *Luff* (1978), 122 Sol. J. 164.

59 Harvey Teff, 'Products Liability in the Pharmaceutical Industry at Common Law' (1973) 20 *McGill L.J.* 102, 120. Similar difficulties existed in other countries. In West Germany criminal proceedings were instituted against company officials but were eventually abandoned in view of a favourable settlement for the children. Henning Sjöström and Robert Nilsson, *Thalidomide and the Power of the Drug Companies* (Harmondsworth: Penguin, 1972), pp. 258ff.

60 Ibid., chs. 3–5; 'Thalidomide: The Story They Suppressed', *Sunday Times*, 27 June 1976, pp. 14–19.

61 cf. *Distillers Co. (Biochemicals) Ltd* v. *Thompson* [1971] A.C. 458, 465–6, 469.

62 *S.* v. *Distillers Co. (Biochemicals) Ltd* [1969] 3 All E.R. 1412; [1970] 1 W.L.R. 114.

63 *In Re Taylor's Application* [1972] 2 Q.B. 369. A constraint on Distillers was their insurance. John A. Franks, 'The Thalidomide Claim: Laws, Fantasy and Reform', (1973) 117 *Sol. J.* 643.

64 *Allen* v. *Distillers Co. (Biochemicals) Ltd*, *The Times*, 3 July 1973. See also *Allen* v. *Distillers Co. (Biochemicals) Ltd* [1974] Q.B. 384.

65 cf. Thomas C. Bartsh *et al.*, *A Class-Action Suit That Worked* (Lexington, Mass.: Lexington, 1978) (antibiotic anti-trust litigation).

66 Now Limitation Act 1980, ss. 11, 14.

67 *Attorney-General* v. *Times Newspapers Ltd* [1974] A.C. 273. Criticised in 1st edition at pp. 155–6. cf. *Schering Chemicals Ltd* v. *Falkman Ltd* [1982] Q.B. 1.

68 *Sunday Times* v. *United Kingdom* (1979) 2 E.H.R.R. 245.

69 Hugh Hebert, 'The Forgotten Drug Disaster', *Guardian*, 3 March 1981, p. 8. The litigation over Primodos was discontinued over the issue of causation: see *Hyman and Williams* v. *Schering Chemicals*, *The Times*, 10 June 1980; [1983] 1 W.L.R. 143; *Guardian*, 3 July 1982, p. 22.

70 *Royal Commission on Civil Liability and Compensation for Personal Injury*, Cmnd. 7054, 1978, pp. 256–7 (the Pearson Commission). The average amount paid is half the average for tort compensation as a whole.

71 But manufacturers may have a defence under the Acts if they have taken

reasonable steps and exercised due diligence, e.g. Consumer Safety
Act 1978, s. 2(6).

72 See Richard A. Epstein, *Modern Products Liability Law* (Westport, Conn.:
Quorum, 1980); Friedrich Kessler, 'Products Liability', (1967) 76 *Yale
L.J.* 887; Marshall S. Shapo, 'A Representational Theory of Consumer
Protection', (1974) 60 *Vir. L. Rev.* 1109.

73 161 A. 2d 69 (1960).

74 377 P. 2d 897 (1963).

75 *Cronin* v. *J. B. E. Olson Corp.*, 501 P. 2d 1153 (1972).

76 *Fields* v. *Volkswagen of America, Inc.*, 555 P. 2d 48 (1976).

77 391 P. 2d 168 (1964).

78 For example, *Sindell* v. *Abbott Laboratories* 607 P. 2d 924 (1980); *Ferrigno* v.
Eli Lilly & Company, 420 A. 2d 1305 (1980). But this may apply in only
very special circumstances.

79 Gary T. Schwartz, 'Foreword: Understanding Products Liability'
(1979) 6 *Calif. L. Rev* 435.

80 Proposal for a Council Directive . . . Concerning Liability for Defective
Products, Submitted by the Commission to the Council, 1 October 1979;
European Convention on Products Liability in Regard to Personal
Injury and Death, European Treaty Series No. 91, 1977; Law Commis-
sion, *Liability for Defective Products* Law Com. No. 82, 1977; *Royal
Commission on Civil Liability and Compensation for Personal Injury*, Cmnd
7054, 1978, pp. 262–74. The draft directive and the Convention are
conveniently located in Miller, op. cit.

81 *Liability for Defective Products*, op. cit., pp. 6–7; 11–12. See also Serge
Galitsky, 'Manufacturers' Liability: An Examination of the Policy and
Social Cost of a New Regime' (1979) 3 *U.N.S.W. L.J.* 145; Richard
Thomas, 'The Consumer Interest in a Strong Products Liability
System', (1982) 1 *Home Economist* 106.

82 See Guido Calabresi and Kenneth C. Bass, 'Right Approach, Wrong
Implications: A Critique of McKean on Products Liability', (1970) 38
U. Chi. L. Rev. 74. Besides, insurance is not available for consumers for
all product-related risks.

83 Ontario Law Reform Commission, *Report on Products Liability* (Toronto:
Ministry of the Attorney-General, 1979), p. 73. cf. James L. Croyle, 'An
Impact Analysis of Judge-Made Products Liability Policies', (1979) 13
Law & Soc. Rev. 949.

84 *Liability for Defective Products*, op. cit., pp. 14–15.

85 EEC, art. 4; Council of Europe, art. 2; Law Commission, p. 17.
Development risks (i.e. defects not knowable in the light of the scientific
knowledge at the time of development) are covered, although the EEC
Draft and the Council of Europe Convention provide that liability is
extinguished ten years after the article is put in circulation. The Pearson
recommendations are discussed in P. S. Atiyah, *Accidents, Compensation*

and the Law, 3rd edn (London: Weidenfeld & Nicolson, 1980), pp. 170–1.

86 EEC Accompanying Memorandum, p. 16; Law Commission, p. 17. The proposed limitation would be in keeping with common law principle: *Levi* v. *Colgate-Palmolive Pty Ltd* (1941) 41 S.R. (N.S.W.) 48.

87 EEC, arts. 1–2; Council of Europe, arts 2–3; Law Commission, pp. 23, 29–30. Producers include importers, component makers and suppliers when they fail to inform the consumer of the identity of the producer.

88 EEC, art. 6, Council of Europe, art. 3(1); Law Commission, p. 33. The EEC Draft and the Council of Europe Treaty allow for non-pecuniary losses (e.g. pain and suffering). The EEC Draft extends to property losses (art. 6), but the Law Commission thinks that this is unnecessarily costly and that consumers should take out their own insurance (e.g. on their homes).

89 Art. 7. The Annex to the Convention allows states to impose limits subject to certain minimum provisions.

90 EEC, art. 5; Council of Europe, art. 4; Law Commission, pp. 31–3.

91 cf. *Green* v. *American Tobacco Co.*, 409 F. 2d 1166 (1969), cert. denied 397 U.S. 911 (1970).

CHAPTER 6

1 The shops survey was carried out by Jane Stapleton and the cars survey by Leonard Goodrich and Karen Booth.

2 The Unfair Contract Terms Act 1977, s. 6(1)(a) makes the condition non-excludable.

3 s. 12(3)–(4).

4 [1923] 2 K.B. 500. Counsel for the seller unsuccessfully argued that being unable to put the seller in *statu quo*, the consumer could only receive damages. See also *Warman* v. *Southern Counties Car Finance Corporation Ltd* [1949] 2 K.B. 576; *Butterworth* v. *Kingsway Motors Ltd* [1954] 1 W.L.R. 1286; [1954] 2 All E.R. 694; *Patten* v. *Thomas Motors Pty Ltd* [1965] N.S.W.R. 1457.

5 s. 21(1).

6 For example, *J. Sargent (Garages) Ltd* v. *Motor Auctions (West Bromwich) Ltd* [1977] R.T.R. 121.

7 *Central Newbury Car Auctions Ltd* v. *Unity Finance Ltd* [1957] 1 Q.B. 371, Denning L. J. dissenting.

8 4 Geo. IV, c. 83. The doctrine of ostensible agency did not cover all transactions by mercantile agents; e.g. pledging.

9 *Staffs Motor Guarantee Ltd* v. *British Wagon Co. Ltd* [1934] 2 K.B. 305; *Beverley Acceptances Ltd* v. *Oakley* [1982] R.T.R. 417.

10 *Newtons of Wembley Ltd* v. *Williams* [1965] 1 Q.B. 560. See also *Magnussen* v. *Flanagan* [1981] 2 N.S.W.L.R. 926 (non-compliance with consumer

protection provisions did not prevent transaction from being within ordinary course of business).

11 *Pearson* v. *Rose and Young Ltd* [1951] 1 K.B. 275; *Stadium Finance Ltd* v. *Robbins* [1962] 2 Q.B. 664.

12 *Heap* v. *Motorists' Advisory Agency Ltd* [1923] 1 K.B. 577. cf. *Robinson Motors Pty Ltd* v. *Fowler* [1982] Qd.R. 374.

13 *Central Newbury Car Auctions Ltd* v. *Unity Finance Ltd* [1957] 1 Q.B. 371, 398; *Beverley Acceptances Ltd* v. *Oakley* [1982] R.T.R. 417, 432–3.

14 *Bishopsgate Motor Finance Corporation Ltd* v. *Transport Brakes Ltd* [1949] 1 K.B. 322. The rule does not apply in Scotland (Sale of Goods Act 1979, s. 22(2) or Wales (Laws in Wales 1542, s. 47), but applies in Australia: *Ward* v. *Stevens* (1886) 12 V.L.R. 378.

15 *Crane* v. *London Dock Co.* (1866) 122 E.R. 847, 849–50.

16 Sale of Goods Act 1979, s. 22.

17 *Clayton* v. *Le Roy* [1911] 2 K.B. 1031, 1047.

18 *Reid* v. *Metropolitan Police Commissioner* [1973] 1 Q.B. 551.

19 s. 24. See *Worcester Works Finance Ltd* v. *Cooden Engineering Co. Ltd* [1972] 1 Q.B. 210. c.f. *Ford Credit Australia Ltd* v. *Auto Trade Auction Pty Ltd* [1982] V.R. 795.

20 s. 25(1).

21 Sale of Goods Act 1893, s. 25(2); *Helby* v. *Matthews* [1895] A.C. 471.

22 Not trade or finance purchasers: *Stevenson* v. *Beverley Bentinck Ltd* [1976] 1 W.L.R. 483; [1976] 2 All E.R. 606. cf. *Gurr and Ainsworth* v. *Esanda Ltd* (1981) 28 S.A.S.R. 297.

23 *Barker* v. *Bell* [1971] 1 W.L.R. 983; [1971] 2 All E.R. 867. See Consumer Credit Act 1974, Schedule 4, para. 22.

24 *Report of the Committee on Consumer Credit*, Cmnd 4596, 1971, vol. 1, p. 213 (hereafter Crowther Committee).

25 s. 23. See *Lewis* v. *Averay* [1972] 1 Q.B. 198.

26 *Twelfth Report (Transfer of Title to Chattels)*, Cmnd 2958, 1966.

27 But traders cannot assume that there is no hire purchase agreement by consulting these services: *Moorgate Mercantile Co. Ltd* v. *Twitchings* [1977] A.C. 890.

28 See Crowther Committee, p. 210.

29 s. 36. There have been difficulties with the system of registration established under Ontario's Personal Property Security Act: Ontario Law Reform Commission, *Report on Sale of Goods*, op. cit., pp. 301–2.

30 [1961] Q.B. 31.

31 Disputes sometimes arise under Police (Property) Act 1897, s. 1(1); Theft Act 1968, s. 28. There are no national figures. The information in this paragraph is derived from an unpublished paper by Inspector Rollins.

32 cf. U.C.C. 2–509.

33 s. 17. The section refers to specific or ascertained goods. By s. 16 no property can pass with unascertained goods until they are ascertained.

34 s. 20 (2), (3). See *Allied Mills Ltd* v. *Gwydir Valley Oilseeds Pty Ltd* [1978] 2 N.S.W.L.R. 26; N. E. Palmer, *Bailment* (Sydney: Law Book, 1979), pp. 282–3.

35 *R. V. Ward Ltd* v. *Bignall* [1967] 1 Q.B. 534, 541, 545. It seems that in the case of an agreement to sell a house with furniture (non-fixtures), property in the furniture does not pass until the conveyance of the interest in land takes effect. *Warren* v. *Forbes* [1959] V.R. 14.

36 *Lambert* v. *G. & C. Finance Corporation Ltd* (1963) 107 Sol. J. 666 Auctions are an exception: property prima facie passes when the hammer falls (see s. 57(2)), although the consumer subsequently signs a form providing that property does not pass until the cheque is met: *Dennant* v. *Skinner and Collom* [1948] 2 K.B. 164.

37 A product is in a deliverable state if it is in a state that the consumer would be bound to take delivery of it under the contract: Sale of Goods Act 1979, s. 61(5).

38 (1920) 53 D.L.R. 228.

39 s. 5(1). Unascertained goods are not defined in the Act.

40 Unreported, *Sunday Times*, 16 November 1975, p. 53. Subsequent to the judgment the receiver for National Westminster agreed to relinquish all claims to the wine.

41 [1970] 1 Lloyd's L.R. 140.

42 At p. 144.

43 *Benjamin's Sale of Goods*, 2nd edn, §. 362.

44 s. 18, r. 5(2).

45 There are difficulties for the consumer if the undertaking to deliver to the consumer's residence is not supported by consideration. Consideration may be the entering of the main contract. Assistance may also be afforded by the rule that property cannot pass until a product is ascertained. Thus if a carrier is to deliver ten washing machines in a day, all of the same brand, and none is singled out as going to a particular consumer, property and risk remain with the retailer until each is unloaded at the consumer's residence. cf. *Healey* v. *Howlett and Sons* [1917] 1 K.B. 337.

46 cf. *Badische Anilin und Soda Fabrik* v. *Basle Chemical Works, Bindschedler* [1898] A.C. 200.

47 s. 18, r. 4.

48 *R* v. *Justelius* [1973] 1 N.S.W.L.R. 471. cf. *Marsh* v. *Hughes-Hallet* [1900] 16 T.L.R. 376; *Poole* v. *Smith's Car Sales (Balham) Ltd* [1962] 1 W.L.R. 744; [1962] 2 All E.R. 482.

49 *Chalmers' Sale of Goods*, 18th edn, p. 150.

50 *Howard* v. *Harris* [1884] 1 Cab. & El. 253; 3 *Eng. & Emp. Dig.* § 2845.

51 Unsolicited Goods and Services Acts 1971 and 1975.

52 Grant Gilmour, 'Products Liability: A Commentary', (1970) 38 *U. Chi. L. Rev.* 103, 112–14.

53 U.C.C. § 2–509.

54 See Ontario Law Reform Commission, *Report on Sale of Goods* (Toronto: Ministry of the Attorney General, 1979), pp. 265–75.

55 In fact instances were rare, but the following are examples of what was recounted. One car trader recalled a recent case of a car being stolen; he had a vague idea, never confirmed by the appropriate documentation, that it was going to a particular consumer. A carpet retailer told of a current prosecution where two fitters had stolen carpet allocated to a particular consumer and a national store recalled an instance where a carpet was damaged when a fitter spilt oil onto it while laying it. I am grateful to the firms and to Professor H. A. L. Cockerell of the City University for their assistance.

56 s. 29(1).

57 *Galbraith and Grant Ltd* v. *Block* [1922] 2 K.B. 155. cf. *E. & D. Thomas* v. *H. S. Alper & Sons* [1953] C.L.Y.§ 3277.

58 s. 32(1)–(2).

59 s. 31(1). cf. *Howell* v. *Evans* (1926) 134 L.T. 570.

60 *Honck* v. *Muller* (1881) 7 Q.B.D. 92, 99.

61 s. 28.

62 s. 41(1).

63 s. 51(2). *Hinde* v. *Liddell* (1875) L.R. 10 Q.B. 265.

64 s. 52. See *Phillips* v. *Lamdin* [1949] 2 K.B. 33 (ornamental door designed by Adam). cf. *Cohen* v. *Roche* [1927] 1 K.B. 169 ('ordinary Hepplewhite furniture'). *H. Jones & Co. Pty Ltd* v. *Talbot* (1948) 22 A.L.J. 381.

65 *Jackson* v. *Chrysler Acceptances Ltd* [1978] R.T.R. 474.

66 s. 10(1).

67 s. 10(2).

68 *Bunge Corp* v. *Tradax SA* [1981] 1 W.L.R. 711; [1981] 2 All E.R. 513; *Amco Enterprises Pty Ltd* v. *Wade* [1968] Qd.R. 445.

69 *McDougall* v. *Aeromarine of Emsworth Ltd* [1958] 1 W.L.R. 1126; [1958] 3 All E.R. 431; *Charles Rickards Ltd* v. *Oppenheim* [1950] 1 K.B. 616.

70 *Barnett* v. *Ira L. & A. C. Berk Pty Ltd* (1952) 52 S.R. (N.S.W.) 268.

71 cf. s. 29(3). *Charnock* v. *Liverpool Corporation* [1968] 1 W.L.R. 1498; [1968] 3 All E.R. 473; *Allen* v. *Danforth Motors Ltd* (1957) 12 D.L.R. (2d) 572.

72 s. 48(3); *R. V. Ward Ltd* v. *Bignall* [1967] 1 Q.B. 534.

73 See Jan Hellner, 'Consequential Loss and Exemption Clauses', (1981) 1 *Oxford J. L. Studies* 13, 30.

74 See *White Trucks Pty Ltd* v. *Riley* (1949) 66 W.N. (N.S.W.) 101; *Commission Car Sales (Hastings) Ltd* v. *Saul* [1957] N.Z.L.R. 144.

75 *Stockloser* v. *Johnson* [1954] 1 Q.B. 476; *Dies* v. *British and International*

Mining and Finance Co. Ltd [1939] 1 K.B. 724.

76 *Galbraith* v. *Mitchenall Estates Ltd* [1965] 2 Q.B. 473. See J. Beatson, 'Discharge for Breach: The Position of Instalments, Deposits and Other Payments Due Before Completion', (1981) 97 *L.Q.R.* 389. cf. Lay-by Sales Act (N.S.W.) 1943, s. 10.

77 *R. V. Ward Ltd* v. *Bignall (supra)*.

78 Thus a private seller cannot claim for loss of profit for he cannot sell an item twice over.

79 s. 50(2).

80 [1957] 2 Q.B. 117.

81 [1955] Ch. 177.

82 *Lazenby Garages Ltd* v. *Wright* [1976] 1 W.L.R. 459; [1976] 2 All E.R. 770.

CHAPTER 7

1   Mortgage credit for the purchase of houses is not dealt with in this book.

2   John Kenneth Galbraith, *The Affluent Society* (Harmondsworth: Penguin, 1970), p. 167.

3   There is an excellent historical study of consumer credit in *Report of the Committee on Consumer Credit*, Cmnd 4596, 1971, vol. 1, ch. 2 [hereafter called Crowther Committee].

4   *Automobile & General Finance Corporation Ltd* v. *Morris, The Times*, 19 June 1929, *per* Acton. J.; (1929) 73 S.J. 451, quoted in E. Campbell-Salmon, *Hire Purchase and Credit Sales* (London: Pitman, 1962), pp. 10–11.

5   I am grateful to Professor Goode for supplying me with a copy of this Table from *Credit*.

6   See, generally, Neil Runcie, *The Economics of Instalment Credit* (Univ. of London Press, 1969); Galbraith, op. cit., Ch. 13.

7   *Lee* v. *Butler* [1893] 2 Q.B. 318.

8   [1895] A.C. 471.

9   For example, *Bridge* v. *Campbell Discount Co. Ltd* [1962] A.C. 600.

10 J. J. McManus, 'The Consumer Credit Act', (1975) 2 *Brit. J. of Law & Soc.* 66, 68.

11 See also R. M. Goode, 'Introductory Survey' in R. M. Goode (ed.), *Consumer Credit* (Leyden: Sijthoff, 1978), p. 19.

12 In practice a finance house will provide credit in a variety of ways.

13 s. 75.

14 *Contra United Dominions Trust* v. *Thomas* [1976] C.L.Y. 1618.

15 See Monopolies and Mergers Commission, *Trading Check Franchise and Financial Services*, H.C. 62, 1981.

16 ss. 16(5)(a), 25, 75. See A. P. Dobson, 'Credit Cards', [1979] *J. Bus. L.* 331, 333. cf. M. G. Bridge, 'Aspects of the Law Relating to Credit Cards

Note to pages 183–187 449

in the United Kingdom and the United States', (1977) 28 *N. Ire. L.Q.* 382.

17 15 U.S.C. §. 1666f(a)(1).

18 Monopolies and Mergers Commission, *Credit Card Franchise Services,* Cmnd 8034, 1980.

20 s. 51. See *Elliot* v. *Director General of Fair Trading* [1980] 1 W.L.R. 977; [1980] I.C.R. 629.

21 s. 84 Oral notification must be followed by written confirmation. s. 84(5). On fraudulent use by the consumer see *R.* v. *Lambie* [1982] A.C. 449.

22 'Credit Cards: Distributing Fraud Loss', (1968) 77 *Yale L. J.* 1418.

23 Crowther Committee, pp. 152–3.

24 Ibid., pp. 184 ff.

25 Ibid., p. 183.

26 *Reform of the Law on Consumer Credit* (1973), Cmnd. 5427 (herafter White Paper).

27 George H. Tipping, 'Reform of the Law on Consumer Credit', *Credit,* vol. 14, 1973, p. 83. See, generally, J. J. McManus, 'The Emergence and Non-Emergence of Legislation', (1978) 5 *British J. Law & Soc.* 185.

28 'The Consumer Credit Act 1974: Its Scope', (1977) 40 *Mod. L. Rev.* 159, 173.

29 See R. M. Goode, *Consumer Credit Legislation* (London: Butterworths, looseleaf); A. G. Guest and M. G. Lloyd, *Encyclopedia of Consumer Credit Law* (London: Sweet & Maxwell, looseleaf); A. L. Diamond, *Commercial and Consumer Credit – An Introduction* (London: Butterworths, 1982).

30 ss. 8(1)–(2). Thus, credit for unincorporated traders may be covered.

31 s. 9(1).

32 ss. 9(4), 10(2), (3)(b)(iii); Consumer Credit (Total Charge for Credit) Regulations 1980, S.I. 1980 No. 51. The ancillary charges are those payable under the transaction but do not include (a) default charges, (b) charges payable even if the transaction were for cash, (c) charges for incidental services or benefits, (d) certain maintenance charges, (e) charges for operating current accounts, (f) certain insurance premiums: r. 5.

33 s. 9(3).

34 s. 15(1). See Norman Palmer and David Yates, 'The Application of the Consumer Credit Act 1974 to Consumer Hire Agreements', (1979) 38 *Cambridge L.J.* 180.

35 s. 12.

36 s. 13.

37 s. 16. Consumer Credit (Exempt Agreements) Order 1980, S.I. 52 as amended. The minimum lending rate has been abolished. See Goode, op. cit., §. l–322.

38 ss. 17, 189.

39 Sex Discrimination Act 1975, s. 29; Race Relations Act 1976, s. 20.

40 [1981] I.C.R. 328.

41 Consumer Credit Act 1974, s. 25(2)(c).

42 Anne Geary, 'Equal Credit Opportunity', (1976) 31 *Bus. L.* 1641; Judy Gray, 'Credit for Women in California', (1975) 22 *UCLA L. Rev* 873; Ralph J. Rohner, 'Equal Credit Opportunity Act', (1979) 34 *Bus. L.* 1423; 'Protection of Unmarried Couples Against Discrimination in Lending Under the Equal Credit Opportunity Act', (1979), 93 *Harv. L.R.* 430.

43 See the examples in National Consumer Council, *Consumers and Credit* (London: National Consumer Council, 1980), pp. 90, 274–6; *Sunday Times*, 31 January 1982, p. 2; Paul Rock, *Making People Pay* (London: Routledge & Kegan Paul, 1973), p. 33.

44 15 U.S.C. s. 1691(a)(2).

45 15 U.S.C. s. 1691(b)(2).

46 See Brian Bell, 'Giving Credit', *Observer*, 15 May 1977, p. 21.

47 County Courts Act 1959, s. 101. At one time its abolition was suggested on economic grounds and because it can result in an invasion of privacy. Just because an original court hearing might be public does not require that the matter should continue to be public indefinitely. Creditors say that its abolition would make credit more costly because other methods would have to be employed to check creditworthiness. These may also constitute a greater invasion of privacy.

48 *Report of the Committee on Privacy*, Cmnd 5012, 1972, p. 49 (Younger Committee).

49 Ibid., p. 78.

50 Ibid., p. 74.

51 Ibid., p. 81.

52 ss. 158–160. cf. Fair Credit Reporting Act (U.S.), 15 U.S.C. §. 1681g, whereby the consumer can also obtain the sources of information and to whom it has been supplied within a certain period.

53 s. 157. See also Consumer Credit (Conduct of Business) (Credit References) Regulations 1977, S.I. 1977 No. 330; Consumer Credit (Credit Reference Agency) Regulations 1977, S.I. 1977 No. 329.

54 See, generally, R. G. Lawson, 'Credit Reference Agencies and the Consumer Credit Act', (1977), 127 *New L. J.* 57; 'California Consumer Reporting Agencies Act: A Proposed Improvement on the Fair Credit Reporting Act', (1975) 26 *Hastings L. J.* 1219.

55 Fair Credit Reports Act 1974–5 (S.A.), s. 6(2)–(3).

56 See Younger Committee, Appendix I; Law Commission, *Breach of Confidence*, Law Comm. No. 110, 1981.

57 See generally Law Reform Commission (Australia), *Privacy and Personal*

Information, Discussion Paper No. 14, 1980.

58 Consumer Credit Act 1974, s. 62(1).

59 s. 63(2).

60 ss. 63(1), 64(1)(b).

61 s. 65. cf. *Eastern Distributors Ltd* v. *Goldring* [1957] 2 Q.B. 600, 612–13.

62 See s. 127; *V. L. Skuce & Co* v. *Cooper* [1975] 1 W.L.R. 593; [1975] 1 All E.R. 612.

63 s. 67. Regulated agreements secured on land are handled differently, s. 58.

64 s. 64. With credit-token agreements the rules are laxer.

65 Crowther Committee, p. 289. See Robert Cuming, 'Consumer Protection – The Itinerant Seller', (1967) 32 *Sask. L. Rev.* 113, 125.

66 s. 68.

67 s. 69.

68 s. 70. For 'linked transactions', s. 19.

69 ss. 69(2)–(3); 72. The provision regarding perishables has the underlying policy intention of not inhibiting consumers from exercising the right to cancel, for example in relation to a freezer where food was also supplied, where if they cancelled they might still have to pay for the perishables: Goode, op. cit., §. 632.

70 s. 73.

71 ss. 60, 74.

72 s. 60. *White Paper*, Appendix 2.

73 *Crowther Committee*, p. 267.

74 *Fair Dealing with Consumers* (Adelaide: Govt Printer, 1975), p. 36.

75 See Jeffrey Davis, 'Protecting Consumers from Overdisclosure and Gobbledygook: An Empirical Look at the Simplification of Consumer Credit Contracts', (1977) 63 *Virg. L.R.* 841.

76 Consumer Credit Act 1974, s. 55.

77 411 U.S. 356 (1973).

78 Consumer Credit Act. ss. 61(1)(a), s. 65.

79 s. 127(1).

80 s. 127(3).

81 *Crowther Committee*, p. 140.

82 Ibid., p. 145.

83 Ibid., p. 150.

84 Unfair Trade Practices Act (Alberta); R.S.A. 1980, s. 4(1)(a).

85 For example, *Report on the Law Relating to Consumer Credit and Moneylending* (Adelaide: Govt Printer, 1969), p. 43. As the Molomby Committee (Committee of the Law Council of Australia, *Report on Fair Consumer Credit Laws* (Melbourne: 1972), para. 8.3.4.) concluded, 'It is socially and commercially wrong for a supplier to receive a commission without the knowledge of the consumer.' cf. *Crowther Committee*, p. 319.

86 R. Else-Mitchell and R. W. Parsons, *Hire-Purchase Law*, 4th edn (Sydney: Law Book, 1968), pp. 203–4.

87 F. R. Oliver and Neil Runcie, 'The Economic Regulation of Instalment Credit in the United Kingdom', Aubrey L. Diamond (ed.), *Instalment Credit* (London: Stevens, 1970).

88 cf. *Galbraith* v. *Mitchenall Estates* [1965] 2 Q.B. 473.

89 *Hawkins Pleas of the Crown*, Book 1, ch. 82. Much of the material in this paragraph is derived from Hugh H. L. Bellot, *The Legal Principles and Practice of Bargains with Moneylenders* (London: Stevens & Haynes, 1906), chs 1–3. See also P. S. Atiyah, *The Rise and Fall of Freedom of Contract* (Oxford: Clarendon, 1979), pp. 66–7, 550–2, 711.

90 Bellot, op. cit., p. 48.

91 National Consumer Council, *Consumers and Credit*, op. cit., pp. 47–9.

92 Ibid., pp. 59–60.

93 ss. 137–40.

94 Hire Purchase Act 1960, s. 26; repealed Commercial Transactions (Miscl. Provisions) Act 1974.

95 Criminal Code, §. 305.1. For the previous law, see Jacob S. Ziegel, (1981) 59 *Can. Bar Rev.* 188.

96 U.C.C.C. §§. 2–201, 3–508. See William D. Warren, 'Consumer Credit Law: Rates, Costs and Benefits', (1975) 27 *Stan. L. Rev.* 951; Robert W. Johnson, 'Regulation of Finance Charges on Consumer Instalment Credit', (1967) 66 *Mich. L. R.* 81.

97 David Cayne and M. J. Trebilcock, 'Market Considerations in the Formation of Consumer Protection Policy', (1973) 23 *U. of Toronto. L. J.* 396, 411–18.

98 National Consumer Council, op. cit., pp. 125–6.

99 Ralph Harris *et al.*, *Hire Purchase in a Free Society*, 3rd edn (London: Institute of Econ. Affairs, 1961), pp. 130–1.

100 s. 10(1); then Hire Purchase Act 1965, s. 16(1).

101 Crowther Report, pp. 279–83.

102 On the meaning of 'like claim': Goode, op. cit., I – §. 680–1; *United Dominions Trust* v. *Taylor* [1980] S.L.T. 28 (Sh. Ct.).

103 s. 75(3).

104 s. 75(4).

105 Provided the Act otherwise applies.

106 Sale of Goods Act 1979, ss. 12–14; Supply of Goods and Services Act 1982, ss. 7–9.

107 ss. 8–10.

108 s. 10(3)(b).

109 *Andrews* v. *Hopkinson* [1957] 1 Q.B. 229.

110 cf. *Porter* v. *General Guarantee Corporation Ltd* [1982] R.T.R. 384, where s. 75 was invoked.

112 *United Dominions Trust Ltd* v. *Kirkwood* [1966] 2 Q.B. 431, 448–89.

113 Vern Countryman, 'The Holder in Due Course and other Anachronisms in Consumer Credit', (1973) 52 *Tex. L. Rev.* 1. See now F.T.C. Trade Regulation Rule, Preservation of Consumers' Claim and Defences, 16 C.F.R. §. 433.

114 ss. 124, 125.

115 s. 123(2). See also s. 125(2).

116 R. M. Goode, *Hire-Purchase Law and Practice,* 2nd edn (London: Butterworths, (1970), pp. 657–61. See also *Lloyds and Scottish Finance Ltd* v. *Prentice* (1977) 121 Sol. J. 847; *The Times,* 3 November 1977.

117 s. 189(1).

118 ss. 94–5. The provisions are also relevant where an asset is sold or traded in by way of part exchange.

119 James H. Hunt, 'The Rule of 78: Hidden Penalty for Prepayment in Consumer Credit Transactions', (1975) 55 *B.U.L.R.,* 331; cf. R. M. Goode, 'Introductory Survey', in R. M. Goode (ed.) *Consumer Credit* (Leyden: Sijhoff, 1978), pp. 73–5.

120 The discussion is concerned with default for non-payment; default may also occur through the bankruptcy or death of the consumer.

121 National Consumer Council, *Consumers and Credit* (London: National Consumer Council, 1980), p. 202.

122 Department of Trade and Industry, *Surveys Carried out for the Committee on Consumer Credit* (London: HMSO, 1971), (hereafter *NOP Survey*).

123 Paul Rock, *Making People Pay* (London: Routledge, 1973), p. 12.

124 pp. 36–7, 139, respectively.

125 p. 232.

126 Rock, op. cit., chs 2–3.

127 Ibid., ch. 1.

128 op. cit., p. 202. See also pp. 300–1.

129 *NOP Survey,* p. 22; David Caplovitz, *Consumers in Trouble* (New York: Free Press, 1974); Michael Trebilcock and Arthur Schulman, 'The Pathology of Credit Breakdown', (1976) 22 *McGill L. J.* 415.

130 For example, *NOP Survey,* p. 23.

131 Ibid., pp. 23–4.

132 Ibid., Tables 279–80. But there was not much difference when consumers were divided into income groups. Social classes AB are managerial, administrative and professional; C_1 is supervisory/clerical etc.; C_2 is skilled manual; D is semi- and unskilled manual; E are state pensioners, etc.

133 Caplovitz, op. cit., ch. 1.

134 Ibid., p. 270.

135 John Blamire and Arthur Izzard, *Debt Counselling* (Birmingham Settlement Money Advice Centre, 1975), p. 5. Check-trading avoids this

because of the close relationship of consumers and the check traders' representatives.

136 Rock's book is a brilliant study of this; op. cit., pp. 70–1, 82–4

137 *Report of the Committee on the Enforcement of Judgment Debts*, 1969, Cmnd 3909, p. 320–1 (hereafter Payne Committee). See also Law Reform Commission of British Columbia, *Report on Debtor-Creditor Relationships, Debt Collection and Collection Agencies*, Project No. 2, 1971, LRC, pp. 8–9; David St. L. Kelly, *Debt Recovery in Australia* (Canberra: AGPS, 1977), p. 25.

138 p. 321.

139 Rock, op. cit., pp. 53–4.

140 A useful review, containing English and United States references, is Bruce Kercher, 'Debt Collection Harassment in Australia', (1978) 5 *Monash U.L.R.* 87; (1979) 5 ibid., 204.

141 *Stubbs Ltd* v. *Russell* [1913] A.C. 386; *Stubbs* v. *Mazure* [1920] A.C. 66. There may also be an action for invasion of privacy in jurisdictions which recognize this as a cause of action: e.g. *Pack* v. *Wise* 155 So. 2d 909 (1963); *Housh* v. *Peth* 133 N.E. 2d 340 (1956).

142 s. 40(1), (3). The County Courts Act 1959, ss. 188–9 prohibits false representations of official documents.

143 See Law Reform Commission of British Columbia, op. cit., pp. 17–19. cf. Trade Practices Act 1974 (Aust.), s. 60.

144 ss. 145(1), (7), 147(1).

145 Gordon Borrie, 'Legal and Administrative Regulation in the United Kingdom of Competition and Consumer Policies', (1982) 5 *UNSW L.J.* 80, 89.

146 *NOP Survey*, p. 25.

147 Blamire and Izzard, op. cit., pp. 39–46.

148 'Debt Merchants', *Focus*, vol. 3, November 1968, p. 5.

149 ss. 145(1)(b), (c), (5), (6), 147(1).

150 [1967] 2 Q.B. 786. See also *Eastern Distributors Ltd* v. *Goldring* [1957] 2 Q.B. 600.

151 See the discussion on title in the previous chapter.

152 ss. 87–8. In proceedings for the possession of an item s. 134(1) must also be complied with.

153 s. 89.

154 s. 93.

155 R. M. Goode and Jacob S. Ziegel, *Hire Purchase and Conditional Sale* (London: British Institute of International & Comparative Law, 1965), p. 110.

156 *Wadham Stringer Finance Ltd* v. *Meaney* [1981] 1 W.L.R. 39; [1980] 3 All E.R. 789.

157 s. 76. See also ss. 86, 87.

158 *Walker* v. *Mason* (1957) 21 W.W.R. 374.

159 *United Dominions Trust* v. *Thomas* [1976] C.L.Y. 1618 (Lambeth Co. Ct). See also *Canadian Acceptance Corp. Ltd.* v. *Regent Park Butcher Shop Ltd* [1969] 3 D.L.R. (3d) 304.

160 ss. 137–40.

161 Crowther Committee, p. 287.

162 Ulf Bernitz, 'Consumer Protection' (1976), 20 *Scandinavian Studies in Law*, 13, 19.

163 For example, *Cramer* v. *Giles* (1883), 26 *Engl. & Emp. Dig.* §. 5271.

164 Contrast the position of those purchasing land on mortgage where relief against forfeiture was possible.

165 s. 12.

166 *Parl. Deb.*, H.C., vol. 330, 10 December 1937, 731.

167 s. 90. See also s. 91.

168 s. 90(5).

169 [1965] 2 Q.B. 205.

170 R. M. Goode, *Consumer Credit Legislation*, op. cit., I–§. 912.

171 Another argument is that s. 173(3) refers back to s. 173(1) in its opening clause. Thus under the general rules of statutory construction it, like s. 173(1), should be confined to terms in agreements.

172 For example, *United Dominions Trust (Commercial) Ltd* v. *Ennis* [1968] 1 Q.B. 54.

173 [1965] 2 Q.B. 205, 212.

174 s. 90(1) prohibits recovery from the debtor, cf. *Bentinck Ltd* v. *Cromwell Engineering Co.* [1971] 1 Q.B. 324.

175 ss. 92(1); 173(3).

176 s. 92(3).

177 Criminal Law Act 1977, s. 6.

178 See *Halsbury's Laws of England*, 4th edn, vol. 4, pp. 242–3, 253, 298 (R. M. Goode).

179 *NOP Survey*, Part 3 (Bills of Sale), p. 3.

180 *Halsbury's Laws of England*, 4th edn, vol. 4, pp. 321–3.

181 For example, Philip Shuchman, 'Profit on Default: An Archival Study of Automobile Repossession and Resale' (1969) 22 *Stan. L. Rev.* 20; Martin B. White, 'Consumer Repossessions and Deficiencies: New Perspectives from New Data', (1982), 23 *B.C.L.R.* 385.

182 Goode, *Hire-Purchase Law and Practice*, op. cit., p. 403.

183 op. cit., p. 54.

184 *United Dominions Trust (Commercial) Ltd* v. *Ennis* [1968] 1 Q.B. 54, 66; cf. *Brady* v. *St Margaret's Trust Ltd* [1963] 2 Q.B. 494.

185 cf. C. Turner, 'Repossession under the Australian "Uniform" Hire Purchase Legislation', (1973) 7 *Syd. L. Rev.* 1, 37–9.

186 Crowther Report, p. 168.

187 [1962] A.C. 600.

188 At common law the rule against penalties seems not to apply when a consumer voluntarily terminates pursuant to contract. Hence in both *Bridge's Case* and *United Dominions Trust (Commercial) Ltd* v. *Ennis* the courts had first to decide whether this had occurred or – as was decided on somewhat dubious interpretations of the facts, but obviously to benefit the consumer – whether the finance house had terminated, before they could decide the validity of the penalty clauses. The situation is anomalous, and Lords Denning and Devlin in *Bridge's case* said that the courts should have the power to strike down penalty clauses no matter how an agreement is terminated. See also *Associated Distributors Ltd* v. *Hall* [1938] 2 K.B. 83. In any event a minimum payment clause will be ineffective if it requires greater payment than under ss. 99–100, discussed below. See s. 173.

Minimum payment clauses have been upheld in *commercial* hiring agreements: *Robophone Facilities Ltd* v. *Blank* [1966] 1 W.L.R. 1428; [1966] 3 All E.R. 128; *I.A.C. (Leasing) Ltd* v. *Humphrey* (1972) 126 C.L.R. 131. For *consumer* hirings: *Galbraith* v. *Mitchenall Estates Ltd* [1965] 2 Q.B. 473, 480; see also Consumer Credit Act 1974, s. 138. The *Robophone Facilities* case principle is inapplicable to most consumer hirings because business can readily rehire – demand exceeds supply in the market – and therefore a penalty clause would not constitute a genuine pre-estimate of loss.

189 (1977) 121 S.J. 270; see also *Anglo-Auto Finance Co. Ltd* v. *James* [1963] 1 W.L.R. 1042; [1963] 3 All E.R. 566.

190 Goode, op. cit., §. 1–887. Goode notes that the second-mentioned might be in breach of s. 3(2) of the Unfair Contract Terms Act 1977.

191 [1963] 2 Q.B. 104.

192 If there is an installation charge, one-half of the total price refers to the aggregate of the installation charge and one-half of the remainder of the total price: s. 100(2).

193 s. 100(4).

194 *Wadham Stringer Finance Ltd* v. *Meany* [1981] 1 W.L.R. 39; [1980] 3 All E.R. 789.

195 *Eshun* v. *Moorgate Mercantile Co.* [1971] 1 W.L.R. 722; [1971] 2 All E.R. 402.

196 *United Dominions Trust (Commercial) Ltd* v. *Ennis* [1968] 1 Q.B. 54.

197 *Overstone Ltd* v. *Shipway* [1962] 1 W.L.R. 117; [1962] 1 All E.R. 52.

198 *Acceptance Co.* v. *Rice* (1961) 111 L.Jo. 424. See Philip Shuchman, 'Condition and Value of Repossessed Automobiles', (1979) 21 *W. & M.L.R.* 15, whose United States study shows that most repossessed cars range from fair or average to good, with poor condition cars almost offset by the number in good condition.

199 *Brady* v. *St. Margaret's Trust Ltd* [1963] 2 Q.B. 494, 500, *per* Lord Denning M.R. with whom Danckwerts and Davies L. JJ. agreed.
200 [1965] 2 Q.B. 473.
201 s. 130(2).
202 s. 129(1).
203 Consumer Transactions Acts 1972–1982, s. 38(1).
204 ss. 38(3)–(7).
205 Credit Tribunal, November 1974.
206 C.C.R., O.39. See John Blamire, 'Administration Orders', [1980] *LAG Bull.*, 241.
207 *Civil Judicial Statistics*, 1980, p. 92.
208 Attachment of Earnings Act 1971, s. 17.
209 Law Reform Commission of British Columbia, *Debtor-Creditor Relationships, Debt Collection and Collection Agents*, Project No. 2, 1971, L.R.C. 4, p. 31.
210 Ronald Sackville, *Law and Poverty in Australia*, Committee of Inquiry into Poverty (Canberra: A.G.P.S., 1975), p. 149ff.
211 Bankruptcy Act 1914, s. 155(a).
212 s. 38(a).
213 *Insolvency: The Regular Payment of Debts*, Report No. 6, 1977. See also *Insolvency Law and Practice*, Cmnd 8558, 1982, pp. 72–87; Ontario Law Reform Commission, *Report on the Enforcement of Judgment Debts and Related Matters* (Toronto: Ministry of the Attorney General, 1981), vol. 1; Debts Repayment Act 1978 (South Australia).
214 County Courts Act 1959, ss. 124, 132.
215 Rock, op. cit., pp. 159, 163.
216 *Vaughan* v. *McKenzie* [1969] 1 Q.B. 557.
217 *Rainbow* v. *Moorgate Properties Ltd* [1975] 1 W.L.R. 788; [1975] 2 All E.R. 821. See Charging Orders Act 1979, s. 1(5).
218 Attachment of Earnings Act 1971.
219 Kelly, op. cit., pp. 47–66.
220 *Billington* v. *Billington* [1974] 2 W.L.R. 53; [1974] 1 All E.R. 546.
221 s. 7(4).
222 Jane Bitten, M. Soc. Sci. Thesis, 1974 (Birmingham), p. 38, n. 16.
223 Employment Standards Act, R.S.O. 1980 c. 137, s. 9; Magistrates (Summary Proceedings) Act 1975 (Victoria), s. 128. See Ontario Law Reform Commission, *Report on the Enforcement of Judgment Debts and Related Matters*, op. cit., vol. 2, pp. 168–71.
224 Trebilcock and Schulman, op. cit., p. 458.
225 For a cogent view to the contrary, see T. G. Ison, *Credit Marketing and Consumer Protection* (London: Croom Helm, 1979), pp. 271–84.
226 s. 113. Wage assignments still seem valid despite the Truck Acts, *Williams* v. *Butlers Ltd* [1975] 1 W.L.R. 946; [1975] 2 All E.R. 889.
227 White, op. cit., pp. 409–10; Jacob S. Ziegel and Benjamin Geva,

Commercial and Consumer Transactions (Toronto: Emond-Montgomery, 1981), pp. 1128–9.

228 Limitation of Civil Rights Act, R.S.S., s. 18(1).

229 op. cit., p. 43. See also Homer Kripke, 'Consumer Credit Regulation: A Creditor-Oriented Viewpoint', (1968) 68 *Col. L. Rev.* 445, 481–2.

230 For example, Consumer Credit Act 1972–1982 (South Aust.), s. 57

231 See William C. Whitford, 'A Critique of the Consumer Credit Collection System', [1979] *Wisc. L.R.* 1047, 1081–6.

232 William C. Whitford and Harold Laufer, 'The Impact of Denying Self-Help Repossession of Automobiles: A Study of the Wisconsin Consumer Act', [1975] *Wisc. L. Rev.* 607.

233 *Revised Manual for Credit Unions' Leaders* (CUNA Mutual Insurance Society, June 1973), p. 10.

234 Ibid., p. 117.

235 J. Carroll Moody and Gilbert C. Fite, *The Credit Union Movement: Origins and Developments 1850–1970* (Univ. of Nebraska, 1971), pp. 354–5.

236 Ibid., pp. 355–6, 399. But for an Australian success: Anthony C. Lupi, 'Credit Unions: A Partial Solution to the Consumer Credit Problems of Low Income Families', (1978) 13 *Aust. J. Social Issues* 51–2 (low-income earners).

237 *World Council of Credit Union's Yearbook 1976* (Madison, Wisconsin), pp. 10–11. See also Peter G. Lumb, 'The Development of Credit Co-operatives within the State of Victoria, Australia', (1981) 14 *Akron L. Rev.* 517; C. S. Axworthy, 'Credit Unions in Canada: The Dilemma of Success' (1981) 31 *U. Tor. L. J.* 72.

238 cf. Federal Credit Union Act, 12 U.S.C. s. 1751ff.

239 Crowther Committee, p. 31.

240 Child Care Act 1980, s. 1(1).

CHAPTER 8

1 H. L. A. Hart, *Punishment and Responsibility* (Oxford: Clarendon, 1968), p. 23.

2 Michael Barkun, *Law without Sanctions* (New Haven, Conn.: Yale Univ. Press, 1968), p. 62.

3 cf. James Willard Hurst, *The Growth of American Law* (Boston: Little, Brown, 1950), p. 389.

4 Hermann Mannheim, *Criminal Justice and Social Reconstruction* (London: Routledge & Kegan Paul, 1946), pp. 166–7.

5 See Colin Howard, *Strict Responsibility* (London: Sweet & Maxwell, 1963).

6 *Sweet* v. *Parsley* [1970] A.C. 132; *Cameron* v. *Holt* (1980) 54 A.L.J.R. 202; 28 A.L.R. 490.

7 For example, *Roberts* v. *Egerton* (1874) L.R. 9 Q.B. 494.

8 *Tesco Supermarkets Ltd* v. *Nattrass* [1972] A.C. 153, 169–70, 183, 189, 194–5, 203; *R.* v. *Imperial Tobacco Products Ltd* (1971) 22 D.L.R. (3d) 51; and *R.* v. *Firestone Stores Ltd* [1972] 2 O.R. 327; *Darwin Bakery Pty Ltd* v. *Sully* (1981) 36 A.L.R. 371.

9 See generally Law Commission, *Report on the Mental Element in Crime*, Law Comm. No. 89 (London: 1978); Law Reform Commission of Canada, *Strict Liability*, Working Paper 2 (Ottawa: 1974); Brian Hogan, 'Strict Liability', [1978] *Crim. L.R.* 593.

10 Miles Smith and Anthony Pearson, 'The Value of Strict Liability', [1969] *Crim. L.R.* 5.

11 Herbert L. Packer, *The Limits of the Criminal Sanction* (Stanford Univ. Press, 1969), p. 359; Sanford H. Kadish, 'Some Observations on the Use of Criminal Sanctions in Enforcing Economic Regulations' (1963) 30 *U. Chic. L.R.* 423, 436–7; David Tench, *Towards a Middle System of Law* (London: Consumers Association, 1981).

12 cf. Frank Pearce, *Crimes of the Powerful* (London: Pluto Press, 1976).

13 Judah Gribetz and Frank P. Grad, 'Housing Code Enforcement: Sanctions and Remedies', (1966) 66 *Col. L.R.* 1254, 1280.

14 For example, *Report from the Select Committee on Merchandise Marks* (1897), c. 346, xi, 29, p. iii.

15 John Martin and George W. Smith, *The Consumer Interest* (London: Pall Mall, 1968), pp. 161–2; cf. *Slatcher* v. *George Mence Smith Ltd* [1951] 2 K.B. 631, 639.

16 *Final Report of the Committee on Consumer Protection*, Cmnd 1781, 1962.

17 Office of Fair Trading, *Review of the Trade Descriptions Act 1968: A Consultative Document*, Appendix. See also *Annual Report of the Director General of Fair Trading 1981* (London: HMSO, 1982), p. 68.

18 *Havering L.B.C.* v. *Stevenson* [1970] 1 W.L.R. 1375; [1970] 3 All E.R. 609. cf. *Blakemore* v. *Bellamy* (1983) 147 J.P. 89.

19 R. G. Lawson, 'The Consultative Document: Some Comments and Proposals', (1975) 125 *New L.J.* 948.

20 For example, *Roberts* v. *Severn Petroleum & Trading Co. Ltd* [1981] R.T.R. 312 (company supplying their petrol to a garage with Esso signs applied a false tank description).

21 *Robertson* v. *Dicicco* [1972] R.T.R. 431; [1972] Crim. L.R. 592.

22 *Tarleton Engineering Co. Ltd* v. *Nattrass* [1973] 1 W.L.R. 1261; [1973] 3 All E.R. 699; *Given* v. *C. V. Holland (Holdings) Pty Ltd* (1977) 15 A.L.R. 439.

23 Motor Vehicle Information and Cost Savings Act 1974, 15 U.S.C. ss. 1984, 1988–9; Motor Car Traders Act 1973 (Victoria), ss. 29–30.

24 *Consumer Difficulties in the Used-Car Sector* (London: Office of Fair Trading, 1980).

25 W.M.C.C., 'The Motor Trade – Time for Action', (1982) 90 *M.R.* 106.

26 For example, *Kensington and Chelsea B.C.* v. *Riley* [1973] R.T.R. 122;

[1973] Crim. L.R. 133; *R.* v. *Viceroy Construction Co. Ltd* (1975) 11 O.R. (2d) 485. cf. *R.* v. *R. M. Lowe Real Estate Ltd* (1978) 40 C.C.C. (2d) 529. See generally Charles F. Swanson, 'Predicting Changes in Consumer Attitudes', in Stuart H. Britt (ed.), *Consumer Behaviour and the Behavioural Sciences* (New York: Wiley, 1966), pp. 563–4.

27 *Southwark L.B.C.* v. *Elderson Industries Ltd* (1981) 89 M.R. 232; *F.T.C.* v. *Standard Education Society* 302 U.S. 112, 116 (1937).

28 *Chidwick* v. *Beer* [1974] R.T.R. 415; [1974] Crim. L.R. 267; *R.* v. *Alexanian & Sons Ltd* (1974) 23 C.C.C. (2d) 249; (1974) 22 C.P.R. (2d) 37; *Pinetrees Lodge Pty Ltd* v. *Atlas International Pty Ltd* (1981) 38 A.L.R. 187, 193.

29 *Holloway* v. *Cross* [1981] 1 All E.R. 1012; [1981] R.T.R. 146.

30 *Riley McKay Pty Ltd* v. *Bannerman* (1977) 15 A.L.R. 561, 570–1.

31 *Furniss* v. *Scholes* [1974] R.T.R. 133; [1974] Crim. L.R. 199.

32 *Florence Mfg Co.* v. *J. C. Dowd & Co.* 178 F. 73, 75 (1910). See also the remarks in the Australian cases *C.R.W. Pty Ltd* v. *Sneddon* [1972] A. R. (N.S.W.) 17, 28; *Parish* v. *World Series Cricket Pty Ltd* (1977) 16 A.L.R. 172, 179, 203; *Henderson* v. *Pioneer Homes Pty Ltd (No. 2)* (1980) 43 F.L.R. 276, 282, 288.

33 (1982) 56 A.L.J.R. 715.

34 Brennan J. decided the case on other grounds. Gibbs C. J. and Mason J. also endorsed an earlier decision of the Federal Court that it is not enough to establish that conduct is confusing or causes people to wonder for it to be misleading: *McWilliam's Wines Pty Ltd* v. *McDonald's System of Australia Pty Ltd* (1980) 33 A.L.R. 394. (McWilliam's use of the expression 'BIG MAC' in advertising one of its brands of wine was not misleading, even though potential purchasers of that wine and/or McDonald's hamburgers might have been confused as to whether there was a business connection between the two companies because of the erroneous assumption that there was a legal restriction on the use of those words.)

35 [1972] 1 W.L.R. 1418; [1972] 3 All E.R. 759.

36 *Fletcher* v. *Sledmore* [1973] R.T.R. 371; [1973] Crim. L.R. 195.

37 Sale of Goods Act 1979, s. 13(3).

38 s. 14(3).

39 See *Louis C. Edwards & Sons (Manchester)* v. *Miller* (1981) 89 M.R. 240, 241 *per* Donaldson L. J.

40 Patrick Forman, *The Trade Descriptions Act 1968: A Lawyer's Progress Report* (London: Consumer Council, 1970), pp. 48–9. See also Office of Fair Trading, *Review of the Trade Descriptions Act 1968*, Cmnd 6628 (London: HMSO, 1976), pp. 44–6.

41 For example, *Royal Baking Powder Co.* v. *F.T.C.*, 281 F.744 (1922).

42 As suggested in *Cottee* v. *Douglas Seaton (Used Cars) Ltd* [1972] 1 W.L.R.

1408; [1972] 3 All E.R. 750.

43 [1974] 1 W.L.R. 1220; [1974] 3 All E.R. 489.

44 [1974] 1 W.L.R. 1220, 1224; [1974] 3 All E.R. 389, 491–2.

45 The court found it unnecessary to decide whether a new car must be the current model. See also *Routledge* v. *Ansa Motors (Chester-Le-Street)* [1980] R.T.R. 1; [1980] Crim. L.R. 65 (vehicle manufactured in 1972, first registered in 1975, described as a 'used 1975' car); *Annand & Thompson Pty Ltd* v. *T.P.C.* (1979) 25 A.L.R. 91 (vehicles completely assembled and ready for registration in January 1975 described as 'new' in 1977); and *John McGrath Motors (Canberra) Pty Ltd* v. *Applebee* (1964) 110 C.L.R. 656.

46 For example, *R.* v. *Hammertons Cars Ltd* [1976] 1 W.L.R. 1243; [1976] 3 All E.R. 758.

47 For example, *Barker* v. *Hargreaves* [1981] R.T.R. 197; [1981] Crim. L.R. 262.

48 *Doble* v. *David Greig Ltd* [1972] 1 W.L.R. 703; [1972] 2 All E.R. 195.

49 *Norman* v. *Bennett* [1974] 1 W.L.R. 1229; [1974] 3 All E.R. 351; *Zawadski* v. *Sleigh* [1975] R.T.R. 113; *R* v. *Hammertons Cars Ltd* [1976] 1 W.L.R. 1243; [1976] 3 All E.R. 758; *Waltham Forest L.B.C.* v. *T. G. Wheatley (Central Garage) (No. 2)* [1978] R.T.R. 333; [1977] Crim. L.R. 761. See, generally, Richard J. Bragg, 'More Mileage in Disclaimers', (1982) 2 *Legal Studies* 172.

50 [1981] R.T.R. 380.

51 *Newman* v. *Hackney L.B.C.* [1982] R.T.R. 296; *R.* v. *King* [1979] Crim. L.R. 122 (Crown Court). There is also the possibility of offences of obtaining property by deception (Theft Act 1968, s. 15), and under the Consumer Transactions (Restrictions on Statements) Order 1976, S.I. 1976 No. 1813 as amended by S.I. 1978 No. 127. See P. Blish-Cheesman, 'Mileage Disclaimers, Effective and Legal', (1982) 90 *M.R.* 121.

52 Philip Kleinman, 'The £86 giveaway', *Sunday Times*, 4 April 1976; 'A £660 million waste of money', ibid., 24 March 1977; Director General of Fair Trading, *Review of the Price Marking (Bargain Offers) Orders 1979* (London: Office of Fair Trading, 1981), Appendix C, para. 3.10.

53 Monopolies Commission, *Recommended Resale Prices* (London: HMSO, 1969), p. 3.

54 Ibid., p. 7.

55 Ibid., p. 19.

56 Ibid., p. 17; Office of Fair Trading, *Bargain Offer Claims* (London: HMSO, 1975), p. 18. See also Price Commission, *Recommended Retail Prices*, Report No. 25, 1977, p. 17.

57 Phoney recommended prices may be caught by ss. 11(1)(b) 11(3)(a), (c). cf. *Coro Inc.* v. *F.T.C.*, 338 F. 2d 149 (1964); *Helbros Watch Co.* v. *F.T.C.*, 310 F. 2d 868 (1962).

58 S.I. 1979, No. 364; S.I. 1979, No. 633; S.I. 1979, No. 1124.
59 Director General of Fair Trading, *Review of the Price Marking (Bargain Offers) Orders* (1979), op. cit., paras 5.9.3–5.10.
60 s. 11 (3)(a)(ii); *House of Holland v. Brent L.B.C.* [1971] 2 Q.B. 304.
61 Office of Fair Trading, *Review of the Trade Descriptions Act* (1968) op. cit., p. 64.
62 Director General of Fair Trading, *Review of the Price Marking (Bargain Offers) Orders* (1979) op. cit., paras 5.3.2, 9.1, 5.10.
63 *Westminster C.C. v. Ray Alan (Manshops) Ltd* [1982] 1 All E.R. 771.
64 See R. G. Lawson, *Advertising and Labelling Laws in the Common Market*, 2nd edn (Bristol: Jordan, 1981), ch. 10: paras 1–4.
65 Consumer Information Act 1969, s. 10(6).
66 *Cheshire County Council Consumer Protection Department*, 1974–5, p. 6.
67 *Doble v. David Greig Ltd* [1972] 1 W.L.R. 703; [1972] 2 All E.R. 195; *Nattrass v. Marks and Spencer Ltd*, 1981, unreported, noted by Peter Clark, ' "De Minimis": How Not to Deal With It', (1981) 145 *J.P.* 753.
68 [1975] Crim. L.R. 53. See also *Heron Service Stations Ltd v. Hunter* (1981) 79 L.G.R. 679; [1981] Crim. L.R. 418 (display boards offering petrol at one price, but the amount being charged higher). In relation to roadside display boards, see Price Marking (Petrol) Order 1980; S.I. 1980, No. 1121.
69 *Miller v. F. A. Sadd & Son Ltd* [1981] 3 All E.R. 265; *Simmons v. Emmett* (1982) 90 M.R. 97.
70 *Simmons v. Emmett* is a good example: a deposit had been paid on flowers for a wedding; when they arrived on the wedding day a higher price was requested. What customer in this type of situation, when the florist refuses to hand the flowers over unless the higher price is paid, will go out and obtain flowers elsewhere and sue the first florist later for return of the deposit?
71 [1978] R.T.R. 397; (1978) 76 L.G.R. 741. See also *Sweeting v. Northern Upholstery Ltd, The Times*, 28 June 1982; (1983) 1 Tr. L. 5 (advertisements offering a particular style suite at £699, silent as to colour, in breach of s. 11(2) because in fact only beige available at that price).
72 *Barnes v. Watts Tyre & Rubber Co. Ltd* (1973) [1978] R.T.R. 405 (Note).
73 *Richards v. Westminster Motors Ltd* (1975) 61 C.A.R. 228; [1976] R.T.R. 88. The Price Marking (Food and Drink on Premises) Order 1979, S.I. 1979, No. 361, requires that in the case of food, or of a service relating to the supply of food, the supply of which is subject to VAT, the price or charge indicated shall be inclusive of the tax (r. 6).
74 [1975] 1 W.L.R. 649; [1975] 2 All E.R. 226.
75 S.I. 1979, No. 364; S.I. 1979, No. 633; S.I. 1979, No. 1124. See Graham Stephenson, 'Bargain Offers', (1980) 88 *M.R.* 99; M. Carlisle, 'Practical Problems Arising from the Price Marking (Bargain Offers) Order 1979',

(1979) 129 *N.L.J.* 815.

76 Examples of these eight categories are respectively: 'Current price, £10.00 – From 30 September, £12.50'; 'Our price £5 – Joe Smith's price £6'; 'Price £110 – 5% discount for cash'; 'Old age pensioners £1.20 – Normal price £1.50'; 'Normal fare £50 – Awayday return £30'; 'When perfect £2 – Fire damaged £1'; '50p each – five for £2'; 'Table £60 – Chairs £30 each – Table and four chairs only £150'. See Director General of Fair Trading, *Review of the Price Marking (Bargain Offers) Orders* (1979), op. cit., para. 1.3.

77 Examples of meaningless price comparisons are use of 'ready-assembled prices', 'special order prices', high single unit prices and future or 'after sale' prices. Ibid., paras 5.4–5.8. See also T. R. French, 'More Than Was Bargained For!', (1981) 89 *M.R.* 80.

77a As with 'bargain price', but not 'special clearance offer' or 'end-of-range clearance price': *West Yorkshire M.C.C.* v. *MFI Furniture Centre Ltd, The Times,* 18 March 1983.

78 op. cit., para. 5.10(a).

79 Similarly, the Canadian Combines Investigation Act, R.S.C. 1970, provides that no person shall, for the purpose of promoting, directly or indirectly, the supply or use of a product or for the purpose of promoting, directly or indirectly, any business interest, by any means whatever make a materially misleading representation to the public concerning the price at which a product or like products have been, are or will be ordinarily sold (s. 36(1)(d)). See also ss. 36.2(1) (double pricing), 37.1(1) (advertised price must be adhered to). See *R.* v. *Alberta Giftwares Ltd* (1973) 36 D.L.R. (3d) 321; *R.* v. *G. Tamblyn Ltd* (1972) 26 D.L.R. (3d) 436.

80 *Darwin Bakery Pty Ltd* v. *Sully* (1981) 36 A.L.R. 371. See also *Guthrie* v. *Doyle Dane & Bernbach Pty Ltd* (1977) 30 F.L.R. 116.

81 *Henderson* v. *Pioneer Homes Pty Ltd (No. 2)* (1980) 43 F.L.R. 276. Note that the proceedings were brought under ss. 53 (e) (price of services) and (g) (effect of a condition).

82 s. 14(2)(b); *MFI Warehouses Ltd* v. *Nattrass* [1973] 1 W.L.R. 307; [1973] 1 All E.R. 762.

83 Op. cit., p. 20.

84 For example, *Bambury* v. *Hounslow L.B.C.* [1971] R.T.R. 1. But see *Westminster C.C.* v. *Ray Alan (Manshops) Ltd* [1982] 1 All E.R. 771, discussed below. cf. *Montgomery Ward & Co.* v. *F.T.C.*, 379 F. 2d 666 (1967).

85 Cf. Trade Practices Act 1974 (Australia), s. 53(f). See *Keehn* v. *Medical Benefits Fund of Australia Ltd* (1977) 14 A.L.R. 77. cf. *Dawson* v. *Motor Tyre Service Pty Ltd* (1981) Trade Practices Reporting Service 314. 238. Services are defined very widely in the Act: s. 4(1).

86 As we have seen, the Price Marking (Bargain Offers) Order applies to services.

87 [1972] 1 W.L.R. 1593; [1973] 1 All E.R. 120.

88 *Review of the Trade Descriptions Act* (1968), op. cit., p. 34.

89 An Office of Fair Trading survey of 6000 people in 1979 found that of the 700 who had taken package holidays in the previous twelve months, 40 per cent had some cause for complaint. However, overall satisfaction was high – 64.5 per cent were 'very satisfied' and 24.7 per cent were 'quite satisfied'.

90 *R.* v. *Clarksons Holidays Ltd* (1972) 57 C.A.R. 38; [1972] Crim. L.R. 653; *Wilson* v. *British Railways Board* (unreported), respectively. See also *Herron* v. *Lunn Poly (Scotland) Ltd* [1972] S.L.T. 2 (Sh. Ct.). cf. *Dawson* v. *World Travel Headquarters Pty Ltd* (1981) Trade Practices Reporting Service 314.83.

91 [1973] 1 W.L.R. 1105; [1973] 2 All E.R. 1233; cf. *Sunair Holidays* v. *Dodd* [1970] 1 W.L.R. 1037; [1970] 2 All E.R. 410.

92 [1973] 1 W.L.R. 1105, 1109; [1973] 2 All E.R. 1233, 1236.

93 [1976] 1 W.L.R. 13; [1976] 1 All E.R. 65.

94 [1973] 1 W.L.R. 1105; [1973] 2 All E.R. 1233.

95 It is arguable that it extends to houses on long leases or for sale; the word is used in these senses by estate agents. See Graham Stephenson, 'Estate Agents and Trade Descriptions', [1980] *Conveyancer*, 249, 254–5.

96 [1970] 2 Q.B. 459.

97 [1970] 2 Q.B. 459, 462.

98 See pp. 373–4 below.

99 15 U.S.C. ss. 1701–20. See also R. M. Friedman, 'Regulation of Interstate Land Sales: Is Full Disclosure Sufficient?' (1980) 20 *Urban L. Ann.* 137.

100 (1980) 30 A.L.R. 189. See also *Videon* v. *Barry Burroughs Pty Ltd* (1981) 37 A.L.R. 365. cf. *R* v. *Viceroy Construction Co. Ltd* (1975) 11 O.R. (2d) 485; *R.* v. *R. M. Lowe Real Estate Ltd* (1978) 40 C.C.C. (2d) 529.

101 Law Commission, *Transfer of Land 'Subject to Contract' Agreements*, Report No. 65 (London: HMSO, 1975); *Review of the Trade Descriptions Act 1968*, op. cit., p. 68.

102 *Edward A. Savory and Associates Ltd* v. *Noel Dawson* (1976) (unreported).

103 David Boies and Paul R. Verkuil, 'Regulation of Supermarket Advertising Practices', (1972) 60 *Georgetown L.J.* 1195.

104 R. C. Mussehl, 'The Neighbourhood Consumer Centre', (1972) 47 *Nôtre Dame L.* 1093, 1099.

105 [1982] 1 All E.R. 771. cf. *R.* v. *Broadway Clothiers Ltd* (1974) 20 C.C.C. (2d) 35, 16 C.P.R. (2d) 267.

106 Ormrod L. J. said that 'services' implies activities ('Hotels or business of all kinds provide services, meaning that they do something for the

customer'), so that facilities means making things available in a more passive sense (p. 774). But why not conclude that facilities implies activities as well, in this case shopping facilities? cf. *Brooks* v. *Club Continental*, 1981, unreported, noted in G. Stephenson, 'False and Misleading Price Comparisons', (1982) 45 *M.L.R.* 710, 712.

107 See also Victoria: Consumer Affairs Act 1972, s. 13(2A); New South Wales: Consumer Protection Act 1969, s. 29A; *Burton* v. *Samuels* (1973) 5 S.A.S.R. 201; New Zealand: Consumer Information Act 1969, s. 10(3); Canada: Combines Investigation Act 1970, s. 37.

108 (1980) 49 F.L.R. 401.

109 (1971) 36 Fed. Reg. 8781. The Federal Trade Commission has also issued guidelines describing unlawful 'bait and switch' practices. 16 C.F.R. 238. See also *Tashof* v. *F.T.C.* 437 F.2d 707 (1970).

110 *Review of the Trade Descriptions Act*, op. cit., p. 42.

111 See, generally, Ernst W. Stieb, *Drug Adulteration Detection and Control in Nineteenth-century Britain* (Madison: Univ. of Wisconsin Press, 1963); Ingeborg Paulus, *The Search for Pure Food* (London: Martin Robertson, 1974); P. S. Atiyah, *The Rise and Fall of Freedom of Contract* (Oxford: Clarendon, 1979), pp. 546–7; F. B. Smith, *The People's Health 1830–1910* (London: Croom Helm, 1979), pp. 203–15. See also F. Engels, *The Condition of the Working-Class in England* (Moscow: Progress Publishers, 1973), pp. 98–100.

112 *R.* v. *Dixon* (1814) 105 E.R. 516.

113 *R.* v. *Kempson* (1893) 28 L.J. 477.

114 *Shillito* v. *Thompson* (1875) 1 Q.B.D. 12.

115 Tea: 11 Geo. 1, c. 30 (1724); 4 Geo. 2, c. 14 (1731); 17 Geo. 3, c. 29 (1766–7). Coffee: 5 Geo. 1, c. 11 (1718); 11 Geo. 1, c. 30 (1724); 43 Geo. 3, c. 129 (1803); cf. 3 Geo. 4, c. 53 (1822). Beer: 56 Geo. 3, c. 58 (1816); 7 & 8, Geo. 4 c. 52 (1827).

116 *Report of the Commissioners of Inland Revenue*, 1870, c. 82, xx, 193, p. 37.

117 51 Hen. 3, st. 6 *(Assise Panis et cervisiae)*.

118 For example, A. H. Hassall, *Adulterations Detected, or, Plain Instructions for the Discovery of Frauds in Food and Medicine* (London: Longmans, 1857).

119 For example, J. Toulmin-Smith, *Local Self-Government and Centralization* (London: Chapman, 1851), p. 335.

120 For example, *Report from the Select Committee on Adulteration of Food etc.*, 1856, 379, viii, 1, p. iv; *Parl. Deb., H.C.*, vol. 209, 6 March 1872, 1507.

121 As in the Licensing Act 1872, 35 & 36 Vict., c. 94, s. 19, Schedule 1.

122 For example, Vic.: Health Act 1958, s. 294.

123 E. Ballard, 'The Work of the Metropolitan Medical Officers of Health', *National Association for the Promotion of Social Science, Papers and Discussions on Public Health* (London: Faithful, 1862), p. 123.

124 J. Burnett, *Plenty and Want. A Social History of Diet in England from 1815 to the Present Day* (London: Nelson, 1966), p. 82. See also *Parl. Deb., H.C.*, vol. 156, 29 February 1860, 2025–6.

125 ss. 3, 4, 9.

126 s. 6.

127 See E. J. Bigwood and A. Gerard, *Fundamental Principles and Objectives of a Comparative Food Law* (Basle: S. Karger, 1968), vol. 2, pp. 58–9.

128 Food and Drugs Act 1955, ss. 1, 2, 8.

129 For example, Vic.: Health Act 1958, ss. 238, 240; Can.: Food and Drugs Act, R.S.C. 1970, s. 4. See *Palmer* v. *B. J. Clarke's (Hampton) Pty Ltd* [1966] V.R. 7.

130 See, for example, Y. H. Hui, *United States Food Laws, Regulation and Standards* (New York: Wiley, 1979).

131 For example, W. J. Bell, *The Sale of Food and Drugs Acts*, 1st edn (London: Shaw, 1886), p. 12.

132 Ibid., p. 69.

133 *Betts* v. *Armstead* (1888) 20 Q.B.D. 771.

134 *Hoyle* v. *Hitchman* (1879) 4 Q.B.D. 233. See also *Pearks, Gunston and Tee Limited* v. *Ward* [1902] 2 K.B. 1; *Rider* v. *Freebody* (1898) 24 V.L.R. 429.

135 For example, *Williams* v. *Friend* [1912] 2 K.B. 471; *A. J. Mills* v. *Williams* (1964) 62 L.G.R. 354; *Goldup* v. *John Manson* [1981] 3 W.L.R. 833; [1981] 3 All E.R. 257.

136 [1974] A.C. 839.

137 See ibid., p. 857.

138 *Plumb* v. *Tritton* (1915) 20 C.L.R. 408; *Ex parte Vaughan* (1911) 11 S.R. (N.S.W.) 250; 28 N.S.W. (W.N.) 71; *Brown* v. *G. J. Coles & Co. Ltd* [1970] V.R. 867, 873.

139 (1982) 84 *British Food J.* 37.

140 *Edwards* v. *Llaethdy Meirion Ltd* [1957] Crim. L.R. 402; (1957) 107 L. Jo. 138.

141 Ibid., *Southworth* v. *Whitewell Dairies Ltd* (1958) 122 J.P. 322.

142 *J. Miller Ltd* v. *Battersea Borough Council* [1956] 1 Q.B. 43; *Minister* v. *Woolworths (Victoria) Ltd* [1974] V.L.R. 514.

143 *David Greig Ltd* v. *Goldfinch* (1961), 105 Sol. J. 367; *Boucher* v. *Tom the Cheap (S.A.) Pty Ltd* (1975) 10 S.A.S.R. 257; *Turner* v. *Owen* [1956] 1 Q.B. 48, 51.

144 Hui, op. cit., pp. 480–2.

145 J. Love, 'Office of Fair Trading and Environmental Health', (1981) 89 *Environmental Health* 42.

146 Even after the Food and Drugs (Amendment) Act 1982, maximum fines are only £1000 on summary conviction.

147 P. Kelly, *Metrology; or An Exposition of Weights and Measures* (London: Lackington, 1816), pp. 33–82; H. J. Chaney, *Our Weights and Measures*

(London: Eyre & Spottiswoode, 1897), pp. 50–5.

148 Weights and Measures, *Letter from the Comptroller-General of the Exchequer to the Secretary of State for the Home Department*, dated 9 February 1859, 188, xxv, 291, p. 2.

149 *O'Keefe's Law of Weights and Measures* (London: Butterworths, 1982), O 38; o 44. (O'Keefe is the standard work on the current law.) See also C. W. Parsley, *Observations on . . . The Measures Weights and Money used in this Country* (London: Egertons Military Library, 1834), p. 81.

150 G. A. Owen, *The Law Relating to Weights and Measures*, 2nd edn (London: Griffin, 1947), p. 71.

151 *Report by the Board of Trade in the Proceedings and Business under the Weights and Measures Act 1878* (1882), c. 331, xxvii, 715, p. 2.

152 *Report from the Select Committee on Short Weight* (1914), Cd 359, x, 337, p. iii–iv. See also Food Council, *Short Weight and Measure in the Sale of Foodstuffs* (1926), Cmd 2591, x, 733.

153 Law Commission, *Criminal Liability of Corporations*, Working Paper No. 44, pp. 34–5.

154 I. A. Muir, 'Tesco Supermarkets, Corporate Liability and Fault', (1973) 5 *N.Z.U.L.R.* 357, 359.

155 See W. B. Fisse, 'Criminal Law and Consumer Protection', in A. J. Duggan and L. W. Darvall (eds), *Consumer Protection Law and Theory* (Sydney: Law Book, 1980), on the imposition of individual as well as corporate liability.

156 421 U.S. 658 (1975). cf. *Pryor* v. *Given* (1980) 30 A.L.R. 189.

157 For example, *Hotchin* v. *Hindmarsh* [1891] 2 Q.B. 181; *Melias Ltd* v. *Preston* [1957] 2 Q.B. 380.

158 *Quere* whether the act or default of the employee must be wrongful. *Lill (K.) Holdings Ltd* v. *White* [1979] R.T.R. 120, 125. cf. *Tesco Supermarkets Ltd* v. *Nattrass* [1972] A.C. 153, 184, 196.

159 *Tesco Supermarkets Ltd* v. *Nattrass* [1972] A.C. 153, 187–8, 193, 200–1.

160 *H. L. Bolten (Engineering) Co. Ltd* v. *T. J. Graham & Sons Ltd* [1957] 1 Q.B. 159, 172.

161 *Mousell Bros Ltd* v. *London & North-Western Railway Company* [1917] 2 K.B. 836; *James & Son Ltd* v. *Smee* [1955] 1 Q.B. 78.

162 *Tesco Supermarkets Ltd* v. *Nattrass* [1972] A.C. 153; *Universal Telecasters Queensland Ltd* v. *Guthrie* (1978) 18 A.L.R. 531 (a case decided on the equivalent of s. 25 of the Trade Descriptions Act 1968, which gives a defence to those whose business it is to publish or arrange for the publication of advertisements).

163 Cf. *Clode* v. *Barnes* [1974] 1 W.L.R. 544; [1974] 1 All E.R. 1166 (partners).

164 *Coupe* v. *Guyett* [1973] 1 W.L.R. 669; [1973] 2 All E.R. 1058. cf. Trade Practices Act 1974 (Aust.), s. 84(1), which provides that where it is

necessary to establish the intention of a body corporate, it is sufficient to show that one of its servants or agents by whom the conduct was engaged in had that intention.

165 The defences can be invoked by individuals as well as companies but in practice are used by the latter.

166 [1972] A.C. 153.

167 R.W.L. Howells, 'A Blow Against Enterprise Liability', (1971) 34 *Mod. L.R.* 676, 679.

168 [1973] *Crim. L.R.* 197.

169 *The Times*, 3 February 1976; (1976) 120 Sol. J. 197.

170 (1970) 68 L.G.R. 256; (1970) 114 Sol J. 147. See also *Taylor* v. *Lawrence Fraser (Bristol) Ltd* (1977) 121 Sol. J. 757; [1978] Crim. L.R. 43; *Garrett* v. *Boots the Chemists Ltd* (1980) 88 M.R. 238. In *R.* v. *Consumers Distributing Co. Ltd* (1980) 57 C.C.C. (2d) 317, 54 C.P.R. (2d) 50, the Ontario Court of Appeal was satisfied that the retailer had taken reasonable precautions and exercised due diligence, even though it did no independent testing of a fuel-saving device, because it had combined information from independent experts, users and other merchants (pp. 324–5, 327).

171 (1973) 71 L.G.R. 477; [1973] Crim. L.R. 538.

172 For example, *Wandsworth L.B.C.* v. *Bentley* [1980] R.T.R. 429; *Stainthorpe* v. *Bailey* [1980] R.T.R. 7; [1979] Crim. L.R. 677. cf. *Crook* v. *Howells Garages (Newport) Ltd* [1980] R.T.R. 434.

173 For example, Food and Drugs Act 1955, s. 115.

174 *Rochdale M.B.C.* v. *F.M.C. (Meat) Ltd* [1980] 1 W.L.R. 461; [1980] 2 All E.R. 303.

175 *Grattidge* v. *Liuzzi* [1969] V.R. 260; *Palmer* v. *R. J. Mercer (Hampton) Pty Ltd* [1970] V.R.32; *Eton Smallgoods Pty Ltd* v. *Boon* [1980] 1 N.S.W.L.R. 543.

176 [1970] 1 Q.B. 573. See also *Tesco Stores Ltd* v. *Roberts* [1974] 1 W.L.R. 1253; [1974] 3 All E.R. 74; *Milk Marketing Board* v. *Hall* [1968] 1 W.L.R. 704; [1968] 2 All E.R. 259; *Walker* v. *Baxter's Butchers Ltd* (1977) 76 L.G.R. 183 [1977] Crim. L.R. 479.

177 Graham Stephenson, 'The Warranty Defence in Consumer Legislation', (1980) 130 *N.L.J.* 1003.

178 [1972] 1 W.L.R. 1487; [1972] 3 All E.R. 738.

179 Food and Drugs Act 1955, s. 3(3).

180 [1974] A.C. 839. Applied *Greater Manchester Council* v. *Lockwood Foods Ltd* [1979] Crim. L. R. 593.

181 For example, p. 860, *per* Lord Cross. See also *Warnock* v. *Johnstone* (1881) 8 R.55.

182 Note prosecutions under the Theft Act 1968; for example, *R.* v. *Hall* [1973] 1 Q.B. 126. *R.* v. *Mandry* [1973] 1 W.L.R. 1232; [1973] 3 All E.R. 996.

183 *Ballard* v. *Sperry Rand Australia Ltd* (1975) 6 A.L.R. 696. Although not overturned, this decision has been thrown into doubt by *Universal Telecasters Queensland Ltd* v. *Guthrie* (1978) 18 A.L.R. 531. See *Videon* v. *Barry Burroughs Pty Ltd* (1981) 37 A.L.R. 365, 387; A. J. Duggan, 'Misleading Advertising and the Publishers' Defence – A Critique of Universal Telecasters (Qld) Limited v. Guthrie', (1978) 6 *A.B.L.R.* 309, 320–2.

184 (London: Macmillan, 1979). cf. John T. Thompson, 'Prosecution Versus Persuasion', (1982) 90 *Environmental Health* 115.

185 *Report from the Select Committee on Adulteration of Food*, 1856, Parl. Pap. 376, viii, 1, p. vii.

186 s. 35. See J. Landis, 'Statutes and the Sources of Law', *Harvard Legal Essays* (Cambridge, Mass.: Harvard Univ. Press, 1934), p. 220.

187 [1939] 2 K.B. 365. See also *Buckley* v. *La Reserve* [1959] Crim. L.R. 451; *H.P. Bulmer Ltd and Showerings Ltd* v. *J. Bollinger S.A. and Champagne Lanson Pere et Fils* [1978] R.P.C. 79; [1977] 2 C.M.L.R. 625.

188 See Peter Cane 'Civil Liability Under the Consumer Safety Act 1978 (U.K.)', (1979) 3 *J. Products Liability* 215. Section 35 of the Powers of Criminal Courts Act 1973 entitles consumers to compensation in the event of conviction. cf. Trade Practices Act 1974 (Aust.), s. 82, which enables a person to recover the loss or damage suffered by conduct of another person in contravention of the consumer protection provisions of the Act. Under s. 80 any person can apply for an injunction against such conduct; this has been used mainly by businesses against their competitors. *Hornsby Building Information Centre Pty Ltd* v. *Sydney Building Information Centre Pty Ltd* (1978) 52 A.L.J.R. 392.

CHAPTER 9

1 Res. 543, in *Eur. Consultative Assembly, 25th Session, Texts Adopted* (1973), p. 2. C(i).

2 See generally William C. Whitford, 'The Functions of Disclosure Regulation in Consumer Transactions', (1973) *Wisc. L.R.* 400. I have drawn on this excellent study at a number of points in the analysis.

3 15 U.S.C. s. 1451.

4 Stephen A. Rhoades, 'Reducing Consumer Ignorance: An Approach and its Effects', (1975) 20 *Antitrust Bull.* 309, 310. See also Howard Beales *et al.*, 'The Efficient Regulation of Consumer Information', (1981) 24 *J. Law & Economics* 491, 501–13.

5 Trade Descriptions (Sealskin Goods) (Information Order), 1980, S.I. 1980 No. 1150; Trade Descriptions (Origin Marking) (Miscellaneous Goods) Order 1981, S.I. 1981 No.121.

6 *Review of the Trade Descriptions Act*, op. cit., p. 86.

7 *Report of the Committee on Consumer Protection* (1962), Cmnd 1781, pp. 89, 90.

8 Ibid., pp. 92, 96.

9 OECD, *Labelling and Comparative Testing* (Paris: 1972), p. 5.

10 Marketing Act 1975, s. 3.

11 Energy Act 1976, s. 15. See Passenger Car Fuel Consumption Order, 1977, S.I. 1977, No.1603. On the accuracy of fuel saving claims: *Trade Practices Commission* v. *Vaponordic (Aust.) Pty Ltd* (1975) 6 A.L.R. 248; *R.* v. *Consumers Distributing Company Ltd* (1980) 57 C.C.C. (2d) 317; 54 C.P.R. (2d) 50.

12 For example, Vic.: Health Act 1958, s. 248.

13 Norbert Reich and H.-W. Micklitz, *Consumer Legislation in the Federal Republic of Germany* (Wokingham, Berks.: Van Nostrand Reinhold, 1981), pp. 60–2.

14 Monroe P. Friedman, 'Consumer Confusion in the Selection of Supermarket Products', (1966) 50 *J. App. Psy.* 529.

15 Council Directive of 15 January 1980 on . . . prepackaged products. 80/232/E.E.C.

16 Weights and Measures Act 1963, Schedule 4 (as amended). For current provisions see *O'Keefe's Law of Weights and Measures*, esp. [1] 336.

17 See Note, 'Federal Regulation of Deceptive Packaging', (1963) 72 *Yale L.J.* 788, 792–3.

18 cf. Benjamin J. Katz, 'Public Policy Towards Consumer Product Information' (Ph.D. Thesis, Univ. of Penn., 1973), chs 5–7.

19 Labelling of durable goods is covered in Chapter 10 on product standards.

20 Hazardous Products (Hazardous Substances) Regulations, Consolidated Regulations of Canada, 1978, vol. 10.

21 Packaging and Labelling of Dangerous Substances Regulations 1978, S.I. 1978, No. 209. See also Upholstered Furniture (Safety) Regulations, 1980, S.I. 1980, No. 725; Cosmetic Products Regulations 1978, S.I. 1978, No. 1354.

22 15 U.S.C. s. 1335.

23 For example, N.S.W.: Cigarettes (Labelling) Act 1972.

24 Page Keeton and Marshall S. Shapo, *Products and the Consumer: Defective and Dangerous Products* (Mineola: Foundation Press, 1970), pp. 67–8.

25 Upheld *Capital Broadcasting Co.* v. *Mitchell* 333 F. Supp. 582 (1971), affirmed 405 U.S. 1000 (1972).

26 The regulations are conveniently collected in *Butterworths Law of Food and Drugs* (London: 1982), vol. 4, section R. See also Eggs (Marketing Standards) Regulations 1973, S.I. 1973, No. 15, as amended; Common Agricultural Policy (Wine) Regulations 1979, S.I. 1979, No. 1094.

27 The Federal Trade Commission in the United States has introduced a trade regulation rule requiring the disclosure of the light output and average laboratory life of light bulbs: 16 C.F.R. s. 409.1.

28 Directive of 26 July 1971 on Textiles. 71/307/EEC as amended (implemented in UK by Textile Products (Indications of Fibre Content)

Regulations 1973, S.I. 1973, No. 2124, as amended by S.I. 1975, No. 928); Textile Labelling Act (Canada); Textile Fiber Products Identification Act, 15 U.S.C. s. 70b (USA); Textile Products Labelling Act 1954 (N.S.W.).

29 *Quality Assurance Symbols, A Survey of Adults* (London: Quality Assurance Council, August 1972), p. 5. See Norbert Reich and H.-W. Micklitz, *Consumer Legislation in the EC Countries* (Wokingham, Berks.: Van Nostrand Reinhold, 1980), pp. 35–6.

30 For example, Weights and Measures Act 1963, s. 33(2).

31 See Weights and Measures Act 1963, s. 33(3).

32 15 U.S.C. s. 1453(a)(4).

33 Packages Act 1969–72 (S.A.), ss. 26, 37. See also 15 U.S.C. s. 1454 (c)(4).

34 Consumer Information Act 1969, s. 10(5). See R. G. Lawson, *The Law of Sale and Hire Purchase in New Zealand* (Wellington: Reed, 1973), p. 255.

35 For example, Trade Descriptions Act 1972.

36 For example, Trade Descriptions (Origin Marking) (Miscellaneous Goods) Order 1981, S.I. 1981, No. 121.

37 Care Labelling of Textile Products and Leather Clothing, 16 C.F.R. 423. For the voluntary system in Europe: P. P. Ashworth, 'Textile Care Labelling' (1978), 2 *J. Cons. Studies & Home Econ.*, 313.

38 437 F.2d 707, 714 (1970).

39 For example, Vic. Health Act 1958, s. 294.

40 Consumer Credit Act 1974, s. 64(1).

41 S.I. 1976, No. 1813 as amended by S.I. 1978, No. 127.

42 [1981] R.T.R. 430; (1981), 125 Sol.J. 255.

43 Food and Drugs Act 1955, s. 6.

44 Directive on the Labelling, Advertising and Presentation of Foodstuffs, 18 December 1978, 79/112/EEC, Art. 2(I)(a)(ii).

45 *The Labelling and Advertising of Foods* (1942–3), Cmd 6482, xi, 113, p. 3.

46 Food Standards Committee, *Second Report on Food Labelling* (London: MAFF, 1980), para. 27.

47 For example, Sale of Food and Drugs Act 1875, ss. 7, 8. See also *Report from the Select Committee on Adulteration of Food Act* (1872), 1874, C.262, vi. 243, p. v.

48 *Report from the Select Committee on Patent Medicines* (1914), Parl. Paper 414, xi. 1.

49 Ministry of Health, *Final Report of the Departmental Committee on the Use of Preservatives and Colouring Matters in Food* (London: HMSO, 1924), p. 45.

50 Weights and Measures (Packaged Goods) Regulations 1979, S.I. No. 1613 as amended.

51 Food Labelling Regulations 1980, S.I. 1980, No. 1849.

52 Stewart Dresner, *Food Labelling* (Consumers' Association, un-

published), p. 1.
53 Ibid.
54 r. 14(3), Schedule 4.
55 r. 13(2).
56 r. 16.
57 *Report of the Committee on Weights and Measures Legislation* (1950–1), Cmnd 8219, xx, 913, p. 76.
58 Home Canned Fruit and Vegetables Order 1950, S.I. No. 675.
59 Local Authorities Joint Advisory Committee on Food Standards, *Code of Practice No. 4: Canned Fruit and Vegetables*.
60 Articles 8(4), 17. The practice in European countries is reviewed in Trade Practices Commission, *Packaging and Labelling Laws in Australia* (Canberra: AGPS, 1977), pp. 211–12.
61 cf. Food Standards Committee, *Report on the Date Marking of Food* (London: HMSO, 1972).
62 Ibid.; *Interim Report of the Steering Group on Food Freshness* (London: HMSO, 1975).
63 Food Labelling Regulations 1980, r. 20(1).
64 r. 20(4).
65 For example, National Food Administration's Implementing Ordinance to the Food Act and the Food Decree 1971 (Sweden), ch. 3, paras 7–8.
66 Food Labelling Regulations 1980, rr. 29–30.
67 r. 35, Schedule 5.
68 r. 36.
69 André Gabor, 'Consumer Oriented Pricing', in David Thorpe, *Research in Retailing and Distribution* (Westmead, Hants.: Saxon, 1974), p. 50.
70 Reich and Micklitz, *Consumer Legislation in the Federal Republic of Germany*, op. cit., pp. 35–7; J. Calais-Auloy *et al.*, *Consumer Legislation in France* (Wokingham, Berks.: Van Nostrand Reinhold, 1981), pp. 83–4.
71 As amended, Price Commission Act 1977, s. 16(1).
72 s. 5.
73 Price Marking (Fruits and Vegetables) Order 1975, S.I. 1975, No. 1317; Price Marking (Cheese) Order 1977, S.I. 1977, No. 1334, as amended by S.I. 1978, No. 133; Price Marking (Meat) Order 1977, S.I. 1977, No. 1412; Price Marking (Food) Order 1978, S.I. 1978, No. 738. Unit pricing is discussed below.
74 Price Marking (Food and Drink on Premises) Order 1979, S.I. 1979, No. 361.
75 Price Marking (Petrol) Order 1980, S.I. 1980, No. 1121. See *South London Tyre and Battery Centre Ltd* v. *Bexley L.B.C.* [1981] R.T.R. 258. See also Tourism (Sleeping Accommodation Price Display) Order 1977, S.I. 1977, No. 1877 made under the Development of Tourism Act 1969.
76 Unit pricing existed specifically during the second world war in Britain

both directly (Meat, (Maximum Retail) Prices Order 1942, S.I. 2460, r. 4) and indirectly (e.g. The Preserves Order 1944, S.I. 841, Part 1). See generally OECD, *Package Standardization Unit Pricing and Deceptive Packaging* (Paris: 1975).

77 Reich and Micklitz, *Consumer Legislation in the EC Countries*, op. cit., p. 25.

78 C. W. J. Granger and A. Billson, 'Consumers' Attitudes towards Package Size and Price', [1972] *J. of Marking Research* 239.

79 Price Marking (Meat and Fish) Order 1974, S.I. 1974, No. 1368, Schedule, para. 4; Price Marking (Prepacked Milk in Vending Machines) Order 1976, S.I. 1976, No. 796, Price Marking (Cheese) Order 1977, as amended, Schedule; Price Marking (Meat) Order 1977, Schedule, paras 2(b), 3.

80 Price Marking (Food) Order 1978, r. 3(1)(b).

81 Price Marking (Petrol) Order 1980.

82 Price Commission Act 1977, s. 18; repealed Competition Act 1980.

83 David Reeson, 'The Economics of Local Price Information Services', (1978) 2 *J. Cons. Studies & Home Econ.* 35.

84 Crowther Committee, p. 259.

85 Consumer Credit Act 1974, s. 46. But a statement like the following would seem not to be covered: 'We have to show 23 per cent but really it is only about 12 per cent flat.'

86 The regulations, discussed below, are made under s. 44. cf. U.S.: Truth in Lending Act, 15 U.S.C. ss. 1601–65; see also Truth in Lending Regulations, 12 C.F.R. s. 226.

87 s. 189(1).

88 s. 167(2).

89 Powers of Criminal Courts Act 1973, s. 35.

90 s. 43. Additional exceptions are contained in the Consumer Credit (Exempt Advertisements) Order 1980, S.I. 1980, No. 53; Consumer Credit (Advertisements) Regulations 1980, S.I. 1980, No. 54, r. 2.

91 s. 151.

92 S.I. 1980, No. 54. The regulations are complex and what follows is a broad outline.

93 S.I. 1980, No. 51.

94 Consumer Credit (Advertisements) Regulations 1980, S.I. 1980, No. 54, Schedule 3.

95 But see rr. 5(1)(e), (g)–(l), excluding certain maintenance charges and insurance premiums. Creditors might abandon many of these charges because they unnecessarily complicate the calculations of the rate of the total charge to credit.

96 *Consumer Credit Tables* (London: HMSO, 1977), parts 1–15.

97 A. E. Vrisakis, 'Comment', in R. Baxt and A. C. Cullen (eds), *Consumer Credit: The Challenge of Change* (Sydney: C.C.H., 1972), p. 299.

98 However, there are specific provisions for calculating the rate of the total charge for credit for disclosure in advertisements relating to certain debtor-creditor-supplier agreements for running account credit. Covered are those under which the debtor agrees to pay a specified amount on specified occasions, there is a credit limit, and the charges for credit are a fixed amount for each transaction or calculated as a proportion of the price payable under a transaction financed by the credit. Two rates must be disclosed for such agreements: first, if the debtor borrows an amount equal to the credit limit at the outset, repays as required, and obtains no further credit; and secondly, if the debtor borrows one-third of the credit limit at the outset, repays as required, and obtains no further credit: Consumer Credit (Advertisements) Regulations 1980, Schedule 2, para. 3(2)–(4).

99 See R. M. Goode, *Hire-Purchase Law and Practice* (London: Butterworths, 1970), pp. 999–1007.

100 s. 45.

101 Richard E. Speidel *et al.*, *Commercial and Consumer Law* (St Paul, Minn.: West, 1974), p. 489.

102 Lewis Mandell, 'Consumer Perception of Incurred Interest Rates', (1971) 26 *J. of Fin.* 1143.

103 William K. Brandt and George S. Day, 'Information Disclosure and Consumer Behaviour: An Empirical Evaluation of Truth in Lending', (1973) 7 *U. of Mich. J.L. Reform* 297.

104 R. M. C. Lourens, 'Informational Aspects', in Baxt and Cullen, op. cit., p. 307. Another American survey indicates an increased awareness of dollar amounts of credit charges rather than annual percentage charges. T. A. Durkin, 'A High-Rate Market for Consumer Loans', in National Commission on Consumer Finance, *Technical Studies* (New York: C.C.H., 1975), vol. 2.

105 R. E. Olley, 'Disclosure and Regulation of Finance Charges and the Cost of Borrowing: An Economist's Viewpoint', in Jacob S. Ziegel and William F. Foster, *Aspects of Comparative Commercial Law* (Montreal: McGill Univ., 1969), p. 201.

106 William D. Starkweather, *Effects of Federal Truth in Lending Legislation on Sales Finance and Consumer Finance Companies* (D. B. A. Thesis, Kent State Univ., 1973), pp. 110, 121.

107 Joyce Epstein, 'Consumer Research', (1979) 3 *J. Cons. Studies & Home Econ.* 269, 272–4, collects some empirical evidence.

108 Kenneth McNeil *et al.*, 'Market Discrimination Against the Poor and the Impact of Consumer Disclosure Laws: The Used Car Industry', (1979) 13 *Law & Soc. Rev.* 695.

109 For example, 'Survey on Food Labelling', *Focus*, vol. 3, February 1969, p. 13; March 1969, p. 21. See also *Understanding Labels: Problems for Poor*

Readers (London: Adult Literacy Support Services Fund, 1980).

110 cf. R. L. Jordan and W. D. Warren, 'Disclosure of Finance Charges: A Rationale' (1966) 64 *Mich. L. Rev.* 1285, 1303, 1306–7.

111 Jonathan M. Landers and Ralph J. Rohner, 'A Functional Analysis of Truth in Lending', (1979) 26 *U.C.L.A. L. Rev.* 711, 715, 725.

112 Arthur Leff, 'Injury, Ignorance and Spite – The Dynamics of Coercive Collection', (1970) 80 *Yale L.J.* 1, 33.

113 Homer Kripke, 'Gesture and Reality in Consumer Credit Reform', (1969) 44 *N.Y.U.L. Rev.* 1, 5–6; Comment, 'Consumer Protection in Michigan; Current Methods and Some Proposals for Reform', (1970) 68 *Mich. L. Rev.* 926, 935–6.

114 Brandt and Day, op. cit., p. 320.

115 James J. White and Frank W. Munger, 'Consumer Sensitivity to Interest Rates: An Empirical Study of New-Car Buyers and Auto Loans', (1971) 69 *Mich. L. Rev.* 1207, 1227.

116 Robert J. Gage, 'The Discriminating Use of Information Disclosure Rules by The Federal Trade Commission', (1979) 26 *U.C.L.A. L. Rev.* 1037, 1041–2.

CHAPTER 10

1 cf. L. C. B. Gower, 'Business', in Morris Ginsberg (ed.), *Law and Opinion in England in the Twentieth Century* (London: Stevens, 1959), p. 160.

2 There are of course others; cf. Road Traffic Act 1972, s. 40(1)(a).

3 *Molony Report*, pp. 29–30.

4 *Interim Report of the Committee on Consumer Protection* (1960), Cmnd 1011, p. 12.

5 *Royal Commission on Civil Liability and Compensation for Personal Injury* (1978), Cmnd 7054, vol. 1, p. 10.

6 For example, S. B. Burman, 'The Use of Legal Services by Victims of Accidents in the Home – A Pilot Study', (1977) 40 *Mod. L. Rev.* 47.

7 There are obvious problems of proof.

8 cf. Health and Safety at Work etc. Act 1974, s. 6(1). Many products used at work are also used in other situations and are subject to this provision.

9 J. Steiner and C. H. L. Kennard, 'Laws and Regulations Prohibiting Commercial Products from Containing Certain Substances', (1975) 49 *A.L.J.* 697.

10 Walter Y. Oi, 'The Economics of Product Safety', (1973) 4 *Bell J. of Econ.* 3, 22.

11 Rag Flock Act 1911; Rag Flock and other Filling Materials Act 1951; Fabrics (Misdescription) Act 1913; Lead Paint (Protection Against Poisoning) Act 1926; Petroleum (Consolidation) Act 1928; Heating Appliances (Fireguards) Act 1952; Oil Burners (Standards) Act 1960.

12 The Consumer Protection Act 1961 was repealed by the Consumer Safety Act 1978, although at the time of writing the repeal had not taken effect.

13 Dangerous Substances and Preparations (Safety) Regulations 1980, S.I. 1980, No. 136. The names of the other regulations follow the products involved. Many are collected in W. H. Thomas, *Encyclopedia of Consumer Law* (London, Sweet & Maxwell, looseleaf). There might be problems of definition in the ambit of the regulations, e.g. *London Export Corporation Ltd* v. *Camden L.B.C.* (1978) 86 M.R. 99 (definition of 'toy').

14 *Consumer Safety: A Consultative Document* (1976), Cmnd 6398, p. 8.

15 15 U.S.C. ss. 2051–83. See Michael T. Fox, 'The Consumer Product Safety Act – Placebo or Panacea?' (1973), 10, *San Diego L.R.*, 814; Laurence P. Feldman, *Consumer Protection*, 2nd edn (St Paul, Minn.: West, 1980), pp. 58–63, 73–94.

16 *Consumer Safety: A Consultative Document*, pp. 28–9.

17 15 U.S.C. s. 2059 (repealed 1981 by Pub. L. 97–135, s. 1210).

18 Department of Prices and Consumer Protection, 'Consumer Safety', *Consumer Information Bulletin*, December 1974, p. 4.

19 cf. 15 U.S.C. ss. 2057–8, 2061, 2064 (United States); Trade Practices Act 1974, s. 62(1), 2(D). See M. S. Madden, 'Consumer Product Safety Act Section 15 and Substantial Product Hazards', (1981) 30 *Catholic U.L. Rev.* 195. The Department of Trade seem to have taken the narrow view that the power to make orders with respect to 'any goods which the Secretary of State considers are not safe' and which are 'described' or 'specified' cannot be used against a particular brand of product, or a product with other distinguishing features, just because tests have shown *some* are unsafe: (1982) 90 M.R. 105. It is difficult to understand why a Secretary of State cannot reasonably conclude that a class of product is unsafe when some of that class have proved unsafe, irrespective of whether all possess the unsafe characteristics.

20 Examples are Nightwear (Safety) Order 1978, S.I. 1978, No. 1728; Balloon-Making Compounds (Safety) Order 1979, S.I. 1979, No. 44; Children's Furniture (Safety) Order 1982, S.I. 1982, No. 523. The second-mentioned Order and the Tear-Gas Capsules (Safety) Order 1979, S.I. 1979, No. 887 have been replaced by the Novelties (Safety) Regulations 1980, S.I. 1980, No. 958.

2 15 U.S.C. s. 2064(b)(d). M. J. Vernon, 'Consumer Product Safety', in A. J. Duggan and L. W. Darvall (eds), *Consumer Protection Law and Theory* (Sydney: Law Book, 1980).

2 (New York: Pocket Books, 1966).

2 ; Ralph Nader and Joseph A. Page, 'Automobile Design and the Judicial Process', (1967) 55 *Calif. L. Rev.* 645, 646n.

24 See, generally, R. C. Cramton, 'Driver Behaviour and Legal Sanctions', (1969) 67 *Mich. L. Rev.* 421; Laurence Ross, 'The Neutralization of

Severe Penalties: Some Traffic Law Studies', (1976) 10 *Law & Soc. Rev.* 403.

25 cf. Note, 'The Automobile Manufacturer's Liability to Pedestrians for Exterior Design', (1973) 71 *Mich. L. Rev.* 1654.

26 15 U.S.C. ss. 1391–1420. See also 15 U.S.C. ss. 1421–6 (tyre safety); ss. 1911–22 (bumper standards).

27 James F. Holderman, 'Auto Design' [1969] *U. Ill. L. For.*, 396, 406; Cf. Hideo Otake, 'Corporate Power in Social Conflict: Vehicle Safety and Japanese Motor Manufacturers', (1982) 10 *Int. J. of Sociology of Law* 75.

28 15 U.S.C. s. 1411–2. See Glen D. Nager, 'Auto Recalls and the Pursuit of Safety: A Commonsense Approach', (1981) 33 *Stanford L. Rev.* 301.

29 Motor Vehicles (Tests) Regulations 1981, S.I. 1981, No. 1694.

30 Motor Vehicles (Construction and Use) Regulations 1978, S.I. 1978, No. 1017, as amended. See John Burke, *Encyclopedia of Road Traffic and Practice* (London: Sweet & Maxwell, looseleaf). EEC standards are being adopted by reference; they are made by regulations under the *Agreement Concerning ... Uniform Conditions of Approval [for] Motor Vehicle Equipment and Parts*, done at Geneva on 20 March 1958, No. 4789, [335] U.N.T.S. 211.

31 *A Summary of International Vehicle Legislation* (London: Society of Motor Manufacturers and Traders Ltd, 1975), vol. 1, p. 1.

32 Motor Car (Safety) Act 1970.

33 G. W. Trinca and B. J. Dooley, 'Effects of Mandatory Seat Belt Wearing ... in Victoria', *Medical J. of Aust.*, 31 May 1975, p. 675; G. M. Mackay, 'Seat Belts in Europe – Their Use and Performance in Collisions' in *International Symposium on Occupant Restraint, Proceedings*, 1981.

34 *Froom* v. *Butcher* [1976] Q.B. 286; *Eagles* v. *Orth* [1975] Qd. R. 197. *Contra* Road Traffic Act 1961, as amended (South Australia), s. 162ab(5).

35 Britain's membership of the European Economic Community, and the consequent obligation to harmonize its food laws with those of the rest of Europe, is also a factor in food control: European Communities Act 1972, Schedule 4B, para. 3(1); see generally *Butterworths Law of Food and Drugs* (London: Butterworths, looseleaf), Section E.

36 ss. 4, 13, 123A.

37 See A. G. Ward, 'The Changing Role of the Food Standard Committee'; B. C. L. Weedon, 'Food Additives and Contaminants and the Role of the FACC', Ministry of Agriculture, Fisheries and Food, *Food Quality and Safety: A Century of Progress* (London: HMSO, 1976).

38 Natural products like salt and sugar can be a danger if used in excess.

39 For example, Customs and Inland Revenue Act 1888, s. 5.

40 *Report of the Departmental Committee on the Use of Preservatives and Colouring Matters in ... Food*, 1902, Cd 833, xxxiv, 579.

41 Minister of Health, *Final Report ... on the Use of Preservatives and Colouring*

Matters in Food (London: HMSO, 1924).

42 S.I. 1925, No. 775.

43 Preservatives in Food Regulations 1979, S.I. 1979, No. 752 as amended.

44 Food Additives and Contaminants Committee, *Report on the Review of the Preservatives in Food Regulations*, 1962 (London: HMSO, 1972), p. 10.

45 James Turner, 'Principles of Food Additive Regulation', Samuel S. Epstein and Richard D. Grundy, *The Legislation of Product Safety* (Cambridge, Mass.: MIT Press, 1974), vol. 2, p. 315.

46 See E. J. Bigwood and A. Gerard, *Fundamental Principles and Objectives of a Comparative Food Law* (Basle: S. Karger, 1967), vol. 1, pp. 36–7.

47 The current regulations are conveniently collected in *Butterworths Law of Food and Drugs* (London: Butterworths, looseleaf).

48 P. S. Elias, 'Legislative Aspects of Artificial Sweeteners and Other Food Additives', in G.B. Birch *et al.*, *Health and Food* (London: Applied Science Publishers, 1972), p. 139.

49 F. N. B. Carpanini and R. F. Crampton, 'The Testing of Food Additives for Safety in Use', in Birch *et al.*, op. cit.

50 Lead in Food Regulations 1979, S.I. 1979, No. 1254. cf. Richard A. Merrill and Michael Schewel, 'FDA Regulation of Environmental Contaminants of Food', (1980) 66 *Virginia L. Rev.* 1357.

51 For example, 21 U.S.C. s. 346a. See Hui, op. cit., pp. 254–79.

52 S.I. 1978, No. 1927, as amended.

53 21 U.S.C. s. 348(c)(3)(A). J. S. Turner, 'The Delaney Anticancer Clause: A Model Environmental Protection Law', (1971) 24 *Van. L. Rev.* 889; Richard A. Merrill, 'Regulating Carcinogens in Food: A Legislator's Guide to the Food Safety Provisions of the Federal Food, Drug, and Cosmetic Act', (1978) 77 *Mich. L. Rev.* 171; James D. Poliquin, 'The Incremental Development of an Extra-Statutory System of Regulation: A Critique of Food and Drug Administration Regulation of Added Poisonous and Deleterious Substances', (1981) 33 *Maine L. Rev.* 103.

54 *Bell* v. *Goddard*, 366 F. 2d 177 (1966).

55 Charles H. Blank, 'The Delaney Clause: Technical Naiveté and Scientific Advocacy in the Formation of Public Health Policies', (1974) 62 *Cal. L. Rev.* 1084, 1087.

56 Wesley E. Forte, 'Definitions and Standards of Identity for Foods', (1967) 14 *UCLA L. Rev.* 796.

57 Butter Regulations 1966, S.I. 1966, No. 1074; Ice Cream (Heat Treatment, etc.) Regulations 1959, S.I. 1959, No. 734.

58 Jam and Similar Products Regulations 1981, S.I. 1981, No. 1063, s. 4, Schedule 1.

59 Bread and Flour Regulations 1963, S.I. 1963, No. 1435.

60 Richard A. Merrill and Earl M. Collier, ' "Like Mother Used to Make" – An Analysis of FDA Food Standards of Identity', (1974) 74 *Col. L. Rev.*

561, 596–7.

61 Ibid., pp. 603–9; Comment, 'The Federal Food Drug and Cosmetic Act as an Experiment in Quality Control', (1969) 20 *Syracuse L. Rev.* 883, 903–9.

62 For example 6 & 7 Will. 4, c. 37 (1836).

63 Sale of Milk Regulations 1901, S.I. 1901, No. 657.

64 Sale of Butter Regulations 1902, S.I. 1902, No. 355.

65 *Interim Report of the Departmental Committee on Butter Regulations* (1902), Cd 944, xx, 123, p. 5.

66 Margarine Act 1887; Sale of Food and Drugs Act 1889, ss. 5–8; Butter and Margarine Act 1907. See now Margarine Regulations 1967, S.I. 1967, No. 1867.

67 For example, Qld: Margarine Act 1958.

68 *Report of the Departmental Committee on the Composition and Description of Food* (1933–4), Cmd 4564, xii, 159, pp. 6–8. cf. *Final Report of the Royal Commission on Arsenical Poisoning from the Consumption of Beer and other Articles of Food and Drink*, Cd 1848, ix, 399, p. 47.

69 *Labelling and Advertising of Foods* (1942–3), Cmd 6482, xi, 113, p. 2.

70 Food Substitutes (Control) Order 1941, S.I. 1941, No. 1606.

71 Defence (Sale of Food) Regulations 1943, S.I. 1943, No. 1553; Food Standards (General Provisions) Order 1944, S.I. 1944, No. 42, as amended. Limited power already existed under the Food and Drugs Act 1938.

72 Food Standards Committee, *Report on the Pre-1955 Compositional Orders* (London: HMSO, 1970), p. 6.

73 Food Standards Committee, *Report on Meat Pies* (London: HMSO, 1963). See also Food Standards Committee, *Report on Meat Products* (London: MAFF, 1980).

74 Food Standards Committee, *Report on Yogurt* (London: HMSO, 1975), p. 10.

75 Food Standards Committee, *Report on Infant Formulae* (London: MAFF, 1981).

76 cf. Food Standards Committee, *Novel Protein Foods* (London: HMSO, 1974). See also Food Standards Committee, *Report on Meat Products* (London: MAFF, 1980).

77 F. G. Davies, *Public Health Inspector's Handbook*, 13th edn (London: Lewis, 1972), p. 246.

78 [1981] 3 W.L.R. 833; [1981] 3 All E.R. 257. See Graham Stephenson, 'The Legal Regulation of the Quality of Food: A Standard Problem', (1982) 132 *N.L.J.* 553; *T. W. Lawrence & Sons Ltd* v. *Burleigh* (1982) 80 L.G.R. 631.

79 21 U.S.C. s. 343(g).

80 Departmental Committee of Inquiry, *The Aberdeen Typhoid Outbreak, 1964*

(1964), Cmnd 2542.
81 Food Hygiene (General) Regulations 1970, S.I. 1970, No. 1172.
82 National Federation of Consumer Groups, *Hygiene in Food Shops – Survey Report* (Birmingham: 1975).
83 Ibid., p. 3.
84 Op. cit., p. 53.
85 *Hampson* v. *Whitehouse* [1971] 2 N.S.W.L.R. 194; *Pitt* v. *Locke* (1960) 125 J.P. 93; (1960) 58 L.G.R. 330.
86 For example, Vic.: Health Act 1958, ss. 224, 227, 229A.
87 See 'Control of Catering Premises', *Environmental Health*, vol. 83, February 1975, p. 65.
88 s. 1.
89 s. 2.
90 s. 3.
91 Public Health Act 1936, s. 83; Public Health Act 1961, s. 41.

CHAPTER 11

1 Office of Fair Trading, *Seeking to Sell Goods Without Revealing that they are being Sold in the Course of a Business* (London: Office of Fair Trading, 1975), p. 29.
2 *Prepayment for Goods*, H.C. Paper 285 (London: HMSO, 1976), p. 12.
3 Office of Fair Trading, *Prepayment in Mail Order Transactions and in Shops* (London: Office of Fair Trading, 1974), p. 20.
4 Since 1975 the Federal Trade Commission in the United States has had an explicit rule-making power to 'define with specificity acts or practices which are unfair or deceptive': Magnuson-Moss Consumer Product Warranties – Federal Trade Commission Improvement Act, 15 U.S.C. §§ 57a(a)(1). The F.T.C. must give public notice and conduct hearings in relation to proposed trade regulation rules. If promulgated trade regulation rules have the force of law: violation constitutes an unfair or deceptive act or practice in breach of section 5(a) of the Federal Trade Commission Act. Knowing violations enable the F.T.C. to seek civil penalties. Prior to 1975 the F.T.C. had issued trade regulation rules; its power to do this was upheld in *National Petroleum Refiners Association* v. *F.T.C.* (1973), 482 F.2d 672: (1974), cert. denied 415 U.S. 951. These pre-1975 rules are still in force.

The F.T.C.'s record since 1975 does not appear brilliant in relation to trade regulation rules. Few rules have been issued: disclosure requirements and prohibitions concerning franchising (not really a Magnuson-Moss rule); labelling and advertising of home insulation; and advertising of ophthalmic goods and services (rule partly set aside). A rule covering proprietary vocation and home-study schools was set aside in

Katharine Gibbs School, Inc. v. *F.T.C.* (1979), 612 F.2d 658, 662. cf. *American Optometric Association* v. *F.T.C.* (1980), 626 F.2d 896. A basis of the decision was that this rule did not define with sufficient specificity the acts and practices found unfair or deceptive. A rule on the sale of used motor vehicles was vetoed by the Congress in May 1982.

F.T.C. trade regulation rules deal with particular practices in relation to particular products, particular practices in a particular segment of trade and particular practices across a whole trade. Rules and proposed rules are conveniently collected in C.C.H., *Trade Regulation Reporter* (Chicago: looseleaf), s. 38, 001.

The F.T.C. also issues 'industry guides' containing its interpretation of the law, which are intended to provide a basis of voluntary abandonment of unlawful practices. The guides do not have the direct force of law, but failure to comply might result in legal action. Similarly, the F.T.C. has also announced its enforcement policy with respect to specific practices.

5 E. N. Gladden, *The Essentials of Public Administration*, 3rd edn (London: Staples, 1964), p. 173.

6 Fair Trading Act 1973, s. 3.

7 ss. 17, 18, 22.

8 ss. 23, 26.

9 s. 13.

10 ss. 14, 19, 21.

11 Office of Fair Trading, *The Purported Exclusion of Inalienable Rights* (London: Office of Fair Trading, 1974).

12 *Rights of Consumers*, H.C. Paper No.6 (London: HMSO, 1974).

13 S.I. 1976, No. 1813, as amended by S.I. 1978, No. 127.

14 R. 3: A person shall not, in the course of a business—

(a) display, at any place where consumer transactions are effected (whether wholly or partly), a notice containing a statement which purports to apply, in relation to consumer transactions effected there, a term which would—

(i) be void by virtue of section 6 . . . of the Unfair Contract Terms Act 1977, or

(ii) be inconsistent with a warranty . . . implied by section 4(1)(c) of the Trading Stamps Act 1964. . . ,

if applied to some or all such consumer transactions;

(b) publish or cause to be published any advertisement which is intended to induce persons to enter into consumer transactions and which contains a statement purporting to apply in relation to such consumer transactions such a term as is mentioned in paragraph (a)(i) or (ii), being a term which would be void by virtue of, or as the case may be, inconsistent with, the provisions so mentioned if applied to some or all of those transactions;

(c) supply to a consumer pursuant to a consumer transaction goods
bearing, or goods in a container bearing, a statement which is a term
of that consumer transaction and which is void by virtue of, or
inconsistent with, the said provisions, or if it were a term of that
transaction, would be so void or inconsistent;

(d) furnish to a consumer in connection with the carrying out of a
consumer transaction or to a person likely, as a consumer, to enter
into such a transaction, a document which includes a statement
which is a term of that transaction and is void or inconsistent as
aforesaid, or, if it were a term of that transaction or were to become a
term of a prospective transaction, would be so void or inconsistent.

See *Hughes* v. *Hall* [1981] R.T.R. 430; (1981) 125 Sol. J. 255.

15 *Annual Report of the Director General of Fair Trading, 1981* (London: HMSO,
1982), p. 24.

16 Office of Fair Trading, *Prepayment in Mail Order Transactions and in Shops*
(London: Office of Fair Trading, 1974). See also *Prepayment for Goods*,
H.C. No. 285 (London: HMSO, 1976).

17 Mail Order Transactions (Information) Order 1976, S.I. 1976, No.
1812. Advertisements by radio, television or film are excluded. cf.
Consumer Affairs Act 1972 (Victoria), s. 13(2B).

18 *Annual Report of the Director General of Fair Trading 1979* (London: HMSO,
1980), p. 21. See also Customers' Prepayments (Protection) Bill 1982.

19 *Seeking to Sell Goods Without Revealing that they are being Sold in the Course of a
Business*, op. cit.; *Disguised Business Sales*, H.C. Paper No. 355 (London:
HMSO, 1976).

20 Business Advertisements (Disclosure) Order 1977, S.I. 1977, No. 1918.
Agents are covered by the Order whether or not they are acting in the
course of a business: r. 2(2). For a report on how extensive the practice is,
and how it is sometimes associated with other serious offences: D.
Sibbert, 'Disguised Trade Sales', (1981), 89 *M.R.* 147.

21 Office of Fair Trading, *Pricing Goods and Services Exclusive of Tax Payable on
Retail Sale* (London: 1975); *VAT Exclusive Prices*, H.C. No. 416 (London:
HMSO, 1977).

22 S.I. 1979, No. 361.

23 Price Marking (Bargain Offers) Order 1979, S.I. 1979, No. 364, as
amended by S.I. 1979, No. 633, and S.I. 1979, No. 1124.

24 ss. 54, 57, 58, 60.

25 For example, 58 Am. Jur. 2d (Occupations etc.) s. 83; *C.C.H. Australian
Consumer Sales and Credit Law Reporter* (Sydney: looseleaf), ss. 17.150–
17.170.

26 Conrad Jameson, *Stamp Trading* (London: HMSO, 1964).

27 *Goodwin* v. *Brebner* [1962] S.A.S.R. 78; *Samuels* v. *Reader's Digest Services*

Pty Ltd (1972), 4 S.A.S.R. 213.

28 cf. Economist Intelligence Unit, *Trading Stamps in the United Kingdom* (London: 1977).

29 OECD, *Annual Reports on Consumer Policy* (Paris: 1974), p. 11.

30 Mock Auctions Act 1961, s.1(3).

31 *Allen* v. *Simmons* [1978] 1 W.L.R. 879; [1978] 3 All E.R. 662. See also *Clements* v. *Rydeheard* [1978] 3 All E.R. 658; *Lomas* v. *Rydeheard* (1975) 119 Sol. J. 233; *The Times*, 21 February 1975.

32 *R.* v. *Ingram* (1976) 64 Crim. App. Rep. 119, 121; But other breaches of criminal law might be committed: A. T. H. Smith, 'Mock Auctions', (1981) 131 *N.L.J.* 49. The Office of Fair Trading has concluded that further regulation is unnecessary. With the cooperation of the national associations of bodies likely to hire premises for mock auctions several local codes of practice have been concluded. Under these consumer protection (trading standards) departments are notified in advance that mock auctions are to be held and those conducting mock auctions undertake to comply with legal requirements and principles of fair trading. Breach of an undertaking would not of itself give rise to legal action; at most it might as a practical matter deter one day sellers from using certain venues.

33 Note, 'Pyramid Schemes, Dare to be Regulated', (1973) 61 *Georgetown L. J.* 1257, 1258–9 (footnotes omitted).

34 Ibid., p. 1260.

35 *Guardian*, 25 September 1974; *Daily Mail*, 25 September 1974.

36 See Michael Head, 'Pyramid Selling Legislation', (1974) 2 *Aust. Bus. L.R.* 167, 169–73; R. G. Lawson, 'Lotteries and Pyramid Selling', (1974) 118 *Sol. J.* 620.

37 For example, Howard N. Solodky, 'Prohibiting Pyramid Sales Schemes: County, State and Federal Approaches to a Persistent Problem', (1975) 24 *Bull. L. Rev.* 877. J. L. Goldring and L. W. Maher, *Consumer Protection Law in Australia*, 2nd edn. (Sydney: Butterworths, 1983), pp. 300–8; Calais-Auloy *et al.*, op. cit., pp. 98–100; Borge Dahl, *Consumer Legislation in Denmark* (Wokingham, Berks.: Van Nostrand Reinhold, 1981), pp. 54–5.

38 Cunningham, op. cit., p. 46.

39 Fair Trading Act 1973, s. 118(1)(c).

40 s. 119.

41 S.I. 1973, No. 1740.

42 *Guardian*, 25 September 1974; *News of the World*, 5 January 1975.

43 *Re Golden Chemicals Products Ltd* [1976] 3 W.L.R. 1; [1976] 2 All E.R. 543; *Re World Wide Household Products, Guardian* 29 September 1976, p. 17.

44 *Trade Practice Act Review Committee* (Canberra: AGPS, 1976) p. 74. In Britain it is illegal to send unsolicited sexual materials; cf. *D.P.P.* v. *Beate*

Uhse (UK) [1974] Q.B. 158.

45 Unsolicited Goods and Services Acts 1971 and 1975, s. 1. The background to the Act is discussed in Judith Gray, 'The Unsolicited Goods and Services Acts 1971 and 1975' [1978], *Pub. Law*, 242. For elsewhere 'Unsolicited Merchandise: State and Federal Remedies for a Consumer Problem', [1970], *Duke L. J.*, 991; Reich and Micklitz, *Consumer Legislation in the E.C. Countries*, op. cit., pp. 70–1; Goldring and Maher, op. cit., pp. 289–98.

46 s. 2. See also s. 3A. Unsolicited Goods and Services (Invoices etc.) Regulations 1975, S.I. 1975, No. 732 (invoice etc. to be regarded as asserting right to payment unless conspicuous statement to contrary).

47 [1973] S.L.T. 170. See also the poorly reasoned *Corfield* v. *World Records Ltd* (1980) 88 M.R. 88. Both decisions call for amendments to the Act: P. J. Thomas, 'The Unsolicited Goods and Services Act, 1971 – Ten Years On', (1981) 89 *M.R.* 242.

48 [1972] A.C. 153.

49 For example, *Report of Select Committee on Patent Medicines* (1914), Parl. Pap. 414, ix, I, p. xxii.

50 Molony Report, p. 243. Confirmed by a subsequent study of the Office of Fair Trading: House of Lords, *Select Committee on the European Communities*, 41st Report, H.L. 227, 1976, Appendix 14.

51 *R* v. *Potger* (1970) 55 C.A.R. 42: See also *Autoplan Home Improvement Ltd* v. *Craggs* (1971) 80 *Monthly Review* 285 (Crown Court).

52 'The Direct Selling Industry Project', (1969) 16 *UCLA L. Rev.* 883, 913.

53   Enterprises may not without prior request contact a consumer in person or by telephone at his residence, place of work or other place not open to the general public for the purpose of obtaining, immediately or at a later date, an offer or acceptance concerning the entering of an agreement.

Cited in Dahl, op. cit., p. 50. There are limited exceptions regarding books, subscriptions to newspapers etc., insurance, subscriptions to rescue or ambulance services, and certain natural products: s. 2(2). Doorstep credit sales are forbidden in Holland, and with hire purchase transactions the seller must generally be registered: E. H. Hondius, *Consumer Legislation in the Netherlands* (Wokingham, Berks.: Van Nostrand Reinhold, 1980), p. 87.

54 For example, Consumer Affairs Act 1972 (Victoria), s. 20A.

55 Act on Trade No. 426 of 11 June 1971; art. 36. See Gustavo Ghidini, *Consumer Legislation in Italy* (Wokingham, Berks.: Van Nostrand Reinhold, 1980), p. 37.

56 *Molony Report*, p. 263.

57 See Byron D. Sher, 'The "Cooling-Off" Period in Door-to-Door Sales', (1968) 15 *UCLA L. Rev.* 717.

58 Molony Report, p. 264.

59 ss. 21, 145(1)(a), (2).

60 There is a cooling-off period for some long-term insurance policies: see p. 490, n. 26, below.

61 Draft Directive on Contracts Negotiated Away from Business Premises, R/113/77. See House of Lords, *Select Committee on the European Communities* (1976), 41st Report, H.L. No. 227.

62 Philip G. Schrag, *Counsel for the Deceived* (New York: Pantheon, 1972), p. 195. See also the valuable discussion in Terence G. Ison, *Credit Marketing and Consumer Protection* (London: Croom Helm, 1979), pp. 107–21.

63 David Cayne and M. J. Trebilcock, 'Marketing Considerations in the Formulation of Consumer Protection Policy', (1973) 23 *U. Tor. L.J.* 396, 423.

64 s. 49(1). See also s. 154 (canvassing of services of credit-brokerage, debt-adjusting and debt-counselling – also banned).

65 Trading Representatives (Disabled Persons) Acts 1958 and 1972.

66 cf. *Kent County Council* v. *Portland House Stationers Ltd* (1974) 82 *Monthly Review* 123 (Crown Court).

67 *Molony Report*, p. 173.

68 Crowther Committee, p. 289.

69 See Michael B. Metzger and Dennis H. Wolkoff, 'Fulfilling a Promise: Extending a Cooling-Off Period to Retail Sales in General', (1974) 58 *Minnesota L. Rev.*, 753.

70 15 U.S.C. s.45(b), (l).

71 Possibly because of *Heater* v. *F.T.C.* 503 F.2d 321 (1974).

72 E. Cox *et al.*, *The Nader Report on the Federal Trade Commission* (New York: Baron, 1969), p. 61.

73 Harrison Wellford, 'The Federal Trade Commission's New Look: A Case Study of Regulatory Revival', in Samuel S. Epstein and Richard D. Grundy (eds), *Consumer Health and Product Hazards* (Cambridge, Mass.: MIT Press, 1974), pp. 335–7.

74 Fair Trading Act 1973, s. 34(1). See, generally, A. J. Gamble, 'Powers of the Director General of Fair Trading', [1978] S.L.T. 113.

75 s. 37. See *Director General of Fair Trading* v. *Smiths Bakeries (Westfield) Ltd*, *The Times*, 12 May 1978.

76 s. 38.

77 s. 40.

78 *Annual Report of the Director General of Fair Trading 1981* (London: HMSO, 1982), p. 23. The assurances, undertakings and orders in any particular year are set out in Appendices to the Director General's annual report. The information in the remainder of this paragraph, including Table 11.1 comes from David Hope, 'Fair Trading Assurances' (1981), 89 *M.R.* 180. In *R.* v. *Director General of Fair Trading ex p. F. H. Taylor & Co.*

Ltd [1981] I.C.R. 292, Donaldson L. J. commented in relation to the Director General's seeking an assurance against a business with thirteen convictions over three years under the Consumer Protection Act 1961: '[T]he only matter for surprise is that he [the Director General] refrained from doing so before April 1979' (at p. 295).

79 *R.* v. *Director General of Fair Trading ex p. F. H. Taylor & Co. Ltd* [1981] I.C.R. 292. Apart from the law of defamation and statutory restrictions, a qualification might be that if the trader's convictions are publicized so too must its 'reasonable explanations' for these. The power of publicity should be used fairly; Part III of the Act is not for driving traders out of business (at pp. 297–8).

80 The Marketing Act 1975: 1418, s. 2.

81 Fair Trading Act 1973, ss. 35, 41.

82 ss. 80, 87. *T.P.C.* v. *Glen Ion* (1975) A.T.P.R. 40–008. cf. 15 U.S.C. s. 57b(a)(2), (b).

83 William A. W. Neilson, 'Administrative Remedies: The Canadian Experience With Assurances of Voluntary Compliance in Provincial Trade Practices Legislation', (1981) 19 *Osgoode Hall L. J.* 153, 154, 172.

84 At common law there is no limit on what a business can charge unless fraud etc. are involved; e.g. *R.* v. *Lawrence* [1971] 1 Q.B. 373 (overcharging; theft).

85 Steven N. S. Cheung, 'A Theory of Price Control', (1974) 17 *J. of L. & Econ.* 53.

86 There can of course be other motives, e.g. to fix a 'just' price; to redistribute wealth.

87 Traditional demand-pull analysis – that inflation occurs because demand exceeds supply – is inappropriate to the current situation when economies are operating far below capacity.

88 See Richard A. Posner, *Economic Analysis of Law*, 1st edn (Boston: Little, Brown, 1972), pp. 169–70.

89 For example, John K. Galbraith, *The New Industrial State* (Harmondsworth: Penguin, 1974), pp. 251–4.

90 Schedule, para. 2(1).

91 G. A. Stephenson and R. P. Harris, 'The Redistributive Effect of Subsidies on Households', *Economic Trends*, No. 289, November 1977, p. 102.

92 S. Witt and G. Newbould, 'The Impact of Food Subsidies', *Nat. West. Bank Q.R.*, August 1976, p. 29.

93 Jose Harris, 'Food and Fairness: The History of Food Subsidies', *New Society*, 2 August 1973, p. 273.

94 J. T. Romans, 'Moral Suasion as an Instrument of Economic Policy', (1966) 56 *Am. Econ. Rev.* 1220.

95 Other examples are Note, 'Administration of Economic Controls: The

Economic Stabilization Act of 1970', (1979) 29 *Case W. Res. L. Rev.*
485; Peter J. Parsons, 'Prices Justification in Australia – The First
Twenty Months', (1975) 6 *Fed. L. Rev.* 367.

96 Prices and Incomes Act 1966, ss. 2–3, 7–8.

97 Allan Fels, *The British Prices and Incomes Board* (Cambridge: Cambridge
Univ. Press, 1972), p. 250; see also Joan Mitchell, *The National Board for
Prices and Incomes* (London: Secker & Warburg, 1972).

98 cf. John T. Dunlop, 'Wage and Price Controls as seen by a Controller',
(1975) 26 *Lab. L. J.* 457.

99 B. Bracewell-Milnes, *Pay and Price Control Guide* (London: Butterworths,
1973), p. 3.

100 'Price Check Shows The Way', *Consumer Info. Bull.*, February–March
1976, pp. 3–6.

101 Ibid., August 1976, p. 5.

102 The two are usually associated, but several countries have tried prices-
only freezes.

103 Legislation usually comes later; it must contain a 'roll-back' clause for
price increases between the announcement and when the law comes into
force.

104 Arnold R. Weber, *In Pursuit of Price Stabilization: The Wage-Price Freeze of
1971* (Washington, D. C.: Brookings Institution, 1973), p. 123.

105 See Alfred Letzler, 'The General Ceiling Price Regulation – Problems of
Coverage and Exclusion', (1954) 19 *L. & Contemp. Prob.* 486; Joseph
Zwerdling, 'Price Techniques', ibid., p. 522. The problems of adminis-
tering one are discussed in Robert A. Kagan, *Regulatory Justice:
Implementing a Wage-Price Freeze* (New York: Russell Sage, 1978).

106 See *Halsbury's Laws of England*, 3rd edn, vol. 39, pp. 82–3; Jules Backman,
Rationing and Price Control in Great Britain (Washington, D.C.: Brookings
Institution, 1943). See also J. K. Galbraith, *A Theory of Price Control*
(Harvard Univ. Press, 1952).

107 George Kantoma, *Price Controls and Business* (Bloomington, Ill.: Principa
Press, 1945).

108 W. David Slawson, 'Price Controls for a Peacetime Economy', (1971) 84
Harv. L. Rev. 1090, 1093.

109 Mainly S. A.: Prices Act 1948, as amended; N.S.W.: Prices Regulation
Act 1948, as amended. See *Bread Manufacturers of New South Wales* v. *Evans*
(1982) 38 A.L.R. 93. A number of maximum price orders were in force in
Britain for subsidized food under the Prices Act 1974, s. 2. See also
Butter and Concentrated Butter Prices Order 1982, S.I. 1982, No. 1169.

110 For example, S.A.: Urban Land (Price Control) Act 1973; *South
Australian Branch of A.M.A.* v. *South Australia* (1973) 6 S.A.S.R. 350;
Samuels v. *Peter F. Burns Pty Ltd* (1976) 14 S.A.S.R. 88.

111 *Southern Australian Cold Stores Ltd.* v. *Electricity Trust of South Australia*

(1965) 115 C.L.R. 247; *Patterson* v. *Lowe* [1955] Q.S.R. 437.

112 For example, Counter-Inflation (Price and Pay Code) Order 1973, S.I. 1973, No. 658, as amended; Counter-Inflation (Price Code) Order 1974, S.I. 2113, as amended; Joan Mitchell, *Price Determination and Prices Policy* (London: George Allen & Unwin, 1978), pp. 174–181 (price code and Price Commission).

113 For example, Counter-Inflation (Price Code) Order 1977, S.I. 1272.

114 Valentine Korah, 'Counter-Inflation Legislation: Whither Parliamentary Sovereignty?', (1976) 92 *L.Q.R.* 42, 54–7.

115 Stephen A. Herman, 'Private Suits for Overcharges under the Economic Stabilization Act', (1972) 39 *U. Chi. L. Rev.* 295.

116 For example, Price Code 1977, s. 37.

117 Robert S. Summers, 'The Technique Element in Law', (1971) 59 *Calif. L. Rev.* 733, 738.

118 15 U.S.C. s. 45(a)(1). See also Gesetz gegen den unlauteren Wettbewerb, [Act Prohibiting Unfair Competition] (West Germany), art. 1; Trade Practices Act 1974 (Australia), ss. 52, 80, 87. See, generally, Richard Craswell, 'The Identification of Unfair Acts and Practices by the Federal Trade Commission', [1981] *Wisc. L. Rev.* 107.

119 So, in Australia, over 80 per cent of actions under s. 52 of the Trade Practices Act 1974 are brought by one business against another, rather than by the Trade Practices Commission or consumers. (A reported case where a consumer succeeded in bringing an action for damages under s. 52 was *New South Wales Real Estate Fund Ltd.* v. *Brookhouse* (1979) 38 F.L.R. 257; Among the actions are those where businesses have marketed a product or used a logo or name similar to that of a rival business. While many of these could be brought as common law proceedings, there are substantive and procedural advantages in proceeding under s. 52. Although there is a relationship between the deception of consumers and injury to other businesses (*Hornsby Building Information Centre Pty Ltd* v. *Sydney Building Information Centre Pty Ltd.* (1978) 52 A.L.J.R. 392, 395 *per* Stephen J.), some s. 52 actions are of no benefit to consumers whatsoever. See, generally, Denis Petkovic, *From Consumer to Business Protection: The Transformation of Section 52 of the Trade Practices Act* (1982, unpublished).

CHAPTER 12

1 Ernst Freund, *Administrative Powers Over Persons and Property* (Chicago Univ. Press, 1928), ch. 8.

2 cf. Charles Reich, 'The New Property', (1964) 73 *Yale L. J.* 733, 741.

3 *Crowther Committee*, vol. 1, p. 255.

4 The best example being licensing through the magistrates courts: A. J. Duggan, 'Occupational Licensing and the Consumer Interest', in Duggan and Darvall (eds), *Consumer Protection Law and Theory*, op. cit., pp. 166–7.

5 Gordon Borrie, 'Licensing Practice under the Consumer Credit Act', [1982] *J. Bus. L.* 91, 100.

6 Richard Arens and Harold D. Lasswell, *In Defence of Public Order* (New York: Columbia University Press, 1961), pp. 224–5.

7 cf. Stewart Macaulay, *Law and the Balance of Power* (New York: Russell Sage, 1966), p. 140.

8 Consumer Credit Act 1981 (N.S.W.), s. 180(8); Credit Act 1981 (Vic.), s. 212(3); Consumer Credit Act 1972–1982 (S.A.), s. 36.

9 Carl H. Fulda, 'Controls of Entry into Business and Professions – A Comparative Analysis', (1973) 8 *Texas Int. L. J.* 109, 121–4.

10 Ibid., pp. 124–6.

11 John J. Gallagher, 'Regulation of Automotive Repair Services', (1971) 56 *Corn. L. R.* 1010, 1019.

12 See Walter Gellhorn, 'The Abuse of Occupational Licensing', (1976) 44 *U. Chi. L. R.* 6.

13 Terence Daintith, 'Public and Private Enterprise in the U.K.', in Wolfgang Friedman (ed.), *Public and Private Enterprise in Mixed Economies* (London: Stevens, 1974), pp. 225ff.

14 Builders Licensing Act 1971, ss. 24, 30A, 34. See P. E. Nolan, 'The Remedy for Unsatisfactory Work Provided by Sections 59 and 60 of the Builders' Registration and Home-Owners' Protection Act 1979', (1982) 7 *Qld Lawyer* 53.

15 N.S.W.: Motor Dealers Act 1974; Vic.: Motor Car Traders Act 1973; Qld: Auctioneers and Agents Act 1971–81, s. 54; S.A.: Second-hand Motor Vehicles Act 1971; W.A.: Motor Vehicle Dealers Act 1973–82. H. G. Lander, 'Motor Car Traders Act 1973', in *Advising the Consumer* (Melbourne: Leo Cussen Institute for Continuing Legal Education, 1978).

16 Director General of Fair Trading, *Consumer Difficulties in the Used-car Section* (London: Office of Fair Trading, 1980), pp. 9–10, 13–15. The written statement about condition would identify the vehicle; state whether or not certain specified major mechanical and safety components require repair or replacement; and state whether or not the mileage reading has been verified. Where it is stated that repair of a particular component is required, the faults and repairs involved must be specified. The statement about repairs would form a trade description which the seller would be required to sign. The legislation would require the pre-sales information report to be displayed inside the windscreen of used cars offered for supply. The statutory mileage information notice

will be: 'This mileage is unverified', affixed adjacent to the mileage reading.

17 Kenneth McNeil *et al.*, 'Market Discrimination Against the Poor and the Impact of Consumer Disclosure Laws: the Used Car Industry', (1979) 13 *Law & Soc. Rev.* 695, 708–10, 712–13.

18 Economic Council of Canada, *Reforming Regulation* (1981), p. 25.

19 cf. *Cinnamond* v. *British Airports Authority* [1980] 1 W.L.R. 582; [1980] 2 All E.R. 368; *Bassam* v. *Green* [1981] R.T.R. 362; [1981] Crim. L.R. 626.

20 For example, Transport Act 1980, s. 64.

21 Monopolies Commission, *A Report on the Public Interest [and] Certain Restrictive Practices . . . Professional Services* (1970), Cmnd 4463.

22 cf. Thomas G. Moore, 'The Purpose of Licensing', (1961) 4 *J. of Law & Econ.* 93.

23 Milton Friedman, *Capitalism and Freedom* (Univ. Chicago Press, 1962), p. 144.

24 Insolvency featured prominently as a justification for licensing in Law Reform Commission, *Insurance Agents and Brokers*, Report No. 16 (Canberra: AGPS, 1980).

25 Insurance Companies Act 1974, s. 63.

26 s. 66.

27 Insurance Companies Regulations 1981, S.I. 1981, No. 1654, rr. 67–9.

28 Department of Trade, *Insurance Intermediaries* (1977), Cmnd 6715, p. 4. cf. Insurance Law Reform Act 1977 (N.Z.), s. 10.

29 Law Reform Committee, *Conditions and Exceptions in Insurance Policies*, Fifth Report (1957), Cmnd 62, p. 5. Law Reform Commission, Insurance Agents and Brokers, op. cit., pp. 15–22.

30 See Dennis Colenutt, 'The Regulation of Insurance Intermediaries in the United Kingdom', (1979) 46 *J. of Risk & Insurance* 77, 80–2.

31 Insurance Brokerage Act 1952, s. 4; cf. *Coenen* v. *Sociaal-Economische Raad* [1976] 1 C.M.L.R. 30. See also, e.g., General Insurance Brokers and Agents Act 1981 (W.A.).

32 *Insurance Intermediaries*, op. cit., p. 3. Many insurance brokers must be licensed under the Consumer Credit Act 1974.

33 Insurance Brokers (Registration) Act 1977, s. 22.

34 *Sorrell* v. *Finch* [1977] A.C. 728. See now Estate Agents Act 1979, s. 16.

35 (1975) 119 S.J. 475. The passage was quoted in news reports.

36 Department of Prices and Consumer Protection, *The Regulation of Estate Agency: A Consultative Document*, November 1975.

37 cf. Larry I. Haft, 'Recovery of Commissions by Unlicensed Real Estate Brokers', (1976) 50 *Dick L. Rev.* 500, 520; Aust.: Law Reform Commission of West Australia; *Report on a Review of the Land Agents Act*, January 1974, Project No. 37.

38 s. 3. Minimum standards of competency can be set by regulation, and

undischarged bankrupts are barred except as employees: ss. 22–3. In addition the Act attempts to protect clients' money paid to estate agents, requires that clients be given information about their liability to pay remuneration and other payments, prohibits pre-contract deposits beyond the prescribed amount, and obliges disclosure by estate agents of any personal interest: ss. 13–16, 18, 19, 21.

39 Civil Aviation Act 1982, ss. 64–71; Civil Aviation (Air Travel Organizers' Licensing) Regulations 1972, S.I. 1972, No. 223, as amended.

40 Similarly in other jurisdictions: Lisa Kennedy, 'The New York Truth in Travel Act', (1975) 8 *Mich. J. L. Reform* 695, 699ff; Reich and Micklitz, *Consumer Legislation in the EC Countries,* op. cit., p. 113; Travel Agents Act 1973 (N.S.W.).

41 *Fifth Report of the Parl. Comm. for Administration, Session* (1974–5).

42 See *Court Line,* H.C. 498 (1975); Department of Trade, *Courtline Limited, Interim Report* (London: HMSO, 1975); *Final Report* (London: HMSO, 1978).

43 Air Travel Reserve Fund Act 1975.

44 Aubrey L. Diamond, 'Consumer Protection for the Air Traveller from the United Kingdom', (1980) 5 *Air Law* 76, 81.

45 Murray Pickering, 'The Control of Insurance Business in Great Britain', [1969] *Wisc. L. Rev.* 1141, 1143.

46 Companies Act 1967, Part II.

47 Insurance Companies Act 1981, Part I.

48 Insurance Companies Act 1974, Part II; Insurance Companies Act 1981, Part II.

49 The Act has only been invoked in three cases: Department of Trade, *Report on the Policyholders Protection Act,* H.C. No. 363 (London: HMSO, 1981), p. 6.

50 For example, *Report from the Select Committee on Money Lending* (1898), 260, x, 101, p. iii.

51 Crowther Committee, pp. 329–34.

52 ss. 21, 145.

53 s. 23(2).

54 s. 23(3). Canvassing cash loans off trade premises is banned completely (s. 49).

55 s. 22.

56 *Annual Report of the Director General of Fair Trading 1981,* op. cit., p. 51.

57 ss. 39–40, 149.

58 s. 25.

59 *Annual Report of the Director General of Fair Trading 1980,* op. cit., p. 31; ibid. (1981), p. 21.

60 s. 27.

61 Borrie, op. cit., pp. 95–6.

62 *Annual Report of the Director General of Fair Trading 1981*, op. cit., p. 51.

63 ss. 34(2), 41, 42. See also the regulations cited in n. 68.

64 Consumer Credit Act 1981 (N.S.W.), s. 168(2); Consumer Credit Act 1972–82 (S.A.), s. 30.

65 Consumer Credit (Period of Standard Licence) (Amendment) Regulations 1979, S.I. 1979, No. 796.

66 ss. 31–2. See also Consumer Credit (Termination of Licenses) Regulations 1976, S.I. 1002, as amended by S.I. 1981, No. 614.

67 Borrie, op. cit., p. 97.

68 ss. 41–2. See Consumer Credit Licensing (Representations) Order 1976, S.I. 191; Consumer Credit Licensing (Appeals) Regulations 1976, S.I. 837.

69 *Report from the Select Committee [on] Examination of Drugs, to Prevent Adulteration* (1747), *Journals* (H.C.), vol. 25, p. 592.

70 *Report from the Select Committee on Adulteration of Food etc.* (1856), Parl. Pap. 379, viii, 1, at p. ix.

71 Pharmacy Act 1868. See now Medicines Act 1968, Part 4.

72 See, generally, H. E. Chapman, *The Law Relating to Medicines* (London: Burt, 1942), pp. 7–14.

73 See Philip Bean, *The Social Control of Drugs* (London: Martin Robertson, 1974), ch. 2.

74 For example, Therapeutic Substances Act 1925.

75 *Report of the Departmental Committee on Therapeutic Substances* (1921), Cmnd 1156, xiii, 331. Control of therapeutic substances is now under the Medicines Act 1968.

76 Pharmacy Act 1868; Poisons and Pharmacy Act 1908. See also Arsenic Act 1851.

77 Poisons Act 1972. See also Farm and Gardens Chemicals Act 1967.

78 For example, S.I. 1978, No. 1 as amended.

79 For example, *Report from Select Committee on Food Products Adulteration* (1896), Parl. Pap. 288, ix, 483, p. xxxviii.

80 Now Therapeutic Goods Act 1966.

81 ss. 65; Part 7. Previously the courts upheld the standards of the B.P., e.g. *White* v. *Bywater* (1887) 19 Q.B.D. 582.

82 *Report from the Select Committee on Patent Medicines* (1914), 414, ix, 1, p. ix.

83 *Parl. Deb.*, H.C., vol. 677, 8 May 1963, 448.

84 Ministry of Health, *Safety of Drugs, Final Report of Joint Sub-Committee of the Standing Medical Advisory Committees* (London: HMSO, 1963).

85 *Forthcoming Legislation on the Safety, Quality, and Description of Drugs and Medicines* (1967), Cmnd 3395, p. 9.

86 Medicines Act 1968, s. 64. See also s. 63.

87 *Parl. Deb.*, H.C., vol. 758, 15 February 1968, 1601.

88 Medicines Act, 1968, ss. 104, 130.

89 Medicines (Specified Articles and Substances) Order 1976, S.I. 1976, No. 968. The composition and labelling of cosmetics is dealt with in provisions made under the Consumer Protection Act 1961 and the European Communities Act 1972: Cosmetic Products Regulations 1978, S.I. 1978, No. 1354.

90 ss. 8, 19(5).

91 s. 31.

92 ss. 7, 19(1).

93 s. 24.

94 From Annual Reports of Committee on Safety of Medicines.

95 s. 19(2).

96 *Committee on the Safety of Medicines, Second Report 1972*, (London: HMSO, 1973), p. 6.

97 21 U.S.C. s. 355(b).

98 Medicines (Application for Product Licences, etc.) Regulations 1971, S.I. 973.

99 Medicines (Standard Provisions for Licenses and Certificates) Regulations 1971, S.I. 972, Schedule.

100 s. 28.

101 Medicines Commission, *Report on the First General Sale List of Medicinal Products for Human Use* (London: HMSO, 1973), p. 7.

102 For example, Price Commission, *Prices, Costs and Margins in the Production and Distribution of Proprietary Non-ethical Medicines*, H.C. No. 469, (1978), pp. 31–2.

103 Medicines Act 1968, ss. 93, 95.

104 Medicines (Labelling and Advertising to the Public) Regulations 1978, S.I. 1978, No. 41.

105 Medicines (Advertising to Medical and Dental Practitioners) Regulations 1978, S.I. 1978, No. 1020.

106 Bureau Européen des Unions de Consumateurs, *Advertising in the United Kingdom and West Germany* (London: Consumers' Association, 1974).

107 Cmnd 7615, 1979, p. 84. See also L. W. Darvall, 'Prescription Drug Advertising: Legal and Voluntary Controls', in Duggan and Darvall (eds), *Consumer Protection Law and Theory*, op. cit.

108 *Report of the Committee of Inquiry into the Relationship of the Pharmaceutical Industry with the National Health Service*, Cmnd 3410, 1967, pp. 131–2.

109 Ibid., p. 68.

110 For example, G. L. Boland, 'Federal Regulation of Prescription Drug and Labelling', (1970) 12 *B. C. Ind. & Com. L. Rev.* 203; L. W. Darvall, 'The Pharmaceutical Industry: Prescription Drug Information Controls in Australia and the United States', (1980) 7 *Monash U.L.R.*, 39.

111 Medicines (Labelling) Regulations 1976, S.I. 1726, as amended.

112 Medicines Commission, *Annual Report 1973*, p. 11.

113 S.I. 1975, No. 2000.

114 Joseph Hanlon, 'Do Tranquillisers cause Birth Defects?', *New Scientist*, vol. 71, 19 August 1976, p. 398.

115 Sam Peltzman, 'An Evaluation of Consumer Protection Legislation: The 1962 Drug Amendments', (1973) 81 *J. Pol. Econ.* 1049; Keith Hartley and Alan Maynard, *The Costs and Benefits of Regulating New Product Development in the UK Pharmaceutical Industry* (London: Office of Health Economics, 1982).

116 Harold A. Clymer, 'The Economic and Regulatory Climate', in Robert B. Helms, *Drug Development and Marketing* (Washington, D.C.: 1975), p. 137.

117 William M. Wardell, 'Developments in the Introduction of New Drugs in the United States and Britain, 1971–4', ibid., p. 165.

118 H. F. Stewart, 'Public Policy and Innovation in the Drug Industry', in D. Black and G. Thomas (eds), *Providing for the Health Services* (London: Croom Helm, 1978), p. 132. See also Arabella Melville and Colin Johnson, *Cured to Death. The Effects of Prescription Drugs* (London: Secker & Warburg, 1982), pp. 38, 52–3.

119 Paul J. Quirk, 'Food and Drug Administration', in James Q. Wilson (ed.), *The Politics of Regulation* (New York: Basic Books, 1981), p. 230. The FDA has been under pressure to loosen controls: ibid., pp. 219ff.

120 See *Innovative Activity in the Pharmaceutical Industry* (London: HMSO, 1973), p. 24.

121 W. Duncan Reekie, *The Economics of the Pharmaceutical Industry* (London: Macmillan, 1975), pp. 102–3.

122 The Monopolies Commission, *Chlordiazepoxide and Diazepam* (1973), H.C. Paper 197.

123 Regulation of Prices (Tranquillizing Drugs) (No. 3) Order 1973, S.I. 1093. See also Emergency Laws (Re-enactments and Repeals) Act 1964, s. 5.

124 *F. Hoffmann-La Roche & Co. AG* v. *Secretary of State for Trade and Industry* [1975] A.C. 295.

125 *Pfizer Corporation* v. *Minister of Health* [1965] A.C. 512.

126 Op. cit., pp. 163ff.

127 Sjostrom and Nilsson, op. cit., p. 132. In 1977 only 14 per cent of NHS prescriptions were by generic names, as opposed to brand or proprietary names: Royal Commission on the National Health Service, op. cit., p. 85.

128 See *Brand Names in Prescribing* (London: Office of Health Economics, 1976).

129 See Henry G. Grabowski and John M. Vernon, 'Substitution Laws and Innovation in the Pharmaceutical Industry', (1979) 43 *Law & Contemp. Prob.* 43.

CHAPTER 13

1 M. J. Trebilcock, 'The Consumer in the Post-Industrial Market-Place', in K. E. Lindgren *et al.*, *The Corporation and Australian Society* (Sydney: Law Book, 1974), p. 324.

2 An unpublished document for the Australian Commission on Poverty.

3 Philip G. Schrag, 'Bleak House 1968: A Report on Consumer Test Litigation' (1969), 44 *NYU L. R.*, 115, 116. cf. Andrew Nicol, 'Outflanking Protective Legislation – Shams and Beyond', (1981) 44 *M.L.R.* 21.

4 [1970] 1 W.L.R. 1053; [1970] 2 All E.R. 774.

5 [1976] Q.B. 513.

6 [1932] A.C. 562.

7 [1938] 4 All E.R. 258.

8 [1963] 2 Q.B. 104.

9 [1965] 2 Q.B. 473.

10 For example, S. M. Waddams, 'Legislation and Contract Law', (1979) 17 *U.W.O. L.R.* 185, Barry J. Reiter, 'The Control of Contract Power', (1981) 1 *Oxford J. Legal Stud.* 347. cf. Edward P. Belobaba, 'The Resolution of Common Law Contract Doctrinal Problems through Legislative and Administrative Intervention', in Barry J. Reiter and John Swan (eds), *Studies in Contract Law* (Toronto: Butterworths, 1980), pp. 432–5.

11 Andrew Rosenfield, 'An Empirical Test of Class-Action Settlement', (1976) 5 *J. of Leg. Stud.* 113.

12 E. Allan Farnsworth, 'Legal Remedies for Breach of Contract', (1970) 70 *Col. L. Rev.* 1145, 1147–8.

13 A. D. Twerski *et al.*, 'The Use and Abuse of Warnings in Product Liability – Design Defect Litigation Comes of Age', (1976) 61 *Corn. L. R.* 495.

14 Martin Shapiro, 'Stability and Change in Judicial Decision-Making', (1965) 2 *Law in Transition Q.* 134; Paul J. Mishkin and Clarence Morris, *On Law in Courts* (New York: Foundation Press, 1965), p. 124; Belobaba, op. cit., pp. 442–50.

15 James Willard Hurst, *Law and the Conditions of Freedom* (Univ. Wisconsin Press, 1956), p. 97.

16 See Chapter 5, note 33.

17 Grant Gilmore, 'Products Liability: A Commentary', (1970) 38 *U. Chi. L. Rev.* 103, 113.

18 Philip G. Schrag, 'On Her Majesty's Secret Service: Protecting the Consumer in New York City', (1971) 80 *Yale L. J.* 1529.

19 David Tench, *Towards a Middle System of Law* (London: Consumers' Association, 1981).

20 Paul A. Baran and Paul M. Sweezy, *Monopoly Capital* (Harmondsworth: Penguin, 1966), p. 74.
21 Michael J. Trebilcock, 'Winners and Losers in the Modern Regulatory System: Must the Consumer Always Lose?, (1975) 13 *Osgoode H. L. J.* 619, 641–3.

INDEX